California Evidentiary Foundations

Third Edition

EDWARD J. IMWINKELRIED
RICHARD C. WYDICK
JAMES E. HOGAN

Professors of Law
University of California
 at Davis School of Law

LEXIS Publishing™

LEXIS®NEXIS® · MARTINDALE-HUBBELL®
MATTHEW BENDER® · MICHIE™· SHEPARD'S®

P.O. Box 7587, Charlottesville, VA 22906-7587

Library of Congress Catalog Card Number 00-100070

ISBN 0-327-10937-8

www.lexis.com

Customer Service: 1-800-446-3410

6305512

DEDICATION

Professor Imwinkelried dedicates his work on this project to Cindy, Molly and Kenny; his parents, the late John and Enes Imwinkelried; and his parents-in-law, the late Mary Jane and Lyman (Brownie) Clark.

PREFACE

Law students in evidence courses often complain that although they can understand evidence doctrines in the abstract, their evidence books do not explain how the doctrines work in the courtroom. Likewise, students in trial techniques courses sometimes complain that they cannot convert evidence law theories into concrete lines of questioning for the courtroom.

Given those complaints, Professor Imwinkelried began an experiment in 1978. He asked his students to read sample evidentiary foundations in texts such as the *American Jurisprudence Proof of Facts* (Bancroft-Whitney Pub. Co.) and *The Trial Manual of Predicate Questions* (National District Attorneys Association). Some students said the sample foundations helped them understand abstract evidence doctrines. But other students commented that many of the sample foundations were too long and complicated. That is understandable because the available texts are written for practitioners rather than law students.

Professor Imwinkelried then resolved to prepare a set of simple foundations for law students and young trial attorneys. That set became *Evidentiary Foundations* (1980). Approximately 140,000 copies of that book have been sold, and it has been used at some 60 law schools.

In 1986, Michie Publishing Company asked Professor Imwinkelried to revise *Evidentiary Foundations*. They suggested expanding the coverage to include some foundations peculiar to criminal prosecutions. For example, how does a prosecutor prove a suspect's consent to a search, or a suspect's waiver of *Miranda* rights? Further, Michie suggested tailoring the revised text to the California Evidence Code to make it especially useful to Californians.

Professor Imwinkelried invited Professors Wydick and Hogan to help with the revision. They have done so and are glad to share whatever blame may be visited upon them by readers.

In previous editions and supplements, we have added new foundations and cases. As in the past, we have included that type of material in this new edition. However, in this edition and future supplements we are adding a different type of material: limiting instructions and closing arguments for certain types of evidence. In our experience, law students and young litigators commonly have difficulty with such doctrines as character evidence. In particular, young litigators often overreach and attempt to elicit improper opinions from the foundational witness. We suspect that the root cause might be that beginners do not fully appreciate what the judge will tell the jury about the evidence or what the attorney himself or herself can say about the evidence during summation. The beginner may mistakenly feel compelled to have the witness verbalize the inference because they do not realize that either the judge or the attorney will articulate the inference. We thought that it would help if we added illustrative instructions and summations. We do not claim that the enclosed summations are models of effective trial advocacy. Rather, our limited intent is to help the beginner understand what can be said about the evidence *after* the witness lays the foundation for the evidence. In this new edition we are adding the material for some of the evidentiary doctrines set out in Chapter 6. For future supplements we plan to add material for the credibility doctrines discussed in Chapters 5 and 10. In the interim, we welcome your comments on the new material.

The three of us join in expressing the hope that *California Evidentiary Foundations* (3rd ed. 2000) will prove helpful to California law students and attorneys.

Edward J. Imwinkelried
Richard C. Wydick
James E. Hogan

Davis, California

ACKNOWLEDGMENTS

The authors would like to express their thanks to:

—their colleagues, Professor Floyd Feeney and Mr. Charles Sevilla, who reviewed and critiqued Chapter 11;

—Michael Wilcox and Jody Wilson, class of 2000; Ronald Richards, class of 1989; Alison Clarke, class of 1996; and Kirsten Lucey, class of 1996, University of California at Davis Law School, who citechecked and proofread the entire manuscript; and

—Beth Chance, Glenda McGlashan, Helen Forsyth, Ann Graham and Kathy Houston who typed the manuscript.

SUMMARY TABLE OF CONTENTS

TABLE OF CONTENTS

Part 1. The Hearsay Definition

Part 2. The Exception for Admissions

Part 3. Hearsay Exceptions That Do Not Require Unavailability

Part 1. The Products of Searches and Seizures

Chapter 1

INTRODUCTION

A. INTRODUCTION

This text illustrates how to apply California evidence law to lay sufficient foundations for the introduction of items of evidence. Most sections of the text use the following format:

- First, you will find a discussion of an evidence doctrine. The discussion focuses on the California Evidence Code, which went into effect January 1, 1967. Since the main purpose of this book is to teach trial technique, rather than evidence law, the discussion is short and contains few case citations. You will find ample case authority in such treatises as B. JEFFERSON, CALIFORNIA EVIDENCE BENCHBOOK (3d ed. 1999) (cited hereafter as JEFFERSON) and B. WITKIN, CALIFORNIA EVIDENCE (3d ed. 1986) (cited hereafter as WITKIN). The discussion refers frequently to the legislative history of the Evidence Code, that is, the California Law Revision Commission, Senate Committee, and Assembly Committee comments on various code sections. Unless otherwise indicated, those comments can be found in the Parker & Sons Publications' version of the Evidence Code.
- Second, you will find the evidence doctrine broken down into a list of foundational elements. These elements are the historical facts and events that constitute the foundation. Each element is numbered.
- Third, you will find a sample foundation for the evidence. Each question in the sample foundation is numbered; the number corresponds to the element of the foundation to which the question relates. Thus, the number will show you how each element converts into concrete questions in the courtroom. In the sample foundations, "J" means judge, "W" means witness, "P" means the proponent of the evidence, "O" means the opponent of the evidence, and "B" means the bailiff or court reporter. The foundations assume that a jury is present. The procedure would be more informal in a bench trial (a trial by judge alone).

B. LAYING A FOUNDATION—IN GENERAL

1. LEGAL RULES

We start with a key procedural rule: The proponent of an item of evidence must ordinarily lay the foundation before formally offering the item into evidence. For example, the proponent of a letter should present proof that the letter is authentic before offering it into evidence. Proof of authenticity is part of the letter's "foundation" or "predicate." The law of evidence makes proof of authenticity a condition to the letter's admission into evidence. Whenever evidence law makes proof of a fact or event a condition to the admission of an item of evidence, that fact or event is part of the foundation for admission of the evidence. California Evidence Code §§ 400-05 use the terms "foundational" or "preliminary" facts.

Ordinarily the proponent must prove all the preliminary facts before the evidence can be admitted. However, California Evidence Code § 320 gives the trial judge discretion to deviate from this rule. The judge may vary the order of proof and admit the evidence subject to subsequent proof of the foundation. There are only two situations in which the judge must require proof of the preliminary facts before admitting the item of evidence. California Evidence Code § 702(a) provides that if the opposing party makes an appropriate objection, the proponent of a lay witness's testimony must *first* prove the witness' personal knowledge of the facts or events about which the witness will testify. Similarly, California Evidence Code § 720(a) specifies that if the opposing party makes an appropriate objection, the proponent of expert testimony must *first* prove that the witness is qualified to testify as an expert.

With those two exceptions, California trial judges have discretion to admit items of evidence before the proponent has proved all the preliminary facts. But judges are understandably reluctant to use this discretion. It is usually more logical to prove the foundation first and then admit the evidence. Moreover, if the judge admits the evidence first subject to later proof of the foundation, the judge is in an awkward position. At the very least, the judge will have to try to "unring the bell" by instructing the jurors to disregard evidence they have already heard. If the judge thinks that an instruction will be ineffective and that the jurors will be unable to ignore the evidence, the judge may have to grant a mistrial. Hence, whenever possible, the proponent should lay the foundation or predicate before formally offering the item of evidence.

2. PRACTICAL RULES

When you draft a line of questioning, you should follow three cardinal rules: be simple, be brief, and be prepared.

First, use the simplest, most easily understood terms you can. *See generally* R. WYDICK, PLAIN ENGLISH FOR LAWYERS 53-64 (3d ed. 1994). As a trial attorney, you must communicate effectively with lay witnesses and jurors. Jonathan Swift condemned the attorneys of his day for using "a peculiar Cant and Jargon of their own that no other mortal can understand. ..." Sadly, many modern trial attorneys commit this literary sin. Even among ordinary words, prefer the simple to the fancy. Do not use "prior" and "subsequent" if "before" and "after" will do the work. Do not use "motor vehicle" if "car" would suffice. Do not use "altercation" if "fight" would do as well. Examining witnesses is a test of your ability to communicate, not your vocabulary.

Second, be brief. Make your questions as short as you can. Rudolph Flesch has pointed out that there is an inverse relation between sentence length and comprehensibility—the longer the sentence, the less likely the reader or hearer will understand. *See* R. FLESCH, HOW TO WRITE PLAIN ENGLISH: A BOOK FOR LAWYERS AND CONSUMERS 20-32 (1979). Experience suggests that in a written passage the *average* length of the sentences should be below 25 words. *See* WYDICK, *supra*, at 33-40. For many people, listening is harder than reading. Thus, some experienced trial lawyers strive to limit the length of their questions to ten or fifteen words. Questions that are longer can be difficult for the witness and the jurors to follow.

Third, be prepared. Both you and your witness must be prepared. If you falter or pause too long, your examination will lose its flow and rhythm. If the witness appears uncertain in answering, the jurors may doubt the quality of the witness' memory. Thus, you should review the contemplated testimony with the witness before trial. You can use the witness' deposition and other pretrial statements to refresh the witness' recollection.

C. LAYING A FOUNDATION ON DIRECT EXAMINATION

The general rules for laying foundations apply to direct examination. The direct examiner should lay a foundation before offering the evidence and should follow the cardinal rules of simplicity, brevity, and preparation. In addition, there are other rules the direct examiner must be familiar with.

1. LEGAL RULES

One such rule is that under the California Evidence Code, the technical rules of evidence do apply to foundational questions. This contrasts with federal practice. Federal Rule of Evidence 104(a) provides: "Preliminary questions concerning ... the admissibility of evidence ... shall be determined by the court. ... In making its determination [the court] is not bound by the rules of evidence except those with respect to privileges." Suppose that the proponent is offering a witness' former testimony given at a prior trial. Part of the foundation for the former testimony exception to the hearsay rule is proof that the witness is now unavailable at the present trial. In federal court, the proponent could ask an investigator on the witness stand to relate a third party's statement that the former witness had moved to Sweden. The third party's statement would usually be inadmissible hearsay; the third party was outside the courtroom when making the statement, and the proponent is offering the statement for the truth of its assertion. However, by virtue of Federal Rule 104(a), the hearsay rule is inapplicable.

The California Evidence Code does not contain a provision like Federal Rule 104(a). The California Supreme Court has not definitively resolved the question, but the consensus is that in California the technical rules such as hearsay do apply. Justice Jefferson takes that position. 1 JEFFERSON § 2.6, at 147. The text and legislative history of the Code support his position. California Evidence Code

§ 454(a)(2) states that when a trial judge is determining the propriety of a judicial notice request, "exclusionary rules of evidence do not apply. ..." That subdivision shows that the drafters knew how to say that they wanted to dispense with the technical evidentiary rules when they meant to, but they did not say it with respect to preliminary fact issues. Further, an early draft of the Code included a provision similar to Federal Rule 104(a), but the California Law Revision Commission deleted it before the legislature acted on the Code. 21 C. WRIGHT & K. GRAHAM, FEDERAL PRACTICE AND PROCEDURE: EVIDENCE § 5055, at 273 n.3 (1977). Hence, if the former testimony hypothetical arose in a California court, the judge should sustain the opponent's hearsay objection to the investigator's testimony about the third party's statement. The proponent cannot use the testimony even to establish a preliminary fact.

A second legal rule to bear in mind is that leading questions are usually forbidden on direct examination. California Evidence Code § 764 defines a leading question as "a question that suggests to the witness the answer that the examining party desires." Since the witness is presumably friendly to the direct examiner, the witness will probably follow the lead. Suppose that the plaintiff's brother was a witness to the accident. The plaintiff alleges that the defendant was speeding. The plaintiff calls her brother as a witness. It would be impermissibly leading for the plaintiff's attorney to ask, "Isn't it true that the defendant was going eighty miles an hour?" There is a serious risk that the witness, the plaintiff's brother, will simply follow the attorney's lead rather than attempt to give the most accurate testimony. On direct examination, the law prefers the attorney to use a nonleading question, such as, "In your opinion, what was the defendant's speed?" California Evidence Code § 767(a) codifies the preference. In pertinent part, that subdivision reads: "Except under special circumstances where the interests of justice otherwise require ... [a] leading question may not be asked of a witness on direct or redirect examination."

Be aware that there are exceptions to the general prohibition of leading questions on direct examination. The Assembly Committee comment to § 767 declares:

> The exception stated at the beginning of the section continues the present law that permits leading questions on direct examination where there is little danger of improper suggestion or where such questions are necessary to obtain relevant evidence. This would permit leading questions on direct examination for preliminary matters, refreshing recollection, and examining handicapped witnesses, expert witnesses, and hostile witnesses.

The California decisions allow leading questions in these and other exceptional circumstances. E. HEAFEY, CALIFORNIA TRIAL OBJECTIONS §§ 13.4-11 (2d ed. 1984) (cited hereafter as HEAFEY).

2. PRACTICAL RULES

Whenever possible, comply with the technical evidentiary rules. Even if the law arguably permits you to depart from those rules in laying a foundation, your departure may prompt an objection. The opponent may not realize that you are correct, or in bad faith the opponent may be searching for a pretext to disrupt your direct examination. The ideal direct examination is flowing and uninterrupted; without distracting objections, the direct examiner gives the witness a chance to tell a coherent story to the jurors. To minimize the risk that the opponent will interrupt your foundation with an objection, follow the technical rules in your foundational questions.

For the same reason, you should use nonleading questions on direct examination. You want to reduce the risk that your foundation will be interrupted by a leading question objection. Moreover, if you have a good witness, you want the witness to do the talking. By using leading questions which must be answered "Yes" or "No," you restrict the witness' opportunity to speak. Worse, the jurors may suspect that you are putting words in the witness' mouth. If the witness projects honesty and intelligence, you want to use open-ended, nonleading questions. The witness should be center stage. Good witnesses can be your most important "exhibits"; to put them on display, you should use openended, nonleading questions.

To ensure that your questions are nonleading, begin as many as possible with the words Who, What, Which, When, Where, How, or Why. These are natural interrogatory words—the words we use in normal conversation to begin a question when we want information but do not know what the answer will be. If you begin a question with one of these words, you will find that it is very difficult to make the question leading. Indeed, many trial judges use the rule of thumb that questions beginning with these words are not leading. In this text, we have tried to begin most questions in the sample (direct examination) foundations with one of these words, printed in capital letters. We hope that reading questions beginning with this kind of word will help you learn to phrase nonleading questions.

But do not begin *every* sentence of direct examination with one of these words. That would make your direct examination annoyingly monotonous. You need variety. When you elicit background information about your witness, you can use imperative sentences; for example, you may command the witness to "Please tell us where you work." To highlight the subdivisions of your direct examination, you may use declarative sentences such as "Now I want to ask you a few questions about what happened at the hospital. " Finally, as we have seen, evidence law sometimes permits you to use gently leading questions on direct examination, and that can add a little variety.

D. LAYING A FOUNDATION ON CROSS-EXAMINATION

You will occasionally encounter a trial judge who believes that an attorney may not introduce an exhibit during the cross-examination of an opposing witness. That belief is erroneous. J. TANFORD, THE TRIAL PROCESS: LAW, TACTICS AND ETHICS 287 (2d ed. 1993). It is true that California Evidence Code § 761 confines cross-examination to matters "within the scope of the direct examination of the witness." But if the exhibit relates to a matter raised on direct examination, "new exhibits properly may be introduced during cross-examination." TANFORD, *supra.* California Evidence Code § 320 gives the judge discretionary control over the order of proof; the permissibility of introducing exhibits during the cross-examination "lies in the discretion of the trial judge." TANFORD, *supra.*

The general rules for laying a foundation apply also on cross-examination, most of them with even greater force. On cross, many judges are reluctant to let the examiner introduce an item of evidence before presenting the foundational proof. The witness is often hostile to the cross-examiner and the judge is more skeptical of the examiner's assurance that the witness will provide the foundation later in the examination. Simplicity and brevity are also vital on cross-examination. The hostile witness will often strain to misinterpret the question. The cross-examiner wants to frame questions that are so clear and so short that they cannot be misinterpreted. In addition to knowing the general rules for laying foundations, the cross-examiner must be cognizant of several special rules.

1. LEGAL RULES

Since the witness is often hostile to the cross-examiner, the law permits leading questions on cross- and recross-examination. California Evidence Code § 767(a)(2) states that "[a] leading question may be asked of a witness on cross-examination or recross-examination."

Although leading questions are permissible on cross, most California trial judges treat argumentative questions as objectionable, as they were at common law. Goff, *Argumentative Questions: Counsel, Protect Your Witness!*, 49 CAL. ST. B.J. 140 (1974). The Code does not specifically forbid argumentative questions. Technically, an objection to an argumentative question invokes the judge's discretionary "control over the mode of interrogation" under Evidence Code § 765. Graham, *California's "Restatement" of Evidence: Some Reflections on Appellate Repair of the Codification Fiasco*, 4 LOY. L.A. L. REV. 279, 282-83 (1971). However, the overwhelming majority of California judges continue to enforce the common-law norm prohibiting argumentative questions. HEAFEY, ch. 14.

An argumentative question is defined as one that challenges the witness about an inference from the facts in the case. Assume that the witness testifies on direct examination that the defendant's car was going eighty miles an hour just before the collision. You want to impeach the witness with a prior inconsistent statement. It would be permissibly leading cross-examination to ask, "Isn't it true that you told your neighbor, Mrs. Ashton, at a party last Sunday that the defendant's car was going only fifty miles an hour?" The cross-examiner may legitimately attempt to force the witness to concede the historical fact of the prior inconsistent statement. Now assume that the witness admits the statement. It would be impermissible argumentative to ask, "How can you reconcile that statement with your testimony on direct examination?" The cross-examiner is not seeking any additional facts; rather, the cross-examiner is challenging the witness about an inference from the facts. Questions such as "How can you expect the jury to believe that?" are similarly argumentative and objectionable. The attorney may argue the inferences during summation or closing argument, but not when questioning witnesses.

2. PRACTICAL RULES

You should avoid argumentative questions for practical as well as legal reasons. If a hostile witness is intelligent, the witness usually will not easily concede the favorable inference you want to draw. An argumentative question may prompt a heated exchange between you and the witness. The lay jurors will probably sympathize with the lay witness, and you may antagonize them by arguing with the witness. Elicit the facts you are certain the witness will concede, but save your inferences for closing argument.

As a general proposition, you should consistently use leading questions on cross-examination. By using narrowly-phrased leading questions, you can virtually testify for the witness. Albert Krieger, the former president of the National Association of Criminal Defense Lawyers, has remarked that under the guise of asking questions, a good cross-examiner actually makes factual assertions and forces the witness to express assent on the record. You ordinarily do not want to give a hostile witness any opening. Do not give that witness an opportunity to explain by asking "Why?" If you want to impeach a witness with a conviction, ask, "Isn't it true that in 1978, a New York court convicted you of perjury,?" If you want to prove a prior inconsistent statement, ask, "Isn't it a fact that right after the fight, you told the officer that the hallway was so dark that you couldn't identify your attacker?" You can preface your questions with "Isn't it true ...?" or "Isn't it a fact ...?" to maintain control over the witness; or you can make a declarative statement and tag a very short sentence such as "Isn't that true?" at the very end of your question.

We have attempted to begin every question in the sample cross-examination foundations with such prefatory language, printed in capital letters. Our purpose is to help you learn to use leading questions on cross-examination. Again, we do not advocate beginning every question with blatantly leading introductory language. Sometimes you will want to use nonleading questions. For instance, you may suspect that an adverse child witness has a memorized story. As the cross-examiner, you might want to pose an open-ended, nonleading question to make the child repeat the story verbatim. In other cases, if the topic is safe, you can use gently leading questions, beginning with Is, Was, or Did. However, the primary failing of neophyte cross-examiners is that they do not lead enough. We have deliberately exaggerated and begun every cross-examination question with blatantly leading language to underscore the importance of maintaining witness control. Exaggeration can be an effective teaching tool.

Finally, remember that your demeanor and tone should ordinarily be friendly, even when you are using narrowly phrased leading questions. You want the opposing witness to cooperate. You will not get that cooperation if your demeanor is combative or offensive. Quite the contrary; if your demeanor is aggressive, the witness will become defensive, and you will have a difficult time eliciting favorable information. You will sometimes want to make a show of righteous indignation at an opposing witness caught in an obvious lie; but especially when you are using the opposing witness to lay a foundation, the wisest tactic is to be friendly and low-key.

Chapter 2

OBJECTIONS AND OFFERS OF PROOF

A. INTRODUCTION

Before you learn how to present evidence, you should learn the opposite—how to keep it out. This chapter discusses: (1) the procedures the opponent uses to object to the admission of the proponent's evidence; and (2) the procedures the proponent uses if the trial judge sustains the opponent's objection. Sections B through E describe the procedures the opponent uses to exclude evidence. Section F illustrates the procedures the proponent uses if the judge sustains an objection by the opponent.

B. PRETRIAL MOTION *IN LIMINE* BY THE OPPONENT

1. THE DOCTRINE

If the opponent anticipates an evidentiary issue that will arise at trial, the opponent need not wait until trial to object. The opponent may object by a pretrial motion *in limine* under California Evidence Code § 402(b). HEAFEY § 1.2. The proponent of evidence may make a motion *in limine* to obtain an advance ruling of the evidence's admissibility, but this kind of motion is more frequently used by the opponent to exclude evidence before the trial begins. For example, the opponent may use the motion to prevent any mention of a civil defendant's liability insurance or a criminal defendant's prior convictions.

There are several tactical reasons why the opponent may employ a motion *in limine*. The most obvious reason is that the objectionable evidence might be highly prejudicial. If the opponent delays objecting until trial, the jurors may hear at least some mention of the evidence, and they may conclude that the opponent is hiding the truth from them. A motion *in limine* precludes the proponent from even mentioning the evidence during trial. Further, the opponent may need an advance ruling to make strategy decisions for trial. Should the criminal defense attorney put the defendant on the stand? If the defendant testifies, the judge may permit the prosecutor to impeach the defendant with prior convictions. But if the judge grants a pretrial motion *in limine* to exclude the convictions, the defense attorney takes no gamble by placing the defendant on the stand. Finally, especially when the attorney is relying on a novel theory to exclude the evidence, making an *in limine* motion can increase the probability that the judge will exclude the evidence because it gives the judge a chance to think through the theory. If the attorney springs the theory on the judge for the first time at trial, the judge will likely reject the theory and admit the evidence. Submitting the motion before trial shows the judge that the attorney has enough confidence in the theory to allow the judge time to think it through.

How does the opponent make a motion *in limine*? As a matter of fairness, the opponent should give advance notice to the proponent, and some judges require it. Some judges also require or strongly prefer that the opponent reduce the motion to writing, but many judges still permit oral motions. The opponent makes the motion either weeks or days before trial, or on the day of trial when the attorneys and the judge meet in the judge's chambers before they walk into open court. The trial judge has discretion whether to entertain the motion; the judge may prefer to rule on the issue during trial. If the judge hears the motion on its merits, there are several possible rulings: (1) The judge may overrule the objection; (2) the judge may forbid the proponent to mention the evidence during the trial; or (3) the judge may enter a preliminary order. A preliminary order prohibits the proponent from mentioning the evidence to the jury without the judge's consent, but it permits the proponent to request a sidebar hearing out of the jury's presence during the trial. At the hearing, the proponent may attempt to persuade the judge to admit the evidence. A preliminary order is appropriate when the judge finds that the evidence is prejudicial, but does not want to rule finally without knowing the final state of the evidence at trial.

In *People v. Collins*, 42 Cal. 3d 378, 722 P.2d 173, 228 Cal. Rptr. 899 (1986), the court held that the denial of a defendant's motion to exclude a prior conviction offered for impeachment is not reviewable on appeal if the defendant does not testify at trial. The defendant based the motion on Evidence Code § 352, and the court reasoned that it could not intelligently apply § 352's balancing test unless it had the benefit of the defendant's actual testimony. The *Collins* court adopted the position taken earlier by the United States Supreme Court in *Luce v. United States*, 469 U.S. 38 (1984). The harm in such cases is purely speculative, making it impossible for the court to weigh the prejudicial effect of any error in denying the motion. *See People v. Rowland*, 4 Cal. 4th 238, 841 P.2d 897, 14 Cal. Rptr. 2d 377 (1992), *cert. denied*, 510 U.S. 846 (1993). In *People v. Renteria*, 6 Cal. App. 4th 1076, 8 Cal. Rptr. 2d 255 (1992), the defendant argued that the *Luce-Collins* rule did not apply because he testified at his first trial. The court could examine the transcript of his prior testimony to determine the effect of the error. The court refused to make this exception, pointing out that the defendant's testimony at the second trial could have varied from prior testimony for any number of reasons. Thus, the harm was still purely speculative. *Id.* at 1082, 8 Cal. Rptr. 2d at 258. In *People v. Washington*, 211 Cal. App. 3d 207, 259 Cal. Rptr. 307 (1989), the trial judge deferred ruling on the defendant's motion to exclude until after the defendant had testified. The court ruled that the deferral did not constitute reversible error. However, the court commented that "this is not the customary practice and in our view should not be encouraged." *Id.* at 214, 259 Cal. Rptr. at 311.

A motion *in limine* can have the effect of a summary judgment on the merits of a case. In *Cottle v. Superior Court*, 3 Cal. App. 4th 1367, 5 Cal. Rptr. 2d 882 (1992), the trial court granted its own pretrial motion *in limine* to exclude all evidence of toxic-tort personal injuries. The motion was made on the ground that no plaintiffs' expert could be found before trial who would testify to any causal link between the toxic waste and the injuries suffered. Thus, plaintiffs could not make a *prima facie* showing of causation. The appellate court invoked the "inherent powers" of a court to control litigation to support the trial court's order. The majority of the appellate court rejected plaintiff's argument that the *in limine* motion was tantamount to a summary judgment on the merits of the case, without following proper summary judgment procedure.

2. ELEMENTS OF A MOTION *IN LIMINE*

The following are the elements of a motion in limine to exclude evidence:

1. The opponent states his or her intent to move in limine to exclude certain evidence.
2. The opponent has reason to believe that the proponent possesses the evidence and will offer the evidence at trial.
3. The opponent briefly states the ground on which the evidence is inadmissible. The opponent must state the ground with the same specificity required for a trial objection. *See* Section C, *infra*.
4. The opponent explains why an ordinary trial objection would not suffice.
5. The opponent presents the legal argument in favor of the motion.

After the proponent's response, the judge rules.

3. SAMPLE MOTION *IN LIMINE*

The fact situation is a tort action.[1] The plaintiff, Mrs. Cantrell, alleges that while she was a guest in a motel owned by the defendant, Hospitality Corporation, she was raped as a proximate cause of the defendant's negligence. Her complaint alleges that she heard a knock on the motel room door. When she asked who was knocking, she heard a muffled voice that sounded like her husband's. When she opened the door for her husband, a rapist forced his way in. The defendant's answer denies any negligence on its part. After the accident, the defendant installed peepholes in the doors of all the units at the motel. The judge has already begun the in-chambers conference before trial. The opponent is the defense attorney.

J   Are there any other matters either of you think we should take up before trial begins?

O   Yes, your Honor. I would like to make a motion *in limine* to absolutely preclude the plaintiff's attorney from mentioning the installation of peepholes in the doors of the motel units after the attack on the plaintiff. (1) About a month ago, we exchanged experts' reports. When I read the report by the plaintiff's safety expert, I noted that he relied on the subsequent installation of the peepholes as one of the bases for his opinion. I assume that the plaintiff is going to attempt to introduce

---

[1]This hypothetical is based in part on the fact situation in Anderson v. Malloy, 700 F.2d 1208 (8th Cir. 1983).

evidence of the installation during the trial. (2) I have given the plaintiff's attorney a week's advance notice of my intention to make this motion. I also gave her a copy of the memorandum of points and authorities, citing the cases I'm relying on as authority.

J (To the plaintiff's attorney) Do you intend to offer evidence about the installation of the peepholes after the attack on your client?

P I most certainly do, your Honor.

O Your Honor, under Evidence Code § 1151 you can't offer evidence of a subsequent repair to prove negligence or fault. (3) We've cited a wealth of authority to that effect in our memo.

J I am familiar with the rule stated in § 1151, but I normally defer ruling on this type of issue until trial.

O I'm aware of that, your Honor. However, I think that you should dispose of this issue before trial begins; a trial objection won't adequately protect my client. Subsequent repair evidence is uniquely prejudicial. If there's any mention of the installation at trial and you ultimately rule the evidence inadmissible, the jurors simply may be unable to follow a curative instruction to disregard the evidence. (4)

P That argument assumes that the evidence is inadmissible, but the truth is that the evidence will be admissible in this case. In our memorandum of points and authorities, we note that the California cases recognize that without violating § 1151, you can offer subsequent repair evidence to prove the feasibility of a safety measure. There's a long line of California authority cited on page three of our memo. The only thing § 1151 forbids is offering subsequent repair evidence to support a generalized inference of negligence or fault. We have here a more specific, alternative theory of logical relevance.

O Your Honor, I want to direct your attention to the last two pages of our memo. I anticipated that the plaintiff's attorney would make this very argument. (5) On pages six and seven, we point out that under California law, you can offer subsequent repair evidence to show feasibility only when there's a genuine dispute over feasibility. Otherwise, the feasibility theory would swallow up § 1151. There's just no issue over feasibility in this case. We certainly don't deny that it would have been physically possible to have installed those peepholes earlier.

P Counsel may claim that they don't deny that now, your Honor, but that was not their position during discovery. I have here a transcript of the deposition of Mr. Hewitt, the defendant's employee who managed the motel in question. On pages fourteen and seventeen of the transcript, he claims that they did everything "humanly possible" to make the motel safe. He used that expression twice during the deposition. Further, he said that peepholes are worthless as a security device; he claimed that they'd only give guests a false sense of security. By saying those things at the deposition, he placed feasibility in issue.

O I can assure you, your Honor, that we don't intend to offer similar testimony at trial. I certainly don't intend to attempt to introduce those passages from Mr. Hewitt's deposition. He may have said that at the deposition, but at the trial there won't be any dispute over feasibility.

J I think that this is an appropriate case for a preliminary rather than an absolute order. I agree that subsequent repair evidence can be prejudicial and that it shouldn't come in unless there's a bona fide dispute over feasibility. However, at this point I don't want to absolutely preclude any use of the evidence; if Mr.

Hewitt gives trial testimony similar to his testimony at the deposition, there may be a genuine controversy over feasibility. Hence, I'm going to enter this preliminary order. I don't want any mention of the subsequent repair in the jury's hearing without my prior permission. (To the plaintiff's attorney) That means that you're not to refer to it during voir dire or opening statement. Further, I want you to caution your witnesses—especially your expert—against volunteering any references to the installation of the peepholes. If at some point during the trial you think that the state of the record demonstrates a genuine issue over feasibility, I want you to request a sidebar conference; out of the jury's hearing, you can make an offer of proof. Then I'll rule on whether you can offer the evidence of the subsequent installation of the peepholes.

C.　OBJECTIONS AT THE TRIAL BY THE OPPONENT

1. THE DOCTRINE

If the opponent does not move *in limine*, or the judge refuses to entertain the motion *in limine*, the opponent must object at trial. The opponent's objection in effect asserts that it is improper to admit the proponent's evidence. The American litigation system is an adversary system; the burden of presenting evidence is on the proponent, and the burden of excluding evidence is on the opponent. In rare cases, an error can be so plain and prejudicial that the judge will exclude the evidence on his or her own motion. However, given our adversary system, the opponent must ordinarily assume the responsibility for excluding evidence by objecting. The courts go to the length of holding that "a party must object at a later trial, though the objection had been overruled at an earlier trial" of the same case. *People v. Neely*, 70 Cal. App. 4th 767, 82 Cal. Rptr. 2d 886, 896, *modified*, 71 Cal. App. 4th 482C (1999).

The general rule requiring objections is subject to three court recognized exceptions. First, if the parties stipulate on the record that the court's denial of an *in limine* motion will be binding at trial, and that the stipulation will be deemed a continuing objection to the evidence, the opponent need not renew the objection at trial; the stipulation will preserve the point for appeal. *People v. Yarbrough*, 227 Cal. App. 3d 1650, 278 Cal. Rptr. 703 (1991). Second, if the pretrial ruling was a binding, statutory ruling—such as a ruling on a motion under § 1538.5 of the California Penal Code—the opponent need not renew the objection at trial to preserve the point for appeal. *See People v. Boyer*, 48 Cal. 3d 247, 768 P.2d 610, 256 Cal. Rptr. 96, *cert. denied*, 493 U.S. 975 (1989). Third, it is unnecessary to make an objection at trial where the motion *in limine* fulfills the requirements of California Evidence Code § 353, that is: The motion is specific, is directed at an identifiable body of evidence, and is made when the judge has adequate time to consider the admissibility of the evidence in context. *People v. Morris*, 53 Cal. 3d 152, 807 P.2d 949, 279 Cal. Rptr. 720, *cert. denied*, 502 U.S. 959 (1991). In other situations, the opponent must object at the trial to preserve the point for appeal. *People v. Jennings*, 46 Cal. 3d 963, 760 P.2d 475, 251 Cal. Rptr. 278

(1988), *cert. denied*, 489 U.S. 1091 (1989). However, the proponent must secure an express ruling on the motion *in limine* in order to preserve the point for appeal. *People v. Ramos*, 15 Cal. 4th 1133, 938 P.2d 950, 64 Cal. Rptr. 2d 892 (1997). In *People v. Williams*, 16 Cal. 4th 153, 940 P.2d 710, 66 Cal. Rptr. 2d 123 (1997), *cert. denied*, 522 U.S. 1150 (1998), the trial court denied defendant's motion *in limine* to exclude evidence of gang membership but promised to hold hearings out of the jury's presence to decide the admissibility of evidence as it was offered at trial. The court's subsequent failure to hold the hearings did not preserve the point for appeal, absent an objection or request for a hearing at trial. The promise to hold the hearings did not bind the court to hold them unprompted by counsel.

An objection must be courteous, timely, and specific. The opponent owes a duty of courtesy to the trial judge. The opponent should stand to state any objection and preface the objection with "Your Honor ...." California Evidence Code § 353(a) provides that an objection must also be "timely." The opponent should state the objection immediately after the improper question and before the witness begins the answer. If an entire line of questioning is improper, the opponent need not object to every question; the Assembly Committee comment to § 353(a) states that "the use of a continuing objection [is] proper. ..." The opponent should ask the court to note a continuing objection to the line of questions. HEAFEY § 4.11.

Finally, an objection must be specific; the opponent must specify both the material that is objectionable and why he or she is objecting. California Evidence Code § 353(a) requires the opponent to designate "the specific ground of the objection. ..." The reason § 353 requires specificity is to enable the proponent of the evidence to cure the asserted defect. *People v. Holt*, 15 Cal. 4th 619, 937 P.2d 213, 63 Cal. Rptr. 2d 782, 813 (1997). No particular form of objection is required, but the objection must be specific enough to alert the trial court to the "nature of the anticipated evidence and the basis on which exclusion is sought," and to afford the proponent an opportunity to establish its admissibility. *Id.* Sufficient specificity of evidence and legal grounds is required for the appellate court to have a record adequate to review for error. *People v. Williams*, 16 Cal. 4th 153, 940 P.2d 710, 66 Cal. Rptr. 2d 123 (1997), *cert. denied*, 522 U.S. 1150 (1998). A party cannot complain on appeal that the evidence was inadmissible for a reason not mentioned in the objection at the trial. *See, e.g., People v. Wheeler*, 4 Cal. 4th 284, 841 P.2d 938, 14 Cal. Rptr. 2d 418 (1992); *People v. Gallego*, 52 Cal. 3d 115, 802 P.2d 169, 276 Cal. Rptr. 679 (1990), *cert. denied*, 502 U.S. 924 (1991). The opponent should identify the objectionable word, phrase, or question. *People v. Dorsey*, 43 Cal. App. 3d 953, 118 Cal. Rptr. 362 (1974), says that the opponent must name the precise element of the foundation that is missing. *See also People v. Wright*, 48 Cal. 3d 168, 189, 768 P.2d 72, 83, 255 Cal. Rptr. 853, 864 (1989), *subsequent op. on reh'g*, 52 Cal. 3d 367, 802 P.2d 221, 276 Cal. Rptr. 731 (1990), *cert. denied*, 502 U.S. 834 (1991) (cites *Dorsey* with approval). Despite *Dorsey*, the better view allows the opponent simply to cite the applicable generic evidentiary doctrine. 1 JEFFERSON § 4.1, at 226-27 (criticizing *Dorsey*). Thus, the opponent can preserve the issue for appeal by stating that the proposed testimony is "not the best evidence" or is "hearsay." In the jury's presence, the opponent can add a word or two, to avoid giving the impression that the opponent is invoking technical rules to hide the truth. For example, the opponent might state that the proponent is "unfairly" leading the witness or attempting to introduce "u n-reliable" hearsay. But the opponent must not make a "speaking objection, " that is, a longwinded speech rather than a brief statement of the legal ground for the objection. Trial judges will not tolerate speaking objections.

If the opponent neglects to make a proper objection, any error in admitting the evidence is generally waived. The opponent cannot rely on that alleged error as a ground for a new trial or a reversal on appeal. The opponent must both object and obtain a ruling on the objection. SeLegue, *Preserving an Objection for Appeal*, CAL. LAWYER 36 (July 1999) (citing *People v. Danielson*, 3 Cal. 4th 691, 13 Cal. Rptr. 2d 1 (1992)). Moreover, a party who objects to evidence under § 352 of the California Evidence Code (discretionary exclusion of relevant evidence) must press the trial judge for a clear ruling. Absent a clear ruling, the party cannot complain on appeal that the trial judge should have excluded the evidence. *See, e.g., People v. Hayes*, 52 Cal. 3d 577, 802 P.2d 376, 276 Cal. Rptr. 874 (1990), *cert. denied*, 502 U.S. 958 (1991); *but see People v. Triplett*, 16 Cal. App. 4th 624, 20 Cal. Rptr. 2d 225 (1993). If the trial judge rules off the record at a sidebar or a chambers conference, "take care to ensure that your objection and the court's ruling get placed on the record." SeLegue, *Preserving an Objection for Appeal*, CAL. LAWYER 36 (July 1999). If the trial judge refuses your request, insert a written "request for ruling" in the record. *Id.* In addition, the otherwise inadmissible material now constitutes "evidence" as defined by California Evidence Code § 140. Since the material is in evidence, the proponent ma y rely on it if the opponent challenges the legal sufficiency of the proponent's evidence to sustain a judgment in the proponent's favor. The California Law Revision Commission's comment on § 140 asserts that "matter which is technically inadmissible under an exclusionary rule is nonetheless evidence and may be considered in support of a judgment if it is ... received ... without proper objection. ..."

2. ELEMENTS OF AN OBJECTION

A proper objection includes the following elements:

1. The opponent addresses the judge.
2. The opponent indicates that he or she is raising an objection.
3. The opponent specifies the objectionable material, i.e., the particular word, phrase, or question.
4. The opponent specifies the legal ground for the objection, that is, the generic evidentiary doctrine the proponent is violating.

3. SAMPLE OBJECTIONS

Some of the opponent's objections will claim violations of substantive evidentiary doctrines. These objections are illustrative.

> Your Honor (1), I object (2) to any testimony by this proposed witness (3) on the ground she is incompetent to be a witness. (4) (*See* Chapter 3, *infra*).

> Your Honor (1), I object (2) to the admission of Exhibit M (3) on the ground that there has been insufficient authentication. (4) (*See* Chapter 4, *infra*).

> Your Honor (1), I object (2) to the admission of that copy (3) on the ground that it is not the best evidence. (4) (*See* Chapter 7, *infra*).

> Your Honor (1), I object (2) to that question (3) on the ground that it calls for improper opinion. (4) (*See* Chapter 8, *infra*).

> Your Honor (1), I object (2) to that question (3) on the ground that it calls for inadmissible hearsay. (4) (*See* Chapter 9, *infra*).

> Your Honor (1), I object (2) to that question (3) on the ground that it calls for a communication protected by the _____ privilege.(4). (*See* Chapter 10, *infra*). *Cf.* C.C.P. §§ 2030(f)(3), 2031(f)(3), 2033(f)(2) (in discovery, a privilege objection must specify the particular privilege relied on).

Most trial objections relate to matters of form rather than of substance. The following are examples of form objections:

> Your Honor (1), I object (2) to that question (3) on the ground that it is vague and ambiguous. (4)

> Your Honor (1), I object (2) to that question (3) on the ground that it is leading.(4)

> Your Honor (1), I object (2) to that question (3) on the ground that it is compound. (4)

> Your Honor (1), I object (2) to that question (3) on the ground that it has already been asked and answered. (4)

Your Honor (1), I object (2) to that question (3) on the ground that it is argumentative. (4)

Your Honor (1), I object (2) to that question (3) on the ground that it calls for a narrative answer. (4)

Chapters 7-16 of HEAFEY compile the case law on form objections.

D.   MOTIONS TO STRIKE AT TRIAL BY THE OPPONENT

1. THE DOCTRINE

In most cases, when the opponent desires to exclude the proponent's evidence, the opponent makes an objection. However, California Evidence Code § 353(a) also permits the use of a motion to strike. In three situations, the opponent must use a motion to strike rather than an objection. The first situation is when the question is proper, but the witness' answer is improper. The second is when the witness answers so rapidly that the opponent does not have a fair opportunity to object. The third is when, after the witness has given apparently proper testimony, it develops that the testimony was improper. For example, on direct examination, the lay witness appears to testify from personal knowledge, but on cross-examination, the witness makes the surprise concession that he was relating what he was told by third parties. In all three instances, the opponent should "move to strike" rather than "object."

Like an objection, a motion to strike must be courteous, timely, and specific. The requirements for objections also applies to motions to strike. If the witness' answer is improper, the opponent should move to strike immediately after the answer and before the next question. If the judge grants the motion, the opponent should then request a curative instruction to disregard; the judge informs the jury that the answer was improper and orders the jurors to disregard the answer. If the witness began the answer before the opponent had a fair opportunity to object to the question, the opponent makes a motion to strike "for the purpose of interposing an objection to the question." If the judge grants the motion, the opponent then objects to the question.

2. ELEMENTS OF A MOTION TO STRIKE

The elements of a motion to strike are roughly the same as those of an objection:

1. The opponent addresses the judge.
2. The opponent indicates that he or she is moving to strike.
3. The opponent specifies what he or she is moving to strike.

4. The opponent specifies the legal ground for the motion.
5. If the judge grants the motion, the opponent requests a curative instruction to disregard.

If the improper material is highly inflammatory, the opponent should seriously consider moving for a mistrial. If the trial judge grants the motion to strike and agrees to give a curative instruction, the opponent should make sure that the trial judge actually remembers to give the instruction. If the opponent fails to remind the judge, he cannot later claim error on appeal. *People v. Heldenburg*, 219 Cal. App. 3d 468, 268 Cal. Rptr. 255 (1990).

3. SAMPLE MOTION TO STRIKE

The fact situation is a burglary prosecution. The defendant has a number of previous burglary arrests. The prosecution witness is the arresting officer. The officer is testifying that he observed the burglary in progress. The proponent is the prosecutor.

P   Officer, WHERE were you when the defendant left the building?
W   I was standing across the street—maybe fifty feet away.
P   WHAT did you observe the defendant do?
W   I saw him place a bag in the truck, look all around, and then enter the truck to start the engine. Knowing the defendant's long arrest record for burglaries, I immediately concluded that he had just completed a burglary.
O   Your Honor (1), I move to strike (2) that last sentence (3) on two grounds. First, the answer is nonresponsive. Second, the answer is clearly improper character evidence. (4)
J   Motion granted. Officer, I want to caution you very strongly just to answer the questions asked.
O   Your Honor, would you please instruct the jury to disregard the answer? (5)
J   Certainly. Ladies and gentlemen of the jury, the officer just made a reference to the defendant's arrest record. I have stricken that statement from the record, and I instruct you to disregard it. The only testimony you may consider is the officer's testimony about what he personally saw the defendant do.

The officer's reference to the defendant's record is so egregiously improper that in this case, the defense attorney should consider moving for a mistrial.

E.   REQUEST BY THE OPPONENT TO TAKE A WITNESS ON VOIR DIRE

1. THE DOCTRINE

There are two types of preliminary facts that condition the admissibility of evidence. One type conditions only the logical relevance of the evidence. For example, if the item of evidence is a letter, one preliminary fact conditioning its admissibility is its authenticity; the letter is inadmissible unless it is authentic. If the letter is not authentic, it has no logical relevance or probative value in the case. When the preliminary fact falls within this category, the judge uses the following procedure. The judge listens to only the proponent's evidence that the preliminary fact exists. Then the judge decides the question of law whether that evidence has sufficient probative value to support a rational jury finding that the fact exists. California Evidence Code § 403(a)(1) provides that "when ... [t]he relevance of the proffered evidence depends on the existence of the preliminary fact, ... the ... evidence is inadmissible unless the court finds that there is evidence sufficient to sustain a finding of the existence of the preliminary fact. ..." Is there enough evidence of authenticity to support a rational finding that the letter is authentic? If there is, the judge admits the letter into evidence. The opponent then offers his evidence negating authenticity. The judge then instructs the jury to decide for itself whether the letter is authentic, and to ignore the letter if they find that it is not authentic.

California Evidence Code § 403(a) states that it applies when "[t]he preliminary fact is the personal knowledge of a witness concerning the subject matter of his testimony [or] ... the authenticity of a writing," and when "[t]he proffered evidence is of a statement or other conduct of a particular person and the preliminary fact is whether that person made the statement or so conducted himself." California Evidence Code § 1222, governing the vicarious admission hearsay exception, extends the § 403 procedure to the preliminary fact that a party to the lawsuit had authorized the hearsay declarant "to make a statement ... for him concerning the subject matter of statement. ..." Likewise, § 1223, controlling the co-conspirator hearsay exception, applies the § 403 procedure to these preliminary facts: that there was a conspiracy, that the defendant and the declarant were conspirators, and that the declarant made the statement in furtherance of the conspiracy.

The other type of preliminary fact conditions the application of doctrines that exclude logically relevant evidence, for example, the best evidence, hearsay, opinion, and privilege rules. These rules exclude relevant evidence either because the evidence presumably is unreliable (such as hearsay) or to promote social policies (such as the protection of privileged communications). If the preliminary fact falls within this category, the judge listens to the preliminary fact evidence on both sides and decides whether the preliminary fact exists. California Evidence Code § 405(a) states that when the preliminary fact falls within this category, the trial judge makes the final decision. Thus, the judge finally decides whether an original document was destroyed, whether an out-of-court declarant was excited when he made a spontaneous statement, whether a witness qualifies as an expert, and whether a communication was intended to be confidential.

When the preliminary fact falls within the second category, the judge must listen to both sides' evidence about the preliminary fact. How does the opponent interrupt the proponent's direct examination to present the contrary evidence? The opponent does so by requesting the judge's permission to take the witness on voir dire. (Voir dire is a French law term that literally means "to speak the truth." In modern usage, it means a preliminary examination of a witness or juror.) In one respect, the voir dire is functionally a cross-examination during the proponent's direct examination; the opponent conducting the voir dire may ordinarily use leading questions. However, the voir dire's limited purpose is to test the competency of the witness or evidence. The voir dire has a narrow scope, and the opponent may not conduct a general cross-examination on the case's merits under the guise of voir dire.

2. SAMPLE REQUEST TO TAKE A WITNESS ON VOIR DIRE

The fact situation is a homicide prosecution. The prosecution witness is an ambulance attendant. The prosecutor hopes to elicit the ambulance attendant's testimony that he heard the victim identify the defendant as the assailant. The prosecutor's theory is that the victim's statement falls within the dying declaration exception to the hearsay rule. The proponent is the prosecutor.

P   WHAT is your occupation?

W   I am an ambulance attendant employed by the emergency ward of General Hospital.

P   WHAT were you doing on the evening of January 19, 1998?

W   I was on duty when we received a call about a shooting at the Senator Hotel downtown.

P   WHAT did you do then?

W   We responded to the call.

P   WHAT did you find when you arrived at the scene?

W   We found Mr. Jones there.

P   WHAT was his condition?

W   He had a very serious gunshot wound. He'd lost a lot of blood. You could hardly make out what he was talking about.

P   WHAT, if anything, did he talk about?

W   He talked about the fight in which he received the wound.

P   WHO did he say had shot him?

O   Your Honor, I object to that question on the ground that it calls for incompetent hearsay.

P   I'm offering it as a dying declaration, your Honor.

O   I request permission to take the witness on voir dire before your Honor rules on my objection.

J   Very well.

O   ISN'T IT TRUE THAT before he died, Mr. Jones said he was going to get the person who had shot him?

W   Yes.

O   ISN'T IT ALSO A FACT THAT he said he wanted to be rushed into surgery as soon as possible?

W   Right.

O Your Honor, the witness' testimony shows that the decedent did not believe that imminent death was certain. The declarant had not abandoned all hope of recovery. For that reason, the dying declaration exception is inapplicable. I renew my objection.

J Objection sustained.

F. OFFER OF PROOF BY THE PROPONENT

1. THE DOCTRINE

Assume that the judge grants the opponent's pretrial motion *in limine* or sustains an objection at trial. The trial judge thus precludes the proponent from pursuing the line of inquiry. What should the proponent do at this point? The answer is that the proponent should make an offer of proof. There are two senses of the expression "offer of proof." The first is the broad, nontechnical meaning; the proponent "offers" proof whenever he or she presents evidence. However, we are now using the expression in the second, technical sense; for the record, the proponent states: (1) what the witness would have testified to, and (2) why the proponent wanted to elicit that testimony. California Evidence Code § 354(a) requires the proponent to ensure that "[t]he substance, purpose, and relevance of the excluded evidence was made known to the court by ... an offer of proof. ..."

Section 354 also lists a number of exceptions to the general requirement. For example, under § 354(a), a formal offer of proof is unnecessary if on its face "the question asked" clearly reveals the substance, purpose, and relevance of the proposed testimony. "For example, in a personal injury matter, no offer of proof was required when a police officer asked if defendant admitted that he did not stop at a stop sign." HEAFEY § 5.7, at 48. Section 354(b) adds that there is no need for an offer if the earlier rulings of the court make an offer "futile." This exception comes into play when the judge makes broad exclusionary rulings barring an entire class of evidence. HEAFEY § 5.6, at 48; *People v. Schmies*, 44 Cal. App. 4th 38 n.9, 51 Cal. Rptr. 2d 185, 195 n.9 (1996); *Castaneda v. Bornstein*, 36 Cal. App. 4th 1818, 43 Cal. Rptr. 2d 10, 16 (1995) ("Where ... an entire class of evidence has been declared inadmissible or the trial court has clearly intimated that it will receive no evidence of a particular type or class or upon a particular issue, an offer of proof is not a prerequisite .... "). Lastly, § 354(c) makes an offer unnecessary when "[t]he evidence was sought by questions asked during cross-examination or recross-examination." Cross-examination is sometimes exploratory, and the cross-examiner may be unable to predict the answer to the question.

Even when one of these exceptions applies, the attorney should ordinarily make an offer of proof. When the proponent makes the offer of proof, it gives the judge a chance to reconsider and to change the ruling. Until the offer of proof, the judge may not have realized where the line of questioning was leading. The offer of proof is also important if there is an appeal. If there is no offer of proof, the appellate court will have a difficult time evaluating the propriety and effect of the judge's ruling. With an offer of proof in the record of trial, the appellate court can better decide whether simply to remand the case or to enter judgment one way or the other. In fact, the courts have held that failing to make an adequate offer of proof precludes appellate review of an exclusion of evidence. *See People v. Hendricks*, 11 Cal. App. 4th 126, 13 Cal. Rptr. 2d 719 (1992); *In re Mark C.*, 7 Cal. App. 4th 433, 8 Cal. Rptr. 2d 856 (1992).

The proponent should make the offer of proof out of the jury's hearing. If the proponent anticipated the unfavorable ruling, the proponent can prepare a written offer of proof for insertion in the record. Otherwise, the proponent usually makes an oral statement at a sidebar conference. If the expected testimony is complex, the proponent may make the offer in question-and-answer form; the proponent actually elicits the testimony from the witness out of the jury's hearing. The judge may insist that the proponent do so if the judge doubts that the witness' testimony will match the proponent's description of it in the offer of proof.

2. ELEMENTS OF AN OFFER OF PROOF

An offer of proof contains the following elements:

1. The proponent asks for permission to approach the bench or for an out-of-court hearing.
2. The proponent states that he or she intends to make an offer of proof.
3. The proponent states what the witness would have testified to if the judge had permitted the proponent to pursue the line of inquiry. "This entails disclosing the specific evidentiary facts to be proved; it is insufficient merely to refer to conclusions, summaries, or ultimate facts." HEAFEY § 5.10, at 50; *People v. Schmies*, 44 Cal. App. 4th 38 n.9, 51 Cal. Rptr. 2d 185, 195 n.9 (1996) ("an offer of proof ... must set forth the actual evidence to be produced and not merely the facts or issues to be addressed and argued"). In the offer, the proponent should predict the witness' probable answer to the question. *United Sav. & Loan Ass in v. Reeder Dev. Corp.*, 57 Cal. App. 3d 282, 129 Cal. Rptr. 113 (1976); B. JEFFERSON, SYNOPSIS OF CALIFORNIA EVIDENCE LAW § 20.1, at 236-37 (1985) (cited hereafter as JEFFERSON SYNOPSIS). *See also People v. Eid*, 31 Cal. App. 4th 114, 36 Cal. Rptr. 2d 835, 841 (1994) (although an offer of proof must be specific, it need not meet the higher standard demanded of a showing of relevancy under Penal Code § 866(a)).
4. The proponent states the purpose for which he or she wanted to offer the testimony. The proponent explains the testimony's logical relevance.
5. If the judge sustained the objection on the ground of a competence doctrine such as hearsay, the proponent explains why the evidence is admissible. The proponent should identify the nonhearsay theory of logical relevance or the pertinent hearsay exception. If the proponent of hearsay evidence fails to inform the court that the evidence falls under a hearsay exception and fails to lay the foundation for that exception, he cannot invoke the exception on ap-

peal. *People v. Livaditis*, 2 Cal. 4th 759, 831 P.2d 297, 9 Cal. Rptr. 2d 72 (1992), *cert. denied*, 507 U.S. 975 (1993).

When you move to sidebar, make certain that the court reporter can hear the conference. Unless the court reporter records the conference, the appellate court will never know what was said. If the excluded evidence is a physical exhibit, the exhibit should be produced, marked for identification, and described fully for the record. HEAFEY § 5.13, at 52.

3. SAMPLE OFFER OF PROOF[2]

The fact situation is a rape prosecution. The defendant denies any intercourse with the alleged victim. The defendant calls Ms. Gerhard as his next witness.

P   WHAT is your name?
W   Jane Gerhard.
P   WHAT is your address?
W   I live at 4502 New Hampshire Street in San Diego.
P   WHAT is your occupation?
W   I am a physician.
P   WHERE did you attend medical school?
W   I attended Stanford Medical School.
P   WHERE are you licensed?
W   In California, New York and Missouri.
P   WHAT, if anything. is your specialty?
W   I specialize in the treatment of venereal disease.
P   HOW many cases of venereal disease have you treated in your practice?
O   Your Honor, I object to this line of questioning on the ground that it is totally irrelevant.
J   I'm inclined to agree. Objection sustained.
P   Your Honor, may we approach the bench? (1)
J   Yes.
P   I would like to make an offer of proof for the record. (2)
J   Very well.
P   If Dr. Gerhard is permitted to testify, she will state that: She examined the alleged victim last week; the alleged victim is now suffering from an advanced state of syphilis chancroids, a venereal disease; at the time of the alleged rape, the disease would have been in a highly infectious and communicable stage; anyone who had intercourse with the alleged victim at that time would probably contract the disease; and the doctor examined the defendant yesterday and found no evidence of the disease. (3) This testimony would be logically relevant to support my client's denial that he had intercourse with the alleged victim. (4)

---

[2]This hypothetical is based on DEPARTMENT OF THE ARMY PAMPHLET 27-10: MILITARY JUSTICE HANDBOOK 205 (1969).

J   Now I can see what you're driving at. I'm going to change my ruling and permit you to pursue this line of inquiry. Now I can see its logical relevance.

P   Dr. Gerhard, let me repeat the question. HOW many cases of venereal disease have you treated in your practice?

Chapter 3

THE COMPETENCY OF WITNESSES

A. INTRODUCTION

Some evidentiary doctrines can keep a prospective witness off the stand alto-gether—they prevent the person from giving any testimony at all. These doctrines govern the competency of the person to be a witness in the case. For example, at common law in some jurisdictions, one spouse is incompetent to testify against the other spouse in a criminal prosecution if the other spouse is the defendant and ob-jects. The defendant spouse can preclude the witness spouse from testifying at all. Even if the witness is competent, other evidentiary doctrines may prevent the wit-ness from testifying to certain facts. Thus, even when the witness spouse is com-petent to testify, he or she may be barred from testifying to privileged, confidential communications with the other spouse. In this chapter, we are concerned with competency doctrines—those that have the more drastic effect of keeping the wit-ness off the stand.

California Evidence Code § 700 announces that "[e]xcept as otherwise pro-vided by statute, every person ... is qualified to be a witness and no person is dis-qualified to testify to any matter." The California Law Revision Commission comment states that § 700 precludes the courts from rendering prospective wit-nesses incompetent on nonstatutory, common-law grounds.

At common law, to prove that the prospective witness is competent, the propo-nent must show that the person possesses the following abilities: (1) to observe—the testimonial quality of perception; (2) to remember—the testimonial quality of memory; (3) to relate—the testimonial quality of narration; and (4) to recognize a duty to tell the truth—the testimonial quality of sincerity. These abilities ensure that the witness' testimony will have at least minimal reliability.

The California Evidence Code modifies the common law. Section 701(a) re-quires that a prospective witness be "[c]apable of expressing himself or herself ... directly or through interpretation by one who can understand him," and § 701(b) adds that the person must be "[c]apable of understanding the duty of a witness to tell the truth." The California Law Revision Commission comment states that § 701 preserves the common-law requirements for proof of the testimonial quali-ties of narration and sincerity and that the trial judge finally decides (under § 405) whether the person possesses these qualities. Thus, cooperating accomplices who have entered into agreements with the prosecution are competent witnesses against a defendant. *People v. Maldonado*, 72 Cal. App. 4th 588, 84 Cal. Rptr. 2d 898 (1999). The agreement might render the accomplice impeachable for bias; but since there is no statute barring the accomplice's testimony, the court cannot for-mulate a common-law competency rule to exclude the testimony.

However, the text of § 701 makes no mention of the testimonial qualities of perception and memory. The next section, § 702, merely demands proof that the witness has personal knowledge of the facts or events he or she proposes to testify about. The Law Revision Commission comment to § 701 explains:

> Section 701 requires the ... [judge] to determine only the prospective witness's capacity to communicate and his understanding of the duty to tell the truth. The missing qualities—the capacity to perceive and to recollect—are determined in a different manner. Because a witness, qualified under Section 701, must have personal knowledge of the facts to which he testifies (Section 702), he must ... have the capacity to perceive and to recollect those facts. But the court may exclude the testimony of a witness for lack of personal knowledge only if no jury could reasonably find that he has such knowledge. See Evidence Code § 403. ... [U]nder the Evidence Code, if there is evidence that the witness has those capacities, the determination of whether he in fact perceived and does recollect is left to the trier of fact. See Evidence Code § 403.

In short, under the California Evidence Code's statutory scheme, the witness must still possess all four qualities. The trial judge finally decides under § 405 whether the person has the qualities of narration and sincerity. But the § 403 procedure applies to the qualities of perception and memory. The Assembly Committee comment to § 405 states that "under this code, the party objecting to a proffered witness has the burden of proving the witness's lack of capacity." *See also Adamson v. Department of Social Services*, 207 Cal. App. 3d 14, 254 Cal. Rptr. 667 (1988). Since competency is in part a § 405 issue, the objecting party has the right to take the witness on voir dire before the judge rules finally on the objection. JEFFERSON SYNOPSIS § 26.2, at 344-45.

Even if the person is competent in the sense that he or she possesses all four qualities, the law may render the person incompetent as a witness. The law may do so to promote some social policy, such as protecting the stability of marriages. As we shall see later in this chapter, to carry out that policy, California law generally allows a married person to refuse to testify in any proceeding to which the other spouse is a party.

How does the opponent challenge the prospective witness' competency? The opponent must object as soon as the person is called to the stand and before the person is sworn as a witness. After objecting, the opponent requests a voir dire of the person concerning his or her qualifications to be a witness. The person ordinarily takes a special oath to answer the voir dire questions about his or her competency. The bailiff or reporter administers this oath: "Do you swear the answers you will give to these questions about your competency to be a witness shall be the truth, the whole truth, and nothing but the truth?"

The judge determines the order of the examinations during voir dire. At the end of the presentation of the evidence, if the judge decides that the person is incompetent, the judge sustains the objection and directs the person to leave the witness stand. If the judge finds the person competent, the judge overrules the objection, and the person then takes the normal oath in the case. Before testifying, every witness must take an oath. *In re Katrina L.*, 200 Cal. App. ad 1288, 1299, 247 Cal. Rptr. 754, 760 (1988). The oath requirement applies even to young children. *Id.*

B.   THE VOIR DIRE OF A CHILD BY THE WITNESS'S PROPONENT

1. THE DOCTRINE

Some jurisdictions use presumptions concerning children's competency to serve as witnesses. For example, the dividing line might be seven, ten, or twelve years of age; if the child is twelve, the child is presumed competent, but if the child is younger, the child is presumed incompetent. The presumption is usually rebuttable; even when the child is presumed incompetent, the proponent may attempt to show that in fact, the child possesses the four requisite qualities.

California has no such presumptions. Evidence Code § 700, as amended in 1985, states that unless otherwise provided by statute, "every person, irrespective of age, is qualified to be a witness. ..." *Adamson v. Department of Social Services,* 207 Cal. App. 3d 14, 254 Cal. Rptr. 667 (1988). The California Law Revision Commission comment on § 701 acknowledged that the statute may permit children of very tender years to testify. The comment approvingly cites the pre-Code decision in *Bradburn v. Peacock*, 135 Cal. App. 2d 161, 164-65, 286 P.2d 972, 974 (1955). That court held that it was error to preclude a child from testifying without conducting a voir dire examination to determine the child's competency.

In most respects, the voir dire of a prospective child witness proceeds in the same fashion as the voir dire of an adult. However, there is one procedural difference. The child need not take a formal oath to testify truthfully about his or her competency; it is sufficient if the child promises not to lie. *People v. Berry*, 260 Cal. App. 2d 649, 67 Cal. Rptr. 312 (1968).

2. ELEMENTS OF THE FOUNDATION

When the opponent challenges the child witness's competency, the proponent must lay a foundation showing that the child possesses the four qualities:

1. The child has the capacity to observe.
2. The child has the capacity to remember.
3. The child has the capacity to relate.
4. The child recognizes a duty to tell the truth.

In *In re Crystal J.*, 218 Cal. App. 3d 596, 267 Cal. Rptr. 105 (1990), a seven-year-old repeatedly stated that he did not know the difference between the truth and a lie. The trial judge ruled the child incompetent as a witness. The appeals court held that the ruling was not an abuse of discretion. The inability at trial to differentiate truth from falsehood relates back to any prior statement sought for use in trial. In *In re Basilio T.*, 4 Cal. App. 4th 155, 5 Cal. Rptr. 2d 450 (1992), a four-year-old child's statements appeared in a social worker's report. This report was relied on at trial, even though the child was judged incompetent as a witness for inability to tell truth from falsehood. The appellate court held that any part of the report relating or relying on the child's statements should have been totally disregarded at trial. *See also Cruetz v. Superior Court (People)*, 49 Cal. App. 4th 822, 56 Cal. Rptr. 2d 870, 873 (1996) (the trial judge properly found that a three-year-old did not satisfy the competency standards set out in Evidence Code § 701).

   In re Nemis M., 50 Cal. App. 4th 1344, 58 Cal. Rptr. 2d 324 (1996) explains that if a witness is found not competent to testify at trial (because of inability to distinguish between truth and falsity, or the like), then that witness's hearsay statements are inadmissible, *unless* the proponent of the hearsay proves that the declarant was competent at the time the hearsay statements were made. In dictum, the *Nemis* court said that this rule does not apply to excited utterances. The court asserted, without benefit of empirical evidence, that the spontaneity of excited utterances gives them credibility, even though the hearsay declarant "might be otherwise incompetent, due to minority or other valid reasons, to testify at trial." *Id.*, 50 Cal. App. 4th at 1353-54, n.8, 58 Cal. Rptr. 2d at 329, n.8. Further, the rule does not apply to hearsay statements that fall within the so-called "child dependency hearsay exception" created in *In re Carmen O.*, 28 Cal. App. 4th 908, 921, 33 Cal. Rptr. 2d 848 (1994) (mentioned in Chapter 9, section Q of this Cumulative Supplement). *Nemis, supra,* 50 Cal. App. 4th at 1353-54, 58 Cal. Rptr. 2d at 329-30. We suspect that the rule would likewise not apply to hearsay statements that fall within California Evidence Code §§ 1253 and 1360, in which the legislature revised and limited the *Carmen O.* exception. *See* Chapter 9, sections M and V.

3. SAMPLE FOUNDATION

   The fact situation is a personal injury action arising from a traffic accident at an intersection. The plaintiff, the proponent, calls a child as a witness. The child witnessed the collision.

P   As his next witness, the plaintiff calls Master James Giannelli.
O   Your Honor, we object to any testimony by this child on the ground that the child is incompetent to be a witness. We request a voir dire examination of the child concerning his competency.
J   Request granted.
P   Your Honor, may I conduct the initial voir dire of Master Giannelli?
J   You may.
P   Master Giannelli, do you promise that the answers you will now give concerning your competency to be a witness will be the truth, the whole truth, and nothing but the truth?
W   I do.
P   WHAT is your name and address?

W My name is Jim Giannelli. I live at 12 Frontage Road in Stockton with my parents.

P James, HOW well do you see? (1)

W I have no problems. I can see real well.

P HOW well do you hear? (1)

W Just great.

P HOW old are you? (2)

W I'm six. I had my birthday last month.

P WHAT day is your birthday? (2)

W It's September 28, just after my mommy's birthday.

P WHERE do you live? (2)

W Like I said, on Frontage Road with my folks.

P HOW long have you lived there? (2)

W Gee. I guess as long as I can remember.

P HOW many brothers and sisters do you have? (2)

W I have one sister.

P WHAT is her name? (2)

W Amy.

P HOW old is Amy? (2)

W She's older than me. She's almost fifteen.

P WHAT school do you go to? (2)

W Horace Mann.

P WHERE is that school located? (2)

W On Fourth Street.

P WHAT grade are you in? (2)

W I'm in the first grade.

P WHO is your teacher? (2)

W Her name is Mrs. Lederer. She's real nice.

P WHAT courses do you take? (3)

W We take arithmetic and English.

P WHAT do you learn in English? (3)

W We learn about words and sentences and stuff.

P WHAT grades do you get in English? (3)

W I do real well. I got an A on the last paper.

P WHAT does "car" mean? (3)

W My dad has one. You drive around in them. They take you places.

P WHAT does "fast" mean? (3)

W Well, when you drive, you should go slow. You can get hurt if you don't go slow, if you go too fast.

P James, WHAT is an "intersection"? (3)

W That's where two streets meet. They sort of come together.

P WHAT is the truth? (4)

W The truth is what really happens—not a story you come up with.

P WHAT is a lie? (4)

W That's when you don't tell the truth.

P WHAT happens when you don't tell the truth. (4)

W Your parents can get real mad at you, and God won't love you.

P HOW do you know that? (4)

W I learned that at Sunday School.

P   WHERE do you go to Sunday School? (4)

W   At our church.

P   WHICH church is that? (4)

W   Holy Comforter on 12th Avenue.

P   WHAT do you learn at Sunday School? (4)

W   We learn that you have to be good. You gotta obey your parents and tell the truth and stuff like that.

P   WHAT is an oath? (4)

W   I promise to tell the truth to the judge.

P   WHAT happens if you don't tell the judge the truth? (4)

W   He can punish you.

P   I have no further questions of Master Giannelli about his competency. Your witness.

O   I have no questions. I renew my objection on the ground that the child is obviously too young to be a witness.

P   Your Honor, I think the child's answers demonstrate the capacities to observe, remember, and relate, and his recognition of a duty to tell the truth.

J   I agree. The objection will be overruled. Please administer the oath to Master Giannelli.

C.   THE OPPONENT'S PRESENTATION OF PSYCHIATRIC TESTIMONY ATTACKING A PROSPECTIVE WITNESS'S COMPETENCY

1. THE DOCTRINE

Trial judges rarely sustain objections to prospective witnesses' competency; a judge will sustain an objection only in an extreme case. For example, even long-term LSD abuse does not necessarily render a person incompetent as a witness. *People v. Eastmon*, 61 Cal. App. 3d 646, 132 Cal. Rptr. 510 (1976). Likewise, even a recent adjudication of incompetency, such as a civil commitment, is not conclusive that a person is incompetent to be a witness. As a practical matter, the opponent needs expert, psychiatric testimony. The objecting party's psychiatrist will have to testify that the person is suffering from a full-fledged psychosis and that the psychosis grossly interferes with one of the testimonial qualities, such as perception or memory. As we have seen, the § 403 procedure applies to the proof of the prospective witness' qualities of perception and memory. Hence, to persuade the judge to rule the prospective witness incompetent for lack of either of those qualities, the psychiatrist's testimony must negate the person's perception or memory as a matter of law. In contrast, the § 405 procedure applies to the prospective witness' narrative capacity and the ability to understand the duty to tell the truth. To persuade the judge to rule the person incompetent for lack of that capacity or that ability, the psychiatrist's testimony merely has to convince the judge as a matter of fact that the person lacks the capacity or ability. For example, in *Stanchfield v. Hamer Toyota, Inc.*, 27 Cal. App. 4th 1495, 44 Cal. Rptr. 2d 565, 571 (1995), the opponent demonstrated that the prospective witness suffered from chronic organic brain syndrome and dementia which caused difficulty with immediate recall and short-term memory, hallucinations, confusion, and confabulation. If a criminal defendant's attorney fails to object to the competency of a witness, the issue is not necessarily waived. One court of appeal has stated that if the record clearly indicates that the witness was incompetent, it is manifestly unfair to uphold a conviction based on the testimony simply because counsel failed to object. *People v. Lyons*, 10 Cal. App. 4th 837, 13 Cal. Rptr. 2d 112 (1992).

2. ELEMENTS OF THE FOUNDATION

The opponent should demonstrate that:

1. The witness is a qualified psychiatrist.
2. The psychiatrist has examined the prospective witness.
3. The prospective witness has certain symptoms.
4. The symptoms lead to the conclusion that the prospective witness is suffering from a psychosis.
5. The psychosis grossly interferes with one or more of the prospective witness's testimonial qualities.

3. SAMPLE FOUNDATION

The fact situation is a rape prosecution. The prosecution calls Ms. Janet Lincoln as a witness. Ms. Lincoln has told the police that she witnessed the rape; her window overlooks the park, and she saw the defendant attack the alleged victim. The defense counsel objects to any testimony by Ms. Lincoln; the counsel contends that she is incompetent to be a witness. The defense counsel has already taken Ms. Lincoln on voir dire.

J   Do you have anything further you'd like to present on the issue of Ms. Lincoln's competency?
O   Yes, your Honor. At this point, I would like to call Dr. Kenneth Rogers.
J   Proceed.
B   Do you swear that the evidence you will give in this case will be the truth, the whole truth, and nothing but the truth? So help you God.
W   I do.
O   WHAT is your name?
W   Kenneth Rogers.
O   WHERE do you live?
W   I reside at 1774 Club Drive in Los Angeles.
O   WHAT is your occupation? (1)
W   I am a physician.
O   WHERE are you licensed to practice medicine? (1)
W   Here in California and New York as well.
O   WHEN did you obtain your license in California? (1)
W   Approximately seventeen years ago.

O   WHAT medical school did you attend? (1)

W   U.C.L.A. I received my M.D. degree in 1970.

O   WHERE did you intern? (1)

W   I interned at U.S.C. Medical Center in California.

O   HOW long did you intern there? (1)

W   Approximately one year.

O   WHAT field of medicine, if any, is your specialty? (1)

W   Psychiatry.

O   WHAT is the subject matter of that specialty? (1)

W   A psychiatrist studies the diseases and disorders of the mind.

O   WHAT special training have you had in psychiatry? (1)

W   I spent three years as a resident in psychiatry.

O   WHERE did you do your residency? (1)

W   At Sutter Memorial in Sacramento.

O   WHAT other special training have you had in psychiatry? (1)

W   I'm a diplomat with the American Board of Psychiatry. I passed the oral and written examinations for the diploma. I've taught psychiatry at two medical schools, and I've written thirteen articles for psychiatric journals.

O   WHO is Janet Lincoln? (2)

W   She's a woman I've had occasion to interview several times.

O   WHY have you interviewed her? (2)

W   One of the local judges, Judge Lopardo, asked me to do so. It was a court appointment.

O   HOW many times did you interview her? (2)

W   Three times.

O   WHEN was the first interview? (2)

W   Approximately three months ago.

O   HOW long did this interview last? (2)

W   Roughly two and a half hours.

O   WHAT was her appearance at the time of the interview? (3)

W   It was rather unkempt. She was rather dirty.

O   WHAT was her general attitude? (3)

W   At first, she seemed rather detached and distant. She became excited and angry whenever I tried to question her about sexual subjects.

O   WHAT, if anything, did she say during the interview? (3)

W   At first she just told me to keep my distance.

O   WHAT did she say then? (3)

W   She said that all men were sex fiends and could not be trusted. She said that as long as she could remember, at least once a day a man had attempted to assault her.

O   HOW would you characterize her statements? (3)

W   They were delusional. A delusion is a belief that a rational person would not entertain under the same circumstances. The person persists in the belief although all the evidence is to the contrary.

O   WHY did she have this belief? (3)

W   She said that voices told her to distrust all men.

O   WHO were the voices? (3)

W   She didn't know.

O   HOW would you characterize those statements? (3)

W They are hallucinations; she has auditory experiences when in fact there is no voice or sound.

O WHAT did you do after you interviewed Ms. Lincoln? (3)

W I tried to gather her history.

O WHAT is a history? (3)

W The background of an illness. You trace it through the years and its various stages.

Q HOW do you customarily gather a history? (3)

A You speak not only with the patient, but with reliable sources such as close family members.

O HOW did you gather Ms. Lincoln's history? (3)

W I spoke with her brother, Vance Lincoln.

O WHO is he? (3)

W He's a certified public accountant in town.

O WHAT was her background or history? (3)

W Evidently she had made numerous rape complaints to the police. In each case, the police or medical investigation had shown the complaint was groundless. She had spent almost a year in a hospital in the East for mental illness. (Vance's statements to Dr. Rogers are being used for a nonhearsay purpose; the doctor is using the statements as part of the basis for his opinion.)

O WHAT did you do then? (3)

W I conducted further interviews with Ms. Lincoln.

O WHAT happened during those interviews? (3)

W She repeated her beliefs. She told me about some incidents in her life—sometimes giving me conflicting stories about the same incident. On several occasions she accused me of making advances toward her. She again became quite restless.

O WHAT, if anything, did you do to lead her to believe that you were making an advance against her? (3)

W Nothing, as far as I could tell. My mere presence seemed to trigger that belief.

O WHAT, if any, diagnosis have you reached of Ms. Lincoln's psychiatric condition? (4)

W I would diagnose her as having a schizophrenic reaction of the paranoid type.

O WHAT does that mean? (4)

W A schizophrenic person has a sort of split personality. Schizophrenics live in two worlds—one the world of fantasy, the other the world of reality. They have lost contact with reality to a severe extent. Ms. Lincoln's disorder manifests itself in paranoid beliefs that men are persecuting and constantly attacking her.

O WHAT leads you to this diagnosis? (4)

W The irrational content of her statements, for one thing. I also consider her appearance and attitude. Finally, I attach particular importance to her delusions and hallucinations. Her history confirms the diagnosis.

O Dr. Rogers, in this case Ms. Lincoln wants to testify about a sexual assault she allegedly observed. WHAT effect, if any, would her psychosis have on her ability to accurately obscene an encounter between a man and a woman? (5)

W The psychosis grossly interferes with that capacity. She sees things that didn't really happen—just as she hears voices when they're not there. Every male-female encounter tends to become an assault in her mind.

O WHAT effect, if any, would her psychosis have on her ability to accurately remember a male-female encounter she had observed? (5)

W It's going to severely distort the memory process. A psychosis of this magnitude is going to attack her abilities to perceive and remember. Her purported recollections will be untrustworthy. In the process of remembering, she'll add assaultive aspects to the encounter.

O Thank you, Doctor. Your witness.

After the prosecutor's cross-examination of Dr. Rogers, the judge would rule on Ms. Lincoln's competency as a witness.

D. THE OPPONENT'S ATTACK ON THE COMPETENCY OF A WITNESS WHOSE MEMORY HAS BEEN ENHANCED BY TRUTH SERUM OR HYPNOSIS

1. THE DOCTRINE

Psychiatrists sometimes use so-called "truth serum," such as sodium pentothal or sodium amytal, to help patients recover repressed memories. During a sodium amytal interview the patient is injected with sodium amytal, a drug that breaks down inhibitions and theoretically allows the patient to answer questions more freely and truthfully. While this may be useful in a therapeutic setting, it is not as useful as a truth-finding device in a legal setting. Sodium amytal puts some patients in highly suggestible state, while others have been able to lie under the drug's influence. *Ramona v. Superior Court*, 57 Cal. App. 4th 107, 66 Cal. Rptr. 2d 766 (1997). It has long been established that any statements made during a sodium amytal interview are inadmissible as a matter of law because, when used as a truth-seeking device, the sodium amytal interview cannot satisfy California's standards for scientific evidence, the so-called *Kelly-Frye* standard, discussed at pages 106-22 of the text. *See Romona,* 57 Cal. App. 4th at 116; *People v. Johnson*, 32 Cal. App. 3d 988, 109 Cal. Rptr. 118 (1973).

In *Ramona*, 57 Cal. App. 4th 107, the court addressed the competency of a witness in a civil trial who had undergone a sodium amytal interview to recover memories of childhood sexual abuse. One issue was the reliability of memories recovered after the interview. Experts testified that memories recovered after a sodium amytal interview were "inherently untrustworthy and unreliable" and subject to contamination. *Id.* at 124. The court found the witness not competent to testify to any memories relating to sexual abuse recovered after the interview, including the "flashbacks" she experienced two years later. *Id.*

Before the sodium amytal interview, the witness had related experiences of "flashbacks" or "visual flashes" of sexual abuse, but she was not certain if they were true memories. In fact, her uncertainty led her to undergo the sodium amytal interview. *Id.* at 111. Because she did not believe that the events in the flashbacks had actually occurred until after the interview, the court held that the witness was not competent to testify to those incidents. *Id.* at 122. She lacked the personal knowledge required by § 702.

During the 1970s, law enforcement agencies throughout the United States began using hypnosis to enhance the memory of eyewitnesses to crimes. The observation of a crime can be a traumatic event. If, for example, a witness has witnessed a brutal attack, the natural tendency is to repress the memory. To overcome that tendency and help eyewitnesses recall relevant details, such as license numbers, law enforcement agencies began using hypnotists to counteract the repression. In addition, some agencies hired hypnotists to train police officers to hypnotize eyewitnesses to increase the witnesses' recall. This practice was very controversial and divided the courts.[1] There are scientific questions about the reliability of hypnotically enhanced memory. Moreover, there is some evidence that after hypnosis, the witness has greater confidence in the quality of his or her memory and may, therefore, be less vulnerable to effective cross-examination.

The issue came to a head in California when the California Supreme Court decided *People v. Shirley*, 31 Cal. 3d 18, 181 Cal. Rptr. 243, 641 P.2d 775 (1982). In *Shirley*, the court came close to holding that after hypnotic enhancement, the eyewitness to a criminal event is completely incompetent to testify at the subsequent trial. The court generally barred testimony by eyewitnesses who had undergone hypnosis. The court expressly recognized only one exception: "[I]f the prosecution should wish to question such a witness on a topic wholly unrelated to the events that were the subject of the hypnotic session, his testimony as to that topic would not be rendered inadmissible by the present rule."

In 1984, the California legislature partially overturned *Shirley*. 2 WITKIN § 900, at 862-63. The legislature enacted California Evidence Code § 795 to allow an eyewitness to testify about facts and events that the eyewitness recalled even before the hypnotic session:

Testimony of Hypnosis Subject; Admissibility; Conditions

(a) The testimony of a witness is not inadmissible in a criminal proceeding by reason of the fact that the witness has previously undergone hypnosis for the purpose of recalling events which are the subject of the witness's testimony, if all of the following conditions are met:

(1) The testimony is limited to those matters which the witness recalled and related prior to the hypnosis.

(2) The substance of the prehypnotic memory was preserved in written, audiotape, or videotape form prior to the hypnosis.

(3) The hypnosis was conducted in accordance with all of the following procedures:

---

[1] In Rock v. Arkansas, 483 U.S. 44 (1987), the United States Supreme Court considered the admissibility of testimony by a defendant whose memory had been hypnotically enhanced. The state court had applied a per se exclusionary rule and barred the defendant from testifying. The Supreme Court reversed. The Court held that the bar violated the defendant's constitutional right to testify. The Court added, however, that a state would be well within its power if it established guidelines to aid trial courts in evaluation of posthypnosis testimony, and that it may be able to show that testimony in a particular case is so unreliable that exclusion is justified.

(A) A written record was made prior to hypnosis documenting the subject's description of the event, and information which was provided to the hypnotist concerning the subject of the matter of the hypnosis.

(B) The subject gave informed consent to the hypnosis.

(C) The hypnosis session, including the pre- and posthypnosis interview, was videotape recorded for subsequent review.

(D) The hypnosis was performed by a licensed medical doctor, psychologist, licensed clinical social worker, or a licensed marriage, family and child counselor experienced in the use of hypnosis and independent of and not in the presence of law enforcement, the prosecution, or the defense.

(4) Prior to admission of the testimony, the court holds a hearing pursuant to Section 402 of the Evidence Code at which the proponent of the evidence proves by clear and convincing evidence that the hypnosis did not so affect the witness as to render the witness's prehypnosis recollection unreliable or to substantially impair the ability to cross-examine the witness concerning the witness's prehypnosis recollection. At the hearing, each side shall have the right to present expert testimony and to cross-examine witnesses.

(b) Nothing in this section shall be construed to limit the ability of a party to attack the credibility of a witness who has undergone hypnosis, or to limit other legal grounds to admit or exclude the testimony of that witness.

Section 795 mandates the use of safeguards initially proposed by Dr. Martin Orne, one of the leading authorities in the field of hypnosis. Even before the California legislature's enactment of § 795, the safeguards had been approved by the New Jersey Supreme Court in *State v. Hurd*, 86 N.J. 525, 432 A.2d 86 (1981). Dr. Orne first proposed the safeguards in an amicus curiae affidavit filed in *Quaglino v. California*, 23 Crim. L. Rep. (BNA) 4018 (Cal. App. 1977), *cert. denied*, 439 U.S. 875 (1978).

Section 795 differs from the normal competency rules in an important procedural aspect. Usually the opponent has the burden of proving the incompetency of a prospective witness. However, § 795 allocates the burden to the proponent who claims that the eyewitness is competent even though the eyewitness has undergone hypnotic enhancement; the wording of § 795(a) states that the witness' testimony is "not inadmissible ... if all of the following conditions are met. ..." Thus, § 795(a) requires the proponent to establish the witness' competency. Section 795 became effective on January 1, 1985, and it operates prospectively only. *People v. Hayes*, 49 Cal. 3d 1260, 783 P.2d 719, 265 Cal. Rptr. 132 (1989). By its terms, § 795 applies only to criminal cases. However, *Shirley* still governs in civil actions. *Schall v. Lockheed Missiles & Space Co.*, 37 Cal. App. 4th 1485, 44 Cal. Rptr. 2d 191 (1995).

2. ELEMENTS OF THE FOUNDATION

Under § 795, the proponent of a witness who has undergone hypnotic enhancement must prove that:

1. The witness remembered some facts or events even before the hypnotic session.
2. The substance of the witness's prehypnotic memory was "preserved in written, audiotape, or videotape form prior to the hypnosis."
3. The witness gave informed consent to the hypnotic session.
4. The session was conducted by a qualified hypnotist.
5. The entire session, including pre- and post-hypnosis interviews, was videotaped.
6. During the session, the hypnotist did not use any techniques or make any suggestions that would "render the witness's prehypnosis recollection unreliable or to substantially impair the ability to cross-examine the witness concerning the witness's prehypnosis recollection."

3. SAMPLE FOUNDATION

The fact situation is a rape prosecution. Allen Furnish, the defendant, is charged with raping Beverly Nunez on December 13. The prosecution intends to call Ms. Nunez as a witness at the trial of the rape case. The defense has made a pretrial motion *in limine* to exclude her testimony. At the hearing on the motion, the prosecutor calls both Ms. Nunez and Dr. Lance Garibaldi.

P   Please state your full name and spell your last name for the record.

W   My name is Beverly Nunez. My surname is spelled N-U-N-E-Z.

P   Ms. Nunez, WHAT happened to you on the evening of December 13 of last year?

W   I was raped.

P   Immediately after the rape, HOW well could you remember all the facts about the rape?

W   I could remember some of them, but I was very vague on others. It was a terrible experience. The truth is that I really wanted to forget as much about that night as possible.

P   WHICH facts could you remember about the event? (1)

W   I remembered the date, the time, the place, and some details about the rapist's appearance.

P   HOW well did you remember those details? (1)

W   I knew them well enough to tell them to the police right after the rape.

P   WHAT, if anything, did the police have you do after you told them those details? (2)

W   They asked me to write them down, so it would be clear to everyone that I remembered those facts immediately after the rape.

P   Your Honor, I request that this be marked People's Exhibit #1 for identification.

J   It will be so marked.

P   Please let the record reflect that I am showing the exhibit to the defense attorney.

J   The record will so reflect.

P   Permission to approach the witness.

J   Granted.

P   Ms. Nunez, I now hand you what has been marked as People's Exhibit #1 for identification. WHAT is it? (2)

W   It's the statement that I gave the police right after the rape.

P   HOW can you recognize it? (2)

W   It's in my own handwriting.

P   WHAT information did you include in that statement? (2)

W   Everything that I could remember at that time about the rape.

P   Your Honor, I now offer People's Exhibit #1 for identification into evidence for the nonhearsay purpose of showing the extent of the witness' prehypnotic memory.

J   (To the defense attorney) Any objection?

O   No, your Honor.

P   Ms. Nunez, WHAT, if anything, did the police suggest that you do to remember some of the other facts about the rape? (3)

W   They suggested that I undergo hypnosis. They told me that sometimes that helped people remember details about traumatic events.

P   HOW did you react to that suggestion? (3)

W   I said that I would agree to that. I certainly wanted to help them track down the rapist.

P   WHAT happened next? (3)

W   The police introduced me to a Dr. Garibaldi, a psychiatrist who uses hypnotism in his practice.

P   WHAT did Dr. Garibaldi tell you? (3)

W   He asked me whether I would agree to undergo hypnosis. He said that he wouldn't do it unless he was certain he had my consent.

P   WHAT did you say to Dr. Garibaldi? (3)

W   I assured him that I consented.

P   Your Honor, I request that this be marked People's Exhibit #2 for identification.

J   It will be so marked.

P   Your Honor, please let the record reflect that I am showing this exhibit to the defense attorney.

J   The record will so reflect.

P   Permission to approach the witness?

J   Granted.

P   Ms. Nunez, I now hand you what has been marked as People's Exhibit #2 for identification. WHAT is it?

W   It's the consent form that Dr. Garibaldi had me sign.

P   HOW can you recognize it? (3)

W   That's my signature, there at the bottom.

P   Your Honor, I now offer People's Exhibit #2 for identification into evidence as People's Exhibit #2.

J   (To the defense attorney) Any objection?

O   None, your Honor.

J   It will be received.

After the defense's cross-examination of Ms. Nunez, the prosecutor would call Dr. Garibaldi as the next witness. The early phase of Dr. Garibaldi's direct examination would be almost identical to the early part of Dr. Rogers' direct examination in the sample foundation in Section C of this chapter. The early phase of the direct examination would establish that Dr. Garibaldi is a licensed physician practicing psychiatry. The direct examination would then continue:

P Doctor, WHAT training, if any, do you have in the use of hypnosis? (4)

W Extensive training.

P WHERE did you obtain this training? (4)

W As I mentioned earlier, I took my residency at the University of Pennsylvania. There I worked with Dr. Martin Orne, one of the world's leading authorities on the subject. I worked very closely with him.

P WHAT practical experience, if any, do you have in using hypnosis? (4)

W I use it regularly in my practice. Many times the root of a patient's psychiatric problem is the memory of an event—perhaps an event from childhood—that the patient has repressed. The memory was so painful that the person tries to get it out of their conscious mind.

P HOW do you use hypnosis in treating that type of patient? (4)

W You can employ hypnosis to overcome the repression. The hypnosis helps the patient remember the event. Once you have the event out in the open, you're in a much better position to diagnose and treat the patient.

P WHAT application does hypnosis have to police investigations? (4)

W You can use the same technique by analogy. Sometimes the witnesses to crimes repress the memory. You can use hypnosis to help them get over that problem and remember facts and details that would be helpful to the police in their investigation.

P Doctor, WHERE were you on the afternoon of December 17 of last year? (3)

W I was in my office.

P WHAT happened that afternoon? (3)

W I got a call from the local police department here in San Jose.

P WHAT did the call concern? (3)

W They wanted me to come down and meet a Ms. Nunez.

P WHY did they want you to meet her? (3)

W They described a rape victim who was having the typical difficulty remembering details about the rape.

P WHAT did they ask you to do? (3)

W They wanted me to talk to her to see if she would agree to undergo hypnosis to help her remember facts that would help them identify the rapist.

P WHAT did you do? (3)

W I agreed to help and went right down to the police station.

P WHAT happened when you arrived there? (3)

W I met Officer Larson first, and then she introduced me to Ms. Nunez.

P WHERE is Ms. Nunez now? (3)

W She's in the courtroom. She testified just before I did.

P WHAT, if anything, did you say to Ms. Nunez? (3)

W I identified myself and explained that I'm a physician practicing psychiatry. I also tried to explain how hypnosis might help her recall some facts about the rape. I asked her point blank whether she would agree to undergo hypnosis for that purpose.

P HOW did she respond? (3)

W She said fine.

P I now hand you what has previously been admitted as People's Exhibit #2. WHAT is it? (3)

W It's her informed consent form.

P HOW do you recognize it? (3)

W It's the standard form that I've developed for use in my office, and I also can generally recognize her signature on it. I saw her sign it.

P HOW long did this initial meeting with Ms. Nunez last?

W About an hour.

P WHAT notes, if any, did you make during the meeting? (5)

W None.

P WHY not? (5)

W There was no need.

P WHY wasn't there any need? (5)

W The standard procedure at that police station is to videotape every contact between the hypnotist and the eyewitness.

P HOW do you know that? (5)

W I've worked with the department before, and in particular I've viewed the tapes of all my sessions with Ms. Nunez.

P HOW much of each session was videotaped? (5)

W Every bit of it.

P WHAT did you do after Ms. Nunez consented to the hypnotic session? (6)

W After ensuring the videotape was set up, I took her into an interview room and actually conducted the session.

P WHO else was present in the room? (6)

W No one else. Just Ms. Nunez and myself.

P HOW did you induce her hypnosis? (6)

W I used relaxation and trance-inducing techniques I learned from Dr. Orne.

P HOW well did they work? (6)

W Very well. She was an excellent subject. After about fifteen minutes, I was confident that she was relaxed and in a hypnotized state.

P WHAT did you do then? (6)

W I questioned her about the rape.

P WHAT did you ask her about? (6)

W First I reviewed with her the facts and details that she remembered after the rape.

P WHAT did you do then? (6)

W Next I moved to the subjects she was having difficulty remembering.

P During this questioning period, HOW did you phrase the questions that you asked her? (6)

W I made a conscious effort to use open-ended, nonleading questions that wouldn't suggest any answers to her.

P WHY did you do that? (6)

W A person in a hypnotic state can be highly suggestible. I wanted to make certain that I got her memory and that I wasn't suggesting any answers to her.

P WHAT suggestions, if any, did you make to her about the rape? (6)

W None.

P WHAT suggestions, if any, did you make to her about her ability to remember facts about the rape? (6)

W None. I always asked her whether she could remember. I never told her or assured her that she could remember before I tried to question her about a detail. If you do that, you put the person under subtle pressure to make up facts even if they can't honestly remember.

P WHAT notes did you make during this session with Ms. Nunez? (5)

W None.

P WHY not? (5)

W Again, because everything was videotaped. I saw them set up the videotape, and since then I've reviewed all the tapes to ensure that they're complete and accurate.

P WHAT other meetings, if any, did you have with Ms. Nunez? (5)

W Really none. After I brought her out of the hypnotic state, we chatted briefly; but I didn't see her again until today when I came to court.

P WHAT notes did you make of that chat? (5)

W I didn't make any because, like every other contact I had with her, the whole thing was videotaped.

P HOW do you know that? (5)

W I've also viewed that tape.

E. THE SPOUSE WITNESS PRIVILEGE

1. THE DOCTRINE

California Evidence Code § 970 establishes one branch of California's spouse witness privilege: "[e]xcept as provided by statute, a married person has a privilege not to testify against his spouse in any proceeding." California Evidence Code § 971 establishes the second branch of the spouse witness privilege:

> [e]xcept as otherwise provided by statute, a married person whose spouse is a party to a proceeding has a privilege not to be called as a witness by an adverse party to that proceeding without the prior express consent of the spouse having the privilege under this section unless the party calling the spouse does so in good faith without knowledge of the marital relationship.

Note that the holder of spouse witness privilege is the spouse who would be testifying (the "witness spouse"), not the spouse against whom the testimony would be given (the "other spouse").

Unless erroneously compelled to testify, the witness spouse waives the privilege by either (1) testifying *against* the other spouse, or (2) if the other spouse is a party, testifying either *for or against* the other spouse. *See* California Evidence Code § 973(a). A waiver at one stage of a proceeding prevents the witness spouse from claiming the privilege at a subsequent stage of that proceeding. Thus, if a wife willingly testifies at her husband's preliminary hearing, she cannot later claim the privilege and refuse to testify at his trial—and that is true even if she was never informed about the privilege or about waiver. *See People v. Resendez*, 12 Cal. App. 4th 98, 15 Cal. Rptr. 2d 575 (1993).

California Evidence Code §§ 972 and 973(b) list a great many exceptions to the spouse witness privilege. For example, the privilege does not apply in the following kinds of cases:

- A proceeding brought by or on behalf of one spouse against the other spouse;
- A civil case brought or defended by one spouse for the immediate benefit of the other spouse or both spouses;
- A proceeding to have one of the spouses committed because of a mental or physical condition;
- A criminal case in which a spouse is charged with a crime against the other spouse or a child, parent, relative, or cohabitant of either spouse;
- A criminal case in which a spouse is charged with bigamy; or
- A criminal case in which a spouse is charged with child neglect or spousal neglect.
- A proceeding arising from a crime that occurred before the spouses where married if the witness spouse learned two things before the marriage: (1) the witness spouse learned about the crime, and (2) the witness spouse learned that the other spouse had been arrested for or charged with the crime.

2. ELEMENTS OF THE FOUNDATION

Even though the holder of the privilege is the witness spouse, the matter is usually called to the court's attention by the other spouse. The other spouse must show that:

1. The witness spouse and the other spouse are married. Cohabitation is insufficient. *People v. Delph*, 94 Cal. App. 3d 411, 156 Cal. Rptr. 422 (1979). However, if there was a ceremonial marriage, the marriage is rebuttably presumed valid under California Evidence Code § 663. A marriage is presumed valid even when it is a second marriage; the court will presume that the first marriage was dissolved. 2 JEFFERSON § 46.3, at 1707-08 (2d ed. 1982).
2. The marriage is still in existence.
3. The witness spouse claims the privilege.

The party who calls the witness spouse to testify must lay a foundation to prove a waiver by the witness spouse or to trigger an exception to the privilege. If the witness spouse claims that the exception does not apply, or that he or she did not waive the privilege, the witness spouse carries the burden of proving the facts that show nonwaiver or inapplicability of the exception. *See People v. Resendez*,

12 Cal. App. 4th 98, 15 Cal. Rptr. 575 (1993). For purpose of the sample foundation, assume that the proponent is attempting to establish that

4. The witness spouse was the victim of the crime with which her spouse is charged (*see* Evidence Code § 972(e)(1)).
5. The witness spouse's expected testimony relates to an event occurring before the marriage (*see* Evidence Code § 972(f)).

3. SAMPLE FOUNDATION

The fact situation is a criminal prosecution. George Nerney, the defendant, is charged with two offenses. The indictment first alleges that on January 12 of this year, the defendant committed a battery against Grenda Kuhns. The second count of the indictment alleges that on July 1 of this year, the defendant committed a battery against Susan Grace. The proponent of the witness is the prosecutor.

P   As their next witness, the People call Ms. Susan Grace.
O   Your Honor, we believe that this witness is incompetent to testify in this case. We would like an out-of-court hearing to determine the witness' competency.
J   Certainly.
J   (To the jurors) Ladies and gentlemen of the jury, the bailiff is going to escort you to the jury room for a few moments while the attorneys and I discuss a matter. (The jurors leave the courtroom.)
O   Your Honor, I object to any testimony by this witness. The witness is married to my client, and I believe that under Evidence Code § 971 this witness refuses to consent to testify in this proceeding. May I voir dire the witness?
J   You may.
O   Ms. Grace, ISN'T IT A FACT THAT in March of this year, you married a George Nerney? (1)
W   Yes.
O   ISN'T IT A FACT THAT George Nerney is the defendant in this case, seated at this table? (1)
W   Yes.
O   ISN'T IT CORRECT THAT there has been no divorce proceeding since the marriage? (2)
W   Yes.
O   Ms. Grace, ISN'T IT TRUE THAT there hasn't been any annulment proceeding since the marriage? (2)
W   Yes.
O   ARE you aware that since your husband is the defendant in this case, you have the right to refuse to testify for the prosecution?
W   Yes.
O   DO you want to testify for the prosecution in this case?
W   Certainly not.
O   Your Honor, I have no further questions.
P   Your Honor, may I voir dire Ms. Grace?
J   Yes. Proceed.

P   WHEN did you marry the defendant? (5)

W   On March 7 of this year.

P   WHO is Grenda Kuhns? (5)

W   She's a desk clerk at a hotel in a town which the defendant and I once visited.

P   WHEN did you visit that hotel? (5)

W   In early January of this year.

P   WHAT, if anything, happened between the defendant and Ms. Kuhns? (5)

W   Unfortunately, they got into an argument, and the defendant punched Ms. Kuhns.

P   WHICH came first—the defendant's argument with Ms. Kuhns or your marriage to the defendant? (5)

W   The argument with Ms. Kuhns. It came first by several months.

P   WHEN did you learn that the defendant had been charged with battering Ms. Kuhns? (5)

W   It was later in the same week as his argument with Ms. Kuhns.

P   WHEN did you learn that the defendant had been arrested on that charge? (5)

W   Again, the same week.

P   WHICH came first—your knowledge of the defendant's arrest or your marriage to the defendant? (5)

W   I learned of the arrest several months before I married the defendant.

P   WHAT, if anything, happened on July 1 of this year? (5)

W   That's when George and I had an argument.

P   WHAT happened during the argument? (4)

W   He slashed me with a knife. He just lost his head.

P   WHOM did he slash? (4)

W   Me.

P   WHO else was involved in this argument? (4)

W   No one else. I was the only other person there, and I was the only one George attacked.

P   Thank you, Ms. Grace. Your Honor, this voir dire examination demonstrates that Ms. Grace is competent to testify about both counts in the indictment. The first count alleges a battery that occurred before her marriage to the defendant. In the second count, she is the victim, and the injured spouse exception obviously applies. The marital privilege does not preclude Ms. Grace from testifying about either count. California Evidence Code § 972(f) applies to the first count, and § 972(e)(1) applies to the second count.

J   I concur. Objection overruled. You may administer the oath to the witness.

F.   JUDGES AND JURORS

1. THE DOCTRINE

Suppose that during the trial, an attorney calls the presiding judge as a witness. At first blush, it might seem obvious that the judge should be incompetent as a witness. The judge is certainly in an awkward position; if there are objections to the questions posed to the judge or motions to strike the judge's answers, the judge must rule on the objections and motions. The jurors may be unsure how much weight to attach to the judge's testimony. Further, the opposing attorney may be reluctant to conduct an aggressive cross-examination. Yet surprisingly, the common-law rule was that the judge is a competent witness.

The drafters of the California Evidence Code have substantially revised the common-law rule. The initial revision occurred in 1965, when the legislature approved Evidence Code § 703. Under § 703(a), when it becomes apparent that the judge may be called as a witness, the judge "shall, in proceedings held out of the presence and hearing of the jury, inform the parties of the information he has concerning the fact or matter about which he will be called to testify." Once the judge discloses the information to the parties, two things can happen. On the one hand, a party may object. When there is an objection, § 703(b) controls. That subdivision states that "[u]pon ... objection, the judge shall declare a mistrial and order the action assigned for trial before another judge. " Subdivision (c) explains the consequences in greater detail. By calling the judge, the proponent is deemed to consent to a mistrial; and by objecting, the opponent is deemed to move for a mistrial. Thus, in a criminal case, double jeopardy will not bar a retrial. On the other hand, all parties may decide against objecting. In that event, § 703(d) governs. That subdivision explains that absent an objection, "the judge presiding at the trial of an action may testify in that trial as a witness." The Assembly Committee comment to § 703 points out that the drafers purposefully included the verb "may" in § 703(d): "[I]f no party objects, the judge is permitted—but not required—to testify."

In 1979, the legislature further revised the common-law rule by adding California Evidence Code § 703.5. Section 703.5 states that

> [n]o person presiding at any judicial ... proceeding shall be competent to testify, in any subsequent civil proceeding, as to any statement or conduct occurring at the prior proceeding, except as to a statement or conduct that could (a) give rise to civil or criminal contempt, (b) constitute a crime, (c) be the subject of investigation by the State Bar or Commission on Judicial Performance, or (d) give rise to disqualification under paragraph (1) or (6) of subdivision (a) of Section 170 of the Code of Civil Procedure.

While § 703 generally renders the judge incompetent as a witness in any case over which the judge is then presiding, § 703.5 severely limits the judge's competency in "any subsequent civil proceeding."

Just as the appearance of the presiding judge as a witness can make it difficult to conduct a fair trial, the appearance of a sitting petit juror as a witness threatens the fairness of the proceeding. Again, the jurors may find it difficult to weigh the testimony, and the opposing attorney will be reluctant to cross-examine vigorously. For those reasons, the California Evidence Code includes § 704, governing jurors' competency. It is strikingly similar to § 703, governing the judge's competency. Section 704(a) states that when it appears that a sitting petit juror might be called as a witness, the juror "shall, in proceedings conducted by the court out of the presence and hearing of the remaining jurors, inform the parties of the information he has concerning any fact or matter about which he will be called to testify." Section 704 operates in roughly the same fashion as § 703; there are two possibilities. One possibility is that a party may object to the juror's appearance as a witness. Section 704(b) states that if there is an objection, "the court shall declare a mistrial and order the action assigned for trial before another jury." Under subdivision (c), by calling the juror, the proponent consents to a mistrial; by objecting, the opponent moves for a mistrial. As with § 703(c), the purpose of § 704(c) is to moot any double jeopardy bar to retrial in criminal cases. The other possibility is that no party will object. If that happens, § 704(d) governs: "In the absence of objection by a party, a juror sworn and impaneled in the trial of an action may be compelled to testify in that trial as a witness."

At inquiries into the validity of verdicts, jurors may testify about the existence of statements, conduct, conditions, or events that would be likely to influence the verdict. They may not, however, testify about the effect these disturbances have on their subjective mental processes. California Evidence Code § 1150(a); *see also People v. Zapien*, 4 Cal. 4th 929, 846 P.2d 704, 17 Cal. Rptr. 2d 122, *cert. denied*, 510 U.S. 919 (1993).

2. SAMPLE ILLUSTRATION OF THE DOCTRINE'S OPERATION

The fact situation is a personal injury action arising from a traffic accident. The plaintiff alleges that she was driving on a public highway in El Cajon, California, and that the defendant driver, traveling in the opposite direction on the same highway, negligently allowed his car to drift into the plaintiff's traffic lane. The case has just been assigned to a judge for trial. The following occurs at a conference in chambers. In this hypothetical, "J" represents judge, "P" the plaintiff's attorney, and "D" the defense attorney.

J   I've called you into chambers after your opening statements to discuss a problem I didn't anticipate. Quite frankly, I've been very busy lately; and I didn't have time to carefully review this file before trial began. I gather from your opening statements that this collision occurred near Lisbon Lane. Is that true?

P   Yes, your Honor. There certainly won't be any dispute over that. In fact, that's one of the stipulations of fact that we intend to submit later for your approval.

J   Well, the problem is this. I don't know whether either of you realize this, but I happen to live on Lisbon Lane.

D   No, your Honor. I don't think that either of us was aware of that.

J   Further, I gather from the openings that there's some dispute whether the foliage in that area is so thick that it might have obstructed the vision of one or both drivers.

P   That's correct. The defense is claiming negligence on the part of my client, Ms. Riley. Our response is going to be in part that she had never driven on Lisbon Lane before and that the unexpected foliage overhanging parts of the road made it very difficult for her to see the oncoming traffic.

J   Is the defense going to dispute that?

D   We definitely are. We'll probably call some neighbors to testify on that issue.

J   To be precise, which neighbors?

D I know that we'll call Mr. Gutierez and Mrs. Johnson.

J Mr. Gutierez lives right next door to me. Mrs. Johnson is two doors down. Is there any possibility that you would want to call additional neighbors, or that the plaintiff will call some neighbors to contradict testimony by those two witnesses?

P Well, your Honor, depending on how the testimony develops, we may want to do that in rebuttal.

J It seems to me that if that occurs, my wife and I would be likely candidates. It might be better for all concerned if I assigned this case to another judge. Is that agreeable?

P Yes, sir.

D I concur, your Honor.

J I want to get this agreement on the record. I take it that you're both familiar with the provisions of Evidence Code § 703.

D Generally, yes.

P Yes, your Honor.

J That section says that if we enter into this agreement, there's consent to a mistrial. That way there's absolutely no bar to retrying the case.

P I think we're both agreeable to that.

D I'd certainly stipulate, your Honor.

J All right. I'll get the court reporter in here to reflect that on the record, and then I'll try to get the case reassigned immediately. You may even be able to go tomorrow if Judge Smith is available.

G. ATTORNEYS

1. THE DOCTRINE

Like judges and jurors, attorneys are competent witnesses at common law. Furthermore, there is no California Evidence Code provision comparable to § 703 or § 704 that restricts the competency of attorneys as witnesses. Thus, as a matter of evidence law, attorneys are competent witnesses and can testify either for or against their clients. *See, e.g., Romeo v. Jumbo Mkt.*, 247 Cal. App. 2d 817, 56 Cal. Rptr. 26 (1967) (attorney can be called by opponent and required to testify to nonprivileged facts that harm his client); 1 JEFFERSON § 26.25.

The rub, of course, is that legal ethics rules constrain an attorney's freedom to testify in a case in which he or she is the trial counsel. In most jurisdictions, the general rule is that an attorney must not serve as trial counsel in a case in which he or she will be a necessary witness. *Compare* ABA Model Rules of Professional Conduct 1.7, 1.9, 1.10, and 3.7 *with* ABA Model Code of Professional Responsibility DR 5-101(B) and 5-102; *see generally* Wydick, *Trial Counsel as Witness: The Code and the Model Rules*, 15 U.C. DAVIS L. REV. 651 (1982). The dual role of trial counsel and witness is said to raise several problems. First, the trier of fact may discount the trial counsel's testimony for obvious bias. Second, the trier of fact may get confused about whether, at a particular point, the trial counsel is speaking as an oath-bound witness or as a zealous advocate. Third, the dual role may hinder the adversary lawyer's efforts to cross-examine. Fourth, the dual role puts the trial counsel in the odd position of arguing in favor of his or her own credibility.

In two major respects, California's legal ethics rule is more lenient than the rules in other jurisdictions: (1) A trial counsel may always testify in front of a judge, as distinct from a jury; and (2) a trial counsel may testify even in front of a jury, if his or her client gives informed, written consent. California Rule of Professional Conduct 5-210 states as follows:

> A member [of the State Bar of California] shall not act as an advocate before a jury which will hear testimony from the member unless:
> (A) The testimony relates to an uncontested matter; or
> (B) The testimony relates to the nature and value of legal services rendered in the case; or
> (C) The member has the informed, written consent of the client. ...

Moreover, the California rule does not prohibit a lawyer from acting as trial counsel in a case in which some other lawyer in his or her law firm will testify as a witness. *See* Discussion following California Rule of Professional Conduct 5-210.

2. ELEMENTS OF THE FOUNDATION

Before a California lawyer agrees to act as trial counsel in a case in which either the client or the adversary will need the lawyer's testimony before a jury on a contested matter, the lawyer should surface the problem with the client. The lawyer should fully inform the client of the disadvantages of the dual role. If the client understands the disadvantages, and nevertheless wants the lawyer as trial counsel, the lawyer should obtain the client's written consent. *See* California Rule of Professional Conduct 5-210. Sometimes, however, the need for the lawyer's testimony arises unexpectedly. In that situation, the lawyer should be prepared to lay the following foundation for his or her testimony on a contested issue:

1. The lawyer fully disclosed to the client the disadvantages of continuing as trial counsel while at the same time testifying as a witness.
2. The client consented to the dual role.
3. The client's consent was in writing.

3. SAMPLE FOUNDATION

The plaintiff, a pedestrian, brought a civil suit against the defendant driver for injuries she suffered when the defendant's automobile struck her in a pedestrian crosswalk. One of defendant's witnesses, Grover Morris, testified that he was riding in defendant's car at the time of the accident, that the defendant was driving very carefully, and that plaintiff dashed into the street against a red light. Quite inadvertently, plaintiff's trial counsel, *C*, overheard the defense counsel improperly coaching Mr. Morris in the courthouse hallway just before Morris testified. *C* overheard Mr. Morris tell the defense counsel that he and the defendant were both drunk at the time of the accident and that the defendant was speeding. *C* then heard the defense counsel tell Morris: "I am angry that you didn't tell me that before, and I don't want you to mention anything about it when you testify, do you get me? Don't say anything about drinking or speeding!" On cross-examination of Morris, *C* laid a proper foundation for the prior inconsistent statement Morris made in the hallway. *See* California Evidence Code §§ 770, 1235. Then, during the plaintiff's rebuttal case, *C* prepared to take the witness stand to testify about the hallway conversation:

C   Your Honor, I request the court's permission to have my associate, *A*, take over the questioning at this point. I will be the next witness for the plaintiff.

O   May we have a conference in chambers, your Honor?

J   Certainly. Ladies and gentlemen of the jury, it's time for your morning coffee break. The bailiff will escort you as usual.

O   (In chambers) I'd like to know what's going on, your Honor. Why is *C* going to be the next witness?

C   Your Honor, before witness Mr. Morris testified, I inadvertently overheard him in the hallway tell *O* that at the time of the accident, he and the defendant were drunk and that the defendant was speeding. I'm the only one who heard it, and I want to offer it as a prior inconsistent statement.

O   Well, this is most irregular, your Honor. It's unethical for counsel to be a witness for his own client.

C   I have my client's written consent right here, your Honor.

J   All right. Speaking of ethics, *O*, when this case is over, I'll be asking you some questions about this hallway conversation. While we are in chambers with the reporter present, let's get this consent business on the record, so that nobody will wonder about it later. You can start asking the questions, *A*.

(After *C* was sworn as a witness by the reporter)

A   *C*, ARE you trial counsel for the plaintiff in this case?

C   Yes, I am.

A   WHY are you testifying as a witness?

C   Yesterday morning, I inadvertently overheard a statement by a defense witness in this case. The statement is relevant, both on the merits and on the credibility of the defense witness, and I am the only person who overheard it.

A   WHAT, if anything, have you told the plaintiff about continuing as trial counsel and testifying about the statement you overheard?

C   Yesterday noon, the plaintiff and you and I went back to our office during the lunch recess. I told the plaintiff what I'd heard and why it helps our case. I then explained the problems of being both trial counsel and witness. First, I explained that you would be taking over the questioning while I was on the stand. I explained that the jury might not believe me because I am an obviously biased witness. I explained that it would look odd for me to be arguing for my own believability when I make the closing argument. Those are the main points I covered.

A   HOW did the plaintiff respond?

C   She asked me some good questions, which indicated to me that she clearly under-
    stood the situation. And she said that, since we were right in the middle of trial,
    she wanted me to continue as her trial counsel.

A   WHAT did you do then?

C   I prepared a client consent letter, signed it, and had the plaintiff sign it.

A   Your Honor, I ask that this document be marked for identification as plaintiff's
    exhibit next in order. I have copies here for *O* and your Honor. *C*, I hand you
    what has been marked as plaintiff's exhibit 13 for identification. DO you recog-
    nize that?

C   Yes, that is the client consent letter I mentioned. I have signed it here at the bot-
    tom, and my client has countersigned it right here, indicating her consent.

A   I move that plaintiff's exhibit 13 for identification be received in evidence.

J   Motion granted. Let's go back in the courtroom. When the jury returns, I'll ex-
    plain that *C* will be testifying and that *A* will be asking the questions. Is that sat-
    isfactory?

A   Yes, your Honor.

H. CRIMINAL DEFENDANT WITNESSES WHO WANT TO TESTIFY AGAINST THEIR ATTORNEY'S WISHES

Criminal defendants have the right to testify at trial, even against their counsel's advice. *People v. Robles*, 2 Cal. 3d 205, 466 P.2d 710, 85 Cal. Rptr. 166
(1970). This right may be waived through counsel (*see, e.g., Siciliano v. Vose*,
834 F.2d 29 (1st Cir. 1987)), or by conduct. People v. Hayes, 229 Cal. App. 3d
1226, 280 Cal. Rptr. 578 (1991). This right must be claimed in a timely fashion
by the defendant if defendant's counsel opposes defendant testifying for himself.
People v. Guillen, 37 Cal. App. 3d 976, 113 Cal. Rptr. 43 (1974), *overruled on
other grounds, People v. Bracamonte*, 119 Cal. App. 3d 644, 174 Cal. Rptr. 191
(1981). The courts, however, have no duty to inform the defendant of the right to
testify, even if the defendant is representing himself. *People v. Jones*, 2 Cal. App.
4th 867, 3 Cal. Rptr. 2d 602 (1992).

I. USE OF "SUPPORT" PERSONS DURING VICTIM'S TESTIMONY

California Penal Code § 868.5 entitles the victims of certain crimes to the presence of two support persons during testimony at the preliminary hearing and at
trial. One of the support persons may also be a witness. In such cases, the support
person shall testify prior to the supported witness. When requesting the use of
support persons, the prosecutor must show that the witness wants the support, and
that the support will be helpful to the witness. The court may deny the request for
support persons if the defendant shows that the support person's presence poses a
substantial risk of influencing or affecting the content of the testimony. The presence of support persons does not, by itself, violate the defendant's right to due
process, but the defendant may be able to show that the presence of a particular

support person, in the context of the particular case, deprives the defendant of a fair trial. *See People v. Adams*, 19 Cal. App. 4th 412, 1552K, 23 Cal. Rptr. 2d 512 (1993). If the defendant objects to the use of a support person, it is critical that the record reflect the basis for the objection. The defendant should always be sure that the identity, positioning, and activities of the support person are included in the record. *People v. Patten*, 9 Cal. App. 4th 1718, 12 Cal. Rptr. 2d 284 (1992).

J. THE OPPONENT'S ATTACK ON AN ACCOMPLICE /WITNESS TESTIFYING UNDER A COERCIVE PLEA AGREEMENT OR GRANT OF IMMUNITY

1. THE DOCTRINE

The use of plea agreements and grants of immunity in exchange for testimony of accomplices seems to be approved by all jurisdictions. *People v. Green* 102 Cal. App. 2d 831, 228 P.2d 867 (1951). However, courts also recognize the potential for unreliable testimony and injustice inherent in this practice. In California, the case of *People v. Medina*, 41 Cal. App. 3d 438, 116 Cal. Rptr. 133 (1974) set the rule for limiting this kind of testimony. In *Medina*, two defendants were convicted on two counts of first degree murder. The key evidence in the prosecution's case was the testimony of three accomplices who had been offered immunity if they testified in a matter that was not "substantially or materially" different from the tape-recorded statements they had already given police. *Id.* at 452. The appeals court reversed the convictions and held that "a defendant is denied a fair trial if the prosecution's case depends substantially on accomplice testimony and the accomplice witness is placed, either by the prosecution or the court, under a strong compulsion to testify in a particular fashion." *Id.* at 455.

It can be argued that any witness who testifies in exchange for lenient treatment is under a strong compulsion to testify in a way that is helpful to the prosecution. In general this risk of unreliable testimony is accepted as long as the bargain between the prosecution and the witness is proper. In order for an accomplice to testify properly under a grant of immunity or a plea agreement, the bargain cannot be "expressly contingent" on the witness either sticking to a particular version, *People v. Garrison* 47 Cal. 3d 746, 765 P.2d 419, 254 Cal. Rptr. 257 (1989); *Medina* 41 Cal. App. 3d 438, or testifying in a way that results in a conviction, *Green*, 102 Cal. App. 2d 831. If the witness is merely required to testify to the truth, the agreement is valid, and the witness will be allowed to testify. *People v. Pinholster*, 1 Cal. 4th 865, 824 P.2d 571, 4 Cal. Rptr. 2d 765 (1992). "[T]he requirements of due process, as explained in *Medina,* are met if the agreement permits the witness to testify freely at trial and to respond to any claim that he breached the agreement by showing that the testimony he gave was a full and truthful account." *People v Fields*, 35 Cal. 3d 329, 673 P.2d 680, 197 Cal. Rptr. 803 (1983).

In order for accomplice testimony to be considered inadmissible, the improper condition must be express. *Garrison*, 47 Cal. 3d 746. So far, the courts have not been willing to find implied coercion. In *Garrison*, the plea agreement required the accomplice to testify "honestly and truthfully," and further required his assurance that his previous statements to the investigating detectives were true. The appeals court did not agree with the defense that this amounted to an agreement contingent on the witness's testimony conforming to his previous statements. *Id.* at 770. In *People v. Allen*, 42 Cal. 3d 1222, 729 P.2d 115, 232 Cal. Rptr. 849 (1986), the defense unsuccessfully argued on appeal that since the accomplice gave several versions of events over the course of several interviews, but a plea agreement was offered only after a particular version, the witness was under a strong compulsion to testify to that version. *Allen*, 42 Cal. 3d at 1253.

On a practical level, this doctrine does not have much effect at the trial level. Both the *Green* and *Medina* decisions, as well as others, suggest that if the issue were addressed at the trial level, the remedy would be to alter the plea agreement, rather than keep the witness off the stand altogether. In *Medina*, the court remanded the case for a new trial with the instruction that the immunity orders for the three witnesses be modified by striking the offending passage. *Medina* 41 Cal. App. 3d at 464. The witnesses' previous testimony could not be used against either the defendants or the witnesses. *Id.* The witnesses were freed of any possible prejudice as a result of their previous testimony. *Id.* The *Green* court remanded for a new trial as well. In *Fields*, 35 Cal. 3d 329, the defense used leading questions on cross-examination to elicit the terms of the bargain the witness had entered into with the prosecution. The witness agreed that it was part of the bargain that she would testify according to what she had told the court reporter the night before. However, the prosecution redeemed her by asking if he, the prosecution, had asked her to testify to the truth, to which she replied "yes." He then asked if he had ever asked her to "testify to a certain story," to which she replied "no." The witness was then allowed to testify. For a recent application of the principles discussed here, see *People v. Garcia*, 56 Cal. App. 4th 1349, 66 Cal. Rptr. 2d 350 (1997).

Chapter 4

LOGICAL RELEVANCE; PERSONAL KNOWLEDGE AND AUTHENTICATION

A. INTRODUCTION

The common law of evidence is imbued with skepticism; it refuses to accept proffered items of evidence at face value. The common law insists that the proponent establish the probative value of the item of evidence. If the proponent offers testimony by a lay eyewitness, the proponent must establish that the witness has personal knowledge of the facts or events the witness intends to testify about. If the proponent offers a physical exhibit, such as a letter or a hammer, the proponent must show the authenticity of the item; the proponent must establish that the object is what the proponent claims it to be. The California Evidence Code continues that tradition of skepticism. Like the common law, the code demands foundational proof of personal knowledge and genuineness. As a general proposition, California Evidence Code § 403 governs the procedure for proving these foundational facts. Subdivision 403(a) states that the § 403 procedure applies when:

> (2) The preliminary fact is the personal knowledge of a witness concerning the subject matter of his testimony; [or]
> (3) The preliminary fact is the authenticity of a writing. ...

The judge listens to the proponent's foundational evidence and admits the testimony so long as, if believed, the evidence would create a permissive inference of personal knowledge or authenticity. The following sections discuss the personal knowledge and authentication doctrines in detail.

When analyzing the admissibility of a piece of evidence, the first question one must ask is whether the evidence is relevant. Evidence that is not relevant is not admissible. California Evidence Code § 350. To be relevant, a piece of evidence must have two qualities. First, it must bear on a disputed issue that is of consequence to the determination of the action. California Evidence Code § 210. Second, it must have probative value, which means that it must have some tendency in reason to prove or disprove the disputed issue. *Id.* In applying this two-part test for relevance, California trial judges have wide discretion, and an appellate court should reverse only for a prejudicial abuse of that discretion. *DePalma v. Westland Software House*, 225 Cal. App. ad 1534, 276 Cal. Rptr. 214 (1990).

Even if a piece of evidence satisfies the two-part test for relevance, the trial judge nevertheless has discretion to exclude it if the trial judge concludes that its "probative value is substantially outweighed by the probability that its admission will (a) necessitate undue consumption of time or (b) create substantial danger of undue prejudice, of confusing the issues, or of misleading the jury." California

Evidence Code § 352. The doctrine expressed in § 352 is sometimes called "legal relevance," and we discuss it further in the introductions to Chapters 5 and 6.

B. THE QUESTIONING OF A LAY WITNESS BY THE PROPONENT TO DEMONSTRATE PERSONAL KNOWLEDGE

1. THE DOCTRINE

All courts agree that a lay witness must have personal or firsthand knowledge of facts or events to testify about them at trial. California Evidence Code § 702 insists upon personal knowledge. Before questioning a lay witness about an event, the proponent should show that the witness has personal knowledge of the event.

2. ELEMENTS OF THE FOUNDATION

The proponent should show that:

1. The witness was in a physical position to perceive the event by sight, sound, touch, smell, taste, or otherwise. Evidence Code §170 broadly defines "perceive" as meaning "to acquire knowledge through [any] sense."
2. The witness actually perceived the event.

3. SAMPLE FOUNDATION

The fact situation is a personal injury action arising from a collision. The witness is a child. The judge has already ruled the child to be a competent witness.

P James, WHERE did you go on Monday, January 21 of this year? (1)
W I went to school.
P WHERE is your school located? (1)
W It's on Fourth Street.
P WHERE on Fourth Street? (1)
W Right at Main Street. There's a big intersection there. There's lots of cars.
P WHAT happened at the intersection that day at about noon? (1)
W There was this big crash.
P WHERE were you at the time of the crash? (1)
W I was standing at that corner.
P WHAT crashed? (2)
W Two cars.
P WHO was driving the cars? (2)
W The man over there in green and that lady over there in yellow.
P Please let the record reflect that the witness has pointed to the plaintiff and defendant.
J It will so reflect.
P HOW do you know they were driving the cars? (2)

W I ran up right after the big noise, and I saw them get out of their cars.

P HOW well could you see the cars? (2)

W I got a good look. They were real close to me when they crashed. I was real scared.

P HOW well could you see the drivers? (2)

W Gee, I got right up close to them. I ran up right after the big noise, and I saw them get out of their cars.

P HOW much time passed between the crash and the time when you ran up to see the drivers? (2)

W Only a couple of seconds.

P James, now I want to ask some questions about how the crash occurred. ...

California Evidence Code § 702(b) states that "[a] witness' personal knowledge of a matter may be shown by any otherwise admissible evidence, including his own testimony." Under the § 403 procedure that governs the foundational proof of personal knowledge, the trial judge does not weigh the credibility of the evidence. The judge takes the foundational evidence at face value and decides whether it is sufficient to support a finding knowledge.

Given the laxity of the test under § 403, judges rarely exclude testimony for the lack of proof of personal knowledge. However, it is critical for the trial attorney to remember that a foundation may be legally sufficient but unconvincing to a jury. Under §§ 403 and 702, the witness need only assert that he or she perceived and remembers the event. However, if the witness is the only witness to the key event in the case, the attorney should elaborate on the foundation to ensure that the jurors find the witness credible. A. TANFORD, THE TRIAL PROCESS: LAW, TACTICS AND ETHICS 253-54 (2d ed. 1993). Have the witness testify to incidental details; detailed knowledge, especially of matters not known to the general public, will go far in persuading the jury that the witness knows whereof he speaks. *Id.* at 254. In addition, elicit the witness's testimony that he or she has some special reason for remembering the facts—the event was important to the witness, or the event seemed sensational to the witness. If the foundation includes proof of a special reason, the jurors are more likely to conclude that the witness's memory is "accurate and long lasting ..." *Id.* at 256-57.

C.   AUTHENTICATION IN GENERAL

California Evidence Code § 1400 states that "[a]uthentication of a writing means ... the introduction of evidence sufficient to sustain a finding that it is the writing that the proponent of the evidence claims it is. ..." Thus, if the proponent claims that the decedent signed a letter, the proponent must prove that the document is a genuine letter signed by the decedent. When the proponent offers a photograph of an intersection, the proponent must show that the photograph accurately depicts the intersection. Or, if the prosecutor alleges that a pistol is the defendant's pistol, the prosecutor must present evidence tracing the pistol to the defendant's possession.

California Evidence Code § 403 states the procedure for determining the evidence's authenticity. The test is whether the proponent has presented sufficient evidence to support a rational jury finding that the letter is genuine or the photograph is accurate. The trial judge looks to only the proponent's evidence and decides that question of law. Of course, the opponent may have controverting evidence. For example, although the proponent has a lay witness prepared to identify a friend's handwriting on a letter, the opponent may have a questioned document expert ready to testify that the letter is a forgery. In this circumstance, the trial judge would admit the letter, and the opponent would present his or her controverting evidence to the jury. The trial judge would instruct the jurors that they must finally decide whether the letter is genuine. *See People v. Marshall*, 13 Cal. 4th 799, 919 P.2d 1280, 53 Cal. Rptr. 2d 347, 364 (1996) ("The proper standard is that of preponderance of the evidence. In other words, the trial court must determine whether the evidence is sufficient to permit the jury to find the preliminary fact to be true by a preponderance of the evidence ... even if the court would personally disagree").

What are the mechanics of presenting physical or documentary evidence? Until the proponent is ready to use the evidence, the proponent should keep the evidence out of the sight of the jury. When the proponent wants to use the evidence, the proponent should first request that the item be marked for identification. Many judges insist that the proponent ask only that "this" be marked for identification. To make the record of trial clearer to the appellate court, other trial judges permit the proponent to use a short description of the exhibit. For example, these judges permit the proponent to request that "this letter" or "this knife" be marked for identification. The court reporter or bailiff handles the marking of the exhibits. Plaintiffs and prosecutors use numbers to identify their exhibits ("plaintiff's exhibit number two for identification"), while defense attorneys use letters ("defense exhibit C for identification"). After the exhibit is marked for identification, the proponent hands the exhibit to the opposing attorney for inspection. It is customary at this point for the proponent to ask that the record reflect that the opposing attorney is examining the exhibit.

The proponent then hands the exhibit to the witness. The proponent should describe the exhibit as an exhibit for identification: "I now hand you prosecution exhibit number seven for identification." It is improper to state, "I now hand you a letter purportedly signed by the defendant"; the proponent's attorney is not a witness, and that description would amount to unsworn testimony. Once the exhibit is in the witness' hands, the proponent asks the witness what it is, thus laying the foundation for the exhibit's admission. At the very least, the foundation usually includes proof of the item's authenticity. When the foundation has been laid, the proponent formally offers the exhibit into evidence. The proponent can "move" the item's admission or "offer defense exhibit G for identification into evidence as defense exhibit G." Some judges prefer a simpler style; rather than insisting that the proponent "offer defense exhibit G for identification into evidence as defense exhibit G." these judges permit the proponent merely to "offer defense exhibit G for identification into evidence."

If there is no objection, or the trial judge overrules the objection, the item is received in evidence. In the case of a letter, the proponent may next request the judge's permission to read, or have the witness read, all or part of the document to the jury. The proponent may request the judge's permission to "publish" or to hand any documentary or physical evidence to the jurors for their inspection. When the proponent has completed using the exhibit, the proponent should hand the exhibit back to the court reporter or bailiff.

D.   THE AUTHENTICATION OF PRIVATE WRITINGS

There are several well-settled techniques for authenticating private writings. These techniques are alternative methods of establishing a writing's authenticity. California Evidence Code §§ 1411-21 list many of these techniques. (If the writing has been lost, Code of Civil Procedure § 1953.10 permits the filing of a special verified petition to establish the existence and authenticity of the writing. *Daddario v. Snow Valley, Inc.*, 36 Cal. App. 4th 1325, 43 Cal. Rptr. 2d 726 (1995).)

The reader should develop the habit of automatically thinking of authentication, best evidence, and hearsay whenever a document is used in the courtroom. Whenever a document is used, the proponent will have to authenticate it. If the document's terms are in issue, the proponent will have to comply with the best evidence rule. Finally, if the proponent seeks to prove that what the document asserts is true, the proponent will have to consider the hearsay rule. In short, the proponent offering a document will often have to lay three separate foundations—authenticity, best evidence, and hearsay. The proponent should thus consult Chapters 7 and 9 as well as this chapter.

1. TESTIMONY OF A WITNESS WHO OBSERVED THE DOCUMENT'S EXECUTION

The proponent can use direct evidence. If a witness observed the document's execution and recognizes the document executed, the witness' testimony is sufficient authentication. California Evidence Code § 1413 specifically states that "[a] writing may be authenticated by anyone who saw the writing made or executed, including a subscribing witness." This is probably the most common method of authenticating a private writing.

The following are the elements of the foundation:

1. Where the witness observed the document's execution.
2. When the witness observed the execution.
3. Who was present.
4. What happened—the document's execution.
5. The witness recognizes the exhibit as the document previously executed.

Assume that one issue in a commercial case is whether the defendant signed a certain check. The defendant's acquaintance, Mr. Bucher, observed the defendant sign the check. The plaintiff is the proponent.

P   WHERE were you on the afternoon of February 4 of this year? (1), (2)

W   I was at the defendant's house.

P   WHO was there? (3)

W   It was just me, the defendant, and his wife, Ruth.

P   WHAT, if anything, happened while you were there? (4)

W   The defendant was writing out some checks to pay his month's bills.

P   Your Honor, I request that this be marked plaintiff's exhibit number seven for identification.

J   It will be so marked.

P   Please let the record reflect that I am showing the exhibit to the opposing counsel.

J   It will so reflect.

P   I request permission to approach the witness.

J   Permission granted.

P   Mr. Bucher, I now hand you plaintiff's exhibit number seven for identification. WHAT is it? (5)

W   It's one of the checks the defendant signed that afternoon.

P   HOW do you recognize it? (6)

W   Well, the defendant handed it to me and asked me to take a look at it. I recognize the signature and other writing on it.

P   HOW long did you have to examine it? (6)

W   About a minute or so.

P   HOW carefully did you examine it? (6)

W   Closely enough to recognize it now.

P   WHAT characteristics of the exhibit are you relying on as the basis for your identification? (6)

W   I remember the amount of the check, the payee, the defendant's rather peculiar signature, and the color of the check.

P   Your Honor, I now offer plaintiff's exhibit number seven for identification into evidence as plaintiff's exhibit number seven.

J   It will be received.

P   I request permission to hand the exhibit to the jurors for their inspection.

J   Permission granted.

2. TESTIMONY OF A WITNESS FAMILIAR WITH THE AUTHOR'S HANDWRITING STYLE

When the proponent cannot find someone who saw the writing executed, the proponent may be able to find someone familiar with the author's handwriting style. Courts usually prohibit opinion testimony by lay witnesses, but lay opinion testimony on handwriting style is traditionally permitted. The primary problem of proof for the proponent is establishing that the witness is sufficiently familiar with the author's handwriting style to recognize that style. Ideally, the witness will have observed the author write by hand on several previous occasions. It is sufficient if the witness has seen the author's handwriting under reliable circumstances. For example, one corporate executive's secretary may have seen documents bearing the signature of another executive of the same corporation on hundreds of prior occasions. Even if the secretary has never seen that second corporate executive sign a document, the secretary is sufficiently familiar with the handwriting style.

California Evidence Code §1416 recognizes this authentication technique. That section reads:

> A witness who is not otherwise qualified to testify as an expert may state his opinion whether a writing is in the handwriting of a supposed writer if the court finds that he has personal knowledge of the handwriting of the supposed writer. Such personal knowledge may be acquired from:
> (a) Having seen the supposed writer write;
> (b) Having seen a writing purporting to be in the handwriting of the supposed writer and upon which the supposed writer has acted or been charged;
> (c) Having received letters in the due course of mail purporting to be from the supposed writer in response to letters duly addressed and mailed by him to the supposed writer; or
> (d) Any other means of obtaining personal knowledge of the handwriting of the supposed writer.

We have previously noted that California Evidence Code § 403 generally governs the procedure for authentication. However, this technique is one of the exceptions to that general rule. The trial judge makes the final decision whether the witness is sufficiently with the handwriting style of the supposed author. The Assembly Committee comment to § 405 states that under § 405, the judge determines "[w]hether a witness is sufficiently acquainted with the handwriting of a person to give an opinion on whether a questioned writing is in that person's handwriting. ..." *See generally* 1 JEFFERSON'S CALIFORNIA EVIDENCE BENCHBOOK § 30.17 (3d ed. 1997).

The foundation is very simple; the elements are:

1. The witness recognized the author's handwriting on the document.
2. The witness is familiar with the author's handwriting style.
3. The witness has a sufficient basis for familiarity.

Now vary the original hypothetical. Assume that the witness, Mr. Bucher, did not observe the check's execution but is familiar with the author's handwriting style:

P   Your Honor, I request that this be marked plaintiff's exhibit number seven for identification.
J   It will be so marked.

P   Please let the record reflect that I am showing the exhibit to the opposing counsel.
J   It will so reflect.
P   I request permission to approach the witness.
J   Request granted.
P   Mr. Bucher, I now hand you plaintiff's exhibit number seven for identification, WHAT is it?
W   It seems to be a check.
P   WHO signed the check? (1)
W   I'd say that the defendant signed it.
P   WHY do you say that? (2)
W   I recognize the defendant's handwriting style on the check.
P   HOW well do you know the defendants handwriting? (3)
W   Very well.
P   HOW did you become familiar with this handwriting? (3)
W   We've been friends for years.
P   HOW many years? (3)
W   About ten.
P   HOW often have you seen the defendant sign his name? (3)
W   Tens, maybe hundreds?
P   Your Honor, I now offer plaintiff's exhibit seven for identification into evidence as plaintiff's exhibit number seven.
J   It will be received.
P   I request permission to hand the exhibit to the jurors for their inspection.
J   Permission granted.

3. THE REPLY LETTER DOCTRINE

The reply letter doctrine assumes that the mails are reliable. Suppose that the witness sent a letter to a certain person. In the due course of mail, the witness receives a letter. The letter purports to be signed by the person to whom the witness sent the first letter, and the second letter purports to respond to the first letter. The courts generally hold that these facts create a sufficient circumstantial inference that the second letter is authentic. Evidence Code §1420 recognizes this authentication technique.

This foundation contains several elements:

1. The witness prepared the first letter.
2. The witness placed the letter in an envelope and properly stamped the envelope.
3. The witness addressed the letter to the author.
4. The witness mailed the letter to the author. There is no need for independent evidence that the author received the letter mailed by the witness. Evidence Code § 641 provides that ''[al letter correctly addressed and properly mailed is presumed to have been received in the ordinary course of mail.''
5. The witness received a letter.
6. The letter arrived in the due course of mail.

7. The second letter referred to the first letter or was responsive to it.
8. The second letter bore the name of the author.
9. The witness recognizes the exhibit as the second letter.
10. The witness specifies the basis on which he recognizes the exhibit.

Our fact situation is a contract case. The plaintiff wants to prove that the defendant sent a letter containing an express warranty of the goods' condition. The plaintiff had not had previous dealings with the defendant, and hence, cannot recognize the defendant's handwriting style. The witness is the plaintiff. The plaintiff has just testified that he had a telephone conversation with the defendant. The plaintiff's attorney is the proponent.

P   WHAT did you do after this telephone conversation? (1)
W   I decided to send the defendant a letter requesting some specific assurances and warranties about the goods.
P   HOW did you do that? (1)
W   I typed it up and then signed it.
P   WHAT did you do with it after you signed it? (2), (3), (4)
W   I stuck it in an envelope. I stamped the envelope, addressed it, and stuck it in the mail.
P   WHERE did you get the defendant's address? (3)
W   Out of the telephone book.
P   WHEN did you mail the letter? (4)
W   I think it was that afternoon. Yes, it was Monday afternoon.
P   WHAT happened then? (5)
W   I got a reply letter.
P   WHEN did the letter arrive? (6)
W   The following Monday.
P   HOW often have you exchanged letters with people in Santa Monica? (6)
W   I've done it hundreds of times in the course of business.
P   HOW long does it usually take to get a reply from Santa Monica? (6)
W   About a week.
P   HOW much time passed between the time you mailed your letter and the time when you received this second letter? (6)
W   About a week. It was right on time.
P   WHY, in your answer a moment ago, did you refer to the second letter as a "reply letter"? (8)
W   Well, it referred to my letter. It said it was going to answer my questions.
P   WHOSE name appeared on this second letter? (8)
W   The defendant's.
P   Your Honor, I request that this be marked plaintiffs exhibit number eight for identification.
J   It will be so marked.
P   Please let the record reflect that I am showing the exhibit to the opposing counsel.
J   It will so reflect.
P   I request permission to approach the witness.
J   Permission granted.

P   I now hand you plaintiff s exhibit number eight for identification. WHAT is it? (9)

W It's the letter I just referred to.

P   HOW can you recognize it? (10)

W I remember the contents, and the letterhead is unique.

P   Your Honor, I now offer plaintiff s exhibit eight for identification into evidence as plaintiffs exhibit eight.

J   It will be received.

P   I request permission to have the witness read the last paragraph and signature block.

J   Permission granted.

P   (To the witness) Please read this passage to the jurors.

W It reads: "I guarantee that it's a first-rate product. Nobody makes a better shingle. They'll last at least fifteen years. Sincerely yours, John Bettencourt."

P   Your Honor, I now request permission to publish the exhibit to the jurors for their inspection.

J   Permission granted.

4. A COMPARISON BY A QUESTIONED DOCUMENT EXPERT

Subsection 2 analyzed lay opinion testimony about the author's handwriting style. Alternatively, California Evidence Code § 1418 allows the proponent to use testimony of a "handwriting expert." Before presenting the questioned document expert, the proponent must authenticate specimens or exemplars—other documents written by the author. The proponent may use any authentication technique other than expert comparison to establish the exemplars' genuineness. The trial judge rules finally on the authenticity of the exemplars. The Assembly Committee comment to California Evidence Code § 405 states that the § 405 procedure governs the proof of the authenticity of the exemplars, and § 1418 refers to exemplars "proved to be genuine to the satisfaction of the court." The proponent then calls the expert to the stand. After qualifying as an expert, the witness will state that before trial, he or she has compared the exemplars with the questioned document. On the basis of this comparison, the expert may testify whether in his or her opinion, the same person who wrote the exemplars wrote the questioned document.

The elements of the foundation are:

1. The proponent authenticates exemplars to the trial judge's satisfaction. At common law, many jurisdictions forbade the use of exemplars prepared *post litem motam*—after the dispute arose. Before the adoption of the Evidence Code, the California courts followed the common law. *People v. Golembiewski*, 25 Cal. App. 2d 115, 76 P.2d 717 (1938). There is authority that the common-law prohibition is still in effect in California. *People v. Najera*, 8 Cal. 3d 504, 512, 503 P.2d 1353, 1359 105 Cal. Rptr. 345, 351 (1972); CAL. CONTINUING ED. BAR, TRIAL ATTORNEY'S EVIDENCE CODE NOTEBOOK ANNOTATED 32 (3d ed. 1982); 2 WITKIN § 914, at 876. How-

ever, Justice Jefferson takes the contrary position. 1 JEFFERSON, § 30.18, at 630.

2. The witness qualifies as a questioned document expert. The California Law Revision Commission comment on § 1418 states that a person may qualify as an expert by technical training or practical experience. The comment mentions an "experienced banker" as a person who could qualify as an expert based on practical experience.

3. The witness testifies that he or she has compared the exemplars with the questioned document.

4. The witness concludes that the same person who wrote the exemplars wrote the questioned document.

5. The witness specifies the basis for the opinion, namely, the similarities between exemplars and the questioned document.

Assume that the proponent has already authenticated the exemplars. Someone who saw the defendant sign two letters authenticated the letters. The letters are marked plaintiff's exhibits three and four. The plaintiff will mark the disputed check as plaintiff's exhibit number five for identification. The plaintiff is the proponent. The next witness is the questioned document expert. The witness has already identified himself as John Glenn and stated his address.

P   WHAT is your occupation? (2)

W   I am a technician with Richard Whaley and Associates.

P   WHAT line of business is that firm in? (2)

W   It is a private forensic laboratory. We do all sorts of scientific work for legal cases.

P   HOW long have you worked there? (2)

W   For about twelve years.

P   WHAT are your duties there? (2)

W   I examine questioned documents.

P   WHAT does a questioned document examiner do? (2)

W   Among other things, we attempt to determine who wrote a document.

P   WHAT is your formal education? (2)

W   I have a Bachelor of Science degree from the University of Santa Clara.

P   WHAT other training, if any, have you had? (2)

W   I attended several two-week courses on questioned document examination at Northwestern University. I've also attended many seminars on the subject sponsored by the Law Enforcement Assistance Administration.

P   HOW long have you been a questioned document examiner? (2)

W   The whole time I've had my present position—roughly seven years.

P   WHAT part of your working time do you devote to questioned document examination? (2)

W   All of it. It's my specialty.

P   HOW often have you testified as an expert on questioned documents? (2)

W   At least one hundred times.

P   WHERE have you testified? (2)

W   Mainly in the courts in this state. However, I've also testified in Nevada, Washington, and Arizona.

P   WHEN was the last time you testified as a questioned document examiner? (2)

W   Last month.

P   WHERE was that? (2)

W   In another courtroom in this same building.

P   I now hand you plaintiff's exhibits numbers three and four and plaintiff's exhibit number five for identification. WHAT are they?

W   They're handwriting specimens.

P   HOW many times have you seen these documents? (3)

W   Once before.

P   WHEN was that? (3)

W   An investigator brought them to my office.

P   WHAT happened when the investigator came to your office? (3)

W   Well, I examined them. I studied them under an optical microscope to determine whether they had a common authorship.

P   HOW long did you study them? (3)

W   I spent the better part of the afternoon, maybe three hours, working on the comparison.

P   HOW did you make the comparison? (3)

W   I studied the documents. I had some blown up into enlarged photographs and studied the enlargements as well.

P   HOW can you recognize these documents as the ones you previously examined? (3)

W   I noted the peculiarities of the handwriting style. They were uniform throughout each document. They're quite distinctive.

P   Do you have an opinion on the question whether the author of exhibits three and four also wrote plaintiff's exhibit five for identification?

W   Yes.

P   WHAT is that opinion? (4)

W   I'm convinced that it was the same author.

P   WHAT is the basis for your opinion? (5)

W   In all, I detected five unique writing characteristics common to all three documents. There was a common misspelling, a spacing peculiarity, the tail on each y, the pronounced loop on each o, and the unique way in which each t is crossed. These characteristics all point to common authorship.

P   Your Honor, I now offer plaintiff's exhibit number five for identification into evidence as plaintiff's exhibit number five.

J   It will be received.

P   I now request permission to hand exhibits three, four and five to the jurors for their inspection.

J   Permission granted.

The Evidence Code does not limit expert testimony to the subject of handwriting identification. Section 1418 refers broadly to testimony by "an expert witness" about the genuineness of "writing." Evidence Code § 250 defines "writing" broadly: "handwriting, typewriting, printing, photostating, photographing, and every other means of recording upon any tangible thing any form of communication ...." The California Law Revision Commission comment to § 1418 explains that in light of the expansive definition of writing in § 250, § 1418 authorizes expert testimony on such topics as the comparison of typewriting specimens.

In federal court, there is now a controversy over the admissibility of questioned document testimony. *United States v. Paul*, 175 F.3d 906 (11th Cir. 1999), *cert. denied*, 120 S. Ct. 535 (1999); *United States v. Jones*, 107 F.3d 1147 (6th Cir. 1997), *cert. denied*, 521 U.S. 1127 (1997); *United States v. Starzecpyzel*, 880 F. Supp. 1027 (S.D.N.Y. 1995). Some courts such as *Starzecpyzel* admit the testimony but do so only with a cautionary instruction that the evidence does not qualify as truly scientific testimony. The crux of the dispute is whether there has been adequate empirical validation of the underlying premises and techniques of questioned document examination. *Cf.* Moenssens, *Handwriting Identification Evidence in the Post-Daubert World: Identifying the Genuine Article and the Genuine Legal Issue: Broader Standards Needed for "Scientific Knowledge,"* 66 U.M.K.C. L. REV. 251 (1997) *with* Risinger, Denbeaux & Saks, *Brave New "Post-Daubert World"—A Reply to Professor Moenssens*, 29 SETON HALL L. REV. 405 (1998). To date, the controversy has not surfaced in any published California opinions, but the question is likely a coming issue in California.

5. OTHER MEANS OF AUTHENTICATING PRIVATE WRITINGS

The sample foundations in Sections 14 illustrate the most common techniques for authenticating private writings. However, those foundations do not exhaust the possibilities. Section 1410 of the Evidence Code prefaces the list of recognized authentication techniques in §§ 1411-21. Section 1410 states that "[n]othing in this article shall be construed to limit the means by which a writing may be authenticated or proved." If the proponent can marshall enough circumstantial evidence to create a permissive inference satisfying Evidence Code §§ 403 and 1400(a), the proponent has met the authentication requirement.

The Evidence Code mentions several authentication techniques in addition to the methods illustrated in Sections 1-4. Under § 1414, the proponent may authenticate a writing by admission—that is, by proof that:

(a) The party against whom it is offered has at any time admitted its authenticity; or

(b) The writing has been acted upon as authentic by the party against whom it is offered.

In addition to allowing comparisons with exemplars by experts, the Code permits comparisons by the trier of fact. Evidence Code § 1417 is in point. As in the case of expert comparisons under § 1418, the trial judge finally decides the question of the genuineness of the exemplars. According to Justice Jefferson, the trial judge then compares the exemplars with the questioned document to determine whether there is sufficient similarity to allow a rational juror to find that the same author wrote all the documents. JEFFERSON SYNOPSIS § 30.3, at 479. If there is sufficient similarity, the judge submits the exemplars and the questioned document to the jurors for their comparison.

Section 1421 recognizes the content method of authentication. To use this method, the proponent must show that "the writing refers to or states matters that are unlikely to be known to anyone other than the person who is claimed by the proponent ... to be the author of the writing."

Section 643 creates a presumption that an ancient document is authentic. Section 643 is limited to a "deed or will or other writing purporting to ... affect an interest in real or personal property. ..." To satisfy § 643, the proponent must demonstrate that the document: is at least thirty years old; is "in such condition as to create no suspicion concerning its authenticity"; was kept in a natural place of custody; and "has been generally acted upon as genuine by persons having an interest in the matter." In proving the age of the document, the proponent may invoke the presumption in Evidence Code § 640 that a writing is correctly dated.

Finally, to some extent, private writings can be self-authenticating under the Evidence Code. Section 1451 provides that "[a] certificate of the acknowledgment" of certain writings is "prima facie evidence of the facts recited in the certificate and the genuineness of the signature of each person by whom the writing purports to have been signed. ..." Section 1451 conditions the admissibility of the writing on compliance with the pertinent sections of Civil Code. Civil Code §§ 1180-1207 govern the acknowledgment procedure. Evidence Code 645.1 also makes some writings self-authenticating. That section, enacted in 1986, reads that "[p]rinted materials, purporting to be a particular newspaper or periodical are presumed to be that newspaper or periodical if regularly issued at average intervals not exceeding three months."

E.   THE AUTHENTICATION OF BUSINESS WRITINGS

1. THE TRADITIONAL METHOD FOR AUTHENTICATING BUSINESS WRITINGS

Authenticating an ordinary business record is a simple matter. The cases teach that proper custody is sufficient authentication for business records. It is sufficient if the witness is familiar with the business' filing system, took the record from the right file, and recognizes the exhibit as the record removed from the files.

The elements of the foundation are:

1. The witness has personal knowledge of the business' filing system.
2. The witness removed a record from a certain file.
3. It was the right file.

4. The witness recognizes the exhibit as the record he or she removed from the files.

5. The witness specifies the basis on which he or she recognizes the exhibit.

In a contract action, the plaintiff's business, Collegiate Clothing Manufacturers, wants to authenticate a bill it prepared in December 2000. The plaintiff calls Ms. Peters as its witness.

P   WHAT is your occupation? (1)

W   I am a chief bookkeeper.

P   WHERE do you work? (1)

W   I work at the plaintiff's main office in Eureka.

P   HOW long have you worked there? (1)

W   About seven years.

P   WHAT are your duties? (1)

W   As chief bookkeeper, I ensure that we have proper records of all the money and goods flowing into and out of the company. I supervise the records' preparation, maintenance, and eventual destruction.

P   HOW well do you know the plaintiff's filing system? (1)

W   I know it backwards and forwards. In fact, I helped design the system.

P   Ms. Peters, WHERE were you this morning? (3)

W   I was picking up the records you asked me to bring to trial today.

P   WHERE did you go to get the files? (4)

W   I went to the file cabinet for our 2000 records. I was particularly interested in the records for December of that year.

P   WHAT did you find in the file? (3)

W   I located all the bills and invoices we needed.

P   Your Honor, I request that this be marked as plaintiff's exhibit number three for identification.

J   It will be so marked.

P   I request permission to approach the witness.

J   Permission granted.

P   Ms. Peters, I now hand you plaintiff's exhibit number three for identification. WHAT is it? (4)

W   It's one of the bills I removed from the file for December 2000.

P   HOW can you recognize it? (5)

W   I recognize the handwriting of the clerk, John Winters, and I can generally recall the contents of each of the bills I took out of the file cabinet.

P   Your Honor, I now offer plaintiff's exhibit number three for identification into evidence as plaintiff's exhibit number three.

J   It will be received.

P   I now request permission to hand the exhibit to the jurors for their inspection.

J   Permission granted.

2. THE SIMPLIFIED, STATUTORY METHOD FOR AUTHENTICATING BUSINESS WRITINGS

The traditional method of authenticating business records can create a problem for the business. Because of the interplay between the authentication and best evidence rules, the business has to surrender original business records to the court. The business may need the records in its daily operations. For that reason, the California legislature enacted Evidence Code §§ 1560-66 creating a simplified method of authenticating business writings.

This method applies only if the business is neither a party to the proceeding nor, in the words of Evidence Code § 1560(b), "the place where any cause of action is alleged to have arisen. ..." If the business receives a subpoena duces tecum for its records, it would ordinarily have to produce original records. Section 1564 permits the subpoenaing party to demand the custodian's personal attendance and the production of the original records; the section prescribes the language the subpoenaing party must use to make that demand. If the subpoenaing party does not use that language, § 1560(b) allows the business to respond by producing copies accompanied by an affidavit satisfying § 1561. If the business itself prepares the copies, it is arguable that it does not have a further obligation to make the originals available for copying. Subdivision 1561(a) prescribes the contents of the affidavit:

(1) The affiant is the duly authorized custodian of the records or other qualified witness and has authority to certify the records.
(2) The copy is a true copy of all the records described in the subpoena.
(3) The records were prepared by the personnel of the business in the ordinary course of business at or near the time of the act, condition, or event,
(4) The records described in the subpoena duces tecum were delivered to the attorney or his or her representative for copying at the custodian's or witness' place of business. ...

The wording of § 1561(a)(4) suggests that even if the business itself makes the copies, the business must make the originals available to the subpoenaing party "for copying." However, if § 1561(a)(4) is construed sensibly, that subdivision probably does not require production of the originals when the business prepares the copies. The copies and accompanying affidavit are delivered to the clerk of the court.

While §§ 1560-61 govern the subpoena procedure during pretrial discovery, § 1562 controls the admissibility of the records at trial. Section 1562 reads:

The copy of the records is admissible in evidence to the same extent as though the original ... were offered and the custodian had been present and testified to the matters stated in the affidavit. The affidavit is admissible as evidence of the matters stated therein pursuant to Section 1561. ...

By way of illustration, suppose that in the last hypothetical Ms. Peters had executed an affidavit and submitted copies rather than appearing at trial with the original records. Suppose further that Ms. Peters' employer is not a party and that the cause of action did not arise at the employer's place of business. The record of trial might reflect the following.

P   Your Honor, I now request that this be marked as plaintiff's exhibit number three for identification.

J   It will be so marked.

P   Please let the record reflect that I am showing the exhibit to opposing counsel.

J   It will so reflect.

P   Your Honor, may we approach the bench?

J   Yes.

P   Your Honor, as you can see from the stamp of the court clerk on this document, this document is part of the official court file for this case. This initial part of the exhibit is an affidavit from a Ms. Peters. As the affidavit indicates, she works for Collegiate Clothing, which is not a party to this suit. The face of the affidavit is in full compliance with Evidence Code § 1561. The other part of the exhibit is a set of copies of business records purporting to come from Collegiate Clothing. Since the affidavit satisfies § 1561, the copies are authenticated under Evidence Code § 1562.

J   The exhibit seems to be in order. Is there any objection?

O   No, your Honor.

P   In that case, your Honor, I offer plaintiff's exhibit number three for identification into evidence as plaintiff's three.

J   The exhibit will be received.

P   I now request permission to hand the exhibit to the jurors for their inspection.

J   Permission granted.

Notice one limitation on this authentication technique. The presumption created by § 1562 applies only to "the matter stated (in the affidavit) pursuant to Section 1561. ..." If the affidavit includes other extraneous statements, the presumption is inapplicable to those statements. HEAFEY § 24.11, at 226.

3. COMPUTER RECORDS

Computer-generated evidence is a species of scientific evidence. The process of generating data by computer is beyond the knowledge of most laypersons. As Section L of this chapter explains, scientific evidence usually requires proof of the validity of the underlying theory and the reliability of the instrument. However, computers are so widely accepted and used that the proponent of computer evidence need not prove those two elements of the foundation; the trial judge will judicially notice the validity of the theory underlying computers and the general reliability of computers. A computer printout is presumed to accurately reflect the content of the computer's memory. California Evidence Code § 1500.5. *See Aguimatang v. California State Lottery*, 234 Cal. App. 3d 769, 286 Cal. Rptr. 57

(1991).

The proponent can authenticate a computer record by proving the reliability of the particular computer used, the dependability of the business' procedures for using the computer, the use of proper procedures to obtain the document offered in court, and the witness' recognition of that document as the readout from the computer.

A computer readout may not be readable by a layperson. The readout may use symbols and terminology that only an expert can understand. If so, after introducing the record, the proponent will have the expert interpret the record for the trier of fact.

The elements of the foundation are these:

1. The business uses a computer.
2. The computer is reliable.
3. The business has a procedure for inserting data into the computer.
4. The procedure has built-in safeguards to ensure accuracy and identify errors.
5. The business keeps the computer in a good state of repair.
6. The witness had the computer print out certain data.
7. The witness used the proper procedures to obtain the printout.
8. The computer was in working order at the time the witness obtained the printout.
9. The witness recognizes the exhibit as the printout.
10. The witness explains how he or she recognizes the printout.
11. If the printout contains strange symbols or terms, the witness explains the symbols or terms for the trier of fact.

Suppose that Acme Corporation brings an antitrust suit against Bechtor, Inc. To prove its damages, Acme wants to show that its gross sales declined from 1994 to 1996. Acme wants to use a computer printout to show its gross sales in those three years. As its witness, Acme calls Mrs. Schons. Acme is the proponent.

P   Mrs. Schons, WHAT is your occupation?
W   I am one of the accountants from Acme Corporation.
P   HOW long have you worked for Acme Corporation?
W   Roughly ten years.
P   HOW long have you worked for Acme Corporation as an accountant?
W   Again, roughly ten years.
P   WHAT are your duties with Acme Corporation?
W   My specialty is the maintenance of our computer records.
P   HOW does Acme maintain its business records? (1)
W   Most of our data is in our computer.
P   WHICH computer do you use? (1)
W   We use a Logan 660-e.
P   HOW long have you used that computer? (2)
W   For the last three years.

P   HOW widely used is that model computer? (2)

W   There are hundreds in use throughout the country. When it was first marketed, it was the top of the line. There's a somewhat more sophisticated model available now, but the 660-e is regarded as one of the most dependable models on the market.

P   WHAT procedure does Acme have for using the computer to maintain its records? (3)

W   When an order comes in from a customer, we ship it straight to the sales department. They check it for accuracy.

P   WHAT does the sales department do with the order then? (3)

W   They send it to the computer center, where the information from the order form is scanned into a computer data file. The computer makes certain that the merchandise is available in inventory and that the purchaser's credit is good. If the order passes those tests, the computer then makes entries on the customer's account and stores data for statistical and management reports.

P   HOW do you know that is the procedure? (3)

W   I helped design the procedure. As I said, computer record maintenance is my specialty.

P   WHAT safeguards, if any, do you use to ensure that your records are accurate? (4)

W   There are double checks at several points. For example, one computer center employee checks the accuracy of the scanned data, and another checks the inventory, credit, and shipment data that the computer generates. Perhaps the most important safeguard is the customers' review of the bills we print out and send them. If anything's wrong, they let us know right away.

P   HOW is the computer maintained? (5)

W   It's checked nightly for any obvious problems. Whenever operators encounter a mechanical problem, they call maintenance immediately. In addition, Logan's technical rep visits the center periodically and checks the system thoroughly.

P   WHERE were you yesterday afternoon? (6)

W   I was at my office.

P   WHAT were you doing there? (6)

W   I was trying to get the data you asked me to bring to court today.

P   WHAT data was that? (6)

W   The total sales figures for 1994 through 1996.

P   HOW did you obtain the data? (6)

W   I had the computer print it out.

P   HOW did you obtain the printout? (7)

W   I went to the terminal, set it in the printout mode, and then requested the sales figures.

P   HOW many times did you request the data from the computer? (7)

W   Twice.

P   WHY did you do it twice? (7)

W   I wanted to make certain I had the right figures.

P   WHAT was the result of your double-check? (7)

W   The computer printed out the same data both times.

P   WHAT condition was the computer in at the time? (8)

W   It seemed to be OK. There were certainly no obvious problems. It had been checked the night before, and we'd used it several times already that day without any difficulty.

P   Your Honor, may this be marked plaintiff's exhibit number ten for identification?

J   It will be so marked.

P   May the record reflect that I am showing exhibit number ten to the opposing attorney?

J   It will so reflect.

P   Request permission to approach the witness.

J   Permission granted.

P   Mrs. Schons, I now hand you plaintiff's exhibit number ten for identification. WHAT is it? (9)

W   It's the second printout I just referred to.

P   HOW can you recognize it? (10)

W   I put my initials and the date in that corner. I can easily recognize them.

P   Your Honor, I now offer plaintiff's exhibit number ten for identification into evidence as plaintiffs exhibit number ten.

J   It will be received.

P   Now, Mrs. Schons, directing your attention to this notation on the exhibit, WHAT does it say there? (11)

W   It reads "MER S."

P   WHAT does that mean? (11)

W   It means sales of merchandise.

P   HOW do you know that? (11)

W   I helped select the symbols and terminology the computer would use in printouts.

P   WHAT are these figures? (11)

W   They're the dollar amounts of sales for the years indicated, for example, $2,675,334 in 1994.

P   Your Honor, may exhibit ten be handed to the jurors for their inspection?

J   Yes.

4. OTHER TECHNIQUES FOR AUTHENTICATING BUSINESS WRITING

The preceding three sample foundations illustrate the most commonly used methods of authenticating business records. However, there are several other techniques that the reader should be familiar with.

Evidence Code § 712 fashions a special technique for qualified experts' affidavits about "the technique used in taking blood samples." The affidavit must be executed by a registered nurse, licensed vocational nurse, licensed clinical laboratory technology, or a clinical laboratory bioanalyst. The party introducing the affidavit must serve a copy of the affidavit on all other parties no fewer than ten days before trial. If there is no objection, the affidavit is admissible without live foundational testimony.

Another technique is recognized in Commercial Code § 1202. That statute applies to purported bills of lading, policies or certificates of insurance, weigher's certificates, inspector's certificates, consular invoices, and "any other document authorized or required by the contract to be issued by a third party." Under § 1202, if the face of the document is "in due form," the document is "presumed to be authentic and genuine. ..."

F.   THE AUTHENTICATION OF OFFICIAL WRITINGS

1. THE DOCTRINE

The government often possesses information relevant to the outcome of civil and criminal actions. Thus, it may become necessary for one of the parties to introduce an official record. For example, prosecutors often have occasion to offer certified copies of abstracts of judgment and Department of Corrections records. *People v. Ruiz,* 69 Cal. App. 4th 1085, 82 Cal. Rptr. 2d 139, 141 (1999) (certified prison records); *People v. Haney*, 26 Cal. App. 4th 472, 31 Cal. Rptr. 2d 547, 549 (1994). Since official records are used quite often, it would be wasteful to require public officials to appear in court to authenticate them. Further, the originals of some official records need to be kept in their proper place, either because they are irreplaceable or because people need easy access to them.

To remedy these problems, almost every jurisdiction treats a properly attested copy of an official record as self-authenticating. The party obtains a copy of the official record from the official custodian, and the custodian attaches an attestation. The attestation reads along these lines: "I, Robert Dondero, certify that I am the County Clerk of San Francisco, California, and that the attached document is a true and accurate copy of an original, official record in my custody." The certificate is signed and often bears the seal of the official's office.. The courts have developed the doctrine that the purported signature or seal of an official is presumed to be authentic.

California law follows this pattern. Evidence Code § 1530(a)(2) provides that when a document purports to be a copy of an original writing in a public entity's custody, there is "prima facie evidence of the existence and contents" of the writing if the copy is properly attested or certified by the custodian or deputy custodian. The California Law Revision Commission comment to § 1530(a)(2) explains that in California practice, a "certificate" requires a seal but an "attestation" does not. Section 1531 adds that whether "a copy of a writing is attested or certified, the attestation or certificate must state in substance that the copy is a correct copy of the original, or of a specified part thereof. ..." Finally, Evidence Code §§ 1452-54 provide that the seals and signatures of certain public officials are presumed genuine. When a proponent offers an attested document, § 1453 initially comes into play: the signature on the attestation is presumed to be authentic. That presumption authenticates the attestation itself. In turn, the attestation authenticates the attached copy under § 1530(a)(2). These sections "reflect[] an implicit policy decision that if a document 'purports' to be signed by a public employee acting in an official capacity, the likelihood of authenticity is sufficiently high that in the absence of evidence to the contrary it should be found authentic." *Poland v. Dept.*

Motor Vehicles, 34 Cal. App. 4th 1128, 40 Cal. Rptr. 2d 693, 699 (1995).

These procedures have wide application. To begin with, the Evidence Code applies them to documents generated by foreign governments. Section 1452's presumption of the authenticity of seals applies to foreign seals, and § 1454's presumption of the genuineness of official signatures extends to signatures of some foreign officials.. Subdivision 1530(a)(3) prescribes detailed requirements for the attestations and certificates needed to authenticate foreign official documents.

Moreover, in some cases the procedures apply to documents that are now in official custody but that were generated by private parties. Section 1600 is illustrative. That section announces that "[t]he record of an instrument ... purporting to affect an interest in property is prima facie evidence of the existence and content of the original recorded document ... if ... [a] statute authorized [the] document to be recorded" in a public office. Suppose that private parties execute a deed and later record the deed in a public office. In subsequent litigation, one of the parties obtained an attested copy of the recordation. The Assembly Committee comment to Evidence Code § 1401 states that "the duly attested ... copy of the record meets the requirement of authentication for the copy itself, for the official record, and for the original deed."

2. ELEMENTS OF THE FOUNDATION

The mechanics of introducing a properly attested copy of an official record are simple. The elements of the foundation include:

1. The document purports to be a copy of an official record.
2. An attestation is attached to the copy.
3. The attestation states that the signatory is a public custodian of official records.
4. The attestation states that the document is a true and accurate copy of an original, official record.
5. The attestation bears a presumptively authentic signature or seal, or both.

3. SAMPLE FOUNDATION

The fact situation is a probate contest. At one point in the trial, the contestant must prove that a Jean Simmons was born in San Francisco, California in 1946. The contestant is the proponent. The contestant is attempting to introduce a copy of a birth certificate in the custody of the San Francisco County Clerk. The hearing is a bench trial without a jury.

P   Your Honor, I request that this be marked contestant's exhibit number four for identification.
J   It will be so marked.
P   Please let the record reflect that I am showing the exhibit to the opposing counsel.

J   The record will so reflect.

P   I now offer contestant's exhibit number four for identification into evidence as contestant's exhibit number four.

O   I object on the ground that there has been insufficient authentication. No sponsoring witness has come forward to verify the authenticity of this document.

J   (To the contestant) What is your response to the objection?

P   Your Honor, live testimony is unnecessary. In California, the purported signatures and seals of public officials are presumed genuine. This document bears both a purported official signature and seal. The signature and seal authenticate the certificate itself. The certificate states that the attached document is a true and accurate copy of an official record in the county clerk's custody. Thus, the certificate serves to authenticate the attached copy.

J   Objection overruled. The exhibit is received.

P   Your Honor, at this point I would like to invite the court's attention to the body of exhibit four.

J   Yes.

P   I would like to point out that it states that a Jean Simmons was born in San Francisco, California on September 19, 1946.

J   I have noted that.

G.   AUTHENTICATION OF "FAXED" DOCUMENTS

1. THE DOCTRINE

Recent years have witnessed a communications revolution, including the advent of electronic and voice mail. Another commonly-used technology is the telephone facsimile (fax) machine. Because many documents are being transmitted in fax form, counsel must know how to authenticate a "faxed" document. Although fax technology is relatively new, the pertinent evidentiary principles are old and well-settled. Section C of this chapter pointed out that whenever the proponent offers an exhibit into evidence, the proponent must lay a preliminary showing that the exhibit is what its proponent claims. The test is whether the proponent has presented sufficient foundational proof to support a rational jury finding that the evidence is authentic.

The application of these principles depends upon the nature of the proponent's claim about the faxed document. The following three fact patterns illustrate the different claims that the proponent might make. First, suppose that the only issue is whether the company that received the fax had notice of certain facts set out in the fax. The proponent is the recipient company. The company calls an employee to testify that the fax arrived on the company's machine. For this purpose, the source of the information is irrelevant; no matter who sent the fax, the employee can testify that the fax arrived. The fax itself gives the company notice of the information. The essential question is *whether the company actually received a fax with certain contents*. The proponent's only claim is that the fax was produced on the company's facsimile machine, and the employee's testimony suffices to prove that claim. If there is a dispute about whether the fax was given to some specific person once it arrived, the company could use habit evidence to show how faxes are handled and delivered. (*See* Chapter 6, Section C for a discussion of habit evidence.)

Turn to the second fact pattern. Again, assume that the issue is whether a particular company received a fax setting out certain information. The issue is whether a fax transmitted by a particular sender reached the alleged recipient's machine. This time, the witness is an employee of the company that sent the fax rather than the company receiving the fax. The employee in question can give the following foundational testimony: His company uses a fax machine, the machine was in proper working order on the occasion in question, before using the machine he looked up the addressee company's fax number in a reliable directory, he dialed that number on the machine, the sheet of paper containing the facts passed through the machine, and the machine generated a transmission report listing the dialed number and indicating that transmission had occurred. The proponent then offers an exhibit. The witness identifies the exhibit as the sheet that passed through the fax machine at the sending or originating end. Many fax machines produce a transmission report when they send a document, listing the date, time, and number of the receiving machine. Such reports can help verify a transmission.

In the foregoing hypothetical, the proponent claims that: (1) the exhibit is the paper that the witness passed through the fax machine at the transmitting end; and (2) that paper is an accurate copy of the document that the other company received at its end. The foundation is adequate to establish that twofold claim. The witness is certainly competent to prove the initial claim. Furthermore, there is an analogy to the telephone directory doctrine. The use of a telephone directory number identifies the speaker at the other end. Similarly, the use of a fax number from a trustworthy directory identifies the recipient of the fax. The judge can judicially notice the general reliability of fax machines. So long as the proponent shows that the machine in question was in working order, the foundation is sufficient to justify the introduction of the exhibit.

Vary the facts again. In this third fact pattern, the issue is the identity of the sender of a fax. The issue is whether a fax that reached a recipient company was transmitted by the alleged sender. Suppose the recipient company is the plaintiff in a contract action and alleges that the defendant company sent it an offer that the plaintiff accepted. The plaintiff is the proponent, and the witness is one of the plaintiff's employees. The employee received the fax in question, and the proponent claims that the fax is an accurate copy of an offer transmitted by the defendant. This fact pattern differs from the preceding versions. In the first fact pattern, the source of the fax was irrelevant; here, the source is critical—if the defendant company was not the source, the defendant has no contract liability to the plaintiff. In the second fact pattern, the witness was an employee of the sending or transmitting company; here, the witness is an employee of the recipient company. Can that employee's testimony suffice to lay the foundation for the exhibit?

Although the fax authentication issue has not arisen in California case law, faxes are being used as exhibits at trial. Authentication of faxes can involve various authentication doctrines. In *People v. Hagan*, 145 Ill. 2d 287, 164 Ill. Dec.

578, 583 N.E.2d 494 (1991), the Illinois Supreme Court addressed the question of the foundational evidence needed to authenticate faxed documents. The court analogized to the foundation requirements for computer records, stating that faxed documents are properly authenticated by the introduction of evidence sufficient to support a finding that the documents received accurately reflect the documents faxed. *Hagan* was a relatively easy case because there was testimony from witnesses at both the sending and receiving ends. However, a proponent could sufficiently identify the sender of a fax even without such an extensive record. For example, the fax received might disclose information known only to one person, the alleged sender. Or, if the recipient of the fax in question had earlier contacted the alleged sender by letter, telephone, or fax, and the fax in question was obviously responsive to the previous contact, the fax could be authenticated by analogy to the reply letter doctrine. For that matter, if the fax in question bore the sender's fax number automatically imprinted on each page and the witness identifies the imprinted digits as the sender's fax number, there might be sufficient authentication.

2. ELEMENTS OF THE FOUNDATION

Suppose that the case falls into the third fact pattern. The following foundation would suffice to authenticate the fax as originating from the alleged sender.

1. The receiving business uses a facsimile machine.
2. The facsimile machine is standard equipment that can both send and receive documents by telephone. The trial judge should judicially notice this proposition.
3. The facsimile machine accurately transmits by telephone to other facsimile machines copies of original documents inserted into the former facsimile machine for transmission, and accurately receives such documents as well.
4. A procedure exists for checking for mechanical and human error.
5. The facsimile machine accurately and automatically records the time and date of transmittal.
6. A fax cover sheet, sent with the faxed document, shows the phone number of the originating facsimile machine and the name of the person to whom the document is directed, as well as the facsimile number of that person.
7. Each fax page received is automatically imprinted with the fax number of the originating machine.
8. The fax number stated on the cover sheet and on the fax pages is the number of the alleged sender.
9. The witness identifies the exhibit as the document received on the addressee's fax machine.

3. SAMPLE FOUNDATION

The fact situation in this scenario is litigation involving an order placed by Acme Widget Company with one of its suppliers, Pesotum Widget Frames, Inc., for 3,000 widget frames. As part of its case, Pesotum wishes to show that a Ms. Baker, a Pesotum employee, received a faxed letter from Acme containing an order for 3,000 widget frames. Pesotum's lawyer is the proponent, and Ms. Baker is the witness.

P　WHERE do you work?

W　At Pesotum Widget Frames, Inc.

P　WHAT is your position there?

W　I am the executive secretary and assistant to the president of Pesotum, George Clinton.

P　As of September 11 of this year, the date in question here, DID Pesotum own a facsimile machine?

W　Yes.

P　As of that date, for HOW long had Pesotum had the facsimile machine?

W　At least three or four years before that date.

P　HOW often, if ever, did you use that machine to either fax documents or receive documents that others had faxed to Pesotum? (4)

W　Dozens—perhaps hundreds—of times, both sending and receiving.

P　WHAT procedure did you use in September of this year when you wished to fax a document to someone? (2), (3), (5), (6), (7)

W　I would fill out a cover sheet indicating the person to whom the document was directed and that person's phone number. The cover sheet would also contain other information, such as the total number of pages being transmitted, the date and time of the transmission, any additional routing information, and a statement that in case of poor transmission the party receiving the document should call me at the number written on the cover sheet so I could send the document again. I would then feed the cover sheet and the document to be transmitted into the facsimile machine. The machine would transmit them to the number I dialed. The machine automatically recorded the time and date of transmittal on the documents being sent. Our model of machine also automatically imprints the fax number on the top of each page.

P　WHAT was the procedure for documents that you received by fax?

W　The same as I described, only in reverse. Then we got the cover sheet that the sender filled out. If the sender uses a fax machine like ours, the originating fax number is automatically imprinted somewhere on the page—either on the very top or the bottom.

P　HAVE you ever had occasion to see original documents that you have either sent or received by your facsimile machine and to compare those documents the faxed documents? (4)

W　Oh, sure. During the course of my handling the paperwork regarding Pesotum's contracts, I often see documents that I have faxed to some third party that are being returned to me by mail with some additional writing on them.

P　HOW closely do the faxed documents resemble the original document? (4)

W They're exact copies. There are no deviations of any kind. In all instances, the machine has accurately transmitted just what appears on the original document.

P To your knowledge, HOW can you alter the fax machine to create a difference between the document being sent and the document received? (3)

W I don't know of any way I could do that.

P More specifically, HOW, if at all, could your facsimile machine be set to alter in any way a document that someone had faxed to you? (3)

W I don't know how that could be done. Absolutely not.

P Directing your attention to September 11 of this year, WHAT, if any, fax transmissions did you receive that day?

W I received one from Acme.

P Your Honor, I request that this be marked as plaintiff's exhibit number four for identification.

J It will be so marked.

(Examining counsel permits opposing counsel to inspect the exhibit.)

P I request permission to approach the witness.

J Permission granted.

P Ms. Baker, I now hand you plaintiff's exhibit number four for identification. WHAT is this exhibit? (9)

W This is the four-page document and the cover sheet that I received on our facsimile machine on September 11. It indicates that it was sent from Acme Widget Company's facsimile machine. Our machine was called and this document was transmitted to it.

P HOW, if at all, does the present condition of the document differ from its condition when you received it on September 11? (9)

W As far as I can tell, it's in exactly the same condition.

P WHAT date, time, and telephone number are imprinted on plaintiff's exhibit number four for identification?

W September 11, 10:15 a.m., and (510) 456-7890.

P WHERE does the fax number appear on those pages? (7)

W To begin with, it's on the originating cover sheet. Moreover, it's been imprinted on each page.

P WHAT is the significance of the date and time—September 11, 10:15 a.m.? (3), (5), (6)

W That's the date and approximate time I can recall receiving the documents from Acme.

P WHOSE telephone number is (510) 456-7890? (8)

W It is the telephone number of Acme Widget Company?

P HOW do you know that? (8)

W I've faxed documents back and forth with them several times. On some occasions, I pick up the phone and talk to one of their people minutes after getting or sending a fax. I'm positive that that's their number.

P Your Honor, I now offer plaintiff's exhibit number four for identification into evidence as plaintiff's four.

H.   THE AUTHENTICATION OF ORAL STATEMENTS

Like written statements, oral statements must be authenticated. A written statement is authenticated by identifying the author. An oral statement is authenticated by identifying the speaker. To do so, the proponent may use several techniques.

1. LAY OPINION TESTIMONY OF A WITNESS FAMILIAR WITH THE SPEAKER'S VOICE

The proponent may use lay opinion testimony to authenticate an oral statement, just as the proponent may use lay opinion testimony to authenticate a writing. For a writing, the witness must testify that he or she is familiar with the author's handwriting style. For an oral statement, the witness must testify that he or she is familiar with the person's voice.

The foundation contains these elements:

1. At a specific time and place, the witness heard a voice.
2. The witness recognized the voice as that of a certain person.
3. The witness is familiar with that person's voice.
4. The witness explains the basis for his or her familiarity with that person's voice.
5. The person made a statement.

The fact situation is a tort action for slander. The plaintiff, Brown, sues the defendant, Nolan. The plaintiff alleges that Nolan slandered the plaintiff during a telephone conversation with Parish. The plaintiff calls Parish to the stand.

P Mr. Parish, WHERE were you on the evening of April 6 of this year? (1)
W I was at home.
P WHAT, if anything, happened while you were at home? (1)
W I received a phone call.
P WHO was the caller? (2)
W It was the defendant, Ms. Nolan.
P HOW do you know that it was Ms. Nolan? (3)
W I recognized her voice, and she said it was Ms. Nolan.
P HOW did you become familiar with her voice? (4)
W We've known each other for years.
P HOW many years? (4)
W Easily fifteen.
P HOW open have you spoken with her? (4)
W I can't answer. We've spoken hundreds of times, I guess. We're neighbors. She telephoned me at least a couple of times a week.
P WHAT condition was your telephone in when you received this call?
W It was in good working condition. There was no static or anything.
P HOW much noise was there in the background?

W None that I could tell. I didn't have the stereo on or anything like that, and I couldn't hear any noise at the other end, other than Ms. Nolan talking.

P WHAT did Ms. Nolan say during this telephone conversation? (5)

W She said that she had a hot item of news for me.

P WHAT was that? (5)

W She said that the plaintiff, Mr. Brown, had paid $6,000 to bribe one of the City Councilmen to get favorable zoning on some commercial property Brown owns.

2. THE TELEPHONE DIRECTORY DOCTRINE

The telephone directory doctrine parallels the reply letter doctrine. Under the reply letter doctrine, the courts trust the reliability of the Post Office.. Under this doctrine, the courts place their faith in the accuracy of telephone directories. Federal Evidence Rule 901(b)(6) describes the doctrine: The proponent may authenticate a "[t]elephone conversation, by evidence that a call was made to the number assigned at the time by the telephone company to a particular person or business, if ... in the case of a person, circumstances, including self-identification, show the person answering to be the one called. ..." The pre-code California cases recognize the same doctrine. 1 WITKIN § 412. This fact pattern creates a circumstantial inference that the person answering was the person the telephone number is assigned to.

The foundation includes these elements:

1. The telephone directory assigns a certain number to the person.
2. The witness called that number.
3. The witness asked for the person to whom the number is assigned.
4. The person answering identified himself or herself as the person to whom the number is assigned.
5. Any other circumstances indicating that the person answering was the person to whom the number was assigned.

The fact situation is a tort action arising from an automobile crash. The expert testimony indicates that the failure of the defendant's brakes caused the crash. One issue is whether the defendant knew his brakes were defective. The plaintiff wants to elicit Mr. Martinez' testimony that he worked on the defendant's car, found the brakes defective, and notified the defendant by telephone. The telephone conversation was Mr. Martinez' only contact with the defendant, Mr. Jackson. The plaintiff is the proponent.

W After examining the brakes, I concluded that they were in dangerous condition.

P WHAT did you do then?

W I decided to notify the owner, this fellow Jackson.

P HOW did you notify him?

W I wanted to phone him and let him know.

P HOW did you do that? (1)

W First I checked the telephone directory to get his number.

P   WHAT did you do then? (2)

W   I called the number.

P   WHERE was the directory when you were dialing? (2)

W   It was right in front of me. I was looking at it as I di aled.

P   WHAT happened next? (3)

W   It rang, and a man answered.

P   WHAT did you say? (3)

W   I asked to speak to Mr. Jackson, the owner of the purple Corvette.

P   HOW did the person answering the phone identify himself? (4)

W   He just said he was Jackson, the person I wanted to talk to.

P   WHAT, if anything, did he say about the Corvette? (5)

W   He told me that he realized that it had some problems.

P   WHAT problems? (5)

W   He mentioned a problem with the exhaust and the windshield wipers.

P   HOW accurate were those statements? (5)

W   The guy was right. I'd looked at the car, and I'd discovered those problems, among others. The guy I was talking with was obviously familiar with the car.

P   WHAT did you say then?

W   I told him about the brakes.

P   Specifically, WHAT did you tell him?

W   I said that they were defective and dangerous. I told him that they could fail anytime and that he should have them repaired immediately.

3. TESTIMONY BY EXPERTS IN VOICEPRINTS OR SOUND SPECTROGRAPHY

The sound spectrography (voiceprint) expert does for speech what the questioned document examiner does for writings. Two theoretical premises underlie sound spectrography. The first premise is that interspeaker variability exceeds intraspeaker variability; even though a person's voice pattern changes from time to time, the voice pattern differences among the speakers are greater than the variations in a single speaker's voice pattern. The second premise is intraspeaker invariant speech: Each voice has unique characteristics that it will invariably display under spectrographic analysis. Most speech scientists accept the first premise, but the second premise is still controversial in scientific circles. Many critics of sound spectrography argue that there has been insufficient experimental verification of the theory of invariant speech. A report of a committee of the National Academy of Sciences found insufficient verification.

The spectrograph instrument itself includes: (1) a magnetic recording device; (2) a variable electronic filter; (3) a paper-carrying drum coupled to the magnetic recording device; and (4) an electronic stylus that marks the paper as the drum rotates. The spectrograph operates in this fashion. The operator starts with a tape of certain, commonly used English cue words—the, and, me, on, is, it, I, a, and you. The cue words are static-state words; the words preceding and following them have little effect on their pronunciation and, hence, on the spectrograms they produce. The operator prepares the tape by having the person read the words into the tape or excerpting the words from a tape of the person's speech. The operator plays the tape repeatedly on the magnetic recording device. The device is attached to the electronic filter; and each time the operator replays the tape, the filter lets another frequency pass through. The frequencies pass through to an electronic stylus; as the frequencies pass through, the stylus marks the paper-carrying drum. The stylus thus produces a spectrogram, a graphic depiction of the voice pattern. The usual spectrogram is a bar spectrogram. The vertical axis is frequency, the horizontal axis is time, and the darkness is the voice's amplitude.

BAR SPECTROGRAPH

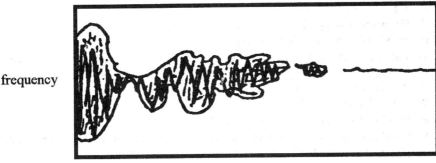

frequency

time

The operator next takes a tape of the unknown voice, for example, the tape of a bomb threat or obscene telephone call. The operator excerpts the same words from the tape of that voice and prepares another spectrogram in the same fashion. The operator then compares the two spectrograms and forms an opinion whether the same voice produced the two spectrograms. Experts vary on the number of points of similarity required for a match; some will accept as few as 16 while others insist upon as many as 33.

Given the division in the scientific community over sound spectrography, it is understandable that the courts are also split. Some courts reject the evidence. In *People v. Kelly*, 17 Cal. ad 24, 130 Cal. Rptr. 144, 549 P.2d 1240 (1976), the California Supreme Court excluded the evidence. Courts in Arizona, the District of Columbia, Indiana, Maryland, Michigan, New Jersey, and Pennsylvania have followed *Kelly*. Other courts continue to accept the evidence. For example, the federal Court of Appeals for the Second Circuit and the Maine Supreme Judicial Court have sustained the admission of sound spectrography as evidence.

The California Supreme Court's holding in *Kelly* is based largely on a view of scientific evidence expressed in an old federal case, *Frye v. United States*, 293 F. 1013 (D.C. Cir. 1923). According to *Frye*, the proponent of testimony based on a scientific technique must establish that the technique is generally accepted within the relevant scientific specialty. *Frye* is no longer good law in the federal courts, thanks to *Daubert v. Merrell Dow Pharmaceuticals, Inc.*, 113 S. Ct. 2786 (1993). (*Daubert* is discussed in more detail in Section M, below.)

In 1994, the California Supreme Court ruled that notwithstanding *Daubert*, it would continue to adhere to *Frye*. *People v. Leahy*, 8 Cal. 4th 587, 34 Cal. Rptr. 2d 663 (1994). Even if the California Supreme Court persists in following *Frye*, it may someday change its mind about sound spectrography and start admitting voiceprint evidence. On that supposition, we offer the following sample foundation for voiceprint evidence.

The elements of a foundation for sound spectrography evidence include:

1.   The tape recordings used to produce the spectrograms are authentic. *See* Section H of this chapter.
2.   The witness is qualified to explain sound spectrography's underlying premises and to conduct the test.
3.   The underlying premises of sound spectrography are interspeaker variability and invariant speech.
4.   Those premises are based on valid scientific methods and principles.
5.   The instrument is the sound spectrograph.
6.   The instrument operates on valid scientific methods and principles.
7.   At a particular time and place, the witness conducted a voiceprint examination.
8.   The witness used the tape recordings mentioned in element #1.
9.   The witness excerpted the cue words from both tapes.
10. The witness used a spectrograph to analyze the tapes of the cue words.
11. The spectrograph was in good working condition at the time.
12. The witness used the proper procedures.
13. The analysis produced two spectrograms.
14. The witness identifies the spectrograms.
15. There are several points of similarity between the two spectrograms.
16. In the witness's opinion, the same voice produced the two spectrograms.

The following is a sample foundation. The fact situation is a bomb threat prosecution. A police officer recorded the threat and authenticated the tape recording as prosecution exhibit number one. Another officer obtained a voice exemplar recording from the defendant; the officer has authenticated that tape recording as prosecution exhibit number two. Thus, the two officers have laid the first element of the foundation. The prosecution now calls Mr. James Cottrell, a sound spectrography expert. The prosecution is the proponent. Mr. Cottrell has already identified himself and stated his address.

P   WHAT is your occupation? (2)
W   I am a member of the staff of the Los Angeles Police Department Crime Laboratory.
P   HOW long have you worked there? (2)
W   For the past six years—ever since I graduated from college.
P   WHERE did you attend college? (2)
W   I attended University of California, Berkeley.

P WHAT was your undergraduate major? (2)

W I was a science major, specializing in speech science and acoustics.

P WHAT are your present duties? (2)

W I do all the sound spectrography or voiceprint analysis for the L.A. Police Department.

P WHAT is sound spectrography (3)

W It's a scientific technique for identifying a speaker.

P WHAT is the basis of this technique? (3)

W It has two premises. One is interspeaker variability.

P WHAT does that mean? (3)

W It means simply that the difference between your and my voice is greater than the fluctuations in my voice. Depending on whether I'm alert or sleepy, my voice pattern changes; but the differences between our two voices are still greater than the changes in my voice pattern from time to time. That's one of the two major premises of sound spectrography.

P WHAT is the other premise? (3)

W Invariant speech.

P WHAT does that mean? (3)

W Each person's voice has some unique characteristics, and you'll always be able to detect those characteristics with the instrument we use, the spectrograph.

P WHAT experiments have been conducted to verify these theories? (3)

W There has been extensive experimentation at Stanford, Michigan State, and a number of industrial laboratories.

P WHAT has been the outcome of these experiments? (3)

W They show that if you have a trained examiner, the examiner will ordinarily be able to determine whether the same voice produced two spectrograms, the charts of the voice patterns.

P HOW high has the error rate been? (3)

W It depends on the type of error you're talking about. If you're talking about false identifications, erroneously identifying a suspect as the person who produced the unknown spectrogram, it's pretty low. If you give the examiner the right to say that a particular test is too close to call, the error rate is likely to be only one or two percent.

P Have the experiments at Stanford, Michigan State, and the industrial labs been written up in scientific journals? (4)

W Yes. There are many articles in well-respected journals that set out various aspects of the subject.

P Have those writings been peer reviewed?

W Oh, yes, all the articles in the journals I referred to are peer reviewed.

P HOW did you apply these theories to a particular case? (5)

W As I said, you use a spectrograph. In our laboratory, we use a Series 700 Sound Spectrograph manufactured by Voiceprint Laboratories in New Jersey.

P WHAT is a sound spectrograph? (5)

W It has four basic components. First, there's a magnetic recording device. Then there's an electronic filter. Third, the machine has a stylus. Finally, it has a paper-carrying drum.

P HOW does the spectrograph operate? (5)

W You put a tape on the recording device. You play it again and again. Every time you play it, the filter lets a different frequency of the voice through. The frequencies activate the stylus, and the stylus marks the paper. The end result is a sort of chart that we call a spectrogram. In effect, it's a visual display of a voice pattern. You compare two charts; and if there are enough points of similarity, you conclude that the same voice produced the two spectrograms and, hence, the two tape recordings.

P   WHAT experiments have been conducted to verify the spectrograph's reliability? (5)

W   Basically the same ones I mentioned before. The researchers have tested both the theory and the instrument. The test results I mentioned before tend to validate the instrument as well.

P   Does the spectrograph employ valid scientific methods and principles? (6)

W   Certainly. The spectrograph itself is basically a very simple measuring and recording machine, and the principles it employs are used in many other kinds of measuring and recording machines that are used for a whole range of purposes.

P   Mr. Cottrell, WHERE were you on the morning of July 17 of this year? (7)

W   I was at my office at the lab.

P   WHAT happened while you were there? (7)

W   A police officer dropped by some tape recordings for spectrographic analysis.

P   I now hand you prosecution exhibits numbers one and two. WHAT are they? (8)

W   They're the tape recordings I was given.

P   HOW can you recognize them? (8)

W   I remember the notations on the containers, and I made these small marks, my initials on the label, on the reels themselves.

P   WHAT did you do with the tapes? (7)

W   I proceeded to conduct the analysis.

P   HOW did you do that? (9)

W   First I had to excerpt common words from both tapes. That took a little while.

P   Then WHAT did you do? (10)

W   One at a time, I put the new tapes of the excerpts on the spectrograph.

P   WHAT condition was your spectrograph in at the time? (11)

W   It was in good working condition.

P   HOW do you know that? (11)

W   I ran through the manufacturer's maintenance checklist before I used the spectrograph. The instrument checked out fine.

P   HOW are you supposed to operate the machine? (12)

W   You let it warm up a bit, mount the tape you're analyzing, activate the machine, and then let it run until the spectrogram is complete.

P   WHAT procedure did you use on this occasion? (12)

W   I followed the proper procedure exactly. I did just what I outlined for you.

P   WHAT was the result of the test? (13)

W   At the end, I had two spectrograms, two visual displays of voice patterns.

P   Your Honor, I request that these be marked prosecution exhibits numbers three and four for identification.

J   They will be so marked.

P   Please let the record reflect that I am showing these exhibits to the opposing attorney.

J   It will so reflect.

P   Mr. Cottrell, I now hand you prosecution exhibit three for identification. WHAT is it? (14)

W It's the spectrogram of that tape, prosecution exhibit number one.

P HOW can you recognize the spectrogram? (14)

W As you can see, on the other side, I marked my initials, the date, and the number of the tape it corresponded to.

P I now hand you prosecution exhibit number four for identification. WHAT is it? (14)

W It's the spectrogram produced by analyzing the other tape, prosecution exhibit number two.

P HOW can you recognize it? (14)

W I made the same sort of notations on the back here.

P Your Honor, I now offer prosecution exhibits three and four for identification into evidence as prosecution exhibits three and four.

J They will be received.

P Mr. Cottrell, WHAT did you do with the spectrograms? (15)

W I compared them.

P WHAT was the result of your comparison? (15)

W I found a large number of points of similarity between the two spectrograms.

P HOW many points of similarity? (15)

W Thirty-two in all.

P Do you have an opinion on the question whether the same voice produced the two spectrograms? (16)

W Yes.

P WHAT is that opinion? (16)

W In my judgment, it was the same voice.

P WHAT is the basis of that opinion? (15)

W Not just the number of points of similarity, but some of them were really unique. I'm confident that the same person who phoned in this bomb threat made this other voice exemplar.

P Request permission to hand exhibits three and four to the jurors for their inspection.

J Permission granted.

4. CALLER IDENTIFICATION

a. The Doctrine

Telephone caller identification service is now widely available. Caller ID units or boxes can be bought from vendors that sell telephone accessories. After buying the unit, the user installs it and orders caller ID service from the telephone company. The telephone company then activates the service. The caller ID information is transmitted as a burst of a model signal to the unit. Once service has been activated, whenever someone places a call to the user, the user's caller ID unit will automatically display the caller's telephone number.[1] More sophisticated caller ID units can timestamp and store the number for later retrieval and printout.

---

[1] Some callers, though, have "blocking." They can block the transmission of their phone number either in all cases or for a particular call. If the caller has the latter type of blocking, he or she

Suppose that at trial the proponent wants to prove that a certain call to the proponent's home or business originated from a certain number. In a contract action, the proponent might be the plaintiff contending that the telephone call (the alleged offer) came from the defendant's corporate headquarters.[2] To help prove up that contention, the plaintiff could rely on caller ID technology.

b. Elements of the Foundation

To lay a proper foundation, the proponent would be required to show the following:

1. In general, caller ID technology is reliable. Caller ID is already in such widespread use that many judges would be willing to judicially notice this proposition under California Evidence Code § 452. The reliability of the technology is both a matter of common knowledge under § 452(g) and a "verifiable certainty" under § 452(h). The problem facing the proponent is that, to date, there are no published opinions upholding an authentication based on caller ID. Given the dearth of precedent, a cautious trial judge might insist that the proponent present live expert testimony to establish this element of the foundation. In that event, the proponent could call a telephone company expert witness under California Evidence Code § 801.
2. Prior to the telephone call in question, the user acquired and installed a caller ID unit or box.
3. The caller ID unit in question is a reliable one. Even if the judge is willing to judicially notice the first element of the foundation, the judge will probably balk at judicially noticing this proposition. To be on the safe side, as on element #1, the proponent could call an expert witness. In this case, the ideal expert would be a representative of the manufacturer. A salesperson at a telephone store would also probably qualify as an expert if he or she had substantial experience with the make and model in question.

    The judge might not demand the appearance of an expert to testify directly to the reliability of the caller ID unit installed at the plaintiff's office. Instead, the judge might well be content with circumstantial proof. For example, one of the plaintiff's agents could testify that: She has used the unit in question for several months or years; when the agent receives a telephone call, the unit regularly displays a telephone number; and on numerous occasions, the circumstances have indicated that the number displayed was the number from which the call originated.

---

must dial a special code at the time of the call in order to prevent the transmission of his or her phone number.

[2]Some callers have PBX, private branch exchanges. If so, the number transmitted to the user might be the main number for the corporation rather than the number of the specific phone which the call was actually originated from.

One could prove this latter fact in a variety of ways. Perhaps when the agent answered, she recognized the voice as that of the person whose number was displayed. Or perhaps the caller disclosed information known only to employees of the business whose number was displayed. Or perhaps at a later time, the user called the number previously displayed by the caller ID unit, and in that subsequent conversation, the respondent referred to the earlier telephone call.

4. On the occasion in question, the caller ID unit displayed a particular telephone number. If the user recalls the number displayed, she can testify to that number on the basis of personal knowledge. If the unit has logging and printout capability, the proponent can offer the printout into evidence so long as the foundational witness can in any manner identify the exhibit as the printout from the user's caller ID unit. If, as is often done in the business world, the user has connected the caller ID unit to a computer that logs incoming calls, the proponent can offer a computer printout.

5. The telephone number in question belongs to a particular person or business. The witness may be able to testify from personal experience that that number belongs to that individual or business. Failing that, the proponent could introduce a telephone directory. Telephone directories fall within the hearsay exception codified in California Evidence Code § 1340. In many cases, the two parties can reach a stipulation that the phone number has been assigned to a particular person or business.

c. Sample Foundation

The fact situation is a civil contract action. The plaintiff, Arnett Corporation, alleges that the defendant, Ballantine Corporation, breached a contract with the plaintiff. The plaintiff contends that on June 15, 2000, the defendant telephoned the plaintiff and placed an order for custom merchandise to be manufactured by the plaintiff. Before trial, the parties stipulated that the main telephone number for the defendant's purchasing department is (916) 752-0727. At a pretrial hearing, the judge accepted the stipulation. In addition, at the same hearing, the judge granted the plaintiff's request that she judicially notice the general reliability of caller identification technology. The next witness is Ms. Amann. Just before calling her, the plaintiff's attorney states:

P Your Honor, as you will recall, at our pretrial conference, you granted our request for judicial notice. I would ask that at this point you instruct the jury on the judicially noticed proposition. (1)

J Very well. Ladies and gentlemen, I am going to give you an instruction now. The instruction is that you are to assume that in general, caller identification units for telephones are reliable. You are to assume that when a unit is working properly, it correctly displays the number of the incoming telephone call. You must assume the truth of that fact even though you will not hear any live testimony about it. All right, let's proceed.

P   Thank you, Your Honor. As our next witness, we call Ms. Holly Amann.

J   Ms. Amann, please approach the witness stand.

     (Ms. Amann is sworn and identifies herself. The plaintiff's direct examination continues.)

P   Ms. Amann, WHERE do you work? (2)

W   I work for Arnett Corporation.

P   HOW long have you worked there? (2)

W   I've been employed there for 15 years.

P   WHAT is your current position with Arnett Corporation? (2)

W   I'm the head of the order department.

P   HOW long have you held that position? (2)

W   I've been in orders for ten years, and I've headed the department for the past three years.

P   WHAT is the job of the order department? (2)

W   We take all the incoming orders for merchandise. We make sure that the order is sent on to records, bookkeeping, and the plant.

P   HOW do you receive these orders? (2)

W   Lots of ways.

P   Such as WHICH ways? (2)

W   We get them by personal contact, e-mail, FAX, telephone—basically, if the means of communication exists, we use it to get orders.

P   WHAT percent of your orders comes over the telephone? (2)

W   The vast majority. Most people still use the good old telephone rather than the fancier stuff like e-mail.

P   WHAT type of telephone equipment do you use in your department? (2)

W   We have a phone hooked to a caller identification unit.

P   HOW long have you had a caller ID unit in your department? (2)

W   We've used one for over three years now.

P   WHAT type of unit do you have? (2)

W   It's a standard caller ID box manufactured by AT & T.

P   WHAT does the unit do? (2)

W   Since we're a business, we use one of the more advanced models.

P   WHAT do you mean by "advanced"? (2), (4)

W   A basic caller ID unit—like the one I have at home—just displays the incoming call number. However, as a business, we need to keep a record of our calls. So we have a caller unit with a history capability.

P   WHAT do you mean by "history capability"? (2), (4)

W   It not only displays the incoming caller number. It also logs or records the number in memory and time-stamps it—indicating the date and time the call came in. At a later point, you can retrieve the number and time stamp from memory; you can either display it again or print it out.

P   HOW reliable is your caller ID unit? (3)

W   It's very trustworthy.

P   HOW do you know that? (3)

W   On many occasions, the information I've gotten from the unit has checked out.

P   HOW has it checked out? (3)

W   Someone will tell me something over the phone, and it will turn out to be true.

P   WHAT would be an example? (3)

W Well, I'll get a call, and someone will tell me to expect an order from their business. Then in a couple of days I'll get that order, and I'll recognize the handwriting on the order. Or they'll say that a check is on the way, and a check will show up from that very company.

P HOW often, if ever, has the caller ID unit malfunctioned? (3)

W As I recall, there was one day in 1999 when it went down. It's not that it malfunctioned in the sense of giving you the wrong number. It shorted and didn't work at all. We immediately called the repairman and got the unit fixed. Since then we've had no problems at all.

P Ms. Amann, WHERE were you on June 15th of 2000? (4)

W I was at work at the office.

P WHAT, if any, telephone calls did you receive that day? (4)

W I got one from a person who said he was a buyer for Ballantine.

P Before that telephone call, HOW much contact, if any, had you had with that person? (4)

W I have to say honestly that I didn't recognize his voice.

P WHO did the caller say he worked for? (4)

W He said he was calling on behalf of Ballantine to place an order.

P At the time of the call, WHAT telephone number was the caller ID unit displaying? (4)

W It was displaying Ballantine's number.

P WHAT is that number? (5)

W It's (916) 752-0727.

P HOW do you know that? (5)

W I've dealt with them on tens of occasions before.

P HOW do you know that the caller ID unit displayed that number? (4)

W As I said, I didn't recognize this person's voice. However, I always make it a practice to check the caller ID display whenever I don't recognize the voice. You have to make sure who you're dealing with. If it hadn't displayed that number, I'd remember that. That would have been a red flag for me.

P WHERE were you before coming to court this afternoon? (4)

W I was at the office.

P WHY were you there? (4)

W You asked me to stop by and print the history log from the caller ID unit for June 15, 2000.

P WHAT did you do? (4)

W I did as you asked. I went to the unit, called up the log for that date, and printed it out.

P Your Honor, I request that this be marked Plaintiff's Exhibit number three for identification. (4)

J It will be so marked.

P Please let the record reflect that I am showing the exhibit to the opposing counsel. (4)

J The record will so reflect.

P Permission to approach the witness? (4)

J Granted.

P Ms. Amann, I now hand you what has just been marked as Plaintiff's Exhibit number three for identification. WHAT is it? (4)

W It's the printout of the history log from the caller ID unit in my department.

P HOW can you recognize it? (4)

W To begin with, I read it as soon as it printed out. I recognize the contents. In addition, just to be on the safe side, I wrote my initials and today's date on the pages. They're right here. I recognize them as well.

P Your Honor, I now offer Plaintiff's Exhibit number three for identification into evidence as Plaintiff's three. (4)

J Any objection?

O No, Your Honor.

J Very well, it will be received.

P Ms. Amann, I'd like you to read to the jury the third entry on the first page. (4)

W Certainly. It reads: "June 15 0930 hours (916) 7520727."

P WHAT does that entry mean? (4)

W It means that at 0930 hours—that is, 9:30 in the morning—we received a telephone call from that number.

P Thank you, Ms. Amann. Your Honor, as you know, at the pretrial hearing you accepted a stipulation between the parties. I would request that at this point, you inform the jury of the stipulation.

J Certainly. Ladies and gentlemen, earlier today the parties "stipulated" to a fact. That term means that they agreed to that fact. You are to assume that that fact is true. The stipulated fact is that (916) 752-0727 is the main telephone number for the defendant's purchasing department. You are to accept the truth of the stipulated fact, just as you are to accept as true the fact I judicially noticed earlier.

I. TAPE RECORDINGS

1. THE DOCTRINE

Like computers, tape recorders present scientific evidence issues. However, the validity of the underlying theory and reliability of recorders in general are so well accepted that the judge will judicially notice those elements of the foundation. Yet, notwithstanding the courts' willingness to notice those foundational elements, the courts have traditionally taken a strict attitude towards tape recordings. The courts realize that tapes can be tampered with. For that reason, the courts generally have insisted on a very complete foundation: the operator's qualifications, the equipment's working condition, custody of the tape, an identification of the speakers on the tape, and finally testimony of someone who heard the conversation that the tape is an accurate reproduction of the conversation. *See People v. Polk*, 47 Cal. App. 4th 944, 54 Cal. Rptr. 2d 921, 926 (1996) ("the court should satisfy itself that [the tapes] are substantially complete and substantially correct as to matters that are material and important").

In the last few years, the courts have begun to liberalize the standards for the admission of tape recordings for two reasons. First, there are now electronic techniques for determining whether a tape has been altered. Pellicano, *Tape Recordings as Evidence*, 7 CAL. LAW. 67 (1990). If the opponent seriously contests a tape's accuracy, the opponent can use an expert to detect the tampering. Second, and more important, the courts have gone back to fundamentals and begun to treat the question of a tape recording's authenticity as a simple question of authentication. A tape recording is a "writing" as broadly defined in Evidence Code § 250, and the test stated in §§ 403 and 1400(a) is controlling. 2 WITKIN § 912, at 874-75. As Section A of this chapter emphasizes, the test for authentication is lax: Has the proponent presented sufficient evidence to support a rational finding of fact that the tape recording is authentic? Given that test, many modern courts no longer insist on the traditional, strict foundation. In truth, the last element of the traditional foundation, standing alone, has sufficient probative value to authenticate the tape. If a witness testifies that he or she heard a conversation and that the tape accurately reproduces the conversation, there is a permissive inference of the tape's genuineness. *People v. Williams*, 16 Cal. 4th 635, 941 P.2d 752, 66 Cal. Rptr. 2d 573 (1997) (audio tape authenticated on detective's testimony that tape was recording of detective's conversation with defendant). Similarly, proof of the other elements of the traditional foundation is sufficient authentication without the last element. Proof of the operator's qualifications, the equipment's working condition, and the tape's custody shows that the tape is an accurate reproduction of some conversation; and in principle, testimony identifying the speakers (by any person familiar with their voices) is sufficient to complete the foundation to authenticate the tape.

In *O'Laskey v. Sortino*, 224 Cal. App. 3d 241, 273 Cal. Rptr. 674 (1990), a litigant offered a written transcript of a tape recording of a conversation between a private investigator and his adversary. The only evidence to authenticate the transcript was a statement by the litigant's attorney that the attorney had listened to the tape recording, and that the transcript accurately reported what was on the tape recording. The attorney was not present during the conversation, so he could not state whether the tape recording itself was an accurate record of the conversation. The court held that the transcript had not been properly authenticated. Absent evidence that the tape recording accurately recorded the conversation, the transcript of the tape recording was useless. *But see People v. Polk*, 47 Cal. App. 4th 944, 54 Cal. Rptr. 2d 921, 927-28 (1996) (adequate authentication of a transcript). (*See also* Chapter 7, concerning secondary evidence.)

2. ELEMENTS OF THE FOUNDATION

The strict, traditional foundation includes the following elements:

1. The operator of the equipment was qualified.
2. The operator recorded a conversation at a certain time and place.
3. The operator used certain equipment to record the conversation.
4. The equipment was in good working order.
5. The operator used proper procedures to record the conversation.
6. The tape was a good reproduction of the conversation.
7. The operator accounts for the tape's custody between the time of taping and the time of trial.

8. The operator recognizes the exhibit as the tape.
9. The tape is still a good reproduction of the conversation.

3. SAMPLE FOUNDATIONS

The first foundation is an example of a strict, traditional foundation. The fact situation is a contract action. The contracting parties were suspicious of each other, and they had a private investigator tape a key negotiating session.

P   WHAT is your occupation? (1)
W   I'm a private investigator.
P   WHO is your employer? (1)
W   I work for the Stead Detective Agency downtown.
P   HOW long have you worked there? (1)
W   For about ten years now.
P   WHAT are your duties for your employer? (1)
W   My real specialty is electronic surveillance and tape recording.
P   HOW long have you worked in that field? (1)
W   About fifteen years.
P   WHEN did you begin working in that field? (1)
W   When I was in the military service.
P   WHICH military service were you in? (1)
W   I was in the Army.
P   WHAT did you do while you were in the service? (1)
W   I specialized in radar.
P   WHAT training did you receive in that specialty? (1)
W   I took a four-month course and was even able to get a first-class license from the Federal Communications Commission.
P   WHAT additional training have you had in the field? (1)
W   Since leaving the service, I've taken ten college level courses in electronics. I've also attended a number of seminars on tape recording and electronic surveillance techniques.
P   WHERE were you on the morning of January 17 of this year? (2)
W   I went to the offices of Atco Corporation.
P   WHY do you do that? (2)
W   The president of the corporation, Mr. Semegen, had asked me to come and record a negotiating session between him and a Mr. Heiser, the head of another corporation.
P   WHAT did you do while you were at the offices of Atco Corporation? (3)
W   I did what I'd been asked to do; I recorded this conversation.
P   WHAT equipment did you use to record the conversation? (3)
W   I used a Uher recorder, microphones, and a seven-inch reel of Ampex audiotape.
P   WHAT do "Uher" and "Ampex" mean? (3)
W   They're tradenames. They are two of the most dependable manufacturers in the field.
P   HOW often had you used that equipment in the past? (3)
W   Hundreds of times. I really trust their equipment; it's very reliable.
P   WHAT condition was the equipment in that morning? (4)

W It was in good condition.
P HOW do you know that? (4)
W Well, I checked out the recorder and microphones. I test recorded some conversation and replayed it; it was a good quality reproduction. I took the tape out of the original wrapper; it was fresh and had never been used before.
P HOW did you use the equipment? (5)
W I followed my standard procedure. First, I plugged the recorder into a wall outlet. Then I attached the mikes. After I'd test recorded some sound on one track—that is, half of the width of the tape, I turned the reel over, threaded the tape again, and set up to record on the second track.
P WHAT did you do then? (5)
W Before I started recording the conversation, I asked the parties, Messrs. Semegen and Heiser, to speak into the microphones. I got the right voice level, and then I was all set to record.
P WHAT happened then? (5)
W They spoke continuously for about half an hour. I then read my name, the date, and the address into the tape. After doing that, I turned off the recorder.
P HOW well did the recorder work during the conversation? (6)
W Very well.
P HOW do you know that? (6)
W In the first place, I didn't experience any technical or mechanical difficulties during the recording session. Secondly, right after the session, I rewound the tape onto the feeder reel and replayed it.
P WHAT happened when you replayed the tape? (6)
W I could hear the recording of the conversation.
P WHAT was the quality of the recording? (6)
W Excellent. As far as I could tell, the recorder picked up everything; and the recording was loud and clear.
P WHAT did you do with the tape after you replayed it? (7)
W I put it in an envelope and wrote my name, parties' names, the date, and address on it.
P WHAT did you do with the envelope? (7)
W I took it back to my office.
P WHERE did you put it in your office? (7)
W In my evidence locker.
P HOW many people have access to the locker? (7)
W Only me. I have a combination lock on it, and I'm the only one who knows the combination.
P WHAT happened to the tape after you placed it in your evidence locker? (7)
W With one exception until today, it's been in the locker the whole time.
P WHAT was that exception? (7)
W You and I took it out several months ago and listened to it.
P WHO was present during that playing of the tape? (7)
W You and I were the only two persons present.
P WHERE were you while the tape was out of the evidence locker? (7)
W I was present the whole time. I took it out, played it for you, and then immediately put it back.
P WHERE has the tape been since then? (7)
W In the locker the whole time.

P   Your Honor, I request that this tape be marked plaintiff's exhibit ten for identification.

J   It will be so marked.

P   May the record reflect that I am showing plaintiff's exhibit number ten for identification to the opposing counsel?

J   It will so reflect.

P   I request permission to approach the witness.

J   Permission granted.

P   I now hand you plaintiff's exhibit number ten for identification. WHAT is it? (8)

W   It's the tape I've been talking about.

P   HOW can you recognize it? (8)

W   I recognize my handwriting. I made those markings on the label on the reel.

P   WHAT condition is the tape recording in? (9)

W   It's in excellent condition.

P   HOW do you know that? (9)

W   When I removed it from the locker this morning, I replayed it.

W   WHAT was the quality of the recording? (9)

W   It hasn't changed at all. It was and is an excellent reproduction of the conversation.

P   Your Honor, I now offer plaintiff's exhibit number ten for identification into evidence as plaintiff's exhibit ten.

J   It will be received.

P   I now request permission to have the bailiff play the exhibit for the jury.

J   Permission granted.

The second foundation is a simple, modern foundation. Here the witness overhead the conversation. Suppose that Mr. Semegen's secretary, Ms. Grant, was present during the negotiating session.

P   WHAT is your occupation?

W   I'm a secretary for Atco Corporation.

P   WHO do you work for?

W   I work directly for the president, Mr. Jason Semegen.

P   HOW long have you worked for him?

W   Easily three years.

P   WHERE were you on the morning of January 17 of this year?

W   I was at the office at work.

P   WHAT happened that morning?

W   Mr. Semegen had a bargaining session with Mr. Heiser.

P   WHERE were you when this session occurred?

W   I was in the room.

P   HOW close were you to them?

W   I was sitting right next to them to take notes.

P   HOW well could you hear the conversation?

W   Just fine.

P   Your Honor, I request that this be marked plaintiff's exhibit number ten for identification.

J   It will be so marked.

P   Please let the record reflect that I am showing plaintiff's exhibit number ten for identification to the opposing counsel.

J   It will so reflect.

P   I request permission to approach the witness.

J   Permission granted.

P   I now hand you plaintiff's exhibit number ten for identification. WHAT is it?

W   It's a tape of the conversation between Mr. Semegen and Mr. Heiser.

P   HOW do you know that?

W   I listened to the tape in the judge's chambers just a few hours ago.

P   WHAT is the quality of the tape recording?

W   It's an excellent reproduction of the conversation as far as I can tell.

P   HOW can you recognize this tape recording as the one you listened to in the judge's chambers?

W   I recognize the marking on the reel, and I've kept it in my possession ever since I listened to it.

P   WHERE have you kept it?

W   I've kept it on my person while I was sitting listening to this trial.

P   HOW long did you have it in your possession?

W   About two hours. I kept it until I put it on your counsel table as I walked to the witness stand just a few minutes ago.

P   Your Honor, I now offer plaintiff's exhibit number ten for identification into evidence as plaintiff's exhibit number ten.

J   It will be received.

P   I request permission to have the bailiff play the tape recording for the jury.

J   Permission granted.

The above foundation illustrates only one of the methods of authenticating a tape recording. Since Evidence Code § 403 governs the question of the sufficiency of the foundational proof of the tape's genuineness, the proponent may use any circumstantial evidence that creates a permissive inference of genuineness. *People v. Fonville*, 35 Cal. App. 3d 693, 111 Cal. Rptr. 53 (1973) is a case in point. In *Fonville*, the police surreptitiously recorded a telephone conversation in jail between the defendant and his uncle. At trial, the prosecution offered a tape recording of the conversation. However, the prosecution did not offer any witnesses to identify the voices on the tape or to vouch that the tape accurately reproduced the conversation. However, on the tape the principal speaker referred to statements the defendant had earlier made to the police. On the one hand, the court conceded that the typical foundation for an audiotape includes testimony by a participant that the tape is a correct reproduction of the earlier conversation. On the other hand, the court emphasized that the proponent of a tape recording is not limited to the recognized methods of authentication. The court pointed out that the tape referred to earlier statements to the police that only the defendant was likely to know about: "They are matters that are unlikely to have been known by anyone other than the appellant. In effect, the conversation proves itself." *Id.* at 709, 111 Cal. Rptr. at 63. In addition, the court emphasized that the jury had already heard the defendant's voice on a properly authenticated tape of his earlier statement to the police. The court held that it was proper for the jurors themselves to compare the tapes to determine whether the defendant was the speaker on the second tape: "There are other ways of identifying a voice than by seeing the speaker ..., and we have concluded that comparing the tapes is one such acceptable method." *Id.*; 3 WITKIN, §1805, at 1766-67.

J.   E-MAIL

Section G discusses telephone facsimile (fax) technology. A fax is a graphic image that is digitized and sent over regular telephone lines by modem. As with a fax, electronic mail (e-mail) poses evidentiary issues.[3] To appreciate the authentication problem posed by e-mail, we must first understand e-mail technology. E-mail is more versatile than fax; it can be sent over a variety of network links, ranging from dialup to fiber optic lines. E-mail is ordinarily text, but other formats can be sent, including graphic images.

The mechanics of a simple e-mail system are straightforward. To send e-mail, the person first opens their e-mail application. The user next sees the e-mail screen, which has two parts: a header and the body.

The visible part of a typical header includes at least three lines. One is a line for the sender's e-mail address. That line has usually been filled in, but it is sometimes a simple matter for the sender to change the entry in that line. The second line is for the recipient's address. An Internet e-mail address consists of a local part and a host part: undername@hostname. The local part is the mailbox, login name, or userID of the intended recipient. The host name indicates the networks serving the user. For example, Professor Imwinkelried's address is "ejimwinkelried@ucdavis.edu." His host is U.C. Davis in the larger educational domain. There are online directory service databases of varying reliability—"white pages"—on the Internet. The third, or subject, line is provided for a brief summary or title of the message.

After completing the heading, the sender composes the body of the message. Once the sender completes the message, he or she ordinarily types "send" or presses a "send" button. Alternatively, the user might press a "queue" button and send queued messages before signing off. The program then routes the message through the computer networks connecting the source (the sender) and destination (the intended recipient). Service providers (servers) intervene between the sender and recipient to transmit the message. After traveling through various servers and networks, the message reaches the recipient's inbox. When that person logs on and checks mail, they will be told, "You have new mail." At that point, the recipient opens the message and reads it. Most programs have a reply feature. To use this feature, the recipient types "reply" or clicks a "reply" button. Depending on the program, the recipient then types the reply immediately before or after the message

---

[3]Note, "When the Postman Beeps Twice: The Admissibility of Electronic Mail Under the Business Records Exception to the Federal Rules of Evidence," 64 FORDH. L. REV. 2285 (1996). *See also* "'God Mail' Authentication and Admissibility of Electronic Mail in Federal Courts," 34 AM. CRIM. L. REV. 1387 (1997).

received. The program then automatically sends the reply to the original sender. The original sender receives a message including both his or her message and recipient's reply.

One fundamental difference between e-mail systems and fax is that it is usually easier to change the e-mail address of the sender. In some e-mail systems, when the sender is completing the heading, it is a simple matter to enter a fictitious name or another name. Subsection 3 in section G noted that some fax machines automatically imprint the sending number on the pages printed out at the recipient's end. Although a sophisticated user of the fax might be able to either disable that function or change the number, doing so requires a level of expertise above and beyond the elementary knowledge needed to send a fax message. Thus, in laying a foundation to show that a fax was sent by a particular person, the proponent can rely in part on the sender's fax address automatically printed on the received form. It is less justifiable to rely on the sender's address appearing in the heading of an e-mail message. With many of the most popular, less sophisticated systems, many persons who use e-mail possess the knowledge needed to change the e-mail address. In short, it is less justifiable to accept an e-mail address at face value than to presume the authenticity of a fax. Accordingly, there is an even greater need to lay additional foundation establishing the authenticity of the message. *See* Jablon, *"God Mail": Authentication and Admissibility of Electronic Mail in Federal Courts*, 34 AM. CRIM. L. REV. 1387 (1997) (arguing for more rigorous standards for the authentication of e-mail).

1. EVIDENTIARY DOCTRINES AND FOUNDATIONAL ELEMENTS

Section G comments that although fax is a relatively new technology, "the pertinent evidentiary principles are old and well-settled." The same comment applies to e-mail. In many instances, the proponent can authenticate an e-mail message by adapting a traditional doctrine:

Reply letter doctrine. Section D.3 discusses the reply doctrine. This doctrine can also be applied by analogy to e-mail. The proponent makes a foundational showing that he or she obtained the address from an online directory or other reliable source, sent an e-mail message to an address obtained from such a source, and in due course received a message responsive in terms to the earlier message. In the context of e-mail and fax, "due course" will ordinarily be a shorter period of time than with conventional mail. When the doctrine is applied to letters, it might take several days for the response to reach the original sender. When the doctrine is applied to e-mail, it might require only a few minutes or hours.

Content. The proponent can authenticate a writing by showing that only the purported author was likely to know the information reflected in the message. That technique also extends to e-mail. There are at least three fact situations in which that technique would come into play. First, the substantive content of the message might be information with which only that person was familiar. Second, if the recipient used the reply feature to respond, the new message may include the sender's original message. Third, if the sender dispatched that message to only one person, its inclusion in the new message indicates that the new message originated with the original recipient.

Cryptography. Alternatively, the proponent can sometimes lay a foundation to authenticate an e-mail message by presenting testimony about the cryptography used in transmitting the message. While it is true that cryptography is employed in only a small percentage of e-mail communication, that percentage is growing. Moreover, many important electronic transactions—the kinds of transactions likely to generate litigation—utilize cryptography.

In most cryptography, the communicating parties use a key which encrypts or scrambles the message. There are two basic types of key cryptography. One is single-key cryptography, where the communicating parties use the same key. The sender utilizes the key to encrypt the message, and the recipient employs the same key to decipher or decrypt it. One difficulty with single-key cryptography is that before using the key, the parties must have a secure communication channel to exchange the key. It can be difficult to obtain access to such a channel. Sending the private key under secure channels can be expensive and slow.

A public/private two-key system provides an additional level of security at the price of some computational complexity. One key is the public key, and the other is the private or secret key. The keys are complementary; each unlocks the code that the other key makes. A person can use commercially available software called Viacrypt which uses PGP (Pretty Good Privacy) to create the two keys.[4] The person who is the key owner will then publish one key and keep the other private. The person can use the private key to send messages that could be sent only by the key owner.[5] Since those messages can be decrypted only by using that person's public key, the fact that recipient successfully opened the message by employing that public key identifies the key owner as the sender.

However, there is a problem: How can the recipient determine that the purported sender is indeed the owner of that public key? "The problem facing [the recipient] in this scenario ... is that there is no more reason to trust an e-mail message purporting to be from Bob that says 'here is my public key' than there is to trust any other e-mail message purporting to come from Bob."[6]

To overcome that problem, a new industry has emerged—the business of certification authorities or CAs.[7] These companies are in the business of verifying that

---

[4]Technically, PGP is a "hybrid" system: The program uses public/private keys encryption to encrypt a session key—a one-time, disposable key—which is then used by IDEA, a strong single-key algorithm, to encrypt the actual message. PGP employs this two-step process because public/private key encryption can be very slow when utilized on long messages.

[5]A. Michael Froomkin, *Flood Control on the Information Ocean: Living with Anonymity, Digital Cash and Distributed Databases*, 15 J. LAW & COMMERCE 395, 419 n.74 (1996) (hereafter cited as Froomkin I); A. Michael Froomkin, *The Essential Role of Trusted Third Parties in Electronic Commerce*, 75 ORE. L. REV. 49, 52 (1996) (hereafter cited as Froomkin II).

[6]Froomkin II, *supra* note 3, at 52.

[7]*Id.* at 49.

a particular person owns a certain public key. Thus, after receiving a request from the person owning the public key, the company would conduct an inquiry to verify the identity of the key owner. Having done so, the company can provide third parties with assurance of the person's ownership of the key by issuing identifying certificates to this effect.[8] A person can request that the CA verify his or her ownership of the public key. After receiving the request, the CA conducts an inquiry to verify the identity of the key owner. Having verified the owner's identity, the CA issues an identifying certificate.[9] In effect, the certificate notarizes the connection between the owner and the public key. "The CA might publish the resulting certificate on a World Wide Web site available to anyone with Internet access, or give the certificate to [the owner], or contract with [the owner] to honor e-mailed requests for the certificate from all comers."[10]

Given this technology, the proponent could authenticate an e-mail message by laying the following foundation:

1. There is a certain CA. In Utah, there is a state statute regulating CAs.[11] However, in most states, CAs are unregulated. The proponent can call a representative of the CA as a witness, introduce the relevant part of a transcript of the representative's deposition, or proffer a stipulation as to the existence and operation of the CA.

2. The CA received a request to verify that a particular person owned a specified public key. The request itself is nonhearsay under Federal Rule 801(a). The request is not a declarative sentence asserting any facts. The CA's record reflecting receipt of the request qualifies as a business entry under Rule 803(6).

3. The CA conducted an inquiry to verify that the person in question owned that public key. The CA might conduct varying levels of inquiry. For instance, VeriSign offers four classes of certificates corresponding with differing levels of inquiry. "Class 1 certificates ... certify only 'the uniqueness of a name or e-mail address.' In contrast, VeriSign will issue a Class 2 certificate, which is more expensive, after receiving 'third party proofing of name, address and other personal information ....'"[12] If the CA has retained the records reflecting the inquiry, the records themselves are admissible under Rule 803(6). If the CA no longer has those records, under Rule 406 the proponent can elicit the representative's testimony about the CA's routine practices for conducting inquiries.

4. As a result of the inquiry, the CA issued an identifying certificate verifying that the person in question owns the specified public key. There are various

---

[8]*Id.* at 60.
[9]*Id.*
[10]*Id.*
[11]Utah Code Ann. § 46-3-309 (1996).
[12]Froomkin II, *supra* note 3, at 58-59.

types of certificates,[13] but for our purpose an identifying certificate is of greatest interest. An identifying certificate establishes the connection or link between a specified public key and a particular person. In essence, the certificate vouches that the person is the key owner. As with the records reflecting the CA's receipt of the request (element #2) and its inquiry (element #3), the certificate itself will qualify as a business entry under Rule 803(6). The CA is not only in the business of conducting the inquiries; another essential part of its business is issuing the certificates and thereby giving third parties assurance of the key owner's identity. (Note that the proponent could dispense with the preceding foundational elements if the opponent were willing to stipulate that the person in question was the owner of the specified public key.)

5. The recipient of the message to be authenticated had previously learned of the person's identity as the owner of the specified public key. The recipient might have obtained the information from any one of many sources, including a telephone call or a page on the World Wide Web. In many cases, in an earlier e-mail message, the recipient received the plain text of the person's public key.[14] The recipient's testimony about his or her discovery of the key owner's identity is not subject to a hearsay objection. The testimony is proffered only for the nonhearsay purpose of explaining the recipient's subsequent conduct under Rule 801(c), namely, later using that public key to decrypt the message in question. On request by the opponent, the trial judge would give the jury a Rule 105 limiting instruction about the nonhearsay status of the recipient's testimony. Of course, the proponent must present independent, admissible evidence of the person's identity as the key owner. However, the prior four foundational elements furnish that evidence.

6. The recipient received the message in question.

7. When the recipient received the message, the recipient used the person's public key to decrypt or decipher the message.

8. When the recipient used the specified public key, the key successfully unscrambled the message.

9. The message identified the key owner as the sender. Standing alone, foundational elements #1–8 support this inference. However, when the message itself identifies the originator, the proponent should elicit this foundational testimony to strengthen the inference.

The proponent would use the above foundation to authenticate an encrypted e-mail message. A variation of this foundation is to present foundational testimony about a digital signature to authenticate an encrypted message.[15] Although the body of the message itself is unencrypted, the sender can use his or her private key

---

[13]*Id.* at 59-65 (identifying certificates, authorizing certificates, transactional certificates, and digital time-stamping devices).

[14]*Id.* at 52.

[15]*Id.* at 54.

to encrypt the digital signature.[16] If the recipient can successfully use the person's public key to decrypt the signature, the circumstances "uniquely identif[y] the sender and connect [] the sender to the exact message."[17]

Action consistent with the message. Suppose that after the receipt of the message the purported sender takes action consistent with the content of the message. In a business context, the action might be the delivery of merchandise mentioned in the message. That conduct could provide circumstantial authentication of the source of the message.

Chain of custody. The chain of custody technique can be used to authenticate a document.[18] Even if a person did not read the letter within an envelope, the person's testimony about the physical handling of the envelope can help establish a chain of custody for the enclosed letter. Suppose, for example, that B testifies that she received an envelope from A and that she later handed it to C. In turn, C testifies that he received the envelope from B and later delivered it to D. D testifies that he accepted the envelope from C, opened it, and found a letter purportedly signed by A. Even though neither B nor C saw the contents of the envelope, their testimony suffices to establish that the letter D received was in fact authored by A.

Analogously, the proponent of an e-mail message may authenticate the message by showing its electronic handling. The proponent can use the business records of all the systems that transmitted the message to trace the message back to the source computer. As long as those records show that each system handled a message originating from the purported sender's computer, it is immaterial that no one at the intermediate systems actually opened and read the message. At the recipient's end, using proper commands, the computer can print out a complete heading, setting out the information indicating the handling of the message between its dispatch and receipt. For example, the computer might print out the following:

```
From aamerson@oxy.eduFri June 7 16:51:49 1996
Received: from guilder.ucdavis.edu by peseta.ucdavis.edu (8.76/UCD3.5.6)
    id QAA24323;Fri, 7 Jun 1996 16:31:30-0700 (PDT)
Received: from bobcat.cc.oxy.edu by guilder:ucdavis.edu (8.7.5/UCD3.5.4)
    id QAA24807;Fri, 7 June 1996 16:31:26-0700 (PDT)
Received (from aamerson@localhost)
    by bobcat.cc.oxy.edu (8.61.11/8.6.11) id QAA21403
    for sdlangford@ucdavis.edu; Fri, 7 June 16:31:22-0700
From Andy Amerson<aamerson@oxy.edu.
```

This string traces a message from Andy Amerson (aamerson@oxy.edu) to Steve Langford (sdlangford@ucdavis.edu). The message initially went from Amerson's computer to bobcat, the e-mail server for Amerson's organization, Occidental College. In turn, the bobcat server routed the message to guilder, the e-mail hub for Langford's organization, the University of California at Davis. Next, guilder

---

[16]*Id.*
[17]*Id.*
[18]*United States v. Thomas*, 54 F.3d 73 (2d Cir. 1995).

routed the message to the peseta network on the Davis campus. Peseta is the e-mail server for that campus. Finally, peseta routed the message to the recipient's e-mail account. Each server in this chain is maintained by a regularly conducted activity such as a department of a college or business. That department generates records documenting the receipt and transmittal of the message in question. When the server receives the message, it assigns the message an identification number and notes the time and date of its processing of the message. Those records should qualify as business entries admissible under Rule 803(6) when testified to by the appropriate custodian or other qualified witnesses. Unless the server's administrator has "flushed" or disposed of the records, the records should still be available to help lay the foundation for an e-mail passage that was handled by the server. Thus, if every other authentication technique fails, the proponent can lay the foundation for an e-mail message by:

1. Having the recipient print out the entire routing of the message.
2. Introducing the routing records for each server that handled the message to verify that the message was processed as the recipient's printout indicates.
3. Establishing that the alleged author had primary or exclusive access to the computer which, according to the records, originated the message.

2. SAMPLE FOUNDATION

Consider a contract lawsuit. The case involves an order placed by the University of California Davis Purchasing Office with one of its suppliers, Intex Company, for computer parts. As part of its case, the University of California wishes to show that Mr. Langford, its employee, received an e-mail message. The message purportedly came from Intex and contained an offer to sell the computer components in question. The university's lawyer is the proponent.

Langford has already taken the stand. During his testimony, he testifies that on September 12, 2000, he received an e-mail message on his personal computer at work; the university hub is "guilder.undavis.edu;" the university server is "peseta.ucdavis.edu;" the message purported to come from Mr. Mishkin, a representative of Intex; the message was an offer to sell computer parts. At the attorney's request, Langford printed out all the routing information for the message; he recognizes the printout as an exhibit. (The printout includes seven entries. Three entries represent Langford's address and the identifications for the university's hub and server. A fourth line of the printout indicates that the message in question was routed by "orgmail.intex.com." That line lists OAA23641 as the identification number for the message and indicates that the message was routed on September 12, 2000 at 2:02 in the afternoon. That line represents Organization Mail, the external server intermediate between the plaintiff's e-mail system and the defendant's. The other three lines correspond to the Internet address and identification identified in the stipulation, *infra*.) The printout is marked as Plaintiff's Exhibit No. 8 for identification.

In addition, the plaintiff introduces a stipulation of fact between the parties. The stipulation is to the effect that on September 12, 2000, Jerome Mishkin was one of the defendant's employees; he is now deceased; as of September 2000, he had been assigned the Internet address "jeromemishkin@ccm.jf.intex.com;" the identification for Intex's server is "ccm.jf.com;" and the identification for Intex's hub is "relay.jf.intex.com." (That address and those identifications correspond with three lines on the heading that Langford printed out.)

The next witness is Ms. Carlton, the employee in charge of records for the Organization Mail company. Organization Mail is an e-mail server for users in the commercial, government, and educational domains.

P   WHAT is your name?
W   My name is Elise Carlton.
P   WHO do you work for?
W   I work for Organization Mail.
P   WHAT is the nature of your company's business?
W   We are an Internet service provider. We're sometimes called an external server. We get e-mail messages from one company or agency and transmit them to another. We take the message from the sender's mail system and transmit it to the intended recipient's system.
P   WHAT is your job title there?
W   I'm chief of records for serving operations.
P   WHAT are your responsibilities as chief?
W   I oversee the generation and maintenance of our records for all the messages which we receive and send on to destination.
P   WHAT kinds of messages do you handle?
W   All kinds—government, commercial, and educational.
P   When your company handles an e-mail message, HOW, if at all, can your firm's handling be reflected at the message's final destination?
W   Well, when they print out the heading at the final destination, the word "orgmail" will be included in an entry indicating that we were a server.
P   When you receive a message for transmission, WHERE, if at all, would the word "orgmail" appear on the message?
W   It automatically becomes a part of the larger heading. It shows that we handled the message.
P   Specifically, WHAT would the heading say about the message?
W   It gives it an identification number and notes the date and time of handling the message.
P   Your Honor, I request that his be marked as plaintiff's exhibit number nine for identification.
J   It will be so marked.
P   Please let the record reflect that I am showing the exhibit to the defense attorney.
J   The record will so reflect.
P   Permission to approach the witness?
J   Granted.
P   Ms. Carlton, I now hand you what has been marked as Plaintiff's exhibit number nine for identification. WHAT is it?
W   It's one of our logs of e-mail messages.

P   WHAT is a "log"?

W   It's a printout of the information relevant to the handling of a message. At the end of every 12-hour period, someone in my office prints out the log listing all messages received or sent on our server system.

P   WHAT does this log show?

W   It documents the handling of messages on a particular date.

P   WHICH date?

W   September 12, 2000.

P   WHAT types of messages does this log list?

W   As I said just a while ago, it lists all the outgoing and incoming messages routed by our server "orgmail" on that date.

P   WHY does your company prepare these logs?

W   For quality control and business reasons. To begin with, the logs help us determine whether our equipment is working properly—that is, whether we're sending messages to the right destinations. Moreover, we obviously have to monitor the volume of traffic for each customer for billing purposes. That's how we determine how much to charge each customer. These logs are absolutely essential in our business.

P   HOW do you prepare these logs?

W   As I said, at the end of each day, we print out our e-mail records and store them.

P   WHO prepares them?

W   One of our employees, one of the people I supervise.

P   HOW often do you prepare this type of record?

W   We do it every day—in fact, twice every day. Again, we do it at the end of every 12-hour period.

P   HOW do you recognize this record?

W   I recognize the contents. You told me that you were interested in the e-mail log for a particular day. I personally went to the file to pull the log. I went to the file cabinet in my office where we store the logs for September 1996. I can vouch that this is the log I took out of the file for that date.

P   Your Honor, I now offer plaintiff's exhibit number nine for identification into evidence as plaintiff's exhibit number nine.

J   Any objection?

O   None, Your Honor.

J   Very well. The exhibit will be received as plaintiff's exhibit number nine.

P   Ms. Carlton, I'd like to take a look at the third entry on the second page of the log.

W   Yes.

P   According to that entry, WHAT message did your server handle on September 12, 2000?

W   According to the entry, we routed a message from the computer used by one of Intex's employees, a person named Jerome Mishkin. The entry is "jeromemiskin@ccm.jf.intex.com."

P   According to your log, WHO was the intended recipient of that message?

W   The log says that the recipient's e-mail address was "sdlangford@ucdavis.edu."

It is true that neither Carlton nor any other Organization Mail employee read the content of the e-mail message handled by her company. However, cumulatively the stipulation and Langford's and Carlton's testimony support a permissive inference that the message Langford received on September 12, 2000 (reflected in Exhibit 9) originated from Mishkin, Intex's employee. Based on the stipulation and the testimony, the plaintiff can now successfully introduce exhibit number eight. The information in a heading can be faked, but the possibility of fabrication goes to the weight of the evidence rather than its admissibility.

K.   DEMONSTRATIVE EVIDENCE

The types of articles we have discussed so far are real or original evidence; the articles have a historical connection with the transaction giving rise to the suit. For example, the document is a will the decedent signed before death, or the item is the very pistol the defendant used during the assault. Sometimes the proponent may use an item even if the item has no connection with the case. *See People v. Barnett*, 17 Cal. 4th 1044, 954 P.2d 384, 74 Cal. Rptr. 2d 121 (1998) (demonstration with objects similar to those used in the crime is proper). Suppose, for example, that the police never found the pistol used in the assault. The trial judge might permit an eyewitness to the assault to use another, similar pistol to illustrate his or her testimony. The courts often refer to this latter type of evidence as demonstrative; the article helps the witness to demonstrate or illustrate oral testimony. The only limits on the use of demonstrative evidence are the trial judge's discretion and the trial attorney's imagination.

1. VERIFICATION OF A DIAGRAM

The verification of a diagram is very similar to the verification of a photograph. The diagram need not be to scale. However, the sponsoring witness must testify that the diagram is generally a "true," "accurate," "good," or "fair" depiction of the scene or object shown. If the diagram is not to scale, the opposing counsel is entitled to a limiting instruction under Evidence Code § 355.

The elements of the foundation are:

1. The diagram depicts a certain area or object.
2. The witness is familiar with that area or object.
3. The witness explains the basis for his or her familiarity with the area or object.
4. In the witness's opinion, the diagram is an accurate depiction of that area or object.

The fact situation is an assault prosecution. The indictment alleges that the defendant attacked the victim, Mr. Williams, in a bathroom in the Senator Hotel in San Diego. The prosecutor wants to use a chart to illustrate the victim's testimony. The witness is the victim. The prosecutor is the proponent. The victim has just testified that he was attacked.

P   WHERE did this attack occur?

W   As I said, it occurred in the bathroom of the second floor of the hotel.

P   Your Honor, I request that this be marked prosecution exhibit number three for identification.

J   It will be so marked.

P   Please let the record reflect that I am showing the exhibit to the defense attorney.

J   It will so reflect.

P   Request permission to approach the witness.

J   Permission granted.

P   Mr. Williams, I hand you prosecution exhibit number three for identification. WHAT is it? (1)

W   It's a chart of the bathroom I was just referring to.

P   HOW do you recognize it? (2)

W   I know that hotel very well.

P   HOW did you become familiar with the hotel? (3)

W   I've lived in it for two years. It's a boarding hotel.

P   HOW many times have you been in that bathroom? (3)

W   Lots of times, I couldn't give you a specific figure.

P   HOW accurate is the diagram? (4)

W   Well, it's not to scale. That's for sure.

P   Otherwise, HOW accurate is the diagram? (4)

W   It's correct. It shows everything in roughly the right place.

P   Your Honor, I now offer prosecution exhibit number three for identification into evidence as prosecution exhibit three.

O   Your Honor, may a limiting instruction be given that the diagram is not to scale?

J   Yes. The exhibit will be received. (To the jurors) Ladies and gentlemen of the jury, the prosecutor is now going to show you a diagram of the bathroom in the Senator Hotel. The witness has testified that the diagram is basically accurate, but the witness also stated that the diagram is not to scale. In deciding what weight to attach to the diagram, you should consider the fact that the diagram is not to scale.

P   I now request permission to hand the diagram to the jurors for their inspection.

J   Permission granted.

2. MARKING A DIAGRAM

To effectively use a diagram, the proponent will sometimes have to have the witness mark on it. The marking will help the jury visualize the testimony. Moreover, the marking will help the appellate court understand the record of trial. Unless the diagram is marked, the record of trial may be confusing to the appellate court; the court will not know where "here" or "there" was on the diagram. The proponent should give the witness specific instructions as to how to mark the diagram. Moreover, in some courtrooms, it is customary to have the record reflect that the witness complied with the proponent's instructions.

To illustrate these techniques, we shall use the original hypothetical:

P Mr. Williams, using the diagram, WHERE were you when the defendant first walked into the bathroom?

W I was standing over here.

P Please take this pen, place a circle where you were standing, and write the number one in the circle.

W (The witness complied.)

P Please let the record reflect that the witness compiled with my instruction.

J The record will so reflect.

P Now, Mr. Williams, in WHAT direction was the defendant walking in when he first entered the room?

W He was going that way.

P Please use the pen again, draw an arrow showing that direction, and write the letter A at the tip of the arrow.

W (The witness.)

P Please let the record reflect that the witness complied w ith my direction.

J The record will so reflect.

Bear in mind one important caveat. Many California trial judges prefer that the diagram be completely marked before it is formally offered into evidence. These judges will not permit any further marking after the exhibit has been received into evidence. If you contemplate using a diagram during a trial, you should inquire about the judge's preference during the chambers conference before the trial begins.

Some attorneys have the witness add a legend at the bottom of the diagram during the marking. For example, the proponent might instruct the witness to indicate at the bottom of the diagram that "capital A represents the defendant." The proponent may eventually ask the judge to send the exhibit to the jury room during deliberations. The legend will help the jurors use the diagram during deliberations.

3. MODELS

The use of models is becoming increasingly common in courtrooms. The proponent may use a skeletal model or a model of a house or machine. Models present more logistical problems for trial courts than simple diagrams. For that reason, some judges are more reluctant to permit their use. Indeed, in some courtrooms, before resorting to a model, the proponent must affirmatively show that the witness needs the model to adequately explain his or her testimony. *See, e.g., People v. Cummings*, 4 Cal. 4th 1233, 1291, 18 Cal. Rptr. 2d 796, 833, 850 P.2d 1 (1993), *cert. denied*, 114 S. Ct. 1576 (1994) (to clarify complex and hotly disputed expert testimony about the path bullets took through victim's body, it was proper to use a mannequin pierced by wooden dowels that illustrated bullet paths).

The foundation for the use of a model should include the following elements:

1. The witness needs the visual aid to explain his or her testimony.
2. The aid depicts a certain scene or object.
3. The witness is familiar with the scene or object.

4. The witness explains the basis for his or her familiarity with the scene or object.
5. In the witness's opinion, the aid is a "true," "accurate," "good," or "fair" model of the scene or object.

The fact situation is a tort action for injuries. The plaintiff, Ms. Graham, suffered extensive bone damage. The next witness is Dr. Miller, a bone specialist. In general terms, Dr. Miller has already described the extensive nature of the bone damage.

P   Now, Doctor, in detail, WHAT are the injuries to Ms. Graham's bones? (1)
W   That question is really difficult answer orally.
P   WHY? (1)
W   Well, in the first place, a large number of bones have been damaged. Secondly, it's sometimes difficult for me to explain the precise location of the bone. Finally, some of the damage is really to the way bones work and fit together. It's hard to put all that into words.
P   HOW could you explain the detailed injuries more effectively? (1)
W   It would be much better if I were permitted to use a skeletal model.
P   Your Honor, I request that this be marked plaintiff's exhibit number seven for identification.
J   It will be so marked.
P   Doctor, I now show you plaintiff's exhibit number seven for identification. WHAT is it? (2)
W   It's the sort of skeletal model I just mentioned.
P   HOW do you know that? (3), (4)
W   I'm not only a medical doctor; I'm a bone specialist. I've studied and used models such as this one for years. In fact, I've consulted with some of the art companies that manufacture these models.
P   HOW accurate is this skeletal model? (5)
W   It's quite good. It depicts the bone structure of a female of the approximate height and build of the plaintiff, Ms. Graham.
P   HOW helpful would this be to illustrate your testimony about the specific bone injuries? (1)
W   Very helpful. I can point to the location of the bones, show you what they look like, and demonstrate how they're supposed to fit together with adjacent bones.

In some jurisdictions, models such as the one in the hypothetical are used without even marking them for identification. That practice makes it difficult for the appellate court to understand the record of trial. Perhaps the prevailing modern practice is at least to mark the model as an exhibit for identification. California follows the prevailing view. In California, if an exhibit is used "only for purposes of illustration," the exhibit is marked for identification but not moved into evidence. Dunn & Crivaro, *Selected Trial Motions*, in CALIFORNIA CRIMINAL LAW: PROCEDURE AND PRACTICE § 31.19, at 785 (1994) (cited hereafter as CALIFORNIA CRIMINAL LAW). If an exhibit is marked only for identification, the exhibit is not sent into the jury room during deliberations. Disco, *Jury Deliberations and*

Verdict, in CALIFORNIA CRIMINAL LAW § 33.8, at 827 (1994).

The proponent does not always have to leave the model in the court's possession after trial. In most jurisdictions, the trial judge has discretion to permit the proponent to substitute a photograph or written description for insertion in the record of trial. If the proponent wishes to do so, after the judge receives the exhibit into evidence, the proponent should state: "I request permission to later substitute a photograph of this model into the record of trial."

L.   THE IDENTIFICATION OF REAL OR ORIGINAL PHYSICAL EVIDENCE

1. THE DOCTRINE

The last section of this chapter discussed demonstrative physical evidence; Demonstrative evidence has two characteristics. On the one hand, it illustrates or demonstrates the witness' testimony. On the other hand, the object itself has no historical connection with the facts of the case; for example, it is not the actual pistol used in the crime.

In contrast, real or original physical evidence has a connection with the case. For example, the prosecutor may contend that it is the very pistol used. If the prosecutor makes that claim, the prosecutor must authenticate the evidence by proving the claim. The prosecutor must demonstrate the object's connection with the case. The process of demonstrating this historical connection is usually termed the identification of the physical evidence. There are two recognized methods of identifying physical evidence.

The first method is ready identifiability. When the article has a unique, one-of-a-kind characteristic, the characteristic makes the article readily identifiable. The foundation is complete if the witness testifies that he or she previously observed the characteristic and presently recalls the characteristic. The identification is sufficient to establish that the exhibit is the object the witness previously observed. Federal Rule of Evidence 901(b)(4) expressly permits identification of an object by its "distinctive characteristics."

Suppose, however, that one of the elements of the foundation for ready identifiability is missing; the object lacks a unique characteristic, the witness did not observe the characteristic on the previous occasion, or the witness cannot presently recall the characteristic. Or suppose that the proponent is interested in the object's condition rather than its simple identity; the proponent might want a laboratory technician to testify about a chemical analysis of the object. In these circumstances, the proponent must establish a chain of custody. Chain of custody is the second method of identifying physical evidence.

The links in the chain are people who handle the object. Other persons who merely have access to the object are not considered links. Thus, even if two other laboratory technicians know the combination to the safe where the witness kept the object, the other technicians are not deemed links. The only link would be the technician who physically handled the object. The proponent would have to account only for that technician's handling of the object.

How does the proponent account for handling? The proponent must show the link's initial receipt of the object, ultimate disposition of the object (retention, destruction, or transfer), and the link's safekeeping of the object between receipt and disposition. The witness can keep the object in a locked safe, a secure evidence container, or any other place where substitution and tampering are unlikely.

Mechanically, the proponent should call each link to the stand in the sequence in which they handled the object. The proponent has the object marked for identification and has each link identify it. However, the proponent does not offer the exhibit into evidence until the last link has testified; at that point, the foundation is complete.

2. ELEMENTS OF THE FOUNDATION

The foundation for ready identifiability is very short.

1. The object has a unique characteristic.
2. The witness observed the characteristic on a previous occasion.
3. The witness identifies the exhibit as the object.
4. The witness rests the identification on his or her present recognition of the characteristic.
5. As best he or she can tell, the exhibit is in the same condition as it was when he or she initially received the object.

The foundation for chain of custody must be laid during the testimony of each link in the chain:

1. The witness initially received the object at a certain time and place.
2. The witness safeguarded the object; the witness testifies circumstances making it unlikely that substitution or tampering occurred.
3. The witness ultimately disposed of the object (retention, destruction, or transfer to another person).
4. As best he or she can tell, the exhibit is the object he or she previously handled.
5. As best he or she can tell, the exhibit is in the same condition as it was when he or she initially received the object.

3. SAMPLE FOUNDATIONS

The fact situation for the ready identifiability foundation is a civil tort case. The complaint alleges that the defendant assaulted the plaintiff with a knife. The witness is a police officer who investigated the complaint. The proponent is the plaintiff. The officer has just testified that he reported to the scene and began inspecting the scene.

P WHAT did you do during this inspection?
W I was looking for any evidence.
P WHAT, if anything, did you find?
W I found a knife answering the description the plaintiff, Ms. Brown, gave me.
P WHERE did you find it?
W Right at the corner of the building where the alleged assault occurred.
P WHAT did you do with the knife? (1)
W I followed standing operating procedure.
P WHAT is that procedure? (1)
W I marked it for identification.
P HOW did you do that? (1)
W In the case of a relatively inexpensive item such as this one, I scratched my initials and the date onto the wooden handle.
P WHEN did you do this? (2)
W As soon as I found it.
P HOW much time passed between your discovery of this knife and your marking it? (2)
W No more than a couple of minutes.
P Your Honor, I request that this be marked plaintiff's exhibit number two for identification.
J It will be so marked.
P Please let the record reflect that I am showing the exhibit to the opposing counsel.
J It will so reflect.
P I request permission to approach the witness.
J Permission granted.
P I now hand you plaintiff's exhibit number two for identification. WHAT is it? (3)
W It's the knife I found.
P HOW can you recognize it? (4)
W As I testified, I marked my initials and the date on the handle. They're right there.
P WHAT condition is the exhibit in? (5)
W It's in good condition.
P HOW has it changed since you found it at the scene? (5)
W It doesn't appear to have changed at all. It seems to be in the same condition.
P Your Honor, I now offer plaintiff's exhibit number two for identification into evidence as plaintiff s exhibit number two.
J It will be received.
P I request permission to hand the exhibit to the jurors for their inspection.
J Permission granted.

The fact situation for the chain of custody foundation is a criminal assault prosecution. The People allege that the defendant, Mr. Morris, used his feet to kick and beat the victim, Mr. Navin. The prosecutor wants to show that the blood grouping of stains on the defendant's shoes matches the victim's blood grouping.

As a predicate for that scientific analysis, the prosecutor must establish a chain of custody for the shoes; the prosecutor must demonstrate that the shoes were in the same condition at the time of analysis as they were when they were seized from the defendant. The seizing police officer, Officer Stevens, has already testified. He testified that he seized the shoes from Morris, kept them safe, and then delivered them to the laboratory technician, Ms. Quinn. Ms. Quinn is the next witness. The prosecutor is the proponent. The shoes have been marked People's exhibit four for identification.

P   WHAT is your occupation?
W   I am a laboratory technician with the Salinas Police Department.
P   HOW long have you worked for the Salinas Police Department.
W   About six years.
P   WHAT are your duties?
W   I specialize In blood and stain analysis.
P   HOW long have you done that sort of work?
W   About six years—ever since I graduated.
P   WHAT school did you graduate from?
W   San Diego State University.
P   WHAT was your major area of study?
W   Chemistry, especially organic chemistry.
P   Ms. Quinn, WHERE were you on the afternoon of November 12 of last year? (1)
W   I was on duty at work at the laboratory.
P   WHAT, if anything, happened that afternoon? (1)
W   Officer Stevens delivered some shoes to me for analysis.
P   WHO is Officer Stevens? (1)
W   He was the last witness in this case.
P   HOW do you know that? (1)
W   I was sitting in the spectators' section over there when he testified.
P   WHAT did you do with the shoes when he delivered them to you? (2)
W   I followed standard practice. The very first thing I did was initial the evidence slip that's attached.
P   WHAT is an evidence slip? (2)
W   It's a chain of custody receipt. You sign off on it when you receive the attached object.
P   WHAT did you do with the shoes after you initialed the evidence slip? (2)
W   I immediately conducted an analysis of some stains on the soles of the shoes.
P   HOW much time passed between his delivery of the shoes and your analysis? (2)
W   Only about five minutes. I wasn't very busy when he walked in.
P   WHAT did you do after you conducted the analysis? (2)
W   I put the shoes in my evidence locker.
P   WHERE is this locker? (2)
W   It's in my work area in the lab.
P   HOW secure is this locker? (2)
W   Well, I have a combination lock on it.
P   WHO knows the combination? (2)
W   Just me and the head of the Fluids section of the lab, Mr. Guinn.
P   WHAT happened to the shoes after you put them in the locker? (3)

W They've just been sitting there until today.

P HOW often have you opened the locker between the time you placed the shoes there and today? (2)

W Probably hundreds of times.

P WHAT procedure do you use to open the locker? (2)

W I use the combination to open it, remove what I want, and immediately close it.

P HOW have the shoes changed since you placed them in the locker? (2)

W They're certainly a little dustier than before, but otherwise they haven't changed.

P Your Honor, I request permission to approach the witness.

J Permission granted.

P I now hand you People's exhibit four for identification. WHAT is it? (4)

W They seem to be the shoes I analyzed.

P HOW can you recognize them? (4)

W I notice my handwriting on the attached slip, and I recognize their general appearance, including the scrapes and the stains on the soles.

P HOW did the shoes get out of the evidence locker? (4)

W I removed them just before coming here to testify.

P WHO has had possession of them since you removed them from the locker? (4)

W I had possession until I got here.

P WHAT did you do then? (4)

W I placed them on your counsel table so you could use them.

P WHAT did you do then? (4)

W I sat in the spectators' area and observed the trial and kept an eye on the shoes.

P HOW often did you leave the room? (4)

W I didn't. I've been here this entire morning, watching the trial and the shoes.

P WHAT condition are the shoes in? (5)

W They seem to be in the same condition as when Officer Stevens delivered them to me.

P WHAT condition are the stains in? (5)

W They're a bit changed because I had to scrape some off to analyze the stains. Otherwise they're in the same condition.

P Your Honor, I now offer People's exhibit number four for identification into evidence as People's exhibit number four.

J They will be received.

P I request permission to hand the exhibit to the jurors for their inspection.

J Request granted. (The jurors inspect the shoes.)

P Now, Ms. Quinn, I'd like to ask you a few questions about your analysis of the shoes.

M. THE VERIFICATION OF PHOTOGRAPHS

1. STILL PHOTOGRAPHS

Like other articles, still photographs must be authenticated or verified. In the past, some courts insisted that the photographer appear as the sponsoring witness. The prevailing modern view is that any person familiar with the scene or object depicted may verify the photograph. California follows this view.

In the past, many jurisdictions also followed the "pictorial testimony" theory for admitting photographs: The photograph merely illustrates the witness' testimony, and the only evidence admitted is the testimony. Suppose, for example, that in a wrongful death action arising from a hit-and-run, the plaintiff attempts to establish that it was the defendant's car that struck and killed the decedent. During the plaintiff's case-in-chief, the defendant's neighbor testifies and verifies a color photograph of the defendant's car. The photograph plainly shows that the defendant's car is red—just as the eyewitnesses to the accident testified that the car that struck the decedent was red. However, the plaintiff's attorney neglects to elicit the neighbor's testimony that the car is red. If the court strictly applied the "pictorial testimony" theory, during closing the plaintiff's attorney could not argue that the defendant's car is red; there would be no substantive evidence in the record of the car's color. The trend in the case law is toward the competing, "silent witness" theory for admitting photographs. If the proponent can authenticate the photograph, the photograph serves as substantive evidence of all the facts clearly shown in the photograph. California has adopted the "silent witness" theory. 2 WITKIN § 841, at 806-08 (citing *People v. Bowley*, 230 Cal. App. 2d 269, 40 Cal. Rptr. 859 (1964)).

The foundational elements are as follows:

1. The witness is familiar with the object or scene.
2. The witness explains the basis for his or her familiarity with the object or scene.
3. The witness recognizes the object or scene in the photograph.
4. The photograph is a "fair," "accurate," "true, " or "good" depiction of the object or scene at the relevant time.

Our fact situation is a tort action arising from a collision. The collision occurred at the intersection of A and Third Streets. The plaintiff calls a witness to verify a photograph of the intersection. The witness has already identified himself as Mr. Donald Adams.

P   WHERE do you work? (2)
W   Downtown.
P   WHERE downtown? (2)
W   I'm a teller at the First National Bank on Third Street.
P   WHERE is the bank located on Third Street? (2)
W   I think it's the 400 block. The bank is between A and B Streets.
P   HOW long have you worked there? (2)
W   A good seven years.
P   Your Honor, I request that this be marked plaintiff's exhibit number three for identification.
J   The record will so reflect.
P   I request permission to approach the witness.
J   Permission granted.
P   I now hand you plaintiff's exhibit number three for identification. WHAT is it? (3)

W It's a photograph of the intersection of A and Third Streets.

P   HOW can you recognize it? (2)

W As I said, I've worked in that area for years.

P   HOW often have you passed that intersection? (2)

W I couldn't give you a figure. I've been there hundreds of times.

P   WHAT perspective or viewpoint does this photograph show? (3)

W Let's see. Third Street runs north-south. A Street runs east-west.

P   From WHICH corner was the photograph apparently taken? (3)

W From the southwest corner.

P   Facing WHICH direction? (3)

W Facing north looking up Third Street.

P   HOW accurate is this photograph? (4)

W Very. It's a good, true depiction as far as I can tell.

P   HOW accurately does it show the intersection as it was at the time of the collision that gave rise to this case? (4)

W Well. It's a good photograph for that purpose. I worked downtown then, and I think it shows roughly how the intersection looked then.

P   HOW has the intersection changed since the collision? (4)

W Some of the signs have changed; businesses come and go. However, the intersection itself really hasn't changed. As best I can recall, it's the same size, the street markings are the same, and traffic flows the same way.

P   Your Honor, I now offer plaintiff's exhibit number three for identification into evidence as plaintiff's exhibit number three.

J   It will be received.

P   I request permission to hand the exhibit to the jurors for their inspection.

J   Permission granted.

2. MOTION PICTURES

Like computers and tape recorders, motion pictures raise scientific evidence issues. Again, the validity of the underlying theory and the general reliability of motion picture cameras are now so well accepted that the judge will judicially notice those two elements of the foundation. As with tape recorders, the courts were initially very conservative in their treatment of motion pictures. Because of possible distortion, the proponent had to lay a very strict foundation: the operator's qualifications, the good working condition of the equipment, the custody of the film, identification of the persons or objects depicted in the film, and testimony by someone present that the film accurately depicts the activity filmed. The law governing the admission of motion pictures has now been liberalized. The testimony of any person present when the activity occurred is sufficient to authenticate the film. Even without the testimony of such a person, the remaining foundational elements have sufficient probative value to verify the film.

The same legal principles govern the authentication of videotapes, that is, visual images recorded on magnetic tape by a video camera. *See* Christopher Mueller and Laird Kirkpatrick, Evidence § 9.14 at 1138-40 (2d ed. 1999); *see also People v. Mayfield*, 14 Cal. 4th 668, 928 P.2d 485, 60 Cal. Rptr. 2d 1, 46 (1997), *cert. denied,* 522 U.S. 839 (1997).

In *People v. Carpenter*, 15 Cal. 4th 312, 935 P.2d 708, 63 Cal. Rptr. 2d 1, 43 (1997), the defendant was alleged to be the "Trailside Killer," who raped and murdered hikers on remote trails in Northern California. The prosecutor's evidence included a 15-minute videotape that depicted various scenes along the trail where one rape and murder took place. The videotape was made long after the crimes, and the trial judge ruled that it did not contain any inflammatory or sensational material. The prosecutor used the tape to "illustrate" the testimony of the victim's male companion, whom the defendant had shot but not killed. The companion directed the making of the videotape, and he narrated the tape as it was played at trial, testifying that it accurately depicted the appearance of the trail on the day of the shooting. Quoting from prior California decisions, the California Supreme Court stated two simple requirements for this kind of use of a videotape:

- First, the trial judge must decide whether the videotape is a "reasonable representation" of what it is alleged to portray; and
- Second, the trial judge must decide whether the videotape would "assist the jurors in their determination of the facts of the case," rather than "serve to mislead them." 15 Cal. 4th at 386, 935 P.2d at 750, 63 Cal. Rptr. 2d at 43.

If those two requirements are met, "the physical conditions which existed at the time the event in question occurred *need not be duplicated with precision*." *Id.* [emphasis added]. Moreover, the proponent *need not* show that no change has occurred between the event and the making of the videotape. *Id.* [emphasis added]. The defendant argued that the videotape was misleading because some of the scenes lasted longer than the actual events, and because the video camera was generally stationary and did not move along the trail as the witness had. The Supreme Court brushed aside those contentions stating: "Differences between real life and a videotape are inevitable and readily apparent to the jury. The videotape illustrated … [the witness's] testimony; it did not replace it." *Id.* Mueller and Kirkpatrick distinguish this "pictorial testimony" use of a photographic film or videotape from what they call the "silent witness" use. *See* Mueller and Kirkpatrick, *supra* at 1138-39. In the "silent witness" use, no human witness is available to testify that he or she observed the scene in question and that the film or videotape accurately depicts the scene. Pictures taken by bank surveillance cameras are a common example. The foundation for the "silent witness" use can be laid by having an appropriate witness: (a) describe the process by which the film or videotape was made; (b) state when and where the film or videotape was made; and (c) testify that the process produces accurate results. *Id.*

The following is a complete, traditional foundation for a photographic film made with a motion picture camera.

1. The operator was qualified to take a motion picture film.
2. The operator filmed a certain activity.

3. The operator used certain equipment to film the activity. Some trial attorneys prefer to present very detailed testimony about the equipment, especially the lens used. As the sample foundation indicates, a general description of the equipment suffices.
4. The equipment was in good working order.
5. The operator used proper procedures to film the activity. Here, again, some attorneys like to offer detailed testimony. Their foundation covers such technical matters as the speed of the film and the lens aperture. General testimony is satisfactory.
6. The operator accounts for the custody of the film and the developed movie.
7. The developed movie was a good reproduction of the activity.
8. The operator recognizes the exhibit as the film he or she took.
9. The film is still a good depiction of the activity.

The fact situation is a tort action. The plaintiff's theory is that the defendant, General Motors, defectively designed the 1999 Chevrolet Camaro. The plaintiff wants to introduce films depicting impact experiments with a 1999 Chevrolet Camaro. The plaintiff calls the photographer who filmed the experiment. The photographer has already identified himself as Mr. Blair McIntosh.

P   WHAT is your occupation? (1)
W   I am a professional photographer.
P   WHERE do you work? (1)
W   I have my own studio at 1333 Flower Street downtown.
P   HOW long have you been a professional photographer? (1)
W   For over twelve years now.
P   HOW did you become a professional photographer? (1)
W   I started working for another professional photographer in Torrance right after graduation from high school.
P   WHAT training have you had as a photographer? (1)
W   I've taken ten college-level courses in photography and attended numerous seminars and training conferences.
P   HOW long have you had your own professional photography business? (1)
W   The last seven years.
P   Mr. McIntosh, WHERE were you on the morning of August 17 of this year? (2)
W   I was at Abbott Laboratories on C Street here in Los Angeles.
P   WHY did you go there? (2)
W   You asked me to go there to film some experiments.
P   WHAT experiments? (2)
W   It was an impact experiment with a 1999 Chevrolet Camaro.
P   WHAT did you do when you arrived at Abbott Laboratories? (2)
W   I carried out my assignment. I introduced myself to the personnel conducting the experiment and proceeded to film their experiment.
P   WHAT equipment did you use? (3)
W   I used a Kodak, ten-millimeter motion picture camera and Kodak film and a standard Kodak lens.
P   HOW widely is this equipment used? (3)

W Lots of professional photographers, especially newspaper photographers, use the very same set of equipment. It's a very reliable set.

P WHAT condition was the equipment in when you filmed the experiment? (4)

W Good, operating condition.

P HOW do you know that? (4)

W I didn't have any mechanical difficulty with the camera or lens during the filming, and I had just given my equipment complete maintenance a week before.

P HOW did you learn to maintain this equipment? (4)

W I attended a maintenance seminar sponsored by Kodak.

P WHAT condition was the film in? (4)

W It was brand new. I had to break the wrapper to take it out of the box.

P HOW did you film the experiment? (5)

W I checked my light meter to make certain that I had the right opening on the lens. Then I set the camera upon the tripod and focused until I had a clear image in my viewer.

P HOW long did it take you to film the experiment? (6)

W Only about twenty minutes.

P WHAT did you do after you filmed the experiment? (6)

W I disassembled my equipment and went back to my studio.

P WHAT did you do after you arrived there? (6)

W It was still early in the day, and I didn't have much else to do, so I developed the film immediately.

P WHERE did you do that? (6)

W In my own darkroom.

P HOW did you learn to develop film? (6)

W My old boss taught me, and I studied developing techniques in many of my college photography courses.

P WHAT did you do after you developed the film? (7)

W I set up a projector and screen to view the film. I then viewed the entire film.

P WHAT was the quality of the film? (7)

W It was excellent. As far as I could tell, it was fine depiction of the experiment.

P WHAT did you do after you viewed the film? (6)

W I put it in my files.

P WHERE did you keep the film after that? (6)

W With one exception, it's been in my files the whole time.

P WHAT was the exception? (6)

W You and I viewed the film two weeks ago.

P WHO was present during the viewing? (6)

W Just the two of us.

P WHERE were you during the viewing? (6)

W I was present during this viewing. (6)

P WHAT did you do with the film after the viewing? (6)

W I put it back in my files.

P Your Honor, I request that this be marked plaintiff's exhibit number five for identification.

J It will be so marked.

P Please let the record reflect that I am showing the exhibit to the opposing counsel.

J The record will so reflect.

P   I request permission to approach the witness.

J   Permission granted.

P   Mr. McIntosh, I now hand you plaintiffs exhibit number five for identification. WHAT is it? (8)

W   It's the motion picture of the experiment.

P   HOW do you recognize it? (8)

W   I recognize my handwriting on the label on reel.

P   HOW did the film get from your files to the courtroom today? (6)

W   I took it out of my files this morning and brought it here myself.

P   WHAT did you do with it after you arrived here? (9)

W   You, the other attorney, the judge, and I viewed the film in the judge's chambers.

P   WHAT condition was the film in? (9)

W   Fine. It's in the same excellent condition it was in after I developed it.

P   WHAT happened to the film after we viewed it in the judge's chambers? (6)

W   I kept it in my possession.

P   WHEN did you surrender possession of it? (6)

W   I put it on your counsel table as I walked u p to the witness stand.

P   Your Honor, I now offer plaintiff's exhibit number five for identification into evidence as plaintiff's exhibit number five for identification into evidence as plaintiff's exhibit number five.

J   It will be received.

P   I request permission to have the bailiff show the motion picture to the jurors.

J   Permission granted.

3. X-RAYS

X-rays are also photographs. In most cases, the counsel stipulate to the authenticity of X-rays in the case. However, occasionally, the proponent will have to authenticate the X-ray. The authentication of an X-ray is a rather peculiar process. No one can testify that he or she saw what the X-ray depicts and verify the X-ray on that theory.

Because of that peculiarity, the proponent must resort to some other authentication technique. Some judges treat X-rays as business records of the hospital; they accept authentication by the testimony of the hospital's X-ray librarian that he or she removed the X-ray from the right file. Other judges view X-ray evidence as presenting both scientific and physical evidence problems; the proponent must show the operator's qualifications, the working order of the X-ray, and a chain of custody for the X-ray cassette. In most hospitals, however, the X-ray technician uses an identification assembly during the X-ray; the assembly is composed of lead letters and numbers and casts a shadow of the letters and numbers on the cassette. In effect, the letters and numbers make the cassette a readily identifiable article.

If the hospital follows the customary practice of using an identification assembly, the complete foundation for the X-ray would include the following elements:

1. The operator was a qualified X-ray technician.
2. The operator filmed a certain part of a person's body at a certain time and place.
3. The operator used certain equipment.
4. The equipment was in good working condition.
5. The operator used the correct procedures.
6. The operator used an identification assembly on the cassette.
7. The operator accounts for the cassette's custody between filming and trial; the chain of custody includes proof of the proper development of the cassette.
8. The witness recognizes the exhibit as the cassette.

The fact situation is a civil action. The plaintiff contends that as a result of the tort, she suffered severe personal injuries, including bone fracture. The plaintiff wishes to introduce an X-ray to depict some of the fractures. The plaintiff calls Mr. Herbert Hain. Mr. Hain has already identified himself.

P   WHAT is your occupation? (1)
W   I am an X-ray technician at Sharp Hospital downtown.
P   HOW long have you worked as an X-ray technician? (1)
W   For seven years.
P   WHAT is your formal education? (1)
W   I have a degree from U.C. Riverside.
P   WHAT was your major field of study? (1)
W   Science.
P   WHAT other training have you had as an X-ray technician? (1)
W   I attended a three-month course at U.C.L.A. Medical School, and I've also attended numerous seminars on the subject.
P   WHERE were you on the afternoon of July 7th of last year? (2)
W   As I recall, I was on duty at the X-ray lab.
P   WHAT, if anything, happened that afternoon? (2)
W   Doctor Bertrand asked me to take the plaintiff's X-ray, and the plaintiff stopped by for the X-ray.
P   WHO is the plaintiff? (2)
W   The woman at the table to the right over there.
P   WHAT is she wearing? (2)
W   The green dress and yellow scarf.
P   Your Honor, please let the record reflect that the witness has identified the plaintiff, Ms. Wohlmuth. (2)
J   It will so reflect.
P   WHAT did you do when Ms. Wohlmuth arrived at the lab? (3)
W   I showed her how to position herself on the table to enable me to get a good X-ray of her right leg.
P   WHAT happened then? (3)
W   Then I set up the equipment.
P   WHAT equipment? (3)
W   The X-ray machine and the cassette with identification assembly.

P   WHAT is the X-ray machine? (3)

W   It's the camera that you use to take an X-ray.

P   WHAT is the cassette? (3)

W   It's the film. The X-rays make the impression on the cassette.

P   WHAT is the identification assembly? (6)

W   It consists of lead numbers and letters. The lead casts shadows on the cassette; you sort of outline the letters and numbers.

P   WHAT are these letters and numbers? (6)

W   The practice varies from hospital to hospital. Some hospitals use the numbers for the patient's file number; each patient has a different file number. We usually spell out the patient's name if it's short and then list the date of the X-ray in numbers.

P   WHAT condition was the equipment in? (4)

W   It was in fine condition.

P   HOW do you know that? (4)

W   I had checked it myself the day before. I always check it Monday morning. I took this X-ray on Tuesday.

P   HOW did you learn to check the equipment? (4)

W   That was one of the subjects we studied at U.C.L.A.

P   HOW did you take the plaintiff's X-ray? (5)

W   After I set up the equipment, I told the plaintiff to position her leg. Then I stepped behind the lead and leaded glass, I viewed the plaintiff during the X-ray. I adjusted the amperage and voltage settings, and then I turned the machine on to make the exposure.

P   WHAT did you do then? (5)

W   I reentered the room and removed the cassette.

P   HAT did you do with the cassette? (7)

W   I put it in a corner in the room and developed it that afternoon.

P   WHAT happened to the cassette between the filming and the development? (7)

W   As far as I know, nothing. It was just there in the room.

P   WHO handled the cassette between the filming and development? (7)

W   As far as I can tell, I was the only one.

P   HOW did you develop the X-ray? (7)

W   I went into the dark room, removed the film from the cassette, and then put it through the developing process.

P   HOW did you learn to develop X-rays? (7)

W   That was another subject we studied in detail at U.C.L.A.

P   WHAT did you do with the film after you developed it? (7)

W   I brought it down to our X-ray records library on the second floor. I filed it under the plaintiff's name.

P   Your Honor, I request that this be marked plaintiff's exhibit number four for identification.

J   It will be so marked.

P   Please let the record reflect that I am showing the exhibit to the opposing counsel.

J   It will so reflect.

P   I request permission to approach the witness.

J   Permission granted.

P   Mr. Hain, I now hand you plaintiff's exhibit number four for identification. WHAT is it? (8)

W   It's the X-ray I took of the plaintiff's leg.

P   HOW can you recognize it? (8)

W   I recognize this type of film, and I see the plaintiff's name and date just as I set them up in the identification assembly. I also recognize the general appearance of the bones depicted.

P   HOW did the film get to court today? (7)

W   I went to the file for that month and looked for the X-ray with the plaintiff's name and the date.

P   HOW many were there? (7)

W   Only the one I took.

P   HOW many times have you used that filing system in the past? (7)

W   Hundreds.

P   WHO taught you how to use the system? (7)

W   The X-ray records librarian herself, Doctor Riley.

P   Your Honor, I now offer plaintiff's exhibit number four for identification into evidence as plaintiff's exhibit number four.

J   It will be received.

The proponent will use the X-ray later during a doctor's testimony. The doctor will testify about the extent of injury and use the X-ray to illustrate the injuries.

N.   THE VALIDATION OF SCIENTIFIC EVIDENCE

1. THE DOCTRINE

At first glance, the validation of scientific evidence appears to be a simple problem of authentication: The proponent need present only sufficient evidence to support a rational jury finding that the underlying theory is valid and the instrument is reliable. It is at least arguable that the validation of scientific evidence should be treated as an Evidence Code § 403 issue. However, the courts have long been suspicious of scientific evidence. In the first place, the courts have sometimes been skeptical of scientists' claims of the virtual infallibility of scientific techniques. Secondly, the courts fear that scientific evidence will overwhelm the jury; the jurors will be so impressed by the scientific evidence that the scientist witness will effectively usurp the jurors' fact-finding duties.

Until the United States Supreme Court's decision in *Daubert v. Merrell Dow Pharmaceuticals, Inc.*, 509 U.S. 579, 113 S. Ct. 2786, 125 L. Ed. 2d 469 (1993), the federal courts and most state courts followed an old federal case, *Frye v. United States*, 293 F. 1013 (D.C. Cir. 1923), which held that the proponent of scientific evidence must show that the theory and instrument have been *generally accepted* in the relevant scientific circles. *Daubert* held that the Federal Rules of Evidence supersede the *Frye* rule. According to *Daubert*, the Federal Rules occupy the field; unless a common-law exclusionary doctrine is specifically incorporated in the Federal Rules, it is no longer the law. Thus, federal courts should no longer use the *Frye* "general acceptance" test as the exclusive criterion to determine the admissibility of scientific evidence. *Daubert* said that Federal Rule 702 establishes that expert testimony must be based on "scientific knowledge." To determine what constitutes "scientific knowledge," a federal judge may still use the indicia of general acceptance, such as publication and peer review, but the federal judge should also consider other facts, such as known rates of error and how the theory has been tested.

Back in 1976, the California Supreme Court adopted a version of the *Frye* rule in *People v. Kelly*, 17 Cal. 3d 24, 130 Cal. Rptr. 144, 549 P.2d 1240 (1976). In California, the general acceptance test is thus called the *Kelly-Frye* rule. In 1994, the California Supreme Court declined to follow *Daubert's* lead. *People v. Leahy*, 8 Cal. 4th 587, 34 Cal. Rptr. 2d 663 (1994). Therefore, *Kelly-Frye* remains the law of California, at least for the present. *See In re Aontee D.*, 25 Cal. App. 4th 167, 30 Cal. Rptr. 2d 176 (1994).

The purported purpose of the *Kelly-Frye* rule is to protect the jury from new scientific techniques that convey a "misleading aura of certainty." *People v. Stoll*, 49 Cal. 3d 1136, 783 P.2d 698, 265 Cal. Rptr. 111 (1989). The court in *Stoll* discerned two themes in the California cases. First, *Kelly-Frye* applies only to evidence that is based on a technique, process, or theory that is "new to science and, even more so, the law." *Id.* (emphasis in original). Second, *Kelly-Frye* applies where the unproven technique, process, or theory appears to provide "some definitive truth which the expert need only accurately recognize and relay to the jury"—in other words, where the evidence has an "undeserved aura of certainty." *Id.*

Kelly-Frye is not limited to physical evidence. It also applies to testimonial evidence that has an undeserved aura of certainty—for example, testimony that has been enhanced by hypnosis. *Id.* However, "absent some special feature which effectively blindsides the jury, expert opinion testimony is not subject to *Kelly-Frye*." *Id.*

The California Supreme Court has not applied *Kelly-Frye* to expert medical testimony, even to the testimony of psychiatrists on subjects as esoteric as reconstitution of a past state of mind, or the prediction of future dangerousness, or the diagnosis of an unusual mental illness. *Id.* In *Stoll*, the Supreme Court held that it was error for the trial judge to apply *Kelly-Frye* to the defendants' expert good character evidence. The expert in that case would have testified that, based on standard tests and personal interviews, the defendant's personality profiles did not include a capacity for deviant sexual behavior with children. *See also People v. Ruiz*, 222 Cal. App. 3d 1241, 272 Cal. Rptr. 368 (1990) (expert's testimony about defendant's capacity for deviant behavior with children); *People v. Harlan*, 222 Cal. App. 3d 439, 271 Cal. Rptr. 653 (1990) (expert testimony about reactions of child abuse victims); *People v. Rowland*, 4 Cal. 4th 238, 841 P.2d 897, 14 Cal. Rptr. 2d 377 (1992), *cert. denied*, 114 S. Ct. 138 (1993) (expert testimony about physical signs of nonconsensual sexual intercourse). A medical diagnosis based on medical literature is not subject to the *Kelly-Frye* test because it is simply an expert opinion developed from knowledge of other cases. *People v. Cegers*, 7 Cal. App. 4th 988, 9 Cal. Rptr. 2d 297 (1992).

Kelly-Frye has been remarkably resilient in California law. One might argue that, as a judge-made rule, *Kelly-Frye* is inconsistent with California Evidence Code § 351, which states that all relevant evidence is admissible except as otherwise provided by *statute*. However, *Kelly* itself was decided nine years after the California Evidence Code went into effect, and it has been followed many times since. Likewise, one might argue that *Kelly-Frye* did not survive Proposition 8, the 1982 voter initiative that made "all relevant evidence" admissible in criminal cases, subject to limited exceptions. However, in *People v; Harris*, 47 Cal. 3d 1047, 767 P.2d 619, 255 Cal. Rptr. 352 (1989), the Supreme Court held that, with respect to character evidence, *Kelly-Frye* survived Proposition 8.

Under *Kelly-Frye*, the foundation for scientific evidence will often require two witnesses. If the theory and instrument are very generally accepted, the judge will judicially notice those elements of the foundation upon a proper timely request by counsel. However, if judicial notice is inapplicable, the proponent will probably have to call an expert with heavy academic credentials to lay those elements of the foundation. The proponent will then call a technician as the second witness to lay the balance of the foundation.

2. ELEMENTS OF THE FOUNDATION

1. Witness #1 is qualified to establish the theory's validity and the instrument's reliability. In *People v. Kelly*, 17 Cal. 3d 24, 39, 549 P.2d 1240, 1250, 130 Cal. Rptr. 144, 154 (1976), the court stated that the witness should ordinarily be a scientist rather than a mere laboratory technician. The court also emphasized that the witness ought to be impartial rather than a person who "has virtually built his career on the reliability of the technique." *Id.* at 38, 549 P.2d at 1249, 130 Cal. Rptr. at 153.
2. The underlying theory is valid.
3. The underlying theory is generally accepted as valid. In *People v. Kelly*, 17 Cal. 3d 24, 37, 549 P.2d 1240, 1248, 130 Cal. Rptr. 144, I52 (1976), the court commented that "it [is] questionable whether the testimony of a single witness alone is ever sufficient to represent, or attest to, the views of an entire scientific community regarding the reliability of a new technique." Suppose that an earlier California case holds that a particular theory has not yet gained general acceptance. In *People v. Harris*, 47 Cal. 3d 1047, 1094, 767 P.2d 619, 649, 255 Cal. Rptr. 352, 382 (1989), the California Supreme Court commented that

> on a proper showing [the proponent of scientific evidence] must from time to time be permitted to demonstrate that advancement in a scientific technique has enhanced its reliability and acceptance in the scientific community and to establish that the advances warrant admission of a previously excluded category of scientific evidence.

Additionally, once a scientific technique has been endorsed in a published appellate opinion, that decision becomes precedent; absent evidence that the prevailing scientific opinion has changed, adjudication on the "general acceptance" prong of the *Kelly* test is not required. *People v. Venegas*, 18 Cal. 4th 47, 954 P.2d 525, 74 Cal. Rptr. 2d 262 (1998); *People v. Wright*, 62 Cal. App. 4th 31, 72 Cal. Rptr. 2d 246 (1998).

4. The instrument is trustworthy.

5. The instrument is generally accepted as trustworthy. In many cases, the proponent will not need live testimony to establish elements #1-5, and the proponent will need only the technician, witness #2. In some cases, the validity and general acceptance of the theory and instrument are judicially noticeable. Evidence Code § 452(h) authorizes trial judges to judicially notice "[facts and propositions that are not reasonably subject to dispute and are capable of immediate and accurate determination by resort to sources of reasonably indisputable accuracy." The Assembly Committee comment to § 452(h) states that subdivision includes "facts which are accepted as established by experts and specialists in the natural, physical, and social sciences. ..."

Or, the legislature may have enacted a statute allowing the admission of testimony based on a particular scientific technique; such statutes obviate the need to produce evidence on the validity issue. For instance, California Family Code §§ 7550-56 authorize the admission of testimony based on certain genetic marker tests in paternity cases. The statutes eliminate the need for the proponent of genetic marker testimony to prove the validity and general acceptance of those tests.

If there is a pertinent statute or if the validity and general acceptance of the theory and instrument are judicially noticeable, the proponent may dispense with live testimony. Under Evidence Code § 457, the proponent should merely request the judge to instruct the jury that they are to assume the validity of the theory and instrument.

6. Witness #2 is qualified to conduct the test results.

7. The instrument witness #2 used was in good working condition.

8. The witness used the instrument in the test.

9. The witness used the proper procedures. In *People v. Venegas*, 18 Cal. 4th 47, 954 P.2d 525, 74 Cal. Rptr. 2d 262 (1998), the California Supreme Court called this the "third prong" of the *Kelly* test. The first prong requires that the reliability of a new scientific technique be established by showing that it has gained acceptance in its field. The second prong requires that any witness testifying about general acceptance be properly qualified as an expert on the subject. The third prong requires that the procedures actually used in the case be in compliance with the methodology and technique that have gained general acceptance. The third prong is thus entirely "case specific." The third prong is part of the test for admissibility—not merely a factor that affects the weight of the evidence. If the evidence meets all three prongs of *Kelly*, it is admissible. However, the opponent can still try to re-

duce the weight of the evidence by showing that the procedures were carried out poorly, for example that samples were mislabeled or contaminated. If these defects are the kind that can readily be understood by the jury, then they can be proven without the help of an expert. *See Venegas*, 18 Cal. 4th at 80-81.

10. The witness states the test result.

3. SAMPLE FOUNDATIONS

a. Radar Speedmeter

The fact situation is a speeding prosecution. The government charges that the defendant, Mr. Berton, was going forty-five miles an hour on a street posted for thirty miles an hour. Officer Jones used a radar speedmeter to clock the defendant. Most jurisdictions judicially notice the validity of the underlying theory and the reliability of speedmeters; but for illustrative purposes, the prosecutor will call a witness to lay those elements of the foundation.

The prosecutor first calls Professor Jerold Harter. The professor first identifies himself.

P   WHAT is your occupation? (1)
W   I teach at the University of San Francisco.
P   WHAT do you teach? (1)
W   I teach physics and electronics.
P   WHAT is your formal education? (1)
W   I have a B.S. from Pepperdine and both a master's and a doctorate from the California Institute of Technology.
P   WHAT was your major area of study? (1)
W   My specialty has been radar and electronics.
P   HOW long have you been teaching? (1)
W   For approximately ten years.
P   WHAT, if anything, have you published? (1)
W   I've published roughly twenty articles, most of them dealing with radar and electronics.
P   Professor, WHAT is the Doppler Shift principle? (2)
W   It's a theory about beams of microwaves. If a beam bounces off an approaching object, the frequency of the beam changes; the change is an increase, and it is proportional to the speed of the approaching object.
P   WHAT experiments, if any, have been conducted to verify this theory? (2)
W   You couldn't count the number. The theory is one of the most fundamental principles in the field.
P   HOW widely is the principle accepted? (3)
W   It's regarded as a truism, a basic principle. Everyone in the field knows about and accepts the principle.
P   Now, professor, WHAT is a radar speedmeter? (4)
W   It's a device for measuring the speed of cars.
P   WHAT are the components of a radar speedmeter? (4)

W It has a component for transmitting a beam of microwaves and another component for receiving.

P HOW does the speedmeter work? (4)

W For example, the transmitter sends a beam toward an approaching vehicle. The beam strikes the vehicle, shifts, and then bounces back to the receiver. The receiver measures the change in frequency, and the speedmeter reads out the speed of the approaching vehicle.

P WHAT experiments, if any, have been conducted to test the reliability of the speedmeter? (4)

W There have been numerous experiments, particularly some at Northwestern and the University of North Carolina.

P WHAT has been the outcome of these experiments? (4)

W If the instrument is in good condition and the operator is qualified, the instrument will give you a very reliable speed estimate.

P HOW widely is the radar speedmeter accepted? (5)

W It's used extensively, and its reliability is almost universally accepted.

The second witness will be the officer who used a radar speedmeter to clock the defendant. The officer has already testified that he arrived at the scene and set up his equipment.

P WHAT equipment were you using? (8)

W A General Electric radar speedmeter.

P WHAT training, if any, have you had in using a speedmeter? (6)

W I spent a week studying the speedmeter at the Police Academy.

P HOW did you study the speedmeter? (6)

W First, we had several lectures on the speedmeter and its operation. Then, we saw demonstrations of its use. Finally, we participated in exercises where we used the speedmeter and more experienced officers double-checked us.

P HOW many times have you used the speedmeter? (6)

W Hundreds of times.

P HOW long have you used a speedmeter? (6)

W I've been assigned to Traffic for three years, and you use the speedmeter almost daily in Traffic detail.

P WHAT did you do after you arrived at the scene? (8)

W I checked to ensure that the speedmeter was in working order.

P WHAT condition was the speedmeter in? (7)

W Good, operational condition.

P HOW do you know that? (7)

W I used a tuning fork test.

P WHAT is the tuning fork test? (7)

W The manufacturer supplies you with several tuning forks. I have thirty-, forty-five-, and sixty-mile-an-hour forks. You set them off, and the speedmeter is supposed to register those speeds.

P HOW did you conduct the test on this occasion? (7)

W I used all three forks, and the machine checked out all three times; it registered the right speed.

P WHAT did you do then? (9)

W I let the machine warm up and then aimed the transmitter down the road.

P   WHAT happened after you aimed the transmitter? (8)

W   I saw the defendant's car approaching.

P   WHO is the defendant? (8)

W   He's the fellow sitting at the table over there.

P   HOW is he dressed? (8)

W   He's wearing a blue suit and red tie.

P   HOW long did you have to observe the defendant at the scene? (8)

W   About three minutes, I saw him as he passed by, and then later, after we stopped him, I talked to him for several minutes.

P   Your Honor, please let the record reflect that the witness has identified the defendant. (8)

J   It will so reflect.

P   WHAT did you do when you saw the defendant's car approaching? (8)

W   I checked to ensure that the speedmeter was on, and then I clocked his car.

P   WHAT does "clocked" mean? (10)

W   It means that I measured his speed.

P   WHAT was the clocking? (10)

W   The speedmeter flashed a signal that his car was going forty-five miles an hour.

The foundation concludes here because the test result, the forty-five-mile-per-hour clocking, is self-explanatory. In some cases, the result is not self-explanatory. Suppose, for example, that the instrument in question produces a chart rather than generating a digital readout. The instrument might be a sound spectrograph. The significance of the spectrogram will not be self-evident to the judge or jurors; an expert must explain its significance. Even when the test yields a numerical result, the meaning of the number may not be obvious. Assume that a laboratory technician at a medical examiner's office conducts a toxicological test which shows that there are fifty micrograms of cyanide per 100 milliliters of blood in a corpse. A technician with exclusively on-the-job experience can be trained to conduct the test. However, the proponent will have to present the testimony of a physician, toxicologist, or pathologist to help the jury understand whether that level of cyanide could have caused the death. Whenever the test result is not self-explanatory, the proponent must lay a more complete foundation, including proof that:

11. The witness, perhaps witness #3, is qualified to interpret the test result.

12. The witness explains the significance of the test result.

b. DNA Testing

The situation for this second sample foundation is a criminal case in which the prosecutor seeks to rely on DNA testing of some blood samples. Samples of blood from the accused and a crime scene stain have already been marked as People's exhibits numbers 1 and 2 for identification during the testimony of an earlier witness, Patrolman Gonzalez. In this hypothetical, three witnesses are required to lay the foundation. Note also that the elements of the foundation are not necessarily developed in numerical sequence. Finally, this sample foundation does not go into detail about the chain of custody, which could be critical in a DNA case. The primary focus here is on demonstrating the scientific principles and methodologies of DNA testing.

P   Please state your full name and spell your last name for the record.

W   My name is John Gilmore. The surname is spelled G-I-L-M-O-R-E.

P   WHAT is your address?

W   I reside at 1433 Macmillan Avenue in Palo Alto, California.

P   WHAT is your occupation? (1)

W   I'm a professor at Stanford University.

P   Please describe your educational background for the ladies and gentlemen of the jury. (1)

W   Well, I received my B.S. from Washington University in St. Louis. I then obtained my master's degree from the same institution.

P   When you studied for that degree, WHAT area of study, if any, did you concentrate in? (1)

W   Molecular biology.

P   WHAT did you do after you obtained your master's degree? (1)

W   I then worked for my Ph.D. I obtained that degree in 1989 from M.I.T.

P   Again, during your study for the doctorate, did you concentrate on any particular area? (1)

W   Certainly.

P   And WHAT was that area? (1)

W   This time I narrowed my focus. I knew that DNA typing was a coming field, so I concentrated not only on molecular biology but more specifically on DNA typing. I wrote my thesis on that topic.

P   WHAT did you do after you received your Ph.D. in 1989? (1)

W   I joined the Stanford faculty. I've taught in the College of Sciences since late 1989.

P   WHAT is your current title? (1)

W   I'm an Associate Professor in the College of Sciences.

P   HOW many times, if ever, have you qualified to testify in court as an expert witness? (1)

W   Many times; I can't tell you exactly how many.

P   WHAT subjects did you testify on?

W   On each occasion, I testified as an expert on DNA.

P   Professor, earlier in your testimony, you used the expression, "DNA typing." In general terms, could you tell us WHAT that is? (2)

W   Certainly. As we all learn in high school biology, DNA is the basic building block of life. Each person's DNA accounts for his or her individuality. Everyone has a certain number of chromosomes. Each chromosome is composed of a DNA molecule. If you think back to high school, you'll remember that the molecule is usually thought of as a double helix—a sort of twisted ladder or spiral staircase.

P   WHAT is this helix or ladder made of? (2)

W   The sides of the ladder are comprised of alternating molecules of sugar and phosphate. However, in DNA typing, what you're really interested in are the rungs of the ladder.

P   WHAT are they made of? (2)

W   What we call nucleotides. There are four: adenine (A), thymine (T), cytosine (C), and guanine (G). Each rung consists of two of these. A always attaches to T. and C always attaches to G. A combination of two forms each rung. The combination is called a base pair.

P   HOW many base pairs does each individual have? (2)

W   Each person has about three billion. Most base pair sequences are common to all human beings; it's what makes us all human beings rather than horses or chimps. However, there are others that vary from person to person—approximately three million of them. They're the so-called polymorphic sites or locations. A person's DNA at any given location on the nucleotide chain wouldn't be unique to that person; but when you consider all three million variable locations, each person's overall sequence is peculiar to that individual. The odds of a random, complete match in nucleotides are astronomical; they run into the trillions. That unique nucleotide sequence is the basis of DNA typing. In a nutshell, that's the underlying theory of DNA typing. With the exception of identical twins, each person's nucleotide sequence is unique.

P   HOW can you use this theory in practice to identify people? (2)

W   There are a number of techniques that implement the theory, but by a wide margin, the one that's most widely used is RFLP—restriction fragment length polymorphism. It's a multistep procedure that enables you to identify some of the parts of the nucleotide sequence that vary from person to person.

P   Your Honor, I request that this be marked People's Exhibit #3 for identification.

(Counsel hands exhibit to court reporter, who marks it and hands it back.)

J   It will be so marked.

P   Please let the record reflect that I am showing the exhibit to the opposing counsel.

J   The record will so reflect.

P   Permission to approach the witness?

J   Granted.

P   Professor, I now hand you what has been marked People's Exhibit #3 for identification. Do you recognize it? (2)

W   Yes.

P   WHAT is it? (2)

W   It's a chart showing the various steps in RFLP. Just an oral description of the technique can be confusing if you don't visualize what's going on.

P   WHO prepared this chart? (2)

W   I did.

P   HOW accurate is the chart? (2)

W   It's a good basic depiction of all of the essential steps in RFLP.

P   Your Honor, I now offer People's Exhibit #3 for identification into evidence as People's #3.

J   Any objection?

O   No, your Honor. The jury may find this exhibit helpful.

J   Very well. It will be received.

P   Your Honor, I would like your permission to distribute a copy of exhibit #3 to each juror. They may find it helpful in following Professor Gilmore's testimony. May I see the copies? And give one to opposing counsel. (Judge and opposing counsel examine copies to ensure that they conform to exhibit.)

P Now, Professor, using exhibit #3, please lead us through this process. (2)

THE RESTRICTION FRAGMENT LENGTH POLYMORPHISM TECHNIQUE

| The DNA Double Helix within the Nucleus of a Cell | The Extraction of the Double Helix from the Nucleus | The Use of Restriction Endonucleases as Biological Scissors to Cut the Double Helix into Fragments | The Use of Electrophoresis to Separate the Fragments by Size | Denaturing the Double Helix into Single Strands | Hybridizing the Single Strands with Complementary Probes | Visualizing the Probes on an Autorad |

W OK. Start on the left-hand margin. That shows the double helix or ladder in the cell. Any cell with a nucleus will contain DNA—for example, white blood cells, sperm, saliva, and those surrounding hair roots. The first thing we've got to do is extract the DNA from the nucleus. Take a look at the second column from the left. We use chemical techniques to extract or remove the DNA.

P WHAT comes next? (2)

W As you can see from the third column from the left, we cut the two sides of the helix, to make some shorter fragments of DNA. We use restriction endonucleases to do that. They function as a sort of biological scissors. Every time they see a certain nucleotide sequence on the DNA, they snip it or cut it. At the end of this stage in the procedure, you've got a number of DNA fragments of varying length. Remember the name of the technique—restriction fragment length polymorphism. You restrict or cut the DNA into fragments. The lengths of the fragments will tend to vary from person to person—again, length of the fragment depends on where the biological scissors cut the DNA, the scissors cut when they see a particular DNA sequence, and overall, each person's nucleotide sequence will be unique. Again, that's true with the single exception of identical twins.

P WHAT is the next step? (2)

W That's electrophoresis. That's used to separate the various fragments from one another, as you can see in the column in the middle of the exhibit. DNA fragments are negatively charged. They're placed in gel. You subject the gel to, say, thirty-two volts of electricity for several hours. Opposites attract; once in the gel, the fragments move toward the positive end. The longer fragments move more slowly than the shorter fragments. So, at the end of this stage, the fragments are arrayed by length from longest to shortest.

P   WHAT do you with this array? (2)

W   To make the array stable enough to work with, you transfer it onto a nylon membrane. It's a technique known as Southern transfer. We don't need to get into that detail now. But at roughly the same time you heat the DNA or treat with a chemical to "denature it." Look at the next column on the chart. As I said before, in the third step, we cut across the two sides of the helix to make the shorter fragments of DNA. Now in the fourth step, we take each fragment of DNA and cut down the middle of its rungs. When you do that, you break each fragment into two single strands. If the rung was A-T, one strand has the A, and the other strand has the T. In nature, DNA is a double helix composed of two strands; now we've denatured it into two single strands.

P   WHAT do you do with the single strands? (2)

W   Now we're ready for hybridization. That means uniting or merging the strands with complementary probes. Look at the next to last column on the exhibit. As I said earlier, A always unites with T. and C must unite with G. If we send in a probe with A and C, and if it unites with the fragment, we know that the fragment has to be T and G. That's why they're called "complementary" probes. The probes are tagged with radioactive material such as phosphorous 32; when they're labeled with this radioactive material, they give off beta radiation.

P   WHY is the radiation important? (2)

W   That's going to enable us to visualize—to see—the fragments. We expose the DNA array to X-ray film in the last step of the procedure. Look at the right hand margin of the exhibit. This step is called autoradiography. The radioactivity produces bands or lines on the film or autorad. You can therefore see where the fragments are. Now you have a visual display of the fragments, again arrayed in order of size, the array for each person tending to be unique because the each person's nucleotide sequence is different.

P   WHY is this procedure called "DNA typing"? (2)

W   The analogy is to fingerprinting. Suppose you have a blood sample found at a crime scene and a sample taken from the accused who's suspected of committing the crime. You'd apply the procedure to both samples to see if the samples matched. You can either visually compare the band patterns on the two autorads or, better still, have a computer make the comparison. In an RFLP test, if they match, you know that at least at the sites tested, the persons have the same nucleotide sequence.

P   WHAT, if anything, have you written about the procedure for conducting an RFLP test? (1)

W   I published an article on the subject in the 1992 issue of BioTechniques magazine. It was co-co-authored with Dr. Munson.

P   Who is Dr. Munson?

W   He's the Ph.D. who heads the DNA testing section of Cellmatch Laboratories in Santa Monica.

P   Your Honor, I request that this be marked People's Exhibit #4 for identification. (Counsel hands to court reporter who marks it as People's exhibit four for identification and hands it back to counsel.)

J   Yes.

P   May the record reflect that I am showing the exhibit to opposing counsel?

J It will so reflect.

P Permission to approach the witness?

J Yes.

P Professor, I hand you what has been marked as People's Exhibit #4 for identification. Can you recognize it?

W I most certainly can.

P WHAT is it? (1)

W It's my article.

P HOW do you recognize it?

W I ought to know the contents, since I cowrote it!

P Your Honor, I offer now the exhibit as People's #4.

J Any objection?

O None, your Honor.

J All right. It will be received, then.

P Professor, HOW well-accepted is the theory underlying DNA typing? (3)

W Universally by anyone who knows anything about molecular biology.

P And HOW well-accepted is the restriction fragment length polymorphism technique? (3)

W Again, almost universally. It's not only employed in universities and colleges; it's also used by hospitals for genetic testing and by crime laboratories throughout the world.

The proponent's second witness establishes the test results in the specific case.

P Please state your full name and spell your last name for the record.

W My name is Ralph Harrison. Harrison is spelled H-A-R-R-I-S-O-N.

P Where do you live, Mr. Harrison?

W I live in Venice, California.

P WHAT is your line of work? (6)

W I'm a DNA genetic marker technician at Cellmatch Company in Santa Monica, California.

P WHAT is your educational background? (6)

W I have a B.S. degree from the University of San Diego.

P WHEN did you receive your degree? (6)

W 1987.

P WHAT did you do after receiving your degree? (6)

W I went right to work for Cellmatch. Initially, I did bloodstain tests and electrophoretic analysis of enzymes and proteins. However, in 1991, when we established our DNA unit, I helped establish the unit with Dr. Andy Munson.

P WHAT special training, if any, did you receive when you joined the unit? (6)

W Dr. Munson conducted an intensive, three-week training program in conjunction with his good friend, Professor John Gilmore. Dr. Gilmore flew down from Stanford and spent two weeks with us going over every step of RFLP testing in great detail.

P I hand you what has already been admitted as People's Exhibit #4. Can you recognize it?

W You bet I do.

P WHAT is it? (9)

W It's the 1992 article about RFLP procedures that Professor Gilmore and Dr. Munson wrote.

P HOW do you recognize it? (9)

W Professor Gilmore distributed it on the first day of class, and we used it throughout his instruction. I know every period and footnote in that article backwards and forwards by now.

P HOW, if at all, do you use the article in your work? (9)

W I use it almost every day. The article has an appendix which is a model protocol or test procedure for conducting RFLP tests. I use that protocol every time I conduct an RFLP test at Cellmatch.

P Now let's shift topics. WHERE were you on the afternoon of June 28 of this year?

W I was at work at Cellmatch.

P WHAT, if anything, happened that afternoon?

W Patrolman Gonzalez from the LAPD stopped by. He delivered two blood samples and asked me to conduct a DNA test.

P I now hand what have previously been marked as People' Exhibits #1 and 2 for identification.

W All right.

P Do you know WHAT these are?

W Yes.

P Could you please tell the jury what they are?

W They're the two samples which Patrolman Gonzalez gave me.

P HOW do you recognize them?

W I know his initials and my initials on the plastic container.

P WHAT did you do with the samples after Patrolman Gonzalez gave them to you? (9)

W I immediately tested them.

P Between the time you received the samples from Patrolman Gonzalez and the time you tested the samples, WHO else handled the samples?

W No one else. I was the only one.

P During that same time, WHEN, if at all, were the samples out of your sight?

W They never were. It had been a quiet day, and I was able to get right to the test. When Gonzalez arrived, I met him at the receptionist's desk; and I went straight from there to my bench in the DNA unit. I conducted the test without almost any delay.

P Your Honor, I now offer People's Exhibits #1 and 2 for identification into evidence.

J Any objection?

O None, your Honor.

J All right. People's Exhibits # 1 and 2 are admitted into evidence.

P Thank you, your Honor. Mr. Harrison, WHAT equipment did you use in the test of these samples? (7), (8)

W There's a variety of stuff. You need some chemicals, the electrophoretic apparatus, the probes, and the autoradiographic equipment.

P WHAT condition were they in when you used them to test Exhibits #1 and 2? (7)

W They all were in good condition.

P HOW do you know that? (7)

W The chemicals and probes were fresh.

P WHAT do you mean by "fresh"? (7)

W   We get a fresh shipment from the manufacturer on Monday morning. I conducted this test on a Monday afternoon. They certainly had not lost any of their potency by then.

P   WHAT about the other apparatus and equipment? (7)

W   We have them serviced every Friday evening after work. Again, I conducted this test on a Monday afternoon. The equipment would have been checked shortly before that, and I know that I didn't encounter any problems in running the tests.

P   HOW did you conduct the test? (9)

W   I did it "by the book"—or I should say "by the article." As I always do, I followed the appendix to the Biotechniques article step by step to ensure that I used the proper protocol.

P   Mr. Harrison, HOW well do you remember the specific occasion when you tested these two samples? (9)

W   I guess I generally do, but I have to admit that I've tested hundreds of these samples and the tests tend to run together in my mind.

P   Your Honor, I request that this be marked People's Exhibit #6 for identification. (Counsel hands exhibit to court reporter, who marks it as People's Exhibit #6 for identification, and returns it to counsel.)

J   All right.

P   May the record please reflect that I am showing the exhibit to opposing counsel. (Counsel shows exhibit to opposing counsel, who briefly examines it.)

J   Yes. Proceed.

P   Permission to approach the witness.

J   Granted.

P   Mr. Harrison, I now show you People's Exhibit #6 for identification. WHAT is it? (9)

W   It's the checklist I used when I ran this test.

P   WHY do you use a checklist? (9)

W   For a couple of reasons. To begin with, I run so many tests that months or years later, I may forget some of the details of the test. This is a record of what I did. Next, I want to be sure that I dot every i and cross every t. Using the checklist is a method of ensuring that I do that.

P   Your Honor, I now offer People's Exhibit #6 for identification into evidence as People's #6.

J   Any objection, counsel?

O   None, your Honor.

J   Then People's Exhibit #6 for identification is received into evidence.

P   WHAT was the result of the test? (10)

W   The test produced two autorads—visual displays of the arrays of DNA fragments in the two samples.

P   Your Honor, I ask that these be marked People's Exhibits #7 and 8 for identification. (Counsel hands exhibits to court reporter, who marks and returns them to counsel.)

J   They have been so marked.

P   Please let the record reflect that I am showing the two exhibits to the defense counsel. (Counsel shows exhibits to opposing counsel.)

J   The record will so reflect.

P   Permission to approach?

J   Go ahead, counsel.

P   Mr. Harrison, I now hand you what have been marked as People's Exhibits #7 and 8 for identification. Do you recognize them?

W   Yes.

P   WHAT are they? (10)

W   They're the autorads produced by the RFLP test of Exhibits #1 and 2. Exhibit #7 is the autorad produced by Exhibit #1, and #8 is the result of the test of Exhibit #2.

P   HOW do you recognize them? (10)

W   I made these notations in the right hand corner of the film.

P   Your Honor, I now offer People's Exhibits #7 and 8 for identification into evidence as Exhibits #7 and 8.

J   Is there any objection?

O   No.

J   Then they will be admitted.

P   Now, Mr. Harrison, WHAT did you do with these two autorads after you developed the film? (10)

W   I compared them.

P   WHAT was the purpose of the comparison? (10)

W   I wanted to see if they matched.

P   WHAT do you mean when you say "match"? (10)

W   If they match, you should have fragments of the same size in the same position on both autorads. In this case, they matched.

P   HOW do you know? (10)

W   I analyzed them both with the naked eye and with an optical microscope. Fragments of identical length were in identical positions on the two autorads. I therefore declared a match.

P   WHAT did you do after declaring a match? (10)

W   I called in Dr. Munson. He's in charge of the next step in the DNA unit, that is, calculating the probability of a random match.

The proponent completes the DNA foundation with a third witness, Dr. Munson. Dr. Munson computes the probability of a random match in DNA markers in the traditional method used by forensic laboratories. He consults database, searches the population frequencies for the defendant's ethnic group, finds the frequency for each DNA marker on the defendant's autorad, and then multiplies the frequencies. In 1991, in *People v. Axell*, 235 Cal. App. 3d 836, 1 Cal. Rptr. 2d 411 (1991), the court approved the admission of testimony about a probability computed in this manner. However, in 1992, the National Research Council (NRC) of the National Academy of Science released a report entitled DNA TECHNOLOGY IN FORENSIC SCIENCE. That report criticized the traditional method of computing the probability. The report pointed out that under the traditional method, databases are divided into three large ethnic groups: Caucasian, Hispanic, and Afro-American. The report noted that there were indications that the population frequencies for the broad categories do not hold true for some subpopulations. For example, the frequencies for Hispanics of Cuban ancestry in Miami might differ from those for Hispanics of Mexican ancestry in Los Angeles. For that reason, the N.R.C. recommended the so-called modified ceiling method of making the computation. Rather than using the frequency for the defendant's ethnic group, the expert: selects the highest frequency for that DNA marker in any ethnic group, raises that number to its 95 percent upper confidence limit, and uses the larger of that number or 10 percent. 2 P. GIANNELLI & E. IMWINKELRIED, SCIENTIFIC EVIDENCE § 18-4(C) (3d ed. 1999). Since the release of that report, several cases have ruled that testimony based on the traditional method is inadmissible; the report created a controversy, precluding a finding of general acceptance required by the *Frye* rule. *People v. Wallace*, 14 Cal. App. 4th 651, 17 Cal. Rptr. 721 (1993); *People v. Barney*, 8 Cal. App. 4th 798, 10 Cal. Rptr. 2d 731 (1992). In several other *Frye* jurisdictions, courts ruled that testimony based on the traditional method of computing the probability is inadmissible. GIANNELLI & IM-WINKELRIED, *supra*, at § 18-5(C).

Although after the 1992 NRC report, *Frye* jurisdictions such as California began to exclude random match probabilities computed in the traditional fashion, the argument was then made that random match probabilities computed under the modified ceiling principle should be admitted. The argument was that such computations are appropriately conservative. A trend developed to accept random match probabilities computed in that manner. In *People v. Venegas*, 18 Cal. 4th 47 at 84-85, 954 P.2d 525, 74 Cal. Rptr. 2d 262 (1998), the Supreme Court held that the NRC's modified ceiling method has gained scientific consensus as being forensically reliable.

In 1996, the NRC released a second report entitled THE EVALUATION OF FORENSIC DNA EVIDENCE. That report pointed out that since the early 1990s there has been extensive research into the population frequencies of DNA markers among subpopulations. The report stated that the more recent scientific research had demonstrated that for the most part, the population frequencies for the large ethnic groups hold true even for subpopulations. The 1996 report added that the fears that led the 1992 report to recommend the modified ceiling principle had proven to be overstated. The 1996 report concluded that it is scientifically valid to compute random match probabilities in the traditional fashion. In light of that report, a new trend has emerged; even in *Frye* jurisdictions such as California, the courts are now accepting probabilities calculated in that manner. GIANNELLI & IMWINKELRIED, *supra*, at § 18-5(C). The California Supreme Court has yet to revisit the issue; but if and when it does, it is highly probable that the court will follow this trend.

An alternative technique for DNA testing that has also acquired general acceptance in the scientific community is polymerase chain reaction matching (PCR). *People v. Wright*, 62 Cal. App. 4th 31, 72 Cal. Rptr. 2d 246 (1998); *People v. Morganti*, 43 Cal. App. 4th 643 at 671, 50 Cal. Rptr. 2d 837 (1996). With PCR matching, a technician compares the genetic structure of a sample and a suspect by amplifying the DNA and checking for the existence or nonexistence of certain specific genetic markers in the two DNA sources. *Wright* at 40 n.1. This method is commonly used when only a small or degraded sample is available. *Morganti* at 662.

A 1999 case approves of the admissibility of testimony about a new generation of DNA tests, short tandem repeat (STR) technology. *People v. Allen*, 72 Cal. App. 4th 1093, 85 Cal. Rptr. 2d 655 (1999). In a STR test, the analyst initially uses PCR to amplify the sample. However, in another respect STR tests resemble RFLP tests; as in RFLP testing, in order to identify the source of the sample the analyst measures fragment length. STR testing is much faster than the RFLP procedure; while an RFLP analysis might take three weeks, a STR analysis can be completed in three days. For the next five to ten years, STR is likely to be the dominant DNA technology. The Convicted Offender DNA database (CODIS), maintained by the federal government, includes the information about each subject's DNA marker at 13 STR loci.

P   Please state your full name and spell your last name for the record.
W   I'm Andrew J. Munson. You spell Munson M-U-N-S-O-N.
P   WHERE you do you live?
W   In Santa Monica.
P   WHERE do you work?
W   I work at the Santa Monica laboratory of Cellmatch, Inc. I am the director of the DNA typing unit of the laboratory.
P   Please tell us your educational background. (11)
W   I attended undergraduate school at the University of California, Davis. I received a basic B.S. degree from U.C.D. Then I obtained my master's degree at Washington University in St. Louis. That's where I met a prior witness, Professor Gilmore. Finally, I obtained a doctorate.
P   WHERE did you obtain that degree? (11)
W   At Yale.
P   WHAT area, if any, did you specialize in during your doctoral program? (11)
W   Population genetics.
P   Could you please tell us WHAT that specialty involves? (11)
W   In part, it involves the application of the laws of statistics to genetics problems.
P   Please give us an example of such a problem. (11), (12)
W   For instance, as in a case like this one, you might be interested in trying to figure out what percentage of the population has a certain DNA marker or a particular set of DNA markers. Population genetics experts attempt to answer that type of problem.
P   Doctor, I hand you what has been admitted as People's Exhibit #7. Do you recognize it?
W   Yes.
P   WHAT is it?
W   It's an autorad that Mr. Harrison gave me to evaluate a few months ago.
P   HOW do you recognize it?
W   I recall the initials and date on this corner of the film.
P   WHAT did you do with this autorad after Mr. Harrison gave it to you? (12)
W   I determined the percentage of the Caucasian population that would have the set of DNA markers depicted on this autorad.
P   WHY did you attempt to determine that percentage in the Caucasian population rather than say, for example, the Hispanic population? (12)

W   I was told by Mr. Harrison that both the perpetrator and the suspect were identified as Caucasian.

O   Objection, your Honor, that amounts to hearsay.

P   Your Honor, we are not offering the statement for the truth of the matter. Instead, we are offering it for the nonhearsay purpose of showing why this witness conducted the study. This is an example of mental input nonhearsay—it was information which the witness acted upon.

J   Objection overruled.

P   WHAT technique did you use to determine the percentage? (2), (12)

W   I used the multiplication or product rule.

P   WHAT is that? (2), (12)

W   Let me give you a simple example. Let's suppose that you want to know what percentage of the Caucasian population has blonde hair and a limp. You check the population frequencies, and you learn the following: Ten percent of the Caucasian population has blonde hair, and one percent has a limp. You multiply the two numbers, ten percent by one percent. The multiplication yields the figure one tenth of one percent. That is the percentage of the Caucasian population that has both characteristics. That's the formula I used in this case.

P   WHY did you use it? (2), (12)

W   You use it when you're analyzing several "independent" factors.

P   WHAT is an "independent" factor? (2), (12)

W   When factors are independent, they don't affect one another. In my example, a person with a limp might have blonde hair, black hair, brown hair, or no hair; the color of the hair doesn't have any effect on the probability that they limp. In contrast, suppose you wanted to know how many Caucasian men not only have a moustache but also have a beard. Those obviously aren't independent factors, and you consequently couldn't use the multiplication or product rule to determine the percentage.

P   Is this multiplication or product rule something you cooked up yourself? (3)

W   Oh, certainly not. It's a standard statistical tool, and it is routinely used in my field, population genetics. It is generally recognized as valid, so long as the population data are sound and so long as the various factors are independent of one another.

P   WHY did you apply the multiplication rule in this case to the various DNA markers shown on the autorad? (2), (12)

W   I was confident that each band, representing a different DNA marker, was independent of the other bands.

P   WHY were you confident of that? (2), (12)

W   Because we use single-locus probes targeting sites on different chromosomes. In early RFLP analysis, they often used multilocus probes. When you do that, the probe hits several locations or sites on the same chromosome. If the sites are close together, they might not be independent; your DNA marker at one location might in fact affect the likelihood you have a particular DNA marker at the nearby site. However, it's generally accepted in biology that when you target sites on separate chromosomes, you have adequate assurance that the bands are independent. We did that in this case.

P   When you use this multiplication rule, exactly WHAT is it that you multiply? (2), (12)

W   You identify each DNA marker, and you insert into the formula the population frequency for that marker for that ethnic group.

P   WHERE did you get the numbers you used in this case? (2), (12)

W   We have an agreement with Lifecodes, one of the largest DNA laboratories in the world. By virtue of their agreement, we can use the population frequencies in their database. They've built up the database over the years, and it now includes the results of thousands of DNA tests of persons of virtually every conceivable ethnic group.

P   HOW many bands or DNA markers did you identify on this autorad, People's Exhibit #7? (12)

W   I could definitely identify four.

P   WHAT did you do once you identified them? (12)

W   I looked up the pertinent frequencies in the Lifecodes database and then inserted those frequencies as four variables in the multiplication rule.

P   When you multiplied those four numbers, WHAT was the result? (12)

W   The multiplication indicated that only one thousandth of one percent of the Caucasian population would possess this set of DNA markers.

O.   COMPUTER ANIMATIONS AND SIMULATIONS

1. THE DOCTRINE

In Section M.2., above, we discussed the use of motion pictures, and in Section N, above, we discussed the use of scientific evidence. We now consider the use of computer animations and simulations, which draw on both of the earlier discussions.

Rather than offering motion pictures or videotapes of historical events, attorneys frequently offer computer animations of the events. Henke, *Admissibility of Computer-Generated Animated Reconstructions and Simulations*, 35 TRIAL LAW. GUIDE 434 (1991); *see also* Tynan, *Evidence in Motion*, CAL. LAW. October 1993, p. 85. A computer animation is the display of a sequence of computer-generated images. The use of computer-generated animation (CGA) is becoming widespread. In a 1992 study, the American Bar Association reported that attorneys at 13 percent of medium-sized litigation firms have already used computer animation. Even more significantly, attorneys at 45 percent of the firms indicated that they intend to use computer animation in the near future. Some law firms now have entire departments devoted to the preparation of trial exhibits, including computer animations.

There are several reasons for the growing use of computer animations. To begin with, when there is no movie or video of the event being litigated, a computer animation is a powerful way to communicate the relevant information to the trier of fact. Absent a movie or video, the proponent might have to rely on static charts or oral testimony to convey a large amount of complex information to the trier of fact. When the proponent relies solely on oral expert testimony, the details may be presented one at a time, but an animation can piece all the details together for the jury. A computer animation in effect condenses the information into a single evidentiary package. Partly due to television, the typical American is a primarily visual learner, and thus, in the short term, many jurors find the animation more understandable than charts or oral testimony. Use of an animation can significantly increase long-term juror retention of the information. Note, *Lights, Camera, Action: Computer-Animated Evidence Gets Its Day in Court*, 34 B.C. L. REV. 1087, 1101 (1993). Furthermore, computer animation technology is becoming more affordable. Krieger, *Sophisticated Computer Graphics Come of Age—And Evidence Will Never Be the Same*, 78 A.B.A.J. 92 (Dec. 1992). In the early days of computer technology, the price of a high-quality animated exhibit might have been as much as $500,000. However, there are now many commercially CAD/CAM (computer assisted design and manufacturing) programs such as Applecrash, Mannequin, and 3D Studio. Some programs even allow the computer operator to scan or digitize external images from artwork or photographs into the computer's memory. Today, the total cost of the hardware and software necessary to generate computer animations can be less than $10,000, and that figure is likely to decrease in the future.

In part, computer animations are becoming popular because the medium is so flexible. The animation can adopt almost any conceivable vantage point or angle. For instance, the animation can depict the perspective of the person behind the wheel of a car or portray an aerial overview of two cars approaching each other. The animation can pan or zoom in. The animation can even display an impossible perspective, that is, the inner working of a piece of machinery. The split screen capability permits the simultaneous display of several perspectives; one perspective can be that of the airplane pilot, and the other that of a ground observer watching the airplane descend for landing. The technology is also flexible in a temporal sense; the animation can be real time, time lapse (accelerated), slow motion (decelerated), or freeze frame. Finally, the animation can be combined with other media. The trial exhibit can begin with a photograph of the actual object involved in the case and then fade or dissolve into a photorealistic-animation. Given this flexibility, animations have already been employed in court to depict a wide range of events, including plane crashes, highway accidents, murders, gas well explosions, product failures, the movement of contaminating particles in the soil, and the progress of diseases.

2. ELEMENTS OF THE FOUNDATION

The foundation depends upon the purposes for which the proponent proffers the animation. The animation can be offered either as illustrative demonstrative evidence or as a substantive computer simulation.

a. Illustrative Evidence

Assume that a lay or expert witness is prepared to describe an event and that the witness did not initially obtain his or her information about the event by viewing any computer animation. A lay witness might simply have seen the accident. Or a scientist might have derived an opinion about the event by merely sitting down, reading the police report of the accident, and applying the laws of physics to the data in the report. Assume further, that after hearing the witness' description of the event before trial, the attorney has a computer animation prepared to depict that description. In that event, the attorney could offer the animation as purely demonstrative evidence to illustrate the witness' description.

When that is the proponent's theory of admissibility, the foundation is minimal. Comment, *Admission of Computer Generated Visual Evidence: Should There Be Clear Standards?*, 6 SOFTWARE L.J. 325, 333-34 (1993). It suffices if the witness testifies that he or she has viewed the animation and that the animation fairly and accurately depicts the witness' version of the event. *People v. Mitchell*, No. 12462 (Cal. Martin County Super Ct. Feb. 19, 1992), is illustrative. Dilworth, *Computer Animations Reach Criminal Court*, 28 TRIAL 26 (Sept. 1992). In that case, the prosecution introduced an animation of a shooting. Crime scene reconstruction expert Lucien Haag testified that the animation accurately illustrated his testimony. In the words of one court,

> The evidence sought to be introduced here is more akin to a chart or diagram than a scientific device. Whether a diagram is hand drawn or mechanically drawn by means of a computer is of no importance. What is important is [that] the presentation ... fairly and accurately reflect the oral testimony offered and that it be an aid to the jury's understanding of the issue.

People v. McHugh, 124 Misc. 2d 559, 476 N.Y.S.2d 721 (1984). As a practical matter, it may be safer to call the animator as well as the lay or expert witness to overcome any objections under California Evidence Code § 352, but if the proponent offers the animation strictly as illustrative evidence, the lay or expert witness can give sufficient sponsoring testimony to authenticate the animation. For instance, after establishing her firsthand knowledge of an event, the witness could testify that she has viewed the animation in question and that the animation accurately depicts the event she observed. That testimony should satisfy California Evidence Code § 403 when the proponent is content to introduce the animation as demonstrative evidence to illustrate testimony by a lay or expert witness.

There are, of course, procedural downsides to proffering the animation purely as an illustrative, demonstrative exhibit. Under California Evidence Code § 355, on the opponent's request, the trial judge will have to give the jury a limiting instruction as to the evidentiary status of the animation. Moreover, in California and many other jurisdictions, illustrative exhibits do not accompany the jury into the deliberation room. *See* Disco, *Jury Deliberations and Verdict*, in CAL. CRIM. L. § 33.8 at 827 (1994); *see also United States v. Wood*, 91-2 USTC 89,574 (9th Cir. 1991); ME. R. EVID. 616; Brain & Broderick, *The Derivative Relevance of Demonstrative Evidence: Charting Its Proper Evidentiary Status*, 25 U.C. DAVIS L. REV. 957, 965-66 (1992); Henke, *supra*, at 444. However, offering the animation for such a limited purpose obviates the need for testimony validating the scientific assumptions programmed into the software that generates the animation.

b. Substantive Evidence

In other cases, though, the proponent will want to offer the animation as substantive evidence. In these cases, it is often said that the proponent is proffering a computer "simulation." Note, *Lights, Camera, Action: Computer Animated Evidence Gets Its Day in Court*, 34 B.C. L. REV. 1087 n.3 (1993). Computer simulation software:

- includes scientific equations and principles such as the laws of Newtonian physics that predict the behavior of, for example, automobiles;
- accepts input of the data such as skidmark length required to apply the scientific principles and equations;
- converts mathematic predictions into still images; and
- subsequently records those images onto a videotape, which can be played back on the computer's screen. *Id.* at 1090 n.33.

When the proponent offers an animation as an accurate computer simulation, the inference of accuracy does not arise from the simulation's correspondence with a description of the same event by any lay or expert witness. Rather, the bases of the inference are the validity of the pertinent scientific principles and the trustworthiness of the input data. Consequently, the foundation for a simulation differs from that for a merely demonstrative, illustrative exhibit; the simulation foundation must include a showing of the principle's validity and the data's trustworthiness. *Commercial Union Insurance Co. v. Boston Edison Co.*, 412 Mass. 545, 591 N.E.2d 165 (1992). If the proponent can lay the necessary foundation, there will be no need for a limiting instruction under California Evidence Code § 355. The judge might decide to read the jury a cautionary instruction against giving the simulation undue weight (*Datskow v. Teledyne Continental Motors*, 826 F. Supp. 677, 685 (W.D.N.Y. 1993)), but it would be inappropriate to deny the simulation the status of substantive evidence. As substantive evidence, the simulation could be taken into the jury room and viewed during deliberation. Henke, *supra*, at 437.

Unfortunately, the published cases offer little specific guidance as to the foundational requirements for computer simulations. Comment, *Admission of Computer Generated Visual Evidence: Should There Be Clear Standards?*, *supra*, at 327. However, in principle, the following foundation should suffice:

1. There are certain valid scientific equations and principles such as the Newtonian laws of motion. At least for the moment in California, these equations and principles will have to pass muster under the *Kelly-Frye* general acceptance test. *See* Section N, above. If the principle or equation in ques-

tion is widely accepted, it may be judicially noticeable, and live testimony on this foundational element would therefore be unnecessary.

2. Computer technology is capable of producing simulations or models based on scientific equations and principles. In some jurisdictions, this proposition is judicially noticeable. *Starr v. Campos*, 134 Ariz. 254, 655 P.2d 794, 797 (1982); Comment, *Admission of Computer Generated Visual Evidence: Should There Be Clear Standards?*, *supra*, at 339.

3. The equations and principles mentioned in foundational element #1 have been programmed into a particular computer program.

4. To generate a mathematical representation, the equations and principles require certain input. The program may require numerical data about measurements of dimensions of objects, human beings, and the environment in which the objects and human beings are moving or acting. For example, to produce a virtual reality (VR) simulation of a room, "everything in the room is measured, and each object's position relative to all other objects—including the VR user—is calculated." Dilworth, *Virtual Reality: Coming Soon to a Courtroom Near You?*, 29 TRIAL 13, 14 (July 1993).

5. The software in question is capable of converting its mathematical predictions of behavior into accurate images. Some programs produce a picture—an individual computer graphic—every thirtieth of a second. When the software is in widespread, commercial use, the judge may treat its widespread acceptance as circumstantial evidence of its accuracy. If a defective program were used widely, presumably the defect would have caused problems for its users, and the program would have been corrected or withdrawn. When the software has not yet come into widespread use, the proponent should present expert testimony vouching for the program's accuracy. For instance, one of the computer experts who helped develop an accident reconstruction program could testify that she had verified the program's accuracy by comparing its output with data from test crashes of automobiles.

6. Someone input all the data needed to use the principles or equations programmed into the software. *Schaeffer v. General Motors Corp.*, 372 Mass. 171, 360 N.E.2d 1062 (Mass. 1977) (the data must be complete).

7. The data input was trustworthy. *Id.* This foundational element reflects "the GIGO principle: garbage in, garbage out." Comment, *Admission of Computer Generated Visual Evidence: Should There Be Clear Standards?*, *supra*, at 346 n.144.

8. The computer operator checked to ensure that the data was properly input. The operator could simply call the data up on the screen and double-check the accuracy of the input data against the police reports that were the source of the data.

9. After inputting the data, the operator asked the computer to generate a simulation or model of the relevant behavior.

10. The computer recorded the images of the simulation on videotape or laser disc. Videotape is more popular. Krieger, *Photorealitic Computer Graph-*

ics: New Horizon for Evidence, 29 TRIAL 46, 48 (Feb. 1993). However, many practitioners prefer laser disc:

> [T]he far better quality is ... laser disc format[].... You get much better definition ... than videotape, plus you have much more flexibility because you can use bar codes to jump to any sequence in the animation.

King, *Animation Seizes Jury, Judge's Attention*, MERRILL'S ILLINOIS LEGAL TIMES 1, 10 (May 1993).

11. The witness on the stand recognizes the videotape or laser disc as the output produced when the operator asked the computer to generate a simulation of the relevant behavior.

In some cases, a single witness is qualified to lay the entire foundation. However, in a given case, multiple witnesses may be necessary: one to validate the pertinent scientific principles and equations, another to verify the part of the program that generates the mathematical representation of behavior, still another to vouch for part of the program that converts the mathematical prediction into visual images, a further witness to describe the collection of the input data, and a final witness to testify to the inputting of the data and the production of the videotape or laser disc.

3. SAMPLE FOUNDATION[19]

The fact situation is a civil tort action. The plaintiffs allege that the defendant negligently lost control of her auto and allowed the auto to drift into a bike lane, where the auto struck and killed the plaintiffs' daughter. The proponent is the defense. The defense calls Professor Thaddeus Grutz as its next witness. Professor Grutz will lay the foundation for a computer animation tending to show that the accident occurred in a manner relieving the defendant from fault.

P   Please state your full name and spell your last name for the record.
W   My name is Thaddeus Grutz. That's G-R-U-T-Z.
P   WHERE do you live?
W   I live and work in Dorrington, California.
P   WHAT is your place of work?
W   I teach in the Engineering Department of California State University, Dorrington.
P   WHAT is your educational background?
W   I obtained my bachelor of science degree in engineering from Iowa State University in 1980.
P   In general terms, WHAT is engineering?

---

[19]The authors wish to express their gratitude to Professor John Kwasnoski of Western New England Technical Consultants, Ludlow, Massachusetts, who reviewed this foundation for technical accuracy.

W Engineers are specialists in using the laws of physics to create machines for human use.

P WHAT did you do after you obtained your bachelor's degree?

W We moved to Ann Arbor, Michigan, so that I could begin my graduate studies at the University of Michigan. I wanted to get my master's degree and then a doctorate. I got the master's in 1982 and the doctorate in 1984.

P WHAT subjects did you study in the course of obtaining those degrees?

W I pretty much specialized in vehicle dynamics.

P WHAT do you mean by the expression, "vehicle dynamics"?

W That's the study of how cars, trucks, and the like, behave as they move and travel down a highway.

P WHAT do you mean by "computer graphics"?

W That's the use of computer programs to create sequences of images that depict the movement of vehicles on a road or highway.

P WHAT licenses, if any, do you hold in California?

W I'm registered as an engineer.

P HOW many professional papers, if any, have you had published?

W Approximately twenty.

P WHAT topics did those papers relate to?

W They all deal with vehicle dynamics, and the vast majority of them relate more specifically to computer animation of vehicle dynamics.

P WHAT professional engineering organizations, if any, do you belong to?

W For years I've been a member of the Society of Automotive Engineers and the American Society of Mechanical Engineers. I've served as the president of the state chapter of the Society of Automotive Engineers.

P WHAT practical experience, if any, do you have in vehicle dynamics?

W I've consulted with major manufacturers such as General Motors and Chrysler on a number of design projects. My contribution was determining how a design change would affect the dynamics of the vehicles in question.

P HOW many times, if ever, have you qualified as an expert witness in a court of law?

W On over forty occasions.

P WHAT topics did you testify about as an expert witness?

W On each occasion, the testimony related to some aspects of vehicle dynamics.

P HOW many times, if ever, did you testify about computer animation of vehicle dynamics?

W The majority of the time.

P WHAT do these computer animations do? (1)

W The ones that I prepare do more than simply illustrate a version of an accident. The ones I develop are intended to use the laws of physics to accurately recreate and portray accidents.

P WHAT laws of physics are you referring to? (1)

W To begin with, you have Newton's laws of motions. Those are fundamental tenets of modern physics. In addition, there are other rules of auto dynamics physics which have been empirically derived.

P WHAT do you mean by "empirically derived"? (1)

W People have conducted experiments to establish that these other propositions are true. You run tests with autos, trucks, and bicycles to prove that the proposition is valid.

P HOW well accepted are these propositions? (1)

W They're universally accepted by engineers in my specialty.

P HOW thoroughly have these propositions been established by the experiments you referred to? (1)

W There are some that are still in the debatable stage, but the ones I use in my computer programs have been proven beyond any doubt.

P HOW can a computer apply these propositions? (2)

W You simply program the principle or equation into the software. The software contains the instructions for the computer, and you include the various principles and equations as part of the instructions. Using these principles and equations, the computer can create a mathematical representation of an auto such as a truck. The simulation program utilizes an "icon" of the vehicle, and the computer simulates the motion of the icon.

P WHAT experience, if any, do you have programming these principles and equations into computer software? (2)

W In large part, that's what I did during my master's and doctoral work at Michigan. I know programming language, and I've developed tens of programs based on the principles of auto dynamics.

P WHAT is "Autodynam"? (3)

W That's the name of a program that I've developed for computer simulations of auto dynamics.

P WHAT laws and equations is that program based on? (3)

W It's one of my most conservative programs.

P WHAT do you mean by "conservative"? (3)

W As I said a little while ago, some propositions about vehicle dynamics are still debatable; the research into the validity of those propositions is still incomplete and inconclusive. None of those propositions is included in Autodynam. It's a conservative program in the sense that it rests on the original laws of motion, propositions deduced directly from those laws, and further propositions that have clearly been established by ample research.

P HOW accurately does Autodynam program state those propositions? (3)

W Not just accurately, but perfectly.

P HOW do you know that? (3)

W To begin with, I have access to a number of databases on actual and test auto crashes. I've checked the results of the program against the databases, and on each occasion the result of using the program has checked out and been confirmed. More importantly, I periodically print out the program itself and review the portion of the program setting out the propositions. I can read programming language; and as a scientist, I also know the propositions. I can personally vouch that the program is 100 percent accurate in that regard. If you input the right information about an accident, you're going to get an accurate reconstruction of the event.

P WHAT do you mean by "input"? (4)

W The laws and equations are general propositions about vehicle dynamics. If you're going to make some findings about a specific accident, you need some of the data about that accident—where the vehicles came to rest, the extent of the damage to the vehicles, the length and direction of skidmarks, the drag factor of the road surface, that sort of thing.

P Suppose that you wanted to use Autodynam to create a computer animation of an accident involving a truck and a bicycle and you wanted to use Autodynam to determine how fast the truck was going. WHAT input would you have to give the computer to determine that? (4)

W I'd need to tell the computer the final resting place of the truck, bicycle, and rider, the extent and nature of any personal injuries suffered by the bicyclist, the extent and location of the damage to the truck and bicycle, the road drag factor, the point where the rider's body first struck the ground, the relative angle of the bicycle and truck at impact, and the length and direction of any skidmarks. Given that information, the computer can create a valid, mathematical representation of the dynamics of the two vehicles.

P All right. You have this mathematical representation in the computer. HOW does the computer convert that into an image on the screen? (5)

W The program also does that. The program creates a sequence of images on the screen. It creates a new picture every thirtieth of a second. Autodynam is a sophisticated program, and its images are photorealistic—they look awfully close to the real thing.

P HOW accurate are these images? (5)

W They're quite accurate.

P HOW do you know that? (5)

W I previously mentioned test crashes. We have a lot of test crashes on videotape. I've often used Autodynam to generate a computer animation and then compared it to a videotape of the same accident. The computer simulation produces amazingly accurate images of the crash.

P Professor, WHERE were you on January 19 of this year? (6)

W I was at my office at the university in Ann Arbor.

P WHAT happened that day? (6)

W That's the day I received the Federal Express package with Xerox copies of all the police reports and depositions in this case.

P WHAT do you mean by "this case"? (6)

W This lawsuit. You had phoned me the week before, and during our telephone conversation I had agreed to use Autodynam to generate a computer simulation of the truck-bicycle collision involved in this lawsuit.

P WHAT reports and depositions did you receive on January 19? (6)

W The stack included the official police report on the accident, the truck driver's deposition, and the deposition of two eyewitnesses to the accident.

P WHAT did you do with the reports? (6)

W I carefully reviewed every page of every document and then extracted the information that Autodynam needs.

P HOW much of the necessary information did you find in the reports? (6)

W They contained all the information the program requires.

P In particular, WHICH reports did you take the information from? (7)

W I gathered all the information from the police report and the eyewitness accounts.

P WHY didn't you take any information from the truck driver's deposition? (7)

W You instructed me not to.

P WHAT reason did I give you? (7)

W You said that you didn't want the simulation to represent simply your client's version of the accident; you said that there might be questions about his bias. So you expressly instructed me to use the police report and the depositions given by the two eyewitnesses who had no connection with either party.

P   WHAT did you do with the information after you extracted it from the report and depositions? (8)

W   I input it.

P   HOW did you do that? (8)

W   I used the computer keyboard.

P   HOW accurately did you input the data? (8)

W   It all was correct.

P   HOW do you know that? (8)

W   You put the data into a particular file on the computer. I called that file back on the screen and double-checked each entry against the original police report and depositions. Every entry was right.

P   WHAT did you do after you double-checked the data input to the computer? (9)

W   I entered a command, directing Autodynam to apply the programmed propositions of physics to that data to first determine where the truck and bicycle collided and then to produce a computer animation showing the point of collision.

P   WHAT happened then? (10)

W   The computer generated the animation that I had requested.

P   HOW, if at all, was the animation recorded? (10)

W   I'm pretty traditional. Some researchers put it on laser disc, but I still like video-tape. So I recorded it on a videotape.

P   Your Honor, request that this be marked Defense Exhibit C for identification.

J   It will be so marked.

P   Permission to approach the witness?

J   Granted.

P   Professor, I now hand you what has been marked Defense Exhibit C for identification. WHAT is it? (11)

W   It's the videotape I just mentioned.

P   HOW do you know that? (11)

W   A couple of ways.

P   Namely?

W   To begin with, I recognize the markings on the label affixed to the tape. That's my handwriting. In my own handwriting, I noted the case name and the date on which I prepared the videotape. In addition, we viewed this tape in its entirety in the judge's chambers about three hours ago, and I recognize the tape as the one Autodynam produced after I input the data about this accident.

P   Your Honor, I now offer Defense Exhibit C for identification into evidence as Defense C.

J   It will be so received.

P   Permission to play the tape for the jury.

J   Granted.

Chapter 5

LIMITATIONS ON CREDIBILITY EVIDENCE

A. INTRODUCTION

As soon as a witness answers one question on direct examination, his or her credibility becomes an issue in the case. Evidence pertinent to the witness's credibility is therefore logically relevant. Evidence Code § 780 contains a long, illustrative list of the types of evidence logically relevant to witnesses' credibility.

However, logical relevance is not enough. The judge might exclude the proposed evidence under Evidence Code § 352. That section reads:

> The court in its discretion may exclude evidence if its probative value is substantially outweighed by the probability that its admission will (a) necessitate undue consumption of time or (b) create substantial danger of undue prejudice, of confusing the issues, or of misleading the jury.

When a judge excludes evidence under § 352, the item is sometimes said to be legally irrelevant. Testimony that is logically relevant only to the witnesses' credibility often raises the dangers mentioned in § 352. The purpose of a trial is to adjudicate the historical merits: Did the civil defendant run the red light, or did the criminal defendant stab the victim? The witnesses' credibility is tangential to the historical merits. To the extent that the jurors focus on the witnesses' credibility, they may lose sight of their primary task. Moreover, credibility evidence can be time-consuming. The witness to be impeached may have testified for only ten minutes, but the opposing attorney may attempt to present three hours of psychiatric testimony about that witness's mental state to impeach the witness.

Thus, the law puts many restrictions on evidence that is relevant only to the witnesses' credibility. The restrictions apply at every stage of credibility analysis: bolstering before attempted impeachment, impeachment, and rehabilitation after impeachment.

The proponent naturally wants to build up the witness's believability or credibility in the jury's eyes. Conversely, the opponent wants to tear it down, to impeach it. The proponent's attempt to build up the witness's credibility before impeachment is called bolstering or supporting the witness's credibility. For example, the proponent might attempt to increase the witness's credibility during the direct examination, before the opponent has cross examined the witness. If the proponent attempts to repair the witness's credibility after impeachment, the proponent is said to be rehabilitating the witness's credibility. If the opponent attempted to impeach during cross-examination, the proponent could attempt to rehabilitate the witness during redirect.

Most of the evidence law dealing with credibility focuses on impeachment. For that reason, most of the sections in this chapter deal with the various impeachment techniques. Some impeachment techniques are limited to cross-examination of the witness to be impeached. The opponent must accept the witness's answer on cross-examination, in the sense that the opponent may not present other evidence to contradict the witness's answer. Section F of this chapter deals with such a technique, proof that the witness has committed bad acts that have not resulted in a conviction.

Other impeachment techniques necessarily entail extrinsic evidence and cannot be used during cross-examination. Sections G, H, and I of this chapter are illustrative. Section G deals with proof that witness #1 has a character trait of untruthfulness. Use of this technique requires that the opponent call witness #2, a character witness, to testify to the bad character of witness #1. Section H deals with polygraph examination. This technique requires a polygraph examiner who will testify that a prior witness flunked an examination. Section I analyzes contradiction impeachment, in which witness #2 contradicts some fact that witness #1 testified to.

The remaining impeachment techniques permit both cross-examination and extrinsic evidence. Sections J-M analyze these techniques: convictions, prior inconsistent statements, bias, and attacks on the witness's mental capacity.

Part 1. Bolstering Before Impeachment

The general common-law rule is that the proponent may not bolster the witness's credibility before any attempted impeachment. The jurors' principal focus should be on the historical issues in the case rather than on the witnesses' credibility. To help the jurors maintain that focus, the common-law excludes evidence of a witness's credibility until the opponent has attacked the witness. Evidence Code § 790 picks up the common law and makes it the general rule in California: "Evidence of the good character of a witness is inadmissible to support his credibility unless evidence of his bad character has been admitted for the purpose of attacking his credibility." The general rule does, however, have exceptions. We discuss three of them in the following sections.

B.   BOLSTERING BEFORE IMPEACHMENT IN CRIMINAL CASES

In 1982, California's voters adopted an initiative measure commonly called "Proposition 8." Proposition 8 was presented to the voters as a "law and order" initiative under the title "Victims' Bill of Rights. " It now appears as Art. I, § 28 of the California Constitution. Section (d) of Proposition 8 states as follows:

> Except as provided by statute hereinafter enacted by a two-thirds vote of the membership in each house of the Legislature, *relevant evidence shall not be excluded in any criminal proceeding.* ... Nothing in this section shall affect

any existing statutory rule of evidence relating to *privilege* or *hearsay* or *Evidence Code, Sections 352, 782, or 1103*. ... (emphasis added).

Proposition 8 had numerous surprising consequences on the law of evidence as applied in criminal cases. One of those surprising consequences was to make the general rule against bolstering before impeachment *inapplicable* in criminal cases. In *People v. Harris*, 47 Cal. 3d 1047, 1080-82, 767 P.2d 619, 640-41, 255 Cal. Rptr. 352, 373-74 (1989), the California Supreme Court held that Proposition 8 repealed Evidence Code § 790 with respect to criminal cases. Thus, a prosecutor is free to offer evidence to support the credibility of a prosecution witness before that witness's credibility has been attacked—and the same freedom should be allowed to the defendant. *Cf. People v. Lankford*, 210 Cal. App. 3d 227, 237, 258 Cal. Rptr. 322, 327 (1989). This freedom does have constraints, however. Proposition 8 specifically preserves the trial judge's discretion under § 352 to exclude evidence if its probative value is substantially outweighed by the danger that it will waste time, create undue prejudice, confuse the issues, or mislead the jury. In applying their § 352 discretion, trial judges should recall the common-sense reason for the rule against bolstering before impeachment—that is, to help keep the proceedings focused on the merits rather than on a tangle of side issues about witness credibility.

C. PRIOR IDENTIFICATION

1. THE DOCTRINE

A second exception to the rule against bolstering before impeachment is the prior identification doctrine. In many jurisdictions, if the witness has already identified a person in court, the proponent may prove that the witness made a pretrial identification of the same person. The prior identification is not admitted as substantive evidence that it was correct; rather, it is admitted for the limited purpose of increasing the witness's credibility. The fact that the witness earlier identified the same person strengthens the witness's credibility—at least the witness is consistent. When the judge admits prior identification evidence on this theory, the opponent is entitled to a limiting instruction that the jury is to use the prior identification only on a bolstering theory, not as substantive evidence.

Some jurisdictions go beyond this view; they permit the proponent to use the prior identification as substantive evidence that the person identified was the perpetrator or actor. California is one of these jurisdictions. Evidence Code § 1238 states:

Evidence of a statement previously made by a witness is not made inadmissible by the hearsay rule if the statement would have been admissible if made by him while testifying and:

(a) The statement is an identification of a party or another who partici-pated in a crime or other occurrence;

(b) The statement was made at a time when the crime or other occur-rence was fresh in the witness's memory; and

(c) The evidence of the statement is offered after the witness testifies that he made the identification and that it was a true reflection of his opinion at that time.

The California Law Revision comment to § 1238 indicates that a proponent may invoke § 1238 even when the witness cannot make an in-court identification of the same person.

2. ELEMENTS OF THE FOUNDATION

The proponent must show that:

1. The witness has made an in-court identification of the person. Even though Evidence Code § 1238 does not require an in-court identification, the proponent will almost always seek one. The testimony is stronger with an in-court identification. Further, if the proponent makes no attempt to elicit an in-court identification, some jurors will be puzzled, perhaps to the extent of disbelieving the out-of-court identification.
2. The witness had a pretrial opportunity to observe the person while the event was still fresh in the witness's memory.
3. The witness had an adequate opportunity to observe the person.
4. The pretrial encounter was conducted in a fair manner.
5. At the pretrial encounter, the witness identified the same person.
6. The witness testifies that his or her earlier identification was a true reflec-tion of his opinion at that time.

3. SAMPLE FOUNDATION

The fact situation is a tort action arising from a hit-and-run accident at 1:00 p.m. on June 13th of last year. The plaintiff calls a witness, Jane Morris. The wit-ness is prepared to testify that the defendant was the driver of the hit-and-run car. She is also ready to testify that she identified the defendant at a lineup at the local police station shortly after the accident. The witness has already described the ac-cident which occurred at noontime. The proponent is the plaintiff.

P   WHAT did the car do after it struck the plaintiff?
W   It sped away from the scene.
P   HOW well did you see the car? (1)
W   Well enough to see both the car and the driver.
P   WHERE is the driver now? (1)
W   He's sitting right here in the courtroom.

P WHERE is he sitting? (1)

W At the end of the table over there to the right.

P HOW is he dressed? (1)

W He's wearing a blue suit, white shirt, and striped tie.

P Your Honor, may the record reflect that the witness has identified the defendant, John Ursin? (1)

J It will so reflect.

P Ms. Morris, HOW many times have you seen the defendant? (2)

W Three times.

P WHAT were those occasions? (2)

W Well, I saw him at the scene of the accident, today in court, and one other time.

P WHAT was that other time? (2)

W It was at a lineup at the police station on New York Street.

P WHEN did this lineup occur? (2)

W It was about 5:00 p.m. the afternoon of the accident.

P HOW well could you remember the accident at the time of the lineup? (2)

W The accident had happened just a couple of hours before, so it was real fresh in my mind.

P WHERE did the police hold this lineup? (2)

W It was on stage in the big room off the entrance.

P HOW was the lighting in the room? (3)

W It was fine.

P HOW close were you to the stage? (3)

W I was only ten feet away.

P HOW were you facing? (3)

W I was facing straight ahead and looking at all the men in the lineup.

P HOW long did the police permit you to observe the lineup? (3)

W They gave me as much time as I wanted. I didn't need long.

P HOW many men were in the lineup? (4)

W There were six.

P HOW were they dressed? (4)

W They were all wearing dark clothes.

P HOW tall were they? (4)

W They were roughly the same height, five ten to six feet.

P WHAT, if anything, did the police say about the men in the lineup? (4)

W They didn't say anything. They just ushered me into the room and asked me if I recognized anyone.

P WHAT did the men in the lineup do while they were on the stage? (4)

W Nothing. They just stood there.

P WHAT happened after the lineup? (5)

W The police asked me if I recognized the driver of the car in the lineup.

P WHAT did you say? (5)

W I told them that I did.

P WHOM did you identify at that lineup? (5)

W The defendant, the same person I just pointed out in court.

P WHY did you identify him at that time? (6)

W At the time, I was convinced that he was the person who was driving that car.

D.   FRESH COMPLAINT

1. THE DOCTRINE

A third exception to the rule against bolstering is the fresh complaint doctrine. Most jurisdictions restrict the doctrine to sex offense cases; a few jurisdictions also recognize the doctrine in burglary and robbery cases. The underlying assumption is that the victim is likely to make an immediate complaint about this type of offense. The freshness helps strengthen the inference of the complainant's truthfulness. Moreover, especially in sex offense cases, there is a crying need for credibility evidence; there are rarely eyewitnesses, and the trial usually becomes a swearing contest.

As noted in Section B. above, Proposition 8 makes the rule against bolstering before impeachment inapplicable in California criminal cases. Even before Proposition 8, California recognized the fresh complaint doctrine in sex offense cases. One modern example is *People v. Snyder*, 14 Cal. App. 4th 1166, 18 Cal. Rptr. 2d 496 (1993).

In applying the doctrine, California courts usually restrict the evidence to proof that the victim complained and identified a particular person as the perpetrator. The other details of the offense are inadmissible. 1 WITKIN § 712. If used to prove that what the victim asserts is true, the fresh complaint would be hearsay, and it should be admitted as substantive evidence only if it falls within an exception to the hearsay rule, such as the spontaneous statements exception. If no hearsay exception applies, the judge, upon request, should instruct the jury to use the fresh complaint only to bolster the victim's credibility, not as evidence that what the victim asserted is true. *See Snyder, supra.*

In *People v. Brown*, 8 Cal. 4th 746, 883 P.2d 949, 35 Cal. Rptr. 2d 407 (1994), the California Supreme Court refused to apply the common-law fresh complaint doctrine because the doctrine rests on the discredited assumption that any true victim will report the offense to someone. However, in the same opinion, the court ruled that under general evidentiary principles, such out-of-court statements may be admitted for the limited, nonhearsay purpose of showing the fact of and circumstances surrounding the victim's disclosure of the assault to others.

2. ELEMENTS OF THE FOUNDATION

The proponent must show that:

1. The victim made a complaint.
2. The victim made the complaint relatively soon after the offense. How soon is soon enough depends on the particular facts of the case and on the victim's situation and perceptions.
3. The victim made the complaint to the authorities or to a person he or she encountered after the offense.

4.   The report stated that the complainant was the victim of an offense.
5.   The report identified the perpetrator of the offense.

3. SAMPLE FOUNDATION

The fact situation is a criminal prosecution for rape. The victim, Ms. McDonald, is on the stand under direct examination by the prosecutor. She has already testified that the defendant, Henry Miles, raped her on a Saturday night in an automobile parked in front of her apartment house, and that after the rape, she broke free and ran into her apartment.

P   WHAT did you do when you got back to your apartment?

W   I was crying. I took a hot bath, and then I just sat in the living room by myself, because my roommate was away for the weekend and I didn't know what to do. I needed to talk to somebody, but I didn't know who to talk to.

P   HOW long did you sit in the living room? (2)

W   Hours and hours. Finally I just went to bed, and I slept.

P   HOW long did you sleep? (2)

W   I don't know, really. I never ate or anything. I just stayed in my bed, like I was numb or dead or something.

P   WHO, other than your roommate, do you know in the apartment house? (2)

W   I don't know anybody else. There are a couple of old ladies and a man that I say hello to, but I don't know their names. There's nobody there that I could really talk to.

P   WHAT happened next?

W   Finally, late Sunday evening, my roommate, Sandy, got home.

P   WHAT was your mental state by that point? (2)

W   Well, by that time I had gotten a grip on myself. I had calmed down. I'd stopped crying. I was in pretty good control.

P   WHAT did you do when Sandy got home? (1), (2), (3), (4)

W   I told her I'd been raped.

P   WHEN did you tell her that? (2)

W   As soon as she walked in.

P   WHO did you say raped you? (5)

W   Henry Miles.

O   Your Honor, I request a limiting instruction under Evidence Code § 355. What she told her roommate is clearly hearsay, and it does not come within the spontaneous statements exception, or any other exception that I can think of.

P   I have no objection to a limiting instruction, your Honor.

J   Very well. Ladies and gentlemen of the jury, you have heard Ms. McDonald testify that she told her roommate, Sandy, about the alleged event. You are not to use her statement to Sandy as evidence that she was raped or that the defendant was the rapist. You are to use it only for whatever value you think it has in supporting Ms. McDonald's credibility as a witness.

Part 2. Impeachment

E.   IMPEACHMENT IN GENERAL

The Evidence Code allows the opposing attorney wide latitude to impeach witnesses. The Code permits the opponent to attack both the proponent's witnesses and the opponent's own witnesses. Under the common-law voucher rule, many jurisdictions limited the opponent's ability to impeach his or her own witnesses. However, Evidence Code § 785 repudiates the voucher rule by stating that "[t]he credibility of a witness may be attacked ... by any party, including the party calling him. " Section 1202 allows the opponent to attack the credibility of a hearsay declarant in the same manner as a live witness.

The Code liberally permits impeachment in another respect. At common law, several impeachment techniques, notably prior inconsistent statements and specific contradiction, were subject to the collateral fact rule. A collateral fact is a fact logically relevant only to the witness credibility with no logical relevance to the historical merits. At common law, if the impeachment related to a collateral fact, the opponent had to take the answer the witness gave on cross-examination; if the witness gave an unfavorable answer, even a perjurious answer, the opponent could not offer other evidence to disprove the answer. The collateral fact rule barred the introduction of extrinsic evidence to prove the inconsistent statement or to contradict the testimony. The drafters of the Code abolished the collateral fact rule. The California Law Revision Commission comment to § 780 asserts that:

> [t]he effect of Section 780 (together with Section 351) is to eliminate this inflexible rule of exclusion. This is not to say that all evidence of a collateral nature offered to attack the credibility of a witness would be admissible. Under Section 352, the court has substantial discretion to exclude collateral evidence. The effect of Section 780 ... is to change the present ... inflexible rule of exclusion to a rule of discretion to be exercised by the trial judge.

We turn now to the specific impeachment techniques commonly used in California courts.

F.   BAD ACTS THAT HAVE NOT RESULTED IN A CONVICTION

1. THE DOCTRINE

Most jurisdictions permit the opponent to impeach the witness with proof that the witness has committed untruthful acts. The opponent may do so even if the acts have not resulted in the witness's conviction of any crime. Federal Rule of Evidence 608(b)(1) states the majority view:

> Specific instances of the conduct of a witness, for the purpose of attacking ... his credibility, other than conviction of crime as provided in rule 609, may not be proved by extrinsic evidence. They may, however, in the discretion of the court, if probative of ... untruthfulness, be inquired into on cross-examination of the witness ... concerning his character for ... untruthfulness ....

The theory of logical relevance is simple: If the witness has lied or cheated in the past, he may lie on the witness stand. Of course, the doctrine is limited to acts that show untruthfulness.

As the Federal Rule indicates, the opponent is restricted to cross-examination. On cross-examination the opponent may inquire whether the witness committed the act. However, the opponent must accept or take the answer, in the sense that the opponent cannot use extrinsic evidence to contradict it. Thus, if witness #1 denies committing the deceitful act, the opponent cannot call witness #2 to testify that he or she saw witness #1 commit the act.

The California Evidence Code adopts a minority view, forbidding this type of impeachment. Evidence Code § 787 states: "Subject to Section 788 [the section authorizing the use of convictions for impeachment], evidence of specific instances of his conduct relevant only as tending to prove a trait of his character is inadmissible to attack ... the credibility of a witness."

California's minority view applies, however, only in *civil* cases; Proposition 8 makes Evidence Code § 787 inapplicable in criminal cases. In *People v. Harris*, 47 Cal. 3d 1047, 1080-83, 767 P.2d 619, 640-42, 255 Cal. Rptr. 352, 373-75 (1989), the California Supreme Court held that on direct examination before an attack on the informant's credibility, a police officer could testify about the informant's reliability "in past cases." *Id.* at 1080, 767 P.2d at 640, 255 Cal. Rptr. at 373. The court specifically rejected the defense argument that § 787 barred such bolstering evidence. More broadly, the court pointed out that there is no language in Proposition 8 preserving the exclusionary rule in § 787. *Id.* at 1082, 767 P.2d at 641, 255 Cal. Rptr. at 374. Thus, Harris indicates that in California criminal cases, one can impeach with prior bad acts that have not resulted in a conviction. *Accord, People v. Wheeler*, 4 Cal. 4th 284, 841 P.2d 938, 14 Cal. Rptr. 2d 418 (1992), which holds that in a California criminal case, the prior bad conduct that underlies a misdemeanor conviction can be used for impeachment, provided that the bad conduct involved moral turpitude and that it bears on the veracity of the witness. [For additional analysis of *Wheeler, see* Section J.3 of this chapter.] In this context "moral turpitude" has been variously defined as conduct indicating bad character, moral depravity, or a readiness to do evil; or conduct involving violence, menace, or threats; or conduct that shows baseness, vileness, or depravity in the private and social duties which a man owes to his fellow men or to society in general. *See People v. Lepolo*, 55 Cal. App. 4th 85, 90, 63 Cal. Rptr. 2d 735, 738 (1997), and cases there cited. Both the prosecution and the defense can resort to this impeachment technique. *People v. Lankford*, 210 Cal. App. 3d 227, 237, 258 Cal. Rptr. 322, 327 (1989). The questioning attorney must reasonably believe that the witness committed the prior bad acts in question. *See People v. Mickle*, 54 Cal. 3d 140, 814 P.2d 290, 284 Cal. Rptr. 511 (1991), *cert. denied*, 503 U.S. 988 (1992).

However, in a California criminal case, the trial judge still has discretion under Evidence Code § 352 to exclude evidence of prior bad acts that have not resulted in a conviction. *See, e.g., People v. Hayes*, 3 Cal. App. 4th 1238, 5 Cal. Rptr. 2d 105 (1992) (spousal rape case in which evidence that the complaining wife was subject to an outstanding arrest warrant for prostitution was properly excluded as unduly prejudicial, degrading, and embarrassing); *People v. Morris*, 53 Cal. 3d 152, 807 P.2d 949, 279 Cal. Rptr. 720, *cert. denied*, 502 U.S. 959 (1991) (evidence of past devil worship excluded as not bearing on witnesses' credibility); *People v. Jennings*, 53 Cal. 3d 334, 807 P.2d 1009, 279 Cal. Rptr. 780, *cert. denied*, 502 U.S. 969 (1991) (failure to report income from prostitution properly excluded as too time consuming on collateral matter).

In *People v. Lepolo,* 55 Cal. App. 4th 85, 63 Cal. Rptr. 2d 735 (1997), the defendant in a brutal murder case had testified on his own behalf. The trial judge allowed the prosecutor to impeach him with evidence that on a prior occasion the defendant had threatened a uniformed police officer by raising a 36-inch machete over his head, pointing at the officer, and yelling "I want that officer." When he was arrested for this misconduct, he explained that the officer had made him mad, that he wanted to "whack [the officer's] head off," and that he hoped to meet the officer again so he could either shoot him or whack his head off. 55 Cal. App. 4th at 89, 63 Cal. Rptr. 2d at 737. The appeals court held that, viewed in context, Lepolo's misconduct and subsequent boastful threats involved moral turpitude, and that the trial judge did not abuse his discretion in allowing it to be used for impeachment.

Section 782 of the Evidence Code prescribes a special procedure when the defendant in certain types of prosecutions offers "evidence of sexual conduct of the complaining victim ... to attack the credibility of the complaining witness ...." The defense must file a pretrial motion, including an offer of proof, describing the conduct in question and "its relevancy in attacking the credibility of the complaining witness." The courts have liberally construed the term "sexual conduct" and thereby increased the special procedural protection afforded the complaining witness. *People v. Franklin*, 25 Cal. App. 4th 328, 30 Cal. Rptr. 2d 376 (1994).

In *People v. Chandler*, 56 Cal. App. 4th 703, 65 Cal. Rptr. 2d 687 (1997), the defendant in a rape case tried to impeach the victim witness by showing that she committed acts of moral turpitude—specifically, exchanging sex for crack cocaine. Two defense witnesses would have testified that they made such exchanges with the victims, but the trial judge refused to let them testify on the sole ground that they were not believable. That ruling was error—lack of believability is not one of the factors the judge can consider under § 352. However, the error was harmless, and the defendant's conviction was affirmed.

2. ELEMENTS OF THE FOUNDATION

The following foundation could be used in a California criminal case, where Evidence Code § 787 does not apply, and where the proponent seeks to impeach one of the opposition's witnesses by showing that the witness committed a prior bad act that demonstrates untruthfulness but that did not result in a criminal conviction.

1. The opposition witness committed the prior bad act.
2. The prior bad act demonstrates untruthfulness.

3. SAMPLE FOUNDATION

The fact situation is a criminal prosecution for armed robbery of a liquor store. Lewis Lee, a California lawyer, happened to be in the store at the time, and has testified as a prosecution witness. In his testimony on direct examination, Lee identified the defendant as the person who committed the armed robbery. The proponent of the impeaching evidence is the defense lawyer, Ms. Dillard, who is now questioning Lee on cross-examination. The opponent of the impeaching evidence is the prosecutor, Ms. West.

P   Mr. Lee, at the start of your testimony, you identified yourself as a California lawyer, DIDN'T YOU?

W   Yes, that's right.

P   You were admitted to practice law in California in 1978, ISN'T THAT COR-RECT?

W   Yes, that was the year I graduated from law school and passed the California bar examination.

P   Mr. Lee, ISN'T IT A FACT that you're not practicing any law these days?

W   I'm taking some time off to do other things.

P   Now this "taking some time off," that ISN'T voluntary on your part, is it?

O   I object, your Honor, on grounds of relevance. May we have a sidebar conference on this, your Honor?

J   Will counsel please approach the bench?

(Sidebar conference.)

J   Ms. Dillard, where is this line of questioning taking us?

P   Your Honor, four months ago, the State Bar of California suspended Mr. Lee from law practice for two years. I have the suspension documents right here, and they state that Mr. Lee was suspended from practice for lying to five different clients about the work he was purporting to do on their cases. Here's a copy of the suspension papers for you, your Honor, and a copy for you, Ms. West.

J   Well, it looks like he was suspended for lying. What do you have to say, Ms. West?

O   I didn't know about this, your Honor. I ask your Honor to exercise her discretion under California Evidence Code § 352 and to end this line of questioning on the ground that it will consume an undue amount of time and divert the jury's attention from the real issues in this case. If we have to get into the facts about what this man said or didn't say to his clients, we could be here for another week.

P   Under Proposition 8, your Honor, I am entitled to use non-conviction bad acts if they show untruthfulness, and this clearly shows untruthfulness.

J   Ms. West, I'm going to deny your § 352 motion for now. I'm going to allow Ms. Dillard to cross-examine, but limited to the fact of suspension and the reason for the suspension, without getting into the background details. If the witness admits the suspension and the reason for it, that will be the end of it. If he doesn't, and if Ms. Dillard then wants to get into extrinsic evidence, I'll be willing to take another look at your § 352 point, Ms. West. You may continue your cross-examination now, Ms. Dillard.

P   Mr. Lee, ISN'T IT A FACT that you are not practicing law at the present time?

W   That is correct.

P   Your license to practice law has been suspended by the State Bar of California, HASN'T IT?

W   Yes. But I will be going back to practice in twenty months.

P   ISN'T IT TRUE, sir, that you were suspended from law practice for lying to some of your clients about the work you were doing for them? (1), (2)

W   Well, that's what the State Bar thought, yes.

P   ISN'T IT TRUE, sir, that the State Bar thought you lied to five different clients on five different occasions? (1), (2)

W   Yes, that's so.

P   I have no further questions at this time, your Honor.

One caveat is appropriate. In the above line of questioning, the trial judge permitted the cross-examiner to inquire not only about the lies to the clients, but also about the State Bar investigation into the alleged lies. Some trial judges restrict the cross-examiner to the former topic. These judges allow the cross-examiner to question directly and bluntly about the witness's untruthful acts, but they do not permit questioning about third party conduct. Thus, while these judges would permit the cross-examiner to ask an employee witness whether he had falsified his business expense account, the cross-examiner could not ask whether the employer fired the witness for that reason. Similarly, although these judges would permit a former student witness to be questioned about whether she had cheated on an examination, the cross-examiner could not inquire whether the school expelled the witness for that reason.

G.   PROOF OF THE CHARACTER TRAIT OF UNTRUTHFULNESS

1. THE DOCTRINE

Under Evidence Code §§ 780(e) and 786, the opponent may impeach the witness by proving that the witness has a character trait of untruthfulness. The opponent uses the character trait as circumstantial proof of conduct—lying on the witness stand. Wydick, *Character Evidence: A Guided Tour of the Grotesque Structure*, 21 U.C. DAVIS L. REV. 123, 173-94 (1987).

This technique is not limited to the cross-examination of the witness to be impeached. Quite the contrary, the opponent usually resorts to extrinsic evidence. To impeach witness #1, the opponent calls witness #2, who testifies that witness #1 has a character trait of untruthfulness. The courts usually term witness #2 a character witness. Under traditional common law, the character witness must restrict his or her testimony to reputation evidence; the character witness describes the witness's reputation for untruthfulness in the community. The modern view, however, is that opinion evidence is also admissible; the character witness may express his or her opinion of witness #1's truthfulness. By the interplay of Evidence Code §§ 786, 787, and 1100, California has embraced the modern view.

2. ELEMENTS OF THE FOUNDATIONS

The foundation varies, depending upon whether the evidence is reputation or opinion. The reputation foundation typically includes these elements:

1. Witness #2 is a member of the same community (residential, business, or social) as witness #1. Although proof of membership in the same community is the normal method by which knowledge of reputation is gained, the California cases recognize other methods. 3 WITKIN § 1937, at 1892. A pre-Code case, *Rios v. Chand*, 130 Cal. App. 2d 833, 280 P.2d 47 (1955), permitted testimony by an investigator sent to the community for the purpose of ascertaining the ... reputation of a person in that community ... by diligent inquiry from ... representative people. ... *Id.* at 839, 280 P.2d at 50.
2. Witness #2 has resided there a substantial period of time.
3. Witness #1 has a reputation for untruthfulness in the community.
4. Witness #2 knows witness #1's reputation for truthfulness.
5. California permits witness #2 to add that given witness #1's reputation, witness #2 would not believe him or her under oath. *People v. Tyler*, 35 Cal. 553, 555 (1868).

The opinion foundation includes the following elements:

1. Witness #2 is personally acquainted with witness #1.
2. Witness #2 knows witness #1 well enough to have formed an opinion of witness #1's truthfulness. One case holds that a *one* month acquaintance is an insufficient basis for an opinion. *People v. Harris*, 270 Cal. App. 2d 863, 76 Cal. Rptr. 130 (1969).
3. Witness #2 has an opinion of witness #1's untruthfulness.
4. Witness #2 has the opinion that witness #1 is an untruthful person.

Again, some courts permit witness #2 to state whether, given that opinion, he or she would believe witness #1 under oath. Since Evidence Code § 1100 uses the generic term "opinion" rather than "lay opinion," in an appropriate case the proponent may offer expert opinion testimony. However, "[t]he use of psychiatric testimony to impeach a witness is generally disfavored." *People v. Marshall*, 13 Cal. 4th 799, 919 P.2d 1280, 55 Cal. Rptr. 2d 347, 365 (1996).

3. SAMPLE FOUNDATIONS

The following is a reputation foundation. The witness to be impeached is Mr. Harding.

P WHO is Mr. Harding?
H He's an acquaintance of mine.
P WHEN is the last time you saw him?
W Here in the courtroom. He testified for the other side a couple of hours ago.
P WHERE does he live? (1)
W Here in San Diego.
P HOW long has Mr. Harding lived in San Diego? (2)
W All his life, I think. I can remember him twenty years back.
P HOW long have you lived here in San Diego? (2)
W All my life.
P HOW many years have you lived here? (2)
W Thirty-seven years.
P Does Mr. Harding have a reputation for truthfulness or untruthfulness in San Diego? (3)
W Yes.
P HOW familiar are you with that reputation?
W Real well. I've been in lots of conversations in which I've heard his name come up.
P WHAT is that reputation? (4)
W It's bad. He's known as an untruthful person.
P Given Mr. Harding's reputation, would you believe him under oath? (5)
W No.

The following is an opinion foundation:

P WHO is Mr. Harding? (1)
W He's an acquaintance of mine.
P WHEN is the last time you saw him?
W Here in the courtroom. He testified for the other side a few hours ago.
P HOW did you come to know him? (2)
W We've lived in the same neighborhood for a long time. I've had a lot of contact with him.
P HOW many years have you known him? (2)
W I'd say easily twenty years.
P In WHAT contexts have you known him? (2)

W As I said, we've lived in the same neighborhood for a long time. I see him around the neighborhood a lot. In addition, we've worked at the same plant together for the last five years.

P HOW often do you talk with him? (2)

W Usually several times a week. We're always bumping into each other.

P Do you have an opinion of his truthfulness? (3)

W Yes.

P WHAT is that opinion? (4)

W In my opinion, he's an untruthful person.

P Given that opinion, would you believe Mr. Harding under oath? (5)

W No.

H. PROOF THAT THE WITNESS HAS FAILED A POLYGRAPH EXAMINATION

1. THE DOCTRINE

Like proof of the character trait of untruthfulness, this impeachment technique requires extrinsic evidence. The opponent calls a polygraph examiner, witness #2, to impeach witness #1. Many people believe that when used by an experienced, competent examiner, the polygraph can be an effective tool for detecting deception. The examiner's diagnosis of deception is logically relevant to show that when the witness gave a certain answer, the witness was lying.

The prevailing view today is still that polygraph evidence is inadmissible. In *United States v. Scheffer*, 523 U.S. 303, 118 S. Ct. 1261, 140 L. Ed. 2d 413 (1998), the U.S. Supreme Court held (8-1) that a criminal defendant has no constitutional right to use favorable polygraph evidence as part of his defense. However, five of the Justices expressed discontent with an evidence rule that excludes polygraph evidence in every case. Most courts premise the inadmissibility of polygraph evidence on *Frye v. United States*, 293 F. 1013 (D.C. Cir. 1923), which held that scientific evidence cannot be admitted without a showing that the principles and techniques it uses are generally accepted within the relevant scientific circle. (As noted in Section N of Chapter 4, *Frye* has now been abandoned in the federal courts. However, most federal courts continue to exclude polygraph evidence under the new *Daubert* standard. *E.g., United States v. Black*, 831 F. Supp. 120 (E.D.N.Y. 1993). After announcing the general acceptance test, the *Frye* court applied the test to a forerunner of the polygraph, the systolic blood pressure deception test, and held the evidence inadmissible. However, since *Frye* in 1923, a great deal of research has been done to advance the state of the polygraphic art. In a significant minority of jurisdictions, the courts now admit polygraph evidence, at least when the parties stipulate to the admission of the evidence.

As explained in Section N of Chapter 4, California continues to be a *Frye* jurisdiction, at least for the moment. In *People v. Wochnick*, 98 Cal. App. 2d 124, 219 P.2d 70 (1950), the California Supreme Court cited *Frye* as the basis for excluding polygraph evidence. In *Witherspoon v. Superior Court*, 133 Cal. App. 3d

24, 183 Cal. Rptr. 615 (1982), an intermediate appellate court held that, even absent a stipulation, the proponent of polygraph evidence was at least entitled to an opportunity to show that the polygraph technique now satisfies *Frye*. The court emphasized that polygraph evidence has improved since *Frye* and *Wochnick*. One optimistic commentator suggested that California courts might soon be admitting polygraph evidence. Comment, *The Polygraph in California: A Heartbeat away from Admissibility*, 14 PAC. L.J. 1113, 1143 (1983).

The California legislature dashed that hope by promptly enacting Evidence Code § 351.1, which states that the results of a polygraph examination, the opinion of a polygraph examiner, an offer to take a polygraph examination, or a failure to take a polygraph examination are inadmissible in criminal and juvenile prosecutions unless all parties stipulate to admissibility. *See, e.g., People v. Morris*, 53 Cal. 3d 152, 807 P.2d 949, 279 Cal. Rptr. 720, *cert. denied*, 502 U.S. 959 (1991) (the defendant in a capital case was not allowed to offer evidence that one witness against him had refused to take a polygraph test and that another had failed a polygraph test); *see also In re Aontae D.*, 25 Cal. App. 4th 167, 30 Cal. Rptr. 2d 176 (1994) (ban on polygraph evidence did not deprive juvenile offender of due process). Note that § 351.1 does not apply to civil cases. In a civil case, the proponent may still attempt to offer polygraph evidence, even without a stipulation. *In re Aontae D.*, 25 Cal. App. 4th 167, 30 Cal. Rptr. 2d 176 (1994) held that § 351.1 applies to a proceeding on a petition for wardship. In such a proceeding, the normal criminal burden of proof governs; the State must prove beyond a reasonable doubt that the juvenile committed a criminal offense.

2. ELEMENTS OF THE FOUNDATION

1. The witness is qualified to establish the underlying principle's validity and the instrument's reliability.
2. The witness is qualified to administer a polygraph examination.
3. The witness is qualified to interpret a polygraph exam result.
4. The underlying principle of polygraphy is valid.
5. The underlying principle is generally accepted as valid.
6. The polygraph instrument is reliable.
7. The instrument is generally accepted as reliable.
8. The examiner tested the subject.
9. When the examiner tested the subject, the witness to be impeached, the instrument was in working order.
10. At the time, the examiner used certain procedures to conduct the test.
11. The procedures used were proper.
12. The subject had a certain result on the test.
13. The results of the test indicate that the subject was lying when he or she made a certain statement.

3. SAMPLE FOUNDATION

The fact situation is a tort action. Ms. Gust sued Mr. Martin for theft of trade secrets. The witness is Mr. Bechtel, a polygraph examiner. Mr. Bechtel is prepared to testify that he examined Mr. Martin. Mr. Bechtel will testify that in his opinion, Mr. Martin was telling the truth when he denied stealing the secrets. The proponent is the defendant.

P WHAT is your name?

W Cleveland Bechtel.

P WHAT is your address?

W 1554 Skinker Boulevard in Millbrae.

P WHAT is your occupation? (1), (2), (3)

W I am a polygraph examiner; I have my own business.

P WHAT is your educational background? (1)

W I have a master's degree in psychology from Stanford.

P WHAT formal training, if any, have you had in polygraphy? (2), (3)

W I attended the Keeler Polygraph Institute in Chicago.

P WHAT is that Institute? (2), (3)

W It's one of the best known and best established polygraph schools in the world.

P WHAT sort of training did you receive there? (2), (3)

W First we had classroom instruction on the underlying principles of polygraph and the instrument, the polygraph. Then we had training in conducting and interpreting polygraph tests. We were given an opportunity to conduct and evaluate tests during the course.

P WHAT experience have you had in the polygraph field? (2), (3)

W After completing my training at Keeler, I worked as an apprentice for a year. I worked for a very experienced examiner. Then I started my own business. I've owned that business for the past twelve years.

P During your career, HOW many polygraph examinations have you conducted? (2), (3)

W Several thousand. Too many to keep count of.

P HOW many times, if any, have you qualified as a polygraph expert in court? (2), (3)

W About fifty times.

P HOW many times in this state? (2), (3)

W Ten times.

P WHEN was the last time? (2), (3)

W About six months ago.

P WHAT is the underlying principle of polygraphy? (4)

W The theory is that conscious deception causes certain physiological changes that the subject has little or no control over blood pressure, pulse rate, breath, and galvanic skin response.

P WHAT experiments, if any, have been conducted to verify the theory? (5)

W Actually, scientists have been working in this area for decades. Almost all of the studies document the theory.

P HOW widely accepted is the theory? (5)

W There's still some controversy, but most people familiar with the area—examiners, psychologists, and psychiatrists—accept the theory.

P WHAT is the polygraph itself? (6)

W It's the instrument the examiner uses. It measures the psychological responses I mentioned. It records them on a graph called the polygram.

P WHAT experiments, if any, have been conducted to test the reliability of the instrument? (7)

W Again, there have been a large number of reported tests. Under typical laboratory conditions, the examiners reach accurate diagnoses in roughly 85 percent of the cases. In field conditions, the accuracy level often reaches the high ninety percents; in field conditions, there is real motivation to deceive, and diagnosing deception is easier.

P HOW widely accepted is the instrument? (7)

W There's been a lot of dispute over the years, but today I think that most experts in the field accept the polygraph. Most knowledgeable people would say that in the hands of a competent, experienced examiner, the polygraph is a reliable instrument for diagnosing deception.

P WHO is George Martin? (8)

W He's the defendant in this case.

P HOW do you know him? (8)

W I had occasion to conduct a polygraph examination of Mr. Mattin several weeks ago.

P WHEN and WHERE did you do that? (8)

W I did that at my office on February 13. It was about ten in the morning. I used my polygraph to test him.

P WHAT condition was the polygraph in when you tested Mr. Martin? (9)

W It was in proper working order.

P HOW did you know that? (9)

W I use a Lafayette polygraph, and the company provides purchasers with a checklist for ensuring the instrument's operational condition. I went through the checklist before the test, and the instrument checked out perfectly.

P HOW did you conduct Mr. Martin's examination? (10)

W I followed the standard operating procedure and took all the steps you're supposed to use.

P HOW are you supposed to conduct an examination? (11)

W First you conduct the pretest interview.

P WHAT is that? (11)

W Before you actually conduct a polygraph examination, you interview the subject. You show the subject the machine, explain its operation, and try to convince the subject that the instrument is effective. You also begin forming your relevant and control questions.

P WHAT are relevant and control questions? (11)

W Relevant questions are the questions about the incident being investigated.

P WHAT would be an example? (11)

W Here, the most relevant question is "Mr. Martin, did you take that file from Ms. Gust's office?"

P WHAT is a control question? (11)

W It's a probable lie question. The subject will probably lie in response.

P WHAT is an example? (11)

W "In your first twenty-five years of life, did you ever steal anything?" The subject is likely to lie and deny stealing.

P HOW do you use the relevant and control questions? (11)

W You compare the responses on the chart to the relevant and control questions. Simply stated, if the subject reacts more to the relevant questions than to the control questions, the person's probably lying. On the other hand, if the subject reacts more to the control questions, the subject is probably telling the truth in his or her responses to the relevant questions.

P HOW did you conduct the test of Mr. Martin? (11)

W I followed the procedure I just described. I conducted a pretest interview and formed my relevant and control questions, including the ones I've already mentioned. Then I ran the test. I spaced the questions about thirty seconds apart to permit the reactions to register fully on the polygram. The test consisted of ten questions, and I ran the test three times during the space of an hour.

P Your Honor, I request that this be marked defense exhibit C for identification.

J It will be so marked.

P Your Honor, please let the record reflect that I am showing the exhibit to the opposing counsel.

J It will so reflect.

P Your Honor, may I have permission to approach the witness?

J Yes.

P Mr. Bechtel, I now hand you defense exhibit C for identification. WHAT is it? (12)

W It's the chart of Mr. Martin's test.

P HOW can you recognize it? (12)

W I recognize my handwriting on it.

P WHAT condition is it in? (12)

W It's in roughly the same condition it was in when I ran the test.

P WHERE has it been since that time? (12)

W In my files. I personally removed it from my files before coming to court.

P Your Honor, I now offer defense exhibit C for identification into evidence as defense exhibit C.

J It will be received.

P Mr. Bechtel, WHAT are the circled areas on exhibit C? (13)

W They're the responses to the control questions, such as the one I mentioned about stealing.

P WHAT are the areas in the squares? (13)

W They're the responses to the relevant questions including the one about the trade secrets.

P WHAT is your diagnosis of that response? (13)

W In my opinion, Mr. Martin was telling the truth when he denied taking the file.

P WHAT is the basis for that opinion? (13)

W The responses to the control questions were fairly mild. There were also mild reactions to the relevant questions. That indicates to me that Mr. Martin was not engaging in conscious deception when he denied stealing the file.

P Your Honor, I request permission to hand exhibit C to the jurors for their personal inspection.

J Yes.

I.   PROOF THAT ANOTHER WITNESS SPECIFICALLY CONTRADICTS THE TESTIMONY OF THE WITNESS TO BE IMPEACHED

Evidence Code § 780(i) states that the opposing attorney may impeach a witness by showing "[t]he ... nonexistence of any fact testified to by him." This impeachment technique is usually termed contradiction. Witness #1 testifies to *fact A*, and the opposing attorney calls witness #2 to testify to *non-A*. The impeaching effect of witness #2's testimony is indirect and inferential: If witness #2 is correct, witness #1 must be mistaken or lying.

Suppose, for example, that plaintiff's witness #1 testifies that the traffic light facing the defendant's car was red. The defense calls witness #2 who testifies that the light facing the defendant's car was green. Since witness #2's testimony is logically relevant to the historical merits, it is admissible both to prove that the light was green and to impeach witness #2 by contradiction.

1. EXTRINSIC EVIDENCE RELEVANT ONLY TO THE WITNESS'S CREDIBILITY

The problem arises when witness #2's testimony is logically relevant only to witness #1's credibility or when there is an independent objection to the testimony such as an objection on character evidence grounds.

Suppose an auto accident occurred in a rural area. During his direct examination witness #1 testified that he was walking near the crossroads where the collision occurred. Witness #1 adds that in the adjacent field, there were at least twenty sheep grazing. During the defense case-in-chief, the defense calls the farmer who owns the field. The farmer is prepared to testify that there were only ten sheep grazing at the time. The farmer's testimony would specifically contradict witness #1's testimony. The farmer's testimony is logically relevant to impeach witness #1; if the farmer is correct, witness #1 erred in perception or memory. However, the farmer's testimony has no logical relevance to the historical merits; the number of sheep in the field has no impact on the facts relating to the auto accident. Before the adoption of the Evidence Code, the collateral fact rule would have mandated the exclusion of the farmer's testimony. *People v. Dice*, 120 Cal. 189, 52 P. 477 (1898).

However, as we have seen, Evidence Code §§ 352 and 780 abolish the collateral fact rule in California. The admission of extrinsic evidence to contradict witness #1 is now governed by § 352. For example, in a 1999 case a trial judge correctly used § 352 to exclude defense evidence in a child molestation case. The defendant wanted to cast doubt on the credibility of the child victim by introducing school records that showed that the victim had learning and personality problems even before the alleged molestation. The records were lengthy and were filled with differing opinions about the victim's problems. Moreover, the records did not specifically contradict any critical part of the prosecution's evidence. Exclusion under

§ 352 was proper. *People v. Pelayo,* 69 Cal. App. 4th 115, 81 Cal. Rptr. 2d 373 (1999).

When applying § 352, the judge weighs the importance of the witness and the strength of the inference that the witness is wrong about the historical merits if the witness is wrong about the detail in question. Suppose that witness #1 is the star witness for one side, and suppose that she testifies to a detail on which she could not possibly have been mistaken, had she really been where she said she was, and had she really seen what she says she saw. To contradict her on the detail is to pull the linchpin of her whole story—even though the detail is not itself relevant to the historical merits. In that situation, the judge ought to exercise the § 352 discretion in favor of admitting extrinsic evidence for the purpose of contradiction. For instance, suppose that in the hypothetical about the sheep in the field, the farmer would testify that the field in question was a flooded rice field, so that any sheep grazing there would need webbed feet. Surely the trial judge should admit the farmer's testimony.

2. OBJECTIONABLE EXTRINSIC EVIDENCE

In section 1, above, we discussed extrinsic testimony that was logically relevant only to witness #1's credibility; the testimony had no independent relevance to the historical merits. The other variation of the problem is where the extrinsic testimony is objectionable, often on character evidence grounds.

Suppose that witness #1 testifies on direct examination that he has never been in trouble with the law and that he always obeys the law. The opposing attorney has proof that the witness has been arrested seventeen times and that the witness has violated the law on numerous occasions. In light of Evidence Code § 787 and the character evidence rules discussed in the next chapter, that proof would ordinarily be objectionable. However, it was improper for witness #1's proponent to elicit the testimony on direct examination; the testimony violated the character evidence rules. The opposing attorney can argue that he or she is now entitled to fight fire with fire. The proponent's violation of the good character evidence rules opened the door, and the opposing attorney may introduce the otherwise objectionable proof on a curative admissibility theory.

The California cases recognize the curative admissibility theory. HEAFEY § 26.5, at 245-46. However, the courts apply the theory with caution and only in special situations. *Id.* The strongest case for applying the theory is when the witness's proponent elicits the testimony on direct examination and the testimony is highly prejudicial to the opposing attorney's case. *Id.* at § 26.6.

J.   PROOF THAT THE WITNESS HAS SUFFERED A CONVICTION

1. THE DOCTRINE

If the witness has been convicted of a crime, the conviction tends to impeach the witness's credibility. The conviction suggests that the witness sometimes disobeys social norms and that he may be violating a norm now by lying. Of course, the conviction has much more probative value if the underlying offense is a crime that involves an element of deceit or fraud, such as perjury or embezzlement.

All jurisdictions recognize this method of impeachment, but they differ on the types of convictions usable to impeach. Most courts allow the opponent to use any felony conviction. Evidence Code § 788 looks simple on its face, and it seems to adopt the prevailing view: "For the purpose of attacking the credibility of a witness, it may be shown by the examination of the witness or by the record of the judgment that he has been convicted of a felony. ..." Penal Code § 17(a) generally defines a felony as a crime that is punishable by death or imprisonment in the state prison. If the judgment of conviction was rendered by a non-California court, the California courts look to the sentence authorized by the other jurisdiction's law to determine whether the conviction is a felony for purpose of Evidence Code § 788. Article, *Impeaching and Rehabilitating a Witness with Character Evidence: Reputation, Opinion, Specific Acts and Prior Convictions*, 9 U.C. DAVIS L. REV. 319, 339-40 (1976). A witness's felony conviction can be used for impeachment before the witness has been sentenced for the crime, even if there is a chance the sentencing court may ultimately impose only a misdemeanor sentence. *People v. Martinez*, 62 Cal. App. 4th 1454, 73 Cal. Rptr. 2d 358 (1998).

2. THE HISTORY OF THE DOCTRINE IN CALIFORNIA

Using criminal convictions to impeach is not as simple as Evidence Code § 788 would make it seem. In 1972, the California Supreme Court decided *People v. Beagle*, 6 Cal. 3d 492, 313 P.2d 1, 99 Cal. Rptr. 313 (1972). The Beagle court announced that trial judges could exercise discretion under Evidence Code § 352 to exclude convictions that otherwise qualified under § 788. As the years passed, the California courts applied *Beagle* more and more rigorously. Some commentators believed that the progeny of *Beagle* essentially limited the scope of § 788 to crimes such as perjury involving dishonesty. Comment, *Proposition 8: California Law After In re Lance W. and People v. Castro*, 12 PEPP. L. REV. 1059, 1101 (1985). Although the line of authority originated in criminal cases, civil practitioners could also invoke the *Beagle* doctrine.

As mentioned in Section B. above, California voters adopted Proposition 8 in 1982. One section of Proposition 8 states: "Any prior felony conviction of any person in any criminal proceeding, whether adult or juvenile, shall subsequently be used without limitation for purposes of impeachment proceeding." CAL. CONST.

ART. 1, § 28(f).

Just as the California Supreme Court refused to read § 788 literally, the court balked at literally interpreting the new language added by Proposition 8. In *People v. Castro*, 38 Cal. 3d 301, 696 P.2d 111, 211 Cal. Rptr. 719 (1985), the court construed Proposition 8. The justices filed several opinions in the case. However, a four-vote majority was mustered for two propositions. Comment, *Proposition 8: California Law After In re Lance W. and People v. Castro, supra,* at 1110. *See also* Imwinkelried & Mendez, *Resurrecting California's Old Law on Character Evidence,* 23 PAC. L.J. 1005, 1017-19 (1992).

- The first proposition is that, even after Proposition 8, § 788 does not authorize the admission of all felonies. The felony must involve moral turpitude. The court quoted Justice Holmes' classic definition of a crime involving moral turpitude as an offense evidencing "the general readiness to do evil" to others. *Id.* at 1105. In determining whether the crime involves moral turpitude, the trial judge must look to the least adjudicated elements of the prior conviction, that is, to the elements of the statutory offense—not to the defendant's actual conduct or to information in the charging document. *See* Chavez & Riggs, *Prior Convictions; Other Bad Acts,* in CALIFORNIA CRIMINAL LAW: PROCEDURE AND PRACTICE § 35.24 at 889 (2d ed. 1994). On the facts in *Castro,* the court held that although possession of heroin for sale involves moral turpitude, simple heroin possession does not. There are now a multitude of lower court decisions determining whether particular crimes involve moral turpitude. *Id.* § 35.24 at 889-91. A list of several of these decisions appears below.
- The second proposition is that even if the crime involves moral turpitude, the trial judge retains discretion under § 352 to exclude the conviction. In another section, Proposition 8 expressly preserves Evidence Code § 352. However, the court added that trial judges were not to use § 352 to reinstate "the rigid black letter rules of exclusion which we had grafted onto the code" after *Beagle.* 38 Cal. 3d at 312, 696 P.2d at 117, 211 Cal. Rptr. at 725. Although Proposition 8 does not apply in civil actions, judges in civil cases may look to *Castro* to help formulate guidelines for judicial weighing under § 352. *Robbins v. Wong,* 27 Cal. App. 4th 261, 32 Cal. Rptr. 2d 337 (1994).

a. Crimes Involving Moral Turpitude

The following crimes have been found to involve moral turpitude:

Arson:
People v. Miles, 172 Cal. App. 3d 474, 218 Cal. Rptr. 378 (1985).

Assault with a deadly weapon:
People v. Thomas, 206 Cal. App. 3d 689, 254 Cal. Rptr. 15 (1988).
People v. Cavazos, 172 Cal. App. 3d 589, 218 Cal. Rptr. 269 (1985).

Assault with intent to commit murder:
People v. Olmedo, 167 Cal. App. 3d 1085, 213 Cal. Rptr. 742 (1985).

Auto theft:
People v. Lang, 49 Cal. 3d 991, 264 Cal. Rptr. 386 (1989).
People v. Zatary, 173 Cal. App. 3d 390, 219 Cal. Rptr. 33 (1985).

Battery upon a police officer:
People v. Lindsay, 209 Cal. App. 3d 849, 257 Cal. Rptr. 529 (1989).
People v. Clarida, 197 Cal. App. 3d 547, 243 Cal. Rptr. 14 (1987).

Burglary:
People v. Muldrow, 202 Cal. App. 3d 636, 248 Cal. Rptr. 89 (1988).
People v. Phillips, 41 Cal. 3d 29, 711 P.2d 423, 222 Cal. Rptr. 127 (1985).

Child molestation:
People v. Massey, 192 Cal. App. 3d 819, 237 Cal. Rptr. 734 (1987).

Child punishment by inhuman corporal means:
People v. Brooks, 3 Cal. App. 4th 669, 4 Cal. Rptr. 2d 570 (1992).

Discharging firearm into inhabited dwelling:
People v. White, 4 Cal. App. 4th 1299, 6 Cal. Rptr. 259 (1992).

Driving with intent to evade pursuing police officers in wanton disregard for the safety of persons or property:
People v. Dewey, 42 Cal. App. 4th 216, 49 Cal. Rptr. 2d 537 (1995).

Escape without force:
People v. Waldecker, 195 Cal. App. 3d 1152, 241 Cal. Rptr. 650 (1987).
People v. Barnett, 17 Cal. 4th 1044, 954 P.2d 384, 74 Cal. Rptr. 2d 121 (1998).

Failure to return to place of confinement:
People v. Lee, 229 Cal. App. 3d 1504, 281 Cal. Rptr. 9 (1991).

False imprisonment:
People v. Cornelio, 207 Cal. App. 3d 1580, 255 Cal. Rptr. 775 (1989).

Felony driving under the influence with 3 or more DUI convictions within 7 years:
People v. Forster, 29 Cal. App. 4th 1746, 35 Cal. Rptr. 2d 705 (1994).

Felony hit-and-run:
People v. Bautista, 217 Cal. App. 3d 1, 265 Cal. Rptr. 661 (1990).

Felony indecent exposure:
People v. Ballard, 13 Cal. App. 4th 687, 16 Cal. Rptr. 2d 624 (1993).

Felony vandalism:
People v. Campbell, 23 Cal. App. 4th 1488, 28 Cal. Rptr. 2d 716 (1994).

Forgery:
People v. Flanagan, 185 Cal. App. 3d 764, 230 Cal. Rptr. 64 (1986).

Keeping a drug house:
People v. Vera, 69 Cal. App. 4th 1100, 82 Cal. Rptr. 2d (1999).

Kidnapping:
People v. Zatary, 173 Cal. App. 3d 390, 219 Cal. Rptr. 33 (1985).

Pimping and pandering:
People v. Jaimez, 184 Cal. App. 3d 146, 228 Cal. Rptr. 852 (1986).

Possession of drugs for sale:
People v. Kwolek, 40 Cal. App. 4th 1521, 48 Cal. Rptr. 2d 325 (1995).
People v. Castro, 38 Cal. 3d 301, 696 P.2d 111, 211 Cal. Rptr. 719 (1985).

Possession of unregistered firearm:
People v. Garrett, 195 Cal. App. 3d 795, 241 Cal. Rptr. 10 (1987).

Prostitution:
People v. Chandler, 56 Cal. App. 4th 703, 65 Cal. Rptr. 2d 687 (1997).

Rape:
People v. Mazza, 175 Cal. App. 3d 836, 221 Cal. Rptr. 640 (1985).
People v. Bonilla, 168 Cal. App. 3d 201, 214 Cal. Rptr. 191 (1985).

Receiving stolen property:
People v. Rodriguez, 177 Cal. App. 3d 174, 222 Cal. Rptr. 809 (1986).

Resisting an executive officer (police officer):
People v. Williams, 72 Cal. App. 4th 1460, 86 Cal. Rptr. 2d 62 (1999).

Robbery:
People v. Hughes, 38 Cal. App. 4th 481, 45 Cal. Rptr. 2d 168 (1995).
People v. Burns, 189 Cal. App. 3d 734, 234 Cal. Rptr. 547 (1987).
People v. Brown, 169 Cal. App. 3d 800, 215 Cal. Rptr. 494 (1985).

Sale of drugs:
People v. Navarez, 169 Cal. App. 3d 936, 215 Cal. Rptr. 519 (1985).

Statutory rape:
People v. Fulcher, 194 Cal. App. 3d 749, 236 Cal. Rptr. 845 (1987)
(*but see People v. Flanagan*, 185 Cal. App. 3d 764, 230 Cal. Rptr. 64 (1986)
[distinction involving good faith belief that minor was of the age of consent]).

Threats to commit a crime involving death or great bodily injury:
People v. Thornton, 3 Cal. App. 4th 419, 4 Cal. Rptr. 2d 519 (1992).

Unlawful driving or taking of a motor vehicle:
People v. Lang, 49 Cal. 3d 991, 264 Cal. Rptr. 386 (1989).

Voluntary manslaughter:
People v. Coad, 181 Cal. App. 3d 1094, 226 Cal. Rptr. 386 (1986).
People v. Partner, 180 Cal. App. 3d 178, 225 Cal. Rptr. 502 (1986).

3. EXTENSION OF THE DOCTRINE TO MISDEMEANOR CONDUCT

In *People v. Wheeler*, 4 Cal. 4th 284, 841 P.2d 938, 14 Cal. Rptr. 2d 418 (1992), the California Supreme Court recognized another of the surprising consequences of Proposition 8. In a criminal case, either side can impeach a witness, not just with felony convictions, but also with conduct that resulted in a misdemeanor conviction, if the conduct involved moral turpitude and if it has a logical bearing on the veracity of the witness. *Id.*, 4 Cal. 4th at 295-97, 14 Cal. Rptr. at 424-25. The trial judge has discretion under § 352, however, to limit or forbid this method of impeachment. *Id.* See also *People v. Cloyd*, 54 Cal. App. 4th 1402, 64 Cal. Rptr. 2d 104 (1997). *Wheeler* adds another bizarre twist: The *underlying conduct* that constitutes the misdemeanor can be proven by competent evidence, but the misdemeanor *conviction itself* cannot be proven. Why not? Because, the court said, the conviction itself is hearsay and does not qualify under any exception to the hearsay rule. *Id.*, 4 Cal. 4th at 297-301, 14 Cal. Rptr. 426-28. (According to the court, felony convictions are admissible over hearsay objection because § 788 supplies its own hearsay exception, but there is no such exception for misdemeanor convictions.) *See generally* Article, *Rush to Judgment: Criminal Propensity Clothed as Credibility Evidence in the Post-Proposition 8 Era of California Criminal Law*, 15 WHITTIER L. REV. 241 (1994); Coleman, *The New Wheeler Case: Witness Impeachment with Prior Misconduct*, CACJ/FORUM, Vol. 20, No. 3, p. 25 (1993).

The dry logic of *Wheeler* is sound, but the result illustrates the mischief done by Proposition 8. To prove the underlying conduct will often be far more time-consuming and distracting than simply to prove the fact of a misdemeanor conviction.

4. APPLYING THE DOCTRINE IN CALIFORNIA

Assume that a witness has testified and that the witness has suffered several felony convictions. Assume, further, that each of the felonies involves moral turpitude. How does the opposing lawyer prove the convictions? And what details about the convictions may the opposing lawyer elicit? The following paragraphs address those issues.

There is no limit to the number or type of prior convictions that can be admitted to impeach a witness. *People v. Johnson*, 233 Cal. App. 3d 425, 284 Cal. Rptr. 579 (1991), *cert. denied*, 503 U.S. 963 (1992). In a criminal case where the defendant testifies on his own behalf, his prior convictions for similar crimes may be used for impeachment, but the potential prejudice must be weighed heavily against admission of the priors. *Id.* Another factor the trial judge may properly consider in deciding whether to exclude a conviction is its age—the longer ago the conviction occurred, the less value it is in assessing the witness's present credibility. Unlike Federal Rule of Evidence 609(b), the California Evidence Code does not contain a presumption that convictions over ten years old are too old to admit. Nonetheless, ten years is an appropriate rough guideline that a trial judge may use in exercising his or her discretion. *People v. Pitts*, 223 Cal. App. 3d 1547, 273 Cal. Rptr. 389 (1990).

How does the opposing lawyer go about proving a felony conviction for impeachment? The opposing lawyer may: (1) cross-examine the witness to be impeached, (2) use extrinsic evidence, or (3) use both cross-examination and extrinsic evidence. The opposing lawyer is not required to lay a foundation on cross-examination as a condition to introducing extrinsic evidence. However, if the opponent does cross-examine the witness and the witness admits having been convicted, the judge may prohibit later use of extrinsic evidence to prove the conviction on the ground that it would be cumulative and a waste of time.

When the opponent resorts to extrinsic evidence, the evidence usually takes the form of an attested or certified copy of the judgment of conviction. A properly attested or certified copy is self-authenticating; the opponent does not need a live, sponsoring witness to authenticate the copy. In rare cases, the opponent will present live testimony such as the testimony of someone who was present in the courtroom when the witness was convicted.

How much detail may the opposing lawyer elicit about a prior felony conviction? Generally, the opposing lawyer may elicit at least the name of the felony, its general nature or elements, and the date and place of the conviction. It is generally not proper, however, to elicit more specific detail about the crime and the surrounding circumstances. *See* Chavez & Riggs, *Prior Convictions; Other Bad Acts*, in CALIFORNIA CRIMINAL LAW: PROCEDURE AND PRACTICE § 35.48 at 892 (2d ed. 1994); *People v. Shea*, 39 Cal. App. 4th 1257, 46 Cal. Rptr. 2d 388

(1995) (other details may become admissible if the defendant attempts to mislead the jury or minimize the facts of the earlier conviction). When admitting evidence of a prior conviction of an identical offense, the court may limit the prosecutor to proving that the defendant was previously convicted of an unspecified felony involving moral turpitude. *People v. Ballard*, 13 Cal. App. 4th 687, 16 Cal. Rptr. 2d 624 (1993).

5. ELEMENTS OF THE FOUNDATION FOR IMPEACHMENT WITH A FELONY CONVICTION

To impeach with a prior felony conviction, the opponent must establish the following foundation:

1. The witness is the person who suffered the felony conviction. The Assembly Committee comment to Evidence Code § 403 states that any evidence sufficient to identify the witness as the person convicted is sufficient to warrant admission of the conviction. *See People v. Theodore*, 121 Cal. App. 2d 17, 28, 262 P.2d 630, 637 (1953) (relying on presumption of identity of person from identity of name). Be careful to review the complete history of the felony conviction. For example, once an Oklahoma conviction had been expunged under that state's statute, "it no longer [was] a viable conviction for impeachment purposes." *People v. Field*, 31 Cal. App. 4th 1778, 37 Cal. Rptr. 2d 803 (1995). A juvenile court adjudication is not considered a conviction. *People v. Renko*, 44 Cal. App. 4th 620, 52 Cal. Rptr. 2d 45, 48 (1996).
2. The conviction is for a felony that involves moral turpitude.
3. The conviction was entered in a certain jurisdiction.
4. The conviction was entered in a certain year.

If the opponent is using a copy of the judgment of conviction, there is another element of the foundation.

5. The copy of the judgment of conviction is authentic.

6. SAMPLE FOUNDATIONS FOR IMPEACHMENT WITH A FELONY CONVICTION

The first sample foundation illustrates cross-examination about a felony conviction. The opponent is the attorney attempting to impeach the witness. The witness is testifying for the plaintiff in a civil action.

O ISN'T IT TRUE THAT you are the same Steven Giles who once was convicted of a felony? (1), (2)
W Yes.
O ISN'T IT A FACT THAT the felony was a robbery? (2)

W Yes.

O ISN'T IT CORRECT THAT you were convicted of that crime in 1998 in New York? (3), (4)

W Yes.

The next foundation illustrates the use of a certified copy of a felony judgment of conviction to impeach. Assume that the witness, Mr. Giles, has already left the stand.

O Your Honor, may this please be marked defense exhibit D for identification?

J It will be so marked.

O Please let the record reflect that I am showing the exhibit to the opposing counsel.

J It will so reflect.

O I now offer defense exhibit D for identification into evidence as defense exhibit D.

P Your Honor, I object on the ground that there's insufficient authentication of this document.

O Your Honor, the exhibit includes a properly executed certificate. The certificate makes the exhibit self-authenticating. (5)

J The objection will be overruled. The exhibit will be received.

O Your Honor, may I read these two sentences to the jury?

J Permission granted. Ladies and gentlemen of the jury, I have just accepted into evidence defense exhibit D. This exhibit is a properly authenticated copy of a judgment of a conviction of crime. You will please bear in mind that the last prosecution witness was Mr. Steven Judson Giles, Jr. You may proceed.

O Ladies and gentlemen, the exhibit reads: "On this day, July 13, 1998, the Supreme Court of the State of New York, Hudson County, the Honorable Paul Lederer presiding, duly found the defendant, Steven Judson Giles, Jr., guilty of the crime of robbery. (1), (2), (3), (4). For this crime, the defendant is hereby sentenced to four years' confinement in the prisons of the State of New York."

7. ELEMENTS OF THE FOUNDATION FOR IMPEACHMENT WITH MISDEMEANOR CONDUCT

The following foundation could be used in a California criminal case where the witness to be impeached has been convicted of a misdemeanor that involves moral turpitude and that demonstrates untruthfulness. *See* the discussion of *Wheeler* in Section J.3., above.

1. The witness to be impeached engaged in conduct that constitutes a misdemeanor.

2. The conduct involved moral turpitude. *See People v. Lee*, 28 Cal. App. 4th 1724, 34 Cal. Rptr. 2d 723 (1994) (if the offense evidences moral turpitude, it is admissible even if the conduct was the subject of a juvenile adjudication so long as the witness has not been released from the penal-

ties and disabilities resulting from the adjudication under California Welfare and Institutions Code § 1772).

3. The conduct has "some logical bearing upon the veracity" of the witness. *Wheeler*, 4 Cal. 4th at 295, 14 Cal. Rptr. at 424.

8. SAMPLE FOUNDATION FOR IMPEACHMENT WITH MISDEMEANOR CONDUCT

The setting is a California criminal case in which witness Wilma Twiggler testified for the prosecution. The defense lawyer, here designated as O, now seeks to impeach her with evidence that, two years ago, she shoplifted some expensive merchandise from a store. Ms. Twiggler was convicted of a misdemeanor and sentenced to eight months in the county jail.

O Ms. Twiggler, you used to live in San Francisco, DIDN'T YOU?

W Yes, that's right.

O You are familiar with Grey & Caughlin, the women's wear shop on Sutter Street in San Francisco, AREN'T YOU?

W Yes.

O Matter of fact, you've gone shopping in that store, HAVEN'T YOU?

P Your Honor, I object on the ground that this is irrelevant.

O May we have a short conference at sidebar, your Honor?

J Yes. Please approach the bench, counsel.

(Sidebar conference.)

J Will defense counsel be good enough to enlighten us on the relevance of this line of questioning?

O Your Honor, two years ago Ms. Twiggler was caught shoplifting expensive merchandise from Grey & Caughlin; she has a misdemeanor conviction that resulted in eight months in county jail. Under *Wheeler*, I'm allowed to explore the underlying conduct; I won't mention the conviction.

P I ask your Honor to exercise her discretion, under Evidence Code § 352, to disallow this line of questioning. Ms. Twiggler had the bad luck to witness the defendant stealing a car. She was public-spirited enough to call the police and now to testify. No earthly purpose can be served by rubbing her nose in this shoplifting incident. How will we ever convince citizens to come forward as witnesses if we give them this kind of treatment?

J I'm sympathetic to that argument, counsel, but shoplifting expensive merchandise does involve moral turpitude and it does bear on the witness's honesty. But I will admonish defense counsel to be quick about it—I see no need to drag this out inch by inch. You may resume your questioning.

O Ms. Twiggler, ISN'T IT TRUE that you shoplifted some property from Grey & Caughlin? (1), (2), (3)

W Yes.

O The item you stole was a $750 silk coat, WASN'T IT? (2), (3)

W Yes.

O You did that only two years ago, DIDN'T YOU? (1)

W Yes.

O I have no further questions at this time, your Honor.

K. PROOF THAT THE WITNESS IS BIASED

1. THE DOCTRINE

Like a conviction, the witness's bias is logically relevant to impeach the witness. Bias may affect the witness consciously or subconsciously. For example, a witness might be prejudiced against persons of the litigant's race, and the prejudice could create a conscious or subconscious bias. The courts grant the opponent great latitude in proving bias. Evidence Code § 780(f) generally permits bias impeachment, and § 722(b) specifically allows the opponent to cross examine an expert witness about the "compensation and expenses paid or to be paid ... by the party calling him. ..."

In fact, the California courts often permit bias impeachment as a method of circumventing other evidentiary rules. For example, there is a general rule that in a civil action, the plaintiff may not prove that the defendant has settled any other claims arising from the same accident. The justification for the rule is that the admission of such evidence would discourage desirable, out-of-court settlements. Suppose, though, that the defendant calls a witness who has settled his or her claim with the defendant. The fact of the settlement is logically relevant and admissible to show the witness's bias in the defendant's favor. The judge could admit the evidence with a limiting instruction. Another illustration is the rule that the plaintiff ordinarily may not prove that the defendant has liability insurance. The admission of such evidence would tempt the jurors to decide the case on an improper basis; they might find in the plaintiff's favor because, in reality, the insurance company will pay the judgment. Assume, however, that the defendant calls one of the insurance company's investigators as a witness. The plaintiff may now prove the defendant's liability insurance. The fact that the witness works for the defendant's liability carrier is logically relevant to show the witness's bias in favor of the defendant. Motive to testify against a defendant can be proved by extrinsic evidence of prior uncharged acts of the defendant. Thus, in *People v. Roberts*, 2 Cal. 4th 271, 826 P.2d 274, 6 Cal. Rptr. 2d 276, *cert. denied*, 113 S. Ct. 436 (1992), the witness testified that his motive for testifying against the defendant was not a payoff offered by the state, but rather that the defendant had put out a contract on the witness's life. A witness may be biased because of fear. *See, e.g., People v. Sanchez*, 58 Cal. App. 4th 1435, 69 Cal. Rptr. 2d 16 (1997) (admitting evidence that members of defendant's gang threatened prosecution witnesses, but acknowledging that evidence about gang membership can be highly prejudicial).

A person might also be biased against the defendant out of a hope for leniency in a case pending against himself. Where an informant witness has offered his information in return for leniency, that is relevant and admissible to show his bias. *People v. Mickle*, 54 Cal. 3d 140, 814 P.2d, 290, 284 Cal. Rptr. 511 (1991), *cert. denied*, 503 U.S. 988 1679 (1992). During pretrial discovery, prosecutors must fully disclose any agreement bearing on a witness's credibility, including the consequences if the witness fails to testify truthfully. The court will exclude any parts of the agreement that do not bear on credibility or that refer to the prosecutor's belief in the witness's veracity. *People v. Fauber*, 2 Cal. 4th 792, 831 P.2d 249, 9 Cal. Rptr. 2d 24 (1992), *cert. denied*, 507 U.S. 1007 (1993).

As with conviction impeachment, the opponent may both cross-examine the witness to be impeached and use extrinsic evidence. On cross-examination, the courts grant the opponent a very wide scope of inquiry. Most jurisdictions require the opponent to lay a foundation on cross-examination as a predicate for extrinsic evidence. These courts reason that as a matter of fairness, the opponent should give the witness an opportunity to explain or deny the impeaching facts. However, California does not require a foundation on cross-examination. 3 WITKIN § 1916, at 1871.

2. ELEMENTS OF THE FOUNDATION

There are no special foundational requirements for bias evidence; the opponent may prove any fact or event logically relevant to show bias. If the impeaching evidence is an event, the foundation usually includes the following elements:

1. Where the event occurred.
2. When the event occurred.
3. Who was present.
4. What occurred.

Some counsel attempt to prove an additional element. They try to get the witness to concede that:

5. The fact or event will tend to bias the witness. Most experienced counsel avoid such attempts. The witness will often not make that concession; and in trying to force the concession, the counsel might seem argumentative. Experienced counsel prefer to invite the jury to draw the inference of bias during closing argument.

3. SAMPLE FOUNDATIONS

The fact situation is a civil suit between Mr. Martinez and Mr. Saltzman. Mr. Martinez calls Mr. Fargo as a witness. After the direct examination, Mr. Saltzman's attorney begins cross-examination. Mr. Saltzman's attorney is the opponent.

O ISN'T IT TRUE THAT on July 4th of last year, you attended a party at Jane Fleming's house? (1), (2)

W Yes.

O ISN'T IT A FACT THAT Ms. Fleming and Mr. Saltzman, the defendant in this case, were at the party? (3)

W Yes.

O ISN'T IT CORRECT THAT during the party, you punched Mr. Saltzman? (4)
W Yes.
O ISN'T IT ALSO TRUE THAT before you left the party, you told Ms. Fleming that you had a strong, personal dislike for Mr. Saltzman? (4)
W Yes.

Assume that the witness had denied the impeaching facts. Then the opponent could present extrinsic evidence such as Ms. Fleming's testimony.

O WHERE were you on the evening of July 4th of last year? (1), (2)
W At my house. I was throwing a party for some friends.
O WHO attended the party? (3)
W There were a lot of people. Mr. Fargo, the last witness, was there. The defendant, Mr. Saltzman, was also in attendance.
O WHAT, if anything, unusual happened during the evening? (4)
W I couldn't believe it, but Mr. Fargo actually punched Mr. Saltzman. They were just standing talking, and all of a sudden Fargo slugged him.
O WHAT happened then? (4)
W I asked Fargo to get out.
O WHAT, if anything, did Mr. Fargo say? (4)
W He said he'd be glad to. He said that he had a strong, personal dislike for Mr. Saltzman and that he, Fargo, wouldn't stay under the same roof as Saltzman. Fargo said if he'd known Saltzman was going to be at the party, he never would have accepted my invitation.

L. PROOF THAT THE WITNESS MADE A PRIOR INCONSISTENT STATEMENT

1. THE DOCTRINE

Suppose that on the morning of January 15 of this year, at the intersection of University and Felton Streets, Mr. Miller's car collided with Ms. Dolan's van. Mr. Miller's car is red, and Ms. Dolan's van is blue. Mr. Williams happened to be standing at a corner of the intersection when the collision occurred. Later that day he had a conversation with his neighbor, Mr. Jensen. During the conversation, he told Mr. Jensen that he witnessed the collision and that the collision occurred because the red car (Mr. Miller's car) ran a red light. Mr. Miller files a personal injury action against Ms. Dolam. At the trial, Mr. Miller calls Mr. Williams as a witness. On direct examination, Mr. Williams testifies that he witnessed the collision and that Ms. Dolan's van caused the accident by running a red light. On cross-examination, may the defense attorney call Mr. Jensen as a defense witness to testify to Mr. Williams' earlier statement?

2. CROSS-EXAMINATION TO ELICIT A WITNESS'S CONCESSION THAT THE WITNESS EARLIER MADE AN INCONSISTENT STATEMENT

As soon as Mr. Williams testifies at the trial, his credibility becomes one of the facts in issue in the case. Common sense suggests that the jury is entitled to know that Mr. Williams made an earlier, inconsistent[1] statement.[2] The fact that he has made inconsistent statements about the same fact calls into question his memory and sincerity. In everyday life, if a person tells us differing stories about the same event, we pause before deciding to believe either story. For that reason, the Evidence Code would permit the defense attorney to cross-examine Mr. Williams about his statement to Mr. Jensen. Sections 769 and 780(h) make it clear that the cross-examination of Williams about the

---

[1] It can be difficult determining whether there is an inconsistency. There need not be a flat, express contradiction; the standard is inconsistency in effect. *People v. Spencer*, 71 Cal. 2d 933, 941, 458 P.2d 43, 50, 80 Cal. Rptr. 99, 106 (1969). Of course, the classic case is the situation in which the witness testifies to *fact A*, but previously asserted *non-A*. All the courts agree that there is sufficient inconsistency in that case. At the polar extreme, suppose that at trial, the witness absolutely refuses to answer questions. Here the prior statement is inadmissible because there is nothing for it to be inconsistent with.

Between these extremes is a gray area that has troubled the courts. Suppose the witness asserts complete lapse of memory or mixes evasive answers and claimed memory lapses. In *People v. Green*, 3 Cal. 3d 981, 92 Cal. Rptr. 494, 479 P.2d 998 (1971), the witness said before trial that the defendant gave him marijuana. At trial, rather than denying that the defendant supplied him with marijuana, the witness gave evasive answers and claimed some memory lapses. The court found that in context, the witness' answers amounted to an implied denial that the defendant furnished marijuana to him. Based on that finding, the court held that there was sufficient inconsistency to allow the prosecutor to impeach the witness with the earlier statement. However, in *People v. Sam*, 71 Cal. 2d 194, 454 P.2d 804, 77 Cal. Rptr. 804, 454 P.2d 700 (1969), all the witness' answers at trial were of the "I cannot remember" variety. The court held that, as in the case of a complete refusal to answer, the witness had for all practical purposes given no testimony. The court therefore forbade the use of earlier statements as prior inconsistent statements. *See also People v. Hawthorne*, 4 Cal. 4th 43, 55-59, 14 Cal. Rptr. 2d 133, 14043, 841 P.2d 118, 125-28 (1992), *cert. denied*, 510 U.S. 1013 (1993). In dictum, *People v. Parks*, 4 Cal. 3d 955, 485 P.2d 257, 95 Cal. Rptr. 193 (1971), states that there is an implied denial if the trial judge finds that the witness is lying in claiming a memory lapse. Such an implied denial creates enough inconsistency to justify the use of prior statements to impeach. In *In re Deon D.*, 208 Cal. App. 3d 953, 256 Cal. Rptr. 490 (1989), the court held that given the balance of the witness' in-court testimony, the witness' refusal to answer certain questions amounted to an implied denial materially inconsistent with his trial testimony. *See also* McWilliams, *Prior Inconsistent Statements*, 3 CAL. DEFENDER 21, 22 (1989); Walla, *When Is a Prior Statement Inconsistent for Purposes of Evidence Code § 1235?*, 4 CAL. DEFENDER 64 (1990); *People v. Arias*, 13 Cal. 4th 92, 913 P.2d 980, 51 Cal. Rptr. 2d 770, 809 (1996) ("When the trial court concludes, on substantial evidence, that … professed lapses of memory are false, evasive devices to avoid truthful answers, it may be admit[ed], as 'inconsistent,' the witness's prior statements describing the events the witness now claims to have forgotten").

[2] Prior inconsistent conduct can also be a basis for impeachment. For example, in some cases, the prosecution may impeach a defense witness by showing the witness 's delay in coming forward with allegedly exculpatory information. *People v. Tauber*, 49 Cal. App. 4th 518, 56 Cal. Rptr. 2d 656, 659-60 (1996).

earlier statement is a proper method of impeachment.

At common law, if Ms. Dolan's attorney forced Williams to concede the earlier statement to Jensen, Mr. Miller's attorney would be entitled to a limiting instruction. In the instruction, the judge would tell the jurors that they could not use Mr. Williams' earlier statement to Jensen as evidence that in fact, Mr. Miller ran a red light; the judge would instruct the jurors that they could consider the evidence only for the limited purpose of deciding whether they want to believe the testimony that it was green. So limited, the evidence would not be subject to a hearsay objection. Quite apart from its truth or falsity, the statement to Jansen is logically relevant; Mr. Williams' credibility is an issue, and the fact that he said one thing at one time and another thing another time about the same subject lowers his credibility. On that reasoning, the common-law courts treated prior inconsistent statements as nonhearsay.

However, in California the impeaching attorney need not be content to offer the prior inconsistent statement for the limited purpose of attacking Williams' credibility. As we shall see in Chapter 9, Evidence Code § 1235 provides that if a statement qualifies as a prior-inconsistent statement of an in-court witness, the statement is admissible as substantive evidence. Hence, under § 1235, Williams' out-of-court statement may be used as evidence that the light was red. The person is available for questioning, and the cross-examiner can ask the witness about both the witness's direct testimony and the witness's earlier statements. Furthermore, the drafters of § 1235 doubted that many jurors can follow a judge's limiting instruction admitting a prior inconsistent statement merely as credibility evidence. [Note that a prior inconsistent statement may be inadmissible as substantive evidence for a reason other than the hearsay rule. For example, in *People v. Macias,* 16 Cal. 4th 739, 941 P.2d 838, 66 Cal. Rptr. 2d 659 (1997), *cert. denied,* 523 U.S. 1084 (1998), the defendant was 16 years old when he killed some people in a car crash. A juvenile fitness hearing was held to determine whether the defendant should be tried as a juvenile or as an adult. In preparation for the hearing, and at the hearing, the defendant made some statements about the crash. Ultimately, he was tried as an adult. For public policy reasons connected to the state and federal privilege against self-incrimination, his prior statements were inadmissible as substantive evidence at his trial. However, at the trial he testified in a manner that was inconsistent with his prior statements. The California Supreme Court held that his prior statements could be used to impeach him, but not as substantive evidence of guilt.]

The opponent seeking to cross examine a witness about a prior inconsistent statement should lay the following foundation:

1. The opponent should get the witness committed to the testimony he gave on direct examination. Unless the opponent does so, the witness may later attempt to explain away the inconsistency by testifying that he or she innocently misspoke. The opponent might attempt to commit the witness by asking directly, ISN'T IT TRUE THAT on direct examination you testified that ...? Many experienced trial attorneys counsel against such direct

questions because they alert the proponent, and often the witness, that the opponent is going to use a prior inconsistent statement. Moreover, on various theories, many trial judges believe that the question is objectionable. In the interests of completeness, we have included the question in the sample foundations, but be aware that this tactic can be dangerous.

2. The witness made an earlier statement at a certain place. (For a written prior inconsistent statement, the place where the witness wrote the document is usually not essential.)

3. The witness made a statement at a certain time.

4. Certain persons were present.

5. The statement was of a certain tenor.

6. The prior statement is more likely to be reliable than the present testimony. In the sample foundations, the opponent attempts to force the witness to concede that the witness's memory was fresher at the time of the inconsistent statement than the memory is at trial. Many experienced counsel prefer not to attempt to force that concession; these counsel elicit the facts about the statement's timing and then argue the relative reliability of the statements during closing argument. These attorneys forgo attempting to force the concession in part because they realize that some judges regard such questions as objectionably argumentative. We have included the question in the sample foundations in the interests of completeness. But, as with element #1, be aware that this tactic can be dangerous.

If the witness made the prior statement at a deposition hearing, the opponent should elicit the following facts: The witness's attorney was present at the deposition (a helpful but not essential condition); a court reporter was also there; the reporter administered an oath to the witness; at the beginning of the deposition, the opposing attorney told the witness that if any question was unclear, the witness should request clarification; the opposing attorney asked whether the witness was experiencing any mental or physical problem that would interfere with testifying at the deposition; the witness assured the attorney that there was none; the reporter later prepared a transcript of the questions and answers at the deposition; the reporter gave the witness a copy of the transcript to review; and the witness signed the transcript without making any changes.

If the statement is written, there is an additional element:

7. If the opponent proposes to hand the writing to the witness, the opponent must first show the writing to the other counsel. The opponent has the choice whether to show the writing to the witness. Evidence Code § 768 reads:

> (a) In examining a witness concerning a writing, it is not necessary to show, read, or disclose to him any part of the writing.

(b) If a writing is shown to the witness, all parties to the action must be given an opportunity to inspect it before any question concerning it may be asked of the witness.

We will now set out two sample foundations. The first foundation is based on the original version of our hypothetical involving Mr. Williams. In this version, the inconsistent statement is oral. In the second version, the inconsistent statement will be a writing. In both cases, the opponent is the defense counsel cross-examining Mr. Williams.

O Mr. Williams, if I correctly understood your testimony on direct examination, my client's car was the car that ran a red light. IS THAT CORRECT? (1)

W Yes.

O ISN'T IT A FACT THAT on the afternoon of the accident, you had a conversation with a Mr. Walter Jensen at your house? (2), (3), (4)

W Yes.

O ISN'T IT CORRECT THAT during that conversation, you discussed the collision between my client's car and the plaintiff's car? (5)

W Right.

O ISN'T IT ALSO TRUE THAT during the conversation, you told Mr. Jensen that it was the defendant's car that had run a red light? (5)

W Yes.

O ISN'T IT A FACT that, in point of time, that conversation was closer to the accident than your testimony today? (6)

W Yes.

O ISN'T IT CORRECT that your memory was fresher then? (6)

W Yes.

P Your Honor, may I please have a limiting instruction that the jurors may use this evidence only in evaluating Mr. Williams' credibility?

O Your Honor, since Mr. Williams is available in court, Evidence Code § 1235 applies, and the jury may use this as substantive evidence.

J I believe the defense counsel is correct. For that reason, I am going to deny the request for a limiting instruction.

Now suppose that Williams made the inconsistent statement in a letter that he mailed to Jensen.

O Mr. Williams, if I correctly understood your testimony on direct examination, my client's car was the car that ran a red light? IS THAT CORRECT? (1)

W Yes.

O Your Honor, may this be marked defense exhibit F for identification?

J It will be so marked.

O Please let the record reflect that I am showing the exhibit to the opposing counsel. (7)

J It will so reflect.

O Mr. Williams, I now hand you defense exhibit F for identification. WHAT is it? (If the exhibit were a deposition transcript, the opponent would show the witness the title page with the witness's name and the signature page with the notary's and the witness's signatures.)

W   It's a letter.

O   ISN'T IT TRUE THAT the letter is in your handwriting?

W   Yes.

O   ISN'T IT A FACT THAT you wrote that letter?

W   Yes.

O   ISN'T IT CORRECT THAT on the day of the collision between my client's car and the plaintiff's car, you wrote that letter at your house? (2), (3)

W   Right.

O   ISN'T IT A FACT THAT you then sent the letter to your friend, Mr. William Jensen? (4)

W   Yes.

O   Let me direct your attention to the third paragraph on page one of the exhibit. (If the exhibit were a deposition transcript, the opponent would specify the page and line numbers: Let me direct your attention to page 13, lines 11 through 20.) Please read that paragraph silently to yourself. ISN'T IT TRUE THAT in that paragraph, you wrote that it was the red car, the plaintiff's car, that ran a red light? (5)

W   Yes.

O   Your Honor, I now offer paragraph three of the exhibit into evidence.

P   Your Honor, this is merely a prior inconsistent statement by a nonparty witness. It can't be admitted as substantive evidence, and I request a jury instruction to that effect.

O   Your Honor, the witness is available for examination. For that reason, under Evidence Code § 1235 this letter can come in as substantive evidence.

J   I agree with the defense attorney. The exhibit will be received.

O   Mr. Williams, ISN'T IT CORRECT THAT, in point of time, the date of the letter was closer to the accident than your testimony today? (6)

W   Yes.

O   ISN'T IT ALSO A FACT THAT your memory was fresher then? (6)

W   Yes.

3. EXTRINSIC EVIDENCE OF A PRIOR INCONSISTENT STATEMENT

In both variations of the hypothetical in the last subsection, the witness obligingly admitted that he made the prior inconsistent statement. When the witness makes that concession, the impeachment is complete. However, if the witness denies the statement, the opponent has a choice. If the statement is in writing and the opponent has not yet shown the writing to the witness, the opponent can immediately confront the witness with the writing and attempt to refresh the witness's memory. Section F of Chapter 9 contains a sample foundation for present recollection refreshed. Alternatively, the opponent may attempt to introduce extrinsic evidence of the inconsistent statement after the witness leaves the stand. Extrinsic evidence, in this context, refers to any other evidence of the inconsistent statement that Ms. Dolan's attorney might offer after Williams leaves the witness stand. For example, if the defense attorney called Mr. Jensen to testify to Williams' oral inconsistent statement, Jensen's testimony would be extrinsic evidence. Or suppose that the defense attorney called another of Mr. Williams' acquaintances, Ms. Bigelow, to identify Williams' handwriting on a written inconsistent statement. Again, the writing would be extrinsic impeachment of Williams. The witness's denial of the inconsistent statement does not make it inadmissible; it is up to the jury to determine the witness's credibility. *People v. Zapien*, 4 Cal. 4th 929, 846 P.2d 704, 17 Cal. Rptr. 2d 122, *cert. denied*, 510 U.S. 919 (1993).

At common law, there were two restrictions on the admissibility of extrinsic evidence of a prior inconsistent statement.

One restriction was the rule that the opponent could present such evidence only if the opponent laid a foundation while cross-examining the witness to be impeached. The theory is that fairness dictates giving the witness an opportunity to explain or deny the impeaching evidence. Common-law judges typically required the cross-examination to mention: the time the statement was made, the place where it was made, the person to whom it was made, and the substance of the statement. The California Evidence Code relaxes the common-law foundational requirement in the following ways. If the opponent is attacking a hearsay declarant's credibility, the Code eliminates any need for a foundation. Evidence Code § 1202 states that an inconsistent statement by the hearsay declarant "is not inadmissible ... though he is not given and has not had an opportunity to explain or to deny such inconsistent statement or ... conduct." If the opponent is attacking an in-court witness's credibility, California Evidence Code § 770(a) allows the use of extrinsic evidence if the witness was cross-examined in a manner that gave him "an opportunity to explain or deny" the prior inconsistent statement. In *People v. Garcia*, 224 Cal. App. 3d 297, 273 Cal. Rptr. 666 (1990), the court said that to satisfy § 770(a), the cross-examination should mention more than one of the following elements: (1) the people involved in the conversation; (2) the time and place of the conversation; and (3) the specific statement that is said to be inconsistent with the witness's trial testimony. In *Garcia*, the cross-examiner asked the witness whether she had "ever told anyone" that she would get the defendant in trouble if he did not give her money. That was insufficient to satisfy § 770(a). Subdivision 770(b) provides that even if there was no foundation on cross, extrinsic evidence of the inconsistent statement is admissible when the witness has not been excused from giving further testimony in the action. Under Evidence Code § 778, the opponent requests that the witness to be impeached be excused subject to recall. If the judge excuses the witness subject to recall, the witness's proponent can later recall the witness to deny the statement or explain away the apparent inconsistency. *See, e.g., People v. Buttles*, 223 Cal. App. 3d 1631, 273 Cal. Rptr. 397 (1990); *People v. Brown*, 35 Cal. App. 4th 1585, 42 Cal. Rptr. 2d 155, 161 (1995) ("the prosecution was entitled to present the evidence of prior statements in one of two ways: By asking Jackson about them and allowing her to explain them, or simply keeping her available for further testimony ...."). Even when there is no foundation on cross and the witness has been permanently excused, the judge retains discretion to admit extrinsic evidence in the interests of justice under § 770.

The California Law Revision Commission comment to § 770 gives this illustration: "[T]he party seeking to introduce the statement may not have learned of its existence until after the witness has left the court and is no longer available to testify."

The common law imposed a further restriction on the admissibility of extrinsic evidence of a prior inconsistent statement. The collateral fact rule decreed that if the statement related to a purely collateral fact, with no relevance to the historical merits, extrinsic evidence was automatically inadmissible. As previously stated, the combined effect of Evidence Code §§ 352 and 780 is to abolish the collateral fact rule in California. Only § 352 remains. If the trial judge believes that the issue is important enough to an assessment of the witness's credibility, the judge may permit the introduction of extrinsic evidence of the prior statement. Unlike the rules for past recollection recorded, where only the adverse party may offer a document into evidence, a document containing an inconsistent statement is admissible no matter which party offers it. *People v. Price*, 1 Cal. 4th 324, 821 P.2d 610, 3 Cal. Rptr. 2d 106 (1991), *cert. denied*, 506 U.S. 851 (1992).

The following three foundations illustrate the presentation of extrinsic evidence of a prior inconsistent statement. For purposes of each foundation, assume that the defense attorney satisfied § 770. Initially suppose that the defense calls Mr. Jensen to testify to Williams' prior, oral inconsistent statement.

O WHERE were you on the afternoon of January 15 of this year? (2), (3)
W At Mr. Williams' house.
O WHO was there? (4)
W Just Mr. Williams and myself.
O WHAT happened while you were there?
W We just talked.
O WHAT did you talk about? (5)
W A lot of things, including the accident he evidently witnessed that morning.
O WHAT did Mr. Williams say about the accident? (5)
W He said that the guy in the red car had clearly caused the accident by running a red light.

In the next variation of the hypothetical, Jensen will authenticate a letter, containing the inconsistent statement, that Williams sent to Jensen.

O Your Honor, may this be marked defense exhibit F for identification?
J It will be so marked.
O Let the record reflect that I am showing the exhibit to the opposing counsel.
J It will so reflect.
O Mr. Jensen, I now hand you defense exhibit F for identification. WHAT is it? (4)
W It's a letter I received.
O WHEN did you receive it? (3)
W It was in January of this year. It arrived in the mail at my apartment. (2)
O WHOSE handwriting is the letter in?
W Mr. Williams'.
O HOW do you know that?

W We've worked together for years in different offices of the same company.

O HOW many times have you seen Mr. Williams' handwriting?

W Hundreds of times. We exchange business memos. Sometimes we'll be at each other's office, and I'll be present when he signs documents.

O HOW familiar are you with his handwriting style?

W Very.

O WHOSE handwriting appears on this letter?

W Mr. Williams'. I'm certain of that.

O Your Honor, I now offer the third paragraph of defense exhibit F for identification into evidence as defense exhibit F.

J It will be received.

O Mr. Jensen, permit me to direct your attention to the second sentence in paragraph three of the exhibit. WHAT does that sentence say? (5)

W It reads: "The guy in the red car ran right through a red light."

O Your Honor, I now request permission to submit the exhibit to the jurors for their inspection.

J Permission granted.

In the final version of the hypothetical, the written statement is in the form of a deposition transcript. The notary public's certificate at the end of the transcript makes the transcript self-authenticating under Evidence Code §§ 1452(f) and 1453(c). "The transcript itself [is] admissible under Evidence Code section 1280, which creates an exception to the hearsay rule ... for official records and writings." *People v. Isais*, 40 Cal. App. 4th 38 n.2, 46 Cal. Rptr. 2d 719, 721 n.2 (1995). After the witness to be impeached leaves the stand, the opponent may request the judge's permission to read the inconsistent passage to the jurors. When the opponent makes the request, the opponent should specify the page and lines to be read. If the transcript has already been filed with the court, there is no need to mark the transcript for identification. However, in many cases, the transcript has not been filed with the court. In that event, the opponent should have the transcript marked for identification:

O Your Honor, I request that this be marked defense exhibit F for identification.

J It will be so marked.

O Please let the record reflect that I am showing the exhibit to the opposing counsel.

J It will so reflect.

O I now offer page eight, lines seventeen through twenty-three, into evidence and request permission to read those lines to the jurors.

J The passage will be admitted, and you may read the passage to the jury.

M.   PROOF THAT THE WITNESS IS DEFICIENT IN THE ABILITY TO OBSERVE, REMEMBER, OR NARRATE

1. THE DOCTRINE

Section A of Chapter 3 listed the elements of competency. To be a competent witness, a person must possess the testimonial qualities of perception, memory, narration, and sincerity. If the opponent can negate one or more of those elements, the person is incompetent; the person cannot testify at all during the trial. However, even if the opponent's evidence does not completely negate one of the elements, the evidence may be logically relevant on an impeachment theory. For example, a color-blind person is a competent witness, but the color blindness is a deficiency that can reduce the value of the witness's testimony.

The courts liberally admit evidence of deficiencies in elements of competency. The courts have admitted evidence that the witness was intoxicated when he or she perceived the event in question, that the witness has a psychiatric disorder affecting his or her testimonial abilities, and that the witness has subnormal intelligence. *See People v. Herring*, 20 Cal. App. 4th 1066, 25 Cal. Rptr. 2d 213 (1993) (borderline mental retardation). The courts' liberality is understandable. Evidence Code § 780(c) explicitly permits the impeaching attorney to attack "[t]he extent of [the witness's] capacity to perceive, to recollect, or to communicate any matter about which he testifies." In spite of this general liberality, courts disfavor the use of psychiatric testimony for impeachment. *People v. Alcala*, 4 Cal. 4th 742, 842 P.2d 1192, 15 Cal. Rptr. 2d 432 (1992), *cert. denied*, 510 U.S. 877 (1993).

Although the courts freely admit evidence impeaching an element of the witness's competency, there are limits. For instance, standing alone, evidence of chronic alcoholism is inadmissible to impeach the witness. Similarly, the opponent cannot offer evidence of drug addiction to impeach the witness unless the opponent is also prepared to present expert testimony that the particular drug in question is likely to affect an element of the witness's competency. *People v. Smith*, 4 Cal. App. 3d 403, 84 Cal. Rptr. 412 (1970); Article, *Impeaching and Rehabilitating a Witness With Character Evidence: Reputation, Opinion, Specific Acts and Prior Convictions*, 9 U.C. DAVIS L. REV. 319, 334 (1976).

As with the last three impeachment methods, the opponent may usually employ either cross-examination or extrinsic evidence. The opponent may also rely on extrinsic evidence and call a psychiatrist to testify that the psychiatrist examined the subject witness and discovered a disorder that calls into question the witness's credibility. Or, on cross-examination, the opponent may attempt to force a witness to concede that he or she was intoxicated at the time of event. The opponent may also cross examine the witness to expose the witness's subnormal intelligence. The opponent may use the "hop, skip and jump" method of cross-examination to do so; the opponent cross examines the witness about a number of events out of chronological sequence. The opponent's hope is that the witness will flounder and the jury will conclude that the witness has a deficient memory. However, many judges believe that subnormal intelligence has relatively little probative value, and they bar extrinsic evidence. The admissibility of extrinsic evidence is entrusted to the judge's discretion under Evidence Code § 352. 3 WITKIN § 1912, at 1867. For example, in *People v. Rodriguez*, 20 Cal. 4th 1, 971 P. 2d 618, 82 Cal. Rptr. 2d 413 (1999), a prosecution witness testified that he saw the murder while he was walking his dog on the roof of his apartment building. The California Supreme Court ruled that the trial judge acted within his discretion in barring one of the two apartment managers from testifying that tenants were not allowed on the roof and that she had not given the witness permission to be up there. The manager's testimony had negligible value in proving that the witness was not in fact on the roof (perhaps with the permission of the other manager, or perhaps with nobody's permission).

An interesting impeachment of a witness's ability to perceive occurred in *People v. Price*, 1 Cal. 4th 324, 821 P.2d 610, 3 Cal. Rptr. 2d 106 (1991), *cert. denied*, 506 U.S. 851 (1992). There, a witness testified that, in his opinion, the defendant was not a violent person. Evidence that the witness dealt in illegal firearms was admitted to show that the witness had an unusual understanding of what it means to be a violent person, thus impeaching his ability to perceive the facts properly.

2. ELEMENTS OF THE FOUNDATION

This impeachment technique often requires proof of a particular historical event such as an occasion when the witness was drunk. The normal foundation will include:

1. Where the event occurred.
2. When the event occurred.
3. Who was present.
4. The alleged defect in the witness's ability to perceive, remember, and relate accurately.
5. The alleged defect may have affected the accuracy of his testimony.

In addition, the technique often requires lay or expert opinion testimony. Chapter 8 illustrates the foundations for lay and expert testimony. When such testimony is necessary, the opponent will also have to establish:

6. The qualifications of the expert, if expert testimony is necessary.
7. The basis for the opinion.
8. The opinion itself.

3. SAMPLE FOUNDATIONS

We will first illustrate cross-examination to attack the witness's ability to perceive the event in question. The fact situation is a tort case arising from a traffic collision. The plaintiff, Ms. Schmitt, sues the defendant, Mr. Jackson. The plaintiff calls a witness, Mr. Malloy. On direct examination, Mr. Malloy testifies that he observed the accident from 150 feet away; he testifies that the defendant swerved into the plaintiff's path. The defendant is the opponent.

O ISN'T IT TRUE THAT on direct examination, you testified that on January 4, at 7:15 p.m. you saw a collision between the plaintiff's and defendant's cars just outside the Sports Arena? (1), (2), (3)

W Yes.

O Mr. Malloy, ISN'T IT CORRECT THAT you are nearsighted? (4)

W Yes.

O ISN'T IT A FACT THAT as a nearsighted person, you have difficulty seeing anything at a distance? (4)

W Yes.

O ISN'T IT CORRECT THAT your doctor has prescribed glasses for you to correct your nearsightedness? (4)

W Yes.

O ISN'T IT ALSO TRUE that when you supposedly saw the collision, you weren't wearing your glasses? (4)

W Yes.

O Finally, ISN'T IT A FACT THAT you were at least 150 feet away from the collision when you supposedly saw it? (5)

W Yes.

Next we turn to an example of extrinsic testimony impeaching a prior witness. Mr. Malloy has left the witness stand. The defendant calls Mr. Thelan. The defendant is still designated the opponent. The defendant is conducting the direct examination of Mr. Thelan.

O WHERE were you on the evening of January 4 of this year? (1), (2)

W I was downtown with Mr. Malloy.

O WHO is Mr. Malloy? (3)

W He's Ed Malloy, the last witness in this case.

O WHAT were you and Mr. Malloy doing? (4)

W We had a bite and some drinks at a bar near the Sports Arena. Then we were going home to our respective wives.

O WHEN did you and Mr. Malloy start drinking? (7)

W At about 5:30 in the early evening.

O HOW many drinks did you have?

W Only one.

O HOW many drinks did Mr. Malloy have? (7)

W He was really putting them away. I'd say he had five before we left.

O WHAT was he drinking? (7)

W   He was having screwdrivers, orange juice and vodka.

O   WHEN did you leave the bar? (7)

W   At about 7. Maybe a little later.

O   WHAT was Mr. Malloy's appearance when you left?

W   His face was a little red.

O   HOW was he acting? (7)

W   Pretty silly. He was stumbling and acting giddy.

O   HOW did his breath smell? (7)

W   He had a strong odor of alcohol on his breath.

O   WHAT was his speech like? (7)

W   It was slurred. He was having trouble pronouncing words.

O   WHAT, if anything, happened after you left the bar?

W   Just down the street a collision occurred.

O   WHAT collision? (7)

W   The collision Ed testified about, the one between the plaintiff and the defendant.

O   WHEN did you see this collision? (5)

W   Maybe five minutes after we left the bar.

O   In your opinion, WHAT was Mr. Malloy's condition when the collision occurred? (5), (8)

W   I hate to say it, but I think he was drunk.

The preceding foundation illustrates lay opinion testimony attacking the witness's credibility. The opponent may also use expert opinion testimony. Section C of Chapter 3 contained a sample foundation for a psychiatrist's testimony. In Chapter 3, the opponent used the testimony to attack the prospective witness's competency. The opponent could use the same foundation to attack the witness's ability to accurately perceive or remember.

Part 3. Rehabilitation After Impeachment

N.   PRIOR CONSISTENT STATEMENT

1. THE DOCTRINE

After the opponent tries to impeach the witness's credibility, the witness proponent may attempt to repair the damage. These attempts are called rehabilitation. One of the most common rehabilitation techniques is proof of a prior consistent statement. The proponent shows that the witness testified to the fact at the time of trial and that witness made a pretrial statement to the same effect. Just as inconsistency can impeach, consistency can rehabilitate. Evidence Code § 780(g) lists proof of a prior consistent statement as a proper method of rehabilitation.

However, the courts do not want trials to bog down with proof of all of the witnesses' pretrial statements. Thus, most jurisdictions impose timing requirements on prior consistent statements. California is no exception. The California timing requirements are found in Evidence Code § 791:

Evidence of a statement previously made by a witness that is consistent with his testimony at the hearing is inadmissible to support his credibility unless it is offered after:

(a) Evidence of a statement made by him that is inconsistent with any part of his testimony at the hearing has been admitted for the purpose of attacking his credibility, and the statement was made before the alleged inconsistent statement; or

(b) An express or implied charge has been made that his testimony at the hearing is recently fabricated or is influenced by bias or other improper motive, and the statement was made before the bias, motive for fabrication, or other improper motive is alleged to have arisen.

The timing requirements under subdivisions (a) and (b) differ; under subdivision (a) the consistent statement must antedate the inconsistent statement while under (b) the statement must antedate the improper motive. Note, *Rehabilitation of the Impeached Witness Through Prior Consistent Statements: An Analysis and Critique of California Evidence Code Section 791*, 50 S. CAL. L. REV. 109, 134 (1976). *See also People v. Johnson*, 3 Cal. 4th 1183, 842 P.2d 1, 14 Cal. Rptr. 2d 702, 719 n.6 (1992), *cert. denied*, 505 U.S. 836 (1993); *People v. Hitchings*, 59 Cal. App. 4th 915, 69 Cal. Rptr. 2d 484 (1997).

2. ELEMENTS OF THE FOUNDATION

Assume that during the cross-examination of the proponent's witness the opposing attorney questioned the witness about a prior inconsistent statement or an improper motive for testifying in the case. The proponent then attempts to introduce a prior consistent statement to rehabilitate the witness's credibility. The statement itself is an event. For that reason, the foundation includes the four normal foundational elements for proof of any event:

1. Where the statement was made.
2. When the statement was made.
3. Who was present.
4. The tenor of the statement.

In addition, if the proponent must comply with a timing requirement, the proponent must show that:

5. The statement preceded (a) the prior inconsistent statement or (b) any motive on the part of the witness to fabricate. In *People v. Andrews*, 49 Cal. 3d 200, 776 P.2d 285, 260 Cal. Rptr. 583 (1989), *cert. denied*, 494 U.S. 1060 (1990), the court discussed the timing requirement. The court stated that in some jurisdictions, to be admissible, the consistent statement must be made before "the existence of any fact which would motivate bias, in-

terest, or corruption on the part of the witness." *Id.* at 211 n.4, 776 P.2d at 291 n.4, 260 Cal. Rptr. at 589 n.4. However, the court held that under § 791, the statement need antedate only "the ... specific motive to fabricate" suggested by the cross-examiner. *Id.* at 210, 776 P.2d at 290, 260 Cal. Rptr. at 588.

3. SAMPLE FOUNDATION

The fact situation is a tort action arising from a collision on December 14. The plaintiff, Mr. Gillis, alleges that the defendant, Ms. Bollack, negligently caused the accident by crossing over into his lane. On direct examination, Mr. Gillis testifies to that effect. On cross-examination, the defense attorney charges that Mr. Gillis fabricated his story. Specifically, the defense attorney asked this question, "ISN'T IT TRUE THAT you never thought of that story until you consulted your attorney, Mr. Clark"? The plaintiff now begins redirect examination. The plaintiff is the proponent.

P   Mr. Gillis, WHAT happened after the accident?
W   The police arrived, and I went down to the nearest station with them.
P   WHERE is the station located? (1)
W   I think it's at the intersection of Elm and Maryland.
P   WHEN did you arrive there? (2)
W   About two hours after the accident. It might have been three in the afternoon.
P   WHO was there? (3)
W   A lot of police officers, myself, and Ms. Bollack.
P   WHO were the officers? (3)
W   There was one named Jorgenson, and then there was Desk Sergeant Allen.
P   WHAT, if anything, did Desk Sergeant Allen do?
W   He questioned me about the accident.
P   Again, on WHAT day did you have this conversation with Desk Sergeant Allen? (2)
W   December 14.
P   WHEN was the first time you ever consulted me about this case? (5)
W   I guess it was three weeks later.
P   So WHICH came first, your conversation with Desk Sergeant Allen or your conversation with me? (5) (Many experienced trial attorneys omit this question. They feel that the timing is obvious and that the question will insult an intelligent judge or juror.)
W   As I just said, my conversation with Allen.
P   WHAT, if anything, did you tell Allen? (4)
W   I told him about the accident. I said that the other driver caused it by coming into my lane. I was minding my own business, and then this car is coming across the lane right at me.

Now assume that in the same fact situation, the defendant attempted a different impeachment technique. On cross-examination, the defendant asked this question, "ISN'T IT TRUE THAT on Christmas Day that year, you told your brother that the accident occurred because your brakes failed"? This question amounts to attempted impeachment by prior inconsistent statement. The foundation would be exactly the same until the last three questions. Now the foundation on redirect would read:

P WHEN did you have the conversation with your brother? (5)

W I'm pretty sure it was on Christmas Day, December 25.

P So WHICH came first, your conversation with Desk Sergeant Allen or your conversation with your brother? (5)

W My conversation with Allen—it was about a week and a half before I saw my brother over the holidays.

P WHAT, if anything, did you tell Allen? (4)

W I told him about the accident. I said that the other driver caused it by coming into my lane. I was minding my own business, and then this car is coming across the lane right at me.

O. PROOF OF THE CHARACTER TRAIT OF TRUTHFULNESS

1. THE DOCTRINE

Many of the impeachment techniques available to the opponent are express or implied attacks on the witness's character. If the opponent calls a character witness to testify to witness #1's character trait of untruthfulness, the testimony is an express attack. If the opponent proves a conviction, there is an implied attack on the witness's character. Even bias impeachment sometimes involves an attack on the witness's character; the proof of bias may be evidence of a corrupt financial motive. In all these cases, under Evidence Code §§ 780(e) and 790, the judge will permit the proponent to rehabilitate by proving a character trait of truthfulness. The sequence would be the following. The proponent, perhaps the plaintiff, calls witness #1 to testify about the historical merits of the case. The opponent then calls witness #2, a character witness; witness #2 testifies that witness #1 has a reputation for untruthfulness. To rehabilitate witness #1, the proponent calls witness #3, another character witness. Witness #3 contradicts witness #2; witness #3 testifies that witness #1 has a good reputation for truthfulness.

In general, the rules governing the opponent's character evidence also apply to the proponent's character evidence. Section F of this chapter outlines those rules. There is only one other point the proponent should bear in mind: Trial judges tend to restrict the proponent's character evidence to the same type, time, and community as the opponent's evidence. If the opponent used reputation evidence, the judge may not permit the proponent to use opinion evidence. The judge may also limit the proponent's character evidence to roughly the same time period and community as the opponent's evidence. If the opponent presented character evidence about the witness's reputation in Sonoma within the past five years, the judge might exclude the proponent's character evidence relating to the witness's reputation in Irvine ten years before. The courts do not want trials to bog down in collateral disputes over a witness's credibility. The proponent should respond in kind to the opponent's attacks on the witness's credibility.

As indicated above, Evidence Code § 790 is the primary source for the restrictions on the admissibility of evidence logically relevant to a witness's character trait of truthfulness. Under § 790, the witness's proponent may not resort to such evidence "unless evidence of [the witness's] bad character has [already] been admitted for the purpose of attacking his credibility." That restriction still obtains in civil cases. However, the restriction no longer applies in criminal cases. In *People v. Taylor*, 180 Cal. App. 3d 622, 225 Cal. Rptr. 733 (1986), the court held that Proposition 8 effected a pro tanto repeal of § 790 as respects criminal cases. In that case, the court held that the defense could offer evidence of the defendant's reputation for truth and veracity even before the prosecution had attempted to impeach the defendant's character trait for truthfulness. In *People v. Harris*, 47 Cal. 3d 1047, 1081, 767 P.2d 619, 640, 255 Cal. Rptr. 352, 373 (1989), the California Supreme Court agreed with the *Taylor* decision.

2. ELEMENTS OF THE FOUNDATION

The foundational elements are generally the same as in Section G of this chapter.

3. SAMPLE FOUNDATION

With one exception, the foundations are the same as in Section G. The exception is that the final answers will be favorable to witness #1 rather than unfavorable. Thus, the reputation foundation would end in this fashion.

P WHAT is the reputation? (4)
W It's good. He's known as a truthful person.
P Given Mr. Harding's reputation, would you believe him under oath? (5)
W Yes.

The opinion foundation would conclude in this fashion:

P WHAT is that opinion? (4)
W In my opinion, he's a truthful person.
P Given that opinion, would you believe Mr. Harding under oath? (5)
W Yes.

P. EXPERT TESTIMONY EXPLAINING AWAY A SEEMINGLY IMPEACHING FACT

The California courts have recognized that expert testimony may be admissible to rehabilitate a witness's credibility. Suppose, for instance, that the witness is the complainant in a child sex abuse prosecution. The witness either delays initially reporting the offense or recants the report. Relying on general notions of typical victim behavior, the lay jurors are likely to treat the delay or recantation as an impeaching act. Comment, *The Admissibility of "Child Sexual Abuse Accommodation Syndrome" in California Criminal Courts*, 17 PAC. L.J. 1361, 1366 (1986). However, there is empirical evidence that, especially when abuse occurs in the family setting, delays and recantations commonly occur. Id. at 1367. Expert testimony, reviewing the empirical evidence, can assist the trier of fact to evaluate the witness's credibility. The evidence usually takes the form of testimony about the Child Sexual Abuse Accommodation Syndrome. This type of expert testimony must be narrowly tailored to address only the credibility issues. *People v. Gilbert*, 5 Cal. App. 4th 1372, 7 Cal. Rptr. 2d 660 (1992).

On the one hand, the California courts have refused to admit this testimony as substantive proof that abuse has occurred. *People v. Archer*, 215 Cal. App. 3d 197, 205 n.2, 263 Cal. Rptr. 486, 490 n.2 (1989). On the other hand, the courts have permitted prosecutors to offer the testimony to rehabilitate a witness's credibility. *People v. Sanchez*, 208 Cal. App. 3d 721, 256 Cal. Rptr. 446, *cert. denied*, 493 U.S. 921 (1989); Carter, *Admissibility of Expert Testimony in Child Sexual Abuse Cases in California: Retire Kelly-Frye and Return to a Traditional Analysis*, 22 LOY. L.A. L. REV. 1103 (1989). The courts have imposed the following conditions on the admissibility of CSAAS testimony:

1. There must be a genuine issue as to the witness's credibility.
2. The prosecutor must identify the myth or misconception about victim behavior that the testimony is designed to rebut. *People v. Sanchez, supra*, 208 Cal. App. 3d at 735, 256 Cal. Rptr. at 454.
3. The testimony itself must focus on that myth or misconception. *People v. Bergschneider*, 211 Cal. App. 3d 144, 259 Cal. Rptr. 219, 227 (1989).
4. The court must instruct the jury sue sponte that the expert's testimony is not intended and should not be used to determine whether the victim's claim is true. *People v. Bowker*, 203 Cal. App. 3d 385, 249 Cal. Rptr. 886 (1988); *People v. Housley*, 6 Cal. App. 4th 947, 8 Cal. Rptr. 2d 431 (1992).

The courts have not confined the use of rehabilitative expert testimony to the admission of CSAAS evidence. In *People v. Stark*, 213 Cal. App. 3d 107, 261 Cal. Rptr. 479 (1989), the defendant was charged with forcible sexual conduct with a child under the age of fourteen. During his testimony, the complainant had difficulty describing the chronology of events. To rehabilitate the complainant's credibility, the prosecutor introduced a school psychologist's testimony. The psychologist testified that although the child was not retarded, he had a learning disability affecting his ability to sequence events and place events in chronological order. The court held that the testimony had been properly admitted under Evidence Code § 780(c).

Chapter 6

LIMITATIONS ON EVIDENCE THAT IS RELEVANT TO THE MERITS OF THE CASE

A.   INTRODUCTION

In the last chapter, we saw that the dangers listed in Evidence Code § 352 can lead to the exclusion of evidence that is logically relevant to the witnesses' credibility. The "legal relevance" doctrine codified in § 352 is not limited to credibility evidence; the doctrine can also apply to evidence that is logically relevant to the historical merits.

The premier danger noted in § 352 is prejudice. In this context, "prejudice" means the evidence's tendency to tempt the jury to decide the case on an improper, usually emotional, basis. For instance, in a homicide prosecution, gruesome photographs of the victim could be excluded if, after viewing them, the jurors could no longer dispassionately evaluate the evidence of guilt or innocence. Most of the types of evidence analyzed in this chapter present the danger of prejudice. Several sections discuss evidence of other misdeeds by a criminal defendant. Such evidence creates a risk that the jurors will convict, not because they are convinced beyond a reasonable doubt of the defendant's commission of the charged crime, but rather because they conclude that the defendant is a bad person who should be behind bars. Evidence of a civil defendant's liability insurance raises a similar danger. Although the evidence of liability may be weak, the jurors may return a plaintiff's verdict because they assume the insurer—the "deep pocket"—will absorb the economic loss.

Simply stated, § 352 embodies the doctrine that the trial judge may exclude logically relevant evidence if, in his or her judgment, the evidence's dangers outweigh its probative value. The judge's application of the doctrine involves several steps. At the outset, the trial judge must determine the probative value of the evidence. How clear is the evidence? How strong is the logical link between the evidence and the fact it is offered to prove? How positive is the witness? These are just some of the questions the judge asks in evaluating probative value. Then the judge identifies the countervailing dangers and finally balances the probative value against the dangers.

Counsel who seeks to have evidence excluded under § 352 should carefully explain to the trial judge, in specific terms, *why* the probative value of the evidence is low, and *why* it is likely to be prejudicial, or *why* it is likely to confuse the issues, mislead the jury, or consume too much time. Further, a judge who uses § 352 to exclude relevant evidence should clearly indicate on the record that he or she has used the balancing test envisioned in § 352 and is exercising the judicial discretion that § 352 contemplates. No special "magic words" are necessary, so long as the record makes clear that the judge did weigh the probative value of the evidence against its dangers and did exercise discretion in favor of exclusion. *See In re Romero C.*, 33 Cal. App. 4th 1838, 40 Cal. Rptr. 2d 85 (1995); *People v. Triplett*, 16 Cal. App. 4th 624, 20 Cal. Rptr. 2d 225 (1993).

The trial judge's discretion under § 352 is broad but not boundless. *Vorse v. Sarsay*, 53 Cal. App. 4th 998, 62 Cal. Rptr. 2d 164 (1997) illustrates a trial judge's misuse of § 352. In *Vorse*, the plaintiff claimed that he and the defendant, together with a non-party named Schmidt, had formed a three-person partnership to purchase a certain business. The defendant later bought the business for his own account, and the plaintiff cried foul. The defendant asserted that the alleged partnership never existed. Schmidt, the non-party, was obviously a key witness, but his pretrial declaration, his deposition, and his trial testimony strongly suggested that the truth was nowhere in him. Midway in Schmidt's trial testimony, counsel met privately with the trial judge concerning a quarrel about Schmidt's pretrial declaration. Instead of resolving the quarrel, the trial judge dismissed Schmidt as a witness and struck his testimony from the record, instructing the jury:

> Ladies and gentlemen, I have discharged the witness. I found that Mr. Schmidt's testimony was not to be believed, and I therefore have stricken it. And I am going to instruct you not to consider anything to which he testified. ... [A]s to what he testified to orally, all of it is to be stricken from your minds.

The Court of Appeal reversed the trial judge, stating that she had misapplied § 352 and misconstrued her role in the fact-finding process. "Prejudice," the appeals court said, does not mean simply "damaging." Every piece of relevant evidence damages the opponent's case, or shores up the proponent's case—that is what makes it relevant. Section 352 is directed to evidence that damages *unfairly*, evidence that evokes "an emotional bias" against one's opponent, or evidence that tempts the jury to prejudge a person or cause on the basis of extraneous factors. *Id.*, 53 Cal. App. 4th at 1008-09, 62 Cal. Rptr. 2d at 170. Schmidt's testimony, if true, would have unusually high probative value, because he was the only non-party who knew whether there was or wasn't a partnership. It was up to the jury, not the trial judge, to determine whether Schmidt's testimony was true or false. In dictum, the appeals court suggested that a trial judge might properly use § 352 to exclude the in-court testimony of a witness if the testimony were "physically impossible" or if "its falsity is apparent without resorting to inferences or deductions." *Id.*, 53 Cal. App. 4th at 1011, 62 Cal. Rptr. 2d at 172. Except in those rare cases of "demonstrable falsity," the credibility of in-court testimony should be left to the jury. *Id.*

For some types of evidence, such as inflammatory photographs, the doctrine codified in § 352 remains highly discretionary. Trial judges resolve the questions case-by-case. *See, e.g., People v. Wilson*, 3 Cal. 4th 926, 838 P.2d 1212, 13 Cal. Rptr. 2d 259 (1992), *cert. denied*, 507 U.S. 1006 (1993). For other types of evidence, including most of those examined in this chapter, relatively rigid rules have evolved.

B.   CHARACTER EVIDENCE

Section G of Chapter 5 discussed evidence of a witness' character trait of truthfulness. Under that theory of admissibility, the opponent uses the witness' character trait of untruthfulness as circumstantial proof of the witness' conduct— lying on the witness stand. We now turn to character evidence on the historical merits of the case. Much of what we said about character on a credibility theory applies here as well. Once again, we are ordinarily using character as circumstantial evidence of conduct. For example, a criminal defendant may introduce testimony that she is a moral, law-abiding person. The defendant wants the jury to infer that if she is that type of person, she would not commit the crime in question. Wydick, *Character Evidence: A Guided Tour of the Grotesque Structure*, 21 U.C. DAVIS L. REV. 123 (1987). Or, in a prosecution for assault, the defendant may introduce evidence that the victim is an aggressive person. The defendant wants the jury to infer that the victim was the aggressor in the fray. Distinguish these situations from the case in which the evidence of the third party's acts is offered to prove the defendant's state of mind rather than the conduct. For example, in a self-defense case, a defendant might offer testimony of threats by third parties associated with the alleged victim in order to establish the defendant's fear. *People v. Minifie*, 13 Cal. 4th 1055, 920 P.2d 1337, 56 Cal. Rptr. 2d 133, 139 (1996). The character evidence prohibition is inapplicable in this case.

The rules governing character evidence on the merits resemble the rules for character evidence of untruthfulness in another respect: the methods of proof. In Chapter 5 you learned that the opponent who presents evidence of the witness' character trait of untruthfulness is usually restricted to reputation and opinion evidence. The same restriction usually applies to character evidence on the historical merits. Thus, under Evidence Code § 1102 the criminal defendant is limited to reputation or opinion evidence of moral, law-abiding character. The major difference in methods of proof is that when the defendant places in issue the character of the victim of an offense, Evidence Code § 1103 (a) permits the defendant to prove specific instances of the victim's conduct.

There are several other differences between the credibility theory for character evidence and the use of character evidence on the historical merits. The following questions highlight those differences.

Whose character is relevant? On a credibility theory, the character of any witness in any type of case can be relevant. Once the person takes the witness stand and gives any testimony in the case, his or her credibility becomes a material fact of consequence. On a character theory on the merits, the rules are quite different. The following statements are over-simplifications, but it is generally true that: (1) due to Evidence Code § 1104, character evidence is inadmissible in civil cases as circumstantial proof of conduct on the merits (*Hinson v. Clairemont Community*

Hosp., 218 Cal. App. 3d 1110, 267 Cal. Rptr. 503 (1990)) and (2) in criminal cases, character evidence is admissible as circumstantial proof of the conduct of only the defendant and the alleged victim.

What part of the person's character is relevant? On a credibility theory, the only relevant character trait is truthfulness. In contrast, on a character theory on the merits, we are usually interested in other parts of the person's character. If the person is the criminal defendant, we may be interested in the defendant's general, moral, law-abiding character. Or we may focus on a specific character trait relevant to the offense, such as peacefulness in an assault prosecution, or honesty in a theft prosecution. Evidence Code § 1102 gives the proponent of character evidence a choice; the proponent may offer evidence of general "character or a (specific relevant) trait of his character. ..."

Finally, when does the person's character become relevant? On a credibility theory, the witness' character trait of truthfulness becomes relevant as soon as the witness gives any testimony in the case. However, in a criminal case, only the defendant may initiate an inquiry into his character as circumstantial evidence of his innocence. The defendant does not initiate that inquiry simply by taking the witness stand. The defendant can initiate the inquiry by presenting proper reputation or opinion testimony under § 1102(a). Alternatively, the defendant can initiate the inquiry by offering objectionable testimony and going into great detail on direct examination about specific instances of good conduct. In either event, after the defense has initiated the inquiry, the prosecution may present rebuttal evidence under § 1102(b). *See, e.g., People v. Morris*, 53 Cal. 3d 152, 807 P.2d 949, 279 Cal. Rptr. 720, *cert. denied*, 502 U.S. 959 (1991).

1. REPUTATION CHARACTER EVIDENCE

The foundation for reputation character evidence on the historical merits is strikingly similar to the foundation for reputation character evidence on credibi lity:

1. The witness is a member of the same community (residential, business, or social) as the defendant. Reputation is a form of aggregate hearsay. One of the hearsay provisions of the Code, § 1324, permits evidence of the defendant's reputation "in the community in which he ... resided or in a group with which he ... habitually associated. ..." In *Orloff v. Los Angeles Turf Club*, 36 Cal. 2d 734, 739, 227 P.2d 449, 453 (1951), the court stated that "evidence of reputation ... may not be shown by witnesses conducting an inquiry. ..." Compare 1 WITKIN § 329, at 301 with 3 WITKIN § 1937, at 1892 (discussing *Rios v. Chand*, 130 Cal. App. 2d 833, 280 P.2d 47 (1955)).

2. The witness has been associated with the community or group for a substantial period of time. In *People v. Pauli*, 58 Cal. App. 594, 596, 209 P. 88, 89 (1922), the court commented that residence in the community for "a few months" might not suffice.

3. The defendant has a reputation for: (a) general, moral, law-abiding character; or (b) a specific, relevant character trait.
4. The witness knows the reputation. Negative evidence is admissible; it is sufficient if the witness testifies that he has never heard a derogatory remark about the defendant's character or character trait. 1 WITKIN, § 328, at 301.
5. The witness states the reputation.

Our fact situation is an assault prosecution. The People have charged Mr. Lowe with a violent assault. During its case-in-chief, the defense calls Mr. Nieman as a character witness. Mr. Nieman has already identified himself. The defense is the proponent.

P   WHO is Mr. Lowe?
W   He's a neighbor of mine.
P   WHEN is the last time you saw him?
W   He's in the courtroom right now.
P   WHERE is he sitting?
W   He's sitting there at the table with you.
P   HOW is he dressed?
W   He's wearing a brown suit and yellow tie.
P   Your Honor, may the record reflect that the witness has identified my client, Mr. Lowe?
J   The record will so reflect.
P   Mr. Nieman, WHERE does Mr. Lowe live? (1)
W   Here in Anaheim.
P   WHERE do you live? (1)
W   I also reside in Anaheim.
P   HOW close do you live to Mr. Lowe? (1)
W   No more than half a block away.
P   HOW long has Mr. Lowe lived in Anaheim? (2)
W   I'd say easily seven years.
P   HOW long have you lived in Anaheim? (2)
W   For the past ten years.
P   Does Mr. Lowe have a reputation for violence or peacefulness in Anaheim? (Or) Does Mr. Lowe have a reputation as a law-breaking or law-abiding person in Anaheim? (3)
W   Yes.
P   Do you know that reputation? (4)
W   Yes.
P   HOW well do you know that reputation? (4)
W   Real well. I've been around many times when his name has come up in a conversation.
P   WHAT is that reputation? (5)
W   He's known as a peaceful person. (Or) He's known as a moral, law-abiding person.

Notice that at the end of this line of questioning, the proponent did not attempt to elicit the witness's testimony that given Mr. Lowe's character, it is less probable that Lowe committed the charged violent assault. That testimony would be inadmissible under the opinion rules. It is unnecessary for the proponent to invite the witness to draw that inference; the judge's subsequent instruction will tell the jury that it may draw that inference, and during summation the proponent may expressly argue in favor of the inference.

When this testimony is admitted, or during the final jury charge, on either or both occasions the judge might tell the jury something like this: "Evidence has been received for the purpose of showing the good character of the defendant for those traits involved in the commission of a crime, of the kind charged here. Good character for the traits involved in the commission of the crime charged may be sufficient by itself to raise a reasonable doubt as to the guilt of a defendant. It may be reasoned that a person of good character as to such traits would not be likely to commit the crime with which the defendant is charged."

During closing argument, the defense attorney could state:

"Ladies and gentlemen, during the trial you heard the testimony of Mr. Nieman. As you'll recall, Mr. Neiman is one of Mr. Lowe's neighbors. They've been neighbors for the better part of a decade; as Mr. Neiman told you, they've both lived in Anaheim for over seven years. Mr. Neiman took the stand and told you that Mr. Lowe has an excellent reputation for peacefulness. In Mr. Neiman's words, Mr. Lowe 'is known as a peaceful person.'

"In a few minutes her Honor will read you the legal instructions that you have to follow during your deliberations. She's going to tell you that in deciding Mr. Lowe's guilt or innocence, you can consider this evidence of Mr. Lowe's good character. In particular, her Honor will instruct you along these lines:

Good character for the traits involved in the commission of the crime charged may be sufficient by itself to raise a reasonable doubt as to the guilt of a defendant. It may be reasoned that a person of good character would not be likely to commit the crime with which the defendant is charged.

Ladies and gentlemen, that instruction makes a lot of sense. Every day in the real world, you make decisions about people based on their character. If they have a bad reputation, you think twice; but if they have a good reputation, you give them the benefit of the doubt. If a person has a good character, it would be 'out of character' for them to violate the law. The uncontradicted evidence in this case—Mr. Nieman's testimony—shows you that Mr. Lowe has an unblemished reputation as a peaceful person. A person has to work hard all his life to earn a good reputation, and you just don't throw away your good name for no reason. Remember what Shakespeare told us:

Who steals my purse steals trash;
But he that filches from me my good name
Robs me of that which not enriches him,
And makes me poor indeed.

The People have charged Mr. Lowe with an assault, a violent offense. Mr. Lowe simply isn't the kind of man who would commit that type of crime; he's a man with an excellent reputation as a peaceful person. And remember again that in her Honor's words, good character 'may be sufficient by itself to raise a reasonable doubt as to the guilt of a defendant.'"

2. OPINION CHARACTER EVIDENCE

This foundation is very similar to the foundation for opinion character evidence on credibility:

1. The witness is personally acquainted with the defendant.
2. The witness knows the defendant well enough to have formed a reliable opinion of the defendant's character. *People v. Harris*, 270 Cal. App. 2d 863, 76 Cal. Rptr. 130 (1969), holds that a one-month acquaintanceship is an inadequate basis for an opinion.
3. The witness has an opinion of the defendant's character. While opinion is usually based on specific observation of conduct, it can also be based on failure to observe conduct. Thus, observations of a person's consistently normal behavior around children can support the opinion that the person does not have the character of a child molester. *People v. McAlpin*, 53 Cal. 3d 1289, 812 P.2d 563, 283 Cal. Rptr. 382 (1991).
4. The witness states his or her opinion.

Assume the same hypothetical assault prosecution.

P WHO is Mr. Lowe? (1)
W He's a neighbor of mine.
P WHEN is the last time you saw him? (1)
W He's in the courtroom right now.
P WHERE is he sitting? (1)
W He's sitting right there at the table with you.
P HOW is he dressed? (1)
W He's wearing a brown suit and yellow tie.
P Your Honor, please let the record reflect that the witness has identified my client, Mr. Lowe.
J It will so reflect.
P Mr. Nieman, WHERE does Mr. Lowe live? (2)
W Here in Anaheim.
P HOW long has he lived here? (2)
W I'd say easily seven years.

P WHERE do you live? (2)

W I also reside in Anaheim.

P HOW close do you live to Mr. Lowe? (2)

W No more than half a mile away.

P HOW long have you lived in Anaheim? (2)

W Over ten years.

P HOW long have you known Mr. Lowe? (2)

W I guess seven years—ever since he moved here.

P HOW did you come to know Mr. Lowe? (2)

W We have several mutual acquaintances, and we both are members of some local clubs, including the Optimists.

P HOW often do you see Mr. Lowe? (2)

W At least once or twice each week.

P HOW well do you know him? (2)

W I consider him a good, close friend.

P Do you have an opinion whether he is a violent or peaceful person? (Or) Do you have an opinion whether he is a law-breaking or law-abiding person? (3)

W Yes.

P WHAT is your opinion? (4)

W In my opinion, he is a peaceful person. (Or) In my opinion, he is a moral, law-abiding person.

The above foundation illustrates lay opinion testimony. Assuming that it meets all the requirements discussed in Chapter 8 on opinion evidence, expert opinion testimony is also admissible. Evidence Code § 1102 uses the generic term "opinion" without differentiating between lay and expert opinions. Before the adoption of the Evidence Code, *People v. Jones*, 42 Cal. 2d 219, 266 P.2d 38 (1954), held that in a sexual offense prosecution, the defense could offer expert psychiatric testimony that the defendant was not a sexual psychopath. The California Law Revision Commission note to § 1102 approvingly cites *Jones*. The California Supreme Court expressly reaffirmed *Jones* in *People v. Stoll*, 49 Cal. 3d 1136, 1153, 1158, 783 P.2d 698, 708, 712, 265 Cal. Rptr. 111, 121, 125 (1989) (a psychologist's testimony that the defendant did not display signs of deviance or abnormality).

After presenting opinion character testimony, the defense counsel could request an instruction like the one set out previously in section B.1. addressing reputation evidence. The defense counsel could also deliver a summation similar to the one illustrated in section B.1. However, a summation discussing opinion evidence would differ slightly from the one discussing reputation evidence. To begin with, the defense attorney would substitute references to opinion for every mention of reputation. Moreover, the attorney would stress that Mr. Nieman knows Mr. Lowe well:

"Mr. Nieman isn't just a passing acquaintance of Mr. Lowe. Mr. Nieman knows him well. The undisputed evidence shows that Mr. Nieman has lived a few blocks from Mr. Lowe for over seven years. They have mutual friends, and they belong to some of the same organizations. In Mr. Nieman's words, they see each other 'at least once or twice each week.' Mr. Nieman knows Mr. Lowe--he knows the type of man Mr. Lowe is. That's why you ought to believe Mr. Nieman when he tells you that Mr. Lowe is not the kind of person who would commit this type of crime."

3. PROOF OF CHARACTER BY SPECIFIC INSTANCES OF CONDUCT

In rare cases, a person's character can itself be a material fact in the case. Assume, for instance, that the plaintiff alleges that the defendant employer negligently entrusted a large truck to an employee driver and that the employee then carelessly collided with the plaintiff. In a negligent entrustment cause of action, the plaintiff must plead and prove that, by character, the employee was a careless driver. In this circumstance, Evidence Code § 1103 permits the parties to prove character by reputation, opinion, and specific acts. A person's character is almost never a material fact during the guilt phase in a criminal case. In *Robinson v. California*, 370 U.S. 660, 666 (1962), the Supreme Court held that the eighth amendment prohibition of cruel and unusual punishment forbids a legislature from criminalizing a status. Consequently, status offenses are unheard of in adult prosecution. Juvenile court is the only setting in which a practitioner is likely to encounter a status offense. *In re Dennis J.*, 72 Cal. App. 3d 755, 140 Cal. Rptr. 463 (1977), superseded in other respects by California Welf. & Inst. Code § 202, as amended in 1984 and 1989.

Evidence Code § 1102 applies when the parties to a criminal case are using character as circumstantial proof of a person's conduct. That section limits the defense and prosecution to reputation and opinion testimony. However, when the person is the victim in a criminal case, § 1103 applies. Subdivision 1103(a) governs when the parties are attempting to prove the victim's nonsexual conduct. Suppose, for example, that a defendant is charged with a violent crime. The defendant may attempt to prove the victim's violent character. The logical relevance is that if the victim has a violent character, that makes it more likely that the victim threw the first punch. Subdivision 1103(a) permits the defense to use the victim's character as circumstantial proof of conduct, and the subdivision allows the defense to resort to specific instances of conduct as well as reputation and opinion. Once the defense has offered such evidence, the prosecution may respond under § 1103(a)(2).

In 1990, the legislature amended § 1103 to prohibit proof of the victim's character by specific instances of conduct. That change proved to be mischievous. The legislature learned of one case in which a woman who was charged with killing her brutal boyfriend was barred from offering the testimony of his former girlfriend that he had once beat her badly enough to cause a miscarriage. In 1991, the legislature amended § 1103 again to restore proof of the victim's character by specific instances of conduct. Further, under the 1991 amendment, if the defendant offers evidence of the victim's violent character, the prosecutor may rebut with evidence that the defendant also has a violent character. *See, e.g., People v. Halsey*, 12 Cal. App. 4th 885, 16 Cal. Rptr. 2d 47 (1993). Section 1103 does not allow evidence of the defendant's character in every case where the defendant claims self-defense. Rather, such evidence may be introduced only when the defendant presents evidence of the victim's violent character to show his reasonable response to the victim's violence. *People v. Blanco*, 10 Cal. App. 4th 1167, 13 Cal. Rptr. 2d 176 (1992).

The elements of the foundation are:

1. Where the event occurred.
2. When the event occurred. The act may even have occurred after the crime the defendant is charged with. *People v. Shoemaker*, 135 Cal. App. 3d 442, 185 Cal. Rptr. 370 (1982).
3. Who was involved?
4. What happened—namely, a violent act by the alleged victim.
5. The circumstances indicating that on the prior occasion, the alleged victim was the aggressor.

Assume that the People charge Mr. Lowe with assaulting Mr. Gilligan on December 1st of last year. During the defense case-in-chief, the defense calls Mr. Nieman as a witness. Mr. Nieman has already identified himself. The defense is the proponent.

P WHERE were you on the evening of December 1st of last year? (1), (2)
W I was at Tarantino's restaurant in downtown Sausalito.
P WHY were you there?
W I was attending a party.
P WHO else was there? (3)
W A number of people, including Mr. Gilligan.
P WHO is Mr. Gilligan? (3)
W He's the complaining witness in this case.
P WHEN did you last see him? (3)
W About an hour ago.
P WHERE was he? (3)
W He was in this courtroom.
P WHAT was he doing? (3)
W He was testifying for the prosecution.
P WHAT, if anything, happened at this party at the restaurant? (4)
W Mostly we just had a good time. There was one unfortunate incident.
P WHAT was that? (4)
W There was a fight.
P WHO was involved in the fight? (4)
W Mr. Gilligan and a Mr. Jones.
P WHERE were you when the fight started? (5)
W I was standing only a few feet away.
P HOW well could you see what happened? (5)
W Very well. I was standing right next to both of them when the fight started.

P HOW did the fight start? (5)
W They were just talking, and then Mr. Gilligan started screaming at Mr. Jones.
P HOW loudly was he screaming? (5)
W At the top of his voice.
P WHAT happened then? (5)
W Mr. Gilligan punched Mr. Jones.
P WHO threw the first punch? (5)
W Mr. Gilligan.
P HOW many punches did he throw? (5)
W He threw five or six.
P WHAT happened then? (5)
W I grabbed Jones, someone else grabbed Gilligan, and we separated them.
P WHAT happened when the other person grabbed Mr. Gilligan? (5)
W He struggled to get free and started calling everyone names.

Notice that at the end of this line of questioning, the proponent does not attempt to elicit the witness's testimony that given Gilligan's violent character, it is more probable that Gilligan started the fight. It would be improper opinion for the witness to draw that inference. Moreover, it is unnecessary for the proponent to invite the witness to draw the inference at this point; in the subsequent instructions the judge will tell the jury that they may decide whether to draw the inference, and in summation the proponent may expressly argue in favor of the inference.

When this testimony is admitted, or during the final jury charge, on either or both occasions the judge might tell the jury the following about the evidence:

"In this case, the defendant claims that Mr. Gilligan was the aggressor. Evidence has been received for the purpose of showing that Mr. Gilligan has a violent character. You may consider that evidence in deciding whether the defendant or Mr. Gilligan was the real aggressor."

During final argument, the defense counsel could state:

"Ladies and gentlemen, as I told you in opening statement, this case boils down to a simple question: Who attacked whom? Did Mr. Lowe start the fight, or was Mr. Gilligan, the so-called victim, the real aggressor? When you discuss that question in the deliberation room, I ask you to remember the testimony by Mr. Nieman. Mr. Nieman testified about another incident involving Mr. Gilligan. It was a relatively recent incident; it happened on December 1st of last year. It started out as a pleasant evening, a party at Tarantino's. Most of us are familiar with that restaurant—it's a great place for a party, good food, nice surroundings, a peaceful atmosphere with a wonderful view of the Bay. But something shattered the peace that evening. A fight broke out. Remember how it broke out. For no good reason, someone just started screaming. Then that same person got violent. With no provocation, he threw one punch, then another, and another—and before it was over, he had thrown five or six punches. Who was that person? Mr.

Nieman told you that it was none other than Mr. Gilligan. Ladies and gentlemen, that incident tells you something about Mr. Gilligan. It shows that he has a violent streak. In a few minutes her Honor will give you the legal instructions that you have to follow during your deliberations. In particular, she is going to tell you that you may consider Mr. Nieman's testimony 'in deciding whether the defendant or Mr. Gilligan was the real aggressor.' I want you to do exactly what her Honor tells you. If you do that, if you consider the evidence of Mr. Gilligan's violent temper, you'll reach the only reasonable conclusion in this case, namely, that Mr. Lowe was the real victim and that the so-called victim, Mr. Gilligan, actually started the fight."

In times past, the law allowed a criminal defendant to attack the chaste character of the alleged victim in a sex offense prosecution. The line of reasoning was that if the alleged victim consented to intercourse on prior occasions, her earlier consent increases the probability that she consented to intercourse with the defendant.

Evidence Code § 1103(c) generally bars the defense from invoking this line of reasoning. As a general proposition, the courts broadly construe "sexual conduct" and thereby increase the protection accorded alleged victims. *People v. Franklin*, 25 Cal. App. 4th 328, 30 Cal. Rptr. 2d 376, 380 (1994). Subdivision 1103(c)(1) provides that with two exceptions, testimony in the form of "opinion evidence, reputation evidence, and evidence of specific instances of the complaining witness' sexual conduct ... is not admissible by the defendant in order to prove consent by the complaining witness." This prohibition does not apply if the alleged crime occurred in a local detention facility or state prison. Evidence Code § 1103(c)(1).

Effective January 1, 1999, Evidence Code § 1103(c)(2) was amended to read that notwithstanding subdivision 1103(c)(3), evidence of the manner in which the victim was dressed at the time of the commission of the offense is not admissible when offered by either party on the issue of consent in a sexual assault prosecution (as defined by subdivision (c)(1)) unless the evidence is determined by the court to be relevant and in the interests of justice. The proponent of the evidence must make an offer of proof outside the presence of the jury and the court must make a ruling on the record. For purposes of this amendment, "manner of dress" does not include the condition of the victim's clothing before, during, or after the commission of the offense.

Subdivision 1103(c)(3) states one exception; the prohibition in § 1103(c)(1) shall not be applicable to evidence of the complaining witness's sexual conduct with the defendant. The defendant may testify to other sexual intercourse with the complainant, or if there was group sex involving the defendant and the complainant, the other participants and observers may testify to the defendant's conduct with the complainant. *People v. Keith*, 118 Cal. App. 3d 973, 173 Cal. Rptr. 704 (1981).

Subdivision 1103(c)(4) sets out another exception. That exception comes into play when "the prosecutor introduces evidence, including testimony of a witness, or the complaining witness as a witness gives testimony, and such evidence or testimony relates to the complaining witness' sexual conduct. ..." In that event, the defense may both cross-examine the prosecution witness and introduce rebuttal testimony. Suppose, for example, that during the complainant's direct examination, the prosecutor elicits the testimony that before the alleged attack, the complainant was a virgin. In many cases, the testimony would be irrelevant; the prosecutor might be overreaching and attempting to generate sympathy for the complainant. In other cases, for example, when proof of a physical injury is an element of the offense, testimony about the complainant's virginity might be relevant. In any event, subdivision 1103(c)(4) would allow the defense to prove an earlier act of intercourse by the complainant even if the act involved a sex partner other than the defendant. The foundation would include these elements:

1. Where the act occurred.
2. When the act occurred.
3. Who was present.
4. What happened.
5. The circumstances showing that the incident tends to rebut the prosecution's testimony.

Assume that the People charge Mr. Lowe with raping Ms. Younger on December 12th of last year. During the defense case-in-chief, the defense calls Mr. Norton as a witness. Mr. Norton has already identified himself. The defense is the proponent.

P   WHERE were you on the evening of November 1st of last year? (1), (2)
W   I was at Gino's bar in downtown Ukiah.
P   WHAT were you doing there?
W   I was hanging out and looking for some women to pick up.
P   WHAT do you mean by "pick up"?
W   I was trying to find someone to have some fun with that night.
P   WHAT happened after you arrived at the bar? (3)
W   I bumped into a woman.
P   WHO was the woman? (3)
W   Ms. Nancy Younger.
P   WHEN did you last see her? (3)
W   Today.
P   WHERE was she? (3)
W   She was testifying for the prosecution a couple of hours ago in this courtroom.
P   WHAT happened after you met Ms. Younger? (4)
W   We spent a couple of hours at the bar and had some drinks.
P   WHAT happened next? (4)
W   We went to my apartment.
P   WHAT happened then? (4)
W   We had a couple more drinks there, and she spent the night.
P   WHAT, if anything, happened that night? (5)
W   We had sex.
P   WHAT do you mean by "we had sex"? (5)

W We had intercourse.

P WHAT was your legal relation to Ms. Younger at that time? (5)

W We didn't have any legal relation. We weren't married or engaged or anything like that.

P HOW long had you known her before she had intercourse with you? (5)

W A couple of hours.

P WHAT force did you use to get her to consent to intercourse? (5)

W None.

P WHAT threats did you make against her? (5)

W None. She did it of her own free will.

P WHAT happened the next morning? (5)

W She just left. I didn't see her again until today when I walked into the courtroom.

Notice that at the end of this line of questioning, the proponent does not ask the witness to opine whether Ms. Younger has a propensity for extra-marital intercourse or whether her propensity increases the probability that she consented to intercourse with the defendant. It would be improper opinion for the witness to attempt to draw those inferences. Moreover, it is unnecessary for the proponent to invite the witness to draw the inferences; in the subsequent instructions the judge will tell the jury that they are to decide whether to draw the inferences, and in summation the proponent may expressly argue in favor of those inferences.

When this testimony is admitted, during the final jury charge, or on both occasions, the judge might tell the jury the following about the evidence:

> "One of the questions in this case is whether Ms. Younger consented to sexual intercourse with the defendant. Evidence has been presented that on another occasion, the alleged victim consented to intercourse with Mr. Norton, another man she was not married to. You may consider that evidence in deciding whether Ms. Younger gave her consent to intercourse with the defendant."

During closing argument, the defense counsel could state:

> "Ladies and gentlemen, as I told you during opening statement, Mr. Lowe admits having sex with Ms. Younger. It's not a crime to have sex with someone. It's a crime only if you force them to have sex with you. And, again as I said during opening, the only real question in this case is whether Ms. Younger agreed to have sex with Mr. Lowe. In a few minutes her Honor will give you the legal instructions that you have to follow during your deliberations in this case. One of those instructions relates to the testimony given by Mr. Norton earlier today. As you'll recall, Mr. Norton told you that in November of last year, he met Ms. Younger at a bar and that later that night they had consensual sex. In her instructions, her Honor will tell you that you can consider Mr. Norton's testimony in deciding whether Ms. Younger consented to having sex with Mr. Lowe. Let's talk about Mr. Norton's testimony. Consider all the striking similarities between Ms.

Younger's contact with Mr. Norton and her contact with Mr. Lowe. The incidents occur very close in time. She ran into Mr. Norton in early November of last year. She met Mr. Lowe in the middle of the following month, December. In both cases, the men are strangers to her. Mr. Norton testified that he'd never met Ms. Younger before that night, just as Mr. Lowe testified and freely admitted that he'd never seen Ms. Younger before. Both men meet her at a local bar and have a couple of drinks with her. On both occasions, she freely agrees to accompany the men to their apartments. And both times she has sex with them at the apartment. Mr. Norton testified in no uncertain terms that Ms. Younger consented to sex that night. Mr. Lowe took the stand, looked you in the eye, and told you flat out that she also consented that night. There are so many parallels between the two incidents that Mr. Norton's testimony corroborates Mr. Lowe's testimony. The evidence shows that she consented in November, and the only reasonable conclusion is that a few weeks later in similar circumstances she consented again. At the very least, given Mr. Norton's testimony, there's reasonable doubt as to the issue of consent."

The above foundation illustrates the operation of Evidence Code § 1103 in a prosecution. In 1985, the legislature decided to apply similar rules to civil actions for sexual harassment, sexual assault, and sexual battery. The rules are prescribed by Evidence Code § 1106. The structure of the two statutes is comparable. Just as § 1103(c)(1) announces a general prohibition, there is a general bar in § 1106(a). Subdivision 1106(b) is the counterpart to § 1103(c)(3); 1106(b) renders the general bar inapplicable to evidence of the plaintiffs sexual conduct with the alleged perpetrator. Subdivision 1106(c) completes the parallel to § 1103. Subdivision 1106(c) permits the defense to rebut after "the plaintiff introduces evidence, including testimony of a witness, or the plaintiff as a witness gives testimony and evidence or testimony relates to the plaintiff's sexual conduct. ..." Subdivision 1106(c) is likely to be used more frequently than § 1103(c)(4). As previously stated, in a rape prosecution, the complainant's prior virginity is usually irrelevant, and the defense will rarely have occasion to offer rebuttal evidence under § 1103(c)(4). In contrast, in a civil action, the plaintiff's prior virginity may be logically relevant to plaintiff's proof of damages in the case. Subdivision 1106(c) applies whether the plaintiff injects the issue properly or improperly. *Patricia C. v. Mark D.*, 12 Cal. App. 4th 1211, 16 Cal. Rptr. 2d 71 (1993) holds that the restrictions set out in § 1106 do not apply to a medical malpractice action involving allegations of psychologist-patient sexual contact.

Another development in this area was the legislature's enactment of § 1108, effective January 1, 1996. Section 1108 is modeled after a relatively new Federal Rule of Evidence provision, that is, Rule 413. According to § 1108(a), "[i]n a criminal action in which the defendant is accused of a sexual offense, evidence of the defendant's commission of another sexual offense or offenses is not made inadmissible by Section 1101, if the evidence is not inadmissible pursuant to Section 352." This language has the effect of selectively abolishing the character evidence prohibition in certain prosecutions. Subdivision (d) defines "sexual offense," and subdivision (b) requires the prosecution to give the defense pretrial notice of its intent to invoke § 1108. In *People v. Fitch*, 55 Cal. App. 4th 172, 63 Cal. Rptr. 2d 753 (1997), the defendant was convicted of raping victim A, partly on the basis of evidence that he had raped victim B five years earlier. He challenged the constitutionality of § 1108, arguing that the due process clause prohibits the use of evidence that the defendant committed a prior sex offense to prove that he committed the sex offense with which he is now charged. The appellate court rejected Fitch's due process challenge, holding that it is not fundamentally unfair to use one sex offense as evidence of a disposition to commit a second sex offense. 55 Cal. App. 4th at 178-84, 63 Cal. Rptr. 2d at 757-59. Moreover, § 1108 expressly makes the use of prior sex offense evidence subject to the trial judge's discretion under § 352, and that reduces the risk that prosecutors will be able to use such evidence unfairly. The court also rejected a challenge under the equal protection clause, holding that § 1108 satisfies the applicable rational-basis analysis. *Accord People v. Davis*, 71 Cal. App. 4th 1492, 84 Cal. Rptr. 2d 628 (1999) (follows *Fitch*).

Under § 1108, the foundation will include the following elements:

1. Where the event occurred.
2. When the event occurred.
3. Who was involved. The prosecution must show that the perpetrator was the defendant.
4. What happened—a sexual offense as defined by § 1108(d).
5. The similarities between the pleaded sexual offense and the unpleaded crime. On its face § 1108 does not require any showing of similarity other than proof that both acts are sexual offenses. However, as a practical matter, the prosecution would almost always want to emphasize the similarities. To begin with, a showing of extensive similarities would make the evidence less vulnerable to an objection under § 352. Moreover, in closing argument, on a character theory the prosecution will urge the jury to treat the unpleaded acts as circumstantial proof of the conduct of the defendant; and the jury will ordinarily find the act more probative on that theory if there are numerous similarities between the pleaded and unpleaded acts. *See, e.g., People v. Soto*, 64 Cal. App. 4th 966, 75 Cal. Rptr. 2d 605 (1998) (defendant charged with molesting his pre-teen niece; trial court correctly admitted evidence that many years earlier he had molested two other pre-teen relatives in a generally similar manner).

Assume that the prosecution charges that the defendant sexually assaulted Ms. Chang on December 2, 1995. The pleading alleges that the assault occurred in the defendant's car in the parking lot of the Castle Restaurant on Huffman Avenue. Ms. Chang has already testified that she knew the defendant because they both were members of a skiing club. Ms. Chang testified that the defendant invited her to dinner and a movie and that he assaulted her in his car after they left the restaurant to attend the movie. Ms. Chang testified that after they both entered the car, the defendant reached over and without permission began kissing her on the mouth and fondling her breasts. Ms. Chang testified that when she resisted, he called her a "prude" and insisted that she exit the car. The defendant then drove away. The next witness is Ms. Leslie. Ms. Leslie has already identified herself. The prosecutor is the proponent.

P   WHERE were you on December 1st of last year?
W   I was at home that evening.
P   WHAT phone calls, if any, did you receive that night?
W   The defendant called me.
P   HOW do you know the defendant? (3), (5)
W   We both belong to the Active 20-30 Club here in Eureka.
P   Before December 1st, HOW long had you known him? (3)
W   About six months.
P   HOW many times had you spoken with him before December 1st? (3)
W   Maybe 10 or 12 times. We had met and chatted at some of the activities sponsored by the club.
P   HOW do you know that it was the defendant who called that night? (3)
W   I recognized his voice.
P   When the defendant called that night, WHAT did he say? (5)
W   He invited me to a dinner and movie the next evening.
P   HOW did you respond to the invitation?
W   I said that I'd be delighted. He seemed like a really sociable, fun guy.
P   WHAT happened the next evening? (2), (5)
W   He picked me up at my condo and initially took me to a local restaurant.
P   WHICH restaurant was that? (1), (5)
W   The Castle Restaurant.
P   WHERE is that restaurant located? (1), (5)
W   It's at the corner of Huffman and 17th.
P   WHAT happened after you arrived at the restaurant? (5)
W   We had a nice time in the restaurant. We both had a good meal, and he was the perfect gentleman while we were there.
P   WHAT happened after you finished eating? (4), (5)
W   We left the restaurant to go to the movie. We stepped outside the restaurant and walked to where we were parked. When we got to the car, he opened my door first. Then he walked over to the driver's side and got into the car.
P   WHAT, if anything, happened then? (4), (5)
W   As soon as he got into the car, without any warning at all, he reaches over, grabs me, and starts kissing me.
P   WHERE did he grab you? (4), (5)
W   He had one arm around my waist, and he put his other hand on my left breast.
P   WHERE did he kiss you? (4), (5)
W   Right on the mouth.
P   WHAT did you do then? (4), (5)
W   I shoved him back as hard as I could, and I told him in no uncertain terms to just knock it off. I was more than angry; I was outraged. I've never had any experience like that.

P   WHAT, if anything, did he say then? (4), (5)

W   To begin with, he acted as if he were upset. He had the nerve to call me a "prude." Then, to top it all off, he basically kicks me out of his car and drives off. I ended up taking a taxi home that night.

P   Ms. Leslie, please think carefully before you answer this question. WHO was the person who did that to you on the evening of December 2nd of last year? (3)

W   It was the defendant right over here.

P   WHERE is he sitting? (3)

W   He's at the table over near the large window.

P   HOW is he dressed? (3)

W   He's wearing a brown suit, white shirt, and red tie.

P   Your Honor, please let the record reflect that the witness has identified the defendant.

J   It will so reflect.

P   Your Honor, I have no further questions of the witness at this time.

Notice that at the end of this line of questioning, the proponent does not attempt to elicit the witness's testimony that the defendant has a propensity to engage in sexual misconduct or that given the propensity, it is more probable that the defendant committed the charged offense. It would be improper opinion for the witness to draw those inferences. Moreover, it is unnecessary for the proponent to invite the witness to draw those inferences; in the subsequent instructions the judge will tell the jury that they are to decide whether to draw the inferences, and during summation the proponent may expressly argue in favor of the inferences.

When this testimony is admitted, during the final jury charge, or on both occasions, the judge would tell the jury the following about the evidence:

"Evidence has been introduced for the purpose of showing that the defendant engaged in a sexual offense on another occasion than that charged in this case. If you find that the defendant committed a prior sexual offense, you may, but are not required, to infer that the defendant had a disposition to commit the same type of sexual offense. If you find that the defendant had this disposition, you may, but are not required to, infer that he was likely to commit and did commit the crime of which he is accused." CAL-JIC 2.50.01

During closing argument, the prosecutor could state:

"Ladies and gentlemen, during the trial you heard the testimony of Ms. Leslie. You heard her describe a sexual assault—an assault made on Ms. Leslie by the defendant in December of last year. In a few minutes his Honor will read you the legal instructions that you have to follow during your deliberations in this case. He is going to tell that in deciding the defendant's guilt or innocence of the sexual attack on Ms. Chang, you can consider Ms. Leslie's testimony. In particular, his Honor is going to tell you the following: If you find that the defendant committed a prior sexual offense, you may, but are not required, to infer that the defendant had a disposition to commit the same type of sexual offense. If you find that the defendant had this disposition, you may, but are not required, to infer that he was likely to commit and did commit the crime of which he is accused.

"Ladies and gentlemen, with that instruction in mind, let's consider Ms. Leslie's testimony. Take a look at this chart. Think of all the striking similarities between the attack on Ms. Chang and the assault on Ms. Leslie: The attack on Ms. Chang occurred on December 2nd of last year. The attack on Ms. Leslie happened one day earlier—the very day before the attack on Ms. Chang. The attack on Ms. Chang occurred at the Castle Restaurant here in town on Huffman Avenue. That's the identical location of the assault on Ms. Leslie. Before the attack, the defendant got to know Ms. Chang because he joined the same ski club she was in. Prior to the assault on Ms. Leslie, he got to know her by joining the same Active 20-30 Club that she was a member of. The defendant invited Ms. Chang to dinner and a movie—the very same invitation he extended to Ms. Leslie. After dinner on the way to the movie, the defendant reaches over and begins trying to kiss Ms. Chang without her permission. That's also exactly what he did to Ms. Leslie. Next, he attempted to fondle Ms. Chang's breasts. He tried the same stunt with Ms. Leslie. When Ms. Chang told him to stop, he had the audacity to call her a 'prude.' That's the very same expression he used when Ms. Leslie told him to knock it off. When it was all over, the defendant dumped Ms. Chang and forced her to find her own way home. That's the very same thing he did with Ms. Leslie. Ask yourselves, ladies and gentlemen: In the words of his Honor's instruction, did the defendant have 'a disposition to commit the same type of sexual offense'? You bet he did. A leopard doesn't change its spots. The defendant did exactly the same thing the day before the attack on Ms. Chang. Ms. Leslie's testimony shows you the type of man the defendant is. He's exactly the kind of person who would commit the assault on Ms. Chang."

In 1996, the legislature carved out another exception to the character evidence prohibition. The legislature did so by enacting Evidence Code § 1109. Subdivision 1109(a) generally provides that "in a criminal action in which the defendant is accused of an offense involving domestic violence, evidence of the defendant's commission of other domestic violence is not made inadmissible by Section 1101, if the evidence is not inadmissible pursuant to Section 352." In *People v. Acosta,* 71 Cal. App. 4th 1206, 84 Cal. Rptr. 2d 370 (1999), the court followed the analysis of *People v. Fitch,* 55 Cal. App. 4th 172, 63 Cal. Rptr. 2d 753 (1997), and upheld § 1109 against challenge under the due process and equal protection clauses. Further, the court held that a prosecutor using § 1109 must prove the prior acts of domestic violence by "a preponderance of the evidence," not "beyond a reasonable doubt." In *People v. Poplar,* 70 Cal. App. 4th 1129, 83 Cal. Rptr. 2d 320 (1999), the defendant was charged with raping his live-in girl friend. The court held that the rape of a live-in partner is a form of domestic violence, thus bringing § 1109 into play and making it proper to admit evidence that the defendant beat up two prior live-in partners.

4. CROSS-EXAMINATION OF A CHARACTER WITNESS

After the defense conducts the direct examination of a character witness, the prosecution has a right to cross-examine the witness.

Suppose that on direct examination, the witness testifies that the defendant has a reputation for peacefulness. Further, assume that the prosecutor knows that the defendant was arrested for a violent battery only two months before the present alleged battery. The traditional view is that during the cross-examination, the prosecutor may ask, "Have you heard a report that the defendant was arrested for battery two years ago? If the witness denies hearing the report, the denial impeaches the witness; the denial indicates that the witness really is not familiar with the defendant's reputation. If the witness admits hearing the report, the admission also impeaches the witness; the admission indicates that the witness has a strange standard for evaluating good reputation. The prosecutor may inquire about reports that the defendant committed, or was arrested for, indicted for, or convicted of a crime. For that matter, the prosecutor may ask about any act that is inconsistent with the character trait the witness testified to; the act need not amount to a crime. Of course, the act must be logically relevant to the character trait the witness testified to on direct examination. Thus, if on direct examination the witness testified to the defendant's character trait of peacefulness, the prosecutor may not inquire about an arrest for mere drunkenness. Finally, the event should be notorious—the type of event that is likely to become known in the community and affect the defendant's reputation. Article, *Have You Heard? cross-examination of a Criminal Defendant's Good Character Witness: A Proposal for Reform*, 9 U.C. DAVIS L. REV. 365, 374-75 (1976). This type of cross-examination is allowed at both the guilt and penalty phases of a trial. *People v. Payton*, 3 Cal. 4th 1050, 839 P.2d 1035, 13 Cal. Rptr. 2d 526 (1992), *cert. denied*, 510 U.S. 1040 (1994).

As we have seen, Evidence Code § 1102 permits the defendant to offer opinion character evidence as well as reputation character evidence. In principle, if the jurisdiction permits opinion character evidence and on direct examination the defense witness expresses an opinion, the prosecutor should no longer have to use the "Have you heard ...?" formula. The prosecutor should be permitted to ask, "Do you know that the defendant was arrested for battery two years ago?" *Id*. at 391-92. If the witness denies knowing about the arrest, the denial indicates that the witness may not know the defendant well. If the witness admits knowing about the arrest, the admission indicates that the witness has a strange personal standard for evaluating good character. When the witness testifies to reputation, what the witness has heard is logically relevant. However, when the witness testifies to his or her own opinion, what the witness knows is logically relevant.

Federal Rule of Evidence 405 governs character evidence in federal trials, and the Advisory Committee's Note to the Rule states that the Committee intended to abolish the old, formal distinctions in the phrasing of the questions on cross-examination. The Note asserts that the Committee intended to "eliminate [the distinctions] as a factor in formulating questions." The legislative history of the Evidence Code is silent on the issue but *People v. Hurd*, 5 Cal. App. 3d 865, 85 Cal. Rptr. 718 (1970), suggests that California courts will no longer rigidly enforce the old distinctions. *See also* 1 JEFFERSON § 28.88.

Of course, the prosecutor must have a good faith basis in fact for inquiring about the incident. The prosecutor cannot simply invent derogatory reports about the defendant. The prosecutor must have a factual basis for believing that, for instance, the defendant committed, was arrested for, was indicted for, or was convicted of the crime. The basis in fact need not be admissible evidence. *Id.* (defendant's "make sheet" listing the defendant's arrests). For example, the prosecutor could use an eyewitness' written statement or a police report as the basis in fact. The statement and report would normally be inadmissible hearsay, but they are sufficient to give the prosecutor a good faith belief that the incident occurred. When the defense attorney challenges the prosecutor to show the basis for the belief that the incident occurred, the prosecutor usually makes a statement for the record outside the jurors' hearing. In some jurisdictions, it is customary for the prosecutor to insert any documentary material into the record; the material is not admitted as a formal exhibit to be submitted to the jury, but it is sometimes marked for identification or marked as an appellate exhibit.

Assume that during cross-examination of a character witness, the prosecutor inquired about an arrest of the defendant for battery. The prosecutor might have used the classic language, "Have you heard a report that the defendant was arrested for battery two years ago?" As opponent, the defense counsel objects:

O Your Honor, may we approach the bench?

J Yes.

O Your Honor, I want to object to the last question on the ground that the prosecutor hasn't shown a good faith basis in fact for believing that this arrest occurred.

P Your Honor, I would like to mark this document as People's appellate exhibit number one.

O What is that document?

P It is an arrest report from the Palo Alto Police Department. The report names the defendant George Larson as the arrestee and states that he was arrested for battery on a Mr. George Langdale.

O That report is inadmissible hearsay.

P That would normally be true, but the material creating the basis in fact for believing the incident occurred need not qualify as admissible evidence. Your Honor, in a sense, it's nonhearsay. What's in issue is whether I have a good faith belief that this incident occurred, and the effect of this report on my state of mind is the production of precisely that belief.

J I agree with the prosecutor. I will receive the appellate exhibit, and the objection to the question will be overruled.

P Mr. Stacey, let me repeat the question. Have you heard a report that the defendant was arrested for battery two years ago?

W No.

Some prosecutors would go further and ask another question:

P If you had heard that report, would it have changed your conclusion that the defendant had a good reputation for peacefulness?

Several California cases have approved this additional question. *People v. Boone*, 126 Cal. App. 2d 746, 273 P.2d 350 (1954); *People v. McKenna*, 11 Cal. 2d 327, 79 P.2d 1065 (1938). However, Witkin believes that the phrasing is "objectionable as calling for an opinion on hypothetical facts. ..." 3 WITKIN § 1896, at 1853.

Notice that at the end of the initial variation of the line of questioning, the proponent does not take a further step and ask: "Well, how then can you say that you know the defendant's reputation well?" It would be objectionably argumentative for the proponent to pose that question. Moreover, it is unnecessary for the proponent to put that question to the witness; in the subsequent instructions the judge will tell the jury that they can decide whether to draw the inference, and during summation the proponent may expressly argue in favor of that inference.

When the cross-examiner asks a character witness about an incident, during the final jury charge, or on both occasions, the judge might tell the jury the following:

> "Where on cross-examination, a witness is asked if he has heard reports of certain conduct of a defendant inconsistent with the traits of good character to which the witness has testified, these questions and the witness's answers to them may be considered only for the purpose of determining the weight to be given to the opinion of the witness or his testimony as to the good reputation of the defendant. These questions and answers are not evidence that the reports are true, and you must not assume from them that the defendant did in fact conduct himself inconsistently with those traits of character."
> CALJIC 2.42

During closing argument, the prosecutor could state:

> "Ladies and gentlemen, as you'll recall, the defense called a Mr. Stacey in an attempt to convince you that Mr. Larson is a peaceful man, not the type of man who would commit the violent battery Mr. Larson is on trial for. In a few minutes, her Honor will read you the legal instructions that you have to follow during your deliberations in this case. One of those instructions deals with Mr. Stacey's character testimony. Her Honor is going to tell you that you don't have to accept Mr. Stacey's direct testimony at face value; it's up to you to decide how much weight, if any, to give it. She's also going to tell that in making that decision, you can consider the way Mr. Stacey

answered my questions on cross-examination. On cross-examination, I asked Mr. Stacey whether he'd heard a report that the defendant had been arrested for battery a mere two years ago. Mr. Stacey said that he'd never heard any such report. Think about that answer. Mr. Stacey expects you to believe that he knows the defendant's reputation for peacefulness well, but he's never heard a report about a battery only two years ago. A battery is a violent crime. A battery is just plain inconsistent with the defendant's supposedly peaceful reputation. Yet Mr. Stacey claims he never heard of the report. That answer tells you that Stacey really doesn't know the defendant's reputation well. If he knew the defendant's reputation as well as he claims, he certainly would have heard about that report. And that's why you should reject Stacey's testimony. Mr. Stacey admitted that he had heard that report. Think about that answer. On the one hand, he testifies that the defendant had a good reputation for peacefulness, and he expects you to believe that he's a good judge of character. On the other hand, he admits that he's heard that the defendant was arrested for battery a mere two years ago. Ladies and gentlemen, Mr. Stacey must have a pretty strange standard for deciding whether someone has a good reputation for peacefulness. When someone is reported to have committed a battery, most reasonable people would say that that person has a terrible reputation for peacefulness. But not Mr. Stacey. Either he has a skewed standard for judging character, or he's simply a biased witness. After all, he conceded on cross-examination that he and the defendant have been good friends for almost ten years. In either case, you just can't trust Stacey's testimony."

C.   HABIT EVIDENCE

1. THE DOCTRINE

The proponent may use habit evidence as circumstantial proof of conduct. Evidence Code § 1105 states the habit evidence doctrine: "Any otherwise admissible evidence of habit or custom is admissible to prove conduct on a specified occasion in conformity with the habit or custom."

Although both character and habit evidence serve as circumstantial proof of conduct, there are major differences between the two theories of admissibility.

The first difference is that, although character evidence is usually admissible only after the criminal defendant initiates the inquiry, under the modern view either party in a civil or criminal case may introduce habit evidence. Some jurisdictions admit habit evidence only if there are no eyewitnesses to the conduct in question or only if there is corroboration of the conduct. However, § 1105 embodies the modern view that habit evidence is always admissible to prove the conduct of a person or business organization. Section 1105 codifies neither the "no eyewitness" rule nor the corroboration requirement. The California Law Revision Commission comment to § 1105 makes it clear the drafters intended to eliminate the "no eyewitness" rule.

The second difference is that while character evidence (in the limited situations in which it is allowed) permits the proponent to prove general character or character traits, habit evidence requires proof of a very specific, frequently repeated behavioral pattern. The Commission comment defines habit as a regular response to a repeated specific situation. For instance, the proponent may prove the precise manner in which a decedent routinely executed right-hand turns or the specific mailing procedure a business customarily used. *See, e.g., Curl v. Superior Court of Fresno County*, 51 Cal. 3d 1292, 801 P.2d 292, 276 Cal. Rptr. 49 (1990) (trial judge's habit of carefully reviewing waiver of constitutional rights when accepting guilty pleas was admissible to prove that defendant's guilty plea was properly accepted). The California courts have been lax in evaluating the specificity of behavioral patterns. In *People v. Memro*, 38 Cal. 3d 658, 681, 700 P.2d 446, 462, 214 Cal. Rptr. 832, 848 (1985), the California Supreme Court assumed that certain police officers' practice of using particular illegal means to obtain confessions could amount to a habit. *See also People v. McPeters*, 2 Cal. 4th 1148, 832 P.2d 146, 9 Cal. Rptr. 2d 834, *modified*, 3 Cal. 4th 678c (1992), *cert. denied*, 507 U.S. 1037 (1993) (allowing evidence of victim's habit of keeping money in envelopes); *People v. Webb*, 6 Cal. 4th 494, 862 P.2d 779, 24 Cal. Rptr. 2d 779, 801 (1993) ("Lori's habit of storing money in baby food jars and envelopes"), *cert. denied*, 513 U.S. 839 (1994).

Finally, the habit and character evidence theories differ in the method of proof. The proponent of character evidence may present reputation evidence. In contrast, the proponent of habit evidence may not use reputation evidence because of the hearsay rule. However, California permits opinion character evidence, and opinion is also the most common method of proving habit. To be qualified to express an opinion on the existence of a habit, the witness must have been familiar with the person or business for a substantial time and must have observed numerous instances of the person's or business' conduct. Lastly, the proponent of character evidence ordinarily may not offer specific instances of the person's conduct. The proponent of habit evidence should be allowed to prove particular acts if the acts are numerous enough and represent a specific enough behavioral pattern to amount to habit. Even without the benefit of a witness' opinion on the existence of a habit, the trier of fact can draw its own conclusion whether a habit exists.

2. ELEMENTS OF THE FOUNDATION

The foundation for opinion habit evidence includes these elements:

1. The witness is familiar with the person or business.
2. The witness has been familiar with the person or business for a substantial period of time.
3. In the witness's opinion, the person or business has a habit, a specific behavioral pattern.

4. The witness has observed the person or business act on numerous occasions.
5. In the overwhelming majority of similar situations, the person or business followed its habit.

3. SAMPLE FOUNDATION

The fact situation is a tort action. The plaintiff sues the decedent's estate on the theory that the decedent negligently caused the traffic accident. The decedent is Mr. Myles. The collision occurred as the decedent was making a right-hand turn at a stop sign at the intersection of 1st and Martin Streets. The decedent turned off 1st Street and began proceeding east on Martin. The estate's personal representative contends that the decedent drove carefully. To support that contention, the representative desires to offer evidence of the decedent's driving habits. To do so, the representative calls Ms. Vincent, an acquaintance of the decedent. The decedent's personal representative is the proponent. Ms. Vincent has already identified herself.

P WHO was Joshua Myles? (1)

W He was a friend of mine. I know that he died in an accident about a year and a half ago.

P HOW long did you know him? (2)

W For about seven years.

P HOW did you come to know him? (2)

W We worked at the same bank. In fact, we were in the same car pool.

P HOW many people were in this car pool? (2)

W Three of us—Joshua, Kathy Jacobs, a teller, and I.

P HOW often did you see the decedent drive a car? (2)

W Hundreds of times. I couldn't give you a precise number.

P WHEN did you see him drive a car? (2)

W He did a lot of the driving in our car pool; he took me to work.

P WHAT route did you take when he drove you to work? (2)

W We drove from our subdivision to downtown. We had to go through the intersection of 1st and Martin Streets where I know this accident happened.

P HOW did you go through the intersection? (2)

W We approached going north on 1st Street. Then we had to turn east onto Martin Street.

P HOW many times a week did the decedent drive you to work? (2)

W Usually twice.

P HOW many weeks during the year did he drive you to work? (2)

W About fifty per year. You have to exclude our vacation times.

P HOW many years were you in this car pool? (2)

W Roughly five years.

P HOW many years was the decedent in this car pool? (2)

W The same—five years.

P WHAT did the decedent do when he came to the stop sign at 1st and Martin? (3)

W He came to a complete stop.

P   HOW regularly did he do that? (5)
W   Always.
P   HOW often did you see him do that? (4)
W   Hundreds of times.
P   HOW did the decedent make right-hand turns after coming to a stop at that intersection? (3)
W   He'd look both ways and start up only after he could see that it was safe.
P   HOW fast did he go immediately after starting up? (3)
W   Usually quite slowly and cautiously.
P   HOW often did you see him make a right-hand turn at that intersection in that manner? (4)
W   All sorts of times.

Notice that at the end of this line of questioning, the proponent does not attempt to elicit the witness's opinion that given Myles' driving habit, it is more probable that he drove in the same manner as alleged in the pleadings. That testimony would amount to an improper opinion. Moreover, it is unnecessary for the proponent to invite the witness to draw the inference; during the subsequent instructions the judge will instruct the jury that they can decide whether to draw that inference, and during summation the proponent may expressly argue in favor of the inference.

When the testimony is admitted, during the final jury charge, or on both occasions the trial judge might tell the jury the following about the evidence:

"Evidence has been presented of the decedent's driving habits. You can infer that a person acts consistently with their personal habits. Thus, you may consider the evidence of the decedent's habits in deciding how the decedent made his right-hand turn on the occasion when his car collided with the plaintiff's car."

During closing argument, the defense attorney could state:

"Ladies and gentlemen, as I told you in opening statement, this case boils down to the question of whether Mr. Myles used due care in making his right-hand turn at 1st and Martin Streets just before the collision with the plaintiff's car. When you discuss that question in the deliberation room, I want you to consider the testimony by Ms. Vincent. She was the witness who testified about Mr. Myles's driving habits. In a few minutes his Honor will give you the legal instructions that you must follow during your deliberations in this case. One of those instructions concerns Ms. Vincent's testimony about one of Mr. Myles's driving habits. In the instruction, his Honor will tell you that you can consider Ms. Vincent's testimony in deciding how Mr. Myles made his right-hand turn that day. How much weight should you give her testimony? Think back to what she told you. She knew Mr. Myles well—for about seven years. They were in the same carpool to work together. Their carpool's route included the intersection of 1st and

Martin, the very intersection where this collision occurred. They both were in the carpool for five years. Each year Mr. Myles drove for the carpool roughly fifty times. It's simple arithmetic: five years, 50 times, over 250 occasions. And on each occasion, Mr. Myles always came to a complete stop at the stop sign. And on every occasion, he looked both ways before entering the intersection and started up only after it was clearly safe. Not just sometimes, not just most of the time, but 'always'—that was the exact word she used. Common sense tells you that you ought to give Ms. Vincent's testimony a lot of weight. If Mr. Myles followed that practice so religiously so many times, it's ridiculous to think that he'd abandon it for no reason on the day he collided with the plaintiff. It's clear what really happened; on that day Mr. Myles exercised reasonable care in making his turn, just as he had literally hundreds of times before at that same intersection. Given his habit at the corner of 1st and Martin, Mr. Myles acted with due care that day, and the plaintiff caused the collision by his own inattention."

D. UNCHARGED MISCONDUCT EVIDENCE IN PROSECUTIONS

1. THE DOCTRINE

Even in rebuttal to defense character evidence, the prosecution may not prove uncharged misconduct (usually other crimes) by the defendant simply to prove that the defendant is a law-breaking, immoral person. However, the prosecution may introduce such evidence for other purposes. As Evidence Code § 1101 states:

(a) Except as provided in this section and in Sections 1102 and 1103, evidence of a person's character or a trait of his or her character (... in the form of ... evidence of specific instances of his or her conduct) is inadmissible when offered to prove his or her conduct on a specified occasion.

(b) Nothing in this section prohibits the admission of evidence that a person committed a crime, civil wrong, or act when relevant to prove some fact (such as motive, opportunity, intent, preparation, plan, knowledge, identity, absence of mistake or accident, or whether a defendant in a prosecution for an unlawful sexual act or attempted unlawful sexual act did not reasonably and in good faith believe that the victim consented) other than his or her disposition to commit such an act.

In *People v. Ewoldt*, 7 Cal. 4th 380, 27 Cal. Rptr. 2d 646, 867 P.2d 757 (1994), the California Supreme Court held that, despite Proposition 8, Evidence Code § 1101 is still in effect. (Proposition 8 is described in Chapter 5, section B.) Thus, under present California law, if uncharged misconduct evidence is logically relevant to a fact in issue other than character, and if the probative value of the evidence is not substantially outweighed by the dangers of undue prejudice, confusion of the issues, and time consumption, the prosecution may introduce the proof of the uncharged act. *See, e.g., People v. Ruiz*, 62 Cal. App. 4th 234, 72 Cal. Rptr. 2d 572 (1998) (although evidence of gang membership is highly prejudicial, and is inadmissible if its only purpose is to prove criminal disposition, the trial court properly admitted evidence of the defendant's gang membership as logically relevant to: 1) show the relationship between defendant and another gang member who had confessed to the crime charged to the defendant; 2) show bias and motive for the confessor to lie—to protect his fellow gang member; and 3) to impeach the confessor, who had claimed he did not know the defendant). *See generally* Roth, *Understanding Admissibility of Prior Bad Acts: A Diagrammatic Approach*, 9 PEPP. L. REV. 297 (1982).

The prosecutor who seeks to use uncharged misconduct evidence must first demonstrate that the evidence is logically relevant to a material fact in issue *other than* the defendant's character—his propensity to do the sort of thing he is now accused of doing. The list of uses in Evidence Code § 1101(b) is not exhaustive; since "such as" prefaces the list, the prosecutor may use any noncharacter theory of logical relevance. For example, if the defendant is charged with a specific intent crime, the defendant's commission of similar, deliberate acts may be logically relevant to prove the specific intent. Or, if the defendant claims entrapment, proof of the defendant's voluntary commission of similar crimes is relevant to rebut the entrapment defense. Or, if the question is who committed the charged crime, and if the prosecution can connect the defendant to other crimes committed with the same unique modus operandi, the evidence of the uncharged crimes is relevant to show that the defendant committed the charged crime. *See, e.g., People v. Erving*, 63 Cal. App. 4th 652, 73 Cal. Rptr. 2d 815 (1998) (evidence of inordinate amount of arson fires in area surrounding defendant's residences over the years was admissible to show identity in arson prosecution).

People v. Ewoldt, supra, illustrates the trickiness of uncharged misconduct evidence. In that case, the defendant was charged with sexually molesting his younger stepdaughter, *J*. The prosecutor offered uncharged misconduct evidence that the defendant had sexually molested his older stepdaughter, *N*, in a generally similar manner more than ten years earlier. The similarities between the two molestations were not distinctive enough to invoke the modus operandi theory, and there was no dispute about either intent or identity. Nonetheless, in a poorly reasoned opinion, the California Supreme Court held that the evidence about the molestation of *N* was admissible to prove a "common design or plan." In a strong dissent, Justice Mosk pinpointed the flaw in the majority's reasoning:

> When there is no issue of identity or intent, and the evidence does not reveal a grand design of which the charged and uncharged crimes are parts, in what way is evidence of a prior uncharged crime of the same nature as the charged crime probative on the ultimate issue of whether defendant committed the charged crime? I submit that it is probative only if we permit the jury to draw the inference from the earlier crime that it is defendant's inclination or nature to commit such crimes, and that this aspect of his character

caused him to commit the charged crimes. *This is nothing but criminal propensity evidence, and should be excluded by section 1101. The majority, in concluding that such evidence is admissible, fail to carry out the basic purpose of section 1101, which is to prohibit the introduction of other crimes evidence to show criminal disposition.*

7 Cal. 4th at 411, 27 Cal. Rptr. 2d at 665, 867 P.2d at 776 (emphasis added). *See also People v. Balcom,* 7 Cal. 4th 414, 27 Cal. Rptr. 2d 666, 867 P.2d 777 (1994), a companion case to *Ewoldt,* in which the majority uses the same flawed reasoning to reach the same unsound conclusion; *People v. Kipp* 18 Cal. 4th 349, 956 P. 2d 1169, 75 Cal. Rptr. 2d 716 (1998) (uncharged rape and murder of one victim used to prove defendant's identity, intent and common plan in a second rape and murder, even though the similarities between the two crimes were general and not particularly distinctive).

The trial judge, of course, has discretionary power to exclude uncharged misconduct evidence if its probative value is substantially outweighed by the danger that it may create undue prejudice, confuse the issues, or consume too much time. That discretionary power ought to be exercised liberally, because uncharged misconduct evidence can be highly prejudicial if the jury misuses it as evidence of the defendant's bad, law-breaking disposition. *See, e.g., Brown v. Smith,* 55 Cal. App. 4th 767, 64 Cal. Rptr. 2d 301 (1997) (in a housing discrimination case where the alleged discrimination was the sexual harassment of a tenant by her landlord, the trial judge ought to have excluded evidence about landlord's general vulgarity and obnoxious behavior toward other female tenants). *See also People v. Harris,* 60 Cal. App. 4th 727, 70 Cal. Rptr. 2d 689 (1998) (in a prosecution for non-violent sexual assault, the trial court ought to have excluded evidence of a burglary that involved a violent, lurid sexual assault, committed by defendant 23 years earlier because the evidence was "remote, inflammatory and nearly irrelevant and likely to confuse the jury").

Prosecutors have no monopoly on the uncharged misconduct theory. Evidence Code § 1101 refers generally to "a person," rather than "an accused" or "a defendant." Thus, defense counsel may also use the uncharged misconduct theory. Suppose, for instance, that the defense has evidence of the complainant's misconduct that is relevant on a noncharacter theory. The evidence would be admissible. *See People v. Steele,* 210 Cal. App. 3d 67, 257 Cal. Rptr. 687 (1989); *see also People v. Clower,* 16 Cal. App. 4th 1737, 21 Cal. Rptr. 2d 38 (1993) (earlier fruitless, warrantless searches as evidence of a pattern of unreasonable searches).

Evidence of misconduct by a third person may be also admissible. For example, in *People v. Loeun,* 17 Cal. 4th 1, 947 P.2d 1313, 69 Cal. Rptr. 2d 776 (1997), the prosecution sought an enhanced penalty under the Street Terrorism Enforcement and Penalty Act (STEP Act). In order to establish the requisite "pattern of criminal gang activity," the prosecution wanted to show that another gang member committed an offense on the same occasion as the charged offense. The California Supreme Court approved the trial judge's admission of the evidence of the other gang member's felonious conduct to justify the STEP Act penalty enhancement.

2. ELEMENTS OF THE FOUNDATION

The typical foundation includes these elements:

1. Where the other act occurred.
2. When the act occurred.
3. What the nature of the act was.
4. The defendant committed the other act. Prior California law was uncertain, but in *People v. Carpenter*, 15 Cal. 4th 312, 935 P.2d 708, 63 Cal. Rptr. 2d 1, 39-41 (1997), the Supreme Court assumed (without discussing the point) that this foundational fact issue is to be decided by the jury under California Evidence Code § 403, not by the judge under § 405. Moreover, *Carpenter* clearly holds that the foundational fact issue is to be decided by the preponderance of the evidence standard—not by the reasonable doubt standard or the clear and convincing evidence standard.
5. The surrounding circumstances making the uncharged act relevant to a disputed issue in the case. The proponent must do more than merely assert an admissible purpose in the abstract. The proponent must demonstrate that the uncharged misconduct has a clear connection to an ultimate disputed fact, without relying on the forbidden character inference. *People v. Valentine*, 207 Cal. App. 3d 697, 703-04, 254 Cal. Rptr. 822, 825 (1988).

Even after the proponent lays a proper foundation, the opponent has a right to a limiting instruction under Evidence Code § 355. The judge must inform the jury that they may not use the evidence as general character evidence; rather, the jury must use the evidence only for the limited purpose for which it was admitted.

3. SAMPLE FOUNDATION

Suppose that the People have charged the defendant, Mr. Standish, with armed robbery. During the prosecution case-in-chief, a single eyewitness identified the defendant as the robber. A police officer also testified on behalf of the prosecution. He testified that he searched the crime scene and found a .32 caliber pistol with the serial number 789444. During the defense case-in-chief, the defendant testified and denied committing the robbery. During the prosecution rebuttal, the prosecution calls Mr. Usher. Mr. Usher has already identified himself. The prosecution is the proponent.

P   WHAT is your occupation?
W   I own a gun store.
P   WHERE were you on March 15th of this year? (1), (2)
W   I was at work at my store.

P   WHAT, if anything, happened that day? (3)
W   I was the victim of a theft that day.
P   WHAT was stolen? (5)
W   A pistol.
P   WHAT pistol? (5)
W   It was a .32 caliber pistol, serial number 789444.
P   HOW do you know that? (5)
W   I handle all my inventory personally, and I refreshed my memory by reviewing my records before trial.
P   HOW was the pistol stolen? (4)
W   A guy came in broad daylight, pretended he was looking to buy, and then grabbed the pistol and ran out the door.
P   HOW well did you see the thief? (4)
W   Very well.
P   HOW close were you to the thief? (4)
W   When he was at the counter, he was only about five feet away.
P   HOW much time did you have to observe the thief? (4)
W   He was in the store for at least a couple of minutes.
P   WHO was the thief?
W   I'm not sure of his name, but I see him in the courtroom right now.
P   WHERE is he sitting? (4)
W   At that table over there.
P   HOW is he dressed? (4)
W   He's wearing a blue suit and green tie.
P   Your Honor, may the record reflect that the witness has identified the defendant?
J   It will so reflect.
O   Your Honor, at this point, I request a limiting instruction.
J   I will grant the request. Ladies and gentlemen of the jury, you have just heard testimony that the defendant stole a pistol, serial number 789444. You may not infer from that evidence that the defendant is generally a bad person and, for that reason, more likely to have committed the armed robbery with which he is charged in this case. However, there is evidence that a pistol with that serial number was found at the robbery scene. You may use Mr. Usher's testimony in deciding whether the defendant had possession of that pistol before the robbery.

Notice that at the end of this line of questioning, the proponent does not attempt to elicit the witness's testimony that it is therefore more likely that the defendant committed the charged offense. That testimony would amount to improper opinion. Moreover, it is unnecessary for the proponent to invite the witness to draw the inference; during the subsequent instructions the judge will instruct the jury that they can decide whether to draw the inference, and during summation the proponent may expressly argue in favor of the inference.

When this testimony is admitted, during the final jury charge, or on both occasions the judge might tell the jury the following about the evidence:

"Evidence has been introduced for the purpose of showing that the defendant committed a crime other than that for which he is on trial. This evidence, if believed, may not be considered by you to prove that defendant is a person of bad character or that he has a disposition to commit crimes. It may be considered by you only for the limited purpose of determining if it tends to show the identity of the person who committed the crime of which the defendant is accused. For the limited purpose for which you may consider this evidence, you must weigh it in the same manner as you do all other evidence in the case. You are not permitted to consider this evidence for any other purpose." CALJIC 2.50

During closing argument, the prosecutor could state:

"Ladies and gentlemen, the key issue in this case is identity. This case boils down to the question of whether the defendant is the person who committed the armed robbery at the liquor store. In deciding that question, I want you to especially remember the testimony of three witnesses. One witness was Officer Salcido. He testified that he arrived at the crime scene a few minutes after the robber made his getaway. Right there on the floor of the liquor store he found People's Exhibit #2—the .32 caliber pistol, serial number 789444, which I'm holding right now. The second witness, the liquor store owner, Mr. Vermont, told you that he doesn't even own a gun, much less keep one at the store. And liquor store customers don't go around throwing guns on the floor of the store. Mr. Vermont told you that when the alarm went off, the robber panicked; Mr. Vincent saw the robber drop this pistol and run out of the store. Ladies and gentlemen, it's undisputed—this *is* the pistol the armed robber used." Now think back to the testimony by the third witness, Mr. Usher. He took the stand and told you that he owns a gun store downtown. He testified that in March of this year, a man came to his store—a man he recognizes as the defendant. Most importantly, he testified that the defendant grabbed a pistol and ran out of the store. Mr. Usher immediately checked his records. And guess what? The missing gun was a .32 caliber pistol, serial number 789444. This is People's Exhibit #3, Mr. Usher's inventory sheet. It lists all the weapons in Mr. Usher's inventory that day. You're going to have this exhibit in the deliberation room. Check it against exhibit #2. You'll see that the number matches perfectly. Ladies and gentlemen, there's only one pistol out there that perfectly fits that description. It's this one. This is the pistol the defendant stole from Mr. Usher, and it's the same one he used to rob Mr. Vermont. Put the testimony by Officer Salcido, Mr. Vermont, and Mr. Usher together, and what do you get? You get the only reasonable conclusion, namely, that the defendant is the man who robbed the liquor store. In a few minutes, her Honor will give you the legal instructions you have to follow during your deliberations. One of those instructions relates to Mr. Usher's testimony. In her Honor's words, you can consider that testimony 'if it tends to show the identity of the person who committed the crime of which the defendant is accused.' I want you to do exactly what her Honor is going to tell you to do. Think about Mr. Usher's testimony when you deliberate on the question of the identity of the robber. If you do that, I'm confident you'll find that the defendant was the robber and that the defendant is guilty as charged."

This hypothetical illustrates the typical use of § 1101(b) in a criminal case. However, § 1101(b) is not limited to other acts by the defendant. Section 1101(b) applies to the conduct of any person. For example, if the conduct in question is logically relevant in the case on a noncharacter theory, the defense may offer evidence of the misconduct of the police. *People v. Davis*, 10 Cal. 4th 463, 896 P.2d 119, 41 Cal. Rptr. 2d 826, *cert. denied*, 516 U.S. 1121 (1996); *People v. Memro*, 38 Cal. 3d 658, 681, 700 P.2d 446, 462, 214 Cal. Rptr. 832, 848 (1985). Or the defense may offer uncharged misconduct by a third party whom the defense claims committed the crime the defendant is charged with. *People v. Hall*, 41 Cal. 3d 826, 718 P.2d 99, 226 Cal. Rptr. 112 (1986); Note, *And Justice for Hall: The Overruling of the Mendez-Arline Standard of Admissibility for Third Party Culpability Evidence in People v. Hall*, 14 W. St. U. L. Rev. 261 (1986).

E.   UNCHARGED MISCONDUCT EVIDENCE IN CIVIL ACTIONS

1. THE DOCTRINE

Subdivision 1101(b) refers not only to evidence of other crimes, but also to evidence of other civil wrongs or other acts. Moreover, while statutes such as § 1102 are expressly limited to criminal actions, there is no such limitation in § 1101(b). Therefore, § 1101(b) applies to civil actions as well as prosecutions. In a prosecution, the People may not use evidence of a defendant's other crimes as evidence of his propensity to commit crimes. Similarly, in a tort action, the plaintiff may not use evidence of a defendant's other torts as evidence of his propensity to act tortiously. For instance, the plaintiff may not argue that the defendant is a careless driver and that his character trait of careless driving increases the likelihood that he ran the red light. To this extent, the criminal and civil cases are parallel.

However, in another respect, the civil cases differ from the criminal cases. As stated in the last section, in contemporary criminal cases the California courts follow the inclusionary approach; they permit the prosecutor to rely on any noncharacter theory of logical relevance. They do so because § 1101(b) prefaces the list of acceptable theories of logical relevance with the words, "such as." In contrast, most civil cases still follow an exclusionary approach; they insist that the proponent of other misconduct in a civil case bring the evidence within a listed pigeonhole, such as proof of a defendant's earlier notice of the existence of a dangerous condition. This approach ignores the plain language of § 1101(b), which is clearly inclusionary, not exclusionary. Nonetheless, California courts have tended to look to § 352 as a source of authority to maintain rigid, common-law restrictions on the admission of a defendant's other torts. The better approach would be to look to the more specific statute, § 1101(b); the proponent of uncharged misconduct in a civil case ought to be permitted to introduce the evidence on any noncharacter theory, just as in criminal cases.

2. ELEMENTS OF THE FOUNDATION

The list of foundational elements is the same as the list for uncharged misconduct evidence in criminal cases:

1. Where the other act occurred.
2. When the act occurred.
3. What the nature of the act was.
4. The defendant committed the other act.
5. The surrounding circumstances make the unpleaded act relevant to the pleaded act. The proponent must convince the trial judge that the act is logically relevant to a material fact other than the defendant's disposition or propensity.

3. SAMPLE FOUNDATION

The fact situation is a wrongful discharge action. The plaintiff, Mr. Morrison, contends that the defendant, Mr. Ziegler, fired him because the plaintiff is black. The complaint alleges that the defendant employed the plaintiff as a Shop Supervisor and that the defendant fired the plaintiff on May 12th of the present year. The defendant purchased the company the year before. As his next witness, the plaintiff calls Mr. Foote. Mr. Foote has identified himself.

P WHERE do you work?
W At the moment I'm unemployed.
P WHAT was your last job? (4), (5)
W I worked for the defendant, Ron Ziegler.
P WHERE is he now? (4)
W In the courtroom. He's sitting at the table to my right. He's got on a brown suit.
P Your Honor, please let the record reflect that the witness has correctly identified the defendant.
J It will so reflect.
P WHAT type of work did you do for the defendant? (5)
W I was a Shop Supervisor for my last four years there. I worked on the assembly line for six years before that.
P WHY did you stop working for him? (3)
W He fired me.
P WHEN did he do that? (2)
W It was on May 6th of this year.
P WHERE did it happen? (1)
W One day over the public address system he just called me into his office. I reported there as soon as I heard the call.

P WHAT happened after you reported to his office? (3)

W He said he was firing me.

P WHAT did you do then? (5)

W I demanded an explanation. I'd put in a lot of good years at that company, and I wanted to know why he was letting me go.

P WHAT, if anything, did the defendant say when you demanded an explanation? (5)

W He said he was letting me go because I was black. He said blacks are not dependable, and, since there were no witnesses to our conversation, he didn't mind telling me the real reason he was giving me my walking papers.

O Your Honor, may we approach the bench?

J Certainly.

O Your Honor, I move to strike this entire line of questioning on the ground that it's irrelevant and that it amounts to bad character evidence.

P May I be heard?

J Yes.

P Your Honor, I'm not going to offer this evidence to support a general inference that the defendant is a bad person. I know that would violate Evidence Code § 1101(a). Rather, I'm offering this evidence on a noncharacter theory of logical relevance. The defendant fired Mr. Foote less than a week before he fired the plaintiff. Like the plaintiff, Mr. Foote is a black man. Given the surrounding circumstances, including the defendant's statements to Mr. Foote, the firing of Mr. Foote shows that the defendant had a racial prejudice that motivated him to fire black employees. In this case, we have to show that the defendant fired the plaintiff because he was black, and this incident with Mr. Foote tends to show the defendant's later intent.

J I agree. Motion to strike denied.

O If you're going to overrule my motion, will you at least give the jury a limiting instruction?

J Of course. I will tell them that they can't use the evidence as proof that your client is a bad person. I'll direct them to consider the evidence only in deciding why your client discharged the plaintiff.

Notice that at the end of this line of questioning, the proponent did not attempt to elicit the witness's testimony that given the prior incident, it is more probable that the defendant's termination of the plaintiff was motivated by racial discrimination. That testimony would amount to improper opinion. Moreover, it is unnecessary for the proponent to invite the witness to draw that inference; during the subsequent instructions the judge will tell the jury that they can decide whether to draw the inference, and during summation the proponent may expressly argue in favor of the inference.

When the testimony is admitted, during the final jury charge, or on both occasions the judge might tell the jury the following about the evidence:

"Evidence has been introduced to show that the defendant discriminated against an employee other than the plaintiff. This evidence, if believed, may not be considered by you to prove that the defendant is a bad person or that he has a disposition to perform illegal acts. It may be considered by you only for the limited purpose of determining if it tends to show that the defendant has a bias against a class of persons that includes the plaintiff. For the limited purpose for which you may consider this evidence, you must weigh it in the same manner as you do all other evidence in the case. You are not permitted to consider this evidence for any other purpose."

During closing argument, the plaintiff's attorney could state:

"Ladies and gentlemen, as I told you in opening statement, there wouldn't be any denying that Mr. Morrison worked for the defendant or that the defendant fired him this May. As I said then, this case was going to boil down to one question: Why did the defendant fire Mr. Morrison? Did the defendant fire Mr. Morrison because Mr. Morrison is an African-American? In a few minutes her Honor will read you the legal instructions that you must follow during your deliberations in this case. One of those instructions relates to some of the key testimony in this case, the testimony given by Mr. Foote. As you'll recall, Mr. Foote told you what happened when the defendant fired him. That firing also occurred in May of this year. In her instruction, her Honor will tell you that you may consider Mr. Foote's testimony in deciding why the defendant let Mr. Morrison go. Mr. Foote told you that, like Mr. Morrison, he had worked for the defendant for years. Like Mr. Morrison, Mr. Foote was called into the defendant's private office. There the defendant flabbergasted Mr. Foote. With absolutely no advance warning, the defendant gives Mr. Foote his walking papers; and to add insult to injury, the defendant told him point blank that he was firing Mr. Foote because he's black! Now think about it, ladies and gentlemen. This all happened in the same month in which the defendant fired Mr. Morrison. And remember that we're talking about racial bias. Racial bias run deep. It takes years for those attitudes to build up, and they last and last and last. You're not a bigot one day and a completely tolerant person the next. If the defendant acted out of racial bias when he fired Mr. Foote, it stands to reason that he did the same thing when he fired Mr. Morrison a mere six days later. Follow her Honor's instruction. Consider Mr. Foote's testimony; and when you do, you'll come to the only reasonable conclusion, namely, that the defendant fired Mr. Morrison out of simple racism."

F. SIMILAR HAPPENINGS EVIDENCE

1. THE DOCTRINE

In the last section, we saw that § 1101 applies in a civil case when a party offers evidence of a person's misdeeds that are not mentioned in the pleadings. Subdivision 1101(a) bars the party from using the misdeeds as circumstantial proof of the person's conduct, but §1101(b) permits the party to use noncharacter theories of logical relevance to introduce evidence of the misdeeds. Whether the case is a prosecution or a civil action, under § 1101 the focus is on the conduct of some person.

In other cases, the focus is on the qualities or properties of a nonperson, usually some kind of physical object. Was a sidewalk cracked at the time the plaintiff slipped and fell? Was a steering wheel's design dangerously defective? To prove the quality of the object, the plaintiff may attempt to introduce evidence of other accidents involving the same or similar objects. Article, *Similar Facts Evidence: Balancing Probative Value Against the Probable Dangers of Admission*, 9 U.C. DAVIS L. REV. 395 (1976). For example, the plaintiff may offer evidence that the day before her mishap, another passerby slipped and fell at the same location on the sidewalk.

On the one hand, § 1101 does not apply directly when a plaintiff offers evidence of such a similar happening. Section 1101 comes into play when the party offers evidence of another incident to prove a person's conduct. The focus is now on the property of something other than a person. On the other hand, like evidence of a person's misdeeds used as circumstantial proof of the person's conduct, evidence of the other slip and fall poses probative dangers. The presentation of the testimony about the other accident may confuse the trier of fact, consume an undue amount of time, and sidetrack the trial. For that reason, although the evidence of other slip and fall is relevant to prove the existence of the crack in the sidewalk, the judge might exclude the evidence under § 352.

In the past, the California courts adopted an exclusionary approach to the admission of evidence of other accidents. The courts announced a general rule that such evidence is inadmissible. The courts recognized only a limited number of exceptions to the general rule; they permitted plaintiffs to introduce evidence of other torts to show that a particular physical condition existed at the time of plaintiff's accident, that the condition was dangerous or defective, and that the condition caused the accident. Further, even if the evidence otherwise fell within an exception to the general exclusionary rule, the plaintiff had to demonstrate that the conditions existing at the time of the pleaded accident were substantially similar to the circumstances surrounding the unpleaded tort. *Id.*

The courts have begun to liberalize the standards for admitting evidence of other torts and accidents. In *Ault v. International Harvester Co.*, 13 Cal. 3d 113, 528 P.2d 1148, 117 Cal. Rptr. 812 (1974), the plaintiff claimed that he was injured when the gear box of the vehicle manufactured by the defendant failed. The plaintiff offered evidence of several other accidents involving the defendant's motor vehicle and seemingly caused by metal fatigue of the aluminum gear box. However, the plaintiff did not introduce any other evidence of the circumstances surrounding the other accidents. On appeal, the California Supreme Court held that the evidence of the other accidents was admissible. Justice Jefferson comments:

In *Ault*, the supreme court created an exception to the general rule on admissibility of evidence of prior or subsequent accidents. This exception permits evidence of a prior or subsequent accident in a defective product strict liability case without a showing of similarity of circumstances or conditions between the other accident and the accident in question. The defect claimed must be a defect in the physical and mechanical characteristics of a product. The evidence of the prior or subsequent accident must establish that the product involved in that accident and the product involved in the accident in question possessed inherent similarities in their physical and mechanical characteristics. Finally, the evidence must establish that the two products possessed similar defects in their physical and mechanical characteristics that caused the two accidents. If these conditions are satisfied, it does not matter that the two accidents may have occurred under substantially different circumstances or conditions. In such a case, the focus is not on the accidents themselves but on the inherent similarity of the physical and mechanical properties of the allegedly defective products.

1 JEFFERSON § 21.67.

Courts severely limit the use of similar happenings evidence in criminal trials. "Profile" evidence is particularly objectionable, and is inadmissible unless there is evidence connecting the defendant to the specific crimes referred to by the testimony. *People v. Martinez*, 10 Cal. App. 4th 1001, 12 Cal. Rptr. 2d 838 (1992).

2. ELEMENTS OF THE FOUNDATION

The foundation is similar to the foundation for evidence of an uncharged crime in a prosecution or tort offered under § 1101(b):

1. Where the other accident occurred.
2. When the accident occurred.
3. What the nature of the accident was.
4. The defendant's responsibility for the accident.
5. The surrounding circumstances making the unpleaded happening relevant to show the property or quality of the object mentioned in the pleading.

3. SAMPLE FOUNDATION[1]

The fact situation is a products liability case arising from a traffic accident. The plaintiff, Ms. Ramachotti, alleges that she purchased a new Cetus sedan and that the car's steering mechanism had a design defect. Specifically, the plaintiff contends that the mechanism had a tendency to freeze in lengthy, uphill sums.

The plaintiff has already testified. During her testimony the plaintiff testified

---

[1] *Adapted from* E. IMWINKELRIED, UNCHARGED MISCONDUCT EVIDENCE § 9:26 (1984). *Reprinted with permission of Clark Boardman Callahan.*

that she was driving north on a freeway and entered an off-ramp leading to the eastbound lane of a street near the freeway. She described the off-ramp as turning to the right, sloping slightly uphill, and being approximately 2000 feet in length. The plaintiff stated that the steering wheel froze when her car was halfway through the off-ramp. During her testimony, the plaintiff used a chart to illustrate her testimony.

The plaintiff's attorney calls Mr. Dorsey to testify about an uncharged accident involving his new Cetus sedan, which was equipped with a stick shift. The purpose of Dorsey's testimony is to show the existence of a defect in the Cetus sedan's steering mechanism.

Assume that the witness has already identified himself. The next part of the direct examination establishes the witness' personal knowledge of the uncharged accident.

P WHERE were you on the morning of September 19?
W I drove from my home in San Lorenzo to downtown Livermore. (1), (2)
P WHO was driving the car?
W I was.

The next part of the direct examination is devoted to showing the similarity of circumstances between the uncharged accident and the accident alleged in the pleading. The plaintiff wants to demonstrate that the physical layout of the site of the uncharged accident is comparable to that of the pleaded accident.

P WHAT route did you take?
W I drove Highway 580 most of the way. (1)
P In WHAT direction were you driving on Highway 580? (1)
W I was traveling east.
P WHEN did you get off Highway 580? (2)
W I tried to get off at the exit for traffic going south on Hanley Avenue.
P HOW can you remember that exit?
W I use it all the time when I go into Livermore.
P Your Honor, I request that this be marked Plaintiff's exhibit number four for identification.
J It will be so marked.
P Please let the record reflect that I am showing the exhibit to the opposing counsel.
J The record will so reflect.
P I request permission to approach the witness.
J Permission granted.
P Mr. Dorsey, I now hand you what has been marked Plaintiff's exhibit number four for identification. WHAT is it? (1)
W It s a map showing Highway 580 and the off-ramp for Hanley going south.
P HOW can you recognize it? (1)
W As I said, I've used that off-ramp lots of times.
P WHEN you enter this off-ramp, in WHAT diction are you traveling?
W At first, you're still going east.

P Please use this blue marker and write "east" at the mouth of the off-ramp.

W Yes.

P Your Honor, please let the record reflect that the witness has complied with my request.

J It will so reflect.

P WHEN you finally reached Hanley, in WHAT direction were you traveling? (1)

W South.

P Please write "south" at the off-ramp's exit.

W Done.

P In WHAT direction were you turning on the off-ramp? (1)

W I was turning to the right.

P HOW long is the off-ramp? (5)

W It's pretty long. It's a gradual thing. It's maybe 2,000 feet.

P HOW does the off-ramp slope? Does it go up to Hanley or down to Hanley? (5)

W It slopes up. You're going up maybe ten feet in all.

P Please draw an arrow from the mouth of the off-ramp to the exit and write "up" next to the arrow.

W OK.

P HOW steep is the slope? (5)

W I'm no engineer, but it's pretty gradual.

P In general, HOW accurate is this exhibit? (1)

W I don't know if it's to scale, but on the whole it seems correct.

P Your Honor, I now offer plaintiff's exhibit number four for identification into evidence as plaintiff s exhibit number four.

J It will be received.

(The plaintiff now begins to invoke process-of-elimination reasoning. To single out the defect in the vehicle's steering as the cause of the accident, the plaintiff questions the witness to negate other possible causes of the accident such as lack of maintenance, speeding, intoxication, poor visibility, and the witness' inattention.)

P Now, Mr. Dorsey, I'd like to ask you a few question about the car you were driving toward this off-ramp. WHERE did you purchase this car? (4)

W From a Cetus dealer in Hayward.

P Was the car new or used?

W New. I was the first owner.

P HOW long had you owned the car before the accident on September 19? (4)

W I'd had it for only two months before this occurred.

P HOW often, if at all, had you had the car serviced before the accident? (4)

W I took it in twice. The first time I took it in about two weeks after buying it, and then I took it in about a week before the accident for the 2,500-mile maintenance under the warranty.

P WHERE did you take the car for service? (4)

W I took it back to the same Cetus dealer that I initially bought it from.

P Mr. Dorsey, to the best of your knowledge, WHAT was the condition of your car on the day of the accident?

W As far as I knew, it was in good working order.

P All right, now let's get back to the exhibit. Could you show us approximately WHERE your car was on the map when you were 1000 feet from the entrance to the off-ramp? (1)

W I'd say right here.

P Please place a dot and "D-1" at that point.

W Here it is.

P At that point, HOW fast were you doing? (5)

W I was doing about fifty-five, but this is the point where I began to slow down.

P WHAT is the posted speed limit along this portion of Highway 580? (5)

W Fifty-five.

P Now please indicate with a dot and "D-2" WHERE you would be when you were 100 feet from the entrance to the off-ramp. (1)

W Right.

P HOW fast were you going then? (5)

W I had slowed to thirty.

P WHAT is the posted speed limit at the entrance to the off-ramp? (5)

W I m pretty sure it's thirty.

P WHAT was the condition of the pavement? (5)

W It was dry.

P WHEN was the last rain? (5)

W Not in weeks.

P HOW well could you see when you reached the mouth of the off-ramp?(5)

W Perfectly.

P WHAT were the lighting conditions at that time? (5)

W It was mid-morning, and it was a beautiful, clear day.

P WHAT, if anything, obstructed your view of the off-ramp? (5)

W Nothing. The only shrubbery in the area is grass. There are no big trees or anything.

P HOW closely were you paying attention to your driving? (5)

W I was watching it close.

P WHY? (5)

W Hanley is a pretty busy street, and I wanted to have good control of my car before I got on a busy thoroughfare like Hanley.

P HOW good was your vision that morning? (5)

W Fine. I have twenty-twenty vision, and I've never worn glasses.

P WHAT was your physical condition? (5)

W Excellent.

P HOW many drinks, if any, had you had that morning? (5)

W None. None at all.

At this point, the plaintiff elicits the description of the accident itself. The plaintiff wants to make the uncharged accident sound as similar as possible to the pleaded accident.

P WHAT happened after you entered the off-ramp? (3)

W At first, everything was going smoothly.

P WHAT happened next?

W About halfway into the turn, the steering wheel just plain froze.

P WHAT do you mean by "froze"? (5)

W   I couldn't move it at all.
P   Please indicate by placing "D-3" WHERE you were when the steering first froze. (1)
W   Right there.
P   HOW fast were you going then? (5)
W   Probably only twenty or twenty-five.
P   WHAT did you do then? (5)
W   I hit the brakes and tried to move the wheel.
P   HOW quickly did you hit the brakes? (5)
W   As soon as I realized I was in trouble—immediately.
P   HOW did the wheel respond? (5)
W   Not at all.
P   WHAT happened after you hit the brakes? (5)
W   I slowed a bit, but it was just too late.
P   WHERE did the car go? (5)
W   It plowed through the railing, flew off the off-ramp, and finally stopped over here.
P   Please mark the resting point of your car with "D-4."
W   Right here.

At this point, the plaintiff elicits the witness' testimony that his automobile contained the same design feature as the plaintiff's.

P   Now the car that you were driving that morning, the car that eventually came to rest at D-4, WHAT was the make of that car? (4), (5)
W   It was a Cetus.
P   WHAT was the model of Cetus? (5)
W   It was the sedan.
P   WHAT was the year of that model? (5)
W   1995.
P   Was the car automatic or stick shift? (5)
W   Stick shift.
P   WHAT, if any, accessories did you have on the car? (5)
W   Other than air-conditioning and radio, there were none. It was a basic 1995 Cetus sedan, right off the showroom floor.
P   Thank you, Mr. Dorsey. (To the defense counsel) Your witness.

G.   LIABILITY INSURANCE

A tort plaintiff ordinarily may not prove that the defendant has liability insurance. There is a weak argument that the defendant's liability coverage is logically relevant to show the defendant's negligence; knowing that he or she has liability insurance, the defendant might be less careful. However, there is a danger that the evidence will tempt the jury to decide the case on an improper basis; the jurors may find for the plaintiff, not because they are convinced of the defendant's fault, but rather because they believe the insurance company can absorb the economic loss better than the plaintiff. Evidence Code § 1155 states the rule:

Evidence that a person was, at the time a harm was suffered by another, insured wholly or partially against loss arising from liability for that harm is inadmissible to prove negligence or other wrongdoing.

The structure of the liability insurance doctrine under § 1155 is similar to the uncharged misconduct doctrine under § 1101. The uncharged misconduct doctrine is two-pronged. One prong is the prohibition of introducing uncharged acts on a character theory of reasoning. The second prong is an authorization to admit uncharged acts on noncharacter theories of relevance. Section 1155 likewise has two prongs. On the one hand, the evidence of the defendant's liability insurance may not be used to support a generalized inference of the defendant's negligence. On the other hand, the plaintiff may use the evidence for other purposes. The following foundations illustrate both the rule and three of the more important exceptions to the rule.

The first fact situation is a tort case. This situation illustrates the rule and the exception for references that are integral parts of an admission. The plaintiff, Ms. Greenwich, sues the defendant, Mr. Fenton. The plaintiff alleges that the defendant's negligent driving caused the collision in which she was injured. The defendant takes the stand and denies driving carelessly. The plaintiff then begins cross-examination. The plaintiff is the opponent.

O Mr. Fenton, ISN'T IT TRUE THAT you carry liability insurance?
P Your Honor, I object to that question on the ground that it calls for evidence of liability insurance.
J Objection sustained.
P Your Honor, I request a curative instruction.
J Yes. Ladies and gentlemen of the jury, you have just heard a reference to possible liability insurance in this case. You are to disregard that reference. You may not speculate whether the defendant has insurance, and you may not consider the possible existence of insurance in your deliberations. You are to decide whether the defendant is liable solely on the basis of the evidence admitted in this case.
P Now, your Honor, I must move for a mistrial. Even the curative instruction won't undo the damage that's already been done.
J Well, I don't think that the reference is serious enough to warrant that. The motion will be denied.

The hypothetical continues.

O Mr. Fenton, ISN'T IT TRUE THAT after the collision, you walked up to my client, Ms. Greenwich?
W Yes.
O DID you have a conversation with her then?
W Yes.
O During that conversation, DIDN'T you tell Ms. Greenwich, Don't worry. If your insurance doesn't cover this, my insurance company will pick up the tab?
P Your Honor, I object to that question on the ground that it calls for evidence of liability insurance.

O   May we approach the bench?

J   Yes.

O   Your Honor, it is well-settled in California that § 1155 does not bar mention of liability insurance when the mention is an integral part of an admission of fault. Section 34.34 of the third edition of Justice Jefferson's Benchbook recognizes the rule, and the rule was applied in *Brainard v. Cotner*, 59 Cal. App. 3d 790, 130 Cal. Rptr. 915 (1976).

P   I agree, your Honor, that § 1155 permits the introduction of the evidence when it's truly an inseverable part of an admission. However, it's not even clear that this statement was intended as an admission of fault. The case in point is *Menefee v. Williams*, 259 Cal. App. 2d 56, 66 Cal. Rptr. 108 (1968). There the defendant allegedly said, "Don't worry. If your insurance doesn't cover this, mine will." The court squarely held that § 1155 barred the evidence.

J   *Menefee* seems much closer on the facts to the instant case. Therefore, I'll sustain the objection.

P   Thank you, your Honor. I request a curative instruction. I'll do that as well, counsel.

The hypothetical continues. The continuation illustrates a second exception. Assume that the defendant called Mr. Graham as a witness. Mr. Graham inspected the accident scene and measured the plaintiff's skidmarks. The skidmarks supported the defendant's theory that the plaintiff caused the accident by speeding. The plaintiff now takes Mr. Graham on cross-examination.

P   Mr. Graham, ISN'T IT TRUE THAT you work for Allied Insurance Company?

W   Yes.

P   AND ISN'T IT ALSO A FACT THAT your company insures the defendant, Mr. Fenton?

O   Your Honor, I object to that question on the ground that it calls for evidence of liability insurance.

P   Your Honor, may we approach the bench?

J   Yes.

P   Your Honor, we are not offering the evidence to support a general inference of negligence on Mr. Fenton's part. Rather, we would offer the evidence to impeach Mr. Graham; the evidence is logically relevant to show Mr. Graham's bias in the defendant's favor. *Hart v. Wielt*, 4 Cal. App. ad 224, 231, 84 Cal. Rptr. 220, 225 (1970), holds that proof of bias is a permissible alternative theory for admitting evidence of liability insurance.

J   The objection is overruled.

P   Mr. Graham, let me repeat the question. ISN'T IT CORRECT THAT your company insures the defendant?

W   Yes.

O   Your Honor, I request a limiting instruction under Evidence Code § 355.

J   Very well. Ladies and gentlemen of the jury, you have just heard evidence that the defendant has liability insurance. You may not consider that evidence in deciding whether the defendant was at fault in the accident. You also should not consider whether the insurance company is in a better economic position to absorb any loss than the plaintiff. I am admitting the evidence for one limited purpose—to shed light on Mr. Graham's credibility. You may consider the fact that Mr. Graham works for Mr. Fenton's insurance company in deciding how much weight to attach to Mr. Graham's testimony.

The hypothetical continues. This version of the hypothetical illustrates another exception to the rule. Now assume that Jennings Trucking Company is the codefendant. The codefendant denies that Fenton is its employee. The codefendant calls Mr. Munster as a witness. Mr. Munster testifies that he is the codefendant's general manager. On direct examination, he testifies that although Fenton once worked for Jennings Trucking Company, he was not an employee at the time of the accident. Suppose that the plaintiff gave Jennings notice to produce its insurance policy and thereby satisfied the best evidence rule. The plaintiff now takes Mr. Munster on cross-examination.

P   Mr. Munster, ISN'T IT TRUE THAT your company carries liability insurance?

O   Your Honor, I object to that question on the ground that it calls for evidence of liability insurance.[2]

P   Your Honor, may we approach the bench?

J   Yes.

P   I offer to prove that if the witness is permitted to answer, the witness will testify that the codefendant's insurance policy listed Mr. Fenton as an employee at the time of the accident. The codefendant denies that Mr. Fenton was its employee at that time, and I am offering the evidence for the limited purpose of showing Mr. Fenton's agency. That purpose is a permissible alternative theory for introducing evidence of liability insurance. The federal counterpart of Evidence Code §1155, Federal Evidence Rule 411, specifically lists proof of agency, ownership, or control as a legitimate purpose for admitting the evidence.

J   The objection will be overruled.

P   Mr. Munster, let me repeat the question. ISN'T IT TRUE THAT your company carries liability insurance?

W   Yes.

P   AND ISN'T IT A FACT THAT appendix II to the policy lists the employees covered by the policy?

W   That's correct.

P   ISN'T IT TRUE THAT at the time of the accident, appendix II to your policy listed Mr. Fenton as one of your employees?

W   That's right.

O   Your Honor, I would like a limiting instruction.

J   Yes. Ladies and gentlemen of the jury, you have just heard a reference to the codefendant's liability insurance. You are not to consider that evidence in deciding whether either defendant acted negligently. You are also not to speculate as to whether the insurance company could absorb the loss resulting from the accident. You are to consider the evidence only for the purpose of deciding whether, at the

---

[2]The defense attorney might also object under Evidence Code § 352. The attorney might argue, for example, that there are several, far less prejudicial ways to prove that Fenton was an employee at the time of the accident.

time of the accident, Mr. Fenton was an employee of Jennings Trucking Company.

H.   IN-COURT EXHIBITIONS

In a personal injury case, the plaintiff's attorney may want the plaintiff to display the injured arm or leg to the jurors. Such an exhibition can be helpful to the jury in determining the damages in the case. Evidence Code § 140 implicitly recognizes the permissibility of exhibitions. That section defines "evidence" as including "material objects, or other things presented to the senses. ..." The California Law Revision Commission comment on § 140 states that the definition encompasses "sights ... such as ... the appearance of a person exhibited to a jury. ..." However, the danger is that the exhibition will inflame the jurors; after viewing a badly mangled limb, the jurors may be unable to dispassionately weigh the evidence on liability or damages.

Under Evidence Code § 352, the trial judge has wide discretion in deciding whether to permit an exhibition. The judge ordinarily considers three factors: (1) whether the object to be exhibited is relevant to the case; (2) whether the jurors need to see the object to understand the oral testimony about the object; and (3) the risk that viewing the object will inflame the jurors' emotions.

The fact situation is a products liability action. The plaintiff, Mr. Jansen, brought the action against Kenway, Inc., which manufactures electrical saws. The plaintiff alleged that the defendant defectively designed the saw, and that the design defect caused the blade to come loose and slice the plaintiff's arms. The plaintiff takes the witness stand; when he does so, the plaintiff is wearing a jacket. The plaintiff has testified about his injuries in general terms. The proponent, the plaintiff's attorney, now wants to exhibit the injuries to the jurors.

P WHAT were your injuries?

W The blade sliced both of my arms very badly.

P Mr. Jansen, would you please take off your jacket and show your arms to the jurors?

O Your Honor, may we approach the bench?

J Certainly.

O Your Honor, I strenuously object to this exhibition.

P Your Honor, the plaintiff's arms were injured in this accident, and it's certainly logically relevant to show the jurors what the arms look like now.

O I admit that the exhibition would be relevant, but I object on the ground that the sight of the plaintiff's badly cut arms will arouse the jurors' emotions and prejudice my client.

P The jurors simply won't understand the extent of the plaintiff's injuries unless they actually see the arms.

J I tend to agree. The objection is overruled. You may proceed with the exhibition.

I.   IN-COURT DEMONSTRATIONS

A demonstration is a step beyond an exhibition. In an exhibition, the proponent merely displays something for the jurors' view. In a demonstration, the proponent demonstrates some physical or mechanical process in action. The California Law Revision Commission comment to Evidence Code § 140 also specifically refers to demonstrations. The proponent may want to demonstrate how poorly the plaintiff can move his limbs or how a particular machine operates. Once again, under § 352 the trial judge has wide discretion in deciding whether to permit the demonstration. In exercising this discretion, the judge looks to three factors relevant to exhibitions plus an additional factor. The fourth factor is the risk that the party demonstrating a physical process may be feigning. A plaintiff can easily feign the extent of his or her disability, and it will be very difficult to expose the feigning plaintiff during cross-examination. Courts will not allow a demonstration unless the proponent can show that the conditions of the demonstration are substantially similar to those of the original event. *People v. Gilbert*, 5 Cal. App. 4th 1372, 7 Cal. Rptr. 2d 660 (1992).

We shall continue the hypothetical in Section H. Suppose that the plaintiff claims that as a result of the saw accident, he can no longer straighten his arms.

P   Mr. Jansen, let me repeat my request. Please show your arms to the jurors.
W   (The witness does so.)
P   HOW has the accident affected your arms?
W   I have a good deal of pain, and I can't straighten them all the way any more.
P   Please show us how far you can straighten your arms.
O   Your Honor, may we approach the bench again?
J   Yes.
O   I hate to object again, your Honor, but I feel compelled to register my objection to this demonstration.
P   Your Honor, this demonstration is indisputably relevant. To show the plaintiffs disability, we have to show the extent to which he's lost the use of his arms.
O   Your Honor, how can I cross-examine a demonstration? There's too great a risk that the plaintiff will be able to feign the extent of his disability.
P   We need this demonstration to help the jury understand our medical testimony about the extent of disability, and the defendant can cross-examine the experts about whether the plaintiff is faking.
J   The objection will be overruled. The demonstration may proceed.

Chapter 7

SECONDARY EVIDENCE RULE

A. REPEAL OF THE BEST EVIDENCE RULE, EFFECTIVE JANUARY 1, 1999

The California legislature repealed California's best evidence rule, effective January 1, 1999. As of that date, new statutes called the "Secondary Evidence Rule" replaced the former best evidence rule. To effect this change, the legislature repealed California Evidence Code §§ 1500-1511 and added §§ 1520-1523 and 1552-1553. The legislature made the changes on recommendation of the California Law Revision Commission. *See* Best Evidence Rule, 26 Cal. L. Revision Comm'n Reports 369 (1996). In support of its recommendation, the Law Revision Commission argued that the old law was hard to understand and apply, and that it had become outmoded in modern times when accurate copying machines are commonplace and when litigants can use pretrial discovery to examine the originals of suspicious writings. *Id.* It remains to be seen whether the new law will be easier to understand and apply.

Part 1 of this chapter analyzes the new Secondary Evidence Rule. Part 2 of this chapter retains the best evidence rule analysis that existed in the Second Edition of this book. Several features of the best evidence rule were continued without substantive change in the Secondary Evidence Rule, as stated in the Law Revision Commission Comments that accompany the repeal of the former statutes. The purpose of retaining the prior analysis is to aid practitioners and jurists as they interpret provisions that are common to both the former and current rules.

Part 1. Secondary Evidence Rule

B. INTRODUCTION

The Secondary Evidence Rule, Evidence Code §§ 1520-1523, became effective January 1, 1999, and replaced the former best evidence rule, repealed §§ 1500-1511. The new rule applies in an action or proceeding commenced before, on, or after January 1, 1999. Nothing in the new law invalidates an evidentiary determination made before January 1, 1999, pursuant to the former best evidence rule. However, if an action or proceeding was pending on January 1, 1999, the proponent of evidence excluded under the former best evidence rule could, before entry of judgment in the action or proceeding, make a new request for admission of the evidence on the basis of the Secondary Evidence Rule.

C.   PROVING THE CONTENT OF A WRITING

1. THE DOCTRINE

The new law authorizes three ways to prove the content of a writing, as follows:

1) **The Original.** First, you may use the original of the writing (assuming, of course, that the original is otherwise admissible). *See* Evidence Code § 1520.

2) **Secondary Evidence.** Second, subject to the exceptions noted below, you may use secondary evidence of the writing (assuming that the secondary evidence is otherwise admissible). *See* Evidence Code § 1521(a). Oddly, the new law does not define the term secondary evidence, but the term appears to mean:

- duplicates, as defined by § 260 (e.g., a photocopy of a birth certificate, a xerographic copy of a contract, an electronic copy of a computer disk, and other copies made by highly accurate methods); plus
- copies made by methods that may or may not be accurate (e.g., a handwritten copy of a police report, a re-typed copy of a lease, a computer disk containing a stenographer's transcription of a letter).

Under the new law, the term secondary evidence does *not* include oral testimony about the content of a writing. The new usage is a departure from the old law. *Compare* Evidence Code §§ 1521(b) and 1523 *with* former Evidence Code § 1505.

In all types of cases—civil, criminal, and miscellaneous—you may *not* use secondary evidence of the writing if your opponent convinces the court that either of the following is true:

- a genuine dispute exists about the material terms of the writing, and justice requires the secondary evidence to be excluded; or
- use of the secondary evidence would be unfair. *See* Evidence Code § 1521(a)(1) and (2).

The term "unfair" is borrowed from former Evidence Code § 1511 and Federal Rule of Evidence 1003, and the California Law Revision Commission suggests using the case law under those statutes as guidance under the new statute. *See* 26 Cal. Law Revision Comm'n at 392. The Commission's comments [*id.* at 393] list some factors a court might consider in deciding whether use of secondary evidence would be unfair:

- Is the proponent using the writing in a manner that could not have been reasonably anticipated?

- Was the original suppressed during discovery?
- Did reasonably diligent discovery efforts fail to turn up the original?
- Does the secondary evidence differ dramatically from the original? (E.g., the original is in color, and the color helps interpret the writing, but the secondary is in black and white.)
- Is the original unavailable? If so, why?
- Is the writing central to the case, or is it merely collateral?

In criminal cases, there is a third reason—in addition to the two reasons stated above—why the court may prohibit you (either as prosecutor or defendant) from using secondary evidence. *See* Evidence Code § 1522(a). The third reason is that you have the original in your custody or control, and you have not made it available for inspection by your adversary before the trial or at the trial. The language of § 1522(a) is hard to understand, but as we interpret it, the third reason will *not* bar you from using secondary evidence in the following situations:

- you are offering secondary evidence that qualifies as a duplicate, as defined in § 260; or
- you are offering secondary evidence of a writing that is not closely related to the controlling issues in the case; or
- you are offering secondary evidence of a writing that is in the custody of a public entity; or
- you are offering a certified or attested copy of a writing that is recorded in a public record, and a statute makes the certified or attested copy evidence of the writing. [The wording of § 1522(a)(4) might suggest that you could use an uncertified, unattested copy, but that makes no sense and is inconsistent with the case law under the predecessor statutes, former Evidence Code § 1507 and former California Code of Civil Procedure § 1855(4). *See also* Federal Rule of Evidence 1005.]

3) **Oral Testimony.** The third way to prove the content of a writing is by the oral testimony of someone who has seen the writing and can remember it well enough to testify about it. *See* Evidence Code § 1523. This is obviously the least accurate way to prove the contents of a writing, and accordingly it is the least favored way under both the old law and the new law. The new law permits you to use oral testimony in these three situations only:

- if you do not have a copy of the writing, and if the original was lost or destroyed without fraudulent intent on your part;
- if you have neither the original nor a copy of the writing, and if either of the following is true:
  - you could not obtain an original or a copy by the court's process or by other means; or

— the writing is not closely related to the controlling issues, and it would be inexpedient to require its production.

- if the writing is voluminous (such as a box full of accounts) and would take a long time to examine in court, and if the significance of the evidence lies in the "general result" rather than the minutiae.

D.   PRESUMPTIONS AND CRIMINAL EXHIBITS

- Evidence Code § 1552 creates a presumption that a computer printout accurately represents the information or program that it purports to represent. The old law was to the same effect.
- Evidence Code § 1553 creates a presumption that a printout of an image stored on a video or digital medium (for example, a printout from a motion picture disk or a videotape) accurately represents the image it purports to represent. The old law was to the same effect.

California Penal Code § 1417.7 provides that the new law will not affect the admissibility of a certified photographic record of criminal case exhibits that have been disposed of.

E.–H.   RESERVED

Part 2. Analysis of Former Best Evidence Rule

I.   INTRODUCTION

The following analysis is a review of the former best evidence rule. As stated previously, it is included to aid practitioners and jurists as they interpret provisions that are common to both the former and current rule. The Law Revision Commission Comments to the new statutes are provided in section 7.C of this chapter. The following Law Revision Commission Comments accompanied the repeal of the prior statutes (§§ 1500-1511) and state which provisions were incorporated into the new rule.

> LAW REVISION COMMISSION COMMENTS:
> Former Section 1500 is superseded by Sections 1520 (proof of content of writing by original), 1521 (Secondary Evidence Rule), 1522 (exclusion of secondary evidence in criminal action) and 1523 (oral testimony of content of writing).
> Section 1500.5 is repealed to reflect the repeal of the Best Evidence Rule. See Section 1521 Comment. Subdivisions (c) and (d) are continued in Section 1552 (computer printout) without substantive change, except that the reference to "best available evidence" is changed to "an accurate representation," due to the replacement of the Best Evidence Rule with the Secondary Evidence Rule.

Section 1500.6 is repealed to reflect the repeal of the Best Evidence Rule. See Section 1521 Comment. The last three sentences of the second paragraph of Section 1500.6 are continued in Section 1553 (printout of images stored on video or digital media) without substantive change, except that the reference to "best available evidence" is changed to "an accurate representation," due to replacement of the Best Evidence Rule with the Secondary Evidence Rule.

Section 1501 is repealed to reflect the repeal of the Best Evidence Rule. See Section 1521 Comment. As to oral testimony of the content of a writing that is lost or has been destroyed, the combined effect of former Sections 1501 and 1505 is continued in Section 1523 (oral testimony of content of writing) without substantive change.

Section 1502 is repealed to reflect the repeal of the Best Evidence Rule. See Section 1521 Comment. As to oral testimony of the content of a writing that was not reasonably procurable, the combined effect of Sections 1502 and 1505 is continued without substantive change in Section 1523 (oral testimony of content of writing).

Section 1503 is repealed to reflect the repeal of the Best Evidence Rule. See Section 1521 Comment. As to oral testimony of the content of a writing, the combined effect of former Section 1505 and the first sentence of subdivision (a) is continued without substantive change in Section 1523 (oral testimony of content of writing). The requirement of the second sentence of subdivision (a) is continued without substantive change in Section 1522 (exclusion of secondary evidence in criminal action), except that Section 1522 applies that requirement to all requests for exclusion of secondary evidence in a criminal action. Subdivision (b) is not continued, because it is subsumed in the general principle that parties are under no obligation to introduce evidence they subpoena. That principle remains unchanged even though the specific language of subdivision (b) is not continued.

Section 1504 is repealed to reflect the repeal of the Best Evidence Rule. See Section 1521 Comment. As to oral testimony of the content of a collateral writing, the combined effect of former Sections 1504 and 1505 is continued without substantive change in Section 1523 (oral testimony of content of writing).

Section 1505 is repealed to reflect the repeal of the Best Evidence Rule. See Section 1521 Comment. Insofar as Section 1505 pertains to oral testimony of the content of a writing, it is continued without substantive change in Section 1523 (oral testimony of content of writing). See Comments to former Sections 1501-1504.

Section 1506 is repealed to reflect the repeal of the Best Evidence Rule. See Section 1521 Comment. As to oral testimony of the content of a writing in the custody of a public entity, the combined effect of former Sections 1506 and 1508 is continued without substantive change in Section 1523 (oral testimony of content of writing).

Section 1507 is repealed to reflect the repeal of the Best Evidence Rule. See Section 1521 Comment. As to oral testimony of the content of a writing that has been recorded in the public records, the combined effect of former Sections 1507 and 1508 is continued without substantive change in Section 1523 (oral testimony of content of writing).

Section 1508 is repealed to reflect the repeal of the Best Evidence Rule. See Section 1521 Comment. Insofar as Section 1508 pertains to oral testimony of the content of a writing, it is continued without substantive change in Section 1523 (oral testimony of content of writing). See Comments to former Sections 1506, 1507.

Section 1509 is repealed to reflect the repeal of the Best Evidence Rule. See Section 1521 Comment. To the extent that Section 1509 provided a means of obtaining production of accounts or other writings for inspection, continuation of that aspect is unnecessary because other statutes afford sufficient opportunities for such inspection. See, e.g., Code Civ. Proc. §§ 1985.3, 1987, 2020, 2031; Penal Code §§ 1054.1, 1054.3. Insofar as Section 1509 pertains to oral testimony of the content of voluminous writings, it is continued without substantive change in Section 1523 (oral testimony of content of writing).

Section 1510 is repealed to reflect the repeal of the Best Evidence Rule. See Section 1521 Comment.

Section 1511 is repealed to reflect the repeal of the Best Evidence Rule. See Section 1521 Comment. Exceptions to the Secondary Evidence Rule are modeled on the exceptions in former Section 1511. See Section 1521(a) & Comment.

At common law, the best evidence rule was referred to as a "competence" doctrine. Competence doctrines exclude relevant evidence. The common law recognized two types of competence doctrines: (1) doctrines that exclude relevant evidence because of doubts about evidence's reliability; and (2) doctrines that exclude relevant evidence to promote an extrinsic social policy. The opinion, hearsay, and best evidence rules fall into the first category. The best evidence rule excludes secondary evidence of a writing's contents; the rule expresses a preference for the more reliable evidence, the writing itself. Former Evidence Code §§ 1500-11 set out the rule.

Briefly, the rule was that when a writing's terms are in issue, the proponent must either (1) produce an original or duplicate or (2) excuse the nonproduction of the originals and duplicates and present an admissible type of secondary evidence. The rule presents five issues: What is a "document" for purposes of the rule? When are a document's terms "in issue"? What is an "original" or "duplicate"? What are the admissible types of secondary evidence? What are adequate excuses for nonproduction?

The proponent can usually defeat a best evidence objection. The proponent can do so because the five issues convert into several different bases for overriding the objection. The judge can overrule the objection on the grounds that the article involved is not a "writing"; or that the writing's terms are not "in issue"; or that the writing's terms are only collaterally "in issue"; or that the evidence offered is an "original"; or that the evidence offered is a "duplicate"; or that there is an adequate excuse for the nonproduction of the originals and duplicates, and the proponent is offering an admissible type of secondary evidence. The following sections illustrate the various grounds for defeating best evidence objections.

J.   THE OBJECT INVOLVED WAS NOT A "WRITING"

The title of the doctrine, "the best evidence rule," was a misnomer. There was no general requirement that the proponent produce or account for the best evidence, in the sense of the "most persuasive" evidence. It is true that Evidence Code § 412 states that "[i]f weaker and less satisfactory evidence is offered when it was within the power of the party to produce stronger and more satisfactory evidence, the evidence offered should be viewed with distrust." That section allows the opponent to comment adversely during closing argument when the proponent offers inferior evidence. However, unlike the best evidence rule, § 412 does not limit the proponent's ability to offer inferior evidence. The best evidence rule was limited to writings; the rationale is that detail is often vital in the analysis of writings. Thus, a more accurate title for the doctrine would have been the "original writing rule."

Former Evidence Code § 1500 stated the basic exclusionary rule: "Except as otherwise provided by statute, no evidence other than the original of a writing is admissible to prove the content of a writing. This section shall be known and may be cited as the best evidence rule." The key term in the statute is the word "writing." Evidence Code § 250 defines the term expansively: "'Writing' means handwriting, typewriting, printing, photostating, photographing, and every other means of recording upon any tangible thing any form of communication or representation, including letters, words, pictures, sounds, or symbols, or combinations thereof." This definition includes not only conventional writings but also tape recordings and photographs. The definition extends even to inscriptions on tombstones, billboards, traffic signs, and chattels. Article, *The Best Evidence Rule: A Critical Appraisal of the Law in California*, 9 U.C. DAVIS L. REV. 257, 261 (1976). In *People v. Archer*, 215 Cal. App. 3d 197, 207, 263 Cal. Rptr. 486, 492 (1989), the court stated that "videotape is properly considered a writing," citing *People v. Moran*, 39 Cal. App. 3d 398, 407, 114 Cal. Rptr. 413, 418 (1974). In the case of computer magnetic storage media, a computer printout of the contents of the storage media is considered an original. California Evidence Code § 255. *See also Aguimatang v. California State Lottery*, 234 Cal. App. 3d 769, 286 Cal. Rptr. 57 (1991). *See* Chapter 4, Section E, Subsection 3, for authentication of computer records. The only point of disagreement seems to be whether the application of the rule to inscribed chattels is mandatory. In *People v. Mastin*, 115 Cal. App. 3d 978, 171 Cal. Rptr. 780 (1981), the court stated that the Evidence Code gives a judge discretion whether to apply the rule to inscribed chattels. However, that language in *Mastin* may be neither holding nor good law. One commentator dismisses the language as dictum. HEAFEY § 24.2, at 222. Apparently the rule's application to inscribed chattels was mandatory. In *People v. Bizieff*, 226 Cal. App. 3d 1689, 277 Cal. Rptr. 678 (1991), the prosecutor wanted to prove that the defendant and an accomplice were in possession of a robbery victim's credit card shortly following the robbery. For that purpose, the prosecutor offered the testimony of a police officer that the victim's name was on a credit card receipt for a gasoline purchase made by defendant's accomplice. The court concluded that the prosecutor was trying to prove the contents of the credit card, not the credit card receipt. The court further concluded that the credit card, an inscribed chattel, was a "writing" within the meaning of California's best evidence rule. The court allowed the prosecutor to use the police officer's testimony. The receipt was a mere "copy" of the credit card, not a "duplicate," because credit card receipts are often poor reproductions, and they do not reproduce all the information on the card. The credit card itself had not been recovered after the robbery, and the credit card receipt had been sent to the gasoline company. Former Evidence Code § 1505 allowed the prosecutor to use the police officer's oral testimony *without* a showing that the prosecutor had used reasonable diligence to retrieve the receipt from the gasoline company.

The fact situation is a drug prosecution. The People have charged that on January 3 of the present year, the defendant had over a pound of cocaine in his possession at his apartment in Placerville. The prosecutor calls the investigating officer, Officer Feeney, to the witness stand. The officer has already testified that he entered the apartment with the defendant's consent and stepped into the defendant's bedroom. The direct examination continues:

P   WHAT, if anything, did you find when you stepped into the bedroom?

O   Objection, your Honor. May we approach the bench?

J   Certainly.

O   Your Honor, I have reason to believe that the witness's answer will be that he found a quantity of cocaine in the room.

P   That is exactly what he is going to testify to.

O   Is the prosecution going to introduce the cocaine into evidence?

P   No. I intend to elicit the oral testimony about the discovery of the cocaine, but I see no need to introduce the drugs themselves.

O   Your Honor, I would like to call your attention to a Florida decision, *G.E.G. v. State*, 417 So. 2d 975 (Fla. 1982). In that case, the Florida Supreme Court extended the best evidence rule and announced that unless there is an excuse, in a drug case the prosecution must produce the drugs in court. The court reasoned that in a drug prosecution, the drugs are just as important as a writing in a contract or property dispute.

P   That may be the law in Florida, your Honor, but it most certainly is not the law in California. Evidence Code § 1500 limits our best evidence rule to "writings," and

drugs do not fall within the statutory definition of "writing" in § 250. Evidence
Code § 351 mandates the admission of relevant evidence that complies with all
the statutory evidentiary requirements. It would violate § 351 to broaden the
scope of the best evidence rule to cover drugs.

J I concur. Drugs are not "writings" under California law, and the best evidence
rule is simply inapplicable. The objection is overruled, and the prosecutor may
proceed to elicit an answer to that question.

A similar situation arose in *People v. McPeters*, 2 Cal. 4th 1148, 832 P.2d
146, 9 Cal. Rptr. 2d 834, *modified*, 3 Cal. 4th 678c (1992), *cert. denied*, 507
U.S. 1037 (1993), where the defense asserted that the best evidence rule required
that the prosecution produce the actual envelope that had been stolen from the
murder victim. The court reaffirmed that the best evidence rule applies only to
proving the contents of a writing, not to proving the existence of a physical object.

K.   THE WRITING'S TERMS ARE NOT "IN ISSUE"

In the words of former Evidence Code §1500, the rule applied only when the
proponent attempted "to prove the content of a writing." There are two situations
in which a writing's terms are "in issue" for purposes of the former best evidence
rule.

The first is when the material facts of consequence automatically place the
writing's terms in issue. For example, in a forgery prosecution, the terms of the
allegedly forged writing are automatically in issue. The same analysis applies in
an action for breach of a written contract.

This differs from the situation in which a fact exists independently of the writing but the writing is convenient evidence of the fact. Thus, a witness who observed payment of a debt may testify to that fact without producing the receipt; the
receipt is merely convenient evidence of payment. A witness who attended a wedding may testify to the marriage without producing the marriage certificate. Again,
the certificate is convenient evidence, but the wedding is a historical event that
occurred independently of the writing. Or suppose that a police officer has heard a
defendant confess. Even if the oral confession was taped or transcribed, the officer
may testify to the oral confession. Rael & Phillips, *Confessions and Admissions*,
in CALIFORNIA CRIMINAL LAW: PROCEDURE AND PRACTICE § 30.26 (2d ed.
1994).

The second situation is when the witness's testimony expressly or impliedly
refers to the contents of the writing. Suppose that the proponent attempting to
prove the marriage cannot find an eyewitness to the ceremony. The proponent instead calls a deputy county clerk to testify to the contents of the marriage certificate on file. The clerk will expressly or impliedly rely upon the writing's contents;
the express or implied reference to the document's contents will trigger the best
evidence rule.

Our hypothetical fact situation is a probate contest. The contestants are challenging the will and claiming by intestate succession. To prove their right to take by intestate succession, they have to show that on March 1, 1965, Joan Merchant married Thomas Kleven. The contestants call Ms. Trudy Guinn, an eyewitness to the marriage. The contestants are the proponents.

P   Ms. Guinn, WHERE were you on March 1, 1965?
W I was in Rochester, New York.
P   WHAT were you doing there?
W I was attending a wedding.
P   WHOSE wedding?
O   Your Honor, I object to that question on the ground that it calls for secondary evidence; the marriage certificate is the best evidence.
P   Your Honor, may I be heard?
J   Yes.
P   The event of the wedding occurred independently of the certificate; a witness could observe the wedding without ever seeing the certificate. This eyewitness is prepared to testify without relying on the certificate. Thus, the certificate's terms are not in issue.
J   Objection overruled.
P   Ms. Guinn, let me repeat the question. WHOSE wedding?
W The marriage of Joan Merchant and Thomas Kleven.
P   HOW can you remember a wedding that occurred that long ago?
W It sticks in my mind because I was Joan's maid of honor. I knew Joan and Tom well, and Joan asked me to stand up with her.

L. THE WRITING'S TERMS ARE ONLY COLLATERAL TO THE MAIN ISSUES

Even if the writing's terms are technically in issue, the judge could dispense with compliance with the former best evidence rule. Sometimes the writing's terms relate to a minor issue in the case, and the judge concludes that it is not worth the time and inconvenience to require the proponent to comply with the best evidence rule. Suppose, for instance, that the opponent wants to impeach the witness with a written prior inconsistent statement. If the opponent is going to use the writing solely to impeach the witness, the judge is likely to hold that the writing is only collateral. The opponent could dispense with compliance with the best evidence rule and use a copy of the written prior inconsistent statement.

Former Evidence Code §1504 recognized this limitation on the scope of the best evidence rule. That statute stated that "[a] copy of a writing is not made inadmissible if the writing is not closely related to the controlling issues and it would be inexpedient to require its production." The California version of this limitation differed from the federal version. Under Federal Rule of Evidence 1004(4), the judge may dispense with compliance with the best evidence rule whenever the writing "is not closely related to a controlling issue." Evidence Code §1504 imposed the additional requirement that it be "inexpedient" to require the production of the original writing. In California, the judge had to consider both the role of the writing and the inconvenience of producing the original. If the judge decided that the role was minor and the inconvenience major, the proponent could use a copy rather than an original or duplicate.

The fact situation is a tort action arising from a hit-and-run accident. The plaintiff, Ms. Difiglia, alleges that the defendant, Mr. Walker, negligently struck her in a crosswalk. The defendant denies that he was the driver. The plaintiff calls Mr. Meese, an eyewitness to the accident. Mr. Meese has just testified that he saw the accident and observed the car's license number. The plaintiff is the proponent.

P   WHAT was that license number?

W   I'm sorry, but I can't remember off hand.

P   WHAT, if anything, might help you remember?

W   Well, I made a note of the license number right after the accident. If I could see that note, I could probably remember.

P   Your Honor, I request that this be marked plaintiff's exhibit number two for identification.

J   It will be so marked

P   Please let the record reflect that I am showing the exhibit to the opposing counsel.

J   It will so reflect.

O   Your Honor, I am going to have to object to the use of this document to refresh the witness's recollection. It's obvious that this is a Xerox[1] copy and not the best evidence.

P   Your Honor, may I be heard?

J   Yes.

P   I intend to use the exhibit solely to refresh the witness's recollection; I am not going to use the exhibit as substantive evidence of its contents. The exhibit is being used only collaterally. The original is at the witness's residence forty miles away. I had asked Mr. Meese to bring the original with him, but he simply forgot to do so. It would be inconvenient to interrupt the trial to get the original.

J   If the witness will testify that is the location of the original, I'll allow you to proceed.

P   Thank you, your Honor.

M.   THE EVIDENCE OFFERED IS AN "ORIGINAL"

1. THE DOCTRINE

If the object involved was a writing and its terms were in issue, the proponent had to comply with the former best evidence rule. The simplest way was by offering an original. In California, the application of the definition of an "original" to

---

[1]Xerox is the registered trademark of the Xerox Corporation. We use the term in this chapter in its trademark sense, not as a generic term.

to computerized records,[2] and photographs,[3] and tape recordings[4] poses special problems. Those problems are discussed in the footnotes. However, the text of this section focuses on the general definition of "original."

The "original" is usually the first writing signed. But the test is not strictly chronological. Suppose that the case is a bomb threat prosecution in which the threat was mailed. The defendant first typed the threat. However, the defendant realized that it would be harder for a questioned document examiner to identify the paper or typewriter if he mailed a copy rather than the original. Consequently, he copied the threat on a Xerox machine and mailed the copy to the bank. For the purposes of the best evidence rule, the copy is the original. Chronologically, it is a copy, but since it is the very document the defendant mailed to the bank, it is the original.

Evidence Code § 255 defines "original" as "the writing itself or any counterpart intended to have the same effect by a person executing or issuing it." Under this definition, there can be more than one "original." The statute does not even require that all the writings be prepared at the same time. The term, "counterpart," implies that a counterpart must be identical to the original—that is, prepared by a reliable, mechanical means such as a Xerox machine. The only other requirement is that the parties intend the counterpart to have the same effect as the original.

Suppose, for example, that shortly before the close of business hours, an

---

[2]The last sentence of Evidence Code § 255 reads: "If data are stored in a computer or similar device, any printout or other output readable by sight, shown to reflect the data accurately, is an 'original.'" Thus, a printout constitutes an "original" if the proponent shows that the printout "reflects the data accurately." In 1983, the legislature enacted Evidence Code § 1500.5 [now repealed] to make the proponent's task easier. Section 1500.5 gave the proponent the benefit of a presumption: "Printed representations of computer information and computer programs will be presumed to be accurate representations of the computer information or computer programs they purport to represent." However, the presumption was rebuttable. After stating the presumption, § 1500.5 continued:

> This presumption ... will be a presumption affecting the burden of producing evidence only. If any party to a judicial proceeding introduces evidence that such a printed representation is inaccurate or unreliable, the party introducing it into evidence will have the burden of proving, by a preponderance of the evidence, that the printed representation is the best available evidence of the existence and content of the computer information or computer programs that it purports to represent.

[3]Evidence Code § 255 contains a special definition of "original" for photographs: "An 'original' of a photograph includes the negative or any print therefrom."

[4]There is a controversy over how the definition in § 255 applies to tape recordings. *People v. Marcus*, 31 Cal. App. 3d 367, 107 Cal. Rptr. 264 (1973), states that the rerecording of a tape can qualify as an original. *People v. Fujita*, 43 Cal. App. 3d 454, 117 Cal. Rptr. 757 (1974), *cert. denied*, 421 U.S. 964 (1975), goes further and characterizes the transcript of a tape recording as original evidence. Given the breadth of § 255, *Marcus* may be correct but *Fujita* appears wrong. Since a rerecording could be created by a reliable, mechanical means of reproduction, the rerecording could be a "counterpart" for purposes of § 255. If the parties created the rerecording for the same purpose as the initial recording, the rerecording would qualify as a "counterpart." However, a transcript would ordinarily have to be typed, and that creates a chance of human error. For that reason, the transcript could not be either a "counterpart" or an "original," even under the broad definition in § 255.

executive is preparing a letter. She types the letter with a carbon copy on pink paper. After removing the letter and carbon from the typewriter, she uses a rubber stamp to place her name in the signature block on the carbon copy. She then walks to the duplicating room and makes a Xerox copy of the letter. She uses her pen to sign both the letter and the Xerox copy. She then mails the signed letter to the addressee's office and the signed Xerox copy to his home. At that point, she realizes that she needs another copy of the letter for her files; the carbon copy has to be sent to Central Files. Unfortunately, the duplicating room is closed now. For that reason, she prepares a handwritten copy of the letter for her own files. In this hypothetical, the initial letter the executive typed and mailed is the original writing. However, the signed Xerox copy mailed to the addressee's home also qualifies as an "original" as defined by Evidence Code § 255. The copy made on the Xerox machine is a counterpart because the executive obviously intended it to serve the same purpose as letter prepared on the typewriter.

2. ELEMENTS OF THE FOUNDATION

The foundation includes these elements:

1. The witness recognizes the writing.
2. The witness specifies how he or she recognizes the writing.
3. The writing is either:
   a. the original, legally significant writing; or
   b. a writing that qualifies as a counterpart and was intended to have the same effect as the original writing.

3. SAMPLE FOUNDATION

The fact situation is a contract action. The plaintiff, Mr. Levine, alleges that the defendant, Mr. Bratton, breached a written employment contract by discharging Levine without cause. The plaintiff's attorney calls the plaintiff to the stand. The plaintiff has already identified himself and described the oral agreement that was later reduced to writing. The plaintiff is the proponent.

P WHAT happened after you reached the oral agreement?

W Mr. Bratton's secretary reduced the agreement to writing.

P WHEN did she do that?

W The very afternoon we reached the agreement. Mr. Bratton had standard forms with blanks, so it didn't take the secretary long to get the contract ready for signature.

P Your Honor, I request that this be marked plaintiff's exhibit number one for identification.

J It will be so marked.

P Please let the record reflect that I am showing the exhibit to the opposing counsel.

J The record will reflect that.

P   I request permission to approach the witness.

J   Granted.

P   Mr. Levine, I now hand you plaintiff's exhibit number one for identification. WHAT is it? (1)

W   It's the contract I was describing.

P   HOW can you recognize it? (2)

W   I can tell by its general appearance and especially by the signatures on page five. I certainly know my own handwriting.

P   HOW many copies of this did you make? (3a)

W   Three. We signed one in ink, and two were carbon copies.

P   WHICH one is this exhibit—the one in ink or one of the carbon copies? (3a)

W   This is the one in ink.

P   WHEN did you sign this one? (3a)

W   We signed it first.

P   HOW did you sign the carbon copies? (3a)

W   The signature just pressed through to them and marked them as we signed the one in ink.

P   Your Honor, I now offer plaintiff's exhibit number one for identification into evidence as plaintiff's exhibit number one.

O   Your Honor, I object to the introduction of the exhibit on the ground that the plaintiff has not accounted for the other documents.

P   Your Honor, may I be heard?

J   Yes.

P   The testimony shows that this exhibit is an original, the very first document the parties signed. Thus, we've complied with the best evidence rule.

J   Objection overruled. The exhibit will be received.

P   I request permission to hand the exhibit to the jurors for their inspection.

J   Permission granted.

N.   THE EVIDENCE OFFERED IS A "DUPLICATE"

1. THE DOCTRINE

The proponent could usually comply with the former best evidence rule by offering a duplicate rather than the original. California now uses the liberal definition of "duplicate" given in the Federal Rules of Evidence.[5] Evidence Code § 260

---

[5]When the California legislature initially adopted the Evidence Code in 1965, the legislature made only a limited inroad on the traditional, common-law definition of duplicate. The legislature included the provisions of the Uniform Photographic Copies of Business and Public Records as Evidence Act in Evidence Code §§ 1550-51. As amended in 1992, § 1550 makes certain kinds of "nonerasable optical image reproduction[s]," as well as "photostatic, microfilm, microcard, miniature photographic or other photographic" copies or reproductions or enlargements admissible as duplicates on one condition. The condition is that the "copy or reproduction was made and preserved as a part of the records of a business ... in the regular course of such business." Section 1551 deals more specifically with prints from photographic films of an original writing. Section 1551 provides that under certain conditions including proof of the original's destruction or loss, the print is admissible as a duplicate. Since the definition of "duplicate" in § 260 is so expansive, today it is rarely necessary for the proponent to invoke §§ 1550-51.

states that "a 'duplicate' is a counterpart produced by the same impression as the original, or from the same matrix, or by means of photography, including enlargements and miniatures, or by mechanical or electronic rerecording, or by chemical reproduction, or by some other equivalent technique which accurately reproduces the original." That definition of "duplicate" requires proof that the document is an identical counterpart prepared by a reliable, mechanical means of reproduction. *People v. Bizieff*, 226 Cal. App. 3d 1689, 277 Cal. Rptr. 678 (1991), holds that a credit card receipt is not a duplicate of the credit card that was used to imprint it, because credit card receipts are frequently poor reproductions, and because they do not reproduce all of the information that is on the card. However, unlike § 255, § 260 does not require that the writing be prepared for the same purpose as the original writing. Think back to the hypothetical in Section E of this chapter—the fact situation in which the business executive prepared a carbon copy of the letter that she mailed. On the one hand, the carbon copy does not satisfy the definition of "original" in § 255; as the file copy, it was not intended to have the same effect as the original and the Xerox copy mailed to the addressee. On the other hand, the carbon copy was "a counterpart prepared by the same impression as the original. ..." Consequently, the carbon copy qualifies as a "duplicate."

If the writing qualifies as a duplicate under § 260, former § 1511 governed its admissibility. Former § 1511 stated: "A duplicate is admissible to the same extent as an original unless (a) a genuine question is raised as to the authenticity of the original or (b) in the circumstances it would be unfair to admit the duplicate in lieu of the original." This wording was borrowed verbatim from Federal Rule of Evidence 1003. Section 1511 "brings California into line with Federal Rule of Evidence [1003] on the admissibility of duplicates." *People v. Garcia*, 201 Cal. App. 3d 324, 328, 247 Cal. Rptr. 94, 97 (1988). The Advisory Committee Note to Rule 1003 describes the circumstances in which the trial judge should treat the document as secondary evidence rather than a duplicate. In *People v. Atkins*, 210 Cal. App. 3d 47, 55, 258 Cal. Rptr. 113, 118 (1989), the court held that a photostatic copy of the certification of an official record is admissible as a duplicate under California Evidence Code § 1511. It is questionable, however, whether this type of bootstrapping is consistent with the plain language of § 1511. One circumstance is the presence of evidence in the record—rather than counsel's mere assertion—that there is a discrepancy between the document and the original. The Note adds that another "reason for requiring the original may be present when only a part of the original is reproduced and the remainder is needed for cross-examination or may disclose matters qualifying the part offered. ..." "The opponent of the evidence has the burden of showing the unfairness; such a claim must be based on substance, not mere speculation that the original might contain some relevant difference." *People v. Garcia*, 201 Cal. App. 3d 324, 328, 247 Cal. Rptr. 94, 98 (1988). The mere fact that the proponent has exclusive possession of the original for several years "raises no issue of authenticity or unfairness of substituting duplicates for the originals." *Id.*

2. ELEMENTS OF THE FOUNDATION

To qualify a writing as a duplicate under Evidence Code § 260, the proponent must establish the following foundational elements:

1. The witness recognizes the writing.
2. The witness specifies the basis on which he or she recognizes the writing.
3. The writing is a copy of the original.
4. The witness states the time when the copy was made. Under § 260, subsequently prepared writings can qualify as duplicates.
5. The copy was made by a reliable, mechanical means of reproduction.

3. SAMPLE FOUNDATION

We shall continue the hypothetical involving the employment contract in the last section. The plaintiff has already stated that the parties reached an oral agreement and had the agreement reduced to writing. The plaintiff is still the proponent.

P HOW many documents did you prepare when you signed the contract?
W Three.
P HOW did the documents differ, if at all?
W We signed one in ink, there was a carbon copy, and we made one other copy.
P WHEN did you prepare the carbon copy?
W When we signed the original.
P WHEN did you prepare the other copy? (4)
W About a week after the signing of the contract.
P HOW did you prepare this other copy? (5)
W I ran it off on my Xerox machine at work.
P WHAT condition was the Xerox machine in when you made the copy? (5)
W It seemed to be in good working condition. I didn't have any mechanical difficulties with the machine.
P WHY did you make this other copy?
W I just wanted to be on the safe side. I wanted one copy, the carbon, at home and the other, the Xerox copy, at my office.
P Your Honor, I request that this be marked plaintiff's exhibit number one for identification.
J It will be so marked.
P Please let the record reflect that I am showing the exhibit to the opposing counsel.
J It will so reflect.
P I request permission to approach the witness.
J Permission granted.
P Mr. Levine, I now hand you plaintiffs exhibit number one for identification. WHAT is it? (1)
W It's the contract.
P HOW can you recognize it? (2)

W I know it by its general appearance and the signatures at the end of page three. I certainly ought to know my own handwriting style.

P Again, HOW many documents did you prepare? (3)

W Three—the ink original, one carbon copy, and one Xerox copy.

P WHICH one is this? (3)

W It's the Xerox copy.

P HOW can you tell? (3)

W It's obviously a Xerox copy rather than an ink or carbon. You can tell by its appearance.

P Your Honor, I now offer plaintiff's exhibit number one for identification into evidence as plaintiff's exhibit number one.

O I object to the introduction of this exhibit on the ground that it is not the best evidence.

P Your Honor, may I be heard?

J Yes.

P The testimony shows that this exhibit is a duplicate, as that term is used in the California Evidence Code. It is true that it was prepared subsequently, but under the law of California, it can still qualify as a duplicate so long as it was made by a mechanical means of reproduction.

J The objection will be overruled, and the exhibit will be received into evidence.

P I request permission to hand the exhibit to the jurors for their inspection.

J Permission granted.

O. EXCUSES FOR THE NONPRODUCTION OF THE ORIGINALS

If the proponent cannot produce an original, the proponent must both establish an excuse for nonproduction and offer authentic secondary evidence of the writing. This section discusses the foundations for the various excuses for nonproduction. The proponent must excuse the nonproduction of all originals before offering secondary evidence. The list of excuses for nonproduction under former law was exhaustive. Former Evidence Code § 1500 read that "[e]xcept as otherwise provided by statute, no evidence other than the original of a writing is admissible to prove the content of a writing." The introductory phrase in former § 1500 made the statutory list of excuses exhaustive—thus, a California trial judge lacked the common-law power to create a new excuse. For example, Federal Rule of Evidence 1007 excuses nonproduction of the original when the proponent can prove the opponent's previous written admission of the contents of the original. Under California law, the proponent cannot invoke that excuse because California has no parallel statute. However, the Evidence Code did recognize the following excuses.

1. THE ORIGINAL IS LOST

Former Evidence Code §1501 stated that "[a] copy of a writing is not made inadmissible by the best evidence rule if the writing is lost ... without fraudulent intent on the part of the proponent of the evidence." Sometimes the witness can testify directly to the original's loss; for example, perhaps the witness saw the original fall into a sewer. In most cases, however, the proponent will have to rely on circumstantial proof of loss: Although the witness conducted a diligent search for the original, the witness could not locate it. Some jurisdictions impose strict rules to determine the search's diligence; the proponent must always search the last known place of custody or contact the last known custodian. However, in California there are no hard-and-fast rules; the trial judge made a discretionary determination of whether the proponent exercised sufficient diligence to locate the original. *See, e.g., People v. Von Villas*, 10 Cal. App. 4th 201, 13 Cal. Rptr. 2d 62 (1992), *cert. denied*, 508 U.S. 975 (1993).

The foundational elements include the following:

1. The witness discovered that the original was lost.
2. The witness then searched for the original.
3. The search was reasonably diligent.
4. Despite the search, the witness could not locate the original.

Our fact situation is a civil action for libel. The plaintiff, Mr. Smythe, alleges that the defendant Wiggins libeled him in a letter that Wiggins sent to Mr. Jackson. The letter has been lost. The plaintiff will use Mr. Jackson's testimony to establish the excuse for nonproduction. Mr. Jackson has already testified about receiving a handwritten letter from the defendant.

P   WHAT did you do with the letter after you received it? (1)
W   I put it in my dresser in our bedroom.
P   WHERE is the letter now? (1)
W   I don't know.
P   WHEN did you discover that the letter was missing? (1)
W   I looked for it three weeks ago when you told me we would be going to trial.
P   HOW did you discover that the letter was missing? (1)
W   I went to the dresser, looked through it, and couldn't find the letter.
P   WHAT did you do then? (2)
W   I searched for the letter.
P   HOW did you conduct this search? (3)
W   I went through each drawer in the dresser very carefully.
P   HOW carefully? (3)
W   I went through it item by item and still couldn't find the letter.
P   WHERE else did you search? (3)
W   I looked all around the room.
P   WHERE else did you look? (3)
W   I checked my desk to see if I might have put it there.
P   WHAT else did you do? (3)
W   I asked my wife if she had seen it.
P   WHAT did she say? (3)
W   She said she hadn't seen it. (Note that her response is being offered for a nonhearsay purpose—to prove the effect on the hearer's state of mind. Given the wife's response, it was reasonable for the witness not to search further.)

P WHAT did you do then? (3)

W I stopped searching.

P WHY did you stop the search? (3)

W I just couldn't think of anywhere else to look.

P WHAT was the outcome of your search? (4)

W I couldn't find it. I just don't know where it got to, and I didn't make a copy of it.

Authentication of the Secondary Evidence

At this point, the proponent authenticates the secondary evidence. *See* Section P.3., *infra*. Assume that the proponent authenticates the witness's recollection of the letter's contents.

P WHAT, if anything, did the letter say about Mr. Smythe?

O Your Honor, I object to that question on the ground that it calls for secondary evidence.

P Your Honor, may I be heard?

J Yes.

P It's true that the witness's recollection is secondary evidence. However, we've established the loss of the original which is an adequate excuse for nonproduction. In addition, the witness says he can remember the substance of the letter.

J The objection will be overruled.

P Mr. Jackson, let me repeat the question. WHAT, if anything, did the letter say about Mr. Smythe?

W It said that he had bribed Councilman Wild in connection with a zoning application.

P WHOSE handwriting was the letter in?

W The defendant's.

2. THE PROPONENT INNOCENTLY DESTROYED THE ORIGINAL

The early common-law view was that if the proponent intentionally destroyed the original, the proponent could not introduce secondary evidence of its contents. However, modern courts realize that intentional destruction can be in perfect good faith. For example, businesses routinely destroy their original records after a number of years; they retain only computer or microfilm copies because they do not want warehouses jammed with voluminous, outdated records. The test under the former best evidence rule was whether the proponent destroyed the original in bad faith. If the proponent destroyed the original intentionally but in good faith, the secondary evidence was admissible. Former Evidence Code § 1501 adopted this doctrine: "A copy of a writing is not made inadmissible by the best evidence rule if the writing ... has been lost without fraudulent intent on the part of the proponent of the evidence." A copy of an original letter destroyed by a prosecution witness is admissible where the prosecution had not contributed to the witness's destruction of the letter. *People v. Morris*, 53 Cal. 3d 152, 807 P.2d 949, 279 Cal. Rptr. 720, *cert. denied*, 502 U.S. 959 (1991).

The foundation includes these elements:

1. The witness had the original.
2. The witness destroyed the original.
3. The destruction was accidental, or the witness's intentional destruction of the original was in good faith.

The fact situation is an antitrust action. Belmar Corporation sues Dutton Corporation for violation of the Cartwright Act. Belmar alleges that over a ten-year period, it overpaid $5,000,000 for certain supplies, due to a fraudulently concealed price-fixing conspiracy among the defendant suppliers. To show its damages, the plaintiff calls its chief records custodian, Ms. Gerst. Ms. Gerst has already identified herself and testified to her familiarity with Belmar's records policies. The proponent is the plaintiff.

P   WHAT, if any, procedures does Belmar use to record purchases of these supplies? (1)
W   We first prepare purchase memoranda.
P   WHAT is a purchase memorandum? (1)
W   It is a record of all the data concerning the purchase—supplier, item, date, amount, and the like.
P   WHO prepares the memorandum? (1)
W   One of the people in bookkeeping.
P   WHAT do they do with the memorandum? (1)
W   They place it in their files.
P   WHAT happens to the memoranda after they are inserted in the files? (2)
W   They're kept there for two years.
P   WHAT happens after two years pass? (2)
W   They're transferred to a records holding area in our warehouse.
P   WHAT happens to the memoranda after they are stored in the warehouse? (2)
W   They're kept there for another two years.
P   WHAT happens after that two-year period passes? (2)
W   We destroy the originals.
P   WHY do you do that? (3)
W   We just don't have enough room to keep the originals. We need our warehouse space for equipment and merchandise, not old documents.
P   Ms. Gerst, WHERE are the purchase memoranda for 1991? (2)
W   They're gone.
P   HOW do you know that? (2)
W   I searched for them in the warehouse and couldn't find them.
P   WHAT happened to them? (3)
W   In all probability, they were destroyed after sitting in the warehouse for the two-year period. As I said, that is our customary practice.
P   WHEN would they have been destroyed? (3)
W   By my estimates, probably in January or February of 1994.
P   WHEN did you first learn about the conspiracy alleged in this law suit? (3)

W In November of 1994.
P WHAT did you know about it in January or February of 1994? (3)
W Nothing.

Authentication of the Secondary Evidence

At this point, the proponent authenticates the secondary evidence.

P Your Honor, I now offer plaintiff's exhibit number three for identification into evidence as plaintiff's exhibit number three.
O Your Honor, I object to the introduction of that exhibit on the ground that this is not the best evidence. The plaintiff intentionally destroyed the originals.
P May I be heard?
J Yes.
P It's true that these summaries are secondary evidence and that the plaintiff intentionally destroyed the original memoranda. However, the witness's testimony shows that the destruction was in good faith; the plaintiff did not destroy the originals for the fraudulent purpose of making them unavailable to the defendant.
J The objection will be overruled, and the exhibit will be received into evidence.

3. THE ORIGINAL IS IN THE POSSESSION OF A THIRD PARTY BEYOND THE REACH OF THE COURT'S COMPULSORY PROCESS

Federal Rule of Evidence 1004(2) provides an excuse for nonproduction if "[n]o original can be obtained by any available judicial process or procedure." Thus, federal law requires the proponent to prove only that the original is beyond the reach of compulsory process. California law was stricter. Former Evidence Code § 1502 stated that "[a] copy of a writing is not made inadmissible by the best evidence rule if the writing was not reasonably procurable by the proponent by use of the court's process or by other available means." The words "other available means," required the proponent to exhaust any reasonably available, informal means of obtaining the original. Article, *The Best Evidence Rule: A Critical Appraisal of the Law in California*, 9 U.C. DAVIS L. REV. 257, 270 (1976). Suppose, for example, that the original is in the possession of a third party overseas, but the proponent has no reason to believe that the third party will be uncooperative. The proponent should phone or write to the third party and request the third party to send the original to the site of the trial.

The foundation includes these elements:

1. A third party has the original.
2. The third party resides in a certain place.
3. That place is beyond the reach of the court's compulsory process.
4. The proponent unsuccessfully requested the third party to send the document to the place of trial, or the circumstances indicate that a request would be futile.

Our fact situation is, again, the civil libel action. The plaintiff, Mr. Smythe, alleges that the defendant, Mr. Wiggins, is guilty of libel. The complaint alleges that the defendant committed the libel in a letter to a Mr. Jackson. The witness is the plaintiff, Mr. Smythe. Mr. Smythe has already identified himself. The plaintiff is the proponent. The place of the trial is San Jose.

P   WHERE were you on the afternoon of January 15th of this year?
W   I visited Bill Jackson at his home in San Jose.
P   WHAT did you do while you visited Mr. Jackson?
W   We talked about some mutual acquaintances.
P   WHICH acquaintances?
W   Several, including the defendant, Mr. Wiggins.
P   WHAT, if anything, did Mr. Jackson say about Mr. Wiggins? (1)
W   He said that Wiggins had just sent him a handwritten letter about me.
P   WHAT was Mr. Jackson's demeanor when he made this statement? (1)
W   He seemed very upset and excited. He said that the letter had come in the mail just a few minutes before I arrived at his house and that the contents of the letter really disturbed him. (This additional testimony probably brings Jackson's statement about receipt of the letter within the excited utterance hearsay exception under Evidence Code § 1209.)
P   WHAT did Mr. Jackson do after he told you about the letter? (1)
W   He showed it to me.
P   WHOSE handwriting was the letter in?
W   Clearly the defendant's.
P   HOW do you know that?
W   I've known the defendant for years, and I've seen his handwriting on innumerable occasions.
P   WHAT did you do after Mr. Jackson showed you the letter? (4)
W   I asked him if I could have it. I told him it made me real angry, and I wanted to use the letter to sue the defendant.
P   HOW did Mr. Jackson respond to your request for the letter? (4)
W   He refused to let me have it. (Mr. Jackson's statement is being used for a non-hearsay purpose. The statement is an operative fact; it is the refusal that satisfies the fourth element of the foundation.) I don't even have a copy.
P   WHY did he refuse to let you have it? (4)
W   He said he didn't want to become involved.
P   WHAT other efforts did you make to persuade Mr. Jackson to give you the letter? (4)
W   I phoned him several times. Each time I asked him to send it to me.
P   WHAT was his answer? (4)
W   He still insists that he won't send it to me.
P   WHERE is Mr. Jackson now? (4)
W   He now lives as a permanent resident in London.
P   HOW do you know that? (4)

W In our last conversation in San Jose, he told me that he was about to move to London for business reasons. (Jackson's statement qualifies as a declaration of present plan under Evidence Code § 1250(a). Subdivision 1250(a)(2) permits the proponent to use Jackson's statement as evidence that Jackson subsequently carried out the plan and moved to London.) In addition, I placed several overseas calls to him.

Authentication of the Secondary Evidence

At this point, the proponent authenticates the witness's oral recollection. *See* Section P.3., *infra*.

P WHAT, if anything, did the letter say about you?

O Your Honor, I object to that question on the ground that the witness's testimony is not the best evidence.

P Your Honor, may I be heard?

J Certainly.

P The testimony shows that a third party, Mr. Jackson, has the original. Mr. Jackson lives in England, and your Honor may judicially notice the fact that under our Code of Civil Procedure, Mr. Jackson is beyond the reach of our compulsory process. Finally, the testimony shows that Mr. Jackson refused to send the original here. The testimony hence establishes an excuse for the original's nonproduction.

J I will judicially notice that and overrule the objection.

P Mr. Smythe, let me repeat the question. WHAT, if anything, did the letter say about you?

W It said that I had bribed Councilman Wild in connection with a zoning application.

P WHOSE handwriting was the letter in?

W The defendant's.

4. THE PARTY-OPPONENT HAS THE ORIGINAL AND FAILS TO PRODUCE IT AFTER NOTICE TO PRODUCE

Former Evidence Code § 1503(a) recognized an excuse for nonproduction of a writing:

> if, at a time when the writing was under the control of the opponent, the opponent was expressly or impliedly notified by the pleadings or otherwise, that the writing would be needed at the hearing, and on request at the hearing the opponent has failed to produce the writing. In a criminal action, the request at the hearing to produce the writing may not be made in the presence of the jury.

The initial problem of proof is establishing that "the writing was under the control of the opponent ...." Sometimes the proponent has direct evidence of this fact. More often the proponent must rely on circumstantial evidence, tracing the original to the party-opponent.

The proponent must also prove that the party-opponent had fair notice that the original would be needed at trial. The proponent can sometimes argue that the terms of the pleadings gave the party-opponent implied notice; the implication would be strong in an action for breach of a written contract. However, to be safe, the proponent should give the party-opponent express notice that the original will be needed at trial.

The foundation includes these elements:

1. The party-opponent has the original.
2. The party-opponent knew that the original would be needed at trial.
3. Before or at trial, the proponent requested the original. Some attorneys make it a general practice to serve a written demand on the opposing attorney.
4. The party-opponent nevertheless failed to produce the original at trial.

The fact situation is a contract action. The plaintiff, Mr. Renfield, alleges that the defendant, Mr. Payntor, warranted that the car the defendant sold plaintiff would get at least twenty miles per gallon on the open highway. The complaint alleges that the defendant breached the warranty because, on the open highway, the car gets only fifteen miles to a gallon. The plaintiff takes the stand. The proponent is the plaintiff. The plaintiff wants to testify that before agreeing to buy the car, he wrote the defendant and made it clear that he did not want the car unless it got at least twenty miles per gallon. The plaintiff has identified himself and described his preliminary oral negotiations with the defendant.

P WHAT did you do after your oral discussion with the defendant? (1)
W I thought about the deal and then decided to write the defendant and outline the parts of the deal I was really insistent on.
P WHEN did you write this letter? (1)
W I wrote it on February 14 of this year.
P WHAT did you do with the letter? (1)
W I mailed it to the defendant.
P HOW did you mail it to him? (1)
W I stuck it in an envelope and addressed it to the defendant.
P WHERE did you get the defendant's address? (1)
W From the telephone book.
P WHAT did you do with the letter after you addressed it? (1)
W I stamped it and deposited it in a mailbox.
P WHAT response, if any, did you receive from the defendant? (1)
W I didn't get any written response.
P WHEN, if ever, did you see the letter again? (1)
W Well, when we sat down to sign the final contract, the defendant pulled it out and showed it to me.
P WHEN was the last time you saw the letter? (1)

W   The day I signed the contract for the car.
P   WHO had the letter? (1)
W   The defendant.
P   WHERE were you on the morning of November 17th of this year? (2)
W   I was here at the courthouse.
P   WHY were you here? (2)
W   We were having a conference in this case.
P   WHO attended the conference? (2)
W   You and I were there. The defendant and his attorney were also there.
P   WHAT happened during the conference? (2)
W   We discussed some aspects of the case.
P   WHAT, if anything, did you tell the defendant during the conference about the letter? (2)
W   I told him that you and I wanted him to bring the letter to trial.
P   WHAT was the defendant's response? (3)
W   He said to forget about the letter. (This statement is being offered for a non-hearsay purpose. The answer is the party-opponent's refusal, the last foundational element.)
P   WHAT, if anything, did you tell the defendant today about the letter? (3)
W   I again asked the defendant for the letter.
P   WHAT was his response? (4)
W   He said he didn't have it.
P   WHAT did you tell the defendant in your letter to him?
O   Your Honor, I object to that question on the ground that it calls for secondary evidence. The letter is the best evidence.
P   Your Honor, may I be heard?
J   Yes.
P   The testimony shows that the defendant was the last known custodian of the letter. The testimony also indicates that the defendant knew we wanted the original letter at trial today. That amounts to an excuse for the letter's nonproduction.
J   The objection will be overruled.
P   Mr. Renfield, let me repeat the question. WHAT did you tell the defendant in your letter to him?
W   I said that unless the car got at least twenty miles a gallon, I didn't want the car at all.

5. VOLUMINOUS OR BULKY RECORDS

Former Evidence Code § 1509 read:

> Secondary evidence, whether written or oral, of the content of a writing is not made inadmissible by the best evidence rule if the writing consists of numerous accounts or other writings that cannot be examined in court without great loss of time, and the evidence sought from them is only the general result of the whole; but the court in its discretion may require that such accounts or other writings be produced for inspection by the adverse party.

See generally Wolfen v. Clinical Data, Inc., 16 Cal. App. 4th 171, 19 Cal. Rptr. 2d 684 (1993).

Section 1509 differed from its federal counterpart, Federal Rule of Evidence 1006. Rule 1006 states that the original or duplicate writings "shall be made available for examination or copying" to the opponent. Thus, Federal Rule 1006 requires proof that the proponent gave the opponent access to the writings. Under former Evidence Code § 1509, the trial judge had discretion whether to order the proponent to make the original writings available to the opponent. Since access is discretionary rather than mandatory, the foundation under § 1509 need not include proof that the proponent gave the opponent access.

Section 1509 permitted either a written summary or an oral summary of the contents of bulky documents, unlike § 1505, which expressed California's general preference for written secondary evidence over oral secondary evidence. *See* Section P.3., *infra.* Ordinarily, a proponent would wish to use a written summary of bulky documents, simply for the sake of convenience and persuasiveness, but §1509 made an oral summary equally permissible. The following foundation is for an oral summary:

1. The original entries would be admissible in evidence.
2. The original entries are so voluminous or bulky that it would be inconvenient for the trier of fact to examine them.
3. The witness was qualified to review the records.
4. The witness reviewed the records.
5. The witness's testimony is a summary of the records.

The fact situation is a civil action to rescind a corporate merger. The Gemini Corporation was to merge into Rohr Corporation. Gemini sues to rescind the merger agreement; the complaint alleges that the contract is voidable because of Rohr's fraud. Specifically, the complaint alleges that the defendant overstated the amount of its yearly sales. The defendant denies that its representations were false. The defendant is attempting to prove the amount of its annual sales. To prove its annual sales, the defendant would probably call two witnesses. The first witness would be the defendant's bookkeeper or records custodian. The first witness would describe the original records and show that they fall within the business entry exception to the hearsay rule. This testimony would lay the first element of the foundation. The witness would conclude by stating that he or she gave the second witness access to the relevant records.

The second witness is Ms. Beer. Ms. Beer has already identified herself. The defendant is the proponent.

P   WHAT is your occupation? (3)
W   I am a certified public accountant.
P   WHERE do you work? (3)
W   I am self-employed. I own my own C.P.A. firm downtown.
P   HOW long have you been a C.P.A.? (3)

W   Roughly ten years.
P   WHAT is your formal education? (3)
W   I have a bachelor's, a master's, and a doctorate.
P   WHAT was your field of study? (3)
W   Accounting.
P   WHAT school awarded you your degrees? (3)
W   Cornell.
P   WHERE were you on April 15 of this year? (4)
W   I went to the offices of Rohr Corporation.
P   WHY did you go there? (4)
W   You asked me to review the corporation's sales records from 1992 to the present.
P   WHAT did you do when you arrived at the corporation's offices? (4)
W   First I met Mr. Gaynor, the head bookkeeper.
P   WHAT did he do?
W   He led me to the office where all the records are kept.
P   WHAT did you do when you arrived at the office? (4)
W   I immediately started reviewing the records to compute the annual sales for each year, starting with 1992.
P   HOW did you do that? (4)
W   I used generally accepted accounting techniques and a calculator to double check my computations.
P   HOW many pages of records did you review? (2)
W   I couldn't give you a precise number. The number would run into the thousands.
P   HOW long did it take you to compute the yearly totals? (2)
W   Five workdays.
P   HOW long is your workday? (2)
W   A solid eight hours a day.
P   Ms. Beer, WHAT was the total amount of Rohr Corporation's sales in 1992? (5)
O   Your Honor, I object to that question on the ground that it calls for secondary evidence. The best evidence would be the records themselves.
P   Your Honor, may I be heard?
J   Yes.
P   Mr. Gaynor's testimony established that the original records would be admissible. Ms. Beer's testimony shows that the original records are too voluminous to be used in the courtroom. Moreover, last month we offered to let the plaintiff's accountants review the records.
J   (To the opposing attorney.) Is that true?
O   Yes, your Honor.
J   I think there's an adequate excuse for nonproduction. The objection will be overruled.
P   Ms. Beer, let me repeat the question. WHAT was the total amount of Rohr Corporation's sales in 1992? (5)
W   It was $5,312,300.

6. THE PRODUCTION OF THE ORIGINAL AT TRIAL

Former Evidence Code § 1510 recognized another excuse for nonproduction: "A copy of a writing is not made inadmissible by the best evidence rule if the writing has been produced at the hearing and made available for inspection by the adverse party." The California Law Revision Commission comment to former § 1510 e xplained the rationale:

> Section 1510 is designed to permit the owner of a writing that is needed for evidence to leave a copy for the court's use and to retain the original in his own possession. The exception is valuable for business records that are needed in the continuing operation of the business. If the original is produced in court for inspection, a copy may be left for the court's use and the original returned to the owner.

The elements of the foundation for this excuse are:

1. The proponent produced a document in court.
2. The document was an original or a duplicate.
3. The proponent made the document available to the opposing party for inspection.

The fact situation is a civil action by a bank to collect on a promissory note executed by the defendant businessperson. The witness is the bank vice president in charge of commercial loans. The witness has already testified that she approved a $320,000 loan to the defendant. Her direct examination continues:

P WHAT, if anything, did you do after you told the defendant that you had approved his loan?

W I had him execute a promissory note.

P WHAT is a promissory note?

W It's a formal written promise to repay the loan.

P Your Honor, I request that these documents be marked plaintiff's exhibits numbers 2 and 3 for identification. (1)

J They will be so marked.

P Please let the record reflect that I am showing both exhibits to the opposing counsel. (3)

J The record will so reflect.

P Permission to approach the witness?

J Granted.

P Ms. Goodpaster, I now hand you what have been marked as plaintiff's exhibits numbers 2 and 3 for identification. WHAT is exhibit 2? (2)

W It's the promissory note that I had the defendant sign.

P HOW can you recognize it? (2)

W To begin with, I know our form note. I ought to; I'm the one who drafted the form. I also recognize the defendant's signature on the note. He's been one of our customers for years, and I've seen tens of documents bearing his signature.

P Now please tell us WHAT exhibit 3 is?

W It's a summary I prepared of the terms of the original note.

P HOW can you tell that?

W I'm looking at both of them right now. The key information is identical—word for word.

P Your Honor, I offer exhibit 3 for identification into evidence as exhibit 3 and request permission to return exhibit 2 for identification to the witness.

O Your Honor, she's said that number 2 is the original. The best evidence rule requires that the plaintiff tender that exhibit into evidence.

P I beg to differ, your Honor. Under Evidence Code § 1510, all we have to do is to produce the original in court and authenticate our secondary evidence. We've done both.

J Objection overruled. Exhibit 3 will be received, and exhibit 2 may be returned to the bank.

7. THE ORIGINAL IS IN OFFICIAL CUSTODY

If the original is in official custody, the original's nonproduction is automatically excused. Former Evidence Code § 1506 stated that "[a] copy of a writing is not made inadmissible by the best evidence rule if the writing is a record or other writing that is in the custody of a public entity. " There are several reasons for this doctrine. First, the removal of the original from official custody might inconvenience other persons who wanted to use the original. Second, the removal would create the risk of the loss of the original. Some jurisdictions restrict the excuse to documents that by statute or regulation cannot lawfully be removed from official custody. California broadly applied the excuse to any document in official custody.

Our fact situation is a probate contest. The contestants claim by intestate succession. To establish their claim, they must prove the marriage between Joan Merchant and Thomas Kleven. The contestants want to offer the marriage certificate to prove the marriage. The proponent does not offer live testimony to authenticate the copy of the certificate; rather, the proponent merely offers a properly attested copy of the original marriage certificate.

P Your Honor, I request that this be marked contestants' exhibit B for identification.

J Granted. It will be so marked.

P Please let the record reflect that I am showing the exhibit to opposing counsel.

J The record will reflect that.

P Your Honor, I now offer contestants' exhibit B for identification into evidence as exhibit B.

O I object to the introduction of this exhibit on best evidence grounds. This is obviously just a Xerox copy.

P Your Honor, it's true that this is a purported copy. However, there is an attached attestation. The attestation is self-authenticating because it is in proper form. The signature and seal are presumptively authentic under Evidence Code §§ 1452-53.

O That may well be, your Honor. However, that merely authenticates it as a copy. It's still only a copy and, therefore, barred by the best evidence rule.

P I agree that this is a copy, your Honor. However, Evidence Code § 1506 states that a copy of a writing "is not made inadmissible by the best evidence rule if the writing is a record or other writing that is in the custody of a public entity." The attestation specifically recites that the original is in official custody. There's thus an excuse for nonproduction.

J　That analysis is correct. The objection will be overruled, and the exhibit will be received.

P　Thank you, your Honor. May I please read the exhibit to the jurors now?

J　Yes.

P　Ladies and gentlemen of the jury, I am about to read to you a document which Her Honor has just admitted into evidence. As you will see when you later have an opportunity to inspect this exhibit, there are two parts to the exhibit. One part reads:

"I, the undersigned, Gregory Villanueva, do hereby attest that I am the deputy city clerk for the City of San Diego, State of California and that the attached document is a true, complete, and correct copy of a marriage certificate in the official custody of my office."

The second part reads:

"On this day, November 3, 1977, in San Diego, California, I, the Honorable Lewis Welsh, married Miss Joan Merchant and Mr. Thomas Klevenin accordance with the laws of the State of California."

P.　ADMISSIBLE TYPES OF SECONDARY EVIDENCE

If the object involved was a writing and the writing's terms were in issue, there were two methods of satisfying the former rule. Sections L and M dealt with the first method: proving that the evidence offered qualified as an original or duplicate. The second method involves two steps: (1) proving an adequate excuse for the nonproduction of all originals; and (2) offering an admissible type of secondary evidence. There were three types of admissible secondary evidence. In Section N.7., we noted one type of secondary evidence: an attested copy. A second type is a copy authenticated by live testimony. A witness testifies that the document is an accurate copy of the original, and the witness can recall the contents of the original well enough to state that the copy is accurate. A third type is oral recollection testimony.

1.　AN ATTESTED COPY

The attestation must bear a signature that is presumptively authentic under Evidence Code § 1453 or a seal that is presumptively genuine under Evidence Code § 1452. Further, the contents of the attestation must comply with Evidence Code § 1531; the attestation "must state in substance that the copy is a correct copy of the original, or of a specified part hereof. ..." If the attestation satisfies all these requirements, under Evidence Code §1530(a), the attested copy is "prima facie evidence of the existence and content" of the original document in official custody. In effect, the attestation makes the copy self-authenticating. As in Section O.7., the proponent may introduce the copy without any sponsoring, live testimony.

2. COPY AUTHENTICATED BY LIVE TESTIMONY

Another permissible type of secondary evidence is a copy authenticated by live testimony. The witness need not have personally prepared the copy. However, the witness must remember the contents of the original, read the copy, and finally testify that the exhibit is an accurate copy of the original. The elements of the foundation are:

1. On a previous occasion, the witness read the original.
2. The witness still remembers the original.
3. As best he or she can tell, the exhibit is an accurate copy of the original.

In *People v. Von Villas*, 10 Cal. App. 4th 201, 13 Cal. Rptr. 2d 62 (1992), *cert. denied*, 508 U.S. 975 (1993), the defense asserted that § 1511 (discussed in Section N, *supra*) applied to the admission of a copy as well as to the admission of duplicates. The Court of Appeals found no error because the defense evidence did not raise a genuine question of the authenticity of the original, thus implying that if there *were* a genuine question of authenticity, a copy would be inadmissible. *Id.*, 10 Cal. App. 4th at 244-45, 13 Cal. Rptr. at 87.

Assume that the original writing is a simple letter that was never in official custody. The fact situation is a continuation of our earlier libel hypothetical. The plaintiff, Mr. Smythe, alleges that the defendant, Mr. Wiggins, is guilty of libel. The complaint alleges that the defendant committed the libel in a letter to Mr. Jackson. The plaintiff calls Mr. Jackson as a witness. Mr. Jackson first testifies that he received the letter in the defendant's handwriting. The plaintiff then establishes an excuse for the nonproduction of the original letter, such as the loss of the letter. Now the proponent attempts to have Mr. Jackson authenticate a handwritten copy of the letter.

P   WHAT did you do when you first received the letter? (1)
W   I read it.
P   HOW carefully did you read it? (1), (2)
W   Very carefully.
P   WHY did you read it carefully? (1), (2)
W   It shocked me. I had to read it several times before I could believe what I saw.
P   HOW many times did you read it? (1), (2)
W   At least three.
P   WHY did you read it three times? (1)
W   Again, it was hard to believe what I read in that letter.
P   HOW well do you remember the contents of the letter? (2)
W   Very well. I can't quote it word for word, but I have a distinct recollection of it.
P   HOW can you remember it so well? (2)

W   Well, it was fairly short; and I read it both carefully and several times.

P   Your Honor, I request that this be marked plaintiff's exhibit number two for identification.

J   It will be so marked.

P   Please let the record reflect that I am showing the exhibit to the opposing counsel.

J   It will so reflect.

P   I request permission to approach the witness.

J   Permission granted.

P   Mr. Jackson, I now hand you plaintiff's exhibit number two for identification. WHAT is it? (3)

W   It's a copy of the letter I was mentioning.

P   HOW do you recognize it? (3)

W   I recognize the general contents and some phrases that stick in my mind.

P   HOW accurate is this copy? (3)

W   As far as I can tell, it's verbatim. It's not the same letter that I saw—that one had different spacing and margins. But the contents seem to be the same.

P   Your Honor, I now offer plaintiff's exhibit number two for identification into evidence as plaintiff's exhibit two.

O   I object to the introduction of this exhibit on the ground that it isn't the best evidence; it's only a secondary copy.

P   Your Honor, may I be heard?

J   Yes.

P   It's true that this is secondary evidence. However, we've established the loss of the original which is an adequate excuse for nonproduction. In addition, the witness has authenticated the copy.

J   The objection will be overruled, and the exhibit will be received into evidence.

P   Mr. Jackson, would you please read the last paragraph of the letter to the jurors?

W   The paragraph reads: "I heard this juicy rumor about our mutual friend, James Smythe. He evidently slipped $2,000 to Councilman Wild to get a favorable ruling on a zoning application. Old Smythe is a lot slicker—and a lot less honest—than I thought."

P   WHOSE handwriting is that letter in?

W   The defendant's, Marvin Wiggins'.

P   I request permission to hand the exhibit to the jurors for their inspection.

J   Granted.

3. ORAL RECOLLECTION TESTIMONY

If the proponent does not have a copy, the proponent can prove the contents of a writing by calling the witness who can testify to his or her recollection of the original's contents. The proponent must establish an excuse for nonproduction of the original and an excuse for nonproduction of a copy. In this latter respect, California and federal law differ. In federal practice, once the proponent establishes an excuse for the nonproduction of the originals, the proponent may generally resort to any type of secondary evidence, copies or oral recollection testimony. California law, however, preferred written copies over oral recollection testimony. Former Evidence Code § 1505 stated that "[i]f the proponent does not have in his possession or under his control a copy of a writing ..., other secondary evidence of the content of the writing is not made inadmissible by the best evidence rule." Section 1505 did not require the proponent to prove an excuse for the nonproduction of all secondary copies; it required only proof that the proponent did not have a copy in his possession or under his control. *See People v. Bizieff*, 226 Cal. App. 3d 1689, 277 Cal. Rptr. 678 (1991).

The foundation includes these elements:

1. On a previous occasion, the witness read the original.
2. The witness still remembers the substance of the original's contents.
3. The witness states the substance of the original's contents.
4. The witness does not have a copy in his possession or control.

We shall continue the libel hypothetical to illustrate this type of secondary evidence. The plaintiff, Mr. Smythe, has already testified. During his direct examination, the plaintiff stated that although Mr. Jackson showed him the letter, Mr. Jackson gave him neither the original letter nor a copy. The witness is Mr. Jackson. Again, assume that the proponent has already established an excuse for nonproduction of the original letter.

P   WHAT did you do when you first received the letter? (1)
W I read it.
P   HOW carefully did you read it? (1), (2)
W Very carefully.
P   WHY did you read it carefully? (1), (2)
W It shocked me. I had to read it several times before I could believe what I saw there.
P   HOW many times did you read it? (1), (2)
W At least three times. Again, it was so hard to believe what I read there.
P   HOW was the letter prepared? Was it printed, written, or typed? (2)
W It was handwritten.
P   HOW well do you remember the contents of the letter? (2)
W Very well. I can't quote it word for word, but I have a distinct recollection.
P   HOW can you remember it so well? (2)
W It was relatively short, and I read it carefully several times.
P   WHAT copies of the letter, if any, do you still have in your possession? (4)
W I'm afraid I don't have any. As I explained before, the original has been mislaid, and I didn't make any copies before it got lost.
P   To the best of your knowledge, WHAT copies, if any, does Mr. Smythe have? (4)
W I know that I didn't give him any.
P   WHAT were the contents of the letter? (3)
W It talked about several things.
P   WHAT, if anything, did the letter say about Mr. Smythe? (3)
O Your Honor, I object to that question on the ground that it calls for secondary evidence.
P   Your Honor, may I be heard?
J   Yes.

P   It's true that the witness's recollection is secondary evidence. However, we've established the loss of the original which is an adequate excuse for the nonproduction of the original. In addition, the witness has testified to the lack of copies and to recalling the contents of the letter.

J   Objection overruled.

P   Mr. Jackson, let me repeat the question. WHAT, if anything, did the letter say about Mr. Smythe? (3)

W   It said that Smythe had bribed Councilman Wild in connection with a zoning application.

Chapter 8

OPINION EVIDENCE

A. INTRODUCTION

Like the secondary evidence rule, the opinion rule is based on doubts about the reliability of a certain type of evidence. The common law distrusts opinions and thus prefers that witnesses restrict their testimony to statements of perceived fact. The witness states the primary, sensory data, and the jurors then draw the inferences or conclusions from the underlying data.

The opinion rule is a general norm rather than an absolute. In two situations, the law allows opinion testimony. First, a lay witness may express an opinion on a subject if the opinion will be helpful to the trier of fact, and if the lay witness cannot verbalize all the underlying data and communicate it to the jury. For example, a witness cannot articulate the complicated sensory impressions that led the witness to conclude that a car was going forty-five miles an hour rather than sixty. Thus, the law permits the lay witness to voice an opinion—the car was going forty-five. Evidence Code § 800 allows this type of lay opinion testimony.

In the second situation, the trier of fact lacks the knowledge or skill to draw the proper inferences from the underlying data. When the subject matter is technical or scientific, the jurors, or the judge as trier of fact, may be unable to evaluate the hard data; lacking expert knowledge and skill, they cannot draw reliable inferences or opinions from the facts. Here too, the law permits opinion testimony: expert opinion testimony. Evidence Code § 801 authorizes such testimony.

B. LAY OPINION TESTIMONY

Evidence Code § 800 governs the admissibility of lay opinion testimony. That section reads:

> If a witness is not testifying as an expert, his testimony in the form of an opinion is limited to such an opinion as is permitted by law, including but not limited to an opinion that is:
> (a) Rationally based on the perception of the witness; and
> (b) Helpful to a clear understanding of his testimony.

The courts have construed § 800 as authorizing three types of lay opinion testimony: (1) collective fact or shorthand rendition opinions; (2) skilled lay observer opinions; and (3) lay opinions authorized by pre-Code case law, such as owners' estimates of the value of their property.

1. COLLECTIVE FACT OPINIONS

The commentators have coined various titles for this doctrine; some call it the collective fact doctrine, and others call it the shorthand rendition doctrine. The elements of the doctrine are these: The witness's opinion is based on perceived facts; the opinion is a type of inference that lay persons often draw; and—the key to the doctrine—the lay witness cannot verbalize the underlying sensory data supporting the opinion. *See Osborn v. Mission Ready Mix*, 224 Cal. App. 3d 104, 112, 273 Cal. Rptr. 457, 461-62 (1990) ("the matters observed by the witness may be too complex or subtle to enable the witness accurately to convey them without resorting to the use of conclusory descriptions"). This doctrine permits opinions on such subjects as height, distance, speed, color, and identity. The trial judge passes on the second and third elements of the doctrine as questions of law. The judge decides whether lay persons commonly draw this type of inference and whether the lay witness would be able to articulate the underlying actual data. For example, the California Law Revision Commission comment to Evidence Code § 870 refers to § 800 and states that §800 "permits a witness to testify to a person's rational or irrational appearance or conduct." Testimony that a person's conduct was "irrational" is a classic illustration of collective fact lay opinion. *See also People v. McAlpin*, 53 Cal. 3d 1289, 812 P.2d 563, 283 Cal. Rptr. 382 (1991) (a lay witness could opine whether the defendant was a sexual deviant); *Visueta v. General Motors Corp.*, 234 Cal. App. 3d 1609, 286 Cal. Rptr. 402, 405 (1991) ("A nonexpert witness cannot express his opinion as to the cause of a particular [traffic] accident."); *People v. Williams*, 3 Cal. App. 4th 1326, 5 Cal. Rptr. 2d 130, 134-35 (1992) (a police officer, who did not qualify as an expert on the subject, could not express a lay opinion on intoxication based on a horizontal gaze nystagmus (HGN) test because "matters beyond common experience are not proper subjects for lay opinion testimony.").

The foundation for the doctrine's first element requires proof that:

1. The witness was in a position to observe.
2. The witness in fact observed.
3. The witness observed enough data to form a reliable opinion.
4. The witness states the opinion.

Our fact situation is a tort action arising from a collision. The plaintiff, Ms. Neuman, alleges that the defendant, Mr. Armato, caused the accident by speeding. The accident occurred on November 17th of last year, at the intersection of Haight and Ashbury Streets. The plaintiff calls Mr. Corona as a witness. Mr. Corona has already identified himself. The plaintiff is the proponent.

P   WHERE were you on the morning of November 17th of last year, at approximately ten o'clock? (1)

W   I was standing at the intersection of Haight and Ashbury Streets in San Francisco.

P HOW were you facing? (1)

W I was ready to enter the crosswalk, so I was facing the intersection itself.

P WHAT, if anything, did you see while you were standing there? (2)

W I saw a red car on Haight Street approaching the intersection.

P WHAT else did you see? (2)

W There was a blue car approaching the intersection on Ashbury Street.

P HOW far was the red car from the intersection when you first saw it? (3)

W A couple of hundred feet away.

P HOW long did you have to observe the red car before it reached the intersection? (3)

W Several seconds. I had a pretty good chance to eyeball it.

P Do you have an opinion of the red car's speed? (4)

W Yes.

P In your opinion, WHAT was the speed of the red car? (4)

W I'd say forty miles an hour. It was moving at a pretty good clip.

P WHAT happened when the red car reached the intersection?

W It hit the blue car.

P WHO was the driver of the red car?

W The fellow sitting at the table over there.

P WHAT is he wearing?

W He's wearing a gray sweater.

P Your Honor, may the record reflect that the witness has identified the defendant, Mr. Armato?

J It will so reflect.

P HOW can you recognize him?

W After the two cars hit, he got out of the car, and I walked over to see what had happened.

P HOW long did you stay at the accident scene?

W About an hour. I talked to the parties and then to the police.

P HOW close were you standing to the defendant?

W At one time, I was talking to him. He was no more than a foot or two away from me.

P WHAT were the lighting conditions?

W It was broad daylight.

P HOW well could you see him?

W Very well.

P WHO was the driver of the blue car?

W That lady over there.

P HOW is she dressed?

W She's wearing a green dress and white shoes.

P Your Honor, please let the record reflect that the witness has identified the plaintiff, Ms. Neuman.

J The record will reflect that.

P HOW can you recognize her?

W She was also at the accident scene. I had a chance to look at and talk with her.

2. SKILLED LAY OBSERVER TESTIMONY

The judge will assume that the witness has enough common, human experience to be able to estimate distance, time, height and the like. That explains why the foundation for collective fact opinion is so brief. However, there is a second category of lay opinion testimony that requires a more extensive foundation; it is sometimes called "skilled lay observer testimony." This category includes lay opinions about a person's voice and handwriting style. A lay witness cannot express an opinion identifying someone's voice unless the witness has often heard that voice. Similarly, a lay witness cannot identify a person's handwriting style unless the witness has often observed that person's writing. In each of these situations, if the witness has had repeated, prior opportunities for observation, the witness qualifies as a skilled lay observer.

The foundation for skilled lay observer testimony includes these elements:

1. The witness is familiar with the person's voice or handwriting style.
2. The witness explains how he or she became familiar.
3. The witness states his or her opinion.

Our fact situation is a commercial case in which one of the issues is whether the defendant signed a certain check. The witness is Mr. Bucher, an acquaintance of the defendant. Mr. Bucher did not observe the check's execution, but he is familiar with the author's handwriting style.

P   Your Honor, I request that this be marked plaintiff's exhibit number seven for identification.

J   It will be so marked.

P   Please let the record reflect that I am showing the exhibit to the opposing counsel.

J   It will so reflect.

P   I request permission to approach the witness.

J   Permission granted.

P   Mr. Bucher, I now hand you plaintiff's exhibit number seven for identification, WHAT is it?

W   It seems to be a check.

P   Do you have an opinion as to who signed the check?

W   Yes.

P   In your opinion, WHO signed the check? (3)

W   I'd say that the defendant signed it.

P   WHY do you say that? (1)

W   I recognize his handwriting style on the check.

P   HOW well do you know the defendant's handwriting style? (1)

W   Very well.

P   HOW did you become familiar with his handwriting style? (2)

W   We've been friends for years.

P   HOW often have you seen the defendant sign his name? (2)

W   Tens, maybe hundreds, of times.

P   Your Honor, I now offer plaintiff's exhibit number seven for identification into evidence as plaintiff's exhibit number seven.
J   It will be received.
P   I request permission to hand the exhibit to the jurors for their inspection.
J   Permission granted.

3. OTHER LAY OPINIONS "PERMITTED BY LAW"

Collective fact and skilled lay observer opinions satisfy the criteria stated in subdivisions 800(a) and 800(b). In both instances, the opinion is based on the witness's perceptions and helpfulness to the jurors. However, some lay opinions are admissible even though they do not meet those criteria. Section 800 purports to authorize the admission of lay "opinion[s] ... permitted by law, including but not limited to" opinions satisfying the criteria in § 800(a)-(b). The California Law Revision Commission comment to § 800 explains that the drafters purposefully chose that language:

> Section 800 does not make inadmissible an opinion that is admissible under existing law, even though the requirements of subdivisions (a) and (b) are not satisfied. Thus, the section does not affect the existing rule that a non-expert witness may give his opinion as to the value of his property or the value of his own services. The words "such an opinion as is permitted by law" in Section 800 make this clear.

Like the pre-Code case law, § 800 authorizes a layperson to opine about the value of his or her own services, personal property, or real property. 1 JEFFERSON § 29.7. Evidence Code § 813 more specifically regulates lay opinion testimony on the value of property. Subdivision (a)(2) authorizes lay opinion testimony by either "the owner or the spouse of the owner," but § 814 restricts the permissible bases of the opinions. Section 814 provides that any opinion about the value of property must be "based on matter perceived by or personally known by the witness or made known to the witness at or before the hearing, whether or not admissible, that is of a type that reasonably may be relied upon by an expert in forming an opinion as to ... value. ..." Thus, even lay opinions must rest on the same bases allowable for expert opinion. Evidence Code §§ 815-23 go into detail about the permissible bases for opinions on value. For example, § 816 indicates that the opinion may rest on data about comparable sales. *See Contra Costa Water Dist. v. Bar-C Properties*, 5 Cal. App. 4th 652, 7 Cal. Rptr. 2d 91, 95-96 (1992) (although an owner may testify about the value of his or her own property, "an owner is bound by the same rules of admissibility as any other witness's; consequently, a property owner could not base his opinion on the residual land value approach to valuation).

The foundation for a lay opinion about value therefore includes these elements:

1. The witness is the owner or the spouse of the owner.
2. There is a proper basis for the opinion.

The fact situation is a suit for the breach of a contract to buy a parcel of realty. The plaintiff is the prospective seller, Mr. Wildman. The defendant is the prospective buyer, Mr. Ruth. The witness is Mr. Wildman. Near the beginning of the direct examination, after identifying himself Mr. Wildman testifies:

P   WHERE do you live? (1)
W   I live at 4032 Fair Oaks in Sacramento.
P   WHAT kind of residence is that—a house, a condominium, or an apartment? (1)
W   It's a house.
P   WHO owns that house? (1)
W   I do.
P   Your Honor, I would like this marked as plaintiff's exhibit number three for identification. (1)
J   It will be so marked.
P   Please let the record reflect that I am showing the exhibit to the opposing counsel. (1)
J   The record will so reflect.
P   Permission to approach the witness?
J   Granted.
P   Mr. Wildman, I now hand you what has been marked plaintiff's exhibit number three for identification. WHAT is it? (1)
W   It's the deed conveying title to the property to me three years ago.
P   HOW do you recognize it? (1)
W   I was there when it was signed. I recognize the contents and the grantor's signature.
P   WHERE did this exhibit come from? (1)
W   I had it in a safety deposit box. You asked me to bring it to trial this morning. Just before I took the witness stand, I placed it on your counsel table. It's been sitting there in view since I walked up here.
P   Your Honor, I now offer plaintiff's exhibit number three into evidence as plaintiff's number three. (1)
J   It will be so received.
P   Mr. Wildman, WHOM does this deed name as the person receiving title to the property? (1)
W   Me.
P   Since obtaining title, to WHOM have you conveyed title? (1)
W   No one. The only contract I've had is the one with the defendant, and we're here today because that fell through. I still hold title to the property.

After Mr. Wildman testifies about the breach of contract, the direct examination shifts to the topic of damages. The plaintiff seeks to recover the difference between the contract price and the market value at the time set for delivery of the deed, January 1 of the present year. To establish the market value, the proponent attempts to elicit Mr. Wildman's opinion based on comparable sales.

P Do you have an opinion about the value of your property on January 1 of this year?

W Yes.

P WHAT is the basis of that opinion? (2)

W Sales of other houses in the same subdivision during the prior year.

P HOW many other such sales do you know of? (2)

W There were seven sales of four-bedroom, two-bath houses in the subdivision during that time period.

P HOW did you learn about those sales? (2)

W I talked to the sellers and the realtors. In each case, I got to see the sales documents showing the price figures. (Were it not for § 814, the references to these conversations and documents might raise hearsay and best evidence problems. However, § 814 states that this type of information, "whether or not admissible," may be used for the limited purpose of establishing the basis of the opinion.)

P HOW did those houses differ from yours?

W Very little. The developer used a standard floor plan for the four-bedroom model in the Fair Oaks subdivision. The exteriors differ—some are sort of country, others are Tudor, and some are identical to mine.

P HOW do you know that those houses have that floor plan? (2)

W At one time or another I've been in each of those houses.

P WHAT is the distance between your house and those houses? (2)

W Two of them are on the very same block. They're all in the same, small subdivision. The one farthest away is about three blocks over.

P WHAT is the approximate distance between your house and the one farthest away? (2)

W Under half a mile.

P HOW old is your house? (2)

W It's five years old.

P HOW old are the other houses? (2)

W The subdivision was built up at the same time. All the houses are five to seven years old.

P HOW does the landscaping of your house differ from that of the other houses? (2)

W They're virtually the same. The developer put in the landscaping, and we all have the same type of landscaping. In front, you typically have three trees and some bushes. The backyards are all lawn. It's a very simple landscaping scheme.

P HOW do you know that those houses have that landscaping scheme? (2)

W I've driven by each front yard tens of times, and at one time or another, I've been in each of the backyards.

P WHAT did those seven houses sell for?

W They all went for between $190,000 and $210,000.

P HOW do you know that?

W Again, I talked to the sellers and realtors, and I saw the sales documents.

P Based on your knowledge of those prices, WHAT is your opinion of the value of your house on January 1 of this year?

W I'd say $200,000. My house is pretty average in terms of curb appeal and upkeep. I don't think it's the most appealing house in the subdivision, and I don't think it's the worst. If everything comparable is going for between $190,000 and $210,000, I'd say split the difference and choose $200,000 as the value of my house on that date.

C.   EXPERT OPINION TESTIMONY

The Evidence Code admits expert opinion testimony as well as lay opinion testimony. Section 801(a) states that expert opinion testimony is admissible on "a subject that is sufficiently beyond common experience that the opinion of an expert would assist the trier of fact." "The jury need not be wholly ignorant of the subject matter of the opinion …; if that were the test, little expert opinion testimony would be heard. Instead, the statute declares that even if the jury has some knowledge of the matter, expert opinion may be admitted whenever it would 'assist' the jury. It will be excluded only when it would add nothing at all to the jury's common fund of information, i.e., when 'the subject of inquiry is one of such common knowledge that men of ordinary education could reach a conclusion as intelligently as the witness.'" *People v. Dillard*, 45 Cal. App. 4th 1417, 53 Cal. Rptr. 2d 456, 461 (1996). Some issues, however, call for legal conclusions and are therefore inherently unfit for expert testimony.

The proponent may use an expert witness in three different ways. First, the proponent may use an expert purely as a fact witness. Suppose that the defendant is on trial for rape. The complaining witness testifies that during the rape, she scratched the rapist's face and drew blood. By chance the defendant visited his doctor the day after the alleged rape. The defendant could call his doctor to testify that there were no scratches on the defendant's face. The witness certainly would not have to be an expert to observe the defendant's face, but it is equally clear that the witness is not barred from testifying to facts solely because he or she is an expert. If a witness acts as both a percipient witness and an expert, her expert testimony is subject to a jury instruction identifying it as such.

Second, the proponent may use the expert to teach the jurors scientific or technical principles they need to evaluate the facts in the case. The expert witness explains the principles without applying them to the specific facts of the case; the jurors themselves apply the principles to the facts. This use of expert testimony is quite common. In *People v. McDonald*, 37 Cal. 3d 351, 690 P.2d 709, 208 Cal. Rptr. 236 (1984), the California Supreme Court ruled that in some cases, a criminal defense attorney may introduce expert psychological testimony about the general unreliability of eyewitness identification. In most cases, the expert in question has not examined or interviewed the eyewitnesses called by the prosecution. The expert describes the weaknesses of eyewitness testimony; then during closing argument, the defense attorney invites the jurors to apply the expert's theories to the facts of the case. For instance, the expert might testify that cross-racial identifications are particularly suspect. The trial judge would ordinarily not permit the expert to testify that the prosecution witnesses were mistaken. However, if there is a cross-racial identification, during summation the defense attorney could ask the jurors to discount the eyewitness testimony because of that factor. In effect, the expert testifies to a general theory, and the trier of fact applies the theory to the facts of the case. *See, e.g., People v. Morgan*, 58 Cal. App. 4th 1210, 68 Cal. Rptr. 2d 772 (1997), where, in order to rehabilitate the victim witness, prosecution expert testified to Battered Women's Syndrome generally but had not met or spoken with victim and gave no opinion on the victim's credibility.

Finally, the proponent may have the expert express an opinion evaluating the significance of the facts of the case. The expert first states the theory and then states an opinion about the merits of the case by applying the theory to the facts of the case. When the expert serves as an evaluator or interpreter of the facts, the direct examination is typically structured as follows. Initially, the witness testifies to the credentials that qualify him or her as an expert. The balance of the direct examination takes the form of a simple syllogism. The major premise is the theory the expert relies on. If the witness is a psychiatrist, the theory may be that the presence of certain symptoms indicates a particular mental disease. The next part of the direct examination is the minor premise, the facts about the instant case. For instance, in this part of the testimony a psychiatrist typically recites the patient's symptoms. Then the expert states the opinion itself. Lastly, an experienced proponent will often have the expert explain in detail the reasoning process underlying the opinion—that is, explain how the theory (the major premise) relates to the facts (the minor premise).

1. THE EXPERT'S QUALIFICATIONS TO FORM THE OPINION

The law permits expert opinion testimony because the expert has the knowledge or skill to draw inferences beyond the capability of the trier of fact. The expert can acquire the knowledge or skill by education, experience, or a combination of both. The expert's background often includes theoretical education plus practical experience.

As Evidence Code § 720 states:

(a) A person is qualified to testify as an expert if he has special knowledge, skill, experience, training, or education sufficient to qualify him as an expert on the subject to which his testimony relates. Against the objection of a party, such special knowledge, skill, experience, training, or education, must be shown before the witness may testify as an expert.

(b) A witness's special knowledge, skill, experience, training, or education may be shown by any otherwise admissible evidence, including his own testimony.

Under Evidence Code § 405, the trial judge finally decides whether the witness is qualified as an expert to express an opinion on the subject. *Martin v. Superior Court (People)*, 230 Cal. App. 3d 1192, 281 Cal. Rptr. 682, 687 (1991); *People v. Leahy*, 8 Cal. 4th 587, 882 P.2d 321, 34 Cal. Rptr. 2d 663 (1994) (a police officer without formal scientific training was unqualified to lay the *Frye* foundation for the horizontal gaze nystagmus (HGN) field sobriety test); *People v. Clark*, 5 Cal. 4th 950, 857 P.2d 1099, 22 Cal. Rptr. 2d 689 (1993) (the witness qualified as an expert on blood spatter), *cert. denied*, 512 U.S. 1253 (1994).

The foundation for the expert's qualifications could include the following elements, but bear in mind that no single element is essential.[1] *See, e.g., Osborn v. Irwin Mem. Blood Bank*, 5 Cal. App. 4th 234, 7 Cal. Rptr. 2d 101, 122-23 (1992) ("work in a particular field is not an absolute prerequisite to qualification as an expert in that field"); *see also Tibor v. Superior Court*, 52 Cal. App. 4th 1359, 1364-65, n.1, 61 Cal. Rptr. 2d 326, 329 n.1 (1997) (on a motion for summary judgment, a declaration of a supposed expert is defective if it fails to show that the declarant has the skill, training, or experience needed to express the opinions stated in the declaration).

1. The witness has acquired degrees from educational institutions.
2. The witness has had other specialized training in this field of expertise.
3. The witness is licensed to practice in the field.
4. The witness has practiced in the field for a substantial period of time.
5. The witness has taught in the field.
6. The witness has published in the field.
7. The witness belongs to professional organizations in the field.
8. The witness has previously testified as an expert on this subject.

Our fact situation is a civil personal injury action. The plaintiff, Mr. Nowick, alleges that the defendant, Mr. Johnson, negligently caused the collision in which Mr. Nowick was injured. The complaint alleges that the plaintiff has suffered severe brain injury as a result of the accident. The plaintiff calls Dr. Worth. The plaintiff is the proponent. Dr. Worth has already identified herself.

P WHAT is your formal education? (1)
W I have a bachelor's degree and a medical degree.
P WHICH undergraduate school did you attend? (1)
W Arizona State University.
P WHAT degree did you obtain there? (1)
W I earned a bachelor of science degree.
P WHAT was your major field of study? (1)
W Biology.
P WHICH medical school did you attend? (1)
W The Johns Hopkins University Medical School in Baltimore.
P WHAT degree did you obtain there? (1)
W My M.D.

---

[1]California Health and Safety Code § 1799.110(c) states special requirements for medical experts in malpractice actions against emergency room doctors. *See, e.g., Zavala v. Board of Trustees of Leland Stanford, Jr. Univ.*, 16 Cal. App. 4th 1755, 20 Cal. Rptr. 2d 768 (1993); *Miranda v. National Emergency Services, Inc.*, 35 Cal. App. 4th 894, 41 Cal. Rptr. 2d 593 (1995) (the prospective witness must have "on the job" experience as an emergency room physician in a locality where emergency care is provided in a manner substantially the same as in the locale where and when the alleged malpractice occurred; in this case, the prospective witness did not qualify, since he was merely a specialist on call to an emergency room).

P WHAT did you do after you graduated from medical school? (2)

W I interned at the University of Southern California Medical Center.

P HOW long was your internship? (2)

W A year.

P WHAT did you do after your internship? (2)

W I became a resident at Gross Hospital in Lexington, Kentucky.

P WHAT is a residency? (2)

W You specialize in a certain field and get practical experience.

P WHAT was your specialty? (2)

W Neurology, brain problems.

P HOW long was your residency? (2)

W Three years.

P WHEN did your residency end? (2)

W In 1979.

P WHAT did you do when your residency ended? (3)

W I moved back here to Los Angeles and began practicing.

P WHAT did you have to do to practice in Los Angeles? (3)

W I had to become licensed in California.

P WHEN did you obtain your license in this state? (3)

W In 1980.

P WHAT did you do after you obtained your license? (4)

W I began my practice, specializing in neurology.

P HOW long have you practiced in this state? (4)

W Since 1980—I've never left California.

P HOW many clients with neurological problems have you treated? (4)

W I can't name a number. By this time, I've probably treated thousands.

P HOW much of your time do you devote to the practice of medicine? (5)

W About 80 percent of my working time.

P WHAT else do you spend your time on? (5)

W For one thing, I teach at the U.C.L.A. Medical School.

P HOW long have you taught there? (5)

W For four years now.

P WHAT courses do you teach? (5)

W I teach three upper division courses in the field of neurology.

P WHAT else do you spend your professional time on? (6)

W I publish with some frequency.

P WHAT journals have published your articles? (6)

W Some of the leading medical and neurological journals, including the A.M.A.
   Journal.

P HOW many articles have you published? (6)

W Nine.

P WHAT topics did you discuss in these articles? (6)

W All the articles relate to neurology.

P WHAT professional organizations do you belong to? (7)

W Several, including the American College of Neurological Specialists and the
   American Board of Neurology.

P HOW do you become a member of the American College? (7)

W You have to have specialized in the neurological field for at least five years.

P HOW do you become a member of the Board? (7)

W   There are strict requirements. You not only have to have practiced for several years; you also have to pass oral and written examinations.

P   HOW often have you testified in court? (8)

W   I'd say at least one hundred cases.

P   HOW many times were you permitted to give expert opinion testimony? (8)

W   Every time.

P   WHAT subjects did you testify on? (8)

W   Most of the time I testified on neurology.

2. THE GENERAL THEORY OR PRINCIPLE THE EXPERT RELIES ON

After describing his or her credentials, the expert often states the major premise—the general theory or principle on which the expert relies. The theory or principle must pass two tests. The first test is stated in Evidence Code § 801(a): the theory or principle must relate "to a subject that is sufficiently beyond the common experience that the opinion of an expert would assist the trier of fact." If the subject is a matter of common knowledge, there is no need for expert testimony. *Compare Loth v. Truck-A-Way Corp.*, 60 Cal. App. 4th 757, 70 Cal. Rptr. 2d 571 (1998) (error in a personal injury case to admit expert testimony on how to value the loss of "enjoyment of life" because that was within the jury's common experience) *with People v. Valdez*, 58 Cal. App. 4th 494, 68 Cal. Rptr. 2d 135 (1997) (culture, habits, and psychology of gangs was beyond common experience).

The second test is stated in Evidence Code 801(b): the expert's testimony must be "based on matter ... that is of a type that reasonably may be relied upon by an expert in forming an opinion" on the subject in question. For example, in *City of San Diego v. Sobke,* 65 Cal. App. 4th 379, 76 Cal. Rptr. 2d 9 (1998), the city condemned part of the defendants' business property for road improvements. In the condemnation proceeding, the defendant property owners tried to prove loss of business good will by offering the testimony of an expert appraiser (who was also a certified public accountant). Instead of valuing the good will before the taking and comparing that figure to the good will after the taking, the expert appraiser devised a different method. He added up the extra business expenses defendant incurred due to the taking, capitalized the total, and asserted that the result equaled the loss of business good will. The appellate court affirmed the trial judge's refusal to let the appraiser testify, holding that his opinion was not based on the type of information that would be used by an expert in the subject in question.

If the expert's opinion testimony is based on a *scientific* principle or theory, it must pass yet a third test—California's *Kelly-Frye* test, which requires that the principle or theory must be *generally accepted* within the scientific field to which it relates. As we explained in Chapter 4 Section N, the federal courts no longer use the general acceptance test, thanks to *Daubert v. Merrell Dow Pharm.*, 509 U.S. 579, 113 S. Ct. 2786, 125 L. Ed. 2d 469 (1993). *See also Kuhmo Tire Co., Ltd. v. Carmichael*, 526 U. S. 137, 119 S. Ct. 1167, 143 L. Ed. 2d 238 (1999) (*Dau-*

bert principle applies also to technological evidence such as that provided by an expert on tire failure). California has not yet modernized its position on scientific evidence, and for the moment *Kelly-Frye* still reigns in California. *See People v. Wash*, 6 Cal. 4th 215, 243 n.9, 24 Cal. Rptr. 2d 421, 861 P.2d 1107 (1993); *see also In re Aontae D.*, 25 Cal. App. 4th 167, 30 Cal. Rptr. 2d 176 (1994).

The *Kelly-Frye* standard applies to the testimony of scientific experts in both criminal and civil cases. *See, e.g., People v. Kelly*, 17 Cal. 3d 24, 130 Cal. Rptr. 144, 549 P.2d 1240 (1976); *Huntingdon v. Crowley*, 64 Cal. 2d 647, 414 P.2d 382, 51 Cal. Rptr. 254 (1966). *Melaleuca, Inc. v. Clark*, 66 Cal. App. 4th 1344, 78 Cal. Rptr. 2d 627 (1998) presents an unusual application of *Kelly-Frye*. Defendant Clark, a purported research scientist who claimed to have discovered the causes and cures for all cancers, and for HIV/AIDS as well, disparaged plaintiff's products by asserting that they contain benzene, a carcinogen. Standard laboratory tests revealed no benzene, but plaintiff said she could detect benzene using her "syncrometer," a detection device of her own invention. The appellate court affirmed the trial judge's refusal to allow plaintiff to support her "truth" defense with expert testimony based on syncrometer readings because her device was not generally accepted in the field of chemical analysis and could not pass muster under *Kelly-Frye*. Further, the standard applies to all species of scientific testimony, whether the testimony rests on an instrumental technique, such as polygraph or a noninstrumental technique employed in psychology.[2]

The *Kelly/Frye* element of the foundation is superfluous if a statute authorizes the receipt of testimony based on a particular scientific technique. 1 P. GIANNELLI & E. IMWINKELRIED, SCIENTIFIC EVIDENCE § 1-3 (2d ed. 1993). "[L]egislative ... recognition relieves the proponent of scientific evidence of the burden of introducing evidence on" this issue. *Id.*, § 1-3, at 7. For example, Evidence Code § 1107 authorizes expert testimony regarding battered women's syndrome, as follows:

---

[2]*See People v. Shirley*, 31 Cal. 3d 18, 34, 641 P.2d 775, 783-84, 181 Cal. Rptr. 243, 641, 252 *cert. denied*, 459 U.S. 860 (1982). *But see People v. Stoll*, 49 Cal. 3d 1136, 783 P.2d 698, 265 Cal. Rptr. 111 (1989), in which the supreme court found harmful error in the trial court's exclusion on *Kelly/Frye* grounds of expert testimony based on psychological tests. The court, following *People v. McDonald*, 37 Cal. 3d 351, 690 P.2d 709, 208 Cal. Rptr. 236 (1984), reasoned that the *Kelly/Frye* standard had never been applied to expert medical testimony. The majority's reasoning, however, ignores the rule's rationale of ensuring reasonable reliability of scientific evidence. In dissent, Chief Justice Lucas argued that "the need for *Kelly/Frye* compliance is even more compelling [where, as here, the testimony is offered] to prove that [defendant] could not have committed [the charged offenses" *People v. Stoll, supra*, 49 Cal. 3d at 1166, 783 P.2d at 717, 265 Cal. Rptr. at 130. According to at least one commentator, though, the prevailing view among the states such as California subscribing to *Frye* is that "soft" scientific evidence such as psychological testimony is exempt from the *Frye* test. Hanson, *James Alphonzo Frye Is Sixty-Five Years Old; Should He Retire?*, 16 WEST ST. U. L. REV. *See also People v. Ward*, 71 Cal. App. 4th 368, 83 Cal. Rptr. 2d 828 (1999) (in action to commit a person to a mental hospital under California's Sexually Violent Predator Act, the expert testimony of psychologists and psychiatrists is not scientific evidence and is thus not subject to *Kelly-Frye*); *Texaco Producing, Inc. v. County of Kern*, 66 Cal. App. 4th 1029, 78 Cal. Rptr. 2d 433 (1998) (*Kelly-Frye* inapplicable to appraisal methods used by county's experts to value oil property for tax purposes).

(a) In a criminal action, expert testimony is admissible by either the prosecution or the defense regarding battered women's syndrome, including the physical, emotional, or mental effects upon the beliefs, perceptions, or behavior of victims of domestic violence, except when offered against a criminal defendant to prove the occurrence of the act or acts of abuse which form the basis of the criminal charge.

(b) The foundation shall be sufficient for admission of this expert testimony if the proponent of the evidence establishes its relevancy and the proper qualifications of the expert witness. Expert opinion testimony on battered women's syndrome shall not be considered a new scientific technique whose reliability is unproven.

To lay the *Kelly-Frye* element of the foundation, the proponent should establish that:

1. The expert used a particular theory to evaluate the facts in the case.
2. The theory in question has been experimentally verified.
3. The theory is generally accepted by the majority of experts in the pertinent scientific specialty.

The fact situation is a rape prosecution. The People allege that the defendant, Mr. Marx, raped the complainant, Ms. Jane Whitlow. During her direct testimony, Ms. Whitlow described the rape and identified the defendant as the rapist. Ms. Whitlow reported the rape to the police the day it happened. On cross-examination, she admitted that the following day, in a conversation with her mother, Ms. Whitlow refused to confirm or deny that there had been a rape. As their next witness, the People call Dr. Herbert Dubowski, a licensed psychiatrist. The People propose to elicit Dr. Dubowski's testimony about rape trauma syndrome (RTS) to rehabilitate Ms. Whitlow's credibility. In *People v. Bledsoe*, 36 Cal. 3d 236, 251, 681 P.2d 291, 301, 203 Cal. Rptr. 450, 460 (1984), the California Supreme Court held that the prosecution may not use the fact that the complainant displays RTS symptoms as substantive evidence that there has been a rape. However, the court indicated that RTS evidence could be used for other purposes, such as rehabilitating the credibility of an impeached complainant. *People v. Roscoe*, 168 Cal. App. 3d 1093, 1099, 215 Cal. Rptr. 45, 49 (1985), applied *Bledsoe* and held RTS evidence admissible "to support the victim's credibility." After stating his credentials, Dr. Dubowski testifies:

P Doctor, WHAT is your specialty? (1)

W For the past few years, I've concentrated my practice and research in the area of rape trauma syndrome.

P WHAT is rape trauma syndrome? (1)

W The theory holds that in most cases, after a rape women cope with that traumatic event in a predictable manner.

P WHAT manner is that? (1)

W Their reaction usually progresses through two phases. The initial stage is the acute phase. They try to come to terms with the physical trauma and the immediate psychological impact. They experience disorganization in their lives. They become confused.

P WHAT do you mean by "confused"? (1)

W They're indecisive. Even if someone asks them point blank about the rape, out of shame or a sense of morality, they are often reluctant to discuss it. Again, that's the acute phase. That's followed by the long-term phase.

P WHAT happens during that phase? (1)

W They begin reorganizing their lives. They may move, change their telephone number, and visit friends and family much more frequently to gain moral support. They often develop phobias. They may have a fear of being alone.

P WHAT research, if any, have you done on rape trauma syndrome? (2)

W I was fortunate enough to participate in the original research done on the subject. Before I moved to San Francisco, I lived in Boston. That's where Burgess and Homstrom did the first intensive study of this subject.

P WHEN and WHERE did they conduct that study? (2)

W Between July 1972 and July 1973, they interviewed all the rape victims admitted to the emergency ward of Boston City Hospital.

P HOW many persons did they study? (2)

W About 150 women were included in the data base.

P WHAT types of women were included in the study? (2)

W All sorts—they were all races. About 70 percent were adult, and the rest were minors. In fact, there were three male children included in the study.

P HOW did the researchers conduct the study? (2)

W They initially interviewed these people, and they then followed up by studying the changes in the life patterns after the traumatic incident.

P WHAT findings did the researchers make? (2)

W In the overwhelming majority of cases, there was a clear pattern.

P WHAT do you mean by "overwhelming majority"? (2)

W I mean about 85 to 90 percent of the cases.

P WHAT was the pattern? (2)

W It was the two stages, the acute and long-term phases, that I described a few moments ago.

P WHAT other research, if any, has been done on rape trauma syndrome? (2)

W There have been several other studies, including Sutherland and Scherl.

P WHAT were the findings in those studies? (2)

W About the same. You can quibble with percentages, but the virtually uniform finding is that in most cases, there is a definite pattern of coping behavior after a rape.

P Doctor, HOW well accepted is rape trauma syndrome? (3)

W It's very well accepted in my field.

P WHAT evidence is there that the syndrome is well accepted? (3)

W The latest editions of the leading, authoritative treatises on psychiatry all mention the syndrome.

P WHAT professional organizations are there in your field? (3)

W One is the APA, the American Psychiatric Association.

P To WHAT extent has the American Psychiatric Association recognized the existence of rape trauma syndrome? (3)

W The APA has an official manual, the Diagnostic and Statistical Manual of Mental Disorders, which lists posttraumatic stress disorder as a recognized syndrome.

P WHAT, if anything, does the manual say about rape trauma syndrome? (3)

W One of the examples of posttraumatic stress disorder in the manual is its application after a rape.

3. THE FACTUAL BASES OF THE EXPERT'S OPINION

The expert should now state the minor premise, the factual data to which the theory will be applied. Evidence Code § 801(b) governs the permissible bases of expert opinions. That subdivision states that an expert opinion may rest on material

> perceived by or personally known to the witness or made known to him at or before the hearing, whether or not admissible, that is of a type that reasonably may be relied upon by an expert in forming an opinion upon the subject to which his testimony relates, unless an expert is precluded by law from using such matter as a basis for his opinion.

Given the wording of § 801(b), there are three possible bases for an expert opinion.

a. Facts the Expert Personally Knows

Evidence Code § 801(b) permits an expert to base an opinion on personal knowledge—facts "perceived by him or personally known" to him. For instance, doctors usually base their opinions in part on conditions and symptoms they personally observed when examining a patient. *See People v. Ramos*, 15 Cal. 4th 1133, 938 P.2d 950, 64 Cal. Rptr. 2d 892 (1997), *cert. denied*, 118 S. Ct. 1315 (1998), where an expert on the general subject of prisons and prisoners was held not qualified to testify to conditions of incarceration of defendant, because expert lacked the personal knowledge of the prison conditions at the relevant time.

The foundation ordinarily includes these elements:

1. Where the witness observed the fact.
2. When the witness observed the fact.
3. Who was present.
4. How the witness observed the fact.
5. A description of the fact(s) observed.

We shall continue our hypothetical with the neurologist, Dr. Worth.

P WHERE were you on the afternoon of July 11th of this year? (1) (2)

W In my office.

P WHAT, if anything, happened that afternoon? (3)

W I conducted an examination of the plaintiff, Mr. Nowick.

P WHO is Mr. Nowick? (3)

W He's the gentleman sitting over there at the end of the table.

P HOW is he dressed? (3)

W He's wearing the white suit with the gray tie.

P Your Honor, please let the record reflect that the witness has correctly identified the plaintiff, Mr. Nowick.

J The record will reflect that.

P WHO was present during this examination? (3)

W Just Mr. Nowick, myself, and my nurse, Ms. Cartwright.

P WHAT happened during the examination? (4)

W I personally examined the plaintiff for any symptoms of brain damage.

P HOW did you conduct the examination? (4)

W I conducted a manual inspection of his cranium and then administered a battery of standard eye and coordination tests.

P HOW long did this examination take? (4)

W A good three hours. I conducted a very thorough examination.

P WHAT, if anything, did you observe during the examination? (5)

W I saw some symptoms and signs of brain damage.

P WHAT were the symptoms? (5)

W For one thing, there was a deep scar on the front, right side of Mr. Nowick's head.

P HOW deep? (5)

W Almost one-eighth of an inch into the surface—easily deep enough to cause some damage.

P WHAT else did you observe? (5)

W There was a sort of vacancy in the plaintiff's eyes, again possibly indicating brain problems. Finally, the plaintiff exhibited real difficulty in the eye-to-hand coordination tests.

b. Hearsay Reports from Third Parties

There is a split of authority whether the expert may rely on reports from third parties, such as other experts, if the reports do not fall within any hearsay exception. The traditional view has been that the expert may not do so. However, the Evidence Code follows the trend that the expert may do so as long as it is customary in the specialty to consider that type of data. The hearsay report is not admitted to prove that what it states is true; the report is admitted for the limited purpose of showing the basis of the expert's opinion. Consequently, under Evidence Code § 355, upon request, the opponent is entitled to a limiting instruction by the trial judge.

Evidence Code § 801(b) states that an expert cannot base an opinion on matter that "an expert is *precluded by law* from using ... as a basis for his opinion." Evidence Code § 160 defines "law" as including decisional law. The California Law Revision Commission comment to § 801(b) expressly states that by decisional law, judges may rule that a particular type of information is "an improper basis for an opinion." The comment gives several examples. On the one hand, the comment states that a physician may rely on "case history recited by the patient or reports from various technicians or other physicians." Likewise, appraisers may "rely on reports of sales and other market data." On the other hand, the comment states that in expressing an opinion about the cause of a fire, arson investigators may not rely on "the statements of bystanders, even though it is customary for investigators to do so." The comment emphasizes that "the courts ... are free to continue to develop specific rules regarding the proper bases for particular types of expert opinion in specific fields." *See, e.g., People v. Parnell*, 16 Cal. App. 4th 862, 20 Cal. Rptr. 2d 302 (1993) (trial judge correctly excluded a psychotherapist's opinion about defendant's mental state at the time of the crime where the opinion was based on statements defendant made under hypnosis).

The foundation for an opinion based on hearsay reports includes these elements:

1. The source of the third party report.
2. The content or tenor of the report.
3. It is customary within the specialty to consider that type of report.
4. The expert actually relied on the report.

Our hypothetical continues:

P Dr. Worth, in addition to the symptoms you personally observed during your examination of Mr. Nowick, WHAT else have you considered? (1)

W For one thing, I talked to Mr. Nowick's family physician, Dr. Stiles.

P WHO is Dr. Stiles? (1)

W Maynard Stiles is a general practitioner here in town.

P HOW long has he been in practice here? (1)

W Maybe fifteen years. He's a well-respected member of our local medical community.

P WHEN did you talk with him? (1)

W The day after I examined the plaintiff.

P WHY did you talk to him? (3)

W I had to get Mr. Nowick's medical history. Specifically, I wanted to know whether he had that scar or displayed the vacant stare or lack of coordination before his car accident.

P WHAT is the importance of the medical history? (3)

W You just can't make an intelligent diagnosis without that.

P WHAT is the customary medical practice concerning the use of medical history? (3)

W I followed the custom here. (4) It would be malpractice not to gather the history and consider it in making your diagnosis. Use of the history is good, accepted practice.

P WHAT did Dr. Stiles tell you about the plaintiff's medical history? (2)

W He gave me a detailed review of his medical records. He said that prior to the accident, there was no scar on the plaintiff's cranium. Further, prior to the collision, the plaintiff had not exhibited the symptoms of either vacancy of stare or lack of coordination.

O Your Honor, I request a limiting instruction.

J Yes. Ladies and gentlemen of the jury, Dr. Worth has just referred to a statement made by a Dr. Stiles. You may not consider Dr. Stiles' statement as proof that before the accident, the plaintiff had no scar or vacant stare or lack of coordination. You may consider Dr. Stiles' statement only for the limited purpose of showing one factor or element Dr. Worth considered in arriving at his opinion.

Evidence Code § 802 states that an expert "may state on direct examination the reasons for his opinion and the matter ... upon which it is based. ..." Justice Jefferson construes § 802 to mean that the expert witness may read into the record the relevant portions of a hearsay document on which he or she relied. 2 JEFFERSON § 29.4, at 1025 (citing *Kelley v. Bailey*, 189 Cal. App. 2d 728, 11 Cal. Rptr. 448 (1961), a pre-Code case). However, in his view, the document should not be formally received as an exhibit, and it should not go to the jury room. *Id.* at 1026. *See also Nortica v. State Compensation Ins. Fund*, 70 Cal. App. 4th 911, 83 Cal. Rptr. 2d 89 (1999) (insurance expert, testifying about defendant insurance company's likely motive for increasing its reserve levels, may rely on an industry trade paper interview in which defendant's president stated the motive for the increase; further, the expert may read parts of the interview to the jury). In *Continental Airlines, Inc. v. McDonnell Douglas Corp.*, 216 Cal. App. 3d 388, 414, 264 Cal. Rptr. 779, 793 (1989), the court held that an expert may rely on matters that are inadmissible hearsay, but may not testify to the details of such matters if they are otherwise inadmissible. *See also People v. Nicolaus*, 54 Cal. 3d 551, 582, 817 P.2d 893, 910, 286 Cal. Rptr. 628, 645 (1991); *Korsak v. Atlas Hotels, Inc.*, 2 Cal. App. 4th 1516, 3 Cal. Rptr. 2d 833 (1992); *People v. Campos*, 32 Cal. App. 4th 304, 38 Cal. Rptr. 2d 113 (1995) (on direct examination, the expert may not reveal the contents of reports prepared by or opinions expressed by nontestifying experts). However, in *People v. Valdez*, 58 Cal. App. 4th 494, 68 Cal. Rptr. 2d 135 (1997), the trial court properly allowed an expert on gangs to relate in detail large amounts of inadmissible hearsay upon which he relied in forming his opinion that the defendant was a member of a street gang.

c. Assumed Facts

Sometimes the testifying expert has neither examined the party nor even talked with an expert who has personally examined the party. The testifying expert may still express an opinion in response to a hypothetical question. In the question, the proponent specifies the facts he or she wants the expert to assume. The expert then relies on expert knowledge and skill to draw a proper inference from those assumed facts. *See generally People v. Sims*, 5 Cal. 4th 405 n.6, 20 Cal. Rptr. 2d 537 n.6, 853 P.2d 992 n.6 (1993), *cert. denied*, 512 U.S. 1253 (1994) (hypothetical question can be framed on any theory that can be deduced from any evidence admitted at trial, including assumption of facts within the limits of the evidence).

There are three major limitations on hypothetical questions. First, the proponent must ordinarily have already introduced evidence sufficient to support a finding that the assumed facts exist. Under Evidence Code § 320, the trial judge may permit the proponent to vary the order of proof and introduce proof of the assumed facts later, but judges seldom let the proponent do so.

Second, the hypothesis must include all the undisputed, material facts. The reason is obvious; if the hypothesis omits critical facts, the ultimate opinion will be misleading rather than helpful. To be sure, the hypothesis need not include all the relevant evidence. HEAFEY § 20.9, at 180. However, the hypothesis must include enough proven facts to support the expert's opinion. 1 JEFFERSON § 29.43. For an illustration of the attendant dangers of expert testimony based on responses to hypothetical questions, *see 580 Folsom Assocs. v. Prometheus Dev. Co.,* 216 Cal. App. 3d 972, 265 Cal. Rptr. 251 (1989), *modified on other grounds,* 223 Cal. App. 3d 1, 272 Cal. Rptr. 227 (1990). The expert's opinion relying on assumed facts not in evidence became worthless when the proponent failed to substantiate its assumptions.

The third and final limitation is that the proponent must state the hypothesis before asking for the opinion. Under § 802, the proponent may usually elicit the opinion before the bases of the opinion. However, the California Law Revision Commission comment to § 802 states that

> the assumed facts upon which his opinion is based must be stated in order to show that the witness has some basis for forming an intelligent opinion and to permit the trier of fact to determine the applicability of the opinion in light of the existence or nonexistence of such facts.

Hypothetical questions can take two forms. In the first form, the proponent specifies the facts the expert is to assume. For example, the proponent could say:

P   Dr. Worth, please assume the following facts as true:
      Number one, in the accident, the plaintiff sustained a cut three inches in length and one-eighth inch in depth on the right, front part of his head. Number two, the plaintiff bled profusely from that cut. Number three, immediately after the accident, the plaintiff began experiencing sharp, painful headaches in the right, front part of his head.

In the second form, the proponent asks the witness to assume the truth of the testimony of another witness or witnesses. Assume, for instance, that the ambulance attendant, Mr. Phelan, has already testified. During his testimony, Phelan stated that he observed the cut on plaintiff's head, noted the bleeding, and heard plaintiff complain about a headache. The plaintiff now calls Dr. Worth.

P   Dr. Worth, WHERE were you this morning?
W   Here in the courtroom.
P   WHAT were you doing?
W   Listening to the testimony.
P   WHOSE testimony did you listen to?
W   Mr. Phelan, the ambulance attendant, was on the stand most of the morning.

P HOW well could you hear his testimony?
W Very well. I had no problems hearing what he was saying.
P Specifically, WHERE were you sitting?
W In the first row reserved for spectators.
P HOW often did you leave the room during Mr. Phelan's testimony?
W I didn't leave; I stayed in the courtroom the whole time.
P Dr. Worth, please assume the truth of Mr. Phelan's testimony about Mr. Nowick's condition immediately after the accident.

Many jurisdictions prohibit the second form of hypothetical question. These courts reason that this form is ambiguous; it is difficult for the jurors to determine the specific facts the expert witness is assuming. Moreover, if the proponent invites the expert to assume the truth of several witnesses' testimony, and if there are any conflicts in the testimony, the proponent is really asking the expert to resolve those conflicts. However, California and some other jurisdictions allow this form of hypothetical question if the assumed testimony is simple and internally consistent. *See* 3 WITKIN § 1850, at 1806; Article, *The Opinion Rule in California and Federal Courts: A Liberal Approach*, 9 U.C. DAVIS L. REV. 233, 248 (1976).

4. EVIDENCE OF AN OUT-OF-COURT EXPERIMENT

Suppose that in a particular case, the central issue is whether a traffic accident occurred in a certain manner. The plaintiff and defendant advance conflicting theories as to how the accident occurred. To corroborate his or her theory, the plaintiff might offer testimony about an out-of-court experiment.[3] The plaintiff would hire an expert to design and conduct an experiment duplicating the conditions existing at the time of the accident in question. Suppose that the result of the experiment indicated that the accident occurred in the manner claimed by the plaintiff. The experiment might be important corroboration for the plaintiff's theory of the case. At trial, the plaintiff could present an expert witness or witnesses to provide an oral description of the experiment. In addition, the plaintiff could offer a photograph[4] or videotape[5] depicting part or all of the experiment.

To lay a proper predicate for evidence of an out-of-court experiment, the proponent must lay the following foundation:

1. The witness possesses the expertise to design and conduct the experiment. The witness must qualify as an expert under California Evidence Code § 801(b). In the accident reconstruction context, the witness might have

---

[3]C. Philip Colver, *The Persuasive Impact of Simulative Experimentation*, 17 TRIAL 64 (Nov. 1981).
[4]*Reed v. Tiffin Motor Homes, Inc.*, 697 F.2d 1192 (4th Cir. 1982).
[5]*Chase v. General Motors Corp.*, 856 F.2d 17 (4th Cir. 1988); *Champeau v. Fruehauf Corp.*, 814 F.2d 1271 (8th Cir. 1987); *Gladhill v. General Motors Corp.*, 743 F.2d 1049 (4th Cir. 1984).

prior experience as a traffic police officer or a background in engineering,[6] notably physics.

2. The proponent asked the witness to design and conduct an experiment. The request itself is not a hearsay statement under California Evidence Code § 225 and § 1200 because it is not offered "to prove the truth of the matter stated." For the same reason, the witness's agreement to carry out the experiment is not a hearsay statement.

3. The witness studied the accident which the proponent asked the witness to duplicate. Under California Evidence Code § 801(b), the expert may gain his or her information about the accident from three sources. First, the expert can rely on personal knowledge. For instance, the expert might personally visit the accident scene or go to the mechanic's shop to inspect the vehicles involved in the accident. Second, the expert could rely on facts that would be posited to the expert at trial in the form of a hypothetical question. When the proponent opts to rely on this source, the proponent will, of course, have to introduce admissible evidence of all the facts stated in the hypothesis posed to the expert. Ordinarily, the trial judge will require that the proponent present the admissible evidence before calling the expert. In many cases, if not most, in wording the hypothesis the proponent specifies the facts that he or she wants the expert to assume. In other cases, the judge exempts the expert from any sequestration order entered under California Evidence Code § 777, and the proponent then invites the expert to assume the truth of the particular testimony the expert has heard in court. Third, the expert may rely on hearsay sources of information. The expert certainly can do so when the hearsay would be independently admissible under exceptions to the hearsay rule. Moreover, by the terms of § 801(b), the expert may even rely on hearsay information that would not be independently admissible so long as that type of information is reasonably relied on by experts in that particular field. Thus, an accident reconstruction expert might testify that she read the police report containing the officer's description of the accident scene.

4. After studying the accident, the witness identified the variables that would have to be duplicated to replicate the accident. In laying this element of the foundation, the witness is testifying as an expert. In an accident reconstruction case, the proponent might be attempting to introduce the expert's testimony about an experiment involving braking distance. The witness would testify that the following factors, among others, determine braking distance: the type of road surface, the wet or dry condition of the surface, the condition of the tire tread, and the amount of pressure which the driver applies to the brake. The witness might explicitly or implicitly rely on a scientific hypothesis about the factors that determine the outcome of the experiment. When the expert relies on a purportedly scientific hypothesis, the expert

---

[6]*Spraker v. Lankin*, 218 Kan. 609, 545 P.2d 352, 353 (1976).

must be prepared to testify to the general acceptance of the hypothesis under *Kelly-Frye*.

5. In designing the experiment, the witness ensured that the experimental conditions were substantially similar to those existing at the time of the accident. The two sets of conditions need not be perfectly identical.[7] The judge has considerable discretion in assessing the degree of similarity between the two sets of conditions,[8] but the judge should ensure similarity in the critical,[9] essential,[10] or salient[11] respects. In most of the published opinions, the appellate court asserts that when the experiment is offered to establish how the particular incident occurred, the trial judge must find substantial similarity.[12] On the other hand, the courts tend to accept a lesser degree of similarity when the experiment is for the limited purpose of demonstrating the operation of a scientific law.[13] If the proponent offered the experimental evidence for the latter purpose, the opponent would be entitled to a limiting instruction under California Evidence Code § 355. In the instruction, the judge would inform the jury that although the experiment illustrates the operation of a scientific law relevant to the accident, the experiment is not intended to duplicate the accident.

6. The witness later conducted the experiment or supervised the experiment. Any instructions the witness issued or received for conducting the experiment would be nonhearsay under California Evidence Code §§ 225 and 1200, since they are imperatives, not statements. Furthermore, even if the witness did not personally conduct every facet of the experiment, he or she could rely on hearsay reports from the other experts participating in the experiment, subject to California Evidence Code §§ 801(b) and 804.

7. The experiment yielded a particular result. The proponent could present the experiment's outcome to the trier of fact in several different ways. The simplest way would be to elicit a description of the outcome from a witness with personal knowledge. In addition, under California Evidence Code §§ 1400 and 1401, the same witness could lay the foundation to authenticate a photograph or videotape of the experiment. The proponent usually prefers incorporating the last method of presentation. A photograph or videotape helps the trier of fact visualize the expert's testimony, and in turn that usually enhances the trier's immediate understanding of the testimony as well as long-term memory.

---

[7] *Patterson v. F.W. Woolworth Co.*, 786 F.2d 874 (8th Cir. 1986); *Moore v. Chesapeake & O. Ry. Co.*, 493 F. Supp. 1252 (S.D. W. Va. 1980).

[8] *Wagner v. International Harvester Co.*, 611 F.2d 224 (8th Cir. 1979); *Wolf by Wolf v. Proctor & Gamble Co.*, 555 F. Supp. 613 (D.N.J. 1982).

[9] *Lawson v. Schumacher & Blum Chevrolet, Inc.*, 687 S.W. 2d 947 (Mo. App. 1985).

[10] *Hawkins v. Scott's Gas of Lowry City, Inc.*, 685 S.W. 2d 247 (Mo. App. 1985).

[11] *Salsberry v. Archibald Plbg. & Heat. Co., Inc.*, 587 S.W. 2d 907 (Mo. App. 1979).

[12] *Cowens v. Siemens-Elema AB*, 837 F.2d 817 (8th Cir. 1988).

[13] *Robinson v. Audi NSU Auto Union, A.G.*, 739 F.2d 1481 (10th Cir. 1984); *Brandt v. French*, 638 F.2d 209 (10th Cir. 1981); *Carr v. Suzuki Motor Co.*, 280 Ark. 1, 655 S.W. 2d 364 (1983).

The fact situation is a civil tort action. The plaintiff alleges that the defendant was driving inattentively and negligently rear-ended the plaintiff's auto. In particular, the complaint alleges that but for the defendant's inattention, the defendant could have stopped his car in time to avoid striking the rear of the plaintiff's car. The proponent is the plaintiff. The plaintiff calls Professor Ernest Kamisar as its next witness. Professor Kamisar will lay the foundation for an experiment about braking distance.

P   Please state your full name and spell your last name for the record.

W   My name is Ernest Kamisar. My last name is spelled K - A - M - I - S - A - R.

P   WHERE do you live?

W   I live in Saratoga, California.

P   WHERE do you work? (1)

W   I teach in the Engineering Department of California State University, San Jose.

P   WHAT is your educational background? (1)

W   I obtained my Bachelor of Science degree in engineering from Iowa State University in 1980.

P   In general terms, WHAT is engineering? (1)

W   Engineers are specialists in using the laws of physics to create machines for human use.

P   WHAT did you do after you obtained your bachelor's degree? (1)

W   We moved to Ann Arbor, Michigan, so I could begin my graduate studies at the University of Michigan. I got the Master's in 1982 and my doctorate in 1984.

P   WHAT subjects did you study in the course of obtaining those degrees? (1)

W   I pretty much specialized in vehicle dynamics.

P   WHAT do you mean by the expression, "vehicle dynamics"? (1)

W   That's the study of how automobiles like cars behave as they move and travel down a highway.

P   WHAT licenses do you hold in the State of California? (1)

W   I'm registered as an engineer.

P   HOW many professional papers, if any, have you had published? (1)

W   Approximately 40.

P   WHAT topics did those papers relate to? (1)

W   They all deal with aspects of vehicle dynamics. The vast majority of them relate to braking.

P   WHAT professional engineering organizations, if any, do you belong to? (1)

W   For years I've been a member of the Society of Automotive Engineers and the American Society of Mechanical Engineers. I've served as the president of the state chapter of the SAE, the Society of Automotive Engineers.

P   WHAT practical experience, if any, do you have in vehicle dynamics? (1)

W   I've consulted with major manufacturers such as General Motors and Chrysler on a number of brake system design projects.

P   HOW many times, if ever, have you testified as an expert witness in a court of law? (1)

W   On over 50 occasions.

P   WHAT topics did you testify about as an expert witness? (1)

W   On every occasion I've testified about braking vehicles, including both passenger cars and trucks.

P Professor, WHERE were you on January 19 of this year? (2)

W I was at my office at the university in San Jose.

P WHAT happened that day? (2)

W That was the day your associate phoned me about this case.

P WHO phoned you? (2)

W Your associate, Ms. Clark.

P WHAT, if anything, did she ask you to do? (2)

W She requested that I study the material about a braking problem in this case with a view to possibly testifying at this trial.

P Specifically, WHAT type of analysis did she ask you to perform? (2)

W Ms. Clark explained that it had been raining the day of the accident and that the defense might contend that the real cause of the accident was the design of the road. She said that the road curves just before the stop sign where the plaintiff's car had stopped. She said that she expected the defense to contend that on a rainy day, given that curve, even an attentive driver wouldn't be able to stop in time to avoid hitting a car sitting at the stop sign.

P WHAT, if anything, did you say to Ms. Clark? (2)

W I agreed to review the problem, conduct the analysis, and testify at trial if necessary.

P WHERE were you earlier today? (3)

W Right here in court.

P WHICH witnesses, if any, did you hear testify? (3)

W I heard the testimony by the witness to the accident, by the mechanic, and by the police officer.

P HOW well do you remember their testimony about the physical layout of this stretch of road, the type of vehicle, and the condition of both the tire tread and the brake lining? (3)

W I recall it well. I was paying special attention to that testimony.

P WHAT exhibits, if any, did you hear read? (3)

W I heard the weather report read into evidence.

P HOW well do you remember the contents of the report? (3)

W Again, I remember it quite well. I was trying to be specially attentive.

P Professor Kamisar, WHEN did you first hear this information about the stretch of road and the vehicle? (3)

W Actually, I got a lot of the information a few days after I spoke with Ms. Clark.

P HOW did you obtain the information? (3)

W A few days later Ms. Clark sent me a Federal Express package containing the material in the case.

P Specifically, WHAT material did that package contain? (3)

W Let's see. As I recall, it included the police reports, a mechanic's reports on the post-accident inspection of both vehicles, a U.S. Weather Service report about the rain the day of the accident, and the depositions of both the plaintiff and the defendant.

P When you analyze braking problems, WHAT type of material do you ordinarily review? (3)

W Exactly the sort of material that Ms. Clark had sent me. I specifically asked her to send me that material.

P HOW many experts in your field make it a practice to consider that type of material? (3)

W Virtually everyone. It would be irresponsible not to gather that type of material.

P WHAT other information, if any, did you gather? (3)

W In March, I went to the accident scene and inspected the stretch of road before I prepared my final design for the experiment.

P WHY did you do that? (3)

W I wanted to measure the coefficient of friction of that stretch of road.

P WHAT is a "coefficient of friction"? (3)

W It's sometimes loosely called the drag factor. In general terms, the type of road surface determines how much horizontal force you need to move an object across the road surface.

P HOW did you determine the coefficient of friction? (3)

W There's an instrument known as a drag sled or box that measures the coefficient. I brought mine with me from San Jose, and I used the sled to personally measure the coefficient on the road surface where the accident occurred.

P Professor, for the balance of your testimony, I want you to take into consideration: (1) the coefficient of friction you personally measured; (2) the truth of the prior testimony about the section of road, the model of car, and the condition of the car's tire tread and brake lining; and (3) the truth of the weather report. (3)

W Very well.

P WHAT, if anything, did you do after studying all this written material and measuring the coefficient of friction? (5)

W At that point, I designed an experiment to duplicate the defendant's attempt to brake just before impact.

P HOW did you do that? (5)

W Whenever you design an experiment like this, you're trying to duplicate the conditions that obtained at the time of the event. You identify the key conditions and try your best to replicate them.

P WHAT are the key conditions? (4)

W In a braking experiment like this, excluding the human factor, they're the following: the type of road and its coefficient of friction, the wet or dry condition of the surface, the condition of the tire tread, the condition of the brake lining, and the type of vehicle. The literature indicates that those are the most important variables.

P You said "excluding the human factor." WHY do you exclude that factor? (4)

W That's what you're trying to determine by this experiment. You're trying to figure out whether an attentive human could have braked in time. You duplicate the physical conditions in order to draw a conclusion about the other condition, namely, the attentiveness of the human being behind the wheel.

P After you identified these key conditions, WHAT did you do? (5)

W I went about trying to duplicate them.

P In particular, HOW did you do that? (5)

W Well, to begin with, we ran our experiment over the very same stretch of road. Then we got hold of another car of the same year, make, and model as the defendant's. We had the tire tread and brake lining modified by a mechanic to ensure that they were essentially identical to the tread and lining on the defendant's car at the time of this accident. Next, after reading the Weather Service report, we waited to conduct the experiment until there had been the same amount of rain on a given day as there had been the day of the accident. As I said, the wet or dry condition of the road surface will affect braking. I hired six test drivers from the automobile plant at Fremont to actually drive the car during the experiment.

P WHEN did you conduct the experiment? (6)

W We had our act together and the weather condition was almost ideal on June 1st. That's when we conducted the experiment.

P HOW did you conduct the experiment? (6)

W We initially coordinated with the Highway Patrol to briefly block off that section of highway. The patrol was very cooperative. I gave a detailed set of instructions to the test drivers. For example, I instructed the drivers to follow a particular route to the stop sign. It was the same route the defendant took that day. I also instructed them to drive at the same speed that the defendant claimed in his deposition. We had an unoccupied car parked at the stop sign in the same position in which the plaintiff had stopped. We didn't tell the test drivers that a car would be stopped there; we didn't want them to anticipate that and get an unfair advantage in braking—a forewarning that the defendant did not have on the day of the accident.

P WHAT happened next? (6)

W We actually ran the experiment. Each driver drove the designated route and turned the curve at the speed indicated by the defendant.

P HOW do you know that they had the right speed? (6)

W Each time we ran the test, there was a researcher in the passenger seat. That person's sole responsibility was ensuring that the test driver hit the curve at the right speed. They did every time.

P Professor, at the time of the accident the defendant was the only occupant of his car. You've just said that during the test, there were both a driver and a researcher in the car. HOW might the presence of the second person have affected the outcome of your case? (6)

W It really wouldn't.

P WHY not? (6)

W To begin with, the researcher's weight wouldn't have affected the braking distance. Moreover, we instructed the researcher to remain both silent and stationary during the test. Their only function was to passively note the speed of the test car when the driver reached the curve.

P WHAT was the result of your experiment? (7)

W On each occasion, the driver stopped well before hitting the rear of the parked car.

P WHAT do you mean by "well before" hitting the car? (7)

W The closest any test vehicle came to striking the car was 30 feet away. In the six tests, the average distance was 46 feet.

P WHAT do you mean by "the average distance"—from where to where? (7)

W From the rear of the vehicle parked at the stop sign to the front of the test vehicle.

P WHO measured the distance? (7)

W I did so myself.

P HOW did you measure the distance? (7)

W I used a type of tape measure officially approved by the Society of Automotive Engineers. It's the most accurate one available on the market.

5. THE STATEMENT OF THE OPINION ITSELF

In the next part of the expert's testimony, the proponent should elicit the expert's opinion. Some jurisdictions insist that the expert vouch that his or her opinion is "reasonably certain." Other jurisdictions demand a "reasonably probable" opinion, meaning that the witness has formed the opinion to a reasonable medical or scientific certainty or probability. Still other jurisdictions have abandoned these formal limitations; so long as the opinion is likely to be helpful to the jurors, these jurisdictions allow an expert to state a possibility, probability, or certainty. The Evidence Code requires no specified degree of probability or certainty. Nevertheless, if the witness can truthfully testify to a certainty or probability, it is obviously good advocacy to make that clear to the trier of fact.

The complete foundation for the opinion includes these elements:

1. The witness has formed an opinion.
2. The witness believes that the opinion is a reasonable medical or scientific certainty or probability. *See, e.g., People v. Cegers*, 7 Cal. App. 4th 988, 9 Cal. Rptr. 2d 297 (1992) ("lack of absolute scientific certainty does not constitute a basis for excluding the opinion"). *See also Ramona v. Superior Court*, 57 Cal. App. 4th 107, 66 Cal. Rptr. 2d 766 (1997) (diagnosis need not be based on certainty but may be based on probability).
3. The witness states the opinion.

The hypothetical fact situation continues:

P   Dr. Worth, do you have an opinion whether Mr. Nowick suffered brain damage as a result of the accident? (1)
W   Yes.
P   HOW sure are you of your opinion? (2)
W   I'm fairly confident in it. I think that any competent neurologist would reach the same conclusion.
P   WHAT is the degree of your certainty? (2)
W   You can't treat this sort of question as an absolute, but I'm reasonably certain of my conclusion.
P   WHAT is that conclusion? (3)
W   In my opinion, Mr. Nowick has suffered permanent brain damage, located in the right, front part of his cranium, as a direct result of the accident.

Just as the Evidence Code rejects a hard-and-fast rule that the expert must vouch for a particular degree of certitude, the Code abandons the old common-law view that the expert may not express an opinion on an ultimate fact. Evidence Code § 805 states that "[t]estimony in the form of an opinion that is otherwise admissible is not objectionable because it embraces the ultimate fact to be decided by the trier of fact." *See People v. Doss*, 4 Cal. App. 4th 1585, 6 Cal. Rptr. 2d 590, 597 (1992) ("It is neither unusual nor impermissible for an expert to testify to an ultimate issue, and such opinions are expressly contemplated by Evidence

Code section 805.") For example, forensic pathologists may testify that the wound pattern on a cadaver indicates homicide rather than suicide or accident. The question whether there was a homicide is obviously an ultimate issue in the case, but the characterization of wound patterns falls within the expertise of a forensic pathologist.[14] *See People v. Erickson,* 57 Cal. App. 4th 1391, 67 Cal. Rptr. 2d 740 (1997) (statute allowing evidence about Battered Women's Syndrome precludes expert from testifying to ultimate issue of defendant's state of mind at time of killing). *But see People v. Valdez,* 58 Cal. App. 4th 494, 68 Cal. Rptr. 2d 135 (1997) (prosecution's expert on gangs was allowed to give his opinion on whether the defendant had "acted for the benefit" of a criminal street gang, an ultimate issue of the gang enhancement allegation).

However, § 805 is not a license for experts to testify on questions of law. If the witness has an adequate background in physics and the laws of motion, the witness can qualify as an expert in accident reconstruction. Given that expertise, the witness can testify about such factual questions as point of impact and velocity. However, the proponent should not attempt to elicit an opinion that a particular driver acted "negligently" or violated a specific section of the Vehicle Code. Those questions are mixed questions of law and fact, and the legal component of the questions exceeds the scientific expertise of the witness. *See Staten v. Superior Court (Bafus),* 45 Cal. App. 4th 1628, 53 Cal. Rptr. 2d 657, 661 (1996) (" 'it is thoroughly established that experts may not give opinions on matters which are essentially within the province of the court to decide'").

6. THE EXPLANATION OF THE OPINION

Evidence law does not require the expert to explain the opinion. However, common sense suggests that unless the expert explains the opinion, the jurors may not be persuaded. The proponent cannot expect the jurors to have a blind faith in the expert. The jury is unlikely to attach much weight to the opinion unless the expert explains the reasoning in plausible, common sense terms. Evidence Code § 802 permits the expert to state the reasons for the opinion. The expert should explain the opinion in general terms and should tie it to the bases the expert previously recited. The opinion will be most persuasive if the expert can show the ju-

---

[14]In criminal cases, California law limits opinion testimony concerning the defendant's mental state at the time of the alleged crime. California Penal Code § 28 prohibits *all* evidence offered to prove that the defendant did or did not have *the capacity* to form a particular mental state, but it permits evidence offered to prove that the defendant did or did not actually form a particular mental state. Further, Penal Code § 29 prohibits an expert witness from testifying at the guilt phase of a criminal trial that the defendant did or did not have a particular mental state at the time of the alleged crime. An expert may testify about the symptoms and consequences of a mental illness, disorder, or defect, but whether the defendant did or did not have a particular mental state at the time of the alleged crime is an ultimate issue that must be left for the trier of fact to decide. *See also* Penal Code § 25, concerning the former California defense of diminished capacity. The history and meaning of these statutes is explained in *People v. Saille,* 54 Cal. 3d 1103, 820 P.2d 588, 2 Cal. Rptr. 2d 364 (1991); *see also People v. Rangel,* 11 Cal. App. 4th 291, 14 Cal. Rptr. Id 529 (1992).

rors why the opinion is firmly grounded on the facts. The proponent wants to demonstrate that the expert's opinion is not only consistent with, but also virtually dictated, by the hard facts of the case.

In short, the foundation for this last part of the expert's testimony consists of two elements:

1. In general terms, the expert explains the opinion.
2. The expert explains the significance of each basis of the opinion. The expert demonstrates how each basis contributes to and supports the opinion.

The hypothetical finally concludes:

P   Dr. Worth, WHY did you reach that conclusion? (1)

W   The symptoms demonstrate brain damage, and the medical history discloses only one possible cause.

P   WHAT symptoms are you referring to? (2)

W   Well, the scar, the vacancy of gaze, and the lack of eye-to-hand coordination.

P   WHAT is the significance of those symptoms? (2)

W   The scar is deep enough to indicate a wound that probably would have applied damaging pressure to the brain. The part of the brain located under the scar is the part that controls vision and eye-to-hand coordination. The other symptoms of vacant stare and lack of manual coordination confirm that pressure in fact was applied with resulting damage.

P   WHAT medical history are you relying on? (2)

W   My consultation with Dr. Stiles and the plaintiff's hospital records.

P   WHAT is the significance of the medical history? (2)

W   It helps establish the causation. The scar was produced by a cut that was apparently inflicted in the accident. The other symptoms not only didn't exist before the accident; they arose immediately after the accident. The timing is almost conclusive in my mind.

7. CROSS-EXAMINATION OF THE EXPERT

Subsections 1-5, above, relate to the direct testimony elicited by the proponent of the expert witness. When the direct examination ends, the cross-examination begins. The scope of the cross-examination of an expert is broad. Evidence Code § 722(b) states that the cross-examiner may inquire about "the compensation and expenses paid or to be paid to an expert witness by the party calling him ...." Section 721 is a more general regulation of the scope of the cross-examination. Effective January 1, 1998, § 721 was amended by the legislature to add subsection (b)(3), which is a third basis for cross-examining an expert witness regarding a scientific, technical, or professional text, treatise, journal, or similar publication, as well as new statutory language about reading portions of the publication into evidence. Section 721 now states:

(a) Subject to subdivision (b), a witness testifying as an expert witness may be cross-examined to the same extent as any other witness and, in addition, may be fully cross-examined as to (1) his or her qualifications, (2) the subject to which his or her expert testimony relates, and (3) the matter upon which his or her opinion is based and the reasons for his or her opinion.

(b) If a witness testifying as an expert testifies in the for m of an opinion, he or she may not be cross-examined in regard to the content or tenor of any scientific, technical, or professional text, treatise, journal, or similar publication unless any of the following occurs:

(1) The witness referred to, considered, or relied upon such publication in arriving at or forming his or her opinion.

(2) The publication has been admitted in evidence.

(3) The publication has been established as a reliable authority by the testimony or admission of the witness or by other expert testimony or by judicial notice.

If admitted, relevant portions of the publication may be read into evidence but may not be received as exhibits.

Under § 721(b), the cross-examiner may use some types of texts to attack the major premise that the expert relies on. *See generally McGarity v. Department of Transportation*, 8 Cal. App. 4th 677, 10 Cal. Rptr. 2d 344 (1992).

Under § 721(b)(2), the cross-examiner may use any text "admitted in ev idence." The California Law Revision Commission comment to § 721 cross-references Evidence Code § 1340, the California version of the learned treatise hearsay exception. Chapter 9 will analyze that exception. If a text has already been admitted into evidence under that exception, the cross-examiner may use that text to question the opposing expert. The Commission states that the cross-examiner may do so "without regard to whether he [the expert] referred to, considered, or relied on it in forming his opi nion."

If the text has not been admitted into evidence, either section 721(b)(1) or (3) controls. Section 721(b)(3) allows the opposing attorney to discredit a expert by showing that the opinion was based on incomplete information. *See People v. Arias*, 13 Cal. 4th 92, 913 P.2d 980, 51 Cal. Rptr. 2d 770 (1996), *cert. denied* 520 U.S. 1251 (1997) (prosecution could use defendant's statements to forensic psychiatrist to discredit expert's opinion that defendant would be able to adjust to prison life without violence). The foundation for invoking subdivision (b)(3) includes the following elements:

1. The witness is familiar with the text. (This element is required only if you are using the expert to authenticate the text.)
2. The publication is a reliable authority.

The fact situation is a homicide prosecution. The People allege that the defendant Morris murdered the victim Ramirez on February 13th of last year. At trial, the People's theory of the case is that the defendant committed the murder at 1:00 p.m. The people call Dr. Graham, a forensic pathologist. On direct examination, Dr. Graham testifies to his opinion that the time of death was 1:00 p.m., "plus or minus two hours or so." On cross-examination, the defense attorneys attempt to attack the accuracy of the time-of-death opinion:

O   Doctor, are you familiar with a Dr. J. F. Burton? (1)

W   Certainly.

O   ISN'T IT TRUE THAT Dr. Burton is the former chief medical examiner for Pontiac, Michigan? (1)

W   Yes.

O   He was an authority on time of death, WASN'T HE? (1)

W   That's true.

O   And he wrote a classic article on the subject entitled "Fallacies in Signs of Death," DIDN'T HE? (1), (2)

W   Yes.

O   That article appeared in the 1974 Journal of Forensic Science. DIDN'T IT? (1),(2)

W   I believe that's true.

O   The journal is the official publication of the American Academy of Forensic Science. CORRECT? (1), (2)

W   Yes.

O   ISN'T IT TRUE that you've been a member of the American Academy since 1970? (1)

W   Yes.

O   And you regularly receive the journal. DON'T YOU? (1)

W   Correct.

O   In fact, when I visited your office three months ago to take your deposition, didn't I see a complete set of all the issues of the journal in your office? (1)

W   Yes. It's one of the leading journals in my field, and I keep all the volumes there for research purposes.

O   In the process of preparing for this case, DID you do some research?

W   Yes.

O   Specifically, DID you refer to Dr. Burton's article?

W   No, I didn't.

O   Your Honor, I request that this be marked as Defense Exhibit D for identification.

J   It will be so marked.

O   Please let the record reflect that I am showing the exhibit to the opposing counsel.

J   The record will so reflect.

O   Your honor may I approach the witness?

J   Yes.

O   Doctor. I now hand you what has been marked as Defense Exhibit D for identification. WHAT is it?

W   It's a copy of the article By Dr. Burton.

O   HOW can you recognize it?

W   I've read it several times over the years.

O I'd like you to turn to the third page, the page numbered 531. To be specific, turn to the third full paragraph on that page.

W Yes.

O ISN'T IT TRUE that in that paragraph, Dr. Burton states ... .

Chapter 9

THE HEARSAY RULE AND ITS EXCEPTIONS

A. INTRODUCTION

The hearsay rule is the last of three major doctrines that are the result of judicial concerns about the reliability of the type or form of the evidence that is offered to prove a relevant fact. The secondary evidence rule, discussed in Chapter 7, manifests judicial misgivings about proving the contents of a writing by any form of evidence other than the original writing itself. The opinion rule, discussed in Chapter 8, is an outgrowth of the courts' reservations about allowing witnesses to describe their perceptions in language that is conclusory and general as opposed to concrete and specific. The hearsay rule, which is the subject of this chapter, reflects judicial worries about allowing people's relevant information to be proved by way of their earlier spoken or written statements instead of via their live testimony in the presence of the trier of fact.

The trial of any case, civil or criminal, is an inquiry into whether certain relevant transactions or events happened in the so-called "outside world." Very often, these happenings will have been perceived (i.e., seen, heard, touched, smelled, or tasted) by one or more human beings. One way, and sometimes the only way, of later establishing what actually took place will be by asking those persons to recall and recount what their perceptions were. But this method of proving a fact is subject to the risks of human fallibility and duplicity.

The fallibility of human beings can come into play in three ways: (1) they may misperceive what happened; (2) even though their initial perception was correct, by the time they are asked to describe it, they may misremember what it was that they perceived; and (3) even their past perception and present memory are correct, their word selection as they narrate their perceptions may be so inartful that their statements are misleading or ambiguous.

Human beings are capable not only of honest error, but also of deliberate deception. Those who initially perceived a traffic light to be red and who still remember seeing that the light was red can nevertheless decide for one reason or another to lie about what they saw. This falsehood could take three forms: (1) "The light was green;" (2) "I did not see the color of the light;" and (3) "I no longer remember the color of the light."

There is, of course, no way to shape the rules of evidence to totally eliminate the twin risks that human beings will supply the court with information that is inaccurate or dishonest. Yet a court system could not function in the vast majority of cases unless it was willing to run these risks and allow facts to be proved by the later recollections of those who claim to have perceived them. When these later recollections are provided by way of the perceiver's live testimony at the trial of the case, the courts have developed three safeguards that, in combination, operate to reduce significantly the danger of inaccuracy and dishonesty. First, witnesses at a trial may not give any information unless and until they expose themselves to the penalties for perjury by taking an oath to testify truthfully. Second, witnesses at trial must testify in the presence of the trier of fact so that their demeanor or "body language" may be observed and factored into the decision of whether they are mistaken or lying in what they say. Third, and most important, at trial, the other parties to the case are given an opportunity to cross-examine them in the presence of the trier of fact.

Cross-examination is the most potent courtroom tool for testing the accuracy or impugning the honesty of the testimony given on direct examination. The cross-examiner may challenge the correctness of witness's initial perceptions, cast doubt on their present ability to recall those perceptions, inquire as to the meaning of the words used by the witnesses during their direct examination, or attack their truthfulness.

Those who have perceived matters that become relevant in later civil or criminal trials usually will have made, other than at the present trial, solicited or unsolicited statements setting forth their memory of their perceptions. Sometimes they or someone else will have recorded their version of the events in writing or on tape. Other times, the only record of their statement is the memory of another human being who heard and still recalls what it was that they said.

A hearsay situation occurs when a litigant undertakes to prove during trial what people perceived, not by presenting their live testimony, but rather by offering their out-of-court statements. These out-of-court statements are deemed hearsay whether they are proved by written or taped records or by the live testimony of other persons who heard and remember them. The vice that inheres in this use of the out-of-court statements is that the speaker's or writer's version of relevant events is presented to the trier of fact without being subjected to all of the credibility safeguards—oath, demeanor, and especially cross-examination—that would attend live testimony by that individual. A strong judicial preference for live testimony over out-of-court statements has resulted in the general rule excluding hearsay evidence.

A common misconception is that the hearsay definition covers any oral or written utterance made "out of court," that is to say, made "other than by a witness while testifying at the [instant] hearing." Actually, the hearsay concept is not that broad. An out-of-court utterance is not even eligible for classification as hearsay unless the speaker or writer was undertaking thereby to "assert" something. In the sense in which the word is used in discussions of the hearsay rule, an utterance is classified as an assertion only when it undertakes to describe the sensory perceptions or the thought processes of the one who makes the utterance. Since some utterances are not asserting either of these things, they are intrinsically incapable of being hearsay. Examples include: a warning: "Please be careful"; an instruction: "Do not use near fire or flame"; an interrogatory: "Where were you last night?"; a greeting: "Good morning!"; an entreaty or plea: "Don't kill me!" *See, e.g., People v. Bolin*, 18 Cal. 4th 297, 320, 75 Cal. Rptr. 2d 412, 428-29, 956 P.2d 374, 390-91 (1998) (witness testified to murder victim's pleas to defendant to spare his life; "[T]he evidence was not hearsay. [The victim's] words were not offered to prove the truth of the statements but the fact of the statements.")

Even when an out-of-court utterance is eligible to be classified as hearsay because it does assert some perception or thought process on the part of the one who spoke or wrote it, a statement may still escape classification as hearsay in the instant proceeding if it is not being used for the purpose of proving that the declarant actually made the perception or entertained the thought asserted. When the out-of-court statement is not being offered to prove the truth of the matter it asserts, but only to prove that the statement itself was made, the trier of fact is not being asked to rely on the credibility of the one who made the statement. Therefore, the need evaporates for the trio of credibility safeguards (oath, demeanor, cross-examination) that would attend live testimony by the speaker or writer.

Even the paradigmatic out-of-court statement, "The traffic light was red," is not per se hearsay. One must always inquire further: What does the proponent of this statement expect to prove with it? On the one hand, if the statement is offered to prove that the light was indeed red, it is being offered for a hearsay purpose because the trier of fact is being asked to accept the word of the declarant that the matter asserted (the red color of the traffic light) was true. On the other hand, if the statement is offered to show not the color of the traffic light, but only that the declarant was alive at the time of making it and was capable of speaking the English language, the identical out-of-court statement would escape hearsay classification. This is so because the statement is not being used to prove the truth of the matter asserted, but simply to prove that the statement itself was spoken or written by the declarant. Use for this purpose does not implicate the credibility of the declarant.

Theoretically, the proponent of an out-of-court statement can always overcome a hearsay objection by offering the statement only to prove that it was made, and not to prove the truth of any matter that it asserts. The price of doing so, however, frequently is to strip the out-of-court statement of all relevancy to the issues in the present litigation. One who proposes to surmount a hearsay objection by this route must be prepared to explain to the court why the mere making of the statement, irrespective of the truth or falsity of what it asserts, is relevant to the material issues in the case. Otherwise, the proponent of the statement is simply jumping out of the frying pan of hearsay into the fire of irrelevancy.

Even if a statement is being used for a hearsay purpose, it may nonetheless be admissible under one of the numerous exceptions to the hearsay rule. Evidence Code §§1220-1341 contain a lengthy list of exceptions. Broadly speaking, most of the exceptions are based on a combination of two factors: (1) the special reliability of a statement, deriving from circumstances attending the making of it that provide an element of trustworthiness that sets it apart from the mine run of hearsay; and (2) a special need to resort to the hearsay declaration instead of proving the matter asserted in it by live testimony.

The elements of the foundation for most hearsay exceptions reflect the reason why that particular type of statement has unusual features of reliability. For instance, the foundation for the declaration against interest exception includes proof that at the time of the statement, the declarant realized that the facts stated were contrary to his or her interest. It is common knowledge that a reasonable person ordinarily would not make a disserving statement unless it were true. Similarly, the foundation for the excited utterance exception requires proof that at the time of the statement, the declarant was in a state of agitation caused by a startling event. Experience teaches that an excited person is unlikely to have the presence of mind to compose a fabricated perception.

Another common denominator of most hearsay exceptions is a special need to resort to the hearsay instead of presenting the declarant's live testimony. Sometimes, that need is an absolute one, resulting from the unavailability of the declarant to provide live testimony. Here, the choice open to the courts is not between live testimony and hearsay; it is between hearsay and nothing at all. The three principal exceptions to the hearsay rule that require a showing of unavailability are former testimony, declarations against interest, and dying declarations.

With most exceptions, the special need to resort to the hearsay is a relative one in the sense that circumstances attending the out-of-court statement have given it a degree of trustworthiness that is comparable, if not superior, to the declarant's live testimony. For example, when an excited person makes a statement about an accident soon after viewing it, we have little reason to doubt that person's sincerity. Thus, the trinity of courtroom credibility safeguards (oath, demeanor, and cross-examination) becomes superfluous. That hearsay statement is at least as reliable a method of obtaining the declarant's information as subsequent live testimony would be. Arguably, the hearsay is more reliable than live testimony at trial, by which time the declarant may have a memory that is faulty or distorted by an awareness of the legal consequences of one version of the events over another. Hence, there is no reason for the law of evidence to insist upon live testimony, even if the declarant is readily available to provide it.

This chapter contains an in-depth coverage of hearsay: the concept itself, the general rule excluding it, and the many exceptions to this rule of exclusion. The chapter is divided into five parts. Part 1 focuses on the elements of the definition of hearsay. The remaining parts address the principal exceptions to the hearsay rule. Part 2 analyzes what might be called the "admissions" package of exceptions, a group of exceptions whose rationale is based not upon the unusual trustworthiness of and special need for the out-of-court statement, but rather upon the declarant's connection to the party against whom the statement is now being offered. Part 3 discusses a host of exceptions that do not require proof of the declarant's unavailability at the time of trial. Part 4 takes up a smaller cluster of exceptions that do require proof of unavailability. Finally, Part 5 discusses the extent to which that the California judiciary has the power to admit reliable, needed hearsay, even if the particular assertion does not fit neatly within one of the exceptions provided in the Evidence Code.

Part 1. The Hearsay Definition

B.   THE DEFINITION OF HEARSAY

As previously stated, the definition of hearsay is relatively narrow. Evidence Code § 1200(a) states that hearsay "is evidence of a statement that was made other than by a witness while testifying at the hearing and that is offered to prove the truth of the matter stated." In turn, § 225 defines "statement" to mean "(a) oral or written verbal expression or (b) nonverbal conduct of a person intended by him as a substitute for oral or written verbal expression." Hence, evidence is hearsay only if three conditions are met: (1) the evidence is an assertive statement or action; (2) the statement was made or the conduct performed out of court; and (3) the evidence is being used to prove the truth of the assertion contained in the statement or signaled by the conduct. When any of these three elements is missing, the evidence is not hearsay, and there is no need to search for a hearsay exception. We shall now examine each element of the hearsay definition.

1. THE EVIDENCE IS AN ASSERTIVE STATEMENT OR ACT

a. Assertive Statements

All courts agree that assertive statements, whether oral or written, fall within the hearsay definition. But not all statements are assertive. Most questions ask for information; they are not assertions. Most imperatives state commands; they do not assert the speaker's perceptions or thoughts. On the other hand, most declaratory sentences are assertions. For instance, "the car ran the red light" asserts directly and expressly that the car ran the red light.

A statement can be assertive even if it is not expressly in the form of a declarative sentence. "An implied statement is inferred from an express statement because it is reasonable to conclude that declarant (1) in fact intended to make such implied statement, or (2) that a reasonable hearer or reader of declarant's express statement would believe that declarant intended by his express statement to make the implied statement." 1 JEFFERSON § 1.2, at 33. Consider, for example, a repairman's bill. JEFFERSON SYNOPSIS § 1.3, at 16. On its face, the bill may consist of isolated phrases and sentence fragments, descriptions of work and dollar figures. However, reasonably construed, the bill represents implied hearsay statements "that the services were rendered and that the dollar figures were the charge for the services." *Id.*

If the proponent wishes to offer a statement in evidence on the theory that it is nonassertive, the foundation usually includes these elements:

1. Where the statement was made.
2. When the statement was made.
3. Who was present at that place and time.

4. The tenor of the statement.

5. A representation (by an offer of proof outside the jury's hearing) that the tenor of the statement is nonassertive.

6. A showing (also during this offer of proof) that the nonassertive statement is logically relevant to some material fact in the case.

Our example is a criminal prosecution in which the People charge that the defendant, Mr. Britton, conspired with one Mr. Cetina to sell heroin, and that the pair actually sold heroin. The witness is Ms. Grace, who, after identifying herself, testifies that she is a government informant who infiltrated the meeting of a drug ring. The prosecutor is the proponent.

P   Ms. Grace, WHERE were you on the evening of January 17, 2000? (1), (2)
W   I was at 70 Aberdeen Court in Capistrano, California.
P   WHO else was there? (3)
W   The defendant, Joe Britton, and a person named Ray Cetina.
P   WHERE are they now? (3)
W   Joe Britton is in the courtroom. I don't know where Cetina is.
P   Specifically, WHERE in the courtroom do you see Joe Britton? (3)
W   At that table over there.
P   HOW is he dressed? (3)
W   He is wearing a brown suit and yellow tie.
P   Your Honor, please let the record reflect that the witness has identified the defendant, Joe Britton.
J   It will so reflect.
P   Ms. Grace, WHAT happened during this meeting? (4)
W   Britton and Cetina made some plans.
P   WHAT plans did they discuss? (4)
O   Your Honor, I object to that question on the ground that it calls for hearsay.
P   Your Honor, may we approach the bench and be heard?
J   Yes.
P   Your Honor, if the witness is permitted to do so, she will testify that she heard Cetina tell the defendant, Joe Britton, to go and get some bags of heroin out of the trunk of a car parked nearby and bring them to him, and that Britton proceeded to do so. (4) Cetina's statement is not and, indeed, could not be hearsay because he didn't assert any fact. The only thing we're interested in is whether he gave Britton the order, and whether Britton carried it out. You might say that Ms. Grace is an "earwitness" to the fact that Cetina gave the order, as well as an eyewitness to Britton's obeying it. (5) The statement of Cetina, coupled with Britton's reaction to it, is logically relevant to prove the existence of a conspiracy between them. (6)
J   The objection will be overruled.
P   Ms. Grace, let me repeat the question. WHAT plans did they discuss? (4)
W   The plans for a drug sale. Cetina ordered Britton to get some bags of heroin out of a car parked nearby and to get them ready for sale.
P   WHAT happened then?
W   Britton left for a couple of minutes and then came back with some bags.
P   WHAT was the appearance of the bags?

W The bags themselves were transparent.
P WHAT, if anything, could you see in the bags?
W There was a white, powdery substance in each bag.

b. Assertive Acts

Sometimes a person intends an act to be a substitute for speech. For instance, one might respond to a question with a nod or a shake of the head, instead of a "yes" or a "no." In principle, these acts should be treated in the same fashion as assertive statements; these acts present the same dangers respecting perception, memory, narration, and sincerity. For this reason, all courts agree that, like assertive statements, assertive acts fall within the hearsay definition. This is recognized in § 225, which defines "statement." Subdivision (b) includes "nonverbal conduct of a person intended by him as a substitute for oral or written verbal expression."

The following situation, occurring during a robbery prosecution, illustrates this aspect of the hearsay definition. The witness is Officer Glancy, who, having first identified himself, has already testified that he investigated the crime and eventually brought the victim, who is now deceased, to the police station. The proponent is the prosecutor.

P WHAT happened when you took the victim, Mr. Clayton, to the police station?
W I talked to him, and then I took him to the lineup room.
P WHAT is the lineup room?
W It's the room in the station where we permit victims and eyewitnesses to view suspects. We hope that they can pick the criminal out of the lineup parade.
P WHAT happened after you took Mr. Clayton into the interview room?
O Your Honor, I object to that question on the ground that it calls for inadmissible hearsay.
P Your Honor, may we approach the bench and be heard?
J Yes.
P Your Honor, the witness is prepared to testify that at a six-person lineup, Mr. Clayton silently pointed with the index finger of his right hand at the defendant. This testimony can't be hearsay because Mr. Clayton didn't say anything. He just lifted his arm and pointed his finger.
O Mr. Clayton obviously intended his act of pointing at the defendant to substitute for a verbal assertion: "That's the fellow who robbed me." The prosecutor apparently concedes that such an oral accusation would be inadmissible hearsay. Since this is so, a gesture performed as a substitute for speech is subject to the same objection. Assertive acts are treated as a type of statement for purposes of the hearsay definition.
J I agree with defense counsel. The objection will be sustained.

c. Nonassertive Acts

The vast majority of actions performed by human beings are of the nonassertive variety. For example, when motorists who have been stopped for a red light now proceed into the intersection, they are not doing so as a way of asserting that the light has just changed to green. The drivers are simply reacting to their perception of that change of the traffic signal. On the other hand, someone who sees this nonassertive conduct on the part of the motorists would doubtless draw the conclusion that the motorists have just seen the light change from red to green.

Suppose that the color of that traffic light at that precise moment becomes a material issue in a lawsuit. One who observed the conduct of the motorists is called to testify to what he saw them do. Would this testimony be hearsay? The evidence is *unlike* hearsay in that it does not entail proof of any assertion about the light's color on the part of the motorists. It is *like* hearsay in that the trier of fact is being asked to find that the light changed to green because it was perceived to have done so by certain individuals who have not come into the courtroom to give live testimony as to what their perceptions were.

The courts that developed the common law of evidence had difficulty in deciding whether nonassertive conduct, offered to prove what the out-of-court actors were perceiving, should be treated as hearsay or as mere circumstantial evidence. The leading decision is *Wright v. Tatham* (Eng. 1837), a case that turned on the mental competency of an English lord at the time he executed his will. As evidence of the testator's competence, the proponent of the will offered to show that near the time the will was signed, several persons had written serious business letters to the testator. The letters, of course, did not assert to the nobleman that the writers considered him competent, nor did their authors intend that the writing and sending of the letters serve as a substitute for an express statement to that effect. Instead, the very fact that these people had written to the lord about such weighty topics was offered as circumstantial evidence that in their previous dealings with him, they had found him to mentally competent. The proponent of the will reasoned that the writers would not have mailed serious letters to the testator-nobleman unless their prior contact with him had led them to believe that he was in possession of his faculties. If his close acquaintances believed him to be competent, this was relevant evidence that he was in fact competent.

The English court, however, ruled that the evidence fell within the hearsay definition. The judges concluded that even though the out-of-court conduct in writing and sending the letters was nonassertive of the fact it was now being offered to prove, this nonassertive conduct nonetheless contained the same dangers that would have led to the exclusion of a direct out-of-court assertion by these people that the nobleman was mentally competent. *Wright v. Tatham* became the principal authority for the traditional common-law view that evidence of a nonassertive act is hearsay if (1) the act is apparently prompted by a certain belief, and (2) the proponent offers the evidence to prove the truth of the belief. Such evidence came to be designated Morgan hearsay.

However, the trend of the modern cases and codifications has been to the contrary. The California Evidence Code excludes nonassertive conduct from its definition of a "statement" in § 225, and hence from its definition of hearsay in § 1200(a). The Senate Committee comment on Evidence Code § 1200 explains the reasons for this position:

[E]vidence of a person's conduct out of court is not inadmissible under the hearsay rule expressed in Section 1200 unless that conduct is clearly assertive in character. Nonassertive conduct is not hearsay. Under the Evidence Code, nonassertive conduct is not regarded as hearsay for two reasons. First, one of the principal reasons for the hearsay rule—to exclude declarations where the veracity of the declarant cannot be tested by cross-examination—does not apply because such conduct, being nonassertive, does not involve the veracity of the declarant. Second, there is frequently a guarantee of the trustworthiness of the inference to be drawn from such conduct because the actor has based his actions on the correctness of his belief, i.e., his actions speak louder than words.

The California courts would consider the letters that were excluded as hearsay in the *Wright* case to be a form of nonhearsay circumstantial evidence that the testator was mentally competent at the time he signed the proffered will. The Federal Rules of Evidence reach essentially the same result. FR Evid. 801(a). *See United States v. Zenni*, 492 F. Supp. 464 (E.D. Ky. 1980).

The following example is drawn from *People v. Nealy*, 228 Cal. App. 3d 447, 279 Cal. Rptr. 36 (1991), in which the defendant was charged with possessing cocaine base for sale. The proponent is the prosecution. The witness is Mary Loomis, one of several police officers who executed a warrant authorizing a search of defendant's apartment. The witness has already identified herself, stated her position on the Oxnard police force, and established that a search warrant was issued for defendant's apartment.

P   WHERE were you on the morning of April 16, 2000?
W   In an apartment at 104 East Pleasant Valley Road in Oxnard, Ventura County, California.
P   WHAT were you doing there?
W   I was one of a group of eight police officers carrying out a search of that apartment.
P   While you were conducting that search, WHAT happened?
W   The phone in the apartment rang at least three different times.
P   WHAT did you do when the telephone would ring?
W   I would pick up the receiver and said "Hello."
P   WHAT, if anything, did the first caller say in response?
O   Your Honor, I object to that question because it calls for inadmissible hearsay.
P   Your Honor, may we approach the bench and be heard?
J   Counsel may approach the bench.
P   Your Honor, if the officer is permitted to answer, she will testify as follows: After she answered the phone, a female voice asked to speak to Shelly. Officer Loomis replied: "Shelly's gone out for a few minutes." The voice then said: "When she gets back, tell her that Regina is looking to buy a 'dove.'" The witness will then testify that in drug nomenclature, the term "dove" means a $20 piece of rock cocaine. I might add that the other two calls were much the same, except the second caller said it was "Tommy" that wanted to buy a "dove" and the third caller, without identifying himself, just said, "I'll call back later. I need two 'doves.'"

Your Honor, it's obvious that these three callers, whoever they were, believed that rock cocaine could be purchased from the defendant, and we think that this is circumstantial evidence that she had been trafficking in cocaine.

O Your Honor, to the extent that this evidence might indicate that the defendant has made prior sales of cocaine to these callers, the People are presenting a series of out-of-court statements from three anonymous declarants. None of these people was under oath. There is no opportunity to see their demeanor. And my client is being deprived of the opportunity to confront and cross-examine them.

P Your Honor, if these callers had expressly asserted that the defendant had sold them cocaine in the past, defense counsel's hearsay objection would be well taken. However, none of them made any such assertion. We are relying on their conduct in trying to buy cocaine from the defendant in the future as circumstantial evidence that has a tendency in reason to make it more probable that she had sold it to them in the past. Their conduct does indeed take the form of out-of-court statements, but the statements themselves do not assert the fact that the People are trying to prove with them. Our Evidence Code has rejected the notion that nonassertive conduct is hearsay.

J I agree with the Assistant District Attorney. The objection will be overruled.

P Officer, WHAT, if anything, did the first caller respond after you picked up the phone and said, "Hello"?

W A female voice asked to speak to Shelly. I told her: "Shelly's gone out for a few minutes." The voice then said: "When she gets back, tell her that Regina is looking to buy a 'dove.'"

P Has your experience on the police force made you familiar with the term "dove"?

W Yes.

P WHAT does that word to mean?

W It is street language describing a $20 piece of rock cocaine.

2. THE STATEMENT WAS MADE OR THE ACT PERFORMED OUT OF COURT

In their discussions of the hearsay concept, judges and lawyers commonly use the shorthand phrase "out-of-court" or, less frequently, the word "extrajudicial" to describe the kind of statements and actions that come within the hearsay definition. Although in most situations either term is useful and acceptable, neither is completely accurate. The precise language is found in the definition of hearsay set forth in § 1200(a) of the Evidence Code. To be eligible for classification as hearsay, the statement must be one that was "made other than by a witness while testifying at the hearing." The phrase "the hearing" is, in turn, defined in § 145 to mean only "the hearing at which a question under this code arises, and not some earlier or later hearing." This means that in-court statements in the form of live testimony at some earlier trial or hearing (even a trial of or hearing in this very case) become out-of-court statements when they are offered in evidence at a later proceeding.

Under the traditional common-law view, an out-of-court assertion does not escape classification as hearsay if it is offered substantively during the declarant's appearance as a witness at trial. Several commentators, among them Professor

Morgan, have argued that the hearsay rule should not apply to any prior statements made by a person who is now on the witness stand and thus subject to cross-examination about that statement. They believe that the time gap between the out-of-court statement and the in-court cross-examination of its declarant is not important enough to forego the probative value of the earlier assertion. Only one jurisdiction, Kansas, has been willing to go this far.

There is an intermediate view: Once a trial witness's earlier out-of-court statement is shown to be admissible for a nonhearsay purpose, that statement should be admitted as substantive evidence as well. The California Evidence Code adopts this compromise view. Under specified circumstances, prior identifications (§ 1238), prior inconsistent statements (§ 1235), and prior consistent statements (§ 1236) are admissible as substantive evidence. It is important to note that each of these provisions refers to a prior statement of a "witness." Therefore, the declarant of the out-of-court statement must now have become a witness at trial before one may take advantage of these changes in the common law. *People v. Williams*, 16 Cal. 3d 663, 128 Cal. Rptr. 888, 547 P.2d 1000 (1976).

This departure from the common law was made for two reasons. First, there is substantial merit in Morgan's broader position that hearsay concerns evaporate whenever a declarant can be subjected to later in-court cross-examination. Second, once a jury has actually heard the content of an out-of-court statement, for example, as an impeaching prior inconsistent statement, it is futile and even confusing to try to prevent the jury from using that statement substantively, that is, for the truth of the matter asserted in the statement.

A litigant who wishes to take advantage of this new approach must first show that the witness's prior statement is admissible on a nonhearsay theory. The proponent would have to lay a complete foundation for use of the statement as a prior identification, or a prior inconsistent statement, or a prior consistent statement. Chapter 5 outlines those foundations.

The following illustration is drawn from a tort action arising from a collision between two autos. Plaintiff contends that on January 17, 2000, defendant caused the collision because he was operating his vehicle at a grossly excessive speed. Defendant maintains that he was not speeding at all. Plaintiff calls as a witness Ms. Gerst, who, after identifying herself, states that she observed the two cars, and expresses her opinion that defendant's car was going 60 miles an hour. Defendant has learned that, a month after the accident, Ms. Gerst told a friend that she thought the defendant was going only 30 miles an hour. Defendant, as proponent, cross-examines as follows:

P ISN'T IT A FACT THAT on February 14, 2000, you discussed the collision with your friend, Charles Gil, who was at a party you were giving at your home?

W Yes.

P ISN'T IT CORRECT THAT during that conversation, you told him that the defendant was going only 30 miles an hour?

W Yes.

O Your Honor, I request a limiting instruction under Evidence Code § 355.

J   What type of limiting instruction?

O   An instruction that the jurors may consider Ms. Gerst's statement to Gil only insofar as it reflects on her credibility; that they are not to consider the statement to Gil as evidence that defendant was indeed traveling at the slower speed.

P   Your Honor, may we approach the bench?

J   Counsel will come to the bench.

P   Your Honor, it would be error to tell the jury that it may not use the statement at the party substantively.

O   Your Honor, defendant is obviously introducing this statement as a prior inconsistent statement to impeach. The jury may properly use the fact that Ms. Gerst has earlier made an estimate of defendant's speed that is different from the one she gave here in the courtroom on direct examination to decide that she is not a reliable source of information as to defendant's speed. That is quite a bit different from using the earlier statement to prove that he was in fact going only 30 miles an hour. That would involve using the out-of-court statement for a hearsay purpose, namely, to establish the truth of the matter asserted.

P   Your Honor, counsel for plaintiff apparently concedes that the statement to Mr. Gil is admissible to impeach Ms. Gerst under § 780(h) of the Evidence Code. What counsel does not seem to realize is that § 1235 has made a drastic change in the previous law of evidence. It has created an exception to the hearsay rule for any out-of-court statement of a witness that is inconsistent with that witness's testimony at trial. Under this provision, the jury is authorized to use the prior statement as substantive evidence that my client was, in fact, traveling at only 30 miles per hour at the time of the collision.

J   I agree with defense counsel. I'm not going to give the requested limiting instruction. Moreover, when I come to instruct the jury at the conclusion of the trial, I shall tell them that they may use prior inconsistent statements of trial witnesses as substantive evidence of the facts asserted in those statements.

3. THE STATEMENT IS OFFERED FOR A HEARSAY PURPOSE

When an out-of-court utterance qualifies as an assertive statement, and is therefore eligible for hearsay classification, this does not necessarily mean the statement will be treated as hearsay when it is offered in evidence. In order to fall within the ban of the hearsay rule, the out-of-court statement must not only assert some "matter;" it must also be offered in evidence for a hearsay purpose, that is to say, for the purpose of proving the truth of that "matter." Quite apart from the truth of the matter a statement asserts, the mere fact that the statement was spoken or written may shed light on one of the material issues in the case. Here it may be helpful to bear in mind the difference between the fact *in* the statement, and the fact *of* the statement. If at trial a statement is being used to prove the fact *in* that statement, the trier of fact is being asked to accept the word of the out-of-court declarant, and the hearsay rule is implicated. On the other hand, if the trier of fact is asked only to accept the fact *of* the statement, it will have before it either the statement itself, if it was written or taped, or the courtroom testimony of some person (an *ear*witness) who is claiming from the stand to have heard and to remember the content of the statement. For example, in *People v. Williams*, 3 Cal. App. 4th 1535, 1541, 5 Cal. Rptr. 2d 372, 375 (1992), defendant at a suppression hearing sought to prove that he resided in the bedroom of the searched premises and thus had standing to assert that the search under attack was an unreasonable invasion of his privacy. He offered evidence that a dresser drawer in the bedroom contained a fishing license in his name and two checks payable to him. The trial magistrate court excluded these items as hearsay. This was held to be error:

> [T]he fishing license and the two checks ... are more likely to be found in the residence of the persons named on those documents than in the residence of any other person. Accordingly, regardless of the truth of any express or implied statement contained in those documents, they are circumstantial evidence that a person with the same name as the defendant resided in the apartment from which they were seized. Therefore, when introduced for the purpose of showing that residency, they are admissible nonhearsay evidence.

See also *People v. Harvey*, 233 Cal. App. 3d 1206, 1219, 285 Cal. Rptr. 158, 166 (1991) (ledgers listing receipts and sales of drugs admissible for the nonhearsay purpose of showing circumstantially that the place where ledgers were found was being used for drug transactions).

The foundation for admitting an out-of-court statement for a nonhearsay purpose includes these elements:

1. Where the statement was made.
2. When the statement was made.
3. Who was present at that place and time.
4. The tenor of the statement.
5. A representation (by an offer of proof outside the jury's hearing) that the statement is being offered only to prove that it was made, and not for the truth of the facts it asserts.
6. A showing (also during this offer of proof) that the mere fact that statement was made is logically relevant to some material fact in the case.

There are three common nonhearsay uses of out-of-court statements that contain assertions. (1) The fact *of* the making of the statement may be circumstantial evidence of the declarant's state of mind. For example, a testator's assertion that her nephew is a caring and generous person may shed light on whether she intended to make a certain gift to him. This is so even if the nephew is, in fact, a selfish wastrel. (2) The fact *of* the statement may be relevant because of its effect on the state of mind of those who heard or read it. For example, if one person is told, even falsely, that his enemy has been threatening to kill him, such a statement would shed light on whether his later killing of that enemy was an act of self-defense. (3) The fact *of* the statement may constitute a verbal act with its own legal consequences, for example, the speaking or writing of assertions that are defamatory.

a. The Statement Is Circumstantial Proof of the Declarant's State of Mind

In many litigation situations, it becomes essential under the substantive law to determine the state of mind that accompanied the performance of certain acts by an individual. That person often will have made statements before, during, and after the performance of the act that reveal circumstantially what his or her state of mind at the critical time was. These statements often contain assertions, the actual truth of which is unimportant. What is important is whether these assertions were made by that particular person, and what the making of them tells us about his or her thought processes. *People v. Ortiz*, 38 Cal. App. 4th 377, 44 Cal. Rptr. 2d 914 (1995) (although the statement did not directly declare a mental state, the fact that the statement was made was circumstantial evidence of a state of mind).

A dispute over the title to real property provides an example. One Joan Furlow owned a large tract of unimproved land worth at least $250,000. In April of 1996, Ms. Furlow executed and handed over to one of her nephews, Garrett Furlow, a deed that purported to convey to him fee simple title to this tract. Ms. Furlow died early in 2000. Her son, who is the executor of her estate, does not dispute the execution of the deed or its delivery to Garrett, but claims that it was actually intended by his mother as a mortgage to secure a $5,000 loan that Garrett had made to her. The nephew acknowledges that he made a loan to Ms. Furlow shortly before the date of the deed, but claims that this was an unsecured loan, totally unconnected with the deed; and that his aunt intended by the deed to make a gift of the land to him. The nephew calls as a witness Ms. Peterson, who, after identifying herself, states that she was a close friend of Joan Furlow for many years. The nephew is the proponent.

P   WHERE were you on April 13, 2000? (1), (2)
W   I was visiting my friend, Joan Furlow, at her house on Dwight Street.
P   WHO else was there? (3)
W   Only the two of us.
P   WHAT happened while you were there? (4)
W   We just had a nice chat.
P   WHAT did you chat about? (4)
W   A lot of things, including Joan's nephew, Garrett.
P   WHAT did Ms. Furlow say about her nephew, Garrett? (4)
O   Your Honor, I object to that question on the ground that it calls for hearsay.
P   Your Honor, may we approach the bench?
J   Yes.
P   Your Honor, if permitted to answer my question, Ms. Peterson will testify that Joan Furlow said that her nephew was a generous and unselfish person, who was always helping other people, and that it was about time for something good to happen to him. (4) I am not seeking to prove that Ms. Furlow was correct in the

things that she asserted to Ms. Peterson about Garrett. I want to offer that testimony for a nonhearsay purpose, namely, as circumstantial proof of Ms. Furlow's deep affection for Garrett. (5) The testimony is logically relevant to show that she had donative intent when she gave him the deed the next day. (6)

J   The objection will be overruled. I will admit the evidence for that nonhearsay purpose.

P   Ms. Peterson, let me repeat the question. WHAT did Ms. Furlow say on that occasion about her nephew, Garrett? (4)

W   She said that Garrett was a generous and unselfish person, who was always helping other people, and that it was about time for something good to happen to him.

O   Your Honor, I request a limiting instruction.

J   Yes. Ladies and gentlemen of the jury, you have just heard Ms. Peterson's testimony about Ms. Furlow's statement to her. I am admitting Ms. Furlow's statement only for whatever light it may shed on Ms. Furlow's feelings for or attitude toward her nephew. It is not being offered as evidence that the nephew actually possessed the characteristics his aunt was attributing to him.

b. The Effect of the Statement on the Mind of the Hearer or Reader

Out-of-court statements are usually made for the purpose of communicating the assertions they contain to some other person. In a subsequent litigation, it often becomes important to show the impact that the hearing or reading of that statement had upon the state of mind of the person to whom it was directed. When an out-of-court statement is offered merely to show its effect on another person, the statement is not being offered for a hearsay purpose and hence is not subject to the hearsay rule. *People v. Mayfield*, 14 Cal. 4th 668, 750-51, 60 Cal. Rptr. 2d 1, 48-49, 928 P.2d 485, 532-33 (1997) (a statement by a bystander to a police officer to the effect that D might be carrying a gun is admissible when there is an issue in the case concerning whether the force used by the officer in his ensuing confrontation with D was excessive); *People v. Sanders*, 11 Cal. 4th 475, 46 Cal. Rptr. 2d 751, 905 P.2d 420 (1995) (the question was whether the store manager had focused and concentrated on the appearance of the perpetrator of a robbery; it was permissible to show that before the robbery, he had read manuals entitled "Hold-Ups and Robberies" and "In the Event of a Robbery," advising employees to study the physical features and clothing of robbers); *Silva v. Lucky Stores, Inc.*, 65 Cal. App. 4th 256, 265, 76 Cal. Rptr. 2d 382, 388 (1998) (defendant-employer's investigator of plaintiff-employee's alleged sexual harassment compiled 15 interviews, some summarized on a witness-interview form, and some in the form of signed statements; plaintiff's hearsay objection was properly overruled: "Where the reasonableness of a person's conduct is at issue, the statements of others on which he acted are admissible.")

Suppose one auto collides with the rear of another auto. The driver of the lead car alleges that driver of the following car, Mike Dolan, was negligent in that he was driving an auto that he knew had defective brakes. Plaintiff calls John Home, who, after identifying himself, testifies that he manages the auto repair shop near the defendant's house, and that on January 14, 2000, which was one week before the collision, defendant dropped off his car for regular maintenance. Plaintiff is the proponent.

P   Mr. Home, WHERE were you on the evening of January 14, 2000? (1), (2)

W   I was at my repair shop.

P   WHO else was there? (3)

W   We had several customers, including Dolan, come in to pick up their cars.

P   WHAT happened when the defendant Dolan came into the shop to get his car? (4)

W   He paid his bill, I gave him the keys, and we talked for a while.

P   WHAT did you talk about? (4)

W   Mostly his car.

P   WHAT did you tell him about the car? (4)

O   Your Honor, I object to that question on the ground that it calls for hearsay.

P   Your Honor, may we approach the bench?

J   Counsel will approach the bench.

P   Your Honor, if permitted to do so, the witness will testify that he told the defendant Dolan that the mechanic who worked on his car had reported that its brakes were slipping badly and that they needed new linings right away. (4) I am not offering this statement to prove that the brakes on defendant's car were in fact defective. I intend to prove the condition of the brakes by the testimony of the mechanic who worked on the car. I am offering Mr. Home's statement about the brakes for a nonhearsay purpose, namely, to show its effect on the defendant's state of mind; it put him on notice of the dangerous condition of his car's brakes. (5) This notice to the defendant is a key element of our theory of his negligence.

J   The objection on the ground of hearsay will be overruled.

P   Mr. Home, let me repeat the question. WHAT did you tell the defendant about his car? (4)

W   I told him that my mechanic who worked on the car had reported that its brakes were slipping badly and that they needed new linings right away.

P   HOW close were you standing to the defendant when you told him that?

W   Only a foot or two away.

P   HOW noisy was the repair shop at the time?

W   It wasn't really noisy at all. Our work day was over.

P   HOW were you facing when you told him about his brakes?

W   I was talking right at him.

P   WHO else was talking to him at the time?

W   No one else. We were the only two talking.

P   HOW did he react when you told him about the bad brakes?

W   He nodded his head, said that he guessed that he better do something about that, got into his car, and drove away.

O   Your Honor, I request a limiting instruction.

J   Yes. Ladies and gentlemen of the jury, you have just heard Mr. Home's testimony that he told the defendant that his brakes were bad. You may not consider this witness's testimony as evidence that in fact the brakes were bad. However, if other evidence in this case establishes that the brakes were indeed defective, then and only then you may consider the testimony of Mr. Horne in deciding whether when the defendant was driving his car on the day of the collision, he knew that its brakes were defective.

See also Bihun v. AT&T Information Systems, 13 Cal. App. 4th 976, 988-89, 16 Cal. Rptr. 2d 787, 792-93 (1993) (in a sexual harassment case, statements to employer concerning other harassing activities of an executive were admissible to prove the "operative fact" of notice).

c. The Statement Is an Operative Fact or Verbal Act

To illustrate this foundation, we shall use a variation of the fact situation in *Hanson v. Johnson*, 161 Minn. 229, 201 N.W. 322 (1924). Plaintiff Hanson owned a farm that he leased to a sharecropper named Schrik, who intended to plant it in corn. Hanson was to receive 40 percent of the corn crop as his rent. Schrik then pledged his share of the corn crop as security for a loan from Cattlemen's Bank.

There were five numbered cribs on the farm for storing corn, and Schrik's harvest filled each of them to capacity. Instead of partitioning this jointly owned corn by a sale, Hanson and Schrik decided to make a partition in kind. They met at the farm one day after the harvest, and Schrik, pointing to crib Nos. 4 and 5, declared: "These two cribs of corn are yours, Mr. Hanson." Hanson responded: "That seems fair to me."

Schrik sells the corn in cribs Nos. 1 and 2 and uses the proceeds to buy himself a new car. When he defaults on his loan, the bank forecloses on its pledge and sells all the corn in cribs Nos. 3, 4, and 5 to satisfy Schrik's debt.

Hanson then sues the Cattleman's Bank for conversion of the corn in cribs Nos. 4 and 5. At trial Hanson takes the witness stand, and, after identifying himself, testifies to the 40-60 percent sharecrop arrangement that he made with Schrik. The plaintiff is the proponent.

P   Mr. Hanson, WHERE were you on the afternoon of July 6, 1999? (1), (2)
W   I was at my farm, the one I had rented to Schrik.
P   WHO else was there? (3)
W   Schrik was the only one around. I didn't see his wife or kids.
P   WHY were you there? (4)
W   It was time to split up the corn crop so we each could have our own share.
P   WHAT arrangement did you and he make to split up that corn crop?
O   Your Honor, I move to strike that question on the ground that it calls for hearsay.
P   Your Honor, may we approach the bench?
J   Yes, counsel may come to the bench.
P   Your Honor, if permitted to do so, Mr. Hanson will testify that his tenant Schrik pointed to cribs Nos. 4 and 5 and said: "These two cribs of corn are yours, Mr. Hanson." My client will further testify that he responded: "That seems fair to me." The witness will indeed be testifying to two out-of-court utterances, one by Schrik, and the other by the witness himself. However, although the phrasing of Schrik seems to be assertive, its meaning is not. Schrik is simply making an oral

offer to partition the corn in a certain way. This is followed by Hanson's statement: "That seems fair to me," which is nothing more than a colloquial way of saying: "I accept your proposal." Under the objective theory of mutual assent, an oral contract results from the mere speaking of these words by these two individuals in this setting. Thus the words of Schrik and of Hanson were really verbal acts; their words, consisting of an offer followed by an acceptance, are the operative facts that create an oral contract. If I may be excused for using the term, the words of Schrik and of Hanson are the *res gestae* of a partition in kind of the corn crop.

J   I agree. The important thing is whether a conversation of this import occurred. If it did, the plaintiff would have become the sole owner of the corn in cribs Nos. 4 and 5. The objection on the ground of hearsay is overruled.

P   Mr. Hanson, let me repeat the question. WHAT arrangement did Mr. Schrik and you make to split up that corn crop? (4)

W   Schrik pointed to crib Nos. 4 and 5 and said: "These two cribs of corn are yours, Mr. Hanson." I replied: "That seems fair to me." A few minutes later, I left.

See also People v. Jimenez, 38 Cal. App. 4th 795, 802, 45 Cal. Rptr. 2d 466, 470 (1995) ("An operative fact, such as words forming an agreement, is not hearsay ....").

Part 2. The Exception for Admissions

C.   ADMISSIONS OF A PARTY-OPPONENT

If a statement is being offered for a hearsay purpose, that is, to prove the truth of the matter it asserts, the proponent must bring it within one of the exceptions to the hearsay rule or it will be excluded. One of the most frequently used exceptions is the one for the admissions of a party-opponent. Under this exception, each party to a lawsuit may offer in evidence against an adverse party any relevant out-of-court statements made by that adverse party.

Commentators have had some difficulty explaining the rationale for the admission exception. Most of the hearsay exceptions are based on some special features of trustworthiness that attended the making of the out-of-court statement. The admission exception does not contain such a requirement. It requires only a statement *by* a party that is being offered *against* that party. To be sure, the vast majority of statements offered under this exception will have a feature that makes them reliable when made, namely, the assertion of facts that were obviously against the interest of the party at the time the statement was made. Although most admissions will be against interest when made, this is not a requirement for this exception. The exception embraces assertions of a party that were neutral or self-serving when made, but have meanwhile become disserving because of later developments.

The real reason for the admissions exception is that the hearsay rule exists not to protect people from their own relevant out-of-court statements, but to protect them from the relevant out-of-court statements of other persons. Because the hearsay rule reflects a judicial concern for the credibility of the declarant of the statement, an objection on the ground of hearsay to one's own out-of-court statement would be a challenge to one's own credibility. In a loose sense of the term, parties to a lawsuit are "estopped" from attacking the reliability of their own statements. There is no need to cross-examine oneself. The party-opponent can take the stand to deny or explain the statement.

Because admissions of a party-opponent do not implicate the concerns reflected in the hearsay rule, some commentators *exempt* admissions of party from the definition of hearsay. Federal Evidence Rule 801(d)(2), for example, states flatly that an admission of a party-opponent "is not hearsay." On the other hand, the California Evidence Code follows the traditional approach: admissions fall within the hearsay *definition* in § 1200(a), but they are then *excepted* from the operation of the hearsay *rule* exceptions by §§ 1220-27. Whether admissions of a party-opponent are *exempted* from the hearsay definition or *excepted* from the hearsay rule, the important thing is that such out-of-court statements are admissible against the one who made them to prove the truth of the matters asserted.

Admissions are of three basic types: personal, adoptive, and vicarious. We attribute a personal admission to the party-opponent because it consists of his or her own words or acts. With an adoptive admission, the actual speaking or writing of the assertive statement is done by someone else, but we impute it to the party-opponent because that party has manifested agreement with what it says. Finally, vicarious admissions are statements of a third person that the party-opponent has neither made nor adopted, but are attributed to the party-opponent because of a legal relationship—principal and agent, employer and employee, fellow conspirator—between that party and the one who actually made the statement. We shall now examine the foundations for these three types of admission in detail.

1. PERSONAL ADMISSIONS

All jurisdictions admit the party-opponent's own personal admissions in civil and criminal cases. Evidence Code § 1220 creates an exception to the hearsay rule for statements "when offered against the declarant in an action to which he is a party in either his individual or representative capacity, regardless of whether the statement was made in his individual or representative capacity."

The attitude of the law of evidence towards personal admissions is very liberal; they are not subject to the hearsay rule, the opinion rule, or the personal knowledge rule. The few restrictions that there are on the admissibility of personal admissions exist to serve some extrinsic social policy. For example, in order to encourage the disposition of criminal cases by pleas of nolo contendere, Penal Code § 1016(3) prohibits the use of that plea "as an admission in any civil suit based upon or growing out of the act upon which the criminal prosecution is based." *See County of Los Angeles v. Civ. Serv. Comm'n*, 39 Cal. App. 4th 620, 629 n.8, 46 Cal. Rptr. 2d 256, 263 n.8 (1995). Another example is found in a decision that predates the adoption of the Evidence Code, *Meyer v. State Bd. of Equalization*, 42 Cal. 2d 376, 385, 267 P.2d 257, 262-63 (1954), in which the

Supreme Court ruled that a superseded pleading in a civil case may not be introduced as an evidentiary admission at trial. Such use would undermine the policy allowing liberal amendment of pleadings. The most significant restriction on the use of an admission comes into play when it falls within one of the evidentiary privileges, such as the attorney-client privilege or the privilege for marital communications, which are discussed in detail in Chapter 10.

a. In Civil Cases

In civil cases, the foundation for personal admissions includes these elements:

1. The witness heard a declarant make a statement.
2. The witness identifies the declarant as the present party-opponent. (Under Evidence Code § 403, the trial judge does not decide whether the party-opponent in fact made the statement, but only whether there is enough evidence to support a finding by the trier of fact that the party-opponent made the statement.)
3. The statement asserts matters that are logically relevant to some material issue in the case. (As a practical matter, the assertion will be inconsistent with the position the party-opponent is taking at trial.)

Our fact situation is a civil tort action. The case arose from a collision on March 19, 2000. The plaintiff, Ms. Langdale, has claimed that the defendant, Mr. Maire, caused the collision by speeding. The speed limit at the place of the collision is 25 miles an hour. Plaintiff calls Officer Hightower, who, after identifying himself, testifies that, in response to a radio message, he proceeded to the accident scene. The proponent is the plaintiff.

P WHAT did you do when you arrived at the scene of the collision?
W I investigated the accident.
P HOW did you investigate the accident? (1)
W I noted the position of the vehicles, examined the road surface and the debris, and interviewed the persons involved.
P WHOM did you interview? (2)
W Ms. Langdale and Mr. Maire.
P WHERE is Mr. Maire now? (2)
W In the courtroom.
P Specifically, WHERE in the courtroom? (2)
W He's sitting at one of the trial tables.
P HOW is he dressed? (2)
W In a green suit and blue tie.
P Your Honor, please let the record reflect that the witness has identified the defendant, Mr. Maire.
J The record will so reflect.
P Officer Hightower, WHAT did the defendant say about the accident? (3)
O Your Honor, I object on the ground that the question calls for hearsay.

P   Your Honor, may I approach the bench and be heard?

J   Yes. Counsel may come to the bench.

P   If permitted to answer, the witness will testify that defendant Maire told him that he guessed the accident was his fault, that he was going "too damn fast." The witness then asked him how fast he was going, and he said: "I wasn't really paying attention. I could have been doing forty miles an hour."

O   Your Honor, in addition to my hearsay objection, I also object on the ground that the statement that he was going "too damn fast" and "could have been doing 40 miles an hour" is nothing more than speculation by someone who says that he has no personal knowledge of his speed.

P   Your Honor, the statement I just described is indeed hearsay. However, it is a statement by the defendant that is being offered against the defendant. Therefore, it falls within the exception to the hearsay rule for admissions of a party-opponent. The assertions in the statement are indeed conclusory and not based on Mr. Maire's personal knowledge. However, a statement that qualifies under the admissions exception is not subject to objection on the ground that it contains an opinion or that the declarant lacked personal knowledge. None of these rules exists to protect Mr. Maire from his own out-of-court statements.

J   The objection will be overruled.

P   Let me repeat the question. WHAT did defendant Maire say about the accident? (3)

W   He told that me that he guessed the accident was his fault, that he was going "too damn fast." I then asked him how fast he was going, and he said: "I wasn't really paying attention. I guess I could have been doing 40 miles an hour."

b. In Criminal Cases

The foundation for prosecutorial use of the out-of-court statements by the accused is more complex than the foundation for admissions in civil cases. This is true because the prosecutor must show that statement was not obtained in violation of the defendant's constitutional rights. The prosecutor must first demonstrate that the confession was voluntary; the Due Process Clauses of the Fifth and the Fourteenth Amendments bar the admission of involuntary confessions. In addition, if the accused was in custody when the statement was made, the prosecutor must demonstrate that the police administered proper *Miranda* warnings informing the accused of the right to remain silent and the right to the assistance of counsel. Finally, the prosecutor must prove that the defendant effectively waived these *Miranda* rights. Chapter 11 is devoted to the constitutional exclusionary rules and contains illustrations of the foundations that show the confession to be voluntary, and compliance with the requirements of the *Miranda* rule.

The admissions exception operates in a one-sided way in criminal cases. The accused is the party-opponent of the People, and therefore the hearsay rule is not an obstacle to the use by the prosecution of the out-of-court statements of the accused. However, the alleged victim of the crime for which the defendant is on trial is not considered to be the party-opponent of the accused. *People v. McLaughlin*, 44 Cal. 435 (1872). The defense must find some other exception to the hearsay rule if it wishes to admit the victim's hearsay statements against the People.

2. ADOPTIVE ADMISSIONS

With a personal admission, the party-opponent is the one who actually speaks or writes a statement; with an adoptive admission, the statement is made by some third party. However, once the statement has been made by this third party, it is in one way or another brought to the attention of the party-opponent, who in some fashion indicates agreement with what was said. In the words of § 1221, the party-opponent "manifest[s] his adoption or his belief in its truth." A party-opponent can manifest assent expressly or impliedly or even by silence. Once that assent has been manifested, the statement is treated just as if the party-opponent had made it in the first instance. For this reason, in criminal cases, the Confrontation Clause does not require that the prosecution establish the independent reliability of a statement that has been adopted by an accused. *People v. Sully*, 53 Cal. 3d 1195, 1232, 812 P.2d 163, 184, 283 Cal. Rptr. 144, 165-66, 812 P.2d 163, 184-85 (1991).

a. Express Adoption

The foundation includes these elements:

1. A declarant made a statement.
2. The declarant made this statement in the party-opponent's presence, or the statement was later brought to the party-opponent's attention.
3. The party-opponent heard and understood the statement.
4. The party-opponent made a statement that expressed agreement with the declarant's statement. *See, e.g., People v. Sohal,* 53 Cal. App. 4th 911, 62 Cal. Rptr. 2d 110 (1997) (D's plea of guilty to assault after hearing the prosecution's description of the facts the State was prepared to prove is an adoptive admission of those facts; therefore, the transcript of the plea hearing may be used in a later case to establish that the assault involved D's personal use of a dangerous weapon).

To illustrate this doctrine, we shall use a tort action involving a hit-and-run accident. On July 1, 1998, the plaintiff, Ms. Waylen, was crossing a street in downtown Santa Barbara when a car struck her and fled the scene. Her complaint alleges that the driver of the car was the defendant, Mr. Benton. Mr. Benton works as a salesclerk at an electronics store in Santa Barbara. He denies any involvement in the accident. In his pretrial deposition, he claimed that he was on vacation in Mexico on the date of the accident. Plaintiff calls as her witness George Nickmeyer, who identifies himself and then testifies that he is the manager of the store where Mr. Benton works. Plaintiff is the proponent.

P   Mr. Nickmeyer, WHAT are your duties as manager?

W   I'm generally in charge of everything—purchasing, finance, personnel—you name it, and I do it at the store. It's a pretty small operation.

P   Please describe your responsibilities with respect to the store's personnel.

W   It's a big area. I make sure that everyone is signed up for fringe benefits, medical plans, and the like. I also keep track of work days and vacations. We don't have an old-fashioned time clock.

P   HOW do you keep track of vacation days? (1)

W   I keep a personal log of when people work and when they're off. Then, at the end of each month, I prepare a summary for each employee and have them verify its accuracy.

P   HOW do you do that? (2), (3)

W   I hand them the statement. At the end of each month, everyone checks by my office to inspect their work and vacation statement. They read it; and if it's correct, then they sign it.

P   Your Honor I request that this be marked plaintiff's exhibit #1 for identification.

J   It will be so marked.

P   Please let the record reflect that I am showing the exhibit to the opposing counsel.

J   The record will so reflect.

P   Permission to approach the witness?

J   Granted.

P   Mr. Nickmeyer, I now hand you plaintiff's exhibit #1 for identification. WHAT is it? (1)

W   It's Brad Benton's work and vacation statement for the month of July 1998.

P   HOW do you recognize it? (1)

W   I was the one who prepared it; I recognize the contents and the form. In addition, I see Brad's signature at the bottom. He's worked for me for over three years.

P   HOW many times have you seen the defendant sign his name? (4)

W   I can't give you a precise number, but I've probably seen him do it dozens of times over the years. As I said, the employees come by at the end of every month to sign these statements right in my presence.

P   HOW was this form prepared? (2), (3), (4)

W   I always do it the same way. I don't want any hassles with them over their vacation time. I call them into the office or they stop by on their own, read the statement while I'm present, and then put their John Hancock on it.

P   Your Honor, I now offer plaintiff's exhibit #1 for identification into evidence.

O   Your Honor, I must object on the ground that this is inadmissible hearsay. There's obviously an inadequate foundation for a business entry.

P   Your Honor, may I be heard?

J   Yes.

P   I'm not offering this exhibit as a business entry. I'm offering it as an adoptive admission. Mr. Nickmeyer prepared the form, but his testimony shows that defendant Benton had an opportunity to read and check it before signing it. By signing it, the defendant manifested his assent to the accuracy of the form. The form lists July 1, 1998 as a workday for the defendant—not a vacation day. (4)

J   Objection overruled. The exhibit will be received into evidence as Plaintiff's #1.

P   Mr. Nickmeyer, let me direct your attention to the extreme, left-hand margin of that exhibit. WHAT is listed on that margin?

W   That margin lists each day of the month.

P   Now let me direct your attention to the middle column of the form and the column on the extreme right-hand margin. WHAT do those columns represent?

W The middle column is for checkmarks indicating workdays. The column on the right is for vacation days. If someone works a particular day, I place a checkmark in the middle of the form. If they're on vacation, I place the check in the right-hand column.

P Please look at the columns for July 1, 1998.

W OK.

P WHERE is the checkmark for July 1st—in the middle or in the right-hand margin?

W It's in the middle.

P Again, WHAT does the middle column represent?

W Workdays.

P Your Honor, I now request permission to circulate the exhibit to the jurors for their inspection.

J Certainly.

b. Implied Adoption by Silence—Tacit Admission

If a person stands silent in the face of an accusation, we may sometimes draw from that silence the inference that the person assents to the accusation. The courts sometimes call this silence a tacit admission. The foundation includes these elements:

1. The declarant made a statement.
2. The statement asserted a fact, usually some accusation against the party-opponent.
3. The declarant made the statement in the party-opponent's presence.
4. The party-opponent heard and apparently understood the statement.
5. The party-opponent had the opportunity to deny the statement.
6. The party-opponent either remained silent or made an evasive or equivocal reply. *People v. Rodrigues*, 8 Cal. 4th 1060, 36 Cal. Rptr. 2d 235, 276, 885 P.2d 1, 42-43 (1994) (the defendant did not "demur" to the statement).
7. Under similar circumstances, a reasonable person would have denied the statement if it was not true. (Under Evidence Code § 403, the trial judge decides only whether there is enough evidence to support a finding by the trier of fact that a reasonable person would have denied the statement.)

Our fact situation is another tort case arising from an auto collision. The plaintiff, Mr. Girard, alleges that the defendant, Ms. Ratner, caused the accident by disregarding a stop sign. The investigating officer was Highway Patrolman Kuns. The plaintiff calls Patrolman Kuns, who identified himself and testified that he responded to the accident. The plaintiff is the proponent.

P WHAT did you do when you went to the scene?

W I immediately sought out the two drivers.

P WHO were the drivers?

W A Ms. Ratner and a Mr. Girard.

P   WHERE is Mr. Girard now?

W   At the trial table over there.

P   HOW is he dressed?

W   He's wearing a gray business suit and blue tie.

P   Your Honor, may the record reflect that the witness has identified the plaintiff?

J   The record will so reflect.

P   WHERE is Ms. Ratner now?

W   At the other trial table there.

P   HOW is she dressed?

W   She has on a pink dress and red shoes.

P   Your Honor, may the record reflect that the witness has now identified the defendant?

J   The record will so reflect.

P   WHERE did you come upon Mr. Girard and Ms. Ratner at the accident scene?

W   They were standing on the northeast corner of the intersection.

P   HOW close were they to each other?

W   Right next to each other.

P   WHAT were they doing?

W   They were talking to each other.

P   WHAT were they talking about?

W   The accident.

P   WHAT, if anything, did Mr. Girard say to Ms. Ratner about the accident?

O   Your Honor, I object to that question on the ground that it calls for self-serving hearsay.

P   Your Honor, may counsel approach the bench?

J   You may.

P   Your Honor, if permitted to do so, the witness will testify that Mr. Girard told Ms. Ratner that she had run a stop sign and that Ms. Ratner made no response; she simply remained silent. I am offering my client's out-of-court statement about the stop sign for a nonhearsay purpose. I simply want to prove that he made the statement and by her silence Ms. Ratner adopted it.

O   Your Honor, there has been no sufficient foundation for an adoptive admission.

P   Your Honor, I was just about to develop that foundation when counsel objected.

J   I will admit the statement and Ms. Ratner's silence subject to a motion to strike if an adequate foundation is not immediately laid.

P   Officer Kuns, let me ask you again. WHAT, if anything, did Mr. Girard say to the defendant about the accident? (1), (2)

W   He told her that she was responsible for the collision because she had run a stop sign. He said that she must be blind as a bat.

P   WHAT language was Mr. Girard speaking in? (4)

W   English.

P   HOW close was Mr. Girard to her when he made that statement? (3)

W   Two feet away at most. As I said, they were standing right next to each other.

P   HOW much noise was there at the time Mr. Girard made that statement about her running a stop sign? (4), (5)

W   It was pretty quiet. The traffic had died down.

P   HOW many other people were talking to Ms. Ratner at that time? (4), (5)

W   No one else.

P   WHOM was Mr. Girard facing when he made the statement? (4), (5)

W   He was looking right at Ms. Ratner.

P   HOW was she facing? (4), (5)

W   She was facing him.

P   WHAT was Mr. Girard's tone of voice? (5), (7)

W   He was obviously agitated.

P   Did he make any threats against Ms. Ratner at that time? (5), (7)

W   No. He was upset, but he was not threatening to do anything about it.

P   WHAT gestures did Mr. Girard make? (5), (7)

W   He was quite animated, but he wasn't making a fist or jabbing a finger in her face. He was just exasperated.

P   WHAT was Ms. Ratner's facial expression immediately after Mr. Girard made the statement about her running a stop sign? (7)

W   She just looked kind of worried.

P   WHERE did she look? (4), (5), (7)

W   She looked down and away from him.

P   WHAT, if anything, did Ms. Ratner then say?

W   Nothing at all. (6)

P   WHAT was her response to Mr. Girard's statement that she had run the stop sign?

W   None. She didn't say anything in response to his remark.

When an accusatory statement is made to the accused in a criminal case while he is in custody, the use of his silence as an adoptive admission implicates his privilege against self-incrimination, especially if he has already been given the *Miranda* warnings, which include mention of his right to remain silent. However, where the statement is made by someone other than a police officer, the accused has no reason to think the police are monitoring the conversation, and he does not indicate that he is invoking his constitutional rights, his silence may still be found to be an adoption of the statement made to him. *See People v. Medina*, 51 Cal. 3d 870, 889-91, 1294, 274 Cal. Rptr. 849, 861-62, 799 P.2d 1282, 1294-95 (1991) (when defendant's sister during a jail visit asked him in private why he had killed three youths, his initial silence was properly submitted to the jury as a possible adoptive admission).

3. VICARIOUS ADMISSIONS

When the party-opponent has entered into certain relationships with another person (for example, an agent, an employee, a co-conspirator), these relationships may become the basis for imputing the out-of-court statements of that other person to the party-opponent. For purposes of the hearsay rule, the statements are treated just as if they had been made personally by the party-opponents, and are often referred to as vicarious admissions. This is true even where it appears that the declarant lacked personal knowledge of matter that was asserted. *See Levy-Zentner Co. v. Southern Pac. Transp. Co.*, 74 Cal. App. 3d 762, 142 Cal. Rptr. 1 (1977).

a. Authorized Admissions

Most vicarious admissions are statements made by an agent and admitted against the principal in a case to which the principal is a party. It is not enough that the declarant was an agent of the party-opponent. He or she must be a "speaking agent," one who was "authorized by the party to make a statement for him concerning the subject matter of the statement." § 1222. The foundation for an authorized admission includes the following elements:

1. The declarant was an agent of the party-opponent.
2. The party-opponent authorized the declarant to make statements on the subject in question. *O'Mary v. Mitsubishi Electronics America, Inc.*, 59 Cal. App. 4th 563, 570–74, 69 Cal. Rptr. 2d 389, 394–96 (1997) (officer who attended meeting at which both the founder and the president of a corporation announced new policy of replacing older employees with younger ones was implicitly authorized to relay this announcement to his subordinates; hence, the testimony of one of those subordinates was admissible to prove the fact of the company's age discrimination policy); *see also Cruey v. Gannett Co.*, 64 Cal. App. 4th 356, 366, 76 Cal. Rptr. 2d 670, 675-76 (1998) (the high place in the hierarchy occupied by the general manager of a corporation's Los Angeles office is "probably sufficient without more to establish that he was authorized to speak on behalf of the company).
3. The statement is logically relevant to a material issue in the case.

Our illustration is a suit to collect on claim under a policy of fire insurance. Grant Mutual insured the premises of Delta Corporation against loss by fire. The insurance policy excluded from its coverage any fire traceable to negligence on the party of Delta's employees. Delta's complaint alleges that in January of 1998, a fire causing $100,000 in damages occurred on the insured premises, and that defendant has wrongfully refused to pay the claim for this damage.

Immediately after the fire occurred, Delta ordered its safety supervisor, Mr. Richards, to investigate and report on the cause of the fire. During the discovery stage of the lawsuit, defendant Grant Mutual obtained a copy of a Mr. Richards' investigation report, in which he concluded that one contributing cause of the fire was the carelessness of two welders employed by Delta, who had cut into a furnace and permitted flames to escape. One year after the fire, Mr. Richards was killed in an auto accident. The witness is Henry Jackson, the general manager of Delta Corporation. The defendant is the proponent. Mr. Jackson has already identified himself.

P   Did you know the late Joseph Richards?
W   Yes, I did.
P   WHERE did he work during the first half of 1998? (1)
W   He worked for Delta Corporation at our main office in San Jose.
P   HOW long did he work for Delta? (1)

W Seven years, give or take a few months.

P WHAT was his job with Delta Corporation? (2)

W He was a safety and accident investigator.

P WHAT were his duties as an accident investigator? (2)

W He would check into the details any incident involving injury or damage and then write up a report about the incident.

P HOW long had he held the position of safety and accident investigator? (2)

W From 1995 until his death early in 1999.

P Did Mr. Richards investigate the fire that damaged the Delta plant in El Cajon? (2)

W Yes, I sent him to El Cajon the day after the fire.

P WHAT was he to do there? (2)

W He was to investigate the fire that had occurred the day before.

P HOW long did he spend investigating the fire? (2)

W The whole day.

P WHAT did he do when finished the investigation? (2)

W He prepared a report of the investigation.

P Was that his normal practice?

W Yes.

P Your Honor, I request that this be marked as defendant's exhibit F for identification.

J It will be so marked.

P Please let the record reflect that I am showing the exhibit to counsel for plaintiff.

J The record will so reflect.

P Your Honor, may I approach the witness?

J Yes, you may.

P Mr. Jackson, I now hand you defense exhibit F for identification. WHAT is it? (2)

W It's the report that Richards prepared on the El Cajon plant fire.

P HOW can you recognize it? (2)

W It's on the company letterhead and I recognize Mr. Richards' signature on the last page.

P WHY did Mr. Richards prepare this particular report? (2)

W It was part of his job.

P Your Honor, I now offer defendant's exhibit F for identification into evidence as defendant's exhibit F.

O Your Honor, plaintiff objects to that report on the ground that it is hearsay.

J Will counsel come to the bench?

P Your Honor, we are primarily interested in that part of the report in which Mr. Richards states his findings as to the origin of the fire. It is, of course, hearsay, but it is admissible against Delta as an authorized admission under § 1222.

O Your Honor, this report is an internal Delta communication. Section 1222 covers only statements that an agent is authorized to make to third parties. Moreover, the part they are interested in violates the opinion and personal knowledge rules. Mr. Richards didn't see the fire start and he had no first-hand knowledge of what caused it.

P Your Honor, California follows the modern trend and extends the authorized admission exception to internal reports of an organization. And it is well established that neither the opinion rule nor the personal knowledge rule are applicable to hearsay statements that qualify as a type of admission of a party-opponent.

J   I agree with defense counsel. The objection will be overruled.

J   The report will be received into evidence as defendant's exhibit F.

P   Mr. Jackson, please turn to page 18 of exhibit F and read finding #4 to the jury.

    (3)

W   The report reads: "Another contributing factor may have been our own employees' carelessness. Two of our welders were evidently working next to the plant's furnace. Evidently the welders mistakenly cut into the furnace, releasing the flames that started the fire."

b. Employee's Admissions

Under the traditional common-law view, which was also the California position before the adoption of the Evidence Code, the statement of an agent or employee would be admissible against a principal or employer only if the declarant was a "speaking agent," that is one expressly or impliedly authorized to make a statement about the subject matter it covered.

Under the emerging view it suffices that the declarant was an employee of the party-opponent and that the statement related to a matter within the scope of that employment. As long as the matter covered by the statement relates to the employee-declarant's duties and how they were performed, and the statement itself was made while the declarant was still employed, it does not matter that the declarant was authorized only to act and not to speak. Federal Evidence Rule 801(d)(2)(D) opts for this view. That Rule authorizes the admission of "a statement by the party's agent or servant concerning a matter within the scope of the agency or employment, made during the existence of the relationship."

Whether the California Evidence Code embraces this modern rule, which has now become the majority view, is unclear. Section § 1224 reads:

> When the liability ... of a party to a civil action is based in whole or in part upon the liability ... of the declarant, ... evidence of a statement made by the declarant is as admissible against the party as it would be if offered against the declarant in an action involving that liability. ...

If read literally, Evidence Code § 1224 would be even more liberal than the modern rule, because it does not articulate a requirement that the statement be made at a time when the declarant is still an agent or employee.

Markley v. Beagle, 66 Cal. 2d 951, 59 Cal. Rptr. 429, 809 P.2d 129 (1967), arose out of trial that took place before the Evidence Code went into effect. It involved a statement by a *former* employee made a year after the accident. The California Supreme Court properly upheld the exclusion of the statement under the traditional common-law view that California was following on the date of the trial. However, Chief Justice Traynor included in his opinion a dictum to the effect that the result would not be any different under § 1224 of the new Evidence Code in suits based on a respondent superior theory. On the other hand, *Labis v. Stopper*, 11 Cal. App. 3d 1003, 89 Cal. Rptr. 926 (1970), a case actually governed by the Evidence Code, limited the *Markley* decision to its facts, and allowed into evidence under § 1224 an apparently unauthorized statement by a member of a painting crew made the same day he had caused a passerby to fall when he moved a drop cloth. Commentators consider the *Labis* case to set forth the correct rule. Article, *Negligence at Work: Employee Admissions in California and Federal Courts*, 9 U.C. DAVIS L. REV. 89, 112 (1976).

Under § 1224, as interpreted in the *Labis* case, the foundation includes these elements:

1. The declarant was an agent or employee of the party-opponent.
2. A description of the scope of that agency or employment.
3. The declarant made the statement while he or she was still an agent or employee.
4. The statement related to the duties of the agent or employee.
5. The matter asserted in the statement is logically relevant to an issue the proponent has a right to prove at trial.

Our fact situation is a tort action arising from an auto collision. Plaintiff Henningsen alleges that Mike Julius, a truck driver for Carrington Co., negligently caused the accident. Plaintiff names only Carrington Co. as defendant. For some reason, neither party calls Mr. Julius as a witness at trial; it is unclear whether he is unavailable. Plaintiff first calls, as an adverse witness under § 776, Ms. Luciano, who is the manager of the Carrington branch where Mr. Julius worked. Plaintiff is the proponent. Ms. Luciano identifies herself and states her job title.

P ISN'T IT TRUE THAT you are the manager of the Carrington branch in Truckee?
W Yes.
P ISN'T IT TRUE THAT Mike Julius was one of your drivers? (1), (3)
W Yes.
P ISN'T IT ALSO TRUE THAT he was employed by Carrington Company on October 13 1998? (2)
W Yes.
P That morning, DID you dispatch him on a trip? DID you send him on a trip for Carrington? (2)
W Yes.
P ISN'T IT TRUE THAT you ordered him to take a load of furniture to Colorado by truck? (2)
W That's right.
P And you told him to start the trip by heading east on Highway 80, ISN'T THAT CORRECT? (3)
W Yes.

As her next witness, the plaintiff calls Officer Blue, who investigated the accident. Officer Blue testifies during this investigation he had a conversation with Mike Julius about two hours after the collision. The questioning by the plaintiff continues:

W Officer Blue, WHAT, if anything, did Mr. Julius tell you about his speed just before the collision? (3), (4)
O Your Honor, I object to that question on the ground that it calls for hearsay.
P Your Honor, may we approach the bench?
J Counsel will approach the bench.
P Your Honor, if permitted to testify, the witness will state that Julius said he was going 70 miles an hour at the time his truck crashed into plaintiff Henningsen's car. I have established that he was driving this truck within the scope of his employment by the defendant Carrington Company. This statement is indeed hearsay, but it qualifies under the exception to the hearsay rule for vicarious admissions by an employee relating to the manner in which he carried out his duties.
O Julius was hired to drive the truck, not to admit liability. There has been no showing that he was authorized by Carrington Co. to say anything to anybody about how fast he was going in his truck.
P Your Honor, the only post-Evidence Code authority on this point is *Labis v. Stopper*, which squarely holds that statements such as this now qualify as vicarious admissions under § 1224. Vicarious admissions are no longer limited to statements of speaking agents. It suffices that an employee is making a statement that relates to the way he was carrying out his employment duties. This statement relates to the speed at which Mr. Julius was driving.
J The objection will be overruled.
P Officer, let me repeat the question. WHAT, if anything, did Mr. Julius tell you about his speed just before the collision? (3), (4)
W He told me he was going about 70 miles an hour, because he was a little behind schedule, and he was trying to make up time.
P WHAT is the posted speed limit on the stretch of highway where the collision occurred?
W Fifty-five miles an hour.

Other vicarious admission statutes may also come into play in civil cases. Section 1225 applies to statements by other holders of the same "right, title, or interest" as the party-opponent. Section 1226 admits a minor child's statement against the plaintiff in an action brought for injury to such minor child. Lastly, § 1227 provides that the decedent's statement is admissible against the plaintiff in a wrongful death action.

c. Admissions of Co-Conspirator

A conspiracy is a partnership in crime. The law of evidence considers that each member of conspiracy is implicitly authorizing the other members to make, during the life of the conspiracy, any statement that will further its objectives. When such a statement is made it is a personal admission as to the conspirator who actually makes it, and a vicarious admission as to all other parties to the conspiracy.

The foundation under § 1223 includes these elements:

1. Two or more people combined to achieve some unlawful objective.
2. A member of that conspiracy made a statement out of court.
3. The conspiracy was in progress at the time this statement was made.
4. The statement in some manner furthered the goals of the conspiracy.
5. The accused was then or later became a member of that conspiracy.

Compare People v. Hardy, 2 Cal. 4th 86, 139-153, 5 Cal. Rptr. 2d 796, 823-33, 825 P.2d 781, 808-18 (1992) (each element of the foundation for a co-conspirator exception established), *with People v. Morales*, 48 Cal. 3d 527, 551-52, 257 Cal. Rptr. 64, 77, 770 P.2d 244, 257 (1989) (none of the elements for the co-conspirator exception established).

It is now clear that in the federal courts, the trial judge acts as the fact finder with respect to these foundational elements, that the judge must be persuaded as to these facts by a preponderance of the evidence, and that he or she may use the probative value of the statements themselves in reaching this finding. *See Bourjaily v. United States*, 483 U.S. 171, 107 S. Ct. 2775, 97 L. Ed. 2d 144 (1987).

The California approach is quite different. Under § 1223(c), the judge's role is limited to a determination of whether the evidence is sufficient to sustain a finding by the jury as to the foundational elements. The jury will be instructed that it may use the statements of a co-conspirator against the accused only if evidence independent of the statements themselves has persuaded them that a conspiracy existed between the declarant and the accused. *People v. Mayfield*, 14 Cal. 4th 668, 740-41, 60 Cal. Rptr. 2d 1, 42, 928 P.2d 485, 526 (1997) (after kidnapped victim stated over the telephone that D had shot him, D took the phone and remarked, "Okay, so now y'all know."); *People v. Jeffrey*, 37 Cal. App. 4th 209, 43 Cal. Rptr. 2d 526 (1995) (the standard is prima facie evidence rather than proof beyond a reasonable doubt or even a preponderance of the evidence). In 1995, CALJIC 6.24 was revised to explicitly tell the jury that "you determine" the foundational facts.

To lay the foundation, the People usually rely on an informer, or on a coconspirator who has turned state's evidence. Our fact situation is a prosecution of George Sherr for possession of cocaine with intent to sell. The indictment alleges that the defendant conspired with one James Blanton to import and sell cocaine. The defense is that the cocaine in question was placed in defendant's basement without his knowledge or consent. The prosecution puts Donald Peterson on the stand. The witness has already identified himself. The prosecution is the proponent.

P   WHAT is your occupation?
W   I am a police officer, a member of the Rancho Santa Fe Police Department.
P   WHAT are your duties?

W I specialize in undercover work for the Narcotics Division.

P HOW long have you done that type of work?

W For the last three years.

P WHERE were you on the evening of September 3, 1999? (1)

W I was at the house of James Blanton near the City Hall in Rancho Santa Fe.

P WHO else was there? (1), (3), (5)

W It was just me, Blanton, and the defendant, George Sherr.

P WHAT happened while you were there? (1)

W Blanton showed me some bags containing a drug. Both Blanton and the defendant referred to it as cocaine.

P WHAT happened after Blanton showed you the bags? (1)

W I pretended to get high on some marijuana. While I doing that, I heard Blanton and defendant discuss plans for getting more cocaine.

P WHAT plans did they discuss? (1)

W Blanton said that he had a contact in Mexico for good cocaine. The defendant then said he could fly down there, pick up the cocaine, and smuggle it back across the border.

P WHEN did they say they would carry out these plans? (2)

W Over the next couple of months.

P WHAT happened after they discussed their plans?

W The defendant took me home.

W WHEN did you next see Blanton?

W About a month later I met him for lunch.

P WHAT happened during the lunch? (4)

W Blanton asked me to help the defendant and him to sell cocaine.

P HOW did he want you to help him? (4)

W He said he wanted me to hide some bags of cocaine in my apartment. He said he thought it would be a good idea to divide up the cache rather than storing it in only one place.

P WHAT, if anything, did he tell you about where the cocaine then was located? (4)

O Your Honor, I object to that question on the ground that it calls for hearsay.

P Your Honor, may we approach the bench?

J Counsel may come to the bench.

P Your Honor, if permitted to do so, the witness will testify that Blanton told him that the defendant had just returned from Mexico with a large amount of cocaine and had hidden it in his basement. Since Blanton and the defendant were then involved in an ongoing conspiracy to sell that cocaine, Blanton's hearsay statement is admissible against the defendant under the co-conspirator exception.

J The objection will be overruled.

P Once again, Officer, WHAT, if anything, did Blanton tell you about where the cocaine then was located? (4)

W He said that the defendant had just returned from Mexico with a planeload of cocaine and had hidden it in his basement.

Suppose one defendant has made an out-of-court statement that implicates both himself and his codefendant. However, this statement is not admissible against the codefendant under § 1223 either because it was made after the conspiracy was over, or because it was a mere narrative statement that in no way furthered the objectives of the conspiracy. May the prosecution introduce the statement as a personal admission against the defendant who made it, provided that the judge gives the jury an instruction that it is not to use it against the codefendant?

In *Bruton v. United States*, 391 U.S. 123, 88 S. Ct. 1620, 20 L. Ed. 2d 476 (1968), the Supreme Court held that, in the event the defendant who made the statement does not testify at the trial, even such restricted use of the statement would violate the confrontation rights of the other defendant. The Court recognized the great probability that, notwithstanding the limiting instruction, the jury will misuse the evidence against that other defendant. The defendant who made the statement is then for all practical purposes an uncross-examined accuser of the other defendant.

People v. Aranda, 63 Cal. 2d 518, 47 Cal. Rptr. 353, 407 P.2d 265 (1965), which predates the *Bruton* case, is the California counterpart to *Bruton*. However, *Aranda* announced a rule is stricter than the one in *Bruton*. It applies to both bench and jury trials, and it applies even if the confessing codefendant testifies. Insofar as the *Aranda* doctrine that would require exclusion even of the hearsay statements of a testifying codefendant's statement, it accords the remaining defendants a broader right to exclude hearsay than required by the Sixth and Fourteenth Amendments. *See Nelson v. O'Neil*, 402 U.S. 622, 91 S. Ct. 1723, 29 L. Ed. 2d 222 (1971).

This feature of *Aranda*, excluding as it did otherwise relevant evidence for reasons not compelled by the federal Constitution, did not survive passage of Proposition 8. *See People v. Boyd*, 222 Cal. App. 3d 541, 562-63, 271 Cal. Rptr. 738, 751-52 (1990):

> Thus, to the extent *Aranda* required exclusion of inculpatory extrajudicial statements of codefendant, even when the codefendant testified and was available for cross-examination at trial, *Aranda* was abrogated by Proposition 8. There is no federal constitutional basis for requiring exclusion of a codefendant's statements when the codefendant testifies at trial and is subject to cross-examination. [Citations omitted.] However, to the extent *Aranda* duplicates the protection available under the federal Constitution, as deemed in *Bruton* and *O'Neil*, the *Aranda* rule survives the passage of Proposition 8. The California rule is now coextensive with the federal rule.

Cf. People v. Mitcham, 1 Cal. 4th 1027, 1045 n.6, 5 Cal. Rptr. 2d 230, 242-43 n.6, 824 P.2d 1277, 1289-90 n.6 (1992) ("Because in the present case [the] codefendant did not testify, the *Bruton* rule applies; we therefore need not and do not determine the extent to which the *Aranda* rule, if broader than the *Bruton* rule, has been abrogated.").

Suppose that although the original statement refers to the defendant as well as the declarant, the prosecutor proposes redacting the defendant's name, and substituting neutral terms such as "the second man." In some jurisdictions, the courts hold that the redaction automatically eliminates the *Bruton* problem. IM-WINKELRIED, GIANNELLI, GILLIGAN & LEDERER, COURTROOM CRIMINAL

EVIDENCE § 1109 (2d ed. 1993). However, in *People v. Orozco*, 20 Cal. App. 4th 1554, 1565-66, 25 Cal. Rptr. 2d 659, 665-66 (1993), the court took a different approach. The court stated that "with respect to the use of neutral terms as substitutes for specific names, there is no hard and fast rule. Rather, the approach should be an analysis on a case-by-case basis within the context of the redacted statement. In those cases wherein the neutral term still obviously refers to the non-declaring defendant, all references to the specific name or any identifying term must be eliminated to satisfy *Bruton*. However, where the use of a neutral term does not compel incriminating implication of the nondeclaring defendant, the statement may properly be used … as long as the trial court provides a sufficient limiting instruction." *See also People v. Fletcher*, 13 Cal. 4th 451, 456, 53 Cal. Rptr. 2d 572, 574, 917 P.2d 187, 189 (1996) (the court refused to adopt a "bright line" rule that redaction by substituting a pronoun or other neutral term is always adequate protection for the defendant's confrontation rights).

Part 3. Hearsay Exceptions That Do Not Require Unavailability

Admissions aside, most hearsay exceptions have a two-part rationale: There is both a circumstantial inference of the statement's trustworthiness, and there is some need to resort to the hearsay. In some cases, the need is absolute: The declarant is dead or otherwise unavailable. In other cases, the need is relative: the out-of-court statement is considered to be at least as trustworthy as any testimony the declarant would give at trial. This part of this chapter analyzes the hearsay exceptions that require only relative need. A common ingredient of these exceptions is a proximity between the time one makes a perception or entertains a thought, and the time that person makes a statement asserting it.

D.   BUSINESS ENTRIES

1. THE DOCTRINE

Business records have special features of reliability. The fact that they are made "in the regular course of business" implies that the declarants (the employees who make the entries) are paid and trained and more or less experienced in perceiving correctly and recording accurately any "act, condition, or event" that they assert in the record. Moreover, these declarants are aware that: (1) the organization that employs them will take future action on the assumption that these records are correct in what they assert; and (2) if the records prove to be incorrect, the error is likely to be traced back to them and result in adverse personnel actions such as demotions, pay deductions, even discharge. Additional trustworthiness is obtained by insisting that the record be made "at or near" the occurrence of the matter that it records, and be based on reliable sources of information.

There is also a special need to resort to hearsay. With many records, the entries are so numerous and made over such a long period of time by so many different employees, that it would be difficult, costly, and disruptive to require a litigant to identify, locate, and subpoena them. Moreover, it would usually be pointless to do so, for the employees are likely now to have at best a very hazy memory of the things that they recorded. Producing them in court is unlikely to yield live testimony about these matters; instead, the proponent will wind up simply transferring the hearsay from the business record exception to the past recollection recorded exception.

Evidence Code §1271 states the California version of the common-law business records doctrine:

> Evidence of a writing made as a record of an act, condition, or event is not made inadmissible by the hearsay rule when offered to prove the act, condition, or event if:
>
> (a) The writing was made in the regular course of a business;
>
> (b) The writing was made at or near the time of the act, condition, or event;
>
> (c) The custodian or other qualified witness testifies to its identity and the mode of its preparation; and
>
> (d) The sources of information and method and time of preparation were such as to indicate its trustworthiness.

Section 1270 contains a broad definition of "business"; it covers "every kind of business, governmental activity, profession, occupation, calling, or operation of institutions, whether carried on for profit or not."

2. ELEMENTS OF THE FOUNDATION

The elements of the foundation for the exception to the hearsay rule for business entries are:

1. The record was prepared by an employee of the business.
2. The entrant (and the informant, where they are not one and the same person) was under a business duty to perceive carefully and record accurately the act, condition, or event covered by the entry.
3. The entrant (or the informant, where they are not one and the same person) had personal knowledge of the act, condition, or event recorded.
4. The entry was written at or near the time of the act, condition or event recorded. Where the record is in the form of a computer printout, it is the entry of the data, not its retrieval, that must occur "at or near" the time of the event recorded. *Aguimatang v. California State Lottery*, 234 Cal. App. 3d 769, 798, 286 Cal. Rptr. 57, 73 (1991).
5. It was a routine practice of the business to make such an entry. Unlike its federal counterpart, Federal Rule of Evidence 803(6), § 1271 does not articulate a requirement that "it was the regular practice of that business

activity to make the memorandum." On occasion, the California courts have admitted under the business record exception a one-time report of a nonrecurring event. 1 JEFFERSON § 4.1, at 210; 1 WITKIN § 766, at 745.

6. The report is in writing.

7. The entry records the happening of some act or event; or if it contains an opinion, it be the sort of conclusion that would be formed by most trained observers of the same data (e.g., "fractured femur"), and not an intensely evaluative and subjective one (e.g., "schizophrenic paranoia") that in all fairness should be tested by cross-examination. *People v. Reyes*, 12 Cal. 3d 486, 502-503, 16 Cal. Rptr. 217, 227, 526 P.2d 255, 285 (1974), where "the Supreme Court held that a psychiatric evaluation did not qualify as a business record because '[t]he psychiatrist's opinion that the [patient] suffered from a sexual psychopathology was merely an opinion, not an act, condition, or event within the meaning of [Evid. Code § 1271] ...'" "a conclusion is neither an act, condition, or event ..."; *see also People v. Campos*, 32 Cal. App. 4th 304, 309, 38 Cal. Rptr. 2d 113, 115-16 (1995).

8. The source of the information in the report is not an employee (e.g., the driver of the truck involved in a collision) who would have had at the time of preparing the report strong motives to misrepresent what happened.

The witness who brings the record need not be the one who made the entry and need not have personal knowledge of the record's preparation. *See County of Sonoma v. Grant W.*, 187 Cal. App. 3d 1439, 1450-52, 232 Cal. Rptr. 471, 477-78 (1986) (foundation for report of analysis of defendant's blood in paternity proceeding could be established through testimony of the laboratory director who did not personally analyze blood sample). In fact, the witness rarely has such knowledge. The witness is usually someone whose duties in the organization include custody and preservation of its records. The witness testifies to his or her connection with the business and then describes the habitual method with which the business prepares and maintains its reports. *See People v. Matthews*, 229 Cal. App. 3d 930, 940, 280 Cal. Rptr. 134, 140 (1991) (foundation for business records exception is lacking where custodian does not describe sources of information and mode of preparation). The proponent lays the foundation for this habitual method by following the procedure outlined in Section C of Chapter 6. The habit evidence has sufficient probative value to support a finding that the business followed that procedure on the occasion in question.

3. SAMPLE FOUNDATION

The foundation for the business record exception may be illustrated by an action for breach of contract, in which plaintiff Armor Corporation has alleged that it delivered 500 stereophonic speakers to Hymark Corporation, which has failed without justification to pay for them. Plaintiff Armor wants to introduce from its records a delivery sheet that indicates that its employees delivered the 500 speakers to the defendant. It calls Mr. James Merton as a witness. Mr. Merton has already identified himself. The plaintiff is the proponent.

P   WHERE do you work?
W   I am the records librarian for Armor Corporation.
P   HOW long have you held that position?
W   About six years.
P   WHAT are your duties as records librarian?
W   I establish company-wide procedures for preparing records. I see to it that our records, once prepared, are properly filed. I'm also in charge of records retirement and destruction.
P   Your Honor, I request that this be marked plaintiff's exhibit #3 for identification.
J   It will be so marked.
P   Please let the record reflect that I am showing the exhibit to the opposing counsel.
J   It will so reflect.
P   I request permission to approach the witness.
J   Permission granted.
P   Mr. Merton, I now hand you plaintiff's #3 for identification. WHAT is it?

Authentication

The complete foundation would include proof of the document's authenticity. See Sections B and C of Chapter 5.

Secondary Evidence

The complete foundation will also include proof of compliance with the secondary evidence rule. See Chapter 7.

Hearsay

P   WHO prepared this document? (1)
W   Well, it seems to have been prepared by Bob Grant.
P   HOW do you know that? (1)
W   I recognize his handwriting style. I've seen his writing on hundreds of occasions.
P   WHO is Bob Grant? (1)
W   He's one of our delivery personnel.
P   In that capacity, WHAT are Mr. Grant's duties? (2)
W   He picks up merchandise in our warehouse in Martinez, makes sure that it gets to the customer, and prepares the paperwork on the delivery.
P   WHICH of your employees is authorized to prepare the paperwork? (3)
W   Only the one who is in charge of that particular delivery. That's the employee who fills out the delivery report or sheet.
P   WHEN does this employee make out the report? (4)
W   They're supposed to make it out as soon as they make the delivery. At the very latest, they make it out later that day when they get back to our office.

P HOW often do your employees prepare these reports? (5)

W Every time they make a delivery. I'd say that they send us fifty to eighty of those delivery sheets each week.

P WHAT form does the report take? (6)

W It's a standard, written report we call a delivery sheet. Like the one we have here, exhibit #3 or whatever the number is.

P WHY do you require that the delivery personnel prepare these reports? (7)

W There are all sorts of business reasons for the reports—accounting, inventory, taxes.

P HOW important are these reports to your company?

W We make our money by selling and delivering our products. We couldn't run an efficient, profitable business unless we keep very, very close tabs on our deliveries. They are the basis on which we bill our customers.

P WHAT would happen if your delivery reports were incorrect?

W Either we'd overbill our customers and they'd be so angry they'd stop buying from us, or we'd underbill. Either way we'd soon go out of business.

P WHAT does the one who makes the delivery do with the report after it is prepared?

W He hands it to someone in our office.

P WHAT does your office do with it?

W We store it in a separate file, including all the delivery sheets for that week.

P WHERE did you find plaintiff's #3 for identification?

W In the file for that week's delivery sheets.

P WHEN did you remove it from that file?

W This morning, just before I left for court.

P Your Honor, I now offer plaintiff's #3 for identification into evidence as plaintiff's exhibit #3.

O Your Honor, I object to the exhibit's introduction on the ground that the exhibit is inadmissible hearsay.

J The objection will be overruled, and the exhibit will be received.

P Mr. Merton, please read the circled part of the exhibit to the jury.

W That part reads: "January 18—delivered 500 stereo speakers to Hymark Corp."

P Your Honor, I request permission to submit the exhibit to the jurors for their personal inspection.

J Permission granted.

Although § 1271 generally authorizes the introduction of business entries, there are other, more specific statutes governing the admission of particular types of business entries. For example, § 712 permits the introduction of a laboratory technologist's affidavit to establish "the technique used in taking blood samples." Section 1315 allows the admission of church records. Although definition of business in § 1270 is certainly broad enough to include a church, § 1315 is not surplusage. It expressly authorizes the admission of church records reflecting facts of family history such as age and relationship. The Law Revision Commission comment to § 1315 observes that:

> [I]t is unlikely that Section 1271 would permit such records to be used as evidence of the age or relationship of the participants, for the business rec-

ords act has been held to authorize business records ... to prove only facts known personally to the recorder of the information or to other employees of the business.

E. OFFICIAL RECORDS

1. THE DOCTRINE

Just as workers in a business usually are careful in gathering and recording information for their employers, public employees presumably are careful in gathering and recording information for the government agency that employs them. For this reason, the common law developed an exception to the hearsay rule for official records. Section 1280, the Evidence Code's version of this exception, provides:

> Evidence of a writing made as a record of an act, condition, or event is not made inadmissible by the hearsay rule when offered to prove the act, condition, or event if:
>
>   (a) The writing was made by and within the scope of duty of a public employee;
>
>   (b) The writing was made at or near the time of the act, condition, or event; and
>
>   (c) The sources of information and method and time of preparation were such as to indicate its trustworthiness.

It is noteworthy that although the wording of § 1280 parallels that of §1271, which deals with business records, the official records exception does not require that a witness from the governmental agency appear in court and testify to the identity and mode of preparation of the public record. Live testimony is unnecessary to lay the foundation for the official record exception to the hearsay rule for two reasons. First, as the comment of the Law Revision Commission to § 1280 points out, the trial judge may take judicial notice of the statute, regulation, or custom requiring the public official to prepare the record. Second, if an attested copy produced in court is fair on its face (complete, with no erasures), this creates a permissive inference that the public employees followed the proper procedures in preparing the particular record. Evidence Code § 664 creates a rebuttable presumption that public officials have properly performed their duties. *See People v. Dunlap*, 18 Cal. App. 4th 1468, 23 Cal. Rptr. 2d 204 (1993); *People v. George*, 30 Cal. App. 4th 262, 273-74, 35 Cal. Rptr. 2d 750, 757 (1994) (citing §§ 664 and 1280 in sustaining the admission of a card used by correctional detention facility personnel to identify lock assignments for inmates).

2. ELEMENTS OF THE FOUNDATION

The foundation for admitting an official record for the purpose of the truth of the matters it asserts includes these elements:

1. The record was prepared at or near the time of the fact or event recorded. *People v. Monreal*, 52 Cal. App. 4th 670, 678, 60 Cal. Rptr. 2d 737, 742 (1997) (probation officer shown to have recorded defendant's statement "at or near the time" defendant made it).
2. The record is in official custody.
3. The record appears on its face to have been prepared in substantial compliance with the prescribed procedures.
4. The preparer was a public official. *People v. Monreal*, 52 Cal. App. 4th 670, 678, 60 Cal. Rptr. 2d 737, 742 (1997) (a probation officer qualifies as a public official under Section 1280).
5. The official had a duty to perceive accurately and record correctly the act, condition, or event.
6. The official had personal knowledge of the act, condition, or event, or received the information recorded from someone in the agency who had personal knowledge. *See People v. Parker*, 8 Cal. App. 4th 114, 10 Cal. Rptr. 2d 38 (1992) (sufficient foundation under official records exception is laid by testimony of one lab tester that notes of another lab tester indicated that normal procedures had been followed for determining whether substance was cocaine); *Gananian v.Zolin*, 33 Cal. App. 4th 634, 639-40, 39 Cal. Rptr. 2d 384, 387 (1995) (although the official preparing the record need not have personal knowledge, there must be a showing that "the written report is based upon the observations of public employees who had a duty to observe the facts and report ... them correctly"). Note, however, that where the act recorded is the official's hearing or reading of an out-of-court statement by someone unconnected with the agency, a party may still use the statement so recorded to prove the truth of any matter it asserts, provided that statement itself qualifies under some exception to the hearsay rule. *See, e.g., People v. Monreal*, 52 Cal. App. 4th 670, 676, 60 Cal. Rptr. 2d 737, 740-741 (1997) (probation officer's report containing accused's admission that his prior assault conviction involved his personal use of a deadly weapon).
7. The entry records the happening of some act or event; or if it contains an opinion, it is the sort of conclusion that would be formed by most trained observers of the same data, and not an intensely evaluative and subjective one (cause of plane crash: pilot error) that in all fairness should be tested by cross-examination. *See Wilson v. Zolin*, 9 Cal. App. 4th 1104, 11 Cal. Rptr. 2d 870 (1992) (result of blood alcohol test may be established by affidavit of officer administering the test).

3. SAMPLE FOUNDATION

The fact situation is a quiet title action. Plaintiff John Thelan and defendant Garrett each claim title to the same parcel of land in Fresno, California. Each is named as grantee in a deed from the same grantor, Paul Peterson, but plaintiff contends that he recorded his deed first. He proposes to offer a properly attested copy of the recordation of the deed in the County Clerk's office. The plaintiff is the proponent.

P Your Honor, I request that this be marked plaintiff's exhibit #4 for identification.

J It will be so marked.

P Please let the record reflect that I am showing the exhibit to the opposing counsel.

J The record will so reflect.

P I now offer plaintiff's #4 for identification into evidence as plaintiff's exhibit #4.

O Your Honor, I object to the introduction of the exhibit on the ground that it is hearsay.

P Your Honor, may we approach the bench?

J Counsel may come to the bench.

O Your Honor, this record asserts as a fact that the deed to plaintiff was recorded on January 13, 1997. It is being offered to prove the truth of that assertion. This record is hearsay.

P Counsel is correct that the record is hearsay. However, it is a hearsay statement by a public employee carrying out a public duty. Thus, the record falls within the official record exception to the hearsay rule.

O There's been no foundation laid to bring this record under that exception. No witness from the County Clerk's office has come to court to testify as to the method and time of the preparation of this record.

P Your Honor, in contrast to the business records exception, live testimony from a sponsoring witness is unnecessary where an official record is offered in evidence. The court may take judicial notice of the Government Code sections that authorize the County Clerk to record deeds relating to land in the County. Moreover, the attached copy is fair on its face; it's complete, and there are no erasures or unexplained marks. The face of the document creates an inference that the public official properly carried out his duties.

J I agree. The objection will be overruled, and the exhibit will be received.

P Your Honor, I request permission to read plaintiff's exhibit #4 to the jury.

J Permission granted.

P Plaintiff's exhibit #4 is a Xerox copy of a page from the records of the Clerk of Fresno County. The exhibit reads: "Date of Recordation: January 13, 1997; Grantor: Paul Peterson; Grantee: John Thelan; Parcel No. 17,886." Your Honor, I now request permission to hand plaintiff's exhibit #4 to the jurors for their inspection.

J Permission granted.

F.   PAST RECOLLECTION RECORDED AND PRESENT RECOLLECTION REFRESHED

This section discusses two related but distinct doctrines of the law of evidence. The first, past recollection recorded, is one of the exceptions to the hearsay rule. The second, present recollection refreshed, is merely a method of jogging the witness's memory.

1. PAST RECOLLECTION RECORDED

Past recollection recorded, like business and officials records, is a documentary exception to the hearsay rule. Suppose that at trial a witness on the stand cannot recall a particular fact or event. However, that witness has at some time in the past recorded in writing his or her recollection of that fact or event. If that written record of the witness's past recollection is offered as evidence of the matter it asserts, the writing is hearsay, and the proponent will need to qualify it under some exception to the hearsay rule.

The witness's inability to recall furnishes the special need to resort to hearsay evidence. If the record was made at or near the time of the event it records, this reduces dramatically the danger that the statement was affected by a faded memory. If to this feature of special reliability, there is added the declarant's live testimony that the record was an effort to record his or her recollection at that time honestly and accurately, the writing qualifies for exception from the general rule that excludes hearsay.

Section 1237(a) of the Evidence Code contains California's formulation of the exception to the hearsay rule for past recollection recorded:

> Evidence of a statement previously made by a witness is not made inadmissible by the hearsay rule if the statement would have been admissible if made by him while testifying, the statement concerns a matter as to which the witness has insufficient present recollection to enable him to testify fully and accurately, and the statement is contained in a writing which:
>
> (1) Was made at a time when the fact recorded in the writing actually occurred or was fresh in the witness's memory;
>
> (2) Was made (i) by the witness himself or under his direction or (ii) by some other person for the purpose of recording the witness's statement at the time it was made;
>
> (3) Is offered after the witness testifies that the statement he made was a true statement of such fact; and
>
> (4) Is offered after the writing is authenticated as a record of the statement.

Although under this exception the writing itself is admitted in evidence, § 1237(b) specifies that it must be "read into evidence" unless an adverse party decides to have it "received into evidence." This restriction is to prevent the proponents from gaining a tactical advantage, in the form of an exhibit that might be taken into the jury room, from the inability of witnesses to recall events during their live testimony.

The foundation for the past recollection recorded exception to the hearsay rule includes these elements:

1. The witness had personal knowledge of the fact or event recorded. *See People v. Lee*, 219 Cal. App. 3d 829, 840, 268 Cal. Rptr. 595, 601 (1990) (citing Treatise); *People v. Cummings*, 4 Cal. 4th 1233, 1292-94, 18 Cal. Rptr. 2d 796, 833-35, 850 P.2d 1, 38-40 (1993) (a document prepared by a police officer was admissible under this doctrine to prove that the defendant made a statement; in turn, the statement then fell within the admission of a party-opponent hearsay exception).
2. The witness while testifying at trial has insufficient present recollection of the fact or event to describe it fully and accurately. Although § 1237(a) does not articulate a requirement that the proponent first try to use the writing to refresh the witness's present recollection, it is arguable that this step is necessary to establish the "insufficiency" of that present recollection.
3. The witness or someone acting at the direction of the witness prepared a record of that fact or event.
4. The witness prepared or verified the record at a time when the fact or event was fresh in his or her memory.
5. The witness vouches for the truth of the matter asserted in the record in one of three ways: (a) the witness now remembers preparing the record and striving to make it accurate; (b) the witness testifies to a habit of carefully making accurate records of that type of information; or (c) the witness recognizes the handwriting on the record and testifies that he or she would not have made or signed the record unless it was accurate.

Our fact situation is a prosecution for a bank robbery. The People charge that the defendant robbed the First National Bank in downtown Tulare. The witness is Jane Millot, who, after identifying herself, has testified that she works as a teller at that bank. The prosecution is the proponent.

P   Ms. Millot, WHERE were you on the morning of February 14, 2000?
W   I was at work at the bank.
P   WHAT happened that morning? (1)
W   The bank was robbed.
P   HOW were the robbers dressed? (1)
W   They all had masks on. That's why I can't identify any faces.
P   WHAT happened immediately after the robbers took the money? (1)
W   They made their getaway.
P   HOW did they make their getaway? (1)
W   In a white car parked in front of the bank.
P   HOW well did you see the car? (1)

W Pretty well. I saw a lot of the details.

P WHAT details? (1)

W For one, I saw the license number.

P WHAT was the license number of the getaway car? (1), (2)

W I can't remember. I know that I saw it, but I can't remember it now.

P WHAT, if anything, might help you remember? (3)

W I made a note on a slip of paper I had at the time.

P WHAT did you note on this slip of paper? (3)

W The license number of the getaway car.

P WHO prepared this slip? (3)

W I did it myself.

P WHEN did you prepare this slip? (4)

W Right after the car got away.

P HOW many minutes passed between the time the car left and the time you wrote on the slip? (4)

W One or two. Not any more than that. I had the slip of paper and a pen in the pocket of my dress.

P HOW clear was your memory of the license number when you wrote the number down? (4), (5)

W It was excellent. I kept repeating to myself the license number until I was able to write it down.

P Your Honor, I request that this be marked as people's exhibit #5 for identification.

J It will be so marked.

P Please let the record reflect that I am showing the exhibit to the opposing counsel.

J The record will so reflect.

P Ms. Millot, I now hand you people's #5 for identification. WHAT is it?

W It's the slip of paper on which I wrote down the license number of the robbers' car.

P HOW can you recognize it?

W I recognize my handwriting.

P Please read the exhibit silently to yourself. (Pause.) Have you done so?

W Yes.

P Now, please hand it to me. (The witness does so.) Your Honor, please let the record reflect that I am holding the exhibit away from the witness and out of her view.

J It will so reflect.

P Ms. Millot, you've had a chance to read the exhibit. Does seeing that slip refresh your memory as to letters and numbers of license plate on the getaway car?

W I still can't remember without the note in front of me.

P WHY can't you remember? (6)

W It's been too long since the robbery. I have a poor memory for numbers anyway. I can't honestly say that I now remember the license number.

P Please read the slip of paper to the jury.

W It reads: "USC 247."

P WHAT do those letters and numbers stand for?

W That's the license number that I saw on the getaway car.

The past recollection recorded exception may be used to admit into evidence a writing that contains double hearsay. Suppose that Able observes some relevant fact and, while his memory of it is still fresh, orally asserts it to Betty. Betty writes down Able's statement while her memory of the statement is still fresh. The writing, often referred to as a cooperative entry, may be used in evidence under the past recollection recorded, but the foundation requires trial testimony both from Able vouching for the accuracy of his oral assertion to Betty, and from Betty vouching for the accuracy of her written assertion as to what Able said to her. *See People v. Cummings*, 4 Cal. 4th 1233, 1292-94, 18 Cal. Rptr. 2d 796, 833-35, 850 P.2d 1, 38-40 (1993); *cf. People v. Dennis*, 17 Cal. 4th 468, 530–531, 71 Cal. Rptr. 2d 680, 717, 950 P.2d 1035, 1072 (1998).

2. PRESENT RECOLLECTION REFRESHED OR REVIVED

When a writing is admitted as past recollection recorded, it is being used for a hearsay purpose. However, sometimes the writing may be used for a nonhearsay purpose, namely, the fact *of* the writing may revive a witness's faded memory of the fact asserted *in* the writing. A writing used for this purpose does not get admitted into evidence unless an adverse party decides to offer it. It is simply a catalyst for jogging the memory of the witness so that he or she can now give live testimony of a present memory of the facts.

Any writing may be used in an effort to refresh a witness's present memory. Unlike the writing required for the past recollection recorded exception, a writing used only to refresh recollection need not have been made by or at the direction of the witness, nor need it have been written at or near the time of the occurrence it records.

No provision of the Evidence Code directly authorizes attempts to refresh the recollection of a witness after the witness has taken the stand and begun to testify; the propriety of this procedure evidently is taken for granted by § 771, which governs the rights of an adverse party with respect to writings used before or during trial testimony to refresh the recollection of a witness.

The foundation for present recollection refreshed or revived is quite simple:

1. The witness testifies to an inability to recall some fact or event.
2. The witness testifies that a certain writing or object could help refresh his or her memory. (California does not require this showing as a formal element of the foundation, but many trial attorneys think that it is good practice to have first mention of the writing or object come from the witness rather than the attorney.)
3. The proponent has the writing marked as an exhibit for identification and shows the writing to the witness.
4. The proponent asks the witness to read the writing silently.

5. The witness testifies that reading the document has revived a forgotten memory of the fact or event.
6. The witness then testifies to his or her recollection of the fact or event.

We can use the same robbery hypothetical to illustrate present recollection refreshed. In this variation of the hypothetical, bank teller Ms. Millot has a somewhat better memory for numbers.

P WHAT was the getaway car's license number? (1)

W I know I saw it, but I can't recall it anymore.

P WHAT, if anything, might help you remember? (2)

W I know that the late Thomas Smoot, the bank guard, wrote the number down on a slip of paper when I called it out to him. It might help if I could see that slip.

P Did you check what Mr. Smoot wrote to see that he had written down correctly what you called out to him?

W No, I never thought to do that.

P Your Honor, I request that this slip of paper be marked as people's exhibit #5 for identification.

J It will be so marked.

P Please let the record reflect that I am showing the exhibit to opposing counsel.

J The record will so reflect.

P I request permission to approach the witness.

J Granted.

P Ms. Millot, I now hand you People's exhibit #5 for identification.

O Your Honor, I object to the prosecutor showing the witness a writing that she didn't make or verify at the time.

P Your Honor, that objection would be valid if I were trying to offer this slip of paper under the past recollection recorded exception to the hearsay rule. I have no intention of doing that. I am simply trying to see whether an inspection of the paper will refresh the witness's memory.

J Objection overruled.

P Once again, Ms. Millot, I now hand you people's exhibit #5 for identification. (3) WHAT is it? (2)

W It's in Mr. Smoot's handwriting. It might be the slip of paper I mentioned.

P Please read the exhibit silently to yourself. (4) (Pause.) Have you done so?

W Yes.

P Now hand it to me. (The witness does so.) Your Honor, please let the record reflect that I am holding the exhibit away from the witness and out of her view.

J It will so reflect.

P Ms. Millot, you've had a chance to read that exhibit to refresh your memory. Now without relying on the exhibit, do you now have an independent memory of the license number that you saw on the robbers' getaway car? (5)

W Yes. I recall now that the letters happened to be the initials of my brother's college, and the numbers were the ages of my three children.

P WHAT do you now remember to have been the letters and numbers on the license that you saw on the robbers' getaway car?

W USC 247.

G. LEARNED TREATISES

1. THE DOCTRINE

In Chapter 8, we pointed out that during their testimony, experts are permitted to cite learned texts and articles in support of the opinions they give. When the text or article is used for that purpose, the opponent is entitled to a limiting instruction under Evidence Code § 355. The trial judge instructs the jury to consider the matter only to shed light on the credibility of the expert's testimony. However, in some cases, the contents of treatises may be used to prove the truth of the matters asserted by their authors. An exception to the hearsay rule for learned treatises is contained in § 1341:

> Historical works, books of science, or art, and published maps or charts, made by persons indifferent between the parties, are not made inadmissible by the hearsay rule when offered to prove facts of general notoriety and interest.

2. ELEMENTS OF THE FOUNDATION

The elements of the foundation required to qualify a statement in a book under the learned treatise exception to the hearsay rule are:

1. The witness is familiar with the literature in some discipline as a practitioner, teacher, or librarian in the field.
2. The author of the text or article is a qualified expert in the field.
3. The text or article relates to an exact science such as physics, chemistry, or mathematics. Although § 1341 does not articulate this limitation, the California courts have construed § 1341 narrowly. HEAFEY §19.26, at 163. California judges are much more likely to apply § 1341 if the text relates to an exact science. JEFFERSON SYNOPSIS § 18.7, at 222.
4. The text is an authoritative, standard work in the field, one that is used in schools teaching the discipline, or consulted by practitioners in that field, or frequently cited in the technical journals relating to the discipline.
5. The specific passage of the treatise that is offered states a fact of such general notoriety and interest that it is practically subject to judicial notice. For example, *People v. Conrad*, 31 Cal. App. 3d 308, 107 Cal. Rptr. 421 (1973), holds that medical propositions stated in the Physicians' Desk Reference do not qualify under § 1341.

3. SAMPLE FOUNDATION

The fact situation is a job discrimination suit. Plaintiff alleges that his employer, Johnston Industries, discriminated against him and denied him a promotion because of race. He wishes to introduce statistical evidence to support his allegations. The witness is Professor Cynthia Gerber.

P WHAT is your educational background? (1)

W I have both a bachelor of science degree and a master's degree.

P In WHAT fields did you obtain your degrees? (1)

W Mathematics. I obtained both degrees at the University of Southern California.

P WHAT is your current position? (1)

W I am a professor in the Statistics Department at the University of San Francisco.

P HOW familiar are you with the literature in the field of mathematics? (1)

W I try to stay on top of it. It's a vast field, and I think I can honestly say that I am very current with the literature.

P WHO are the Wonacotts? (2)

W They are the authors of one of the most widely used texts in the field of statistics.

P WHAT is their background? (2)

W They are both respected teachers and scholars in the field of statistics.

P Your Honor, I request that this be marked plaintiff's exhibit #4 for identification.

J It will be so marked.

P Please let the record reflect that I am showing the exhibit to opposing counsel.

J The record will so reflect.

P Permission to approach the witness?

J Granted.

P Professor, I now hand you what has been marked as plaintiff's exhibit #4 for identification. WHAT is it? (3)

W It's the latest edition of the Wonacotts' text on statistics.

P HOW do you recognize it? (3)

W I have my own copy of it, and I use it as a textbook in one of my upper division courses at U.S.F.

P WHAT is the subject matter of this text? (3)

W Statistics, a branch of mathematics.

P HOW widely used is this text? (4)

W It may be the most extensively used text in the field. To the best of my knowledge, it's the most popular text for teaching undergraduates. You also see it cited all the time in the professional journals for statisticians.

P I'd like to call your attention to page 141. Please read that page silently to yourself. (5)

W Yes. I've read it.

P WHAT is the topic of that page? (5)

W This is the page on which the Wonacotts discuss the method of computing a standard deviation.

P HOW well accepted is that method? (5)

W It's universally accepted.

P Your Honor, I would now like to offer into evidence page 141 of Plaintiff's Exhibit #4 for identification.

J Is there any objection?

O None, your Honor, just so long as you give a limiting instruction.

P Your Honor, this page qualifies under the exception to hearsay rule for learned treatises set forth in Evidence Code § 1341. It's not simply being offered to show the basis for some expert's opinion. For that reason, a limiting instruction would not be proper.

J   I agree. The passage will be admitted under § 1341.

P   Before I have the witness read and explain the passage, I request permission to distribute these exact, Xerox copies of the page marked exhibits 4-A through 4-L to the jurors.

O   I object, your Honor. You can merely read the page to the jurors; it can't be handed to them.

P   If this were federal court, your Honor, that objection would be well taken. Their Rule 803(18) prohibits submitting the text itself to the jurors. However, there is no prohibition in § 1341.

J   Objection overruled. You may proceed.

H.   JUDGMENTS

1. THE DOCTRINE

In some cases, under the doctrines of res judicata or collateral estoppel, an earlier judgment may bind the parties in the current trial. In other cases, the proponent may want to introduce a judgment as evidence of a fact that was impliedly determined in the earlier trial. Offered for this purpose, the judgment embodies a hearsay statement by the trier of fact in the earlier case. *See People v. Cummings*, 4 Cal. 4th 1233, 1294-95, 18 Cal. Rptr. 2d 796, 835-36, 850 P.2d 1, 39-40 (1993).

California recognizes a limited exception to the hearsay rule for judgments. Section 1300 provides:

> Evidence of a final judgment adjudging a person guilty of a crime punishable as a felony is not made inadmissible by the hearsay rule when offered in a civil action to prove any fact essential to the judgment whether or not the judgment was based on a plea of nolo contendere.

See County of Los Angeles v. Civ. Serv. Comm'n, 39 Cal. App. 4th 620, 632, 46 Cal. Rptr. 2d 256, 265 (1995) ("The exception applies even if the judgment was based upon a plea of nolo contendere"). At trial, the proponent will ordinarily offer documentary evidence, that is, an attested copy of the prior judgment.

When a judgment satisfies § 1300, the judgment is admissible as evidence of any relevant fact that the trier of fact in the earlier case necessarily found to be true in reaching that judgment. However, although the judgment may be considered as some evidence of the fact it is offered to prove, it does not create a presumption that that fact is true. Section 639 provides:

> A judgment, when not conclusive, is presumed to correctly determine or set forth the rights of the parties, but there is no presumption that the facts essential to the judgment have been correctly determined.

2. ELEMENTS OF THE FOUNDATION

The foundation for the exception to the hearsay rule for judgments includes these elements:

1. A person has been convicted of a crime.
2. That conviction is now final.
3. The conviction was for a crime punishable as a felony.
4. In that earlier trial, the fact that the judgment is now being offered to prove was one that the trier of fact in that case had to resolve in order for that judgment to be rendered. In a simple case, an attested copy of a single-count indictment will be sufficient. If the earlier case was more complex, the proponent may have to offer at least a partial record of the trial in addition to the indictment.
5. The trier of fact resolved the fact in a particular way.
6. The present proceeding is a civil case.

3. SAMPLE FOUNDATION

The fact situation is a tort action, in which the plaintiff, Tilton is claiming that James Waltz, a truck driver employed by defendant Keyshun Motor Express, drove one of its trucks into an auto occupied by plaintiff's wife, Priscilla, inflicting fatal injuries. The accident occurred a few feet on the Nevada side of the border near Lake Tahoe. Shortly after the accident, Nevada tried and convicted the truck driver, Waltz, for vehicular manslaughter, a crime carrying a maximum punishment of ten years in prison. Plaintiff wants to offer the judgment of conviction to prove that it was Waltz who struck and killed his wife.

J   You may call your next witness.

P   Your Honor, at this time, I would like to have these two exhibits marked as plaintiff's exhibits #9 and #10 for identification.

J   They will be so marked.

P   Please let the record reflect that I am showing the exhibits to opposing counsel.

J   The record will so reflect.

O   Objection, your Honor, inadequate foundation.

P   Permission to approach the bench?

J   Granted.

P   Your Honor, I now offer these exhibits into evidence as plaintiff's exhibits #9 and #10. As you can see, both documents purport to be official records and bear proper certificates. They are, therefore, authenticated under Evidence Code § 1530. Moreover, as your Honor can see from the face of both documents, both name the defendant's driver, James Waltz, as the criminal defendant, and my client's late wife, Priscilla Tilton, as the victim of the crime. California law recognizes an inference of identity of person from identity of names. That inference is sufficient to identify the criminal defendant and the crime victim as the same persons involved in this civil action. Thus, the person who suffered the conviction was the defendant's employee. (1)

O Your Honor, I don't have any problem with their authenticity or with the identity of the two persons named. My objection is that these documents, if offered to prove that Waltz is the one who killed plaintiff's wife, are hearsay statements by a Nevada judge, based on a hearsay verdict by a Nevada jury.

P Your Honor, exhibit #10 shows on its face that the final judgment and sentence have been entered. (2) I have here an official copy of the Nevada statutes. Since the text purports to be published by public authority, it is self-authenticating under Evidence Code § 644. Page 422 shows that under Nevada law, the maximum imposable punishment for vehicular manslaughter is ten years' imprisonment. The judgment convicting Waltz was therefore for a felony under California law. (3)

O I'm also willing to concede that, your Honor, but it's still hearsay.

P If I may continue. Your Honor, if you examine exhibit #9, the indictment in the case, you will see that its only count charged Waltz with the vehicular manslaughter of my client's wife at the same time and place specified in the complaint in this civil case. An essential fact in issue in the Nevada prosecution was whether Waltz struck and killed Ms. Tilton at that time and place. (4) Since the Nevada jury returned a guilty verdict, they must have found that fact to be true. (5) Under Evidence Code § 1300, the judgment is admissible as evidence of that fact in this civil case. (6)

J I agree. Objection overruled. Both exhibits #9 and #10 will be admitted.

P I request permission to read the exhibits and then publish them to the jurors.

J Granted.

I. SPONTANEOUS OR EXCITED UTTERANCES

1. THE DOCTRINE

When people perceive startling occurrences, they usually become excited. This excitement temporarily suspends their powers of reflection. Accordingly, when they speak about the startling occurrence while they are still under the stress of that excitement, their statements have unusual features of reliability that set them apart from the general run of hearsay. Excited utterances have long escaped the operation of the hearsay rule. Initially admitted under the rubric *res gestae*, they are now recognized as one of the exceptions to the hearsay rule. The California version of this exception is found in Evidence Code § 1240:

> Evidence of a statement is not made inadmissible by the hearsay rule if the statement:
>   (a) Purports to narrate, describe, or explain an act, condition, or event perceived by the declarant; and
>   (b) Was made spontaneously while the declarant was under the stress of excitement caused by such perception.

As a source of information about that startling event, an excited utterance is at least as reliable as would be the declarant's later live testimony. Consequently, no showing of the unavailability of the declarant is required in order to admit an excited utterance. For that matter, the declarant need not be a competent witness. "It is well established that the spontaneous hearsay declarations of minors who were not competent to testify in court concerning sexual molestation are admissible pursuant to Evidence Code section 1240." *People v. Daily*, 49 Cal. App. 4th 543, 552, 56 Cal. Rptr. 2d 787, 792 (1996); *see also In re Cindy L.*, 17 Cal. 4th 15, 69 Cal. Rptr. 2d 803, 947 P.2d 1340 (1997).

Although § 1240 requires that the statement be "made spontaneously," this does not mean that it must be blurted out; as long as the declarant is still excited, the statement may be in response to a nonsuggestive question. *See People v. Farmer*, 47 Cal. 3d 888, 903-904, 254 Cal. Rptr. 508, 518, 765 P.2d 940 (1989).

In criminal cases, excited utterances are considered one of the "firmly rooted" exceptions to the hearsay rule, and thus bear sufficient indicia of reliability to pass muster under the Confrontation Clause. *See People v. Trimble*, 5 Cal. App. 4th 1225, 1235, 7 Cal. Rptr. 2d 450, 456 (1992). Moreover, the Confrontation Clause does not require a showing of the unavailability of the declarant. *White v. Illinois*, 502 U.S. 346, 355 n.8, 112 S. Ct. 736, 742 n.8, 116 L. Ed. 848, 859 n.8 (1992); *People v. Dennis*, 17 Cal. 4th 468, 529, 71 Cal. Rptr. 2d 680, 715–716, 950 P.2d 1035, 1070–71 (1998).

2. ELEMENTS OF THE FOUNDATION

The foundation for the exception to the hearsay rule for excited or spontaneous statements includes the following elements:

1. An event that would likely excite its participants or observers has occurred. With this hearsay exception, "bootstrapping" is generally allowed: The happening of the startling event may be proved by the very excited utterance that "purports" to describe it. 1 JEFFERSON § 13.1, at 372-73. *People v. Roybal*, 19 Cal. 4th 481, 515-17, 79 Cal. Rptr. 2d 487, 508-509, 966 P.2d 521, 542-43 (1998) (arriving home, a husband discovered the body of his murdered wife; he immediately made a 911 call and shortly thereafter the first officer to arrive tape-recorded his statement; *held:* both statements qualify as spontaneous statements); *People v. Dennis*, 17 Cal. 4th 468, 528, 71 Cal. Rptr. 2d 680, 715–716, 950 P.2d 1035, 1070 (1998) (the violent murder of one's mother is certainly a startling event; statements by her 4-year-old daughter later that night concerning the murderer's threats to kill her if she identified him qualify as spontaneous declarations).
2. The declarant had personal knowledge of the event. The declarant can be unidentified at the time of trial so long as there is sufficient proof that the declarant was an eyewitness with personal knowledge. *See People v. Provencio*, 210 Cal. App. 3d 290, 303, 258 Cal. Rptr. 330, 337 (1989) (uni-

dentified child at burglary scene excitedly identifies fleeing figure as the defendant).

3. The statement is about the startling event.
4. The declarant made the statement while he or she was in a state of nervous excitement. Section 405 applies to this element of the foundation. If there is a factual dispute as to whether the declarant was still excited, the trial judge resolves it. "[I]f a statement meets the requirements of spontaneity and lack of opportunity for reflection ..., it does not become inadmissible because the declarant failed to mention, recall, or confirm it later upon calmer occasions." *People v. Arias*, 13 Cal. 4th 92, 150, 51 Cal. Rptr. 2d 770, 808, 913 P.2d 980, 1018 (1996).

3. SAMPLE FOUNDATION

Our fact situation is a tort action arising from a collision at an intersection. Plaintiff was driving a sedan. Defendant was driving a convertible. The issue is which car was facing and ran a red light. Plaintiff calls one Mr. Reynolds as a witness. Mr. Reynolds has already identified himself. The plaintiff is the proponent.

P   WHERE were you on the afternoon of March 13, 1999? (1)
W   I was in downtown Oxnard at the intersection of Cedar Street and Sixth Avenue.
P   WHY were you there? (1)
W   I just happened to be walking my dog.
P   WHAT, if anything, happened at the intersection while you were there? (1)
W   Two autos collided in the intersection.
P   HOW noisy was the collision? (1)
W   It was an awful, shattering sound.
P   HOW many bystanders were there? (1)
W   I'd say that there were about twenty people in the immediate vicinity.
P   WHAT was their reaction to the collision? (1)
W   We all were shocked. It happened so fast, and the noise was so loud. And as soon as we looked, we could see that some people were injured and bleeding.
P   WHO else besides yourself was in the crowd of bystanders? (2)
W   There were a number of people mingling around, but there was one guy in particular who stuck in my mind.
P   WHAT was his name? (2)
W   I never got his name.
P   WHAT did he look like?
W   He was a male Caucasian, maybe thirty or thirty-five.
P   WHERE was he at the time of the collision? (2)
W   Standing right next to me.
P   HOW was he facing? (2)
W   He was looking right into the intersection. He was evidently waiting for the light to change to walk across.
P   WHAT was his condition right after the collision? (4)
W   He was just like the rest of us—shocked and frightened.

P   WHAT was his facial expression? (4)

W   He had his mouth open. I guess he was dumbfounded at first.

P   WHAT was his tone of voice? (4)

W   He was shouting in a loud voice.

P   WHAT were his gestures? (4)

W   He was pointing at the wreck and gesturing wildly.

P   WHAT, if anything, did he say about the accident? (3)

O   Your Honor, I object to that question on the ground that it calls for hearsay.

P   Your Honor, may I be heard?

J   Yes.

P   Although the statement is hearsay, it clearly falls within the exception to the hearsay rule for spontaneous statements.

J   I agree. The objection will be overruled.

P   Mr. Reynolds, let me repeat the question. WHAT, if anything, did this man say about the accident? (3)

W   He said that the fellow in the convertible had gone right through the red light.

J.   CONTEMPORANEOUS STATEMENTS

1. THE DOCTRINE

The spontaneity of the statement is the basic rationale for the spontaneous statement exception. The statement's contemporaneity can also serve as proof of the declarant's sincerity; the fact that the declarant makes the statement at roughly the same time the event occurs is some evidence of the statement's reliability.

Some jurisdictions have recognized a broad exception for any statement that reflects a declarant's present sense impression. *Houston Oxygen Co. v. Davis*, 139 Tex. 1, 161 S.W.2d 474 (1942), is the seminal case. The Federal Rules of Evidence codify this broad exception in Rule 803(1). *See People v. Hines,* 15 Cal. 4th 997, 1036, 64 Cal. Rptr. 2d 594, 622, 938 P.2d 388, 416 (1997).

Evidence Code § 1241's heading, "Contemporaneous Statement," suggests that § 1241 is comparable to 803(1), but in truth § 1241 is much narrower. Evidence Code § 5 cautions that "section headings do not in any manner affect the scope, meaning, or intent of the provisions of this code." The text and legislative history of each code section are determinative. The text of § 1241 reads:

> Evidence of a statement is not made inadmissible by the hearsay rule if the statement:
>   (a) is offered to explain, qualify, or make understandable conduct of the declarant; and
>   (b) was made while the declarant was engaged in such conduct.

Part of the legislative history of § 1241, the Assembly comment, states: "Under existing law, where a person's conduct or act is relevant but is equivocal or ambiguous it may be admitted to explain and make the conduct or act understandable." The comment makes no mention of *Houston Oxygen* or its progeny; rather, the comment cites former Code of Civil Procedure § 1850 as the basis for the "existing law." Given this legislative history, both Jefferson and Witkin conclude that § 1241 applies only when the declarant's conduct is equivocal or ambiguous. 1 JEFFERSON § 13.2, at 378; 1 WITKIN § 723, at 706. *See also People v. Hines,* 15 Cal. 4th 997, 1034 n.4, 64 Cal. Rptr. 2d 594, 621 n.4, 938 P.2d 388, 415 n.4 (1997).

Witkin points out that so interpreted, § 1241's scope is essentially limited to "verbal acts." *Id.* In subsection B.3. of this chapter, we noted that the courts sometimes use the expression "verbal act" to describe out-of-court statements such as an offer or a slander admitted on the nonhearsay theory that legal consequences flow directly from their utterance. The Assembly Committee comment declares that before the adoption of the Evidence Code, the courts sometimes used the "verbal act" theory to justify the admission of hearsay statements. The comment concludes by stating that "[s]ection 1241 removes any doubt that might otherwise exist concerning the admissibility of such evidence under the hearsay rule."

2. ELEMENTS OF THE FOUNDATION

On the assumption that the courts will continue to apply § 1241 narrowly, the proponent must lay this foundation:

1. The declarant engages in certain conduct.
2. The conduct was inherently equivocal or ambiguous.
3. The declarant made a statement while or shortly after the declarant engaged in the conduct.
4. The nature of the statement was such that it helps remove the ambiguity about the declarant's conduct.

3. SAMPLE FOUNDATION

Mecchi v. Picchi, 245 Cal. App. 2d 470, 54 Cal. Rptr. 1 (1966), was one of the first cases in which the California courts applied § 1241. Witkin cites *Mecchi* as an illustration of the scope of § 1241. The following hypothetical is based in part on Mecchi. The case is a quiet title action. Before his death, a father gave his daughters the deed to a parcel of realty. The daughters are the plaintiffs in the quiet title action. The decedent's wife, the daughters' stepmother, is the defendant. Her answer alleges that her husband conveyed the parcel to the daughters in consideration of their promise to him that they would later transfer some stock in a family corporation to their father. The answer also alleges that the daughters breached this promise. At trial, the plaintiffs call Mr. Grannuci as a witness. He has already identified himself and stated that he was a good friend of the decedent.

P Mr. Grannuci, WHERE were you on the morning of November 13, 1999?
W I first went to Tomaso's (the father's) house.
P WHY did you do that?

H He asked me to drive him down to his lawyer's office. He couldn't drive anymore, and the attorney's office was way downtown on Folsom Street.

P WHAT did you do after you went to Tomaso's house?

W I drove him to the office. We got there about 11:30 a.m.

P WHO was there?

W It was just me, Tomaso, the lawyer, and Tomaso's two daughters.

P WHO are his daughters?

W Gina and Maria.

P WHERE are they now?

W They're in the courtroom. They're the young ladies at the table to your left. One is dressed in green, and the other is wearing a blue dress. I've known them since they were little babies.

P Your Honor, please let the record reflect that the witness has identified the plaintiffs.

J It will so reflect.

P Mr. Grannuci, WHAT happened after everyone arrived at the lawyer's office?

W The lawyer pulled some document out of her desk and told Tomaso that the deed was ready.

P WHAT, if anything, did Tomaso do then? (1), (2)

W He handed the document to his daughters.

P WHAT else, if anything, happened? (3)

W He gave a little speech. He said it was a proud moment for him to be able to give the deed to his girls.

P WHEN did he make this speech? (3)

W Just as he was handing the deed to the girls—he still had the document in his hand at the time.

P WHAT, if anything, did he say about his reason for giving the deed to his daughters? (4)

W He said that he wanted me and his lawyer to know that there were no strings or promises attached to this deed. He was giving it to his girls purely out of the goodness of his heart.

O Your Honor, may we approach the bench?

J Yes.

O Your Honor, I have to move to strike the reference to the decedent's statement that there were no strings or promises attached to the deed. I agree that under Evidence Code § 1250, the plaintiffs can introduce the decedent's declarations of existing state of mind such as a profession of affection for his daughters, but that statute isn't broad enough to permit the introduction of the statements about strings or promises.

P Your Honor, may I be heard?

J Certainly.

P I'm not relying on § 1250. Rather, I'm relying on § 1241. The act of handing someone a deed is inherently ambiguous; the transaction could be a gift, a mortgage, or a sale. At roughly the same time that the decedent was engaging in his equivocal conduct, he made a statement. That statement helps to explain his conduct and make it understandable. I think that § 1241 is broad enough to allow me to introduce the statement that there were no strings or promises.

J I agree. I'm denying the motion to strike on the authority of § 1241.

K.   DECLARATIONS OF PRESENT STATE OF MIND OR EMOTION

1.   —OFFERED TO PROVE DECLARANT'S STATE OF MIND OR EMOTION

In many lawsuits, it becomes essential under the applicable substantive law to determine what was the state of some person's mind at a particular time. For example, when Aunt Hattie delivered a valuable necklace to her niece, did she intend a loan or a gift? The state of a person's mind is invisible; it cannot be perceived by other people. When the state of someone's mind becomes a material issue in a lawsuit, attorneys usually must resort to circumstantial evidence in an effort to establish what that mental state was. For example, if Aunt Hattie delivered the necklace on her niece's eighteenth birthday, this would be circumstantial evidence that Aunt Hattie intended to make a gift of the necklace to the niece.

Sometimes a person will directly state, orally or in writing, what is on his or her mind at that particular moment. If it later becomes necessary to determine in court what that person's mental state was at that earlier time, an oral or written statement purporting to reveal it would have much probative value. The problem is that such a statement is hearsay: It is made out of court, it asserts the speaker's or writer's state of mind to be such-and-such, and it is being offered to prove the truth of that assertion. Its probative value then depends upon the credibility of the declarant, and just as one may lie about one's perceptions, one may also lie about the state of one's mind. People are perfectly capable of stating that they have intentions or feel emotions that they do not in fact have or feel.

The common law of evidence has long admitted statements of someone's then existing mental or emotional state when that becomes a material issue in litigation. At first, the courts camouflaged what they were doing by calling such statements part of the *res gestae*. Nowadays, it is generally recognized that a statement asserting the then-existing mental or emotional state of the declarant is excepted from the operation of the hearsay rule. Accordingly, Evidence Code § 1250(a) provides:

> Subject to Section 1252 [i.e., unless "made under circumstances such as to indicate its lack of trustworthiness"], evidence of a statement of the declarant's then existing state of mind [or] emotion ... (including a statement of intent, plan, motive, design [or] mental feeling is not made inadmissible by the hearsay rule when:
>
> (1) The evidence is offered to prove the declarant's state of mind [or] emotion ... at that time or at any other time when it is itself an issue in the action. ...

Ideally, the declarant will make the statement asserting his or her mental state at the very time that is pivotal under the substantive law. For example, Aunt Hattie will state: "I am giving you this necklace as a birthday present," as she hands it over to her niece. However, if the statement is made sometime before or after that pivotal moment, it may still be offered as circumstantial evidence of what the declarant's unspoken state of mind was at the critical time. For example, if one week before the niece's birthday, Aunt Hattie stated to someone: "I'm going to give my niece a necklace for her birthday," this earlier donative intent, as evidenced by Aunt Hattie's hearsay statement, would be circumstantial evidence of what Aunt Hattie intended a week later when she silently handed the necklace to her niece. This is simply a recognition of the common sense notion of continuity in time of states of mind; they often do not spring into existence at the moment of the statement, and evaporate as soon as the statement has been made.

The foundation for admitting an out-of-court statement under the exception to the hearsay rule for statements of present state of mind is as follows:

1. Where the statement was made.
2. When the statement was made in relation to the time that is pivotal under the substantive law involved in the lawsuit.
3. Who was present.
4. Who made the statement.
5. The tenor of the statement.
6. The lack of any circumstances indicating that the statement was not trustworthy.

Our fact situation is a quiet title action. Plaintiff Sheila Morris has sued defendant Winters. Plaintiff claims title to a tract of land from the original titleholder, Forest Morris, her grandfather. Plaintiff claims that on December 25, 1992, her grandfather gave her a deed to the property as a Christmas present. Plaintiff calls Thomas Morris, her brother, as a witness. Plaintiff is the prop onent.

P WHERE were you on December 25, 1992? (1), (2)
W I was at our family Christmas party at Santa Monica.
P WHO else was there? (3), (6)
W All the close relatives, including grandfather and my sister, Sheila Morris.
P WHAT, if anything, unusual happened during the party?
W As an unexpected Christmas gift, grandfather handed Sheila a deed to our land in Santa Cruz.
P WHAT, if anything, did he do when he handed her the deed? (4)
W Well, he did say something.
P WHAT did he say? (5)
W He said that he wanted her to have the land because, ever since she was a little girl, she had loved to vacation there.

2. —OFFERED TO PROVE DECLARANT'S SUBSEQUENT CONDUCT

Sometimes a person will make a statement asserting his or her present intention to engage in certain conduct in the future. ("I am going to New York next week." "I'll kill Victor the next time I see him.") *See People v. Majors,* 18 Cal. 4th 385, 403-405, 75 Cal. Rptr. 2d 684, 696-98, 956 P.2d 1137, 1149-51 (1998) (murder victim's statements on the night he was killed that he was about to conduct a drug deal with people from Arizona are admissible as circumstantial evidence that he met with people from Arizona later that night); *People v. Jones,* 13 Cal. 4th 535, 54 Cal. Rptr. 2d 42, 50-51, 917 P.2d 1165, 1173-74 (1996) (the murder victim stated that she was going to another city with the defendant). If indeed the declarant did entertain the intent or plan that he or she was asserting, common sense tells us that his formation of this intent or plan has some tendency in reason to prove that he later carried it out. Evidence Code § 1250, which sets forth the hearsay exception for statements of present mental state, explicitly authorizes use of the statement as circumstantial evidence that the plan was later carried out by the declarant:

> Subject to Section 1252 [i.e., unless "made under circumstances such as to indicate its lack of trustworthiness"], evidence of a statement of the declarant's then existing state of mind [or] emotion ... (including a statement of intent, plan, motive, design [or] mental feeling ...) is not made inadmissible by the hearsay rule when:
>
> (1) ...
>
> (2) The evidence is offered to prove or explain acts or conduct of the declarant.

The foundation for admitting a statement of present state of mind to prove the declarant's subsequent conduct is as follows:

1. Where the statement was made.
2. When the statement was made in relation to the time that is pivotal under the substantive law involved in the lawsuit.
3. Who was present.
4. Who made the statement.
5. The tenor of the statement.
6. The lack of any circumstances indicating that the statement was not trustworthy.

The fact situation is a burglary prosecution. The People allege that defendant Waylen burglarized a drugstore in Los Angeles on August 17, 1999. The defense is alibi. Defendant and his girlfriend testified that he was with her in San Francisco on the day of the burglary. Now defendant calls one Farnsworth as a witness. Farnsworth has already identified himself. Defendant is the proponent:

P Mr. Farnsworth, WHERE were you on the evening of August 15, 1999? (1), (2)
W I was at a party at a friend's house here in Los Angeles.
P WHO else was at the party?
W A lot of people, including the defendant, Michael Waylen. (3)
P WHERE is the defendant now?
W He's in the courtroom.
P Specifically, WHERE in the courtroom?
W He's sitting at that trial table.
P HOW is he dressed?
W He's wearing a gray sweater and black pants.
P Your Honor, please let the record reflect that the witness has identified the defendant, Michael Waylan.
J It will so reflect.
P Mr. Farnsworth, WHAT happened during the party? (4), (6)
W It was just a quiet party. I drank a little and talked with some friends.
P WHOM did you talk with? (4)
W I had a nice long talk with Michael, the defendant.
P WHAT did you talk about? (5)
W A lot of things, especially his plans for the future.
P WHAT, if anything, did the defendant say about his immediate plans? (5)
O Your Honor, I object to that last question on the ground that it calls for self-serving hearsay.
P Your Honor, may we approach the bench to be heard?
J Counsel may come to the bench.
P Your Honor, if permitted to testify, the witness will state that during this conversation at that party defendant said that he intended to visit his girlfriend in San Francisco on the upcoming weekend. Insofar as it is hearsay, defendant's statement of his plan to visit his girlfriend comes within the exception to the hearsay rule for statements of present state of mind. And if he did then have such a plan on August 15th, that is some evidence that he carried it out and went to San Francisco.
J The objection will be overruled.
P WHAT, if anything, did the defendant say about his immediate plans? (5)
W He said that on the upcoming weekend he was going to visit his girlfriend, Norma, in San Francisco.
P WHICH weekend was he referring to? (5)
W The weekend of August 17th and 18th.

L.   DECLARATIONS OF PRESENT BODILY CONDITION

Just as people make out-of-court assertions as to what is then on their mind, so also they quite frequently make out-of-court assertions concerning the state of their bodily health. These statements, made at the time the person is experiencing pain or some other bodily condition, certainly have probative value when the bodily condition at that time becomes a material issue in later litigation. However, when such a statement is used as evidence that the declarant was indeed feeling that pain, it falls within the definition of hearsay.

Recognizing that, as a source of information about a person's bodily condition at that earlier time, such statements are at least as reliable as the declarant's live testimony at a later trial, the common law has recognized an exception to the hearsay rule for statements of present bodily condition. Section 1250(a) recognizes this exception:

> Subject to Section 1252 [i.e., unless "made under circumstances such as to indicate its lack of trustworthiness"], evidence of a statement of ... the declarant's then existing ... physical sensation (including a statement of ... pain or bodily health) is not made inadmissible by the hearsay rule when:
>
> (1) The evidence is offered to prove the declarant's ... physical sensation at that time or at any other time when it is itself an issue in the action. ...

Although § 1250(a) states no such hard and fast rule, it is likely that its incorporation of § 1252's ban of statements made under untrustworthy circumstances would preclude use of statements to a doctor consulted solely for the purpose of testifying as an expert at trial.

The foundation for the exception to the hearsay rule for statements of present bodily condition includes these elements:

1. Where the statement was made.
2. When the statement was made.
3. Who was present.
4. Who made the statement.
5. Whom the statement was made.
6. The tenor of the statement: the declarant's then existing bodily condition.

The following fact situation is illustrative of this exception. Plaintiff, Ms. Gillette, brings a product liability action against defendant, Miller Pharmaceuticals, in which she alleges that defendant sold her a defective medication, which caused her serious internal injuries. She seeks damages that include compensation for pain and suffering. At the trial, plaintiff calls Dr. Wright as a witness. The plaintiff is the proponent:

P Dr. Wright, WHERE were you on the afternoon of January 28, 1999? (1), (2)
W In my office.
P WHO else was there? (3)
W The plaintiff, Ms. Joan Gillette.
P WHERE is the plaintiff now? (3)
W In this courtroom.
P Specifically, WHERE in the courtroom? (3)
W She's sitting next you at that trial table.

P   HOW is she dressed? (3)

W   She's wearing a white blouse and a green skirt.

P   Your Honor, please let the record reflect that the witness correctly identified plaintiff.

J   It will so reflect.

P   WHAT happened while the plaintiff was at your office? (3)

W   I examined her.

P   WHAT, if anything, did she say to you about her physical condition during the examination? (4), (5), (6)

O   Your Honor, I object to that question on the ground that it calls for self-serving hearsay.

P   Your Honor, may we approach the bench?

J   Counsel may come to the bench.

P   Your Honor, I concede that my question calls for hearsay. However, if permitted to testify, Dr. Wright will state that plaintiff told him that she was then in excruciating pain. That statement qualifies as a declaration of present bodily condition under § 1250.

O   Your Honor, I request permission to take the witness on voir dire before you rule on my objection.

J   Permission granted.

O   Dr. Wright, ISN'T IT TRUE THAT you didn't give Ms. Gillette any medicine during this examination?

W   No, I didn't.

O   ISN'T IT A FACT THAT the plaintiff never asked you for medication? (5)

W   She did not.

O   ISN'T IT TRUE THAT you never prescribed any treatment for her? (5)

W   That's correct.

O   AND ISN'T IT CORRECT THAT the plaintiff told you that she was consulting you at her attorney's direction so that you could testify at this trial? (5)

W   Yes, that's so.

O   Your Honor, I renew my objection. It's clear that Dr. Wright is a physician consulted solely for purposes of testimony. Ms. Gillette knew that what she told the doctor would not be acted upon by him in the form of any treatment or medication. She had an incentive to dramatize, exaggerate, even fabricate her pain. The hearsay statement is excludable under § 1252 because it was made in circumstances that indicate a lack of trustworthiness.

J   The objection will be sustained.

M.   STATEMENTS BY CHILD VICTIMS

1. THE DOCTRINE

In 1995, two new hearsay exceptions took effect. One is set out in Evidence Code § 1253. The first sentence of § 1253 is modeled after Federal Rule of Evidence 803(4). That sentence generally permits the introduction of a "statement ... made for purposes of medical diagnosis or treatment and describ[ing] medical history, or past or present symptoms, pain, or sensations, or the inception or general character of the cause or external source thereof insofar as reasonably pertinent to diagnosis or treatment." However, the second sentence of § 1253 narrows the scope of the statute to "only ... a statement made by a victim who is a minor at the time of the proceeding, provided the statement was made when the victim was under the age of 12 describing any act, or attempted act, of child abuse or neglect." *Cf., In re Carmen O.*, 28 Cal. App. 4th 908, 33 Cal. Rptr. 2d 848 (1994).

The legislature also added § 1360. Section 1360 differs from § 1253 in several respects. Whereas § 1253 applies in any type of proceeding, § 1360 applies only "[i]n a criminal prosecution where the victim is a minor." Moreover, whereas § 1253 requires a foundational showing that the statement was made for a specific purpose, that is, "for purposes of medical diagnosis or treatment." Section 1360 requires no such showing. In addition, unlike § 1253, § 1360 imposes a general requirement that the proponent demonstrate that "the time, content, and circumstances of the statement provide sufficient indicia of reliability." Section 1360 also imposes special procedural requirements absent from § 1253. In particular, § 1360(a)(3) specifies that the child "either: (A) Testifies at the proceedings. [or] (B) Is unavailable as a witness, in which case the statement may be admitted only if there is evidence of the child abuse or neglect that corroborates the statement made by the child." Section 1360(b) adds that the proponent of the statement must give the opposition advance notice of the proponent's intent to invoke § 1360.

2. ELEMENTS OF THE FOUNDATION

Under § 1253, the foundation includes these elements:

1. The statement was made by a proper declarant. That person must satisfy two criteria: He or she must have been under the age of 12 at the time of the statement, and he or she must still be a minor at the time of the proceeding in question. *See, e.g., People v. Brodit*, 61 Cal. App. 4th 1312, 72 Cal. Rptr. 2d 154 (1998) (statements of nine-year-old child abuse victim).
2. The declarant made the statement for a medical motive. Like Federal Rule 803(4), § 1253 refers, in the alternative, to "purposes of medical diagnosis or treatment." Ordinarily, that part of the victim's statement that identifies the perpetrator of the abuse is not made "for the purpose of medical diagnosis or treatment. However, where the abuser is a member of the victim's family or household, his or her identity is usually pertinent to the proper treatment of the victim." *People v. Brodit*, 61 Cal. App. 4th 1312, 1331, 72 Cal. Rptr. 2d 154, 165 (1998). A diagnosis for purpose of trial evidently suffices.

   The Advisory Committee Note to Federal Rule 803(4) expressly repudiates the "[c]onventional doctrine ... exclud(ing) from the hearsay exception, as not within its guarantee of truthfulness, statements to a physician consulted only for the purpose of enabling him to testify." Although the statutory language does not restrict the class of persons the statement may be made to, the identity of the addressee is a factor in determining whether the declarant spoke for a medical motive. It is easiest to find such a motive when the statement is directly addressed to a physician. The Advisory Committee Note indicates that under Rule 803(4), the judge can also find a motive when the addressee is a hospital attendant, ambulance driver, or even family member if the understanding was that that addressee will eventually relay the information to a physician.

3. The subject-matter of the statement was proper. Under § 1253, the statement must "describ[e] any act, or attempted act, of child abuse or neglect." Section 1253 concludes by defining those terms as "hav[ing] the meanings provided in subdivision (c) of Section 1360. In addition, 'child abuse' means any act proscribed by Chapter 5 (commencing with Section 281) of Title 9 of Part I of the Penal Code committed against a minor."

The foundation under § 1360 differs from § 1253. To invoke § 1360, the proponent may lay the following elements:

1. The proceeding falls within the scope of § 1360. Again, § 1360(a) indicates that this exception is available only "[i]n a criminal prosecution where the victim is a minor." *See, e.g., People v. Brodit*, 61 Cal. App. 4th 1312, 1329–1330, 72 Cal. Rptr. 2d 154, 163–164 (1998).

2. The statement was made by a proper declarant. The declarant must satisfy two criteria: The declarant must be the victim alleged in the accusatory pleading, and the declarant must have been under the age of 12 when the statement was made. *See, e.g., People v. Brodit*, 61 Cal. App. 4th 1312, 1329–1330, 72 Cal. Rptr. 2d 154, 163–164 (1998).

3. The subject-matter of the statement was proper. Under § 1360, the statement must "describ[e] any act of child abuse or neglect performed with or on the child ... or ... any attempted act of child abuse or neglect with or on the child ...." Subdivision 1360(c) sets out definitions of "child abuse" and "child neglect."

4. "[T]he time, content, and circumstances of the statement provide sufficient indicia of reliability." As previously stated, the hearsay rule guards against the probative dangers of perception, memory, narrative ability, and sincerity. The time of the statement—the period of time between the alleged event and the time of the statement—affects the magnitude of the risk of memory problems; generally, the longer the period, the greater is the danger of misrecollection. The content of the statement is relevant to two dangers. To begin with, the content of the statement should relate to a fact or event of which the declarant had firsthand knowledge. Further, the language of the statement relates to the risk of a danger in narration; the simpler the wording, the less the risk that the declarant expressed the meaning inaptly. Finally, the circumstances bear upon the question of whether the declarant had a motivation to be truthful or lie. Notice that this element dovetails with the second element of the § 1253 foundation; if the declarant had a medical

motive to speak, there is a stronger inference of sincerity. *See, e.g., People v. Brodit*, 61 Cal. App. 4th 1312, 1329–1330, 72 Cal. Rptr. 2d 154, 163–164 (1998).

5. Finally, the proponent must show either that "there is evidence of the child abuse or neglect that corroborates the statement made by the child."

3. SAMPLE FOUNDATION

The fact situation is a child abuse prosecution. The defendant is Paul Leslie. The prosecution alleges that the defendant abused his minor son, Walter. The prosecution calls Dr. Kevin Amar as its next witness.

P   Please state your full name and spell your last name for the record.

W   My name is Kevin Amar. My surname is spelled A - M - A - R.

P   Doctor Amar, WHERE do you live?

W   I live right here in Santa Monica.

P   WHAT is your occupation?

W   I am a licensed physician and psychiatrist in this state.

P   WHAT is your educational background?

W   I received my M.D. degree from Stanford University. I then did my internship at U.S.C. Medical Center. I next spent three years as a resident in psychiatry in New York. Since returning to California, I have specialized in pediatric psychiatry.

P   WHERE were you on the afternoon of November 12th last year?

W   That was the afternoon when the social worker, Ms. Lucey, brought Walter Leslie by my office.

P   WHERE is Walter right now?

W   He's in the courtroom. He's sitting in the first row of the spectators' area of the courtroom.

P   HOW is he dressed?

W   He's wearing a blue suit, white shirt, and green tie.

P   Your Honor, please let the record reflect that the witness has identified Walter Leslie, the alleged victim in this case.

J   The record will so reflect.

P   Doctor Amar, when Walter arrived, HOW did you identify yourself to him?

W   I told him that I was Doctor Amar and that I was going to talk to him to see if I could help him.

P   During the rest of the meeting, HOW did he refer to you?

W   As I recall, he called me either "Doctor" or "Doctor Amar."

P   After you identified yourself, WHAT did you tell him about the purpose of your interview with him?

W   I told him that I wanted to talk to him to see if I could help him. I told him that I heard that he was having some emotional problems, and I wanted to see if I could help him overcome those problems.

P   WHAT, if anything, did he say about his reason for coming to see you?

W   He said that Ms. Lucey had told him that I was a doctor and he had agreed to visit me to obtain some medical advice about his problems.

(During this part of the direct examination, the prosecutor would elicit Walter's statements generally describing his emotional problems and the abuse which caused the problems. The direct examination continues.)

P   According to Walter, WHEN did these events occur?

W   He said that they had all happened in the prior two months.

P   WHAT, if anything, did you ask Walter about the identity of the person who had abused him?

W   I asked him point-blank who did it.

P   WHY did you do that?

W   I needed to know about that for both diagnostic and therapeutic purposes.

P   Please be more specific. HOW could the identity of the abuser affect your diagnosis in Walter's case?

W   Well, to confirm a diagnosis, you need to review the case history to see if it contains an indication of symptoms appropriate for that diagnosis. When the abuser is a family member—someone the child has trusted and who then betrayed the child—you expect different symptoms than those you encounter when the child is abused by a stranger. In cases of abuse by a stranger, you may find a phobia about leaving the house and going out into public. In cases of abuse by a family member, you'll often have a phobia about remaining in the home.

P   And HOW might the identity of the abuser affect the treatment prescribed in Walter's case?

W   If the abuser is a family member likely to remain in the household, you have to consider the drastic step of having the child removed from the home environment and at least temporarily placed in foster care. That's a big step, since it's so disruptive of the family unit; and you ordinarily wouldn't recommend that intervention as part of the treatment except in cases of intrafamily abuse.

P   When you asked Walter about the identity of the abuser, WHAT did you tell him about your reason for wanting to know that?

W   That's such a delicate subject that you want to try to put the patient at ease as much as possible. Before I put the question to Walter, I explained that my medical advice would depend on who had abused him. In very general terms, I told him that I'd make one type of recommendation if the person were a stranger and a different recommendation if the person were a friend or family member.

P   When you asked him about the identity of the abuser, HOW did you word your question?

W   I tried to choose simple terms, since I knew I was speaking with a minor. I said something like, "Walter, please tell me who did those things to you."

P   Doctor Amar, WHOM did Walter name as the person who had been abusing him?

W   His father, Paul Leslie.

P   To the best of your recollection, WHAT were Walter's exact words?

W   He began to sob, but he clearly said, "My daddy, Paul."

Given appropriate additional facts, this testimony could be admissible under both § 1253 and § 1360. The testimony could be admitted under § 1253 if Walter were under the age of 12 at the time of the incident and still a minor at the time of the proceeding. The testimony could also be introduced under § 1360 on the following assumptions: Either Walter testified at the proceeding, or he was unavailable within the meaning of that term in Evidence Code § 240 and there was some corroboration for his statement.

Part 4. Hearsay Exceptions That Require Unavailability

In Sections D-M, we discussed the major hearsay exceptions that do not include as part of their foundation a showing that the hearsay declarant is in one way or another unavailable to testify at trial (however, see possible unavailability requirement of child victims under Evidence Code § 1360, discussed in Section M of this chapter). In Sections N-U, we will analyze the exceptions that do require proof of the declarant's unavailability as a trial witness.

Evidence Code § 240(a) contains a definition of the phrase "unavailable as a witness," which is then used in a number of the statutes defining hearsay exceptions. The categories of unavailability sort into two broad groupings: (1) those where the declarant is not physically present at the trial because of: (a) death; (b) disabling physical illness or infirmity; (c) disabling mental illness or infirmity; (d) location beyond the reach of the court's subpoena power; or (e) whereabouts unknown even after diligent search; and (2) those where the declarant is physically in court but (a) is disqualified from testifying, usually because of incompetence to comprehend an oath; or (b) is blocked from testifying by some claim of privilege.

On its face, § 240(a) purports to deem a hearsay declarant unavailable any time that person is situated outside the borders of the state. This presents no problem in civil cases, or indeed in criminal cases where hearsay is offered by the accused against the prosecution. However, in *Barber v. Page*, 390 U.S. 719 (1968), the Supreme Court held that the Confrontation Clause requires the prosecution to make a good faith, reasonable effort to induce a witness located in a sister state to voluntarily attend the trial. It is not enough to show that the witness is technically beyond the reach of compulsory process. If the declarant is located in a state that has adopted the Uniform Act to Secure the Attendance of Witnesses from Without the State in Criminal Cases, the prosecution must have tried unsuccessfully to avail itself of these procedures.

Notable omissions from this list are two categories that are included in the definition of unavailability set forth in the Federal Rules of Evidence: (1) persistent refusal to testify about the subject matter of the earlier statement even after the trial court orders a response, [Rule 804(b)(2)]; and (2) present lack of memory of the matter earlier asserted in the out-of-court statement [Rule 804(b)(3)]. To some extent, the California courts have compensated for the Legislature's failure to include contumacious refusal to testify and memory loss among the categories of unavailability listed in § 240. For example, in *People v. Rojas*, 15 Cal. 3d 540, 125 Cal. Rptr. 357, 542 P.2d 229 (1975), the California Supreme Court deemed "mental infirmity" in § 240(a)(3) to cover a witness's fear to testify because of threats against his own safety and that of his family. And in *People v. Alcala*, 4 Cal. 4th 742, 777-80, 15 Cal. Rptr. 2d 432, 452-54, 842 P.2d 1192, 1212-14 (1992), the court found a "mental infirmity" in a witness's memory loss traceable to a stress-related disability that had intervened between the time of the hearsay statement and the time of the trial.

In *People v. Reed,* 13 Cal. 4th 217, 226-227, 52 Cal. Rptr. 2d 106, 112, 914 P.2d 184-90 (1996), the Supreme Court held that Evidence Code § 240 should not be interpreted "so strictly as to preclude unlisted variants of unavailability. Rather, courts have given the statutes a realistic construction consistent with their purpose, i.e., to ensure that certain types of hearsay, including former testimony, are admitted only when no preferable version of the evidence, in the form of live testimony, is legally and physically available." See also *People v. Lopez,* 64 Cal. App. 4th 1122, 76 Cal. Rptr. 2d 38 (1998) (since Penal Code § 1337(4) allows a conditional examination of a witness who "is about to leave the state," later use of that testimony at trial if the witness is then out of state falls under *Reed's* flexible, pragmatic approach to the "unavailability" concept). In *People v. Sul*, 122 Cal. App. 3d 355, 175 Cal. Rptr. 893 (1981), a witness simply defied a court order to answer certain questions. The court acknowledged that conduct of the witness "is not covered by any of the provisions of Evidence Code section 240." *Id.* at 362, 175 Cal. Rptr. at 897. It then suggested that the witness's wrongful refusal would render him unavailable "if the court makes a finding of unavailability ... after taking reasonable steps to induce the witness to testify." *Id.* at 364-65, 175 Cal. Rptr. at 899. *See also People v. Francis*, 200 Cal. App. 3d 579, 587, 245 Cal. Rptr. 923, 927-28 (1988) ("A witness who is physically available yet refuses to testify, after the court has used all available avenues to coerce such testimony, is unavailable. This is true even though such a witness does not fit neatly into one of the subdivisions of Evidence Code section 240.").

N.   FORMER TESTIMONY

1. THE DOCTRINE

The definition of hearsay contained in § 1200(a) covers any statement "other than by a witness while testifying at the hearing." Section 145, in turn, restricts the phrase "the hearing" to the one "at which a question under this code arises, and not some earlier or later hearing." This means that a transcript of live testimony given at an earlier proceeding—even at a previous trial or hearing of this very case—is considered hearsay when it is offered in lieu of the declarant's live testimony at the present trial.

Obtaining a person's relevant information out of a transcript of his or her testimony at a former proceeding is clearly inferior to procuring it by live testimony at the instant trial. To be sure, the earlier testimony was given under oath, and there may have been an opportunity to cross-examine the witness, but the present trier of fact is being denied the opportunity to observe the demeanor of the declarant during direct and cross-examination. Accordingly, if the one who testified on the earlier occasion is available to provide live testimony in the instant proceeding, an attempt to use instead that person's former testimony can be blocked by an objection under the hearsay rule. Given a choice between obtaining a person's relevant information by live testimony, or by hearsay in the form of former testimony, the court system opts for and insists upon the live testimony.

Although former testimony is hearsay and inferior to live testimony, it often possesses features of special reliability that will lead the courts to permit its use in the exigency created when the person who gave the testimony on the earlier occasion is shown to be "unavailable as a witness" at the instant hearing. Here the court's choice is different than the one described above. The choice is between using a very reliable form of hearsay, and forgoing altogether the relevant information known to the now unavailable declarant.

Former testimony has two features of special reliability. First, it was given under oath. Second, the former testimony must have been presented (1) either by the party against whom it is now offered; or (2) against a party who had the right and opportunity to cross-examine the declarant with an interest and motive that is similar to that which the party would have at the present trial.

The original common-law version of the former testimony exception contained a strict requirement of identity of parties. This meant that the parties involved in present trial had to be the same as those who were involved in the proceeding at which the earlier testimony was given. This requirement was soon relaxed somewhat by requiring only that both the party offering the former testimony and the party against whom it is being offered each have been parties to the earlier proceeding. The presence or absence of additional parties made no difference.

An intermediate view gradually has come into vogue. Under this approach, it no longer matters whether the party offering the former testimony was a party to the earlier proceeding. The important thing is that the party against whom it is now being offered was a party to the earlier proceeding. Sometimes that party will have presented the earlier testimony. More often, the testimony will have been offered against that party whose motive and interest for thorough cross-examination at the earlier proceeding will have been similar to that at the present trial. In either event, the former testimony is admissible in the present proceeding in the event the one who gave it is shown now to be "unavailable as a witness." Suppose that several passengers are injured when an airplane crashes during landing. Passengers *A* and *B* file separate suits against the airline. In trial #1, passenger *A* introduces the testimony of a safety engineer. The airline then has the opportunity to subject the engineer to cross-examination. Subsequently, in trial #2, passenger *B*, after showing that the expert engineer has died, offers the testimony given during *A*'s trial against the airline. The former testimony is admissible against the airline because it was given in a setting where the airline had a motive and interest in cross-examining the engineer that is similar to the motive and interest it would now have if the engineer were available for live testimony at *B*'s trial. This intermediate view is reflected in § 1291(a):

> Evidence of former testimony is not made inadmissible by the hearsay rule if the declarant is unavailable as a witness and:

(1) The former testimony is offered against a person who offered it in evidence in his own behalf on the former occasion or against the successor in interest of such person; or

(2) The party against whom the former testimony is offered was a party to the action or proceeding in which the testimony was given and had the right and opportunity to cross-examine the declarant with an interest and motive similar to that which he has at the hearing.

Although the Evidence Code adopts the intermediate view, it then takes a significant step beyond it. Suppose that in our plane crash hypothetical, when passenger A's case came to trial, the engineer had testified for the airline. When passenger B's case comes to trial, it develops that the engineer has become, in one way or another, "unavailable as a witness" within the meaning of § 240. May the airline offer the engineer's earlier testimony against passenger B? On the one hand, passenger B has had no opportunity to cross-examine the engineer. On the other hand, passenger A did have that opportunity, and his motive and interest in doing so was similar to that which passenger B now has. In the emergency presented by the unavailability of the engineer, the former testimony is reliable enough for consideration by the trier of fact at the second trial. Accordingly, § 1292(a) provides:

Evidence of former testimony is not made inadmissible by the hearsay rule if:

(1) The declarant is unavailable as a witness;

(2) The former testimony is offered in a civil action; and

(3) The issue is such that the party to the action or proceeding in which the former testimony was given had the right and opportunity to cross-examine the declarant with an interest and motive similar to that which the party against whom the testimony is offered has at the hearing.

The notion that cross-examination by proxy may suffice to surmount a hearsay objection to the earlier testimony is expressly confined to civil cases. § 1292(a)(2). This limitation is doubtless traceable to concerns that in criminal trials, the Confrontation Clause would be implicated if evidence were admitted against an accused simply because some similarly interested person had had an opportunity to cross-examine the witness.

2. ELEMENTS OF THE FOUNDATION

The foundation for use of testimony given at another hearing under the former testimony exception to the hearsay rule varies depending on whether the proponent is offering the former testimony against (1) one who presented it at that earlier hearing; or (2) one against whom it was presented at that earlier hearing; or (3) one who was not a party to that earlier hearing.

(1) Against One Who Earlier Presented the Testimony

1. Hearing #1 was a former trial or hearing of the instant action; or another action; or a proceeding to determine a controversy conducted by a federal agency or some public entity in the United States; or an arbitration proceeding. *See* § 1290.
2. The party against whom the prior testimony is offered was a party to hearing #1.
3. That party offered the testimony of the witness at hearing #1.
4. The person who testified at hearing #1 has become "unavailable as a witness" at hearing #2.
5. There is properly authenticated proof of the prior testimony: a transcript certified by the reporter; or the reporter's reading of his or her notes; or the testimony of a person who heard and recollects the earlier testimony.

(2) Against One Against Whom the Testimony Was Presented

1. Hearing #1 was a former trial or hearing of the instant action; or another action; or a proceeding to determine a controversy conducted by a federal agency or some public entity in the United States; or an arbitration proceeding. *See* § 1290.
2. The party against whom the prior testimony is offered was a party to hearing #1.
3. That party had the opportunity to cross-examine the witness at hearing #1. *People v. Jones,* 66 Cal. App. 4th 760, 768, 78 Cal. Rptr. 2d 265, 270 (1998) (at his initial trial for murder the defendant was erroneously denied his constitutional right to represent himself; at his re-trial the defendant, now representing himself, objected to the prosecution's use of the first trial testimony of three now unavailable witnesses; *held:* although the denial to defendant of his constitutional right to self-representation prevented him from personally cross-examining these witnesses at the first trial, this does not necessarily mean that his right to effective cross-examination was denied; "the constitutional defect was *not* directly related to the effectiveness of the cross-examination. Appointed counsel presumably can conduct a *more* effective cross-examination than a self-represented one can. . . . [D]efendant never explained precisely *what* he would have done differently. Therefore, he never showed his cross-examination would have been any more effective.").
4. That party's motive and interest for cross-examination of the witness at hearing #1 was similar to that party's current motive. *People v. Lepe,* 57 Cal. App. 4th 977, 984, 67 Cal. Rptr. 2d 525, 529 (1997) ("Counsel's motive for the cross-examination in this case was the same at the preliminary hearing because, in both instances, defendant's counsel was seeking to show the bias of the witness and his motive to lie"); *People v.*

Samayoa, 15 Cal. 4th 795, 850, 64 Cal. Rptr. 2d 400, 437, 938 P.2d 2, 39 (1997) (motive to cross-examine need only be "similar," not "identical").

5. The person who testified at hearing #1 has become "unavailable as a witness" at hearing #2.
6. There is properly authenticated proof of the prior testimony: a transcript certified by the reporter; or the reporter's reading of his or her notes; or the testimony of a person who heard and recollects the earlier testimony.

(3) Against One Not a Party to Earlier Proceeding

1. Hearing #1 was another action; or a proceeding to determine a controversy conducted by a federal agency or some public entity in the United States; or an arbitration proceeding. *See* § 1290.
2. The current hearing is a civil action.
3. The party against whom the prior testimony was offered at hearing #1 had an opportunity to cross-examine the witness.
4. That party's motive and interest for cross-examination of the witness at hearing #1 was similar to the motive and interest for cross-examination of the party against whom the former testimony is being offered in the present case. *See Gatton v. A.P. Green Services, Inc.,* 64 Cal. App. 4th 688, 75 Cal. Rptr. 2d 523 (1998) (asbestos company defendants in earlier civil case, to which the present defendant was not a party, did not have an interest in rebutting a deponent's testimony in that earlier case that the present defendant's product was installed in the plant where plaintiffs claim their decedent was exposed to the asbestos that caused his fatal disease).
5. The person who testified at hearing #1 has become "unavailable as a witness" at hearing #2.
6. There is properly authenticated proof of the prior testimony: a transcript certified by the reporter; or the reporter's reading of his or her notes; or the testimony of a person who heard and recollects the earlier testimony.

3. SAMPLE FOUNDATIONS

a. Illustrations of "Unavailability" Element

Section 240 lists the various situations that will qualify to make a declarant "unavailable as a witness" as that term is used in §§ 1291-1292, California's version of the former testimony exception to the hearsay rule. Suppose, for example, that the proponent wants to demonstrate that the whereabouts of the one who testified at the earlier proceeding are now unknown. The proponent might call a process server as a witness:

P WHAT is your name?
W Michael Senet.
P WHERE do you live?

W At 1440 Alsworth Street here in Fresno.

P HOW long have you lived there?

W For the past five years.

P WHAT is your occupation?

W I am a process server.

P WHERE do you work?

W I work for the Speedy Process Service Company downtown.

P HOW long have you worked there?

W Three years.

P HOW long have you been a process server?

W Three years.

P Mr. Senet, WHERE were you on the morning of January 17 of this year?

W I stopped by your office.

P WHY did you visit my office?

W You had phoned and asked me to pick up a subpoena.

P WHO was the subpoena for?

W John Milton.

P WHAT was his address?

W Both the subpoena and the telephone directory listed his address as 40 Oxford Street, Apartment 201.

P WHAT did you do after you picked up the subpoena?

W I went directly to the address given.

P WHAT happened when you arrived there?

W I inquired whether he still lived there.

P WHAT was the result of your inquiry?

O Your Honor, I object to that question on the ground that it calls for hearsay.

P Your Honor. may we approach the bench?

J Counsel may come to the bench.

P Your Honor, I offer to prove that this witness will testify that the manager said Mr. Milton had moved. I want to use the testimony for a nonhearsay purpose, its effect on the process server's state of mind. The issue is whether the process server acted reasonably and diligently. We have to judge his diligence in light of the information about Mr. Milton he was given by other persons such as the apartment manager.

J The objection will be overruled.

P Mr. Senet, let me repeat the question. WHAT was the result of your inquiry at Mr. Milton's apartment?

W The manager said he had moved.

P WHAT was Mr. Milton's new address?

W Unfortunately, he did not leave a forwarding address.

P WHAT did you do then?

W Over the next few days I contacted other companies and agencies that might have Milton's new address.

P WHICH companies and agencies did you contact?

W To list just some, I talked to people at the telephone company, the gas company, the electric company, and the welfare department.

P WHAT was the result of your contact with these companies and agencies?

W It was negative. None of them knew where I could locate Mr. Milton.

P HOW many hours did you spend talking to people at these companies and agencies?

W Over the period of days, I'd estimate I spent at least ten full hours trying to hunt him down.

P Mr. Senet, WHERE is Mr. Milton now?

W I'm afraid that I have no idea.

See People v. Sanders, 11 Cal. 4th 475, 522-25, 46 Cal. Rptr. 2d 751, 775-77, 905 P.2d 420, 450-52 (1995) (the defense did not make a diligent, good faith search to secure a witness's presence; even though the defense knew that the individual was "not ... a totally reliable person," the defense made no effort to subpoena the witness until well into trial; the defense did make a single phone call to her former work number and several visits to her former address, but it did not appear that any relatives, friends, or coworkers had been contacted); *People v. Lopez,* 64 Cal. App. 4th 1122, 76 Cal. Rptr 2d 38 (1998) ("due diligence" shown where prosecution subpoenaed crime victim for trial, launched investigation into her whereabouts when she did return telephone calls, and did not learn until eve of trial a possible address in Las Vegas to which she had gone); *People v. Lepe,* 57 Cal. App. 4th 977, 986, 67 Cal. Rptr. 2d 525, 530 (1997) (search for missing witness was "diligent" when it commenced two months before trial, and included checks of DMV, arrest, and incarceration records, interviews with his relatives, and spot visits to various places associated with him); *People v. Wise,* 25 Cal. App. 4th 339, 30 Cal. Rptr. 2d 413, 415-16 (1994) (the prosecution exercised due diligence; "the witness was a citizen-victim. He was not facing criminal charges and the record does not indicate any reason for the prosecution to believe he would disappear").

Suppose that in a suit for personal injuries arising out of a traffic accident, plaintiff wants to show that one Mr. Green, who was a passenger in his car, is beyond the reach of compulsory process and refuses to voluntarily come to the site of trial. At the first trial of the case, Mr. Green testified on behalf of plaintiff. This trial resulted in a judgment for plaintiff, but on appeal this was reversed and a new trial ordered. After the first trial, Mr. Green moved from California to Minnesota. At trial #2, plaintiff, desiring to offer Mr. Green's testimony at the earlier trial, takes the stand to establish his unavailability:

P WHO were your witnesses at the first trial in this case?

W Myself, Officer Halston, and a Mr. Ted Green.

P WHERE does Mr. Green live now?

W In St. Paul, Minnesota.

P HOW do you know that?

W For one thing, I've received letters from him postmarked St. Paul, Minnesota.

P HOW do you know the letters came from Mr. Green?

W I recognized his handwriting.

P HOW did you recognize his handwriting?

W I'm familiar with it. We worked together for several years, and I saw his handwriting on numerous occasions.

P WHAT else makes you think he now lives in Minnesota?
W I tried to contact him by telephone. I went through the operator in St. Paul and eventually reached him.
P HOW do you know you were speaking with Mr. Green?
W I recognized his voice just as I recognized his handwriting.

The proponent could end the questioning here, because under § 240(a)(4), a declarant is unavailable if he or she is beyond the reach of compulsory process. However, to impress the judge and jurors with his good faith, the proponent continues:

P WHERE is Mr. Green today?
W I don't know for sure.
P WHERE was he when you last spoke with him?
W In St. Paul.
P WHY isn't he here today to testify?
W He refused to come.
P HOW do you know that?
W I asked him to come during our last telephone conversation, and he said he was too tied up with his business to come.
P HOW do you know that?
W I phoned him several times. I even volunteered to pick up the tab for his airline ticket. He just won't cooperate.

b. The Other Elements of the Foundation

We shall first illustrate the testimony of a spectator who happens to remember the substance of the witness's testimony at hearing #1. Our fact situation is a homicide prosecution. The People charge that Joe Gentile murdered his wife. An eyewitness to the killing, John Walton, testified at the preliminary hearing. Walton died after the hearing and before the trial. The prosecution has already established Walton's unavailability by introducing a properly attested death certificate. Now the prosecutor calls Pamela Martin to lay the other elements of the foundation. The prosecutor is the proponent. Ms. Martin has already identified herself.

P Ms. Martin, WHERE were you on the afternoon of March 12, 2000?
W I was in another courtroom in this building.
P WHAT were you doing there?
W I was a spectator at a court proceeding.
P WHY were you there?
W I had read a lot about the case in the papers, and I was interested in watching it.
P WHAT proceeding did you see on the afternoon of March 12, 2000? (2), (3), (4)
W It was the preliminary hearing in this case.
P WHO was there attending the hearing? (2)
W For one, the defendant himself, Mr. Gentile.
P WHERE is Mr. Gentile now? (2)
W He's in the courtroom right now.

P Specifically, WHERE in the courtroom? (2)

W Over there at the end of that table.

P HOW is he dressed? (2)

W He's wearing a blue suit, white shirt, and red tie.

P Your Honor, please let the record reflect that the witness has identified the defendant.

J It will so reflect.

P WHAT happened at this hearing you attended on March 12th? (1)

W They called witnesses to testify.

P WHAT did they do when they first called the witnesses to the stand? (3)

W They would take an oath.

P WHO questioned the witnesses? (3)

W Usually the prosecutor would start, and then the defense counsel would ask questions.

P WHO asked questions on behalf of the defendan t? (3)

W An attorney. I honestly can't remember her name.

P WHO were the witnesses that day?

W There were three who stand out in my mind.

P WHO were they?

W A police officer named Strait, a doctor, and an eyewitness. The eyewitness was on the stand most of the day.

P WHO was the eyewitness?

W His name was John Walton.

P HOW long was he on the stand?

W About three hours.

P HOW much of his testimony did you hear?

W All of it.

P HOW often did you leave the room while he was on the stand?

W I didn't. I wanted to hear all of it. It was very interesting.

P HOW well could you hear Mr. Walton while he testified?

W Very well. I didn't have any problem hearing him.

P HOW loudly was he speaking?

W In a normal voice, but his voice carried well.

P HOW close were you sitting to him while he was on the stand?

W About 15 feet away. I was in the very first row for the spectators.

P HOW well do you remember his testimony?

W Very well. I was very interested.

P WHAT did he say during his testimony?

O Your Honor, I object to that question on the ground that it calls for hearsay.

P Your Honor, may we approach the bench?

J Yes.

P Your Honor, I concede that the testimony will be hearsay. However, it falls within the former testimony exception. The witness's testimony shows that there was oath, cross-examination, and counsel at the preliminary hearing. Since it was the preliminary hearing in this case, there's obviously sufficient identity of issues and parties. Finally, the death certificate shows that the former witness is now unavailable.

J   The objection will be overruled.

P   Ms. Martin, let me repeat the question. WHAT did Mr. Walton say during his testimony?

We shall now illustrate the use of a properly attested transcript of the former testimony. To do so, we shall continue the same hypothetical. In this variation of the hypothetical, there is a documentary transcript of the preliminary hearing. Assume that the prosecutor has already introduced Mr. Walton s death certificate.

P   Your Honor, I request that this be marked People's exhibit #7 for identification.

J   It will be so marked.

P   Please let the record reflect that I am showing the exhibit to the opposing counsel.

J   The record will so reflect.

P   I now offer People's exhibit #7 for identification into evidence as People's exhibit #7.

O   Your Honor, I object to the introduction of the exhibit on the ground that the exhibit is hearsay.

P   Your Honor, may we approach the bench?

J   Yes.

P   Your Honor, I concede that exhibit is hearsay; but it is a properly certified transcript, and it falls within the former testimony exception.

O   Where is the foundation for the former testimony exception?

P   The transcript purports to be the record of the preliminary hearing in this case. There is obviously identity of issues and parties. I've already introduced Mr. Walton's death certificate, showing his unavailability. Page 2 of the transcript shows that the defendant had counsel at the hearing; page 142 shows that the defense had an opportunity to cross-examine Mr. Walton.

J   I agree. The objection will be overruled, and the exhibit will be received.

P   Your Honor, I request permission to read pages 22-53 to the jurors. I shall read the questions, and my clerk will take the witness stand and read the answers.

J   Permission granted.

O. SWORN STATEMENTS REGARDING GANG-RELATED CRIMES

1. THE DOCTRINE

Article 2.5 (§§ 1231-1231.4) of the Evidence Code provides a new exception to the hearsay rule, entitled "Sworn Statements Regarding Gang-Related Crimes." This exception features a unique and narrow "unavailability" requirement, namely, that the declarant must be deceased and have died from other than natural causes. The declarant's hearsay statements must have been made under oath or affirmation, as well satisfying a distinct set of additional requirements listed in § 1231. Also unique under this new exception is that a peace officer may administer and certify oaths for purposes of this new article, which may include the taking of a sworn affidavit.

The following quotation is the text of the statutes, followed by a statement of legislative intent that accompanied the Act.

Article 2.5 Sworn Statements Regarding Gang-Related Crimes

§ 1231. Evidence of a prior statement made by a declarant is not made inadmissible by the hearsay rule if the declarant is deceased and the proponent introducing the statement establishes each of the following:

(a) The statement relates to acts or events relevant to a criminal prosecution under provisions of the California Street Terrorism Enforcement and Prevention Act (Chapter 11 (commencing with Section 186.20) of Title 7 of Part 1 of the Penal Code).

(b) A verbatim transcript, copy, or record of the statement exists. A record may include a statement preserved by means of an audio or video recording or equivalent technology.

(c) The statement relates to acts or events within the personal knowledge of the declarant.

(d) The statement was made under oath or affirmation in an affidavit; or was made at a deposition, preliminary hearing, grand jury hearing, or other proceeding in compliance with law, and was made under penalty of perjury.

(e) The declarant died from other than natural causes.

(f) The statement was made under circumstances that would indicate its trustworthiness and render the declarant's statement particularly worthy of belief. For purposes of this subdivision, circumstances relevant to the issue of trustworthiness include, but are not limited to, all of the following:

(1) Whether the statement was made in contemplation of a pending or anticipated criminal or civil matter, in which the declarant had an interest, other than as a witness.

(2) Whether the declarant had a bias or motive for fabricating the statement, and the extent of any bias or motive.

(3) Whether the statement is corroborated by evidence other than statements that are admissible only pursuant to this section.

(4) Whether the statement was a statement against the declarant's interest.

§ 1231.1 A statement is admissible pursuant to Section 1231 only if the proponent of the statement makes known to the adverse party the intention to offer the statement and the particulars of the statement sufficiently in advance of the proceedings to provide the adverse party with a fair opportunity to prepare to meet the statement.

§ 1231.2 A peace officer may administer and certify oaths for purposes of this article.

§ 1231.3 Any law enforcement officer testifying as to any hearsay statement pursuant to this article shall either have five years of law enforcement experience or have completed a training course certified by the Commission on Peace Officer Standards and Training which includes training in the investigation and reporting of cases and testifying at preliminary hearings and trials.

§ 1231.4 If evidence of a prior statement is introduced pursuant to this article, the jury may not be told that the declarant died from other than natural causes, but shall merely be told that the declarant is unavailable.

Pursuant to Stats. 1997, ch. 499, § 2:

This act shall not affect other evidentiary requirements, including, but not limited to, Sections 351 and 352 of the Evidence Code, shall not impair a party's right to attack the credibility of the declarant pursuant to Section 1202 of the Evidence Code, shall not affect the defendant's right to discovery for purposes of producing rebuttal evidence attacking the declarant's credibility, and shall not be used in a manner inconsistent with the defendant's right to due process and to confront witnesses under the United States or California Constitution.

P. DECLARATIONS AGAINST INTEREST

1. THE DOCTRINE

When a person makes an out-of-court statement that asserts some fact that is against his or her interest, that statement has a feature of special reliability that sets it apart from raw hearsay. Because it is against that person's interest for the fact to be true, he or she is most unlikely to falsely claim that the fact is true. Moreover, when the fact perceived runs contrary to one's interest, there is a special incentive to check the accuracy of the initial perception, to be sure of one's memory of it before speaking or writing about it, and to be careful in the choice of words used to describe it.

Standing alone, this unusual feature of reliability flowing from the against-interest nature of an out-of-court statement does not suffice to remove it from the exclusion of the hearsay rule. Our system of evidence still prefers that the declarant come to court, take the stand, and provide the trier of fact with sworn, cross-examined testimony about the fact he or she claims to have perceived. However, the law's attitude changes in the event that the declarant has become "unavailable as a witness." Given the choice between such reliable hearsay, and forgoing the declarant's information altogether, the common law of evidence gradually became more and more willing to admit an out-of-court declaration that asserts as a fact something that was then against the declarant's interest.

California's version of the exception to the hearsay rule for declarations against interest is found in § 1230:

> Evidence of a statement by a declarant having sufficient knowledge of the subject is not made inadmissible by the hearsay rule if the declarant is unavailable as a witness and the statement, when made, was so far contrary to the declarant's pecuniary or proprietary interest, or so far subjected him to the risk of civil or criminal liability, or so far tended to render invalid a claim by him against another, or created such a risk of making him an object of hatred, ridicule, or social disgrace in the community, that a reasonable man in his position would not have made the statement unless he believed it to be true.

Section 1230 is broad enough to permit the admission of declarations against penal interest against the accused in a criminal case. *People v. Greenberger*, 58 Cal. App. 4th 298, 329, 68 Cal. Rptr. 2d 61, 77 (1997) upheld its constitutionality against a challenge that this application of the statute violated the Confrontation Clause: "In order for a statement to qualify as a declaration against penal interest the statement must be genuinely and specifically inculpatory of the declarant; this provides the 'particularized guarantee of trustworthiness' or 'indicia of reliability' that permits its admission in evidence without the constitutional requirement of cross-examination. Therefore, the determination that the statement fall within this hearsay exception also satisfies the requirements of the confrontation clause."

Moreover, if a statement by X, who is not a party to a criminal case, would be admissible against the accused because it was against X's interest at the time it was made, the result should be no different if declarant X is a codefendant: "Since declarations against interest may be admitted in evidence without doing violence to the confrontation clause, we see no reason why such declarations, when made by a codefendant, should not also be admissible." 58 Cal. App. 4th at 332, 68 Cal. Rptr. 2d at 79. *See also People v. Fuentes*, 61 Cal. App. 4th 956, 72 Cal. Rptr. 2d 237 (1998).

Admissions of a party-opponent differ from declarations against interest in three major ways. First, an admission need not be against the interest of the declarant at the time it is made. Second, the declarant of an admission need not be shown to be unavailable to provide live testimony at the time of the trial. Third, an, admission need not be based on the personal knowledge of the declarant.

2. ELEMENTS OF THE FOUNDATION

The foundation for the exception to the hearsay rule for declarations against interest includes the following elements:

1. At the time of making the statement, the declarant actually realized that the fact being asserted was one that was contrary to his or her interest. Read

literally, § 1230 eliminates this common-law element of the foundation. It appears that the standard is an objective one: only a reasonable person, not necessarily the specific declarant, need realize that the statement is against interest. Article, *Declarations Against Interest in California arid Federal Courts*, 9 U.C. DAVIS L. REV. 119, 138 (1976). However, proof of the declarant's subjective belief will increase the weight of the evidence in the jury's mind, and the proponent should attempt to lay this element of the common-law foundation. Even a statement by a third party admitting that he, and not the defendant, had committed a murder will not automatically qualify as a declaration against interest. "In determining whether a statement is truly against interest .... the court must take into account not just the words but the circumstances under which they were uttered, the possible motivation of the declarant, and the declarant's relationship to the defendant." *People v. Frierson*, 53 Cal. 3d 730, 745, 280 Cal. Rptr. 440, 448, 808 P.2d 1197, 1205 (1991); *People v. Lucas*, 12 Cal. 4th 415, 907 P.2d 373, 48 Cal. Rptr. 2d 525, 554-55, 907 P.2d 373, 402-403 (1995).

2. The interest to which the statement is contrary is one that qualifies under the law of evidence. All jurisdictions recognize pecuniary and proprietary interest, and most jurisdictions have expanded those categories to admit any statement that would subject the declarant to civil liability. Many jurisdictions now recognize penal interest, and a few admit statements contrary to social interest. California is one of those few.

3. The declarant has now become "unavailable as a witness" as that term is defined in § 240(a).

In some jurisdictions, if the defense offers a third party's confession to the crime for which the defendant is on trial on the theory that the confession is a declaration against interest, there must be clear corroboration that the third party committed the crime. *See* Federal Rule of Evidence 803(b)(3). This is not a part of the foundation under § 1230. Moreover, it is not part of the foundation that the trial judge be persuaded as to the credibility of the trial witness who is claiming that the declarant made a statement against interest. *See People v. Cudjo*, 6 Cal. 4th 585, 609, 25 Cal. Rptr. 2d 390, 405, 863 P.2d 635, 650 (1993) ("[D]oubts about the credibility of the in-court witness should be left for the jury's resolution; such doubts do not afford a ground for refusing to admit evidence under the hearsay exception for statements against penal interest.")

Sometimes the same statement will assert several facts. Some of the facts will be against the declarant's interest, but other facts will be either neutral or self-serving. May the statement be used to prove the truth of the neutral or self-serving facts? Some jurisdictions consider that the declaration against interest exception embraces not only the disserving facts, but also the "collateral facts" that are self-serving or neutral to the declarant's interest. They reason that if one is making a statement that includes a fact that is against his or her interest, one is probably in a truth-telling state of mind during the entire statement.

California decisions reject the "collateral statement" rule. They admit only those parts of a statement that were "specifically disserving" to the declarant's interest. The United States Supreme Court has reached essentially the same conclusion in its interpretation of Federal Rule of Evidence 804(b)(3). *Williamson v. United States*, 512 U.S. 594, 114 S. Ct. 2431, 129 L. Ed. 2d 476 (1994). In *Williamson*, the majority ruled that the only portions of the declaration which are admissible are those which are inculpatory to the declarant himself or herself. Under *Williamson*, the trial judge must analyze the statement "sentence by sentence." *United States v. Canan*, 48 F.3d 954, 960 (6th Cir. 1995). The analysis must be "segmented" rather than "aggregate." *United States v. Sims*, 879 F. Supp. 828, 835 (N.D. Ill. 1995).

While it remains true that the declaration-against-interest exception applies only those portions of a statement that are against the interest of the declarant, "[t]his is not to say that a statement that incriminates the declarant *and also inculpates the nondeclarant* cannot be specifically disserving of the declarant's penal interest." *People v. Greenberger*, 58 Cal. App. 4th 298, 335, 68 Cal. Rptr. 2d 61, 81 (1997) (italics added) (statements admitting a relationship between the declarant and another person are admissible against that other person if the existence of the relationship was against the declarant's penal interest).

3. SAMPLE FOUNDATION

Our fact situation is a robbery prosecution. The People allege that the defendant, Bosley, robbed the Midland Stereo Store in Bodega Bay on February 17, 1994. The defense theory is that one Bennett actually committed the robbery. Called as a trial witness, Bennett properly claimed the privilege against self-incrimination and refused to answer any questions about the robbery. His refusal renders him "unavailable as a witness" under § 240(a). As his next witness, the defendant calls William Store. Mr. Store has already identified himself. The defendant is the proponent.

P WHAT is your occupation?
W I am a member of the Bodega Bay Police Department.
P HOW long have you held that position?
W For about eight years.
P WHERE were you on the morning of February 19, 2000?
W I was on duty at the station.
P WHAT happened while you were on duty that morning?
W Some patrolmen brought in a suspect for questioning.
P WHO was the suspect?
W A Gregory Bennett.
P WHEN was the last time you saw Mr. Bennett?
W A few moments ago.
P WHERE was he then?
W He was on the witness stand. He's the fellow who just left the stand.
P WHAT happened after the patrolmen brought in Mr. Bennett?
W As is my custom, I first informed him of his rights.

P WHAT rights did you tell him about? (1), (2)

W I told him he had a privilege against self-incrimination and a right to counsel.

P WHAT was his condition when you informed him of his rights? (1)

W He seemed OK. He was alert, and there didn't seem to be anything physically wrong with him.

P HOW did he react when you informed him of his rights? (1)

W He seemed concerned.

P WHAT did you do after you informed Mr. Bennett of his rights? (1)

W I asked him if he understood his rights.

P HOW did he respond? (1)

W He said he understood them, and then he gave me some factual information I wanted.

P WHAT did you do after you spoke with Mr. Bennett? (4)

W I attempted to verify some of the facts Mr. Bennett had told me.

P WHAT facts? (4)

W He told me about the location of some of the stolen property, some receivers and speakers.

P WHAT did Mr. Bennett say about the location of the stolen property? (4)

W He said that several of the stolen receivers and speakers were in his apartment.

P WHAT steps did you take to verify his statement? (4)

W With his consent, I visited and searched his apartment.

P WHAT did you find in his apartment? (4)

W I found his personal effects. In addition, I found several receivers and speakers. I checked the serial numbers against the list supplied by Midland Stereo. The numbers matched.

P Mr. Store, during your questioning of Mr. Bennett, WHO did he say robbed the Midland Stereo Store on February 17, 1994?

O Your Honor, I object to that question on the ground that it calls for hearsay.

P Your Honor, may we approach the bench?

J Yes.

P Your Honor, if permitted to do so, the witness will testify that Mr. Bennett confessed to the very robbery for which my client is now on trial. In light of the warnings Officer Store gave Bennett, Bennett must have realized his confession was contrary to his penal interest. Although it is not essential, there happens to be corroboration that Bennett was involved in the robbery; some of the stolen property was found in his apartment. Finally, Bennett's refusal to answer makes him unavailable.

J The objection will be overruled.

P Officer Store, let me repeat the question. WHO did Mr. Bennett say robbed the Midland Stereo Store?

W He said that he did.

Q. DYING DECLARATIONS

1. THE DOCTRINE

When a person believes that he or she is about to die, and then makes a statement concerning the cause and circumstances of that impending death, that statement, to be sure, is hearsay, but it is hearsay that arguably possesses an unusual level of reliability. One who believes in a life after death probably will be reluctant to enter eternity with a serious lie on his or her lips. And aside from one's religious beliefs, one is not likely to want one's last act on Earth to be a falsehood. When we add to this special feature of reliability a special need to resort to the statement in the event that the declarant dies, we have the ingredients that led to the common law's recognition of an exception to the hearsay rule for dying declarations.

The common law version of this exception restricted its use to prosecutions for the criminal homicide of the declarant. However, the modern California version permits it to be used not only in all criminal cases, but in civil cases as well. Section 1242 provides:

> Evidence of a statement made by a dying person respecting the cause and circumstances of his death is not made inadmissible by the hearsay rule if the statement was made upon his personal knowledge and under a sense of immediately impending death.

2. ELEMENTS OF THE FOUNDATION

The foundation for the exception to the hearsay rule for dying declarations is as follows:

1. At the time of the statement, the declarant had "a sense of immediately impending death," that is to say, had abandoned all hope of recovery and was convinced that death was imminent. Sometimes this belief can be proved by the declarant's direct statements, which, though also hearsay, are admissible under the exception to the hearsay rule for statements of present mental state. *See People v. Sims*, 5 Cal. 4th 405, 458, 20 Cal. Rptr. 2d 537, 570, 853 P.2d 992, 1025 (1993). Often the requisite belief is proven circumstantially from the nature of the wound, the administration of the last rites, the making of a will, or statements by third persons such as doctors or nurses that one's death is certain and near. These latter statements would not be hearsay because they are offered only to show the effect that they had on the one who heard them.
2. The declarant had personal knowledge of the facts asserted. Section 1242 expressly imposes this requirement.
3. The facts asserted in the statement describe the cause or circumstances of the event that has brought the declarant to point of imminent death. *See People v. Gatson*, 60 Cal. App. 4th 1020, 70 Cal. Rptr. 2d 729 (1998) (where defendant fatally shoots declarant, her hospital-room statement, that defendant was "robbing" her at the time, made under a sense of impending death, qualifies as a description of the cause and circumstances of her death, and thus may be used as evidence that she was killed during the per-

petration of a felony). Descriptions of previous quarrels or fights between the declarant and the defendant fall outside the scope of the exception.

4. The declarant is now dead.

3. SAMPLE FOUNDATION

The fact situation is a homicide prosecution. Defendant James Ireland has been indicted for the murder of Grace Shafer. The prosecution calls one Turner as a witness. Turner has already identified himself. The prosecutor is the proponent.

P WHAT is your occupation?
W I am a physician.
P WHERE are you licensed to practice medicine?
W In three states, including here in California.
P WHERE were you on the morning of February 22, 2000?
W I was in my office in Irvine.
P WHAT happened that morning?
W I received an emergency call.
P WHAT was the nature of the call?
W Someone was hurt very badly, and they needed immediate medical attention.
P WHAT did you do after you received this call?
W I jumped in my car and drove to 1444 Garnet Street.
P WHAT did you find there?
W I found several police surrounding a very badly injured person.
P WHO was that person?
W A Ms. Grace Shafer.
P HOW do you know that's who it was?
W She identified herself, and I also checked the ID that she had in her purse.
P WHAT condition was she in? (1)
W Very bad. She had several stab wounds.
P HOW many stab wounds?
W Five.
P WHERE were the wounds? (2)
W In her chest.
P HOW deep were the wounds? (1)
W Some were several inches deep.
P HOW much blood was she losing? (1)
W She was bleeding profusely.
P WHERE was she bleeding? (1)
W All over the chest area.
P WHAT did you do after you discovered these wounds? (4)
W I helped her as best I could; and when I realized that she was dying, I tried to make her as comfortable as possible.
P WHAT, if anything, did you tell her about her condition? (1)
O Your Honor, I object to that question on the ground that it calls for hearsay.
P Your Honor, may we approach the bench?
J Yes.

P   Your Honor, I offer to prove that the witness will testify that he told Ms. Shafer that she was dying. I want to use that statement for a nonhearsay purpose, namely, to show its effect on her state of mind. His statement helped produce a sense of imminent death in her mind. That is part of the foundation for the dying declaration I ultimately want to offer. The rest of the foundation will include proof that Ms. Shafer is now dead and that at the time of the statement, she sensed imminent death.

J   The objection is overruled. You may proceed.

P   Dr. Turner, let me repeat the question. WHAT, if anything, did you tell Ms. Shafer about her condition? (1)

W   I was honest with her. She asked me what her chances were, and I told her she was dying.

P   HOW did she respond? (1)

W   She looked frightened. Then she sighed very deeply.

P   WHAT happened then? (1)

W   She asked that I contact a Catholic priest. She said that she wanted to receive the last rites of her church before she died.

P   WHAT happened then? (1)

W   The priest arrived and administered the sacrament. Then the priest and I accompanied her in the ambulance taking her to the hospital.

P   WHAT, if anything, did she say about the cause of her death?

W   She said someone had stabbed her with a knife.

P   WHAT, if anything, did she say about the place where the stabbing occurred? (2)

W   She said that it had been in that room where I examined her.

P   WHAT were the lighting conditions in the room where you found her? (2)

W   They were excellent. To begin with, the lights were on in the room. In addition, the shades were up, it was almost noon at the time, and light was streaming in the windows as well.

P   HOW fresh were her wounds? (2)

W   They were only an hour or so old.

P   HOW could you tell that? (2)

W   Even the blood that had fallen on dry, solid surfaces hadn't begun to dry yet. The stabbing must have occurred in the middle of the morning, maybe 10:30 or 11:00 a.m.

P   Did she say who had stabbed her?

W   Yes, she did. (3)

P   WHO did she say stabbed her?

W   She said it was Jim Ireland. (3)

P   Doctor, WHERE is Ms. Shafer now? (4)

W   She's dead.

P   HOW do you know that? (4)

W   She died in the ambulance on the way to the hospital. I was at her side when she died.

R. DECLARATIONS OF PAST BODILY, MENTAL, OR EMOTIONAL CONDITION

The Evidence Code contains a broad hearsay exception for assertions of past bodily, mental, or emotional condition. Section 1251 provides:

> Subject to Section 1252, evidence of a statement of the declarant's state of mind, emotion, or physical sensation (including a statement of intent, plan, motive, design, mental feeling, pain, or bodily health) at a time prior to the statement is not made inadmissible by the hearsay rule if:
> (a) The declarant is unavailable as a witness; and
> (b) The evidence is offered to prove such prior state of mind, emotion, or physical sensation when it is itself an issue in the action and the evidence is not offered to prove any fact other than such state of mind, emotion, or physical sensation.

Under § 1251, the bodily, emotional, or mental state must "itself [be] an issue in the action." In a survival tort action, the physical pain the decedent suffered before dying is an issue. In a suit for punitive damages against a decedent's estate, the decedent's earlier malice toward the plaintiff would be an issue. In a respondeat superior tort action, the plaintiff must show that the defendant's employee acted within the scope of the employment; hence, the employee's prior intent to serve the employer's purposes would be an issue. Article, *State of Mind: The Elusive Exception*, 9 U.C. DAVIS L. REV. 199, 225 (1976). In each of these types of lawsuits, the pleadings place the mental, emotional, or physical state in issue.

In these cases, there are only two foundational requirements for invoking § 1252:

1. The statement must purport to refer to the declarant's earlier physical, emotional, or mental state. Suppose, for example, that the witness is a physician who examined the declarant patient on February 13th, two days after the accident. The proponent might ask, "WHAT, if anything, did she say was the level of her pain right after the accident?"
2. At the time of trial, the declarant is "unavailable as a witness" within the meaning of § 240(a).

S. STATEMENTS ABOUT A DECLARANT'S WILL

Every factual assertion is implicitly a statement of one's present memory or belief. For example, when someone says: "The light was red for northbound traffic," that person is really saying: "I have in mind at this moment a memory of the color of the light for northbound traffic, and my memory is that the light was red." If statements of present memory and belief were admissible as evidence of the fact remembered or believed, the exception for statements of present state of mind would virtually swallow the hearsay rule. Accordingly, Section 1250, which defines that exception, expressly prohibits the use of statement of present "memory or belief" for the purpose of proving the fact that the declarant is claiming to remember or believe.

In one case, however, the common law and the Evidence Code relent and admit statements of memory to prove the fact remembered: statements about a declarant's will. When the issue arises, the declarant is usually dead, and there is an acute need for evidence of the declarant's state of mind. That need accounts for Evidence Code § 1260:

> (a) Evidence of a statement made by a declarant who is unavailable as a witness that he has or has not made a will, or has or has not revoked his will, or that identifies his will, is not made inadmissible by the hearsay rule.
>
> (b) Evidence of a statement is inadmissible under this section if the statement was made under circumstances such as to indicate its lack of trustworthiness.

To lay a foundation under § 1260, the proponent must establish the following elements:

1. The declarant made an assertion about the execution, identity, or revocation of his or her will. The proponent must phrase the question to elicit an answer describing a declaration about one of those topics. For instance, the proponent could ask, WHAT, if anything, did she say about whether she had made out a will?
2. The declarant is dead or otherwise unavailable to testify at the time of trial.

T.   STATEMENTS BY VICTIMS OF PHYSICAL ABUSE

1. THE DOCTRINE

Evidence Code § 1370 contains a special hearsay exception for statements made by victims of physical injury, either actual or threatened. This exception superficially resembles the one for spontaneous or excited utterances in that it regulates the topic or content of the statements it covers: they must "narrate, describe, or explain" either the infliction of physical injury or the threats to do so. Compare § 1370(a)(1) with § 1240(a). However, this exception is in some respects more generous and in others more restrictive than the one for spontaneous statements.

Section 1370 is more generous than § 1240 in that it does not require that at the time of the statement, the declarant must still be under the stress created by the physical force or the threat of it. Instead, it requires only that the statement be made "at or near the time" the physical injury was inflicted or threatened. Moreover, the statute indicates that a statement that otherwise qualifies under its provisions may be considered "near" if it is made no more than five years after the actions it describes. § 1370(a)(3).

Section 1370 is more restrictive than § 1240 in several respects. First, it is not enough that the declarant have perceived the infliction or the threat of physical injury. The declarant must be the one on whom the injury was inflicted or to whom the threat was made. § 1370(a)(1). Second, while that the declarant of an excited utterance need not be "unavailable" to provide live testimony, this new exception imposes this requirement of unavailability for victims of physical violence or threats. § 1370(a)(2). Third, the exception seeks to assure that the statement that was actually made and the statement that is offered in evidence be one and the same. To this end, it lists three alternate safeguards: (1) The statement must have been "made in writing," which implies that the victim must have been the author; or (2) it must have been recorded electronically; or (3) if it is an oral, unrecorded statement, then it must have been made to some law enforcement official. § 1370(a)(5).

The excited utterance exception gets its special reliability from the fact that it is made more or less spontaneously while the declarant is still under the stress of the excitement caused by the perception of a startling event. The new exception substitutes for this assurance a generalized requirement that the statement by the abuse victim have been made "under circumstances that would indicate its trustworthiness." § 1370(a)(4). It then proceeds to provide a nonexclusive list of three circumstances that bear upon the trustworthiness of a victim's statements concerning physical abuse: (1) whether the statement was made to aid in some pending or prospective lawsuit in which the victim was interested; (2) the extent of any bias or motive that might have led the putative physical abuse victim to fabricate the accusation; and (3) whether the facts in the statement are corroborated by other admissible evidence.

This new exception was upheld against a Confrontation Clause attack in *People v. Hernandez*, 71 Cal. App 4th 417, 424, 83 Cal. Rptr. 2d 747, 952 (1999), which involved statements made by the live-in girlfriend of the defendant in which she described to a police officer the brutal beating the defendant had administered to her. The court noted, however, that any suggestion that the requisite trustworthiness could be found mainly in the corroboration of the victim's accusation by other evidence would run afoul of the Sixth Amendment: "While we agree with [defendant] that, under *Idaho v. Wright*, 497 U.S. 805, 110 S. Ct. 3139, 111 L. Ed. 2d 638 (1990), corroboration by other evidence is not a legitimate component of trustworthiness, its presence in [§ 1370] does not render the statute unconstitutional because the section still requires the essential indicia of trustworthiness and it suggests other legitimate factors which may establish that. Absent a case where the trial court relied heavily upon the presence of corroborating evidence in making its determination that the statement bears indicia of reliability, the confrontation clause would not be violated." 71 Cal. App. 4th at 424, 83 Cal. Rptr. 2d at 752.

U.   STATEMENTS BY VICTIMS OF ELDER ABUSE

1. THE DOCTRINE

Effective January 1, 2000, the Legislature enacted yet another specific exception the hearsay rule: statements by specified elder and dependent adults who are victims of abuse. The exception, contained in Evidence Code 1380, applies only to criminal proceedings involving elder and dependent abuse as defined in Penal Code § 368. The declarant must be unavailable as defined by § 240, and as stated under § 1380(a), all of the following elements must be true:

(1) The party offering the statement has made a showing of particularized guarantees of trustworthiness regarding the statement, the statement was made under circumstances which indicate its trustworthiness, and the statement was not the result of promise, inducement, threat, or coercion. In making its determination, the court may consider only the circumstances that surround the making of the statement and that render the declarant particularly worthy of belief.

(2) There is no evidence that the unavailability of the declarant was caused by, aided by, solicited by, or procured on behalf of, the party who is offering the statement.

(3) The entire statement has been memorialized in a videotape recording made by a law enforcement official, prior to the death or disabling of the declarant.

(4) The statement was made by the victim of the alleged violation.

(5) The statement is supported by corroborative evidence.

(6) The victim of the alleged violation is an individual who meets both of the following requirements:

(A) Was 65 years of age or older or was a dependent adult when the alleged violation or attempted violation occurred.

(B) At the time of any criminal proceeding, including, but not limited to, a preliminary hearing or trial, regarding the alleged violation or attempted violation, is either deceased or suffers from the infirmities of aging as manifested by advanced age or organic brain damage, or other physical, mental, or emotional dysfunction, to the extent that the ability of the person to provide adequately for the person's own care or protection is impaired.

The prosecution, if intending to invoke this exception, must serve written notice upon the defendant at least 10 days prior to the hearing or trial, unless good cause is shown; and a showing of good cause entitles the defendant to a reasonable continuance. Evidence Code § 1380(b). If a statement under this section is offered during trial, the court's determination of the victim's unavailability must be made out of the presence of the jury.

If the defendant elects to testify at the hearing on a motion brought pursuant to this section, the court must exclude from the examination every person except the clerk, the court reporter, the bailiff, the prosecutor, the investigating officer, the defendant and his or her counsel, an investigator for the defendant, and the officer having custody of the defendant. The defendant's testimony at the hearing is not admissible in any other proceeding except the hearing brought on the motion, and if a transcript is made of the defendant's testimony, it must be sealed and transmitted to the clerk of the court in which the action is pending. Evidence Code § 1380(c).

Part 5. A Residual Hearsay Exception

V. A RESIDUAL HEARSAY EXCEPTION

1. THE DOCTRINE

The list of hearsay exceptions covered Section B through U of this chapter is not all-inclusive. The Evidence Code itself articulates additional hearsay exceptions:

(1) Sections 1312-16 set out a series of exceptions for hearsay statements about family history. The exceptions include family and community reputation, and statements in family records, church records, and vital statistics certificates. *See People v. Riley*, 45 Cal. App. 4th 351, 52 Cal. Rptr. 2d 670 (1996) (a victim's pregnancy calendar).

(2) Sections 1320-24 create several exceptions for hearsay in the form of reputation. The reputation can relate to community history or property rights.

(3) Sections 1330-31 recognize hearsay exceptions for recitals in dispositive instruments and ancient writings.

(4) Section 1340 codifies an exception for commercial lists such as directories and registers.

(5) Section 1350, added to the Evidence Code in 1985, creates a witness-protection exception to the hearsay rule for statements by a declarant who has been kidnapped or killed at the instance of the accused for the purpose of preventing his or her arrest or prosecution. Thus, a criminal defendant who has a prosecution witness kidnapped or killed forfeits the protection of the hearsay rule and the Confrontation Clause.

The Federal Rules of Evidence contain a residual exception, Rule 807. This rule authorizes the trial judge to admit an item of hearsay that is "not specifically covered" by any of the defined exceptions, but which has "equivalent circumstantial guarantees of trustworthiness." An adverse party is entitled to advance notice of the proponent's intent to offer hearsay under this residual exception.

In contrast to the Federal Rules of Evidence, the California Evidence Code does not expressly confer a residuum of discretion on the trial judge to admit hearsay that falls outside its defined exceptions. However, the Evidence Code does obliquely confer such discretion. Section 1200(b) states: "Except as provided by law, hearsay evidence is inadmissible." Section 160 of the Code defines "law" as including "decisional law." The Senate Committee comment to § 1200 points out that, construed together, §§ 160 and 1200 permit the California courts to recognize hearsay exceptions "in addition to those exceptions expressed in the statutes." *See In re Malinda S.*, 51 Cal. 3d 368, 376, 272 Cal. Rptr. 787, 791, 795 P.2d 1244, 1248 (1990), where, in the course of holding that Welfare Code § 281 and California Rule of Court 1450(c) implicitly create an exception to the hearsay rule for social studies offered in juvenile proceedings, the Court remarked: "[E]xceptions to the hearsay rule are not limited to those enumerated in the Evidence Code; they may also be found in other codes and decisional law." The California Supreme Court has now explicitly held that "appellate courts do in fact have the power to create new exceptions to the hearsay rule not found in the Evidence Code." *In re Cindy L.*, 17 Cal. 4th 15, 25, 69 Cal. Rptr. 2d 803, 809, 947 P.2d 1340, 1346 (1997). This power is appropriately exercised for "classes of evidence for which there is a substantial need, and which possess an intrinsic reliability that enable them to surmount constitutional and other objections that generally apply to hearsay evidence." 17 Cal. 4th at 28, 69 Cal. Rptr. 2d at 811.

Although the courts have rarely exercised their power under § 1200, they have done so to create an exception to allow the use of medical and repair bills to corroborate a plaintiff's testimony that they have been paid. *See PG & E v. G. W. Thomas Drayage & Rigging Co.*, 69 Cal. 2d 33, 69 Cal. Rptr. 561, 442 P.2d 641 (1968); *Jones v. Dumrichob*, 63 Cal. App. 4th 1258, 1267, 74 Cal. Rptr. 2d 607, 612–613 (1998).

In *In re Carmen O.*, 28 Cal. App. 4th 908, 918-22, 33 Cal. Rptr. 2d 848, 853-56 (1994), the court exercised its residual power to recognize a "child dependency hearsay exception." This court-created hearsay exception requires a showing (1) that the minor-declarant was *competent* at the time of making the out-of-court statement, and (2) that the circumstances attending the statement contain adequate indicators of its *reliability*.

Competency requires attention to the following attributes of the child: (a) the ability to differentiate between truth and falsehood, (b) the capacity to observe the matters the statement purports to describe, (c) an adequate intelligence, (d) an adequate memory, (e) the ability to communicate, and (f) an appreciation of the obligation to speak the truth.

Reliability arises from a number of factors, including: (a) the extent to which the minor's youthfulness reduces the likelihood of a fabrication or imagination of the events described, (b) the spontaneity of the statement as opposed to its being prompted by suggestive or leading questions, (c) independent corroborative evidence, (d) internal consistency, (e) unsophisticated wording of the statement, thus indicating no one coached the child, (f) absence of accusations against others, and (g) absence of a motive for the child to lie or exaggerate. *See In re Nemis M.*, 50 Cal. App. 4th 1344, 1353-54, 58 Cal. Rptr. 2d 324, 329-330 (1996).

In 1995, in part in response to the *Carmen O.* decision, the legislature formally added §§ 1253 and 1360 to the Evidence Code. *See* Section M of this chapter.

2. "CHILD DEPENDENCY" EXCEPTION

Investigations of child molestation cases frequently turn up accusatory hearsay statements by the victims. Although some of these statements are admissible as "spontaneous utterances," "fresh complaints," or "statements of physical sensation," many of them do not qualify under these exceptions to the hearsay rule. In child dependency proceedings, there is often a substantial need for statements by the child victims that do not fit within these narrow traditional hearsay exceptions. The California Supreme Court has identified three particular difficulties that attend efforts to prove child sexual abuse: "the frequent lack of physical evidence, the limited verbal and cognitive abilities of child victims, the fact that children are often unable or unwilling to act as witnesses because of the intimidation of the courtroom setting and the reluctance to testify against their parents." *In re Cindy L.*, 17 Cal. 4th 15, 28, 69 Cal. Rptr. 2d 803, 811–12, 947 P.2d 1340, 1348-49 (1997).

This practical need in child dependency proceedings to use out-of-court statements by the victims in child dependency proceedings does not justify their wholesale exemption from the hearsay rule. It does, however, warrant special treatment of any such statements that were made in circumstances that fortify the reliability of what the child said. In the *Cindy L.* case, the Court recognized a non-statutory "child hearsay" exception for statements if three conditions are met. First, the statements must have been made under circumstances that provide *indicia of their reliability*. Second, either the child must be *available* for cross-examination, or there must be other evidence *corroborating* the statements made by the child. Finally, there must be *adequate notice* to other interested parties of the intent to introduce the hearsay evidence. 17 Cal. 4th at 29–30, 69 Cal. Rptr. 2d at 812–13, 947 P.2d at 1349-50.

Indicia of reliability can be found in a number of factors: (a) the extent to which the minor's youthfulness reduces the likelihood of a fabrication or imagination of the events described; (b) the spontaneity of the statement as opposed to its being prompted by suggestive or leading questions; (c) its consistency, both internally and with later statements; (d) the unsophisticated wording of the statement, indicating that no one coached the child; (e) the absence of accusations against others; and (f) the absence of a motive for the child to lie or exaggerate. *Cf. People v. Brodit*, 61 Cal. App. 4th 1312, 1330, 72 Cal. Rptr. 2d 154, 164 (1998).

The admissibility of the hearsay statements of the child, Cindy L., presented an additional problem: the trial judge had found her incompetent to testify at the hearing, not because of fear or intimidation, but because she did not then have sufficient ability to distinguish between truth and falsity. While this certainly was a relevant circumstance in evaluating the reliability of her earlier, hearsay statements, the Court held that it did not create an absolute bar to a finding that they were reliable: "[T]he fact of the child's incompetence to testify does not prevent a court from finding that the various circumstances surrounding the statement—not only its spontaneity, but also the precociousness of the child's knowledge of sexual matters, the lack of motive to lie, and other factors outlined above—[may] lead to the conclusion that the statement bears special indicia of reliability and is therefore admissible." 17 Cal. 4th at 35, 69 Cal. Rptr. 2d at 816, 947 P.2d at 1353.

Chapter 10

STATUTORY PRIVILEGES AND SIMILAR DOCTRINES

A. INTRODUCTION

In the past three chapters, we have examined rules excluding unreliable evidence: secondary evidence, opinion, and hearsay rules. The evidence is logically relevant, but the courts doubt the reliability of secondary evidence, opinions, and hearsay statements. We now turn to a type of doctrine which excludes evidence to promote an extrinsic social policy. The privileges for confidential communications epitomize this doctrine. *See generally* JAMES E. HOGAN & GREGORY S. WEBER, CALIFORNIA CIVIL DISCOVERY (5th ed. 1999) (cited hereafter as HOGAN). Suppose that a party makes damaging admissions in a letter to his or her attorney. The party had firsthand, personal knowledge of the facts admitted. The admissions are not only logically relevant; they are highly reliable, since the party had personal knowledge of the facts. However, the judge would exclude the letter on the ground that the letter is a privileged communication. As a matter of policy, the courts want to assure clients that they can disclose all the facts to their attorneys in confidence. With fuller disclosure from their clients, attorneys can render more effective service. The courts believe that this policy is important enough to warrant excluding even relevant, reliable evidence.

Similar reasoning underlies the government privileges. Modern government needs a vast amount of information to perform its tasks, especially its regulatory functions, and sometimes the government cannot obtain information from particular sources without assuring confidentiality. The government's interest is even more compelling when the government information qualifies as a military or state secret. The information may be highly relevant and thoroughly trustworthy, but the public interest in maintaining the information's secrecy outweighs the parties' interest in disclosure.

B. PRIVILEGES FOR CONFIDENTIAL COMMUNICATIONS—IN GENERAL

The law of privileges for confidential communications can be abstracted thus: *In some types of proceedings, the holder has certain privileges with respect to privileged information unless (1) the holder has waived the privilege or (2) there is an applicable exception to the privilege.* This abstract raises six issues.

Types of Proceedings

The first issue is in what types of proceedings privileges apply. Generally, the privileges apply in any proceeding in which testimony can be compelled. Evidence Code § 901 sets out a broad definition of "proceeding," including arbitration and legislative hearings. A few privileges have a peculiar, limited scope. For instance, § 998 provides that the physician-patient privilege is inapplicable in criminal prosecutions. The protection for proceedings of hospital peer review committees is similarly inapplicable in prosecutions. *People v. Superior Court (Memorial Med. Center)*, 234 Cal. App. 3d 363, 286 Cal. Rptr. 478 (1991). With such rare exceptions, the privileges apply in all legal proceedings.

Holder

The second issue is who is the holder of the privilege. Even if the testimony would be damaging to an accused, he or she may not vicariously assert a third party's privilege to block the admission of the testimony.[1] In the case of a corporation, the client is the entity, not the shareholders.[2] The original holder is the intended beneficiary of the privacy. Thus, the client is the holder of the attorney-client privilege,[3] the patient the holder of the psychotherapist-patient privilege, and both spouses the holders of the spousal privilege. If the original holder of the privilege becomes mentally incompetent, that person's conservator or guardian becomes the successor holder. If the original holder dies, the personal representative (the executor or administrator) becomes a successor holder.[4] The privilege finally terminates when the personal representative is discharged.[5]

Lastly, the holder's agent may sometimes assert the privilege on the holder's behalf. The client may actually authorize the attorney to claim the attorney-client privilege for the client at a particular hearing. Further, the Evidence Code *requires* attorneys, physicians, and psychotherapists to claim the privilege on the holder's

---

[1]*People v. Barnett*, 17 Cal. 4th 1044, 954 P.2d 384, 74 Cal. Rptr. 2d 121, 181 (1998).

[2]*National Football League v. Superior Court*, 65 Cal. App. 4th 100, 75 Cal. Rptr. 2d 893 (1998) (there is no shareholder exception to the corporate attorney-client privilege).

[3]*Fletcher v. Alameda County Superior Court*, 44 Cal. App. 4th 773, 52 Cal. Rptr. 2d 65 (1996) (the client was the trustee, and the client's sons did not gain the status of clients simply because they were the beneficiaries of the trust).

[4]The privileges seem to be "suspended" in the interim between the original holder's death and the personal representative's appointment. HEAFEY § 35.16, at 379. *See also Hale v. Superior Court (DeFelice)*, 28 Cal. App. 4th 1421, 34 Cal. Rptr. 2d 279, 280 (1994) ("Hale's death" is "irrelevant; the privilege was Hale's, it continues after her death, and only her personal representative can waive it").

[5]"Even after ... discharge of the personal representative, it may be possible to revive the privilege by reopening the estate and having a personal representative again appointed." *Id.* at § 35.16, at 380. *See also Rittenhouse v. Superior Ct.*, 235 Cal. App. 3d 1584, 1 Cal. Rptr. 2d 595, 597-99 (1991). If the original holder was a trustee in his or her capacity as such, the power to assert the attorney-client privilege passes to a successor trustee when the successor assumes the office. *Moeller v. Superior Court*, 16 Cal. 4th 1124, 947 P.2d 279, 69 Cal. Rptr. 2d 317 (1997).

behalf in the holder's absence, unless the holder has waived or instructed otherwise. Evidence Code §§ 955, 994(c), 995, 1015.

Nature of Privilege

The third issue is what is the nature of the privilege. The privilege can encompass three rights. The first right is the personal right to refuse to disclose the privileged information. A judge may neither find the holder in contempt nor impose discovery sanctions on the holder if the holder is properly invoking a privilege. The second right is the right to prevent third parties from making disclosure. The recipient of the communication, the attorney, physician, or cleric, is clearly bound. Unlike the common law, the Evidence Code gives the holder the right to silence eavesdroppers and interceptors as well. The third and final right is the right to preclude the opposing counsel and the judge from commenting on the invocation of the privilege. In roughly half the jurisdictions, the opposing counsel may argue that since the holder invoked a privilege to suppress the information, the information probably would have been unfavorable. Roughly half the jurisdictions prohibit such comment; they reason that it is inconsistent, on the one hand, to grant the privilege and, on the other hand, to permit adverse inferences from the privilege's invocation. Evidence Code § 913 adopts the latter view. That section prohibits adverse comment in both civil and criminal actions.

Although most California privileges follow this pattern and confer all three rights on the holder, there are deviations from the pattern. For example, under Evidence Code § 1034, the cleric's solitary right is "a privilege to refuse to disclose a penitential communication ...." The protection for news reporters is even more limited. Evidence Code § 1070 gives them only an immunity from contempt. *See SCI-Sacramento v. Superior Court*, 54 Cal. App. 4th 654, 62 Cal. Rptr. 2d 868 (1997). Even when § 1070 applies, the judge may still impose discovery sanctions if the reporter is a party to the suit.

Privileged Information

The fourth issue is the most difficult: What is privileged information? Simply stated, privileged information is *a confidential communication between properly related parties and incident to the relation*. This presents several subissues.

What is a "communication"? Oral and written statements fall within the definition of "communication."[6] These statements are intended to convey meaning to the hearer or reader. In most cases, the Evidence Code limits the protective scope of privileges to such statements. For example, in California, the spousal privilege applies only to oral and written statements exchanged between the spouses. The prevailing view is that the privilege does not apply to one spouse's nonassertive conduct observed by the other spouse. *People v. Bradford*, 70 Cal. 2d 333, 450

---

[6]*Wellpoint Health Networks v. Superior Court*, 59 Cal. App. 4th 110, 68 Cal. Rptr. 2d 844, 850 (1997)("The attorney-client privilege covers all forms of communication ....").

P.2d 46, 74 Cal. Rptr. 726 (1969), *cert. denied*, 399 U.S. 911 (1970). *But see Rubio v. Superior Court*, 202 Cal. App. 3d 1343, 249 Cal. Rptr. 419 (1988) (the marital privilege applied to a videotape depicting the husband and wife engaged in a sexual act). Nor does the privilege cloak either the fact that a privileged conversation occurred or the identity of the persons conversing. *State Farm Fire & Cas. v. Superior Court*, 54 Cal. App. 4th 625, 62 Cal. Rptr. 2d 834, *modified*, 97 C.D.O.S. 3262 (1997). To be protected, a written statement must come into existence as a communication between the parties; if the writing was created earlier, it does not become privileged merely because it has been turned over to an attorney or spouse. *Wellpoint Health Networks v. Superior Court*, 59 Cal. App. 4th 110, 68 Cal. Rptr. 2d 844, 850 (1997).

However, in some cases, the Code extends the protective scope of a privilege to include information that ordinarily would not be considered a "communication." Evidence Code §§ 992 and 1012 extend the physician-patient and psychotherapist-patient privileges to virtually all information the professional gains by examining the patient. Further, §§ 952, 992, and 1012 apply the attorney-client, physician-patient, and psychotherapist-patient privileges to even unexpressed opinions the professional forms about the client or patient.

When is a communication "confidential"? Confidentiality entails two elements: (1) physical privacy; and (2) an intent on the holder's part to maintain secrecy. The holder must not only have had the latter intent; the intent must also be based on a reasonable expectation of privacy. *People v. von Villas*, 11 Cal. App. 4th 175, 15 Cal. Rptr. 2d 112, 138 (1992). For practical reasons, the courts have allowed nurses, clerks, secretaries, and the like, to be present without destroying confidentiality; the courts realize that attorneys and physicians use assistants to conduct their professional work. Evidence Code § 952 states that the attorney-client privilege is still applicable if the third party was "present to further the interest of the client in the consultation ...." The California Law Revision Commission comment to § 952 explains that the privilege applies to a statement

> even though it is made in the presence of another person—such as a spouse, parent, business associate, or joint client—who is present to further the interest of the client in the consultation. The words refer, too, to another person and his attorney who may meet with the client and his attorney in regard to a matter of joint concern.

For example, in *Lovett v. Superior Court*, 203 Cal. App. 3d 521, 250 Cal. Rptr. 25 (1988), the court extended the psychotherapist-patient privilege to communications among the patients participating in a group therapy session.

Section 917 creates a general presumption that communications between such persons as a client and an attorney are intended to remain confidential.[7] However,

---

[7] Because of the confidentiality requirement, the courts ordinarily do not apply the privilege to the client's or patient's name or fee arrangements. In the typical case, there is no intention that the information remain confidential. However, there is California authority suggesting that in

the presumption is rebuttable.

Even if there was physical privacy at the time of the communication, the communication is unprivileged if the holder intended subsequent disclosure outside the circle of confidence. Suppose that the client gave the attorney information to include in a pleading to be filed with the court. The obvious intent to disclose ought to be enough to rebut the presumption of confidentiality.

When does a communication occur "between properly related parties"?
The legislature has decided to create privileges to protect confidential communications between parties standing in the following relations: attorney-client, spouses,[8] physician-patient, psychotherapist-patient, clergy-penitent, sexual assault victim-counselor, and domestic violence victim-counselor. All these privileges are set out in the Evidence Code. On the basis of the guarantee of confidentiality in Welfare and Institutions Code § 10950, the courts have also recognized a privilege for communications between welfare recipients and their representatives at administrative hearings. *Welfare Rights Organization v. Crisan*, 33 Cal. 3d 766, 661 P.2d 1073, 190 Cal. Rptr. 919 (1983). In some cases, the professional privileges attach even if the professional is not licensed in California. Sections 950, 990, and in part 1010 provide that the legal and medical privileges apply so long as the layperson reasonably believes that the professional is licensed to practice in any state or nation.

However, California courts cannot create new privileges by case law. *Scottsdale Ins. Co. v. Superior Court*, 59 Cal. App. 4th 263, 69 Cal. Rptr. 2d 112, 117 (1997); *Cloud v. Superior Court (Western Atlas)*, 50 Cal. App. 4th 1552, 58 Cal. Rptr. 2d 365 (1996); *Roberts v. City of Palmdale*, 5 Cal. 4th 363, 853 P.2d 496, 20 Cal. Rptr. 2d 330 (1993). Evidence Code § 911 provides that there are no privileges "[e]xcept as ... provided by statute." There are no statutory privileges for the parent-child relationship or unmarried cohabitants, and the courts have consequently refused to recognize any privilege for those relations. *People v. Delph*, 94 Cal. App. 3d 411, 156 Cal. Rptr. 422 (1979) (unmarried persons living together); *In re W.*, 59 Cal. App. 3d 745, 130 Cal. Rptr. 913 (1976);

---

exceptional cases, the privileges would apply to this information. For example, the attorney-client privilege might protect the client's identity if the disclosure of the identity would lead to the client's prosecution for the very conduct which he or she sought counseling about. 2 JEFFERSON § 40.1, at 1427; 2 WITKIN § 1120, at 1059-60. Similarly, the medical privileges might attach at least when the revelation of the patient's name would, in effect, disclose the treatment the patient received. JEFFERSON § 37.1, at 1361; HEAFEY § 37.3, at 410; *Scull v. Superior Ct.*, 206 Cal. App. 3d 784, 789, 254 Cal. Rptr. 24, 26 (1988) ("It is well-settled in California that the mere disclosure of the patient's identity violates the psychotherapist-patient privilege. The rationale for this rule is that the harm to the patient's interest of privacy is exacerbated by the stigma that society often attaches to mental illness"). Even when the client is mailing a letter to his or her attorney, the letter is unprivileged if the client knows that third parties will read the letter. *People v. Mickey*, 54 Cal. ad 612, 818 P.2d 84, 286 Cal. Rptr. 801, 819 (1991).

[8]Although California does not recognize common-law marriage, a California court will apply the spousal privilege if another jurisdiction's law governs the validity of the parties' marriage and that law recognizes such marriages. *People v. Badgett*, 10 Cal. 4th 330, 895 P.2d 877, 41 Cal. Rptr. 2d 635, 655 (1995).

People v. Gallego, 52 Cal. 3d 115, 176-77, 802 P.2d 169, 199, 276 Cal. Rptr. 679, 709 (1990), *cert. denied*, 502 U.S. 924 (1991):

> whatever their nature, defendant's communications with Charlene were not marital communications. [D]efendant was married to Carol Turks in Nevada in 1967, and ... he never legally dissolved that marriage. Defendant's subsequent marriage to Charlene were illegal and void .... and thus he had no right to assert the marital privilege.

Although § 911 generally precludes the recognition of non-statutory privileges, the court can still do so when the privilege has a constitutional basis. In *Garstang v. Superior Court*, 39 Cal. App. 4th 526, 46 Cal. Rptr. 2d 84 (1995), the court employed that theory to create a privilege for communications during mediation sessions before an ombudsperson employed by a private educational institution. The court cited to the inalienable right of privacy stated in Article I, § 1 of the California Constitution.

It is sometimes difficult to determine whether a communication is between properly related persons. Suppose, for example, that the client is an entity such as a corporation. The corporation must communicate with its attorney through its employees. When is a statement from its employee to its attorney deemed a communication between the attorney and the corporate client? The leading California precedent is *D.I. Chadbourne, Inc. v. Superior Court*, 60 Cal. 2d 723, 388 P.2d 700, 36 Cal. Rptr. 468 (1964). In that case, the California Supreme Court laid down a detailed set of rules governing communications between corporate counsel and the corporation's employees. There is a summary of the rules in 2 JEFFERSON § 40.2. "When the employee of a defendant corporation is also a defendant in his own right (or is a person who may be charged with liability), his statement regarding the facts with which he or his employer may be charged ... is entitled to the attorney-client privilege on the same basis as it would be entitled thereto if the employer-employee relationship did not exist. When such an employee is not a codefendant (or the person who may be charged with liability), his communication should not be ... privileged unless, under all the circumstances of the case, he is the natural person to be speaking for the corporation ...." *Martin v. Worker's Compensation Appeals Bd.*, 59 Cal. App. 4th 333, 69 Cal. Rptr. 2d 138, 143 (1997). If the employee was a participant in the accident or transaction and the entity requests the employee to submit a statement to corporate counsel, the employee is an appropriate spokesperson; and the statement is protected. If the employee merely witnessed the event and possesses the same information "that a nonemployee witness ... would have," there is no privilege. JEFFERSON at 1453. If the employee was neither a participant nor a witness, the privilege attaches only when the employee is the natural spokesperson for the entity. *Id.* at 1457. For example, suppose that the head nurse at a hospital neither participates in nor witnesses an accident on the premises. The head nurse might nevertheless be the natural person to prepare an investigative report for the hospital's attorney. The privilege would apply to the report. *See also Upjohn Co. v. United States*, 449

U.S. 383 (1981).

Or, assume that the attorney hires an expert to prepare for trial, and the expert questions the client. Are the communications among the attorney, expert, and client protected by the attorney-client privilege? The issue is whether the communications are considered communications between attorney and client. Evidence Code § 952 states that the attorney-client privilege applies to any communication "reasonably necessary for the transmission of the information or the accomplishment of the purpose for which the lawyer is consulted ..." The Law Revision Commission comment to § 952 explains that the section applies when the "lawyer ... [has the] client reveal information to an expert consultant in order that the lawyer may adequately advise his client." The section applies even if the attorney is not physically present at the meeting between the client and the expert. This theory applies when two conditions are present. First, there must be some private information emanating from the client—information such as his or her physical condition or confidential financial records. 2 JEFFERSON § 40.1, at 1423; *Andrade v. Superior Court (People)*, 46 Cal. App. 4th 1609, 54 Cal. Rptr. 2d 504, 506-07 (1996) (the assistance of a physician). Second, the attorney and client must need the expert's assistance to properly evaluate the information. If the client himself is an expert, the client and attorney do not need an expert intermediary. 2 WITKIN § 1128, at 1069.

When does a communication occur "incident to the relationship"? It is not enough that the communication occur between an attorney and his or her client. The client must be consulting the attorney in his or her professional capacity. This requires the court to examine the purpose of the communication. Why did the client consult the attorney? If the client was seeking legal services, the communication satisfies the incidence requirement. Thus, the privilege attaches when the client seeks the attorney's advice as a counselor or planner. *Wellpoint Health Networks v. Superior Court,* 59 Cal. App. 4th 110, 68 Cal. Rptr. 2d 844, 850 (1997) ("the privilege applies not only to communications made in anticipation of litigation, but also to legal advice when no litigation is threatened"). If an insured gives a statement to the insurer on the understanding that the statement will be sent to an insurance defense attorney in the event of litigation, the privilege attaches. *Soltani-Rastegar v. Superior Court*, 208 Cal. App. 3d 424, 428, 256 Cal. Rptr. 255, 258 (1989). "The fact that litigation was only a threat on the horizon and that attorneys had not yet been selected does not convert the purpose of the transmission." *Id.* Under Evidence Code § 405, the judge makes a final determination of the primary purpose of the communication. 2 WITKIN § 1136, at 1077; *People v. Cabral*, 12 Cal. App. 4th 820, 15 Cal. Rptr. 2d 1866, 870 (1993) ("the test is the dominant purpose;" although a court should liberally protect a privilege that has attached, "the privilege is to be strictly construed" when there is genuine doubt as to whether the privilege attached); *People v. Gionis*, 9 Cal. 4th 1196, 892 P.2d 1199, 40 Cal. Rptr. 2d 456 (1995) (the attorney had already told the defendant that he refused to represent him; after that statement, the defendant had to appreciate that he was consulting the attorney merely as a friend).

In some respects, the incidence requirement in California is more liberal than elsewhere. In many jurisdictions, for example, the medical privileges apply only when the patient consults the professional for treatment. The Senate Committee comment to § 991 points out that the California physician-patient privilege applies even if the patient consults the physician solely for diagnosis "in contemplation of some legal proceeding." *But see In re Tabatha G.*, 45 Cal. App. 4th 1159, 53 Cal. Rptr. 2d 93 (1996) (in a juvenile court proceeding to determine whether Tina's parental rights should be terminated, a Dr. Volcani, Ph.D., conducted a "bonding" study of the relationship between Tina and the child, Tabatha; the psychotherapist privilege did not apply because "the purpose of the bonding study was to obtain evidence of the existence and nature of [the] relationship between Tina and Tabatha;" "Tina was not ... seeking a diagnosis or treatment of a mental or emotional condition nor was any scientific research involved"). Section 1011 extends the psychotherapist privilege to persons who participate in "scientific research on mental or emotional problems." Further, the Law Revision Commission comment to § 1032 emphasizes that the California penitent-clergy privilege is not limited to confessions, as the privilege is in many states.

Waiver

The fifth issue is waiver. If a holder invokes the right type of privilege in the right type of proceeding to suppress the right type of communication, there is a prima facie case for privilege. However, the opposing counsel can still defeat the privilege by showing that the holder has waived it. Evidence Code § 912(a) states that a waiver occurs when a holder

> without coercion, has disclosed a significant part of the communication or has consented to such disclosure made by anyone. Consent to disclosure is manifested by any statement or other conduct of the holder of the privilege indicating consent to the disclosure, including failure to claim the privilege in any proceeding in which the holder has the legal standing and opportunity to claim the privilege.

The waiver thus can occur inside or outside court. For example, on direct examination by his or her attorney, the holder may have revealed a significant part of the privileged communication. The disclosure waives the privilege for the entire communication. The holder can also waive by voluntarily disclosing the privileged communication to a third party outside the courtroom. Not every out-of-court disclosure is a waiver because the disclosure itself might be privileged; a husband might tell his wife what he previously told his attorney.

Exception

The sixth and final issue is whether there is any exception to the privilege's scope. The opponent can defeat a privilege by showing either waiver or an exception. It may not serve the purpose of the privilege to apply it in a particular situation, or there may be a countervailing interest that overrides the privilege. In Section E of this chapter, we shall illustrate several important exceptions to the privilege's scope.

C. PRIVILEGES FOR CONFIDENTIAL COMMUNICATIONS—INVOKING A PRIVILEGE

1. ELEMENTS OF THE FOUNDATION

The claimant has the burden of proving the existence of the elements of the prima facie case for privilege. *People v. Cabral*, 12 Cal. App. 4th 820, 15 Cal. Rptr. 2d 866, 869-70 (1993) (although a court should liberally protect a privilege which has attached, "the privilege is to be strictly construed" when there is genuine doubt as to whether the privilege attached). The prima facie case for privilege includes these elements:

1. The privilege applies in this type of proceeding. The judge determines this by examining the pleadings in the case.
2. The claimant of the privilege is asserting the right type of privilege. If it is not obvious from the context, the claimant must specify the right he or she is claiming, that is, the right to personally refuse to disclose, the right to prevent a third party from disclosing, or the right to preclude comment on the invocation of the privilege.
3. The claimant is a proper holder.
4. The communication the claimant seeks to suppress is privileged.
   a. It was a communication.
   b. It was confidential.
   c. It occurred between properly related parties.
   d. It was incident to the relation.

2. SAMPLE FOUNDATION

Our first situation is a tort action arising from a collision. The plaintiff, Ms. Campbell, alleges that the defendant, Mr. Harris, caused the accident by speeding. Mr. Harris takes the stand during the defense case-in-chief. On direct examination, he testifies that he was going only twenty miles an hour, five miles under the speed limit. On cross-examination, the following occurs. The plaintiff's attorney is the proponent:

P Mr. Harris, ISN'T IT A FACT THAT you testified on direct examination that you were going only twenty miles an hour before the collision?
W Yes.
P ISN'T IT TRUE, Mr. Harris, THAT when you spoke with Mr. Riley, you told him that you were going thirty-five miles an hour?

O   Your Honor, I object to that question on the ground that it calls for a privileged attorney-client communication. (2) I request permission to take the witness on voir dire examination.

J   Permission granted.

O   Mr. Harris, WHO is this Mr. Riley? (4c)

W   He's a long-time friend of mine.

O   WHAT is his occupation? (4c)

W   He's an attorney.

O   HOW do you know he is an attorney? (4c)

W   His office door says attorney, he has a law degree and bar admission certificates on his wall, and he's represented my family in court before.

O   WHERE and WHEN did you talk to Mr. Riley about this case?

W   I think the first time was January 12 or 13 of 1993, just after the accident occurred.

O   WHAT happened during that meeting? (4a)

W   I told him about the accident.

O   Precisely, HOW did you give him information about the accident? (4a)

W   I told him about it. I didn't put it in writing or anything like that.

O   HOW many people were present when you had this meeting with Mr. Riley? (4b)

W   Just the two of us. Just me and my attorney.

O   HOW many doors are there to his office? (4b)

W   Just one.

O   WHAT position was the door in while you talked with him? (4b)

W   It was closed.

O   After you told him about the accident, to WHOM did you authorize him to give the information? (4b)

W   No one.

O   WHAT did you want him to do with the information? (4b)

W   Keep it secret, of course. He was my attorney.

O   WHY did you talk to him that day? (4d)

W   I thought I might need legal help. Even at the accident scene, the plaintiff said something about suing.

O   In WHAT capacity did you consult Mr. Riley? (4d), (2)

W   I was talking to him as an attorney, not just a family friend.

O   Your Honor, I have no further questions on voir dire. I renew my objection and assert my client's privilege to refuse to disclose his communications with his attorney. (2)

J   Objection sustained.

D.   PRIVILEGES FOR CONFIDENTIAL COMMUNICATIONS—DEFEATING A PRIVILEGE BY PROVING WAIVER

1. IN-COURT WAIVER

If the party opposing the privilege claim is going to argue an in-court waiver, that party must be prepared to point to the testimony that effected the waiver. The following is a continuation of the immediately preceding tort hypothetical. The plaintiff is the proponent.

P   Mr. Harris, ISN'T IT A FACT THAT when you first spoke with your family attorney, Mr. Riley, you told him that you were going thirty-five miles an hour?

O   Your Honor, I object to that question on the ground that it calls for a privileged attorney-client communication.

P   Your Honor, may we approach the bench?

J   Yes.

P   Your Honor, I concede that this communication would ordinarily be privileged. However, I contend that the defendant has already waived the privilege. I would request that the court reporter read the last question and answer on direct examination.

J   Very well.

CR   It'll take me just a second to find the passage. Yes, here it is. My notes show that the last question was: "What was your speed just before the collision?" The last answer was: "I was going at a safe rate of speed. That's what I told my attorney, Mr. Riley, when I first discussed the accident with him, and it's the same story I'm telling today. That's the truth."

P   This shows that on direct examination, the defendant expressly revealed his previous conversation with his attorney about the collision. That waives the privilege.

J   I agree. The objection is overruled.

P   Mr. Harris, let me repeat the question. ISN'T IT TRUE THAT you told your attorney that you were going thirty-five miles an hour?

W   Yes.

There can be a valid in-court waiver even if the holder is not advised about the privilege before the answer which effects the waiver. *People v. Barnett*, 17 Cal. 4th 1044, 954 P.2d 384, 74 Cal. Rptr. 2d 121, 181 (1998). An in-court waiver at the initial trial in a case may preclude invoking the privilege at a second trial of the same case. In *People v. Haskett*, 52 Cal. 3d 210, 242-43, 801 P.2d 323, 341-42, 276 Cal. Rptr. 80, 98-99 (1990), *cert. denied*, 502 U.S. 822 (1991), the defendant waived the psychotherapist privilege at the penalty phase of the first trial of his case. The court held that the waiver was also effective at the second penalty trial.

2. OUT-OF-COURT WAIVER

If the party opposing the privilege relies on the theory of out-of-court waiver, the party should lay the following foundation:

1. Where the out-of-court statement was made. The waiver can occur during pretrial discovery. *Scottsdale Ins. Co. v. Superior Court*, 59 Cal. App. 4th 263, 69 Cal. Rptr. 2d 112, 119 (1997) ("We conclude that failure to include an objection expressly based upon attorney-client privilege in the initial response [to a production request] results in waiver of the attorney-client privilege").

2. When the statement was made.

3. To whom the statement was made.

4. The holder knew that the addressee was outside the circle of confidence. The California cases do not explicitly require this element, but proof of this element strengthens the inference of the holder's intent to waive. If the holder makes the statement to an allied party in the litigation, there is a strong argument that the court should treat the allied party as being within the circle of confidence. Kopta, *Applying the Attorney-Client and Work Product Privileges to Allied Party Exchanges of Information in California*, 36 UCLA L. REV. 151 (1988).

5. The holder disclosed or consented to the disclosure of a significant part of the information to the addressee.[9]

6. The disclosure was voluntary. According to some authorities, a voluntary, albeit inadvertent, revelation of privileged information effects a waiver. *Aeroject-General Corp. v. Transport Indemnity Ins.*, 18 Cal. App. 4th 996, 22 Cal. Rptr. 2d 862 (1993).

We continue the hypothetical. Now the proponent will attempt to show that the holder waived the privilege by an out-of-court disclosure.

P Mr. Harris, ISN'T IT A FACT THAT when you first spoke with your family attorney, Mr. Riley, you told him that you were going thirty-five miles an hour?

O Your Honor, I object to that question on the ground that it calls for privileged attorney-client information.

P Your Honor, I request permission to take the witness on voir dire examination before you rule on the objection.

J Granted.

P Mr. Harris, ISN'T IT TRUE THAT on January 19 of this year, you had dinner with your cousin, James Carol? (1), (2), (3)

W Yes.

P ISN'T IT CORRECT THAT during this dinner, you discussed the accident with your cousin? (3)

W Yes.

P ISN'T IT A FACT THAT at the time, you knew your cousin wasn't working for your attorney in this case? (5)

W Right.

P ISN'T IT TRUE THAT during the discussion with your cousin, you described the conversation with your attorney? (5)

W Yes.

---

[9]In *Southern Cal. Gas Co. v. Public Utils. Comm'n*, 50 Cal. 3d 31, 40, 784 P.2d 1373, 1379, 265 Cal. Rptr. 801, 807 (1990), the California supreme court held that there was no nonstatutory waiver of the attorney-client privilege because the holder did not put "its attorney's advice or state of mind" in issue. In dictum, the court also stated that there was no statutory waiver (under CAL. EVID. CODE § 912): "disclosure of the fact of its attorneys review ... and the conclusions arrived at by its attorneys ... was not an express waiver. ..." *Id.* at 49, 784 P.2d at 1384, 265 Cal. Rptr. at 812. *See also People v. Tamborrino*, 215 Cal. App. 3d 575, 263 Cal. Rptr. 731 (1989); *Raytheon Co. v. Superior Ct.*, 208 Cal. App. 3d 683, 256 Cal. Rptr. 425 (1989).

P   And no one forced you to tell that to your cousin. DID THEY? (6)

W   No.

P   And no one made any threats to make you tell your cousin. ISN'T THAT TRUE? (6)

W   Yes.

P   Your Honor, I have no further questions on voir dire.

J   I see. The objection will be overruled.

P   Mr. Harris, let me repeat the question. ISN'T IT CORRECT THAT you told your attorney that you were going thirty-five miles an hour?

W   Yes.

In 1990, in *People v. Clark*, 50 Cal. 3d 583, 789 P.2d 127, 268 Cal. Rptr. 399, *modified*, 50 Cal. 3d 1157, *cert. denied*, 498 U.S. 973 (1990), the court arguably recognized a new, nontraditional type of waiver. In *Clark*, the defendant made confidential communications to a psychotherapist. Evidence Code § 1024 creates a special exception to the psychotherapist privilege; that section permits the psychotherapist to make disclosure when he or she "reasonably believes" that the patient poses a threat to himself or another and that disclosure "is necessary to prevent the threatened danger." Relying on that special exception, the psychotherapist in question revealed a confidential communication in the specific nature of a threat. The defendant later attempted to invoke the privilege to suppress testimony about the communication. The court stated that it was unnecessary for it to decide whether the defendant had somehow waived the privilege or even whether the psychotherapist had properly resorted to § 1024. The court simply asserted that "[t]he reason for the privilege—protecting the patient's right to privacy ...— and thus the privilege itself, disappear once the communication is no longer confidential." *Id.* at 620, 789 P.2d at 151, 268 Cal. Rptr. at 423. In effect, the court held that the psychotherapist's disclosure waived the privilege.

The *Clark* decision is debatable. The Evidence Code recognizes two methods of defeating a privilege which has otherwise attached; the opposing party may either establish a waiver satisfying the requirements of the Code or prove facts triggering a special exception set out in the Code. In *Clark*, the court rejected the privilege claim even though the opposing party had done neither. Moreover, the reasoning in *Clark* seems at odds with Evidence Code § 919. That section provides that a holder may later assert a privilege if disclosure was earlier "erroneously ... required to be made." Even if the disclosure was erroneously compelled, the opposing party could argue that the revelation vitiated the holder's privacy interest and that therefore, "[t]he reason for the privilege ... and thus the privilege itself, disappear. ..." The very existence of § 919 calls into question the validity of the *Clark* court's reasoning.

Despite the dubious reasoning in *Clark*, in 1991 the California Supreme Court appeared to adhere to *Clark* in *People v. Wharton*, 53 Cal. 3d 522, 809 P.2d 290, 280 Cal. Rptr. 631, 653-54 (1991), *cert. denied*, 502 U.S. 1038 (1992). Furthermore, in the same year the lower courts began invoking the *Clark* theory. *E.g.*, *People v. Johnson*, 233 Cal. App. 3d 425, 284 Cal. Rptr. 579, 584 (1991) (since in an earlier proceeding the defendant was charged with a crime against his spouse, the injured spouse exception codified in Evidence Code § 980 applied; pursuant to that exception, the defendant's wife testified against him at the preliminary hearing in that earlier case; the court ruled that the testimony was admissible against the defendant in a later proceeding; in justifying its ruling, the court stated that "[t]he reason for the privilege ... ceased to operate when confidentiality was lost. See *People v. Clark.* ..."), *cert. denied*, 503 U.S. 963 (1992).

However, in 1992, the Supreme Court reconsidered the broad language in *Clark*. In *Menendez v. Superior Court*, 3 Cal. 4th 435, 11 Cal. Rptr. 2d 92, 834 P.2d 786 (1992), the court criticized a trial judge who adopted a broad, literal reading of *Clark*. The court rejected the general proposition that an otherwise privileged communication loses its protected status simply because the communication is no longer confidential due to a disclosure. *Id.* at 450, 11 Cal. Rptr. 2d at 100-02, 834 P.2d at 793. The court stated that "only the patient has the power to waive the privilege in any part" and "only the patient has the power to cause the privilege to go out of existence in its entirety." *Id.* at 449, 11 Cal. Rptr. 2d at 100, 834 P.2d at 794. The court indicated that "*Clark* holds only that when a psychotherapist discloses a patient's threat to the patient's intended victim in a so-called '*Tarasoff* warning' ... the disclosed threat is not covered by the privilege." *Id.* at 447, 11 Cal. Rptr. 2d at 99, 834 P.2d at 793.

Even when the court finds a waiver in the traditional sense, the holder may still possibly prevail by persuading the court that the waiver is limited in scope. *Rodriguez v. Superior Court*, 14 Cal. App. 4th 1260, 1270, 18 Cal. Rptr. 2d 120, 126 (1993) ("waiver as to one aspect of a protected relationship"). *People v. Superior Court (Broderick)*, 231 Cal. App. 3d 584, 282 Cal. Rptr. 418, 422 (1991) recognizes this possibility:

> In considering the psychotherapist-patient privilege the court at the second hearing made a general finding that Betty had waived her privilege based on the doctors either having testified in earlier court proceedings or, if they did not testify, other doctors who did testify relying on their reports. ... The court did not make any inquiry whether the privilege had been waived as to specific doctors or as to all of the material sought from that doctor. While it may be that the privilege has been waived as to many if not all of the doctors and as to much if not all of the material, we consider the procedure followed by the court to be inadequate.

In 1996, one court indicated that the party opposing the privilege must establish any alleged waiver by "clear and convincing evidence." *Wells Fargo Bank, N.A. v. Superior Court (Boltwood)*, 49 Cal. App. 4th 1320, 57 Cal. Rptr. 2d 335, 345 (1996).

E. PRIVILEGES FOR CONFIDENTIAL COMMUNICATIONS—DEFEATING A PRIVILEGE BY PROVING AN EXCEPTION

As previously stated, the various privileges have numerous exceptions. On the one hand, the clergy-penitent privilege has no exceptions. JEFFERSON SYNOPSIS § 39.1, at 633. On the other hand, many of the privileges are riddled with exceptions. By way of example, there is an injured spouse exception to the spousal privilege. *People v. Johnson*, 233 Cal. App. 3d 425, 284 Cal. Rptr. 579 (1991), *cert. denied*, 503 U.S. 963 (1992). For its part, the psychotherapist privilege is subject to both a child abuse reporting exception, (*Roe v. Superior Court*, 229 Cal. App. 3d 832, 280 Cal. Rptr. 380 (1991)), and a dangerous patient exception. *People v. Wharton*, 53 Cal. 3d 522, 809 P.2d 290, 280 Cal. Rptr. 631 (1991) (if the exception came into play and the psychotherapist warned the threatened victim, the patient may not assert the privilege later; the privilege is unavailable later even when the patient has killed the victim and there is no future harm to be avoided; "From that point forward, section 1024 provides, 'There is no privilege. ...'"), *cert. denied*, 502 U.S. 1038 (1992); *Menendez v. Superior Court*, 3 Cal. 4th 435, 11 Cal. Rptr. 2d 92, 102, 834 P.2d 786 (1992). The exception

> does not demand that the patient must be dangerous to a person other than the psychotherapist. ... Nor does it demand that the psychotherapist must actually disclose the relevant communication or even issue a warning. [I]n Wharton, we made plain that the exception was 'not keyed to ... disclosure' or warning, but to the 'existence of the specified factual predicate,' viz., reasonable cause for belief in the dangerousness of the patient and the necessity of disclosure.

For that matter, even the attorney-client privilege is subject to several exceptions. *E.g., Smith, Smith & Kring v. Superior Court*, 60 Cal. App. 4th 573, 70 Cal. Rptr. 2d 507, 511 (1997) (an "allegation of legal malpractice against [a law firm] necessarily waives all claims of confidentiality as to them. See Evid. Code § 958 ...."). The only exceptions recognized in California are the statutory ones. 2 WITKIN § 1072; *Shannon v. Superior Court*, 217 Cal. App. 3d 986, 997-98, 266 Cal. Rptr. 242, 249 (1990) (rejecting the trial court's creation of a "necessity" exception to the attorney-client privilege). *But see County of Alameda v. Superior Court*, 192 Cal. App. 3d 1064, 237 Cal. Rptr. 780 (1987) (judicially created exception to psychotherapist-patient privilege). The following subsections illustrate some of the more important exceptions. As these subsections exemplify, the party opposing the claim of privilege often relies on voir dire examination to show the factual predicate for the exception.

1. FUTURE CRIMES OR FRAUDS

The legislature will not permit holders to abuse and pervert the privileges. For that reason, the Code usually denies a privilege claim if the party opposing the claim shows that at the time of the communication, the holder sought the information or advice to facilitate the commission of a future crime or fraud. The foundation for this exception usually requires proof that:

1. At the time of the communication, the holder knew that the contemplated course of conduct was illegal or fraudulent. The proposed Federal Rule of Evidence 503(d)(1) used the language, "knew or reasonably should have known."
2. The purpose of the communication was to obtain information or advice to facilitate the commission of a future crime or fraud. As the California Law Revision Commission comment to § 981 explains, the exception "does not permit disclosure of communications that merely reveal a plan to commit a fraud or crime; it permits disclosure only of communications made to enable to aid anyone to commit or plan to commit a crime or fraud." In *People v. Clark*, 50 Cal. 3d 583, 789 P.2d 127, 268 Cal. Rptr. 399, *modified*, 50 Cal. 3d 1157, *cert. denied*, 498 U.S. 973 (1990), the California Supreme Court said that the crime/fraud exception does not apply when the client merely threatens future criminal conduct and does not seek the attorney's aid in carrying out the threat. The crime/fraud exception to the attorney-client privilege "requires an intention on the part of the client to abuse the attorney-client relationship." *Id.* at 623, 789 P.2d at 153, 268 Cal. Rptr. at 425 (citing *Glade v. Superior Court*, 76 Cal. App. 3d 738, 746, 143 Cal. Rptr. 119 (1978)); *State Farm Fire & Cas. v. Superior Court*, 54 Cal. App. 4th 625, 62 Cal. Rptr. 2d 834, 848, *modified*, 97 C.D.O.S. 3262 (1997) ("it is the intent of the client upon which attention must be focused and not that of the lawyers").

Before the Evidence Code, some California courts recognized the exception so long as there was a prima facie case or permissive inference of the existence of the improper intent in the holder's mind; the courts did so in part out of recognition of the difficulty of proving the holder's state of mind. HEAFEY § 35.20, at 383. It is arguable that the procedure stated in Evidence Code § 405 is now controlling. *Id.* However, California courts continue to apply the prima facie showing standard. *BP Alaska Exploration, Inc. v. Superior Court*, 199 Cal. App. 3d 1240, 245 Cal. Rptr. 682 (1988). Under either view, it is insufficient for the opponent to simply assert that the holder had fraud in mind; the opponent must establish "some foundation in fact" for the assertion. *Id.* at 1262, 245 Cal. Rptr. at 696. Some courts caution that the doctrine is "a very limited exception" and that the opponent "bears the burden of proof. ..." *Geilim v. Superior Court (People)*, 234 Cal. App. 3d 166, 285 Cal. Rptr. 602, 607 (1991); *Wells Fargo Bank, N.A. v. Superior Court*

(*Boltwood*), 49 Cal. App. 4th 1320, 57 Cal. Rptr. 2d 335, 347 (1996) (there was "only ... speculation" that there had been misconduct by the trustee); *State Farm Fire & Cas. v. Superior Court*, 54 Cal. App. 4th 625, 62 Cal. Rptr. 2d 834, 847, *modified*, 97 C.D.O.S. 3262 (1997) (the court cites two cases holding that "the showing of probable cause to issue a search warrant did not rise to the level of a prima facie showing to establish the crime/fraud exception").

Our fact situation is a prosecution for willful tax evasion. Suppose that California law requires that the purchaser of goods pay a 4 percent sales tax unless the goods are intended for interstate shipment. If the goods are intended for interstate shipment, the purchaser obtains a tax exemption form from the seller and submits the completed form to the Franchise Tax Board. The People allege that in August 1993, the defendant, Mr. Lloyd Marx, purchased goods for intrastate shipment and willfully evaded the tax. The goods were 230 air conditioners. The defendant took the stand during his case-in-chief. On direct examination, the defendant admits that he purchased the air conditioners and neither paid the tax nor filed the exemption form. However, he also testifies that he did not understand the procedures for filing the form and claiming the exemption. The following occurs on cross-examination. The proponent is the prosecutor. The prosecutor is attempting to prove willfulness.

P Mr. Marx, ISN'T IT TRUE THAT in June 1999, you spoke with Mr. Felton of the local office of the Franchise Tax Board? (1)
W Yes.
P ISN'T IT A FACT THAT during this conversation, you asked him whether you had to pay a sales tax on purchases for intrastate shipments? (1)
W Right.
P AND DIDN'T HE tell you that you had to do so? (1)
W Yes.
P ISN'T IT CORRECT THAT on July 1, 1999, you entered into a contract for the sale of air conditioners to Johnson Construction Company? (2)
W Yes.
P ISN'T IT TRUE THAT Johnson has its office in this city and state—Cupertino, California? (2)
W Yes.
P ISN'T IT A FACT THAT you promised to deliver the air conditioners in September to their office in this state? (2)
W Yes.
P ISN'T IT CORRECT THAT the number of air conditioners you promised to sell them was 230? (2)
W Yes.
P AND ISN'T THAT the exact number of air conditioners you bought on August 1, 1999? (2)
W Yes.

Later, during the prosecution rebuttal, the prosecutor calls Ms. Celia Waylan as a witness. The prosecutor is still the proponent. Ms. Waylan has already identified herself and stated that she is an attorney.

P Ms. Waylan, WHERE were you on the morning of July 20, 1999?

W I was in my office.

P WHERE is your office?

W Downtown on High Street.

P WHAT happened that morning?

W I had a visit from a client.

P WHO was that client?

W It was the defendant, Mr. Marx.

P WHERE is Mr. Marx now?

W In this courtroom.

P Specifically, WHERE in the courtroom?

W He's sitting right there.

P HOW is he dressed?

W In plaid slacks and a blue shirt.

P Your Honor, please let the record reflect that the witness has identified the defendant.

J It will so reflect.

P WHAT happened when the defendant came to your office that morning?

W He asked for some advice.

P WHAT advice?

O Your Honor, I object to that question on the ground that it calls for privileged attorney-client information.

P Your Honor, may we approach the bench?

J Yes.

P Your Honor, I concede that Ms. Waylan is an attorney and that the defendant consulted her as such. However, I offer to prove that the witness will testify that the defendant asked how he could evade paying a tax or filing a form on a shipment. She will further testify that she advised him that there was no way to avoid paying or filing. This conversation occurred in July, well before the purchase of the air conditioners in August. She will finally testify that he said that she obviously misunderstood his question and that he wanted her advice as to the best way to evade the law without getting caught. Since the defendant had already talked with Mr. Felton and had already entered into an intrastate shipment contract, the inference is that the defendant sought Ms. Waylan's advice to facilitate a future crime.

J I think there's a sufficient showing to invoke the exception. I shall overrule the objection.

P Ms. Waylan, WHAT advice did the defendant ask for?

W He asked how he could get around paying a tax or filing a form.

P WHAT did you tell him?

W I said that there wasn't; he had to do one or the other. If the goods were destined for intrastate sale, he had to pay the tax. If the goods were destined for interstate shipment, he had to file a form with the state. It was one or the other.

P WHAT did the defendant say then?

W He told me that I'd obviously misunderstood his question. He said that he'd already entered into a contract for an intrastate shipment and that he wanted my advice as to how to evade the law without getting caught.

Evidence Code § 956 recognizes this exception to the attorney-client privilege. There are similar exceptions to the medical privileges. Evidence Code §§ 997, 1018. *But see People v. Superior Court (Bauman & Rose)*, 37 Cal. App. 4th 1757, 44 Cal. Rptr. 2d 734 (1995) (refusing to recognize a similar exception to the work product protection); *State Farm Fire & Cas. v. Superior Court*, 54 Cal. App. 4th 625, 62 Cal. Rptr. 2d 834, 851, *modified*, 97 C.D.O.S. 3262 (1997).

2. JOINT CONSULTATION

If two parties consult an attorney about a common problem, there is an attorney-client privilege. Either party may assert that privilege against a third party. What happens, though, if the parties have a falling out and sue each other? May one party claim the privilege against the other party? In this situation, the courts have generally denied the privilege. The courts reason that there was no confidentiality as between the two parties; they freely communicated with each other and the attorney. This exception is codified in Evidence Code § 962. The joint consultation exception applies even if the two clients do not meet with the attorney at the same time. *Glacier General Assurance Co. v. Superior Court of Los Angeles County*, 95 Cal. App. 3d 836, 157 Cal. Rptr. 435 (1979). However, in the typical case the clients and the attorney meet together. To establish the joint consultation exception to the privilege in a typical case, the party opposing the claim should show that:

1. They both met with the attorney. Suppose that an insurance company issues a policy to an insured. The insured later makes a claim under the policy. In the insured's absence, the insurer consults an attorney about the coverage question. On these facts, the attorney does not represent the insured; the insurer has not hired the attorney to defend any lawsuit brought against the insured. Consequently, the insured cannot invoke "the 'joint client' exception" to obtain confidential communications between the insurer and the attorney. *State Farm Fire & Cas. Co. v. Superior Court*, 206 Cal. App. 3d 1428, 1432, 254 Cal. Rptr. 543, 545 (1988). *Rockwell Intern. v. Superior Court*, 26 Cal. App. 4th 1255, 32 Cal. Rptr. 2d 153, 159-60 (1994) distinguishes the Illinois authorities applying this exception so long as there is commonality of interest between the parties. *Rockwell* reads the California cases as restricting the exception to situations in which both parties retain the attorney to represent them.
2. They met with the attorney at a certain time.
3. They met with the attorney at a certain place.
4. The party claiming the privilege knew that the other party was present.
5. The party claiming the privilege voluntarily participated in the joint consultation.
6. The purpose of the consultation was to seek legal advice.
7. The advice related to a common problem.

Our fact situation is a contract action. The plaintiff, Mr. Zikes, sues the defendant, Mr. Adams, on a contract. The contract provides that the defendant was to pay the plaintiff a percentage of the receipts of the defendant's business in exchange for the plaintiff's investment in the business. The central dispute in the case is over the meaning of the term "receipts." The plaintiff contends that the term means gross receipts, while the defendant asserts that the term means net receipts after deducting certain expenses. The plaintiff takes the stand during his case-in-chief. The following occurs on cross-examination. The proponent is the defendant.

P Mr. Zikes, ISN'T IT TRUE THAT you entered this contract on February 14, 1999?

W Yes.

P ISN'T IT A FACT THAT before you entered this contract, you consulted an attorney?

W Yes.

P ISN'T IT TRUE THAT that attorney was Marcia Harris?

W Yes.

P ISN'T IT CORRECT THAT you met with Ms. Harris at her office on February 12, 1999? (1), (2), (3)

W Yes.

P ISN'T IT TRUE THAT the defendant, Mr. Adams, was also present? (1)

W Yes.

P And no one forced you to attend the meeting with Mr. Adams. DID THEY? (5)

W No.

P And no one threatened you if you didn't attend the meeting. DID THEY? (5)

W No.

P ISN'T IT TRUE THAT at this meeting, you both spoke with Ms. Harris about the contract? (6), (7)

W Yes.

P AND ISN'T IT A FACT THAT you both asked for her advice about drafting the contract? (6), (7)

W Yes.

P ISN'T IT CORRECT THAT during this meeting, you told her that the receipts should be computed after deducting salary expenses?

O Your Honor, I object to that question on the ground that it calls for privileged information.

P Your Honor, may we approach the bench?

J Yes.

P Your Honor, the record shows that this meeting was a joint consultation with the attorney. The plaintiff and defendant jointly consulted Ms. Harris about a common problem, and the plaintiff cannot assert the privilege against the defendant.

J I concur. The objection will be overruled.

P Mr. Zikes, let me repeat the question. ISN'T IT A FACT that during your meeting with the attorney, you told her that the receipts should be computed after deducting salary expenses?

W Yes.

3. THE PATIENT LITIGANT EXCEPTION

One of the most important exceptions to the medical privilege is the patient-litigant exception. If the patient sues and tenders the issue of his or her condition, the patient loses the privilege for communications relevant to that condition. The theory is that it would be unfair to permit the patient litigant to suppress such highly relevant information when it is the patient who tendered the issue. To decide whether this exception applies in a particular case, the judge must examine the complaint and determine whether the complaint tenders an issue of physical or mental condition to which the communication is logically relevant. *Rittenhouse v. Superior Court*, 235 Cal. App. 3d 1584, 1 Cal. Rptr. 2d 595, 599 (1991) ("The issue ... was injected into these proceedings by Stanford itself, not petitioner. Petitioner has done nothing more than respond to factual allegations made in Stanford's contest. This is not a 'tender' within the meaning of section 996."). The subject-matter of the communication must be directly relevant to the specific condition that the patient puts in issue. *In re Lifschutz*, 2 Cal. 3d 415, 431, 467 P.2d 557, 567, 85 Cal. Rptr. 829, 839 (1970). "However, the courts vary in how vigorous they apply the rule." In *Davis v. Superior Court (Williams)*, 7 Cal. App. 4th 1008, 9 Cal. Rptr. 2d 331, 335-36 (1992), a "garden-variety ... personal injury action" in which plaintiff prayed for damages for pain and suffering, the court held that the prayer did not "ipso facto place mental condition in issue" and permit discovery of the plaintiff's psychotherapy records. Similarly, in *Allison v. Worker's Compensation Appeals Board*, 72 Cal. App .4th 654, 84 Cal. Rptr. 2d 915 (1999), the court held that in the case of a worker's compensation claimant, the exception was limited to the alleged work-related injury and did not extend to a general inquiry into her hospitalization history. However, in *Slagle v. Superior Court*, 211 Cal. App. 3d 1309, 260 Cal. Rptr. 122 (1989), the court construed the patient-litigant exception (California Evidence Code § 999) expansively. The dissent argued forcefully that allowing the defendant to discover prior records concerning an injury for which plaintiff did not seek damages was inconsistent with the clear and unambiguous language of § 999. *Id.* at 1315, 260 Cal. Rptr. at 126.

Our fact situation is a tort action in which the plaintiff claims extensive personal injuries. In particular, the complaint prays for $30,000 in damages for pain and suffering. The defendant calls Dr. Metal as a witness. Dr. Metal identifies himself and states that he formerly treated the plaintiff. He testifies that he examined the plaintiff two days after the accident. The defendant is the proponent.

P   Dr. Metal, during the examination, WHAT, if anything, did the plaintiff say about his pain?

O   Your Honor, I object to that question on the ground that it calls for privileged information.

P   Your Honor, may we approach the bench?

J   Yes.

P   Your Honor, I offer to prove that the witness will testify that the plaintiff said his pain was not intense. On page nine of his complaint, the plaintiff prays for

$30,000 in damages for pain and suffering. As a litigant, the plaintiff tendered the issue of the extent of his pain. The statement he made to his physician is logically relevant to his condition and pain.

J   The objection is overruled.

P   Dr. Metal, let me repeat the question, WHAT, if anything, did the plaintiff say about his pain?

W   He said it wasn't very intense. He felt it occasionally, but it bothered him only off and on and then only slightly.

Although the medical privileges have express, statutory patient-litigant exceptions (§§ 996, 1016), there is no comparable provision in the statu tes governing the attorney-client privilege. *People v. Lines*, 13 Cal. 3d 500, 531 P.2d 793, 119 Cal. Rptr. 225 (1975). However, suppose that the client is a securities dealer who sells stock without registration. It develops that registration was necessary, and a buyer later sues the dealer for damages, including punitive damages. The dealer defends in part on the ground that she acted in good faith, specifically, in reliance on counsel's advice. In this hypothetical, the attorney's advice should obviously be discoverable. Article, *Limitations on California Professional Privileges; Waiver Principles and the Policies They Promote*, 9 U.C. DAVIS L. REV. 477, 519 (1976). However, the discovery should not be rationalized by torturing the wording of the attorney-client statutes. Rather, discovery should be permitted on the straightforward theory that the client waives the privilege by placing the attorney's advice in issue. *Id.* at 518-19; *People v. Clark*, 5 Cal. 4th 950, 857 P.2d 1099, 22 Cal. Rptr. 2d 689 (1993).

F.   THE WORK PRODUCT PROTECTION

1. THE CONDITIONAL WORK PRODUCT PROTECTION

In the three previous sections we examined the privileges for confidential communications. Because of the requirements discussed there, the attorney-client privilege does not protect such material as a witness's statement, a nonmedical expert's report, or a model prepared for trial. These materials are not communica tions between an attorney and client, and consequently, they fall outside the privilege.

However, ours is an adversary system, and most attorneys find it distasteful to disclose their trial preparation materials to opposing counsel. In addition, many judges believe that trial preparation materials deserve some protection; it strikes them as unfair to permit the opposing counsel to reap the benefit of the other attorney's factual investigation and legal research. Since the attorney-client privilege does not protect these materials, attorneys and courts looked elsewhere for a new rationale to protect trial preparation materials.

In the leading case of *Hickman v. Taylor*, 329 U.S. 495 (1947), the Supreme Court created a new evidentiary doctrine, the work product protection to protect trial preparation materials. The Court commented: "Proper preparation of a client's case demands that [the lawyer] assemble information, sift what he considers to be the relevant from the irrelevant facts, prepare his legal theories and plan his strategy without undue and needless interference." *Id.* at 511. The Court emphasized that it was not creating an absolute privilege:

> We do not mean to say that all written materials obtained or prepared by an adversary's counsel with an eye toward litigation are necessarily free from discovery in all cases. Where relevant and non-privileged facts remain hidden in an attorney's file and where production of those facts is essential to the preparation of one's case, discovery may properly be had.

Id.

Ultimately, the Supreme Court adopted Federal Rule of Civil Procedure 26(b)(3), stating and refining the *Hickman* doctrine:

> Subject to the provisions of subdivision (b)(4) of this rule, a party may obtain discovery of documents and tangible things otherwise discoverable under subdivision (b)(1) of this rule and prepared in anticipation of litigation or for trial by or for another party or by or for that other party's representative (including the other party's attorney, consultant, surety, indemnitor, insurer or agent) only upon a showing that the party seeking discovery has substantial need of the materials in the preparation of the party's case and that the party is unable without undue hardship to obtain the substantial equivalent of the materials by other means.

California also recognizes the work product doctrine. 2 HOGAN ch. 13. Code of Civil Procedure § 2018 reads:

> (a) It is the policy of the state to: (1) preserve the rights of attorneys to prepare cases for trial with that degree of privacy necessary to encourage them to prepare their cases thoroughly and to investigate not only the favorable but the unfavorable aspects of those cases; and (2) to prevent attorneys from taking undue advantage of their adversary's industry and efforts.
>
> (b) Subject to subdivision (c), the work product of an attorney shall not be discoverable unless the court determines that denial of discovery will unfairly prejudice the party seeking discovery in preparing that party's claim or defense or will result in an injustice.
>
> (c) Any writing that reflects an attorney's impressions, conclusions, opinions, or legal research or theories will not be discoverable under any circumstances.

Prior to the passage of Proposition 115, the California judicial opinions had extended the work product protection to criminal cases. *Izazaga v. Superior Court*, 54 Cal. 3d 356, 815 P.2d 304, 285 Cal. Rptr. 231, 248, *modified*, 54 Cal. 3d 611 (1991); *People v. Municipal Court for San Francisco Judicial Dist.*, 89 Cal.

App. 3d 739, 153 Cal. Rptr. 69 (1979). Proposition 115 added § 1054.6 to the Penal Code. That section provides: "Neither the defendant nor the prosecuting attorney is required to disclose any materials or information which are work product as defined in subdivision (c) of Section 2018 of the Code of Civil Procedure. ..."

The party invoking the work product privilege must establish the following foundational elements:

1. The party is invoking the privilege in the right type of proceeding. The privilege can be asserted not only in the litigation that prompted the creation of the material; the privilege may also be exercised in later litigation. JEFFERSON SYNOPSIS § 41.2, at 671.

2. The party is asserting the right type of privilege. The work product privilege is the personal right to refuse to disclose the material during pretrial discovery or at trial.

3. The party claiming the privilege is a proper holder. The courts treat the attorney and the client as holders. In most of the decided cases, the attorney has asserted the privilege. Before the passage of Proposition 115, the cases were split over the question of whether a prosecutor may assert the work product privilege. Some cases refused to allow a prosecutor to do so on the rationale that the prosecutor does not have a client in the orthodox sense. 2 JEFFERSON § 41.2, at 1500-01 (collecting the cases).

4. The information the party seeks to suppress is work product material. To qualify as work product material, the information must satisfy three requirements.

   a. The information is derivative rather than primary material. Comment, 6 SW. U.L. REV. 677 (1974). Primary material is material historically connected to the case such as the actual brake from the car involved in an accident. An example of derivative material would be a model of the brake. Primary material would be the witness's knowledge of the accident; a party cannot invoke the work product privilege to prevent the opposing counsel from deposing a witness. However, the witness's written statement would be derivative material. 2 HOGAN § 13.8. *See also In re Jeanette H.*, 225 Cal. App. 3d 25, 32, 275 Cal. Rptr. 9, 13 (1990) ("the great weight of authority holds" that lists of intended witnesses are conditionally protected work product material). In short, the attorney's effort and imagination play a role in the creation of derivative material.

   b. The information is the work product of an attorney or someone working with the attorney. A few jurisdictions still insist that the attorney personally prepare the material. However, that requirement interferes with the manner in which attorneys customarily conduct their business. They often use clerks, investigators, and the client to gather information and prepare reports. For that reason, California now extends the privilege to information collected by the attorney's agent. 2 HOGAN at § 13.1.

    c. The material must be prepared in anticipation of litigation. Suit need not be filed; but when the material is prepared, the client and attorney must anticipate litigation.

To date, the courts have restricted the conditional protection to physical material, including written statements and exhibits. However, it could be argued that the protection should extend to oral testimony that would divulge investigatory activities on behalf of a litigant. *People v. Melton*, 44 Cal. 3d 713, 742-43, 750 P.2d 741, 756-57, 244 Cal. Rptr. 867, 883, *cert. denied*, 488 U.S. 934 (1988).

Since this protection is conditional, the opposing party seeking discovery can defeat the protection under § 2018 (b). The opposing party can do so by showing that:

5. The information is logically relevant to the material facts of consequence in the case.
6. The information is highly relevant to the outcome of the case. The opponent should argue that the information relates to the central or one of the central issues in the case.
7. There is no reasonably available, alternative source for the information. Either there is no alternative source at all, or resort to the alternative source would involve prohibitive expense or inconvenience.

This showing should be made with independently admissible evidence. *County of Los Angeles v. Superior Court*, 222 Cal. App. 3d 647, 654 n.4, 271 Cal. Rptr. 698, 702 n.4 (the attorney's declaration contained incompetent hearsay), *review. denied*, 1990 Cal. LEXIS 4578 (1990).

The work-product privilege issue ordinarily arises during pretrial discovery; one party seeks discovery of a document, and the opposing party resists discovery by claiming the privilege. Given the pretrial context, attorneys usually present their supporting facts in declarations rather than eliciting live testimony. To illustrate the doctrine, we shall present first a claimant's declaration, then a sample foundation for the claimant in the unlikely eventuality the claimant uses live testimony, and finally the opponent's affidavit. In our hypothetical, the party seeking discovery desires an accident reconstruction report. The party resisting discovery is the plaintiff, Ms. Leonard. The expert was Professor Suarez. When the plaintiff submitted this, the attorney would simultaneously submit a declaration memorandum of points and authorities. The memorandum would cite the statutes and cases granting the material work product privilege. 2 HOGAN ch. 13 reviews the statutes and case law.

Declaration

1. My name is Stephen Metzger. I reside at 452 Madison Street, San Diego, California. I am an attorney with the firm of Luce, Gray, Forward, and Ames, 433 B Street, San Diego, California.

2. I represent Ms. Adrienne Leonard, the plaintiff in *Leonard v. Morton*, civil action number 1778 now pending in San Diego Superior Court (1).

3. The defendant has moved for the production of a report submitted to me by Professor Paul Suarez. My client and I hereby claim the work product privilege, (3) and on that ground we refuse to surrender Professor Suarez' report to the defendant. (2)

4. On February 14, 1999, I decided that I needed an expert evaluation of the physical evidence left at the scene of the collision between the defendant's van and my client's car on February 11, 1999. (4c) In her complaint, my client alleges that the defendant's car drifted into her lane and that the point of impact was in her lane. The defendant's answer denies these allegations, and I lack the expertise in physics and the laws of motion to evaluate the physical evidence left at the accident scene. Consequently, on February 15, 1999, I telephoned Professor Paul Suarez who teaches in the Physics Department at the University of California, San Diego. I have used him in several prior cases as an accident reconstruction expert. I told Professor Suarez that I needed an expert evaluation of the accident scene as part of my pretrial preparation; I asked him for a confidential report on that subject. He agreed to prepare the report and submit it to me. (4b) On February 16, 1999, Professor Suarez and I visited the accident scene, and on February 20, 1999, he submitted his personal written report to me. (4a) The report recites his findings and conclusions as to the manner in which the collision occurred. I have maintained the report's confidentiality; the only persons who have viewed the report are Professor Suarez, my client, and myself. At the present time, I have not decided whether to call Professor Suarez as a witness at trial.

I declare under penalty of perjury that the above statements are true and correct.

This declaration was executed on April 2, 1999, at San Diego, San Diego County, California.

/s/ Stephen Metzger

In some instances, the party asserting the work product protection might present live testimony in opposition to the motion for the production of the protected report. Or the party might offer live testimony if the other side subpoenas the report's author and the party moves pretrial to quash the subpoena or objects at trial. *Cf. Williamson v. Superior Court of Los Angeles County*, 21 Cal. 3d 829,

582 P.2d 126, 148 Cal. Rptr. 39 (1978); *Lindsay v. Lipson*, 367 Mich. 1, 116 N.W.2d 60 (1962). In the following example, the witness is Professor Suarez. He has already identified himself and stated his occupation. The plaintiff, the party resisting discovery, is the proponent.

P Professor, WHERE were you on the morning of February 15, 1999?

W I was in my office at the U.C.S.D. campus in La Jolla.

P WHAT happened that morning?

W I received a telephone call from you.

P WHAT was said during this telephone call? (4a)

W You told me that you wanted an expert evaluation of the scene of the accident between your client and the defendant.

P WHAT was the purpose of this evaluation? (4c)

W At least your stated purpose was that you needed it as part of your pretrial preparation.

P WHAT was your response when I asked you to conduct the evaluation? (4b)

W I agreed to do so.

P WHAT happened then?

W I met you and visited the accident scene on February 16.

P Please be specific. WHERE did you go?

W I went to the intersection of C and 5th Streets where this accident supposedly occurred.

P WHAT did you do after you visited the accident scene? (4a)

W I prepared a report.

P WHAT form was the report in? (4a)

W It was a typed, four-page document.

P WHAT did you do with the report?

W I gave the original and two copies to you.

P HOW many copies were there?

W Three.

P WHAT did you do with the other copy?

W I have it in my files.

P WHO has access to your files?

W Only myself.

P WHOM have you shown the report to?

W Only you.

P WHY haven't you shown the report to other people?

W You instructed me to keep it confidential, and I've carried out your instructions.

P WHAT role will you have at the trial in this case?

W I do not intend to testify in this case. You have not asked me to. For my part, I have not agreed to or indicated any willingness to do so.

Finally, the following is the format for declaration by the party seeking discovery:

Declaration

1. My name is James Gamer. I reside at 7076 Vista Way, Del Mar, California. I am the attorney with the firm of Sullivan and Archer, 1234 1st Street, San Diego, California.

2. I represent Mr. Philip Morton, the defendant in *Leonard v. Morton*, civil action number 1778 now pending in San Diego Superior Court.

3. We have moved for the production of a report submitted by Professor Paul Suarez to the plaintiff's attorney, Mr. Stephen Metzger. The subject of the report is an expert evaluation of the physical evidence left at the scene of the collision between the plaintiff's car and my client's van at the intersection of C and 5th Streets in downtown San Diego. The report is logically relevant to the material facts in this case. On page 12 of the plaintiff's complaint, she alleges that my client's van drifted into her traffic lane and the point of impact was in her lane. Page 4 of the defendant's answer denies those allegations. Thus, the point of impact is a material fact of consequence in this case, and Professor Suarez' accident reconstruction report undoubtedly discusses point of impact. (5)

4. The information contained in Professor Suarez' report may be highly relevant to the outcome of this case. If the jury finds as a matter of fact that my client's van drifted into the plaintiff's lane, that fact alone may persuade the jurors to conclude that my client was negligent. However, if the jury finds as a matter of fact that the point of impact was in my client's lane, again that fact alone may convince the jurors that the plaintiff's own carelessness caused the accident. (6)

5. There is no reasonably available, alternative source for this information. In the first place, Professor Suarez is widely regarded as the leading accident reconstruction expert in San Diego County. During the past five years, our own law firm has used him more often than any other accident reconstruction witness in our cases. His report would be more authoritative than any other local expert's report. Secondly, Professor Suarez' report may contain a more detailed description of the physical evidence at the accident than any other report. Page 4 of the February 12, 1999 San Diego Police Department Accident Report filed in this case states that there was "a good deal of debris," but neither the report's narrative section nor the attached diagram indicates the nature or specific location of the debris. Mr. Morton did not employ this law firm until March 13, 1999. We immediately hired an accident reconstruction expert, but she was unable to visit the accident scene until March 16, 1999—weeks after the accident. I accompanied her to the scene; but when we did so, we could not locate any skidmarks,

gouge marks, or debris clearly attributable to the accident. In contrast, Professor Suarez visited the scene only a few days after the collision. Hence, Professor Suarez' report may be the only source for critical information about the accident scene.

I declare under penalty of perjury that the above statements are true and correct.

This declaration was executed on April 15, 1999, at San Diego, San Diego County, California.

_____

/s/ James Gamer

Even when the protection attaches and the party seeking discovery does not override the protection before trial, there may be a waiver if the protected party presents testimony from the source of the material. In one case, the California Supreme Court assumed *arguendo* that the protection applies to testimony about investigatory activities on a defendant's behalf. However, the court added that since the defendant called the investigator as a trial witness, the defendant "could not suppress as privileged, damaging evidence which was within the scope of his direct examination." *People v. Melton*, 44 Cal. 3d 713, 74243, 750 P.2d 741, 756-57, 244 Cal. Rptr. 867, 883, *cert. denied*, 488 U.S. 934 (1988).

2. THE ABSOLUTE WORK PRODUCT PROTECTION

The common-law work product protection is conditional; the party seeking discovery can overcome the protection by showing a compelling need for the information. However, by statute, some jurisdictions recognize an absolute work product privilege for certain types of very sensitive trial preparation materials. Federal Rule of Civil Procedure 26(b) is illustrative. After stating the conditional work product privilege, the Rule continues: "In ordering discovery of such material when the required showing has been made, the court shall protect against disclosure of the mental impressions, conclusions, opinions, or legal theories of an attorney or other representative of a party concerning the litigation." California also recognizes an absolute privilege. 2 HOGAN § 13.2. Code of Civil Procedure § 2018(d) declares that writings reflecting "an attorney's impressions, conclusions, opinions, or legal research or theories" are not discoverable "under any circumstances." Those materials are absolutely protected; even if the party seeking discovery shows a compelling need for the material, the material cannot be discovered. The problem is purely definitional; if the material falls within one of the categories listed in the statute, the discovery motion must be denied. When a party seeks discovery of such material, the party claiming the absolute work product privilege usually responds by affidavit setting out the facts allegedly triggering the absolute privilege.

Until 1990, there was a split of authority over whether the opinion work product statute bars discovery even by a former client in a malpractice action. The California Supreme Court had refused to review the two conflicting cases on the issue. In *Neeb v. Superior Court*, 214 Cal. App. 3d 693, 262 Cal. Rptr. 887 (1989), disclosure was denied. In *Platt v. Superior Court*, 214 Cal. App. 3d 779, 783, 263 Cal. Rptr. 32, 34 (1989), however, the court ordered disclosure, criticizing *Neeb* for "reach[ing] an incorrect conclusion because it fails to consider ... its holding in light of other statutes and rules requiring attorneys to deliver their work product to former clients." *Platt* concluded that "[t]he entire context of the absolute work product protection first enacted in 1963 was to prevent inappropriate discovery by third-party adversaries." *Id.* at 790, 263 Cal. Rptr. at 39. In 1990, the legislature amended Code of Civil Procedure § 2018 to resolve this dispute. The legislature did so by adding a new subdivision (f) to the statute:

> In an action between an attorney and his or her client or former client, no work product privilege under this section exists if the work product is relevant to an issue of breach by the attorney of a duty to the attorney's client arising out of the attorney-client relationship.

The amendment was intended to codify *Platt* and overturn *Neeb*. Slind-Flor, *Debate on Work Product Rages*, NAT'L L.J., Dec. 17, 1990, at 3, 26. The split of authority persists, though; § 2018 applies only in actions between the attorney, and his or her client, and the issue can rise in other contexts such as a lawsuit between the attorney's present and former clients. *Metro Goldwyn-Mayer, Inc. v. Superior Court*, 25 Cal. App. 4th 242, 30 Cal. Rptr. 2d 371 (1994).

With one exception, the foundation for absolute work product privilege is roughly the same as the foundation for conditional work product privilege:

1. The party is invoking the privilege in the right type of proceeding. The judge examines the pleadings on file to determine whether the case is the right type of action.
2. The party is asserting the right type of protection. The privilege is the personal right to refuse to disclose the material during pretrial discovery or at a trial.
3. The party claiming the privilege is a proper holder. The courts treat the attorney and the client as holders.
4. This is the exceptional element. The claimant must show that the information the party seeks to suppress is absolutely protected.
   a. The material reflects the attorney's creative thought process. A memorandum summarizing the attorney's impressions of a witness or outlining the attorney's legal theories would be absolutely protected.
   b. The material is the work product of an attorney. In the case of absolutely protected material, most courts require that the attorney personally prepare the material. However, if part of an expert's report reflects the attorney's impressions, opinions, or theories, that part of the report is

absolutely privileged. *National Steel Products Co. v. Superior Court*, 164 Cal. App. 3d 476, 489, 210 Cal. Rptr. 535, 542 (1985).

c. The material was prepared in anticipation of litigation.

The following is a declaration an attorney might file to assert absolute work product privilege:

Declaration

1. My name is Peter Mehalick. I reside at 1333 Cape May Street, San Diego, California. I am an attorney with the firm of Seltzer, Muns, and Mason, 2444 4th Street, San Diego, California.

2. I represent Ms. Michelle Lucerne, the plaintiff in Lucerne v. Rodriguez, civil action number 1997 now pending in San Diego Superior Court. (1)

3. The defendant has moved for the production of the witness statement of Mr. Giles Folsom, an eyewitness to the collision that gave rise to this suit. The defendant's motion specifically stated that the defendant desired Mr. Folsom's statement "and all attachments." My client and I hereby claim the absolute work product privilege, (3) and on that ground we refuse to surrender one attachment, a memorandum that I personally prepared and that is dated February 17, 1999. (2)

4. On February 16, 1999, I interviewed Mr. Folsom at my office in downtown San Diego. I interviewed Mr. Folsom because I realized that we might call him as a witness at trial. (4c) We had filed suit before I interviewed Mr. Folsom. (4c) After the interview, I had my secretary type a copy of his statement and submit it to him for his signature. My secretary did so before he left my office, and I have his signed statement dated February 16, 1999. We do not oppose the discovery of that witness statement; the parties have entered into a stipulation for the exchange of witness statements. However, the next day, February 17, 1999, I dictated a memorandum for file. (4b) The memorandum outlines my impressions of Mr. Folsom as a potential witness. (4a) Given the memorandum's contents, the memorandum is entitled to absolute work product privilege. Although the memorandum is presently physically attached to Mr. Folsom's witness statement, the memorandum is not discoverable.

I declare under penalty of perjury that the above statements are true and correct.

This declaration was executed on May 13, 1999 at San Diego, San Diego County, California.

_____

/s/ Peter Mehalick

As in the previous hypothetical, when the attorney submitted this, the attorney would also submit a memorandum of law. The memorandum should mention the statutes and cases conferring absolute work product privilege. At oral argument on the discovery motion, the attorney would use the memorandum as the source of law and the declaration as the source of facts.

At this time, it is unsettled whether the crime-fraud exception applies to material otherwise entitled to absolute work product protection. The absolute protection vindicates the attorney's personal "need for privacy." *BP Alaska Exploration, Inc. v. Superior Court*, 199 Cal. App. 3d 1240, 1260, 245 Cal. Rptr. 682, 695 (1988). The attorney arguably should not forfeit his or her privacy simply because the client contemplated criminal or fraudulent conduct. However, there is agreement that absolute work product protection can be defeated by proof of a waiver. *Id.* Thus, the protection would be lost "by *the attorney's* voluntary disclosure or consent to disclosure of the writing to a person other than the client who has no interest in maintaining the confidentiality of the contents of the writing." *Id.* at 1261, 245 Cal. Rptr. at 695 (emphasis in the original).

G. GOVERNMENT PRIVILEGES—MILITARY AND STATE SECRETS

1. THE DOCTRINE

Military and state secrets affect the vital interest of the country. The magnitude of the interest justifies creating an evidentiary privilege to cloak these secrets. Following the English precedents, the United States Supreme Court recognized a privilege for military and state secrets in *United States v. Reynolds*, 345 U.S. 1 (1953). The Court created an absolute privilege; if the material falls within the definition of military or state secret, the material is not discoverable even if the party seeking discovery can demonstrate a compelling need for the information.

The most troublesome problem has been defining military and state secrets. Although no court has developed a simple definition of these terms, one commentator—now a federal judge—has offered a relatively comprehensive list of the types of materials falling within the definition:

The specific areas of sensitive information appear to be: (a) The plans and capabilities of specific combat operations; (b) the official estimates of the military plans and capabilities of potential enemy nations; (c) the existence, design, and production of new weapons or equipment or the existence and results of research programs specifically directed toward producing new weapons and equipment; (d) the existence and nature of special ways and means of organizing combat operations; (e) the identity and location of vulnerable areas such as production facilities, critical supply depots, or weapons installations; (f) the existence and nature of clandestine intelligence operations; (g) the keys to communication codes; and (h) the existence and nature of international agreements relative to military plans and capabilities and the exchange of intelligence.

Zagel, *The State Secrets Privilege*, 50 MINN. L. REV. 875, 884-85 (1966).

The *Reynolds* decision creates an absolute privilege. On its face, Evidence Code § 1040(a)(1) recognizes absolute privilege only when "[d]isclosure is forbidden by an act of the Congress of the United States or a statute of this state. ..." Nevertheless, the California courts seem willing to enforce the common-law *Reynolds* privilege for military and state secrets. *Rubin v. City of Los Angeles*, 190 Cal. App. 3d 560, 235 Cal. Rptr. 516 (1987). The courts have stressed that only the federal government may assert the privilege. *Id.* at 577, 235 Cal. Rptr. at 524.

2. ELEMENTS OF THE FOUNDATION

The government can assert this privilege in any type of proceeding. The foundation includes these elements:

1. The government is asserting the right type of privilege. The government may refuse to disclose the information and prevent a third party from making unauthorized disclosure.
2. The claimant asserting the privilege is authorized to do so. The claimant is ordinarily the federal official in charge of the department with jurisdiction over the information. *See Rubin, supra.* The head of the department should make a formal, written claim of privilege.
3. The information the claimant seeks to suppress is a military or state secret. The written claim should indicate the general nature of the privileged information and assert that the government department has maintained the confidentiality of the information.

3. SAMPLE FOUNDATION

The fact situation is a suit arising from a plane crash. Winfield Aircraft Company was testing a plane with a new guidance system for air-to-air missiles. The plane crashed during the test, and the test pilot was killed. The pilot's widow brings a wrongful death action against the company. If the United States anticipated claiming the military secret privilege, the federal attorney monitoring the case should contact the appropriate federal official before trial and have that official prepare a formal, written claim of privilege.

CITY OF WASHINGTON   )
) AFFIDAVIT
DISTRICT OF COLUMBIA   )

I, the undersigned, being duly sworn, depose and say that:

1. My name is John R. Overholt. I reside at 230 Fellmeth Drive, Arlington, Virginia. I am the Secretary of Defense of the United States. (2) My offices are in the Pentagon at the nation's capital.
2. *Jennings v. Infield Aircraft Co.*, civil action C1477, is now pending in California Superior Court in San Jose.
3. It is my understanding that the plaintiff seeks to discover information about the guidance system for air-to-air missiles installed in the airplane involved in the crash that gave rise to this suit. That information is within the jurisdiction of my government agency, and I hereby claim the military secret privilege for such information. (2) On that ground, I refuse to disclose the information and request that the court preclude any third party from disclosing the information. (1)
4. This new guidance system has been in development for the past seven years. The system incorporates new features which, to the best of my knowledge, foreign countries neither use nor have the knowledge of. (3) If perfected, the system would give our planes a decided advantage in aerial combat. (3) The disclosure of this information would significantly harm our national defense interests. (3) To date, our department has maintained the secrecy of this information. (3) The information has been classified COSMIC TOP SECRET, and only persons with both a proper security clearance and a proven need to know have had access to this information. (3)

/s/ John R. Overholt

On September 19, 1999, before the undersigned, a Notary Public for the District of Columbia, personally appeared John R. Overholt, known to me to be the person whose name is subscribed to the within instrument, and acknowledge that he executed the same.

/s/ Marcia Gallagher
Notary Public
My license expires October 19, 2004

At trial, the United States has intervened to assert its privilege. The plaintiff's attorney calls Mr. Garrett Winslow as a witness. Winslow identifies himself and states that he is Winfield's chief engineer in charge of the development of the new guidance system. The plaintiff is the proponent. The plaintiff is examining Mr. Winslow as a hostile witness. An Assistant United States Attorney is present to protect the United States' interests. She is the objecting attorney, *O*. Since the written claim of privilege will not be tendered to the jury, it will be inserted in the record of trial, but it will not be offered as a formal exhibit.

P   Mr. Winslow, ISN'T IT TRUE THAT before this crash, the model of plane involved had a perfect safety record?

W   Yes.

P   ISN'T IT ALSO TRUE THAT you installed a new guidance system for missiles on this plane just before the test?

W   Yes.

P   IN FACT, WASN'T the very purpose of the flight to test the new guidance system?

W   Yes.

P   Please describe this guidance system for us.

O   Your Honor, I object to that question on the ground that it calls for privileged information. May we approach the bench?

J   Yes.

O   Your Honor, I request that this be marked defense exhibit C for identification.

J   It will be so marked.

O   Your Honor, please let the record reflect that I am showing the exhibit to the opposing counsel.

J   It will so reflect.

O   Your Honor, since this document is properly notarized and bears the purported signature of a public official, it is self-authenticating. The exhibit is a formal claim of the military secret privilege for the information about the guidance system.

J   Give me a minute to read the exhibit. The claim seems to be in proper order.

P   Your Honor, my client has a compelling need for that information. We contend that that guidance system caused this accident.

O   The military secret privilege is absolute. So long as the information falls within the definition of military secret, the information is not discoverable. Secretary Overholt's affidavit clearly shows that this information falls within the definition.

J   I think you're right. The objection will be sustained.

H.   GOVERNMENT PRIVILEGE—ABSOLUTELY PRIVILEGED MATERIAL

Subdivision 1040(b)(1) is the only Evidence Code provision conferring an absolute privilege. 2 HOGAN § 12.33. That subdivision recognizes a privilege only when "[d]isclosure is forbidden by an act of Congress of the United States or a statute of this state. ..." *Richards v. Superior Court of Los Angeles County,* 258

Cal. App. 2d 635, 65 Cal. Rptr. 917 (1968), illustrates the operation of § 1040(b)(1). In *Richards*, a personal injury defendant subpoenaed the records of a medical examination of the plaintiff. The examination had been conducted by a doctor on behalf of the State Department of Employment. Although the plaintiff consented to the release of the documents, the department refused to comply with the subpoena. The department cited Unemployment Insurance Code § 2714 as the basis for its refusal. The court construed § 2714 as absolutely forbidding the disclosure of the records and therefore invoked § 1040(b)(1). Similarly, Vehicle and Safety Code § 20013 provides that "[n]o ... [required] accident report shall be used as evidence in any trial, civil or criminal. ..." The statute does not privilege the oral statements which drivers make to the police officer who later prepares the report. *People v. Misner*, 134 Cal. App. 2d 377, 285 P.2d 938 (1955). However, by virtue of § 20013, the report itself is inadmissible. *See* Title, *Police Accident Reports*, 43 CAL. ST. BAR. J. 711 (1968).

When a party relies on a statute such as § 1040(b)(1), the primary problems are issues of statutory construction: (1) Does the statute forbid disclosure? and (2) If so, to what types of information does the statute apply? If the judge construes the statute as forbidding disclosure, the privilege must submit declarations showing that the information in question is the type the statute covers.

I. GOVERNMENT PRIVILEGES—MINOR GOVERNMENT SECRETS

1. THE DOCTRINE

Military and state secrets are such major government secrets that the courts have granted them an absolute evidentiary privilege. Other, lesser government secrets also warrant a measure of protection. Minor government secrets are usually subject to a conditional privilege; the secret is ordinarily privileged, but the party seeking disclosure can defeat the privilege by demonstrating a compelling need for the information.

The definition of a minor government secret varies from jurisdiction to jurisdiction. The federal courts have adopted a relatively narrow definition. In *Ackerly v. Ley*, 420 F.2d 1336, 1340 (D.C. Cir. 1969), the court referred to "the familiar doctrine that the Executive branch is privileged not to disclose intra-governmental documents reflecting advisory opinions, recommendations, and deliberations comprising part of a process by which governmental decisions are formulated." The federal courts have attempted to protect the secrecy of the decisionmaking process. The courts reason that the ultimate government decision will be of higher quality if public officials are candid in their policy discussions and that officials are more likely to be candid if they know that the decisionmaking process is confidential. The federal courts consequently limit their minor government secret privilege to documents that are an integral part of a government decisionmaking process. The federal predecisional, deliberative process privilege does not extend to factual, historical data the government collects from private sources.

In contrast, Evidence Code § 1040(b)(2) sometimes cloaks even factual information with the protection of a qualified privilege. Subdivision 1040(b)(2) reads:

> A public entity has a privilege to refuse to disclose official information, and to prevent another from disclosing official information, if the privilege is claimed by a person authorized by the public entity to do so and ... [d]isclosure of the information is against the public interest because there is a necessity for preserving the confidentiality of the information that outweighs the necessity for disclosure in the interest of justice. ... In determining whether disclosure of the information is against the public interest, the interest of the public entity as a party in the outcome of the proceeding may not be considered.

In other words, a minor government secret privilege attaches if the government shows that: (1) it has a legitimate need for a certain type of information; and (2) it cannot be assured of a free flow of information unless it assures confidentiality to the sources of information. While the federal privilege attempts to foster the free flow of dialogue within government, the primary purpose of § 1040(b)(2) is to promote the flow of information to government.

Section 1040(b)(2) protects various types of information. The courts have applied it to letters to the state parole board, reports to licensing agencies, and complaints to the state bar. 2 WITKIN §§ 1240-42. There is authority applying § 1040 to confidential information about a surveillance location. Sawyer, *The Claim of Privilege Under Evidence Code Section 1040 for the Location of a Police Officer's Surveillance*, CACJ FORUM 33, Vol. 21, No. 2 (1994); *In re Sergio M.*, 13 Cal. App. 4th 809, 16 Cal. Rptr. 2d 701 (1993); *People v. Walker*, 230 Cal. App. 3d 230, 282 Cal. Rptr. 12, 15-16, *modified*, 230 Cal. App. 3d 1071 (1991). Moreover, there is a conditional privilege covering information in the personnel files of law enforcement officers. *Hackett v. Superior Court (Glin)*, 13 Cal. App. 4th 96, 16 Cal. Rptr. 2d 405 (1993) (construing Evidence Code § 1043 and Penal Code § 832.7-.8).

Even if the government makes out a prima facie case that a conditional privilege applies, the party seeking disclosure can defeat the privilege by showing an overriding need for the information. The party shows need in the same fashion as a party seeking to defeat a conditional work product protection. Moreover, the party can defeat the privilege by showing a waiver. *People v. Roberts*, 2 Cal. 4th 271, 826 P.2d 274, 6 Cal. Rptr. 2d 276, 290 ("the information requested was no longer confidential; the defense had learned of it"), *modified*, 2 Cal. 4th 758 (1992).

2. ELEMENTS OF THE FOUNDATION

To establish a prima facie case for invoking the minor government secret privilege, the party opposing disclosure must show these foundational elements:

1. The person claiming the privilege is authorized to do so. The government is the holder of the privilege. The judge will usually permit any government agent, including the prosecutor, to claim the privilege.
2. The right type of privilege is being claimed. The government may refuse to disclose the information and prevent a third party from making disclosure.
3. The information is privileged. The claimant must show that:
   a. The government has a legitimate need for this type of information; and
   b. The government cannot obtain a free flow of this type of information unless it asserts its sources confidentiality. It is ideal if the government agent expressly assures confidentiality to the source, but an express assurance is not essential. HEAFEY § 42.3, at 479.

To defeat the privilege, the party seeking disclosure must show that:

4. The information is logically relevant to the material facts of consequence in the case.
5. The information is important to the outcome of the case. The party should argue that the information relates to a central issue in the case.
6. There is no reasonably available, alternative source for the information.

3. SAMPLE FOUNDATION

The fact situation is a wrongful death action. The plaintiffs are the surviving relatives of the decedent, Andrew Kaye. The defendant is Gary Shelton. The complaint alleges that the defendant and a Mr. Michaels fatally shot Andrew Kaye during a civil rights rally in early 1998. The defendant's answer denied all involvement in the shooting. Michaels was tried, convicted, and sentenced in late 1998. The plaintiff's civil action against Shelton comes to trial today. During their case-in-chief, the plaintiffs called Ms. Martha McGill. She testified that she witnessed the shooting. She identified the defendant as one of the assailants. During the defense case-in-chief, the defendant calls Mr. Daniel Riley as a witness. Mr. Riley identifies himself and states that he is an employee of the California Board of Prison Terms. Riley testifies that he prepared a parole report on Michaels when the Board was considering Michaels' parole application. The defendant hopes to prove that Riley interviewed Ms. McGill and that during the interview, Ms. McGill said that although she could recognize Michaels as one killer, she could not identify the other assailant. The defendant is the proponent. The opponent is a Deputy Attorney General. When Riley was subpoenaed, he notified the Office of the Attorney General; and the State entered an appearance for the purpose of asserting the minor government secret privilege.

P   When you prepared this report, WHOM did you interview?
W   Several people.
P   Specifically WHOM?

W A Genevieve Morton, Brian Michaels, and a Ms. McGill, who witnessed the shooting itself.

P WHAT is Ms. McGill's full name?

W Martha McGill.

P WHAT was her occupation?

W She was the cashier at a store near the killing.

P WHAT did she say during her interview?

O Your Honor, I object to that question on the ground that it calls for privileged information. I request permission to take the witness on voir dire.

J Permission granted.

O Mr. Riley, WHY did you interview Ms. McGill? (3a)

W I wanted to get some information about the robbery.

O WHY did you need that information? (3a)

W Actually it's the Board who needs it. The Board wants to know as much as they can about the gravity of the crime to determine an appropriate release date.

O HOW do you get the information? (3a)

W I interview the witnesses to the crime.

O WHERE and WHEN did you interview Ms. McGill? (3b)

W In my office three months ago.

O WHO else was there? (3b)

W Only the two of us.

O HOW many doors does your office have? (3b)

W Two.

O WHAT position were they in at the time of the interview? (3b)

W They were both closed.

O WHAT, if anything, did you tell Ms. McGill at the beginning of the interview? (3d)

W I thanked her for taking the time to stop by. I told her that her information would be very helpful to the Board, and I assured her that we would keep the interview confidential to the extent possible.

O WHY did you give her that assurance? (3b)

W People are often reluctant to talk to the parole officials.

O WHY? (3b)

W Most obvious reason is that they're afraid of reprisals from the criminal. We always tell interviewees that we'll keep the information confidential as far as possible.

O WHAT did you do after you interviewed Ms. McGill? (3b)

W I summarized her statements and included them in the report.

O WHOM did you give the report to? (3b)

W The Board.

O HOW did you deliver it to them? (3b)

W I hand delivered it to them in a sealed envelope.

O WHO else have you shown the report to? (b)

W No one.

O WHY haven't you shown it to anyone? (3b)

W I want to keep my promise to the interviewees that the information will be confidential. Once word gets out that you don't keep that promise, the sources of information dry up.

O Your Honor, I have no further questions of this witness on voir dire. May we approach the bench?

J Yes.

O Your Honor, it's clear at this point that the witness was gathering information which the government has a legitimate need for. It's also the type of information that the government can't gather unless it assures its sources confidentiality. For that reason, Evidence Code § 1040(b)(2) applies here.

J I agree. The objection will be sustained.

If the party seeking disclosure wants to overcome the conditional privilege, the party should file a declaration. The declaration should detail the logical relevance of the information, the party's need for declaration information, and the unavailability of alternative proof. The party should use the same format as James Garner's declaration in Section F.1 of this chapter. Paragraph 3 of that declaration explains the logical relevance of the information sought. Paragraph 4 shows that the information relates to a pivotal issue in the case. Finally, paragraph 5 demonstrates that it would be difficult or impossible for the party to obtain substitute evidence.

J. GOVERNMENT PRIVILEGES—AN INFORMANT'S IDENTITY

1. THE DOCTRINE

The last section discussed the qualified privilege for minor government secrets. This section deals with a particular application of those rules: the government privilege for an informer's identity. In many cases, an informant would not report a law violation unless the government assured his or her confidentiality. The informant sometimes fears reprisals from the criminal, and other times the informant does not want to expose his or her own involvement in the crime to public scrutiny. To encourage reports of law violations, the courts have created a conditional privilege for the informant's identity. The privilege ordinarily does not protect the informant's report; given its narrow purpose, the privilege protects only the identity of a person who confidentially reports a law violation to law enforcement authorities. The contents of the report are protected only when their disclosure would tend to reveal the informant's identity. *People v. Seibel*, 219 Cal. App. 3d 1279, 269 Cal. Rptr. 313 (1990). Evidence Code § 1041(a)-(b) broadly defines an informant as anyone who confidentially reports a law violation to a "law enforcement officer ... or [a] representative of an ... agency charged with the administration of enforcement of the law. ..." *See* 2 HOGAN ch. 20.

The informant's identity is not absolutely privileged. Section 1041(a)(2) requires the judge to balance the public interest in preserving confidentiality against "the necessity for disclosure in the interest of justice. ..." Although the subdivision uses vague terminology, other statutes and the judicial gloss on the subdivision contain helpful guidance.

In many cases, it is predictable that the judge will uphold the privilege and deny the defense disclosure of the informant's identity. For example, suppose that the judge concludes that the informant's information is relevant only to the legality of a search or seizure, and that the search or seizure was conducted pursuant to a warrant. Evidence Code § 1042(b) provides that in this circumstance, "the public entity ... is not required to reveal ... the identity of [the] informer in order to establish the legality of the search" or seizure. Next, assume that the search or seizure was warrantless, the police contacted an informant before conducting the search or seizure, the informant's information is relevant only to the legality of the intrusion, but there is ample probable cause for the intrusion apart from the informant's report. Again, the judge will strike the balance in favor of maintaining confidentiality. Or lastly, suppose alternatively that the intrusion is warrantless but that the informant's report is an essential part of the showing of probable cause. Evidence Code § 1042(c) is apposite. Under that subdivision, the judge has discretion to uphold confidentiality and deny disclosure "if the judge ... [concludes], based upon evidence produced in open court, ... that such information was received from a reliable informant. ..." The judge's conclusion that the informant was reliable makes it unnecessary to divulge the informant's identity.

In contrast, there are several fact situations in which the judge customarily orders disclosure. One is when the prosecution cannot rely on either § 1042(b) or § 1042(c): The intrusion was warrantless, the informant's report is an essential part of the showing of probable cause, and there is insufficient evidence of the informant's reliability. The second is when, in the words of § 1042(d), the informant is "a material witness on the issue of guilt. ..." Under *Roviaro v. United States*, 353 U.S. 53 (1957), the defendant has a due process right to discover the identity of a percipient witness to facts and events determining the merits of a prosecution. Subdivision 1042(d) recognizes that right and allows the defense discovery when "nondisclosure might deprive the defendant of a fair trial." The California cases require that defendants invoking *Roviaro* establish "a reasonable possibility that the informer could give testimony on the issue of defendant's guilt or innocence which might result in defendant's exoneration. ..." JEFFERSON SYNOPSIS § 43.1, at 697; *People v. Lizarraga*, 219 Cal. App. 3d 476, 482, 268 Cal. Rptr. 262, 266 (1990). The informant must be able to exonerate the defendant of the charged offense; it is not enough that the informant was a percipient witness to some uncharged criminal acts. *In re Benny S.*, 230 Cal. App. 3d, 102, 281 Cal. Rptr. 2d 1, 3-4 (1991). The defendant can satisfy the requirement by showing that the informant was a participant in the crime or a nonparticipating material witness. 2 WITKIN §§ 1269-70. On the one hand, the defense need not show that the informant's testimony would probably be favorable. JEFFERSON SYNOPSIS § 43.1, at 697. On the other hand, the defense must show that the informant possesses information about the merits of the case; it is not enough to demonstrate that the informant was a tipster who pointed the finger of suspicion at the defendant. McKinstry & Clay, *Motion to Disclose the Informant*, in CALIFORNIA CRIMINAL LAW § 21.3, at 433. In *People v. Otte*, 214 Cal. App. 3d 1522, 1536, 263 Cal. Rptr. 393, 401 (1989), *cert. denied sub nom.*

Gordon v. California, 499 U.S. 913 (1991), the court refused to allow disclosure of the informant's identity because "[d]efense counsel presented only the bare unsupported assertion that the informant was a material witness."

2. ELEMENTS OF THE FOUNDATION

The foundation for the privilege itself includes these elements:

1. The privilege applies in this type of proceeding. Most of the cases recognizing the privilege are criminal prosecutions. However, the issue can arise in civil actions such as actions for libel or malicious prosecution.
2. The person claiming the privilege is authorized to do so. The government is the holder of the privilege. The courts usually permit the government's agents, including prosecutors, to invoke the privilege on the government's behalf.
3. The right type of privilege is being claimed. The government can refuse to disclose the informer's identity and can prevent another person from disclosing it. However, under § 1041(c) the government cannot silence the informer; if the informer is brave or foolhardy enough to admit his or her identity, the government loses the privilege.
4. The information is privileged. Again, in most cases the only privileged information is the informer's identity.
   a. A person made a confidential report.
   b. The subject of the report was a violation of law.
   c. The person made the report to a law enforcement agency such as the police, a prosecutor's office, an administrative agency charged with enforcing the law, or a legislative committee investigating law enforcement.

The foundation for the percipient witness exception is quite simple. The defendant shows that the informer was in a physical position—the proper time and place—to observe the facts determining guilt or innocence.

3. SAMPLE FOUNDATION

Our fact situation is a drug prosecution. The People allege that the defendant, Ms. Jane Moreland, wrongfully sold heroin to a Mr. Vincent Styles. The prosecution calls Officer Lopardo as a witness. Officer Lopardo testifies that he was hiding in the house where the alleged sale occurred and observed the sale. Then cross-examination begins. The defense attorney is the proponent.

P   Officer Lopardo, ISN'T IT TRUE THAT someone else was with you when you observed the alleged heroin sale?
W   Yes.
P   WHO was that other person?

O Your Honor, I object to that question on the ground that it calls for privileged information. May we approach the bench?

J Yes.

O Your Honor, on behalf of the government, I claim the privilege for the identity of an informer. (2), (3) I request permission to take the witness on voir dire examinations.

J Permission granted.

O WHEN did you first meet the person who was with you in the house?

W About two months before.

O WHAT happened when you met this person? (4b)

W He told me that he thought a drug sale was going to occur in the neighborhood within the next few months.

O WHERE did he make this report? (4c)

W At the local police station.

O WHOM did he report it to? (4c)

W To me.

O HOW were you dressed at the time? (4c)

W I was wearing my regular police uniform.

O WHO else was present when he made this report? (4a)

W No one else. Just the two of us.

O WHERE did this conversation occur? (4a)

W In a room in the station.

O HOW many doors did the room have? (4a)

W Only one.

O WHAT position was the door in when you met this person? (4a)

W It was closed.

O WHAT, if any, assurances did you give the informant when he made this report to you? (4a)

W I told him that I wouldn't disclose his identity to anyone.

O To WHOM have you revealed his identity? (4a)

W No one. I've worked with him directly. I haven't even revealed his identity to the desk sergeant. I'm the informer's only contact.

O Your Honor, I have no further questions on voir dire. I renew my claim of the privilege for an informer's identity.

Now the defense counsel will attempt to lay the foundation for the percipient witness exception.

P Your Honor, may I also voir dire the witness?

J Very well.

P Officer Lopardo, ISN'T IT TRUE THAT this person accompanied you to the house where the alleged sale occurred?

W Yes.

P ISN'T IT A FACT THAT the informer was standing next to you when you observed the alleged sale?

W Yes.

P ISN'T IT CORRECT THAT most of the time the informer was facing in the same direction as you?

W Yes.

P   Your Honor, I have no further questions on voir dire examination. Although the privilege for the informer's identity applies in this case, the informer was a percipient witness who viewed the very transaction that the defendant's guilt or innocence depends on.

J   I concur. I am going to order the prosecutor to produce the informer in my chambers tomorrow morning. At that time I shall question the informer and determine whether his testimony would be helpful to the defense. If his testimony would be favorable, I'll order that the prosecution disclose his identity. Court will be recessed. The prosecutor, the informer, and I will meet in my chambers at 9:00 a.m. tomorrow morning. Open court will convene at 10:30 a.m.

The above hypothetical represents a simplified version of the process of litigating the applicability of the informant's privilege. In many cases, the litigation is a three-step process. McKinstry, *Motion to Disclose the Informant*, in CALIFORNIA CRIMINAL LAW § 21.1, at 431.

The initial step occurs in open court. *Id*. At this stage, the defense attempts to show that there is a person whose testimony would be material in the case.

Even if the defense makes that showing, the judge does not automatically order the disclosure of the person's identity. The judge may (and upon prosecution request, must) take the second step, an in camera hearing. Evidence Code § 1042(d) states that the hearing will be held "outside the presence of the defendant and his counsel." Although the defense cannot attend the hearing, the defense can submit questions to be posed to the informant. *Id*. at § 21.9, at 436. At the hearing, any witnesses, including the informant, are sworn. *Id*. Subdivision 1042(d) provides that "[a] reporter shall be present at the ... hearing. Any transcription of the proceedings shall be ordered sealed by the court, and only a court may have access to the contents." At the hearing, the prosecution can attempt to show, *inter alia*, that: The person in question was a confidential informant; the informant was not a percipient witness to the merits; or there are substantial reasons for preserving the informant's confidentiality such as an ongoing investigation or threats against the informant. *Id*.

The third step is an adversary hearing in open court. *Id*. at § 21.10, at 437. At this step, the judge hears counsel's legal argument and makes the final order. For a discussion of the mechanics of these hearings, *see People v. Ruiz,* App. 4th 1485, 12 Cal. Rptr. 2d 234 (1992).

K.   JURORS' STATEMENTS ABOUT THEIR VERDICT AND THEIR DELIBERATIONS

1. THE DOCTRINE

The last four sections of this chapter analyzed government privileges—evidentiary doctrines that promote public policies and that can be asserted only by the government. This section addresses a rule that also helps vindicate a government policy but that private parties can assert at trial. There is a general policy of secrecy surrounding jury deliberations. We want to encourage citizens to serve as jurors. There would be a disincentive to jury service if disappointed litigants could harass jurors. The purpose of Evidence Code § 1150 is to remove litigants' motivation to harass jurors. Section 1150 reads:

> (a) Upon an inquiry as to the validity of a verdict, any otherwise admissible evidence may be received as to statements made, or conduct, conditions, or events occurring, either within or without the jury room, of such a character as is likely to have influenced the verdict improperly. No evidence is admissible to show the effect of such statement, conduct, condition, or event upon a juror either in influencing him to assent to or dissent from the verdict or concerning the mental process by which it was determined.
>
> (b) Nothing in this code affects the law relating to the competence of a juror to give evidence to impeach or support a verdict.

Section 1150 generally prohibits jurors from testifying or furnishing affidavits about "the mental processes by which [the verdict] was determined." *People v. Burnett*, 71 Cal. App. 4th 151, 183 n. 13, 83 Cal. Rptr. 2d 629, 649 n. 13 (1999).

Subdivision (b) makes it clear that § 1150 does not regulate the grounds for new trial. The recognized grounds for a new trial are enumerated in statutes such as Code of Civil Procedure § 657. *Garfoot v. Avila*, 213 Cal. App. 3d 1205, 261 Cal. Rptr. 924 (1989), illustrates the courts' refusal to recognize new grounds for a new trial. Nor does § 1150 prescribe the form in which evidentiary matter is presented to a judge ruling on a new trial motion. At the hearing on a new trial motion, judges rarely hear live testimony. Code of Civil Procedure § 658 announces the general rule that a new trial motion "must be made upon affidavits. ..." The cumulative effect of §§ 657-58 is that the evidentiary basis for a new trial motion must be logically relevant to a recognized ground for new trial and must be presented in affidavit form.

However, even if the evidentiary material satisfies Code of Civil Procedure §§ 657-58, the material must also comply with Evidence Code § 1150. Section 1150 is quite limited. In the first place, § 1150 is much less drastic than the competency rule stated in Evidence Code § 704. As noted in Section F of Chapter 3, § 704 normally precludes a juror sitting in the case from testifying before the other jurors during the trial. In contrast, § 1150 does not render the juror incompetent to testify; in more limited fashion, § 1150 prevents the juror from giving live testimony or presenting an affidavit on certain topics.

Moreover, § 1150's list of prohibited topics is narrower than similar lists in many other jurisdictions. The traditional "Mansfield Rule" is that jurors may not provide affidavits or live testimony about their own misconduct. Many jurisdictions follow the lead of Federal Rule of Evidence 606(b). Rule 606(b) generally follows the traditional view and carves out only two exceptions: "a juror may testify on the question whether extraneous prejudicial information was improperly brought to the jury's attention or whether any outside influence was improperly brought to bear upon any juror." *E.g., People v. Holloway*, 50 Cal. 3d 1098,

1109, 790 P.2d 1327, 1332, 269 Cal. Rptr. 530, 535 (1990) ("a paper ... communicated to the jury").

Section 1150 is a more radical departure from the Mansfield Rule than Rule 606(b). The leading precedent is *People v. Hutchinson*, 71 Cal. 2d 342, 455 P.2d 132, 78 Cal. Rptr. 196 (1969). *Hutchinson* interprets § 1150 as permitting any "evidence of objective statements, conduct, or events. ..." 2 JEFFERSON § 34.1, at 1278. Under § 1150, the juror may furnish evidence about any overt acts or statements that could be observed and corroborated by another person. HEAFEY § 18.30, at 135; JEFFERSON SYNOPSIS § 34.1, at 559-61; *In re Hamilton*, 20 Cal. 4th 273, 975 P. 2d 600, 84 Cal. Rptr. 2d 403 (1999) (any overt event or circumstance open to corroboration by sight, hearing, or the other senses); *Vomaska v. City of San Diego*, 55 Cal. App. 4th 905, 64 Cal. Rptr. 2d 492, 494 (1997) ("objectively ascertainable statements, conduct, conditions or events"). There continues to be a good deal of litigation over the proper interpretation of § 1150. *See People v. Sanchez*, 62 Cal. App. 4th 460, 72 Cal. Rptr. 2d 782 (1998) (the jurors' declarations tended to show that they misunderstood the judge's instructions; the declarations showed mere "'deliberative error' in the jury's collective mental process— confusion, misunderstanding, and misinterpretation of the law .... The mere fact that such mental process was manifested in conversation between jurors during deliberations does not alter this rule;" the court specifically cites *Mesecher, infra*); *People v. Duran*, 50 Cal. App. 4th 103, 57 Cal. Rptr. 2d 635, 640 (1996) ("Evidence Code 1150 may be violated 'not only by the admission of jurors' testimony describing their own mental processes, but also by permitting testimony concerning statements made by jurors in the course of their deliberations. In rare circumstances a statement by a juror during deliberations may itself be an act of misconduct, in which case evidence of that statement is admissible. But when a juror in the course of deliberations gives the reasons for his or her vote, the words are simply a reflection of the juror's mental processes. Consideration of such a statement as evidence of those processes is barred by Evidence Code section 1150'"); *Mesecher v. County of San Diego*, 9 Cal. App. 4th 1677, 12 Cal. Rptr. 2d 279, 281-83 (1992) (the jurors' declarations indicated that the jurors misunderstood the judge's instruction; the declarations thus established mere collective deliberative error rather than an express or implied agreement to disregard the instruction); *People v. Perez*, 4 Cal. App. 4th 893, 909, 6 Cal. Rptr. 2d 141, 149 (1992) ("the jury had explicitly or implicitly agreed to disregard the court's express instruction not to consider or discuss Perez's failure to take the witness stand. Such jury discussion is admissible to impeach the verdict under the express provisions of Evidence Code § 1150."); *People v. Hill*, 3 Cal. App. 4th 16, 4 Cal. Rptr. 2d 258, 264-66 (1992) ("Evidence Code § 1150(a) 'thus makes a distinction between proof of overt acts, objectively ascertainable, and proof of the subjective reasoning processes of the individual juror. ...'"; "evidence that the jurors misunderstood the judge's instructions, were influenced by an improper remark of a fellow juror, assented under an erroneous belief that the judge would use clemency or had the legal right to vary the sentence, or had been influenced by inadmissible evidence" is inadmissible); *Smoketree-Lake Murray, Ltd. v. Mills Concrete Con-*

struction Co., 234 Cal. App. 3d 1724, 286 Cal. Rptr. 435, 450-51 (1991) (Evidence Code § 1150 does not permit juror testimony about "deliberative error"; "The declarations indicate, at most, confusion or misunderstanding by the jury in the process of deliberating, in determining how to reach a verdict using the instructions given to them by the court." *Ford v. Bennacka*, 226 Cal. App. 3d 330, 334, 276 Cal. Rptr. 513, 515 (1990) (after citing *Hutchinson*, the court cautioned that "[i]n spite of the perception that, in recent times, the law concerning the ability of jurors to impeach a verdict has been liberalized, the process must be carefully scrutinized and controlled"). The California cases also recognize an exception to § 1150 when the evidence supports a "claim[] that a juror's preexisting bias was concealed on voir dire." *In re Hamilton*, 20 Cal. 4th 273, 298 n. 20, 975 P. 2d 600, 616 n. 20, 84 Cal. Rptr. 2d 403, 419 n. 20 (1999).

The question has arisen as to whether §1150 survived the passage of Proposition 8. One court has ruled that § 1150 is still in effect. *People v. Hill*, 3 Cal. App. 4th 16, 4 Cal. Rptr. 2d 258 (1992). The court reasoned that § 1150 is more than a limitation on the evidence admissible to prove jury misconduct. The court argued that, more fundamentally, § 1150 renders the jurors' subjective thought processes "immaterial." Even after Proposition 8, an item of evidence must be relevant and material in order to be admissible.

2. ELEMENTS OF THE FOUNDATION

In drafting an affidavit to support or oppose a new trial motion, the attorney should include the following foundational elements:

1. The affiant was a juror in the case in question.
2. The affiant describes objective information—some fact or event that the affiant perceived.
3. The information is logically relevant to prove or disprove a recognized ground for new trial.

Even when the attorney can lay a satisfactory foundation for proving the objective fact or event, the attorney may not take the next step and present a juror's testimony or affidavit describing his or her reaction to the fact or event. Rather, the attorney invokes a presumption of prejudice. *In re Carpenter*, 9 Cal. 4th 634, 889 P.2d 985, 38 Cal. Rptr. 2d 665, 676, *modified*, 10 Cal. 4th 256a, *cert. denied sub nom. Carpenter v. Gomez*, 516 U.S. 981 (1995).

3. SAMPLE FOUNDATION

Our fact situation is the hearing on a new trial motion after a defense verdict in a personal injury action. The plaintiff, Ms. Sylvia Hernandez, sued the defendant, Gregory Hirsch, for damages. Her complaint alleges that the defendant was negligently driving his car, permitted his car to drift into Ms. Hernandez' traffic lane, and struck her car. At trial, the plaintiff relied primarily on expert testimony by an accident reconstructionist, Professor Herbert Mandelker. The trial resulted in a defense verdict, and the plaintiff then filed a new trial motion. In support of her motion, the plaintiff submits the following affidavit:

STATE OF CALIFORNIA   )
) AFFIDAVIT
COUNTY OF SAN DIEGO   )

I, the undersigned, being duly sworn, depose and say that:

1. My name is Edward Lowenthal. I reside at 3174 LaValencia Avenue, San Diego, California.
2. Between August 13 and August 29, 1999, I served as a petit juror in the case of *Hernandez v. Hirsch*, tried in California Superior Court in downtown San Diego. (1)
3. On August 28, 1999, after hearing all the evidence in the case, the other jurors and I retired to deliberate. A Mr. Peter Frankel was a member of the jury. At noon on August 28, we broke for lunch. When we gathered again after lunch, Mr. Frankel said that there was something he thought we all should see. At that point, he reached into his pocket and took out several Xerox pages. He said that as he was listening to the testimony by the plaintiff's expert, Professor Mandelker, "something didn't sound right" to him. He added that for that reason, during our lunch break he stopped by a local library and consulted a text on accident reconstruction. He did not identify the text. However, he said that he had browsed through the text and identified the pages explaining how accident reconstruction experts determine point of impact. He said that he had copied the six most important pages and wanted us all to have a look at those pages. He then circulated the six pages to the other jurors. As he was doing that, he said that the material on the pages showed that Professor Mandelker's testimony "was just plain wrong." With the exception of myself, all the other jurors handled the pages and purported to read the pages. I was the last juror to be handed the pages, and I refused to accept them. I told Mr. Frankel and the other jurors that I did not think we should look at those pages; I said that the judge had told us to consider only the evidence we heard in the courtroom. I handed the pages back to Mr. Frankel. He put the pages on the table in the middle of the jury room. During the deliberations, Mr. Frankel and two other jurors—I believe Ms. Macintosh and Mr. Juenger—referred to the pages. On each occasion, they said that the pages showed that Professor Mandeiker was in error. At the end of the discussion of the evidence in the case, Mr. Frankel picked up the Xerox pages and put

them back in his pocket. That is the last I ever saw of those pages.
I do not know where they are now. (2), (3)

_____

/s/ Edward Lowenthal

On September 1, 1999, before the undersigned, a Notary Public for the
State of California, personally appeared Edward Lowenthal, known to
me to be the person whose name is subscribed to the within instrument,
and acknowledged that he executed the same.

_____

/s/ Linda Draper
Notary Public
My license expires May 2, 2004

L.   SUBSEQUENT REPAIRS

1. THE DOCTRINE

Evidence Code § 1151 states the subsequent repair doctrine: "When, after the
occurrence of an event, remedial or precautionary measures are taken which, if
taken previously, would have tended to make the event less likely to occur,
evidence of such subsequent measures is inadmissible to prove negligence or
culpable conduct in connection with the event." Although the doctrine is usually
not characterized as a "privilege," the doctrine is similar to a privilege in several
respects. First, the rationale for the doctrine is an extrinsic social policy. The
privileges for relationships such as attorney-client are designed to encourage
communication between properly related parties; the underlying reasoning is that
there would be a disincentive to communication if the client realized that the
attorney could disclose the client's revelations. The rationale for the subsequent
repair doctrine is analogous. The Law Revision Committee comment to § 1151
explains that if people realized that repairs could be used against them as evidence
in subsequent trials, that realization "would substantially discourage persons from
making repairs. ..." Second, just as a privilege can be asserted only by the
intended beneficiary of the confidentiality, the California courts have held that
only the person making the repair may invoke § 1151. *Magnante v. Pettibone-
Wood Mfg. Co.*, 183 Cal. App. 3d 764, 767-68, 228 Cal. Rptr. 420, 422-23
(1986).[10] Thus, in effect the subsequent repair doctrine is a privilege with a holder.

_____

[10]In *Santilli v. Otis Elev. Co.*, 215 Cal. App. 3d 210, 263 Cal. Rptr. 496 (1989), the court
interpreted § 1151 to exclude evidence of subsequent repairs by a nonparty. Although nominally a
nonparty, plaintiff's employer was directly affected by the judgment: His liability for a workmen's
compensation claim would be reduced by the amount of employee's strict liability recovery
against the product manufacturer. Thus, the rationale of the remedial conduct rule supported application of the statute to the nonparty, who might have been discouraged from making subsequent repairs for fear of monetary loss.

Like many exclusionary doctrines, this doctrine bans the evidence only when the evidence is offered for a particular, forbidden purpose; in the words of § 1151, the evidence is inadmissible when the proponent offers the evidence "to prove negligence or culpable conduct in connection with the event." The exclusionary rule bans the evidence when the proponent's only theory of logical relevance is the general inference that the defendant was negligent or culpable. If the proponent can articulate a different theory of logical relevance, the rule is inapplicable. The federal analogue to § 1151, Federal Rule of Evidence 407, adds: "This rule does not require the exclusion of evidence of subsequent measures when offered for another purpose, such as proving ownership, control, or feasibility of precautionary measures, if controverted, or impeachment." *See Alcaraz v. Vece*, 14 Cal. 4th 1149, 929 P.2d 1239, 60 Cal. Rptr. 2d 448, 460-61 (1997) ("the issue of control of the premises"). If the proponent identifies a theory of logical relevance other than a general inference of negligence or fault, the opponent is entitled to a limiting instruction under Evidence Code § 355; the trial judge informs the jury of the permissible and impermissible uses of the evidence.

California law requires a limiting instruction about subsequent repair evidence in another situation. In *Ault v. International Harvester Co.*, 13 Cal. 3d 113, 528 P.2d 1148, 117 Cal. Rptr. 812 (1974), the California Supreme Court held that § 1151 does not apply to strict product liability actions. The Court stated that strict product liability does not constitute "culpable conduct" within the meaning of § 1151. Moreover, the court reasoned that the policy rationale of § 1151 is inapplicable to strict product liability actions brought against mass manufacturers. The manufacturer's potential exposure to tort liability is great enough to compel the manufacturer to redesign the product in any event; the admissibility of a subsequent repair in a particular case will not deter the manufacturer from making design changes or repairs. Suppose a case in which the plaintiff sues a defendant manufacturer and alleges both negligence and strict product liability. Evidence of the product's redesign is inadmissible to show negligence but admissible to show that the product was defectively designed. The defendant would be entitled to a limiting instruction, specifying the proper and improper uses of the evidence.

2. ELEMENTS OF THE FOUNDATION

The party attempting to exclude the repair evidence should lay the following foundation:

1. The defendant took certain action.
2. The defendant took the action as a safety measure.
3. The defendant took the action after the accident that gave rise to the suit.

The party can assert this doctrine pretrial by a motion *in limine*. If the issue arises at trial, the party can conduct voir dire examination to lay the foundation.

If the party seeking to introduce the evidence is going to invoke an alternative theory of logical relevance, the party must make a proper offer of proof. The offer of proof should include these elements:

4. What the witness will testify to if the judge permits the proponent to pursue the line of inquiry.
5. The evidence is logically relevant to some issue other than the general question of negligence or fault.
6. The issue the evidence relates to is disputed in the case. Many judges insist upon this showing as a separate element of the foundation. The Federal Rules explicitly impose this requirement. The evidence will always be relevant to show the feasibility of repairs; if the courts did not require that the issue be disputed, the feasibility theory of logical relevance would swallow the exclusionary rule. The proponent of the evidence should point to the opponent's specific evidence or contention that puts the issue in dispute. The California courts have adopted the requirement by construing § 1151 in light of Evidence Code § 352.

As previously stated, if the proponent of the evidence successfully invokes an alternative theory of logical relevance, the opponent has the right to insist that the judge give the jurors a limiting instruction.

3. SAMPLE FOUNDATIONS

Our fact situation illustrates the general rule. The fact situation is a tort action arising from a slip and fall on the entrance to a department store. The plaintiff, Mr. Jarvis, alleges that the defendant, Merrill Department Store, had a dangerous slope on its entrance. During the defense case-in-chief, the defense calls Ms. Fenton as a witness. Ms. Fenton identifies herself and states that she was a Merrill employee on duty the day of the accident. She is the manager of the store where the accident occurred. She describes the day, including her conversation with the plaintiff after the slip and fall. On cross-examination, the following occurs. The proponent is the plaintiff.

P   Ms. Fenton, ISN'T IT TRUE THAT one week after the plaintiff's accident, your employer hired a contractor to reduce the slope on the entrance?
O   Your honor, I object to that question on the ground that it calls for evidence of subsequent repair.
J   Objection sustained.
O   Your Honor, will you please give the jury a curative instruction?
J   Yes. Ladies and gentlemen of the jury, the plaintiff's attorney just referred to a change made in the entrance to the defendant's store. I am instructing you to disregard that reference. You may not even speculate whether there were any subsequent changes. The only issue before you is whether the defendant was negligent at the time the accident occurred.

If the defendant thought that the reference would taint the rest of the case, the defendant would next move for a mistrial. Many trial judges feel very strongly about this matter. They will rebuke the questioner—often, even before an objection. These same judges frequently grant the mistrial motion.

O   Your Honor, I now move for a mistrial.

If there is any doubt about the soundness of the objection, the opponent should request permission to take the witness on voir dire outside the jury's hearing to lay a complete foundation. Suppose that the scenario began in this fashion.

P   Ms. Fenton, ISN'T IT TRUE THAT one week after the plaintiff's accident, the Merrill Company hired a contractor to reduce the slope on the entrance?

O   Your Honor, I object to that question. May we approach the bench?

J   Yes.

O   Your Honor, I object to that question on the ground that it calls for evidence of a subsequent repair. I request that you excuse the jurors and permit me to voir dire the witness before you rule on my objection.

J   Very well. Ladies and gentlemen of the jury, I am going to excuse you from the courtroom for a few moments. The bailiff will escort you to the jury room. (The jurors leave.)

O   Ms. Fenton, WHAT did your employer hire this contractor to do? (1)

W   The boss hired a Mr. Darby to reduce the angle of the slope on the entrance.

O   WHY did they do that? (2)

W   We did it as a safety measure. We wanted to ensure that there wouldn't be a recurrence of the accident. We're concerned about the safety of our customers.

O   WHEN did they hire Mr. Darby? (3)

W   In late February of 1993.

O   WHEN did the plaintiff's accident occur? (3)

W   In early February. I think it was February 2.

O   Your Honor, I have no further voir dire questions of this witness. I renew my objection.

J   The objection will be sustained.

The second fact situation is a suit against a railroad company. The plaintiff, Hughes Corporation, sues the California Central Railroad. The plaintiff alleges that the defendant's train derailed near the plaintiff's plant and caused extensive property damage. The defendant's answer alleges that the cause of the derailment was the defective condition of the track and that under the railroad's contract with another adjacent landowner, Laredo Company, Laredo was responsible for maintaining the track. The plaintiff calls Mr. Karl as a witness. Mr. Karl identifies himself and states that he is one of the plaintiff's employees. He is prepared to testify that on December 3, 1998, the day after the accident, one of the defendant's work crews repaired the track. The proponent is the plaintiff.

P   Mr. Karl, WHERE were you on December 3, 1998?

W   I was at work at our main plant in Grass Valley.

P WHAT happened that day?

W I was working outside, trying to repair some of the damage caused by the derailment the day before.

P WHAT, if anything, did you see while you were outside?

W I saw some of the defendant's employees arrive.

P HOW do you know that they were the defendant's employees?

W They all had coveralls on, and the coveralls had the defendant's name on them. They drove to the site in a truck with the defendant's name on the side.

P WHAT were the defendant's employees doing?

O Your Honor, I object to that question. May we approach the bench?

J Yes.

O Your Honor, I suspect that the plaintiff is attempting to elicit inadmissible evidence of subsequent repairs to the track.

J (To the plaintiff's attorney.) Is that your intention?

P Your Honor, I do intend to try to prove a subsequent repair. However, I contend that the evidence is admissible. I offer to prove that the witness will testify that he saw the defendant's employees repair the track. (4) The evidence is logically relevant to prove that the defendant had control of the track and thus a duty to keep the track in a state of good repair. (5) The defendant's answer specifically denied that it had control of the track or a duty to repair. (6) The defendant's general manager testified to that effect yesterday afternoon. (6) The evidence should be admitted for the limited purpose of proving the defendant's control of the track.

J I agree. The objection is overruled.

P Mr. Karl, let me repeat the question. WHAT were the defendant's employees doing?

W They were repairing the track.

O Your Honor, I request a limiting instruction.

J Granted. Ladies and gentlemen of the jury, you have just heard evidence that the day after the accident, the defendant's employees were repairing the track. You are not to use that evidence as proof that the defendant was careless at the time of the accident. You may use the evidence only in deciding whether the defendant had control of the track and a duty to keep it in good repair.

In the last hypothetical, the judge admitted the subsequent repair evidence as proof on the historical merits of the case. As the next hypothetical illustrates, the evidence can also be used for impeachment purposes. Revisit the first hypothetical. Suppose that Ms. Fenton was the store manager. On direct examination, she testifies that she considered the slope "perfectly safe." The proponent is the plaintiff.

P Ms. Fenton, ISN'T IT TRUE that one week after the plaintiff's accident, you hired a contractor to reduce the slope on the entrance?

O Your Honor, I object to that question on the ground that it calls for evidence of a subsequent repair.

P Your Honor, may we approach the bench?

J Yes.

P   Your Honor, I do intend to prove a subsequent repair. However, I contend that the evidence is admissible. I offer to prove that the witness will testify that as store manager, she was in charge of maintenance of the store and that she personally authorized the repair. (4) The evidence is logically relevant to impeach her credibility. On direct examination, she expressed her opinion that the slope was "perfectly safe." As volume 3, sections 1888-89 of the third edition of Witkin point out, this evidence qualifies as prior inconsistent conduct. (5) Since this witness has testified, her credibility is in issue. In fact, she is one of the key witnesses for the defense. (6)

On this state of the record, the trial judge would probably be justified in admitting the evidence. However, as the cited sections of WITKIN point out, the appellate courts give the trial judges wide latitude in ruling on such evidence. Under § 352, the judge might be permitted to exclude the evidence without committing error.

M.   COMPROMISE STATEMENTS

1. STATEMENTS DURING CIVIL SETTLEMENT NEGOTIATIONS

The courts have long favored the out-of-court settlement of legal claims. That attitude has become even more pronounced in recent years; the trial courts are so badly backlogged that it is imperative to encourage out-of-court settlements. The attitude expresses itself in a doctrine excluding statements made during civil settlement negotiations. The courts reason that if negotiators know that their statements are inadmissible, their discussions will be more candid and, hopefully, more successful. This reasoning led to the enactment of Evidence Code §§ 1152-54. Section 1152 protects potential defendants. Section 1152 reads:

> (a) Evidence that a person has, in compromise or from humanitarian motives, furnished or offered or promised to furnish money or any other thing, act, or service to another who has sustained or will sustain or claims that he has sustained or will sustain loss or damage, as well as any conduct or statements made in negotiation thereof, is inadmissible to prove his liability for the loss or damage or any part of it.
>
> (b) This section does not affect the admissibility of evidence of:
>
> (1) Partial satisfaction of an asserted claim or demand without questioning its validity when such evidence is offered to prove the validity of the claim; or
>
> (2) A debtor's payment or promise to pay all or part of his preexisting debt when such evidence is offered to prove the creation of a new duty on his part or a revival of his preexisting duty.

(*People v. Muniz*, 213 Cal. App. 3d 1508, 1515, 262 Cal. Rptr. 743, 746 (1989), held that in a criminal trial § 1152 does not operate to exclude the defendant's offer to pay the victim's medical expenses as evidence of defendant's guilt.)

Section 1154 protects potential plaintiffs:

> Evidence that a person has accepted or offered or promised to accept a sum of money or any other thing, act, or service in satisfaction of a claim, as well as any conduct or statements made in negotiation thereof, is inadmissible to prove the invalidity of the claim or any part of it.

Like the subsequent repair rule, §§ 1152-54 are similar to a privilege doctrine. Just as the attorney-client privilege and the subsequent repair doctrine attempt to promote extrinsic social policies, §§ 1152-54 are calculated to encourage out-of-court settlements. Sections 1152-54 may resemble a privilege in another respect. It is true that if read literally, the statutes seem to permit any party to the litigation to object on the ground of a violation of the statutes. 23 C. WRIGHT & K. GRAHAM, FEDERAL PRACTICE AND PROCEDURE: EVIDENCE § 5303, at 191 n.15 (1978) ("[a] literal reading of Cal. Evid. Code § 1152"). However, in principle, there is a strong argument that only a party to the negotiations should be able to invoke the statutes. Many of the leading commentators support this argument. *Id.* at § 5303, at 191-92; 2 D. LOUISELL & C. MUELLER, FEDERAL EVIDENCE § 171 (1985); Slough, *Relevancy Unraveled—Part III: Remote and Prejudicial Evidence,* 5 KAN. L. REV. 657. 721 (1957). If the California courts ultimately accept this argument, §§ 1152-54 will operate as privileges with a holder.

Like the subsequent repair rule, this doctrine does not exclude evidence for *all* purposes. In the words of § 1152, the plaintiff may not offer the defendant's compromise statements to "prove his liability for the loss or damage. ..." Section 1154 similarly forbids the defendant from offering the plaintiff's compromise statements "to prove the invalidity of the claim. ..." Again, however, the proponent may offer the evidence on other theories of logical relevance. The federal statute, Rule of Evidence 408, adds: "This rule ... does not require exclusion when the evidence is offered for another purpose, such as proving bias or prejudice of a witness, negating a contention of undue delay, or proving an effort to obstruct a criminal investigation or prosecution."

The party attempting to exclude the evidence should lay this foundation:

1. At the time of the statement, there was a dispute over the existence or extent of civil liability. The dispute can relate to a tort claim or a contract claim. *Zeitounian v. Farmers Ins. Group*, 25 Cal. App. 4th 929, 30 Cal. Rptr. 2d 882 (1994).

2. The party made the statement for the purpose of settling the dispute. The exclusionary rule does not attach if the party makes an admission independently of settlement negotiations, for example, after the negotiations end. 2 JEFFERSON § 34.3, at 1289-92.

3. The subject matter of the statement is within the doctrine. All jurisdictions protect an offer to settle. However, some jurisdictions protect an accompanying statement of facts only if the speaker specifically states it as a hypothetical or "without prejudice." The California cases do not require this. Further, the cases construe § 1152-54 as applying to a party's settlement with third parties. 1 WITKIN § 437. The text of § 1152 supports this construction; the statute refers to settlement negotiations with "another." Suppose, for instance, that the defendant has already settled with plaintiff #1. At the trial between plaintiff #2 and the defendant, plaintiff #2 may not use the earlier settlement as evidence of the defendant's liability.

The party attempting to introduce the evidence must be ready to make an offer of proof. In the offer of proof, the party should state:

4. What the witness will testify to if the judge permits the party to pursue the line of questioning.
5. The evidence is logically relevant to some issue other than the general question of the claim's validity. *E.g., Carney v. SCWAR*, 221 Cal. App. 3d 1009, 1024, 271 Cal. Rptr. 30, 39 (1990):

> In this case, ... the letter was not introduced to prove Karen's "liability" for any "loss or damage." The letter was admitted as evidence regarding the truth or falsity of the statements in the SCWAR newsletter as part of Carney's effort to establish SCWAR's liability. [T]he plain language of the statute provides that evidence of a settlement is inadmissible to prove liability of the settling party, and ... Karen's letter was not admitted to establish her liability. ...

6. The issue the evidence relates to is a disputed question in the case.

The first fact situation is a tort action for personal injuries. The plaintiff, Mr. James Stone, sues the defendant, Ms. Rachel Damer. The plaintiff alleges that the defendant caused a collision and that in the collision, the plaintiff suffered injuries in the amount of $100,000. The plaintiff takes the witness stand to testify in his own behalf. On cross-examination, the following occurs. The proponent is the defendant.

P Mr. Stone, ISN'T IT TRUE THAT in your complaint in this case, you claim that you've suffered $100,000 in damages?
W Yes.
P ISN'T IT A FACT THAT on February 17, 1999, you were at my office?
W Right.
P ISN'T IT CORRECT THAT while you were there, you offered to settle your whole claim for only $15,000?
O Your Honor, I object to that question. May we approach the bench?

J   Yes.

O   Your Honor, I object to that question on the ground that it calls for an inadmissible compromise statement. I request permission to voir dire the witness before you rule on my objection. I request that you excuse the jurors.

J   Yes. Ladies and gentlemen of the jury, I am going to ask you to leave the courtroom for a few minutes. The bailiff will accompany you to the deliberation room.

O   Mr. Stone, WHY did you go to the opposing attorney's office on February 17? (2)

W   I went there with my attorney to discuss my claim against his client.

O   WHAT was your claim? (1)

W   I took the position that Ms. Damer was at fault in the accident and caused my injuries.

O   WHAT was your belief about the validity of this claim? (1)

W   I thought I was in the right, I thought the claim was valid. As I remember the accident, I had the green light.

O   WHAT did the defendant say about your claim? (1)

W   She denied that she was at fault.

O   WHAT was the purpose of the meeting on February 17? (2)

W   We wanted to see if we could settle without going to trial.

O   WHY did you want to settle if you thought that your claim was valid? (2)

W   You told me that juries are unpredictable and that sometimes it's better to be conservative and accept less money than you ask for in your complaint. I still thought that I had a good claim, but that's why I was willing to talk about settling.

O   Your Honor, I have no further voir dire questions. The witness's testimony shows that there was a dispute over his claim's validity and that he made his offer in a bona fide effort to compromise. The question I'm objecting to calls for the settlement offer itself. (3) The question is objectionable.

J   The objection is sustained. (As in the case of subsequent repair evidence, the opponent should consider moving for a mistrial. Moreover, since the proponent attorney had personal knowledge of the facts rendering the evidence inadmissible, the attorney may be guilty of misconduct. See the discussion of assigning misconduct in HEAFEY ch. 29.)

The second fact situation is a contract action. The plaintiff, Mr. John Peterson, sues the defendant, Jerris Construction Company. In its answer, the defendant alleges that the plaintiff did not reasonably mitigate damages; the answer alleges that after the defendant's breach, the plaintiff delayed three months before looking for another contractor. The plaintiff takes the witness stand in his own behalf. The plaintiff has already testified to the contract's formation and the defendant's breach. The plaintiff is the proponent.

P   WHAT happened after the defendant's work crew walked off the site?

W   The next day, I contacted Mr. Garner, the defendant's president.

P   WHAT happened when you contacted him?

W   He and I discussed how we might settle my claim against his company.

O   Your Honor, I move to strike the last answer. May we approach the bench?

J   By all means.

O   Your Honor, the answer refers to inadmissible compromise negotiations.

P   Your Honor, may I be heard?

J   Yes.

P   I offer to prove that the witness will testify that the parties began settlement negotiations that day and that the negotiations continued for over two months. (4) The testimony is logically relevant to explain the plaintiff's delay in hiring another contractor. (5) In its answer, the defendant alleged that the plaintiff did not properly mitigate damages. (6) The evidence is admissible for the limited purpose of rebutting the defendant's allegation.

J   Motion denied.

P   Mr. Peterson, permit me to repeat the question. WHAT happened when you contacted Mr. Garner?

W   We discussed settling my claim against his company.

P   HOW long did these discussions last?

W   On and off for over two months. I kept trying to get them back on the project; I wanted a warehouse, not a lawsuit.

O   Your Honor, I request a limiting instruction.

J   Granted. Ladies and gentlemen of the jury, you've just heard testimony about settlement negotiations between the plaintiff and defendant. You are not to use the evidence of the defendant's willingness to negotiate as an admission of liability. You are to use this evidence only for the limited purpose of deciding whether the plaintiff acted with reasonable speed in finding a new contractor to finish the project. The defendant claims that the plaintiff did not. The plaintiff offers these pending settlement negotiations as an explanation for his delay in hiring a new contractor.

In recent years, the backlogged trial court calendars have changed the attitude of the courts and legislatures toward alternative dispute resolution (ADR) mechanisms. There is now a widespread perception that potential civil litigants should be encouraged to resort to ADR techniques. Section 1119 encourages this resort to ADR by creating a limited privilege for statements made during mediation proceedings. In *Ryan v. Garcia*, 27 Cal. App. 4th 1006, 33 Cal. Rptr. 2d 158, 160-62 (1994), the court interpreted § 1119's predecessor (§ 1152.5) expansively; the court read the statute as extending to statements made at a meeting convened to recite the terms of a settlement which has already been successfully negotiated. *See also Rinaker v. Superior Court*, 62 Cal. App. 4th 155, 74 Cal. Rptr. 2d 464 (1998) (both the participants and the mediator may assert the privilege, but it can be waived); Biderman & Gonzalez, *Mediation: The Changed Rules of Evidentiary Privilege*, CAL. LAWYER 30 (June 1999) (the privilege now extends to "even mediation intake consultation;" the privilege "cloaks all discussions related to mediation, starting with the first phone call to the mediator's office, including any preliminary discussions about potential mediation with an adversary and any inquiries you make about a mediator. During the course of the mediation, all statements, other communications, negotiations, or settlement discussions—whether oral or written, including those made outside the presence of the mediator—are privileged"). *But see Regents of the University of California v. Sumner*, 42 Cal. App. 4th 1209, 50 Cal. Rptr. 2d 200, 202-03 (1996) (questioning *Ryan*).

2. STATEMENTS DURING PLEA BARGAINING NEGOTIATIONS

The last subsection examined the doctrine excluding statements made during civil settlement negotiations. The reason for that doctrine is that the courts want to encourage out-of-court settlements and save court time. For a similar reason, many jurisdictions recognize a parallel doctrine excluding statements made during criminal plea bargaining negotiations. Evidence Code § 1153 places California among the jurisdictions following the doctrine. Section 1153 reads:

> Evidence of a plea of guilty, later withdrawn, or of an offer to plead guilty to the crime charged or to any other crime, made by the defendant in a criminal action is inadmissible in any action or in any proceeding of any nature, including proceedings before agencies, commissions, boards, and tribunals.[11]

The defendant attempting to invoke this doctrine must lay this foundation:

1. At a certain time and place, the defendant met with the authorities, that is, the police, the prosecutor, or the judge.
2. The defendant believed that the purpose of the meeting was plea bargaining. In *People v. Posten*, 108 Cal. App. 3d 633, 166 Cal. Rptr. 661 (1980), the defendant made an incriminating statement to a police officer while the officer was transporting the defendant by train from Virginia. The court found that the statement was an unsolicited admission. Given the finding, the court held § 1153 inapplicable. Likewise, *People v. Magana*, 17 Cal. App. 4th 1371, 22 Cal. Rptr. 2d 59 (1993), ruled that § 1153 is inapplicable to both statements made to transporting police officers and statements made in anger to the trial judge.
3. The defendant's belief was reasonable. The authorities' statements and conduct reasonably led the defendant to that belief.
4. The defendant made the statement during the plea bargaining session.
5. The subject-matter of the statement was proper. On its face, § 1153 applies only to withdrawn guilty pleas and "offer(s) to plead guilty." Unlike

---

[11]It has been suggested that Proposition 8 may have abolished Evidence Code § 1153. Butterworth & Horne, *Pleas and Case Settlement*, CALIFORNIA CRIMINAL LAW: PROCEDURE AND PRACTICE § 10.39, at 225 (2d ed. 1994) (citing *People v. Pacchioli*, 9 Cal. App. 4th 1331, 12 Cal. Rptr. 2d 156 (1992) and *People v. Goodner*, 7 Cal. App. 4th 1324, 9 Cal. Rptr. 2d 543 (1992); Trask & Polis, *Pleas and Case Settlement*, in CALIFORNIA CRIMINAL LAW § 10.25, at 190 (1986). However, as we previously noted, Article I, § 28(d) of the California Constitution states that "[n]othing in this section shall affect any existing statutory rule of evidence relating to privilege. ..." Section 1153 arguably operates as a privilege: To vindicate the extrinsic social policy of encouraging plea bargaining, a defendant holder is given the right to exclude certain logically relevant information. If the courts read "privilege" in § 28(d) in a functional fashion, they could treat § 1153 as a privilege expressly preserved by Proposition 8.

§§ 1152 and 1153.5, § 1153 makes no mention of accompanying statements of fact. However, *People v. Tanner*, 45 Cal. App. 3d 345, 119 Cal. Rptr. 407 (1975), extends the protection of § 1153 to such statements.[12]

Our fact situation is a medical fraud prosecution. The People allege that the defendant, Mr. George Aston, is a pharmacist and knowingly filled fraudulent prescriptions for doctors receiving medical payments from the state. The indictment alleges that the defendant filled excessive prescriptions and prescriptions for fictitious patients. Since this is a white-collar crime prosecution, the defendant was not in custody. The government's primary interest was convicting the doctors with whom the defendant conspired. Prior to trial, the defendant makes a motion *in limine* to suppress certain statements he made to the prosecutor during a meeting at the prosecutor's office. The defense counsel was present at the meeting. Since the defendant was not in custody and there is no evidence of force or threats, the defense counsel cannot argue *Miranda* or the voluntariness doctrine. Rather, the defense counsel rests the motion squarely on the doctrine excluding statements made during plea bargaining negotiations. The defense counsel calls the defendant as a witness in support of the motion. The defendant has already identified himself. The defendant is the proponent.

P　Mr. Aston, WHERE were you on the afternoon of April 3, 1999? (1)

W　I went to the D.A.'s office in downtown Oakland.

P　WHO else was there? (1)

W　You were there, and the other person present was a Deputy D.A.

P　WHO was that? (1)

W　I think her name was Hester Martin.

P　WHAT was the purpose of this meeting? (2)

W　Plea bargaining. I hoped to get some concessions, maybe even immunity.

P　WHY did you think that was the purpose of the meeting? (2)

W　You told me that before we got there.

P　WHAT, if anything, did Ms. Martin say about the purpose of the meeting? (3)

W　When we got there, she said that she wanted to be honest with me. She said that I was just a small fish and that they were really interested in nailing all the doctors I had filled false prescriptions for. She said that if I came clean, they might give me a break. She even mentioned some sort of immunity.

P　WHAT did you say then? (4), (5)

W　With your permission, I told her about my involvement with the doctors. I said that I'd be willing to repeat those statements in court for full immunity.

P　HOW did Ms. Martin respond to your offer?

W　She said that she'd have to talk it over with her boss, Mr. Ching, before giving us a final answer.

P　WHAT was the final answer?

---

[12]Justice Jefferson has criticized *Tanner*. 2 JEFFERSON § 34.5, at 1299. He points out that Evidence Code § 351 mandates that "[e]xcept as otherwise provided by statute, all relevant evidence is admissible." He argues that § 351 deprives the courts of the power to expand the scope of § 1153.

W My attorney and I met with Ms. Martin again about three days later. She said that her boss would OK some sentence concessions but wouldn't buy immunity.

P WHAT, if anything, did you say then?

W I told her that it was too bad because you and I had agreed that I'd talk only if I got immunity.

P WHAT happened to your plea bargaining with the District Attorney's office?

W That conversation ended the negotiations.

P Your Honor, I have no further questions of the defendant. I renew my motion to preclude any reference to my client's statements during the plea bargaining session at the District Attorney's office.

J I shall grant the motion.

According to *People v. Cummings*, 4 Cal. 4th 1233, 850 P.2d 1, 18 Cal. Rptr. 2d 796 (1993), the defendant can waive the protection of §1153. In *Cummings*, the prosecution made the waiver a precondition to its willingness to discuss the possible disposition of charges with the defendant. Moreover, *People v. Johnson*, 42 Cal. App. 4th 831, 50 Cal. Rptr. 2d 17, 20 (1996) permits the prosecution to use otherwise privileged statements for the purpose of impeachment. At first blush, it might appear that the court went quite far in permitting that use. In *Johnson*, the testimony impeached was given by a defense expert rather than the defendant himself. However, the expert testified to statements made by the defendant; and in phrasing its holding, the court emphasized that the allowable use of the evidence was "to impeach evidence of ... statements of the defendant ...."

Chapter 11

CONSTITUTIONAL PRIVILEGES—THE EXCLUSIONARY RULES

A. INTRODUCTION

The last chapter dealt with statutory privileges and analogous rules. This chapter takes up the topic of constitutional privileges, the exclusionary rules created to protect a defendant's Fourth, Fifth, and Sixth Amendment rights. There are sophisticated treaties and texts analyzing the exclusionary rules: W. LAFAVE, SEARCH AND SEIZURE: A TREATISE ON THE FOURTH AMENDMENT (2d ed. 1987) (4 vols.), W. LAFAVE & J. ISRAEL, CRIMINAL PROCEDURE (1984) (3 vols.), and C. WHITEBREAD & C. SLOBOGIN, CRIMINAL PROCEDURE (3d ed. 1993). There are also helpful case finders such as BELL'S SEARCHES, SEIZURES, AND BUGGING COMPENDIUM (1985). The purpose of this chapter is to illustrate some of the more common foundations that a prosecutor would have to lay to satisfy the exclusionary rules. This chapter is divided into three parts. The first part addresses primarily Fourth Amendment issues: the restrictions the Constitution imposes on the admissibility of products of searches and seizures. The next part analyzes confession problems—both the admissibility of out-of-court confessions and prosecutors' attempts to elicit judicial confessions from testifying defendants. The third part discusses the limitations on eyewitness testimony. For purposes of the sample foundations, please assume that the testimony is being given at a pretrial hearing such as a hearing on a motion to suppress.

The topic of the procedures for motion practice is itself an important subject. *E.g.*, *People v. Glenn*, 56 Cal. App. 4th 886, 65 Cal. Rptr. 2d 797 (1997) (even if an earlier suppression motion was granted in a prior proceeding, the People have the right to relitigate the motion after moving to dismiss the first prosecution and filing a new complaint). Penal Code § 1538.5 governs when the basis of the motion is a Fourth Amendment argument. There is a detailed discussion of procedure under § 1538.5 in A. BELL, BELL'S MOTION MANUAL ON 1538.5 PROCEDURE (J. Blackmer, ed. 1986). The manual discusses such questions as the timing of the motion and the differences in motion practice between felony and misdemeanor cases. Suppose, however, that the basis of the motion is a Fifth or Sixth Amendment contention. In that event, § 1538.5 does not apply directly; the procedural devices for raising those contentions include objections at preliminary hearings, Penal Code § 995 motions, and common-law motions to exclude. Rael & Phillips, *Confessions and Admissions*, in CALIFORNIA CRIMINAL LAW §§ 30:7-13 (2d ed. 1994) presents a good overview of those procedural devices. For the balance of this chapter, you may assume that the issue is being litigated at a pretrial hearing. Furthermore, please assume that the defense has specified the nature of its Fourth, Fifth, or Sixth Amendment contention. For that reason, the testimony in each hypothetical in this chapter focuses on a particular Fourth, Fifth, or Sixth Amendment doctrine.

Part 1. The Products of Searches and Seizures

B.   IN GENERAL

The Fourth Amendment generally forbids unreasonable searches. There is a similar prohibition in article I, § 13 of the California Constitution. Before the adoption of Proposition 8, the California courts had invoked the state constitution to impose many restrictions on searches and seizures that the United States Supreme Court had balked at mandating under the Fourth Amendment. However, in *In re Lance W.*, 37 Cal. 3d 873, 888, 694 P.2d 744, 753, 210 Cal. Rptr. 631, 640 (1985), the California Supreme Court construed Proposition 8 as requiring the California courts to exclude the products of searches and seizures only when mandated by the Fourth Amendment or a statute passed after June 1, 1982 by two-thirds of each house of the legislature. As a result of the adoption of Proposition 8, California courts can no longer exclude the products of searches and seizures on independent state grounds. *People v. Ford*, 4 Cal. App. 4th 32, 5 Cal. Rptr. 2d 189 (1992) (the nonconsensual withdrawal of blood from a DUI arrestee in violation of provisions of the Business and Professions Code); *People v. Trapane*, 1 Cal. App. 4th Supp. 10, 3 Cal. Rptr. 2d 423 (App. Dep't Super. Ct. 1991) (a warrantless misdemeanor arrest in violation of state statute); *People v. Sullivan*, 234 Cal. App. 3d 56, 285 Cal. Rptr. 553 (1991) (the speed trap exclusion codified in Vehicle Code § 40803(a)); *People v. Boyd*, 224 Cal. App. 3d 736, 742, 274 Cal. Rptr. 100, 103 (1990). The product must be inadmissible on federal grounds, that is, violative of the Fourth Amendment or a federal statute applicable to the states. *People v. Otto*, 2 Cal. 4th 1088, 9 Cal. Rptr. 2d 596, 831 P.2d 1178 (1992) (the federal wiretapping statute); *People v. Murtha*, 235 Cal. App. 3d 1688, 1 Cal. Rptr. 2d 788, 791-93 (1991) (the statutory restrictions on the interception of telephone communications in Title III of the Omnibus Crime Control and Safe Streets Act, 18 U.S.C. §§ 2510 *et seq.*). For that reason, this part of the chapter relies primarily on United States Supreme Court precedents.

(In June 1990, the electorate passed Proposition 115. That proposition included language to the effect that

[i]n criminal cases the right of a defendant to ... be free from unreasonable searches and seizures ... shall be construed by the courts of this state in a manner consistent with the Constitution of the United States. This Constitution shall not be construed by the courts to afford greater rights to criminal defendants than those afforded by the Constitution of the United States.

...

However, on procedural grounds, the California Supreme Court invalidated this provision of Proposition 115. *Raven v. Deukmejian*, 52 Cal. 3d 336, 801 P.2d 1077, 276 Cal. Rptr. 326 (1990).)

The Fourth Amendment precedents address two fundamental topics: The first topic is the rules governing the legality of searches and seizures. In some instances, the prosecutor need not justify a search or seizure. For example, as we shall see in the next section, the Fourth Amendment is inapplicable if the person conducting the search is a private citizen rather than a government agent. Even when there is sufficient government involvement to trigger the Fourth Amendment, the prosecutor may not have to establish any incriminating facts individualized to the defendant to validate the search. For instance, the prosecutor may be able to justify the seizure on the ground that the defendant abandoned the personal property or that the seizure occurred in an open field. In other cases, however, the prosecutor must prove inculpatory facts particularized to the defendant. By way of illustration, the prosecutor must demonstrate founded or reasonable suspicion to justify a stop or frisk. If the intrusion amounts to a full-fledged arrest or search, the prosecutor must go further and establish probable cause.

The second topic is the scope of the exclusionary rule barring the admission of the products of illegal searches and seizures. Even if an illegal search or seizure has occurred, the prosecutor may be able to introduce a product of the search or seizure. Sections P and Q show how a prosecutor can use the inevitable discovery and good faith doctrines to do so.

C.   THE SEARCH AND SEIZURE OF THE DEFENDANT'S PROPERTY BY A PRIVATE CITIZEN

1. THE DOCTRINE

The Fourth Amendment restricts only those searches conducted and seizures made by the government agents. In contrast, before the passage of Proposition 8, the California Supreme Court had held that the exclusionary rule under the state constitution applies to private security guards effecting statutorily authorized citizen's arrests. *People v. Zelinski*, 24 Cal. 3d 357, 594 P.2d 1000, 155 Cal. Rptr. 575 (1979). However, several courts have held that by virtue of Proposition 8, the state exclusionary rule is now limited to intrusions by government agents. *In re Christopher H.*, 227 Cal. App. 3d 1567, 278 Cal. Rptr. 577 (1991); *People v. Taylor*, 222 Cal. App. 3d 612, 271 Cal. Rptr. 785 (1990); *People v. Warren*, 219 Cal. App. 3d 619, 268 Cal. Rptr. 381 (1990) (search of package by the operator of a private shipping and receiving business); *People v. Brouillette*, 210 Cal. App. 3d 842, 258 Cal. Rptr. 635 (1989) (search by private security guard). Suppose, for example, that a private citizen searches another citizen's property, discovers contraband, and then turns the contraband over to the police. If there was no government involvement in the initial search, the Fourth Amendment is inapplicable. 1

W. Lafave, Search and Seizure: A Treatise on the Fourth Amendment § 1.8 (2d ed. 1987).

2. ELEMENTS OF THE FOUNDATION

A prosecutor attempting to introduce the product of a search and seizure under this doctrine must prove the following foundational elements:

1. Someone searched the defendant's property.
2. That person acted as a private citizen.
3. During the search, the person seized certain personal property or made certain incriminating observations. If the prosecutor wants to offer seized personal property, the prosecutor will have to authenticate it. Section J of Chapter 4 discusses the principal methods of identifying items of physical evidence.
4. The scope of the later government intrusion was essentially the same as the scope of the private citizen's intrusion. To prove this, the prosecutor will probably have to call the police officer to whom the private citizen surrendered the personal property. In *United States v. Jacobsen*, 466 U.S. 109 (1984), a private carrier's employee discovered white powder in a damaged package. The employee called a DEA agent, who immediately conducted a simple field test to determine whether the substance was cocaine. The Supreme Court held that the warrantless test was lawful because it did not significantly expand the scope of the earlier private intrusion. However, in *People v. Leichty*, 205 Cal. App. 3d 914, 252 Cal. Rptr. 669 (1988), *cert. denied*, 490 U.S. 1095 (1989), the court distinguished *Jacobsen* and held the warrantless testing illegal. In *Leichty*, the crime laboratory conducted sophisticated tests the day after the discovery of the contraband by a private party. The court held that the testing in *Leichty* significantly expanded the scope of the earlier intrusion and necessitated a warrant. *But see People v. Coston*, 221 Cal. App. 3d 898, 905, 271 Cal. Rptr. 25, 28-29 (1990) (criticizing *Leichty*).

3. SAMPLE FOUNDATION

The People have charged the defendant Green with illegal possession of heroin. The witness is Mr. Winston Farrell. Mr. Farrell has already testified that he is a porter at the St. Gregory Hotel in San Francisco. The proponent is the prosecutor:

P   WHERE were you on the morning of July 13, 1999?
W   I was on duty in the hotel lobby.
P   WHAT happened that morning?
W   People were checking in and out. I remember one customer who checked in in particular.
P   WHO is that?

W The defendant Green over there.

P WHERE is he sitting?

W At the table farther from the jury box.

P HOW is he dressed?

W He's wearing a blue suit with a yellow tie.

P Your Honor, please let the record reflect that the witness has identified the defendant, Thomas Green.

J The record will so reflect.

P WHAT happened after the defendant checked in? (1)

W He gave me his suitcases and told me to take them up to his room while he went to park his car.

P WHAT did you do after he gave you the suitcases? (1)

W I got into the elevator and started taking his suitcases to the 14th floor where his room was. I guess he didn't have the suitcases locked properly. When the elevator got to the 14th floor and I started to pick them up to walk to his room, one came partially open; and I saw two plastic bags.

P WHAT was the appearance of the bags? (1)

W The bags were clear, and you could see the contents.

P WHAT was the appearance of the contents? (1)

W They were a white powdery substance. It looked to me as if it might be heroin.

P WHY do you say that? (1)

W Two weeks before, the head of the hotel security had given us a block of instruction on illegal drugs. She told us to be on the lookout for that sort of junk. She showed us photographs of various illegal drugs, and this stuff looked just like the heroin in the photo she showed us.

P WHAT did you do after the bags fell out of the defendant's luggage? (3)

W I reached in and grabbed them and took them and the luggage downstairs. I immediately called the police.

P WHY did you do that? (2)

W I don't want that sort of stuff going on in the hotel.

P WHEN did you first contact the police—before or after you met the defendant? (2)

W Afterwards.

P WHO else was present when you discovered the bags containing the powder? (2)

W No one—it was just me.

P After you called the police, WHAT happened? (3)

W They came.

P WHAT were their names? (3)

W Officers Brannon and Ramirez.

P WHERE are they now? (3)

W I don't know where Brannon is, but I see Ramirez sitting in the first row over there in uniform.

P WHAT did you do after the two police officers arrived? (3)

W I gave them the luggage and the bags containing the white powder.

D.   THE SEIZURE OF PROPERTY ABANDONED BY THE DEFENDANT

1. THE DOCTRINE

If a defendant voluntarily abandons property, the defendant relinquishes any protected expectation of privacy in the property. The central problem for the prosecutor is establishing that the defendant's physical act was not prompted by an illegal search or surveillance.

2. ELEMENTS OF THE FOUNDATION

The foundation includes these elements:

1. The defendant physically abandoned the property. *See In re Baraka H.*, 6 Cal. App. 4th 1039, 8 Cal. Rptr. 2d 221, 227 (1992) ("Abandonment here ... is not meant in the strict property-right sense. ... In essence, what is abandoned is not necessarily the defendant's property right, but his reasonable expectation of privacy therein. ..."); *People v. Dasilva*, 207 Cal. App. 3d 43, 48, 254 Cal. Rptr. 563, 565-66 (1989) ("It is settled law that a disclaimer of proprietary or possessory interest in the area searched or the evidence discovered terminates the legitimate expectations of privacy over such area or items."); *People v. Dees*, 221 Cal. App. 3d 588, 594-95, 270 Cal. Rptr. 554, 557 (1990) ("[A] total disclaimer of any interest in the area or item searched at the time of the search ... will preclude a successful challenge to the legality of that search.").
2. The defendant performed the act voluntarily. In many cases, when a police officer approaches, the defendant throws contraband to the ground. The act is involuntary if it was the result of illegal action by the police. In *People v. Washington*, 192 Cal. App. 3d 1120, 236 Cal. Rptr. 840 (1987), when the police sighted the defendant, they began chasing him; they did so before there was even reasonable suspicion that he had committed a crime. When the defendant saw the police chasing him, he ran. As he ran, he discarded bundles of illegal drugs. The police picked up the bundles. The court held that the police had illegally seized the drugs. The court reasoned that since the police chase indicated to the defendant that they intended to prevent him from leaving, the chase amounted to a stop. Since the police chased the defendant before they had even reasonable suspicion, the chase was illegal. The seizure was therefore a product of illegal police action. However, in *People v. Nickleberry*, 221 Cal. App. 3d 63, 69, 270 Cal. Rptr. 269, 272 (1990) (citing *Michigan v. Chesternut*, 486 U.S. 567 (1988)), the court ruled that the defendant discarded the rock cocaine before he was detained. In *California v. Hodari D.*, 499 U.S. 621 (1991), the United States Supreme Court held that a person is not "seized" under the Fourth Amendment

until he or she is either physically restrained by or submits to the police. "A suspect's fleeing and police pursuit—even though a reasonable person in the suspect's position might believe that he was not 'free' to leave—is not a 'seizure.'" *See People v. Arangure*, 230 Cal. App. 3d 1302, 282 Cal. Rptr. 51, 54 (1991); *People v. Johnson*, 231 Cal. App. 3d 1, 282 Cal. Rptr. 114, 118 (1991); *People v. Deutsch*, 44 Cal. App. 4th 1224, 52 Cal. Rptr. 2d 366 (1996) (the defendant had renounced any expectation of privacy in her discarded garbage).

3. The police lawfully proceeded to the location where the property was abandoned. If the location is a public street, the police officer does not need a warrant to walk over and pick up the property.

4. The police seized the abandoned item. Once again, the prosecutor must authenticate the physical evidence.

3. SAMPLE FOUNDATION

The People have charged the defendant Nerney with carrying an unlicensed, concealed weapon. The witness is Officer Grant. Officer Grant has already testified that on the morning of July 3, 1999, he was on duty on foot patrol near the corner of Third and Market Streets in downtown San Francisco. The proponent is the prosecutor.

P   WHAT, if anything, unusual happened that morning?
W   I saw someone approach the northwest corner, and I noticed that he had a suspicious looking bulge in the front of his jacket.
P   WHO was that person?
W   The defendant.
P   WHERE is he sitting now?
W   He's the fellow in the green shirt at the table to my right.
P   Your Honor, please let the record reflect that the witness has identified the defendant, Walter Nerney.
J   The record will so reflect.
P   WHAT happened next?
W   He was walking along, and then he caught sight of me.
P   HOW were you dressed?
W   I was in full uniform, as I am now.
P   WHAT did he do then?
W   He looked at me for a second or two. Then he abruptly turned and walked in the other direction.
P   WHAT did you do? (2)
W   I just stood and watched him carefully.
P   WHAT happened next? (1)
W   Next, I saw his left hand reach down and throw something on the ground.
P   WHERE was he standing at the time? (3)
W   On the public sidewalk.
P   WHAT happened to the thing he threw down?
W   It just fell to the ground.

P WHERE did it land? (3)

W It was also on the public sidewalk.

P HOW could you tell that the defendant threw the object down? (4)

W I saw his hand move, and I saw an object fall from his hand.

P WHAT did you do then? (4)

W I walked over quickly and picked it up.

P WHAT was the object? (4)

W It was a pistol.

P HOW would you describe the pistol? (4)

W It was a police special with serial number A14744.

P HOW can you remember the number? (4)

W I have an almost photographic memory for numbers. It's easy for me to remember serial numbers.

P Your Honor, I request that this be marked People's exhibit #1 for identification.

J It will be so marked.

P Please let the record reflect that I am showing the exhibit to the defense attorney.

J The record will so reflect.

P Permission to approach the witness?

J Granted.

P Officer, I now hand you People's exhibit #1 for identification. WHAT is it? (4)

W It's the pistol I picked up after the defendant threw it down.

P HOW can you recognize it? (4)

W I recognize the general type of weapon and the serial number—just like I said, A14744.

P Officer, WHAT did you say to the defendant before he threw his pistol to the ground? (2)

W Nothing.

P HOW far away from the defendant were you when he thre w the pistol down? (2)

W About twenty feet or so.

P WHAT gestures did you make toward him before he threw the pistol down? (2)

W None. I just stood there and watched him carefully.

P WHAT were you doing when he threw the pistol down? (2)

W Nothing—I didn't chase him or even make a move toward him. I was just watching the guy.

E.   THE SEIZURE OF PROPERTY IN AN OPEN FIELD OWNED BY THE DEFENDANT

1. THE DOCTRINE

The Fourth Amendment protects both a person's residence and the curtilage, the area immediately adjacent to the house and used in connection with the house. *People v. Thompson*, 221 Cal. App. 3d 923, 941, 270 Cal. Rptr. 863, 873 (1990) ("the backyard was part of the cartilage of the residence. ..."). However, in *Hester v. United States*, 265 U.S. 57 (1924), the Supreme Court held that the Fourth Amendment does not protect property located in an open field. In *Oliver v. United States*, 466 U.S. 170 (1984), the Court reaffirmed that the Fourth Amendment does not forbid the seizure of property situated in an open field, even if the police commit a technical trespass under state law by entering the field. Moreover, in *People v. Freeman*, 219 Cal. App. 3d 894, 902, 268 Cal. Rptr. 603, 607 (1990), the court stated that if the police have a vantage point in an open field, they may make "observations of the curtilage" without violating the Fourth Amendment.

2. THE ELEMENTS OF THE DOCTRINE

1. The defendant's property was an open field. The prosecutor usually establishes the fact by process of elimination—that is, the prosecutor shows that the location was neither a residence house nor the area immediately connected to the residence. *United States v. Dunn*, 480 U.S. 294 (1987). The prosecutor may introduce a chart or diagram of the defendant's property for this purpose.
2. The police searched the open field.
3. The police discovered and seized certain property in the open field. The prosecutor must authenticate the physical evidence.

3. SAMPLE FOUNDATION

The People have charged the defendant Wyatt with bank robbery. The People allege that on October 13, 1999, the defendant robbed the Bank of America branch in Downey, California. The witness is Officer Crystal. She has already testified that she drove to the defendant's farm in a rural area of Downey on a tip that the defendant was involved in the robbery. The prosecutor is the proponent:

P   HOW did you get to the defendant's farm?
W   I drove there on Highway 111.
P   WHERE is the defendant's farm?
W   It's right by the Highway 74 turnoff from 111. It's just south of 111.
P   HOW well do you know the area? (1)
W   Quite well. I've been on the police force in that area for thirteen years.
P   HOW well do you know the defendant's farm? (1)
W   I know the lay of the land pretty well.
P   HOW did you become acquainted with the layout of the farm? (1)
W   I hunt in that area, and I often hunt on the farm right next to the defendant's. You get a good view of the defendant's place from Garney's farm. Garney is a good buddy of mine, and I've hunted on his property tens of times.
P   Your Honor, I request that this be marked People's exhibit #2 for identification.
J   It will be so marked.
P   Please let the record reflect that I am showing this to opposing counsel.
J   The record will so reflect.
P   I request permission to approach the witness.
J   Granted.
P   Officer Crystal, I now hand you what has been marked as People's exhibit #2 for identification. WHAT is it? (1)

W It's a bare bones diagram of the defendant's farm.

P HOW well does the diagram depict the area? (1)

W All the features it shows are correct—Highway 111 running along the northern border, Highway 74 cutting down the eastern border, and the square shape of the piece of property. It's not to scale; but other than that, it's accurate.

P WHAT buildings are located on the property? (1)

W There are only three. The main residence, a barn, and a little storage shed. They're all located on the western edge of the property.

P Please take this black marker and indicate their location with a capital R for the residence, a capital B for barn, and a capital S for shed. Your Honor, please let the record reflect that the witness has complied with my request.

J It will so reflect.

P HOW are those buildings connected? (1)

W There are paths from the residence house to both the barn and the shed. There's a wooden fence around all three buildings. All three buildings are located in a small area on the western edge of the property, and they're all surrounded by this fence.

P Please use the black marker to indicate the paths with Ps, and then please use this red marker to draw the fence around all three buildings. Your Honor, please let the record reflect that the witness has complied with my request.

J The record will also reflect that.

P Officer Crystal, please describe the eastern half of this farm. (1)

W It's nothing but a big, uncultivated field. There aren't even many weeds.

P HOW is the field separated from the buildings on the western edge of the property? (1)

W The fence—the one I drew in red—cuts those buildings off from the field.

P WHAT paths, if any, connect the field to the buildings? (1)

W As far as I know, there aren't any. The paths from the residence house dead end at the shed and the barn. The paths don't continue into the field.

P HOW is the field separated from the highway? (1)

W There's a short, maybe three foot wire fence around the edge of the entire property, including the field.

P To WHAT extent does the fence block the view of the field from the highway? (1)

W Really not at all. It's an insubstantial, three-strand fence that you can see right through.

P On the morning of October 28, 1999 when you drove to the defendant's farm, WHERE did you park your car? (2)

W Right here near the northeast corner of the property.

P WHY did you do that? (2)

W As I was approaching the property from Highway 74, I thought I noticed something peculiar in the middle of the field.

P WHAT? (2)

W As I recalled, it was just an empty field; but when I approached it that morning, there was something piled in the middle of the field that I hadn't noticed before.

P Please use the green marker and indicate the location where you parked with C1.

W Right there.

P Thank you. WHAT did you do after you parked? (2)

W I walked to the pile in the field.

P   HOW did you get onto the defendant's property? (2)

W   I stepped over the fence here.

P   Please mark that location with C2.

W   There. This is where I stepped over the fence.

P   Thank you. WHAT did you do after you stepped over the fence? (2)

W   I walked straight towards the pile.

P   Please indicate your path with an arrow and mark that arrow C3.

W   OK.

P   WHAT happened then?

W   I reached the pile.

P   Please mark that location with C4. (3)

W   Right here at the end of the arrow.

P   Your Honor, I now offer People's exhibit #2 for identification into evidence as People's exhibit #2.

J   It will be received.

P   WHAT, if anything, did you find at the pile? (3)

W   There was a cardboard box with the top open. Inside I could see some discarded cloth bags.

P   WHAT type of bags were they? (3)

W   They were bank bags. There were three bags, and they all bore the inscription, "Bank of America, Downey."

P   Your Honor, I request that these be marked People's exhibits #3, 4, and 5. (The prosecutor would continue the foundation to identify the three bank bags.)

F.   THE DEFENDANT'S STANDING TO CHALLENGE THE GOVERNMENT INTRUSION

1. THE DOCTRINE

Assume that the defense establishes that there was a government search or seizure. Does the defendant automatically have a right to challenge the legality of the search or seizure? In federal practice, the answer has always been No. In *Jones v. United States*, 362 U.S. 257, 261 (1960), the Supreme Court announced that only "a victim of a search or seizure, one against whom the search was directed," has standing to challenge the intrusion. The United States Supreme Court has consistently rejected defense arguments for third party or vicarious standing. As the Court commented in *Alderman v. United States*, 394 U.S. 165, 174-75 (1969), "[W]e are not convinced that the additional benefit of extending the exclusionary rule to other defendants would justify further encroachment upon the public interest in prosecuting those accused of crime and having them acquitted or convicted on the basis of all the evidence which exposes the truth."

For three decades, however, the California courts followed the vicarious standing doctrine. The California Supreme Court embraced the doctrine in *People v. Martin*, 45 Cal. 2d 755, 290 P.2d 855 (1955). The court reasoned that the traditional bar on third-party standing "virtually invites law enforcement officers to violate the rights of third parties and to trade the escape of a criminal whose rights are violated for the conviction of others by the use of the evidence illegally obtained against them." However, as previously stated, in 1982 the California voters approved Proposition 8, an initiative amending the state constitution. In 1985, the California Supreme Court construed Proposition 8 as abolishing the vicarious standing doctrine. *In re Lance W.*, 37 Cal. 3d 873, 694 P.2d 744, 210 Cal. Rptr. 631 (1985). *See People v. Madrid*, 7 Cal. App. 4th 1888, 9 Cal. Rptr. 2d 798 (1992) (neither defendant's "marital relationship" to occupant of auto nor alleged conspiracy with occupant gave her standing to challenge search of auto).

In light of *In re Lance W.*, unless the California legislature passes a contrary statute by a two-thirds vote in each house, California courts must now apply the federal standing rules. The early federal standing cases often turned on "subtle distinctions, developed and refined by the common law in evolving the body of private property law." *Jones v. United States*, 362 U.S. 257, 266 (1960). However, the Supreme Court has since abandoned that property-oriented mode of analysis. The Court's standing decisions now focus on the question of whether the government intrusion invaded a personal expectation of privacy by the defendant. The Court has explicitly analyzed standing questions in those terms in cases such as *Mancusi v. DeForte*, 392 U.S. 364 (1968), *Combs v. United States*, 408 U.S. 224 (1972), and *Rakas v. Illinois*, 439 U.S. 128 (1978).

Decisions such as *Mancusi* and *Rakas* formally announced a new substantive test for standing. In *People v. Martins*, 228 Cal. App. 3d 1632, 279 Cal. Rptr. 687, 689 (1991), *cert. denied*, 502 U.S. 1061 (1992), the court interpreted the *Rakas* decision as going to the length of disapproving "of the use of the term 'standing'. ..." The decisions are also significant in another respect because in a practical sense, they represent a tightening of the standards the defendant must meet to prove standing. The *Jones* decision at least suggested that a person has standing to challenge a search of premises so long as he or she was legitimately present on the premises at the time of the search. *Jones v. United States*, 362 U.S. 257, 267 (1960). However in *Rakas*, the Court retrenched and held that a mere casual visitor—in that case, a passenger in a car—lacks standing. *But see People v. Bell*, 43 Cal. App. 4th 754, 51 Cal. Rptr. 2d 115 (1996) (since a traffic stop results in the detention of both the driver and every passenger, a passenger had standing to challenge the scope of the driver's detention). In *People v. Koury*, 214 Cal. App. 3d 676, 262 Cal. Rptr. 870 (1989), the court likewise held that without more, mere legitimate presence on the searched premises does not confer standing. *Accord People v. Jackson*, 7 Cal. App. 4th 1367, 10 Cal. Rptr. 2d 5, 7-8 (1992) (although defendant was a passenger in the auto, he had neither a possessory nor other interest in either the wallet seized or the place from which the wallet was recovered); *People v. Williams*, 3 Cal. App. 4th 1535, 5 Cal. Rptr. 2d 372, 374 (1992). Certainly, a car thief lacks standing to challenge an allegedly illegal search of the stolen car. *People v. Melnyk*, 4 Cal. App. 4th 1532, 6 Cal. Rptr. 2d 570 (1992). Similarly, a person who obtains a hotel room through the use of a stolen credit card number lacks standing to challenge a search of the room. *People v. Satz*, 61 Cal. App. 4th 322, 71 Cal. Rptr. 2d 433 (1998). In another early standing case, *United States v. Jeffers*, 342 U.S. 48 (1951), the Court indicated that a defendant has standing to challenge a search of personalty he owns even when the search occurs on premises in which he has no interest. However, applying expectation of privacy analysis, the Court reached a contrary result in *Rawlings v. Kentucky*, 448 U. S. 98 (1980). There the defendant claimed an ownership interest in drugs seized from a female companion's purse. The Court denied the defendant standing to attack the legality of the search of the purse. The Court stated that even if the defendant owned the drugs, he had not established a "legitimate expectation of privacy in the purse." In its latest pronouncement on standing, *Minnesota v. Carter*, 525 U. S. 83 (1998), the Supreme Court denied standing to a defendant who was in another person's apartment for a short time solely for the purpose of packaging cocaine. The Court stressed that the defendant had been only an overnight guest at the apartment and that the drug transaction in question was both of relatively short duration and purely commercial in nature.

In short, it is now much more difficult for a defendant to attain standing to challenge the legality of a government intrusion. A defense attorney seeking to establish standing should make the strongest possible showing of the defendant's personal nexus to both the place searched and any object seized. *E.g., People v. Henderson*, 220 Cal. App. 3d 1632, 270 Cal. Rptr. 248 (1990) (defense counsel established that defendant was authorized to stay at condo for three or four days, enjoyed unencumbered access to premises, had stayed there overnight, and had joint control of bathroom where a meth laboratory was located). In some cases, a sufficiently strong nexus to the object searched will suffice to confer standing. *People v. Ybarra*, 233 Cal. App. 3d 1353, 285 Cal. Rptr. 200 (1991) (defendant retained key to padlocked tool box). The nexus can take the form of an ownership interest, a formal possessory interest, or extensive exclusive, permissive use. Although property rights are no longer determinative of standing analysis, the existence of an ownership or possessory interest can be an important indicium of a personal expectation of privacy.

2. ELEMENTS OF THE FOUNDATION

The required foundation varies with the type of nexus that the defendant is attempting to establish. Suppose, for example, that the defendant claims ownership of the premises searched or the property seized. When the defendant claims ownership of realty, the defense ideally should introduce the deed to the realty. In doing so, there is no hearsay problem. The contents of the deed are offered for a nonhearsay purpose; the statements in the deed are operative facts or verbal acts because the legal consequence of transfer of title flows directly from the fact that the grantor wrote those words. In contrast, the defense attorney must comply with the best evidence and authentication rules. There are several permissible methods of authenticating the deed: If the defendant observed the execution of the deed, the defendant can authenticate the deed under Evidence Code § 1410; or if the original deed is in official custody, the defense can obtain an attested or certified copy that would be self-authenticating under Evidence Code § 1530(a)(2). Similarly, the defense can usually surmount a best evidence objection. A retained copy of the deed will often qualify as an original under Evidence Code § 255 or a duplicate under § 260. Even if the retained copy is considered secondary e vidence, Evidence Code § 1522 recognizes an excuse for nonproduction when the original writing is in the custody of a public entity.

The analysis is similar when the defendant claims a possessory interest evidenced by a document such as a written lease. The defense should have little difficulty authenticating the writing or complying with the best evidence rule. The hearsay rule is inapplicable because the writing is introduced for a nonhearsay purpose; the contents of the writing are operative facts because the transfer of the right to possession flows directly from the fact that the landlord used those words.

Lastly, assume that the nexus the defense claims is extensive, permissive use of the premises or property. Typically, the grant of permission will be oral; for example, a homeowner might orally give the defendant babysitter control over the premises (*People v. Moreno*, 2 Cal. App. 4th 577, 3 Cal. Rptr. 2d 66 (1992)), or a friend of the defendant might orally grant the defendant permission to store some of the defendant's personal property in a closet at the friend's house. The defendant can testify to the grant of permissive, exclusive use without violating the hearsay rule. Once again, the grantor's words are being offered for a nonhearsay purpose; they are a verbal act because they are the grant of permission itself. The defendant should not only testify to the initial grant of permission; the defendant should then add that relying on that grant, he or she then made extensive use of the premises or property. The defendant ordinarily has personal knowledge of the extent of his use of the premises or property, and he is therefore competent to describe the use under Evidence Code § 702. Technically, the "one witness" rule stated in Evidence Code § 411 applies to the question of the defendant's testimony that he had oral permission and made substantial use of the premises or property; if the judge chooses to believe the defendant's testimony, that testimony standing alone is legally sufficient to support the findings of fact required to establish standing. As a practical matter, however, many judges are more dubious of claims of oral permission than of claims documented by a deed or written lease. For that reason, the defense attorney should offer testimony corroborating the defendant's claims of permission and substantial use. The person who granted permission may supply corroboration, and corroboration could likewise be furnished by third parties who heard the oral grant of permission or who observed the defendant making use of the premises or property.

Before setting out a sample foundation for standing, we should add one cautionary note for defense attorneys. On the one hand, defense attorneys should always be prepared to establish standing. On the other hand, in many, if not most, cases it is inadvisable for the defense to raise the standing issue. The prosecution ordinarily must raise the issue. *Steagald v. United States*, 451 U.S. 204, 208-09 (1981). If the prosecution fails to do so, the issue is waived. *People v. Greenwood*, 182 Cal. App. 3d 729, 227 Cal. Rptr. 539 (1986), *rev'd on other grounds*, 486 U.S. 35 (1988). There are many pitfalls for the defense in litigating standing. The defense testimony about standing may furnish the prosecution with important investigative leads. For the same reason, even when they do litigate standing, many defense counsel present only the bare minimum testimony needed to demonstrate standing. In light of the tactical considerations peculiar to his or her case, a defense attorney might go into less detail about standing than the testimony in the following foundation.

3. SAMPLE FOUNDATION

The People have charged the defendant, Mr. Browning, with knowing possession of cocaine. The cocaine was found in a knapsack in a closet in a house owned by Mr. Irving. The police discovered the cocaine during a warrantless search of Irving's house on the afternoon of July 3, 1993. The defendant has taken the stand to testify to both the occurrence of the intrusion and his standing to attack the intrusion.[1] The defense attorney is conducting the direct examination. The defense attorney will attempt to elicit the defendant's testimony describing several indicia of expectation of privacy: (1) the defendant's legitimate presence on the premises at the time of the search; (2) the defendant's permissive, exclusive, and extensive use of the closet where the cocaine was found; and (3) the defendant's ownership of the knapsack in which the cocaine was discovered. The testimony should make it clear that the indicia existed at the time of the intrusion. It is not enough to show that the defendant had an ownership or possessory interest at a time preceding the search; the defendant must retain the interest at the time of the search. *People v. Workman*, 209 Cal. App. 3d 687, 257 Cal. Rptr. 753 (1989).

P Mr. Browning, WHERE were you on the afternoon of July 3, 1999? (1)

W I was at the home of a good friend of mine, Charles Irving.

P WHERE is that home located? (1)

W The address is 4177 Golden Field here in Sacramento.

P WHY were you there? (1)

W I go to school at Sacramento State, which is just a couple of blocks away. I often stop by early in the afternoon because Charlie's house is on my way home.

P HOW did you get into the house that afternoon? (1)

W Charlie let me in. I just rang the bell, and he came to the door to open it for me.

W WHAT, if anything, unusual happened that afternoon at Mr. Irving's house?

W Well, two police arrived, arrested Charlie, and conducted a search while I was there.

P HOW do you know that?

W I was still there when they arrived, and I saw the whole thing with my own eyes.

P WHAT did the police do?

W They told Charlie that he was under arrest, and then they conducted a search of the whole house.

P Specifically, WHERE did they search? (2)

---

[1]According to one appellate court, the trial judge has discretion to require the defense to establish standing before the prosecution comes forward with evidence showing the reasonableness of a challenged warrantless search. *People v. Contreras*, 210 Cal. App. 3d 450, 258 Cal. Rptr. 361(1989). This opinion was depublished. 1990 Cal. LEXIS 661.

W They rummaged around everywhere, but the thing that really concerned me was that they pried into the closet in the guest room of Charlie's house.

P WHERE is that closet located? (2)

W The guest room is the southern most room in the house. The closet is on the southern wall of that room.

P HOW would you describe the closet? (2)

W It has a single wooden door with a door handle that you can lock from the outside.

P WHAT do you mean by "from the outside"? (2)

W When you're standing in the room, you can push in the knob to lock the door handle.

P WHY did it concern you when the police looked into that closet? (2)

W That's my closet.

P WHY do you call it your closet? (2)

W About a year ago, I told Charlie that I didn't have enough storage space at the little studio apartment I rent. As a student, I also don't have enough money to pay the monthly fee for mini-storage. So I asked Charlie whether I could store some stuff at his house.

P WHAT, if anything, did Mr. Irving say when you told him that? (2)

W He said that he'd be glad to help. He said that the closet in the guest room was absolutely empty and that I was welcome to use it.

P WHAT, if anything, did you say when Mr. Irving made that offer? (2)

W I thanked him very much for being so kind. But then I added that I'm sort of a private person and that if I put stuff in the closet, I hope that he'd just leave it alone.

P WHAT, if anything, did Mr. Irving say then? (2)

W He said that that was perfectly agreeable. I think his words were that it would be as if it was my closet. He assured me that he wouldn't poke around in my things.

P WHAT did you do after Mr. Irving told you that? (2)

W The next day I moved some stuff from my apartment to the closet in Charlie's house.

P HOW many things did you move over? (2)

W Enough to fill the closet. Including my knapsack.

P HOW long had you used the closet before July 3, 1999? (2)

W I had been using it for about six months.

P HOW regularly had you used it? (2)

W Throughout that whole period. I didn't find any other storage space; after I put the stuff there, I left it there for those six months.

P To the best of your knowledge, HOW often, if ever, did Mr. Irving go into the closet without your permission?

W Never.

P WHY do you say that?

W Well, whenever I looked into the closet, there was never any indication that anyone else had been in there. Nothing was ever out of place. It was always just as I had left it.

P Now let's return to July 3, 1993. WHAT did the police do after they opened the door to the closet in the guest room? (3)

W They went through my stuff, including my knapsack.

P WHY do you call it your knapsack? (3)

W   It belongs to me. I bought that about two years ago.

P   WHERE did you buy it? (3)

W   At the Price Club store here in Sacramento.

P   WHAT proof do you have that the knapsack is yours? (3)

W   I obviously don't have the sales receipt; I threw that away long ago. However, right after I bought it, I put my name on a cloth tag and sewed the tag into the knapsack.

P   Mr. Browning, I now hand you what has already been received into evidence as People's Exhibit No. 2. WHAT is it? (3)

W   It's my knapsack.

P   HOW can you recognize it? (3)

W   Right there—just as I said. It's the tag with my name on it.

P   WHO else uses that knapsack?

W   No one else used it with my permission and knowledge. For example, Charlie never asked for permission to put anything in there. The knapsack contains some cooking stuff and some books and some linen—all stuff that belonged to me.

G.   THE SEIZURE OF THE DEFENDANT'S PROPERTY DURING THE INVENTORY OF THE DEFENDANT'S AUTOMOBILE

1. THE DOCTRINE

In the prior four sections, we analyzed arguments that obviate any need for the prosecutor to establish a justification for the seizure of the property that will be introduced as evidence. Based on the law discussed in those four sections, the prosecutor can argue that: There was no search or seizure; even if there was, there was insufficient government involvement in the intrusion to trigger the Fourth Amendment; or even if there was a government intrusion, the defendant lacks standing to challenge the legality of the intrusion. When the prosecutor prevails on any of these theories, the seized property is not subject to exclusion on Fourth Amendment grounds. The defense usually has the burden of going forward to establish that a government intrusion occurred and that the defendant has standing to challenge the intrusion.

For the balance of this part of the chapter, we shall assume that the defendant has established standing and the occurrence of a government intrusion. On that assumption, the prosecutor must advance a justification for the seizure. Although the justification often takes the form of incriminating information about the particular defendant, that is not always the case. There can, for example, be an administrative justification for the search. *See* Hall, *The Inventory Search (Part I)*, F.B.I. LAW ENF. BULL., Aug. 2, 1987, at 26; Hall, *The Inventory Search (Conclusion)*, F.B.I. LAW ENF. BULL., Sept. 1987, at 25. Suppose that the defendant unlawfully parks his car so as to obstruct traffic. The traffic obstruction justifies the police in moving and impounding the car. Once the police take the car, a number of interests come into play. As a bailee of the car, the police department has some liability to the defendant; the police should protect the government from claims liability. In addition, apart from claims of liability, the police can safeguard the defendant's property; the defendant is a citizen entitled to police protection. Further, if the car contains any dangerous instrumentalities, the car should be secured to prevent those instrumentalities from falling into the wrong hands. In *South Dakota v. Opperman*, 428 U.S. 364 (1976), and *Colorado v. Bertine*, 479 U.S. 367 (1987), the Supreme Court held that these interests permit a police inventory of a lawfully impounded car. In *Opperman*, the police impounded the defendant's car for parking violations. During the ensuing inventory, the police found incriminating evidence in a closed but unlocked glove compartment. The Court held that the seizure of the evidence was proper, even though under state law, the government would have been protected from claims liability if the police had merely closed and locked the car. It is ideal when there is statutory authority for the impound; but absent statutory authority, the police may nevertheless rely on their "community caretaking function" recognized in *Cady v. Dombrowski*, 413 U.S. 433, 441 (1973).

2. ELEMENTS OF THE FOUNDATION

To rely on the inventory doctrine, the prosecutor must establish the following elements:

1. There was a legitimate basis for impounding the vehicle. Standing alone, the arrest of the driver is an insufficient basis. *See People v. Scigliano*, 196 Cal. App. 3d 26, 30-31, 241 Cal. Rptr. 546, 548-50 (1987) (discussing the limited scope of Vehicle Code § 22651). However, if the car is illegally parked, obstructing traffic, or subject to forfeiture for some reason, the police may properly take possession of the car. *See People v. Benites*, 9 Cal. App. 4th 309, 11 Cal. Rptr. 2d 512 (1992) (neither driver nor passenger had a valid driver's license, and auto was parked on a lonely, isolated stretch of road miles from town); *People v. Green*, 46 Cal. App. 4th 367, 54 Cal. Rptr. 2d 12, 15 (1996) ("In choosing to impound ... a vehicle the police must exercise their discretion ... on the basis of something other than suspicion of evidence of criminal activity"); *People v. Salcero*, 6 Cal. App. 4th 720, 8 Cal. Rptr. 2d 578, 579-80 (1992). An impoundment inventory pursuant to a pretextual traffic stop is unreasonable. *People v. Aguilar*, 228 Cal. App. 3d 1049, 279 Cal. Rptr. 246 (1991).
2. The police conducting the search follow a bona fide administrative procedure. Ideally, the police department has put the procedure in a regulation. The prosecutor can introduce the regulation into evidence. Although the procedure must be standardized, it need not be reduced to written form. *People v. Steeley*, 210 Cal. App. 3d 887, 258 Cal. Rptr. 699 (1989).
3. The scope of the search was reasonable. In *Mozzetti v. Superior Court of Sacramento County*, 4 Cal. 3d 699, 484 P.2d 84, 94 Cal. Rptr. 412 (1971), the California Supreme Court held that even after a lawful impoundment of

an automobile, the police may inventory only the personal effects in plain sight. The court reasoned that the only substantial government interest at stake is the protection of the government from claims liability. The court stressed that as an involuntary bailee, the government has limited claims liability. *Mozzetti* antedated Proposition 8. As previously stated, Proposition 8 generally brings California search and seizure rules into conformity with federal search and seizure rules. In *Opperman*, the Supreme Court upheld the inventory seizure of property that was not in plain sight. Hence, after Proposition 8, *Mozzetti* is probably no longer good law. *People v. Scigliano*, 196 Cal. App. 3d 26, 241 Cal. Rptr. 546 (1987). *Bertine* authorized police intrusions into closed containers discovered during the inventory, and Proposition 8 arguably "compel[s California courts] to follow ... *Bertine*." *People v. Scigliano, supra*, at 550.

4. During the search, the police seized the item in question. The prosecutor must authenticate the item of physical evidence.

3. SAMPLE FOUNDATION

The People have charged the defendant, Mr. Hopkins with the burglary of a gun store. The People allege that the defendant burglarized the store on the evening of May 12, 1999. The owner of the store has already testified. During his testimony, the prosecutor introduced a list describing the missing weapons. The description includes the serial number of each missing weapon. The second witness was Officer Muloney. Muloney testified that while he was driving on a public street in Vacaville, California, he noticed a car stopped, partially blocking a lane of traffic. He testified that he found the defendant slumped behind the wheel. The officer adds that the defendant was obviously intoxicated. He arrested the defendant and called the Vacaville Police Department Impound Lot to seize the car. The next witness is Officer Graham. She testifies that she was the officer on duty at the lot on the evening of May 12, 1999. The prosecutor is the proponent.

P WHAT, if anything, unusual happened that evening? (1)
W I got the phone call from Officer Muloney to pick up a car stopped in a traffic lane on Grant Street.
P HOW do you know that the caller was Officer Muloney? (1)
W We've worked together for years. I know his voice very well.
P WHAT did you do after you received the call? (1)
W I grabbed the tow truck and drove over to Grant Street to pick up the car.
P WHAT did you find when you arrived at Grant Street? (1)
W Just as Muloney had told me, this car was stopped part of the way into a traffic lane. Muloney was just driving off with the defendant in his patrol car.
P WHERE is the defendant now? (1)
W He's over there. He's the guy in the orange jumpsuit at the table to my right.
P Your Honor, please let the record reflect that the witness has identified the defendant, Bruce Hopkins.
J The record will so reflect.

P   WHAT did you do after you found the car in the traffic lane? (1)

W   I followed the standard operating procedure.

P   WHAT is that procedure? (1)

W   I hooked it up to the tow truck and took it back to the impound lot.

P   WHAT did you do when you reached the lot? (2)

W   I continued to follow standard procedure and inventoried the contents of the car.

P   WHY did you do that? (2)

W   Our department has a regulation requiring me to do that.

P   Your Honor, I request that this be marked People's exhibit #3 for identification.

J   It will be so marked.

P   Please let the record reflect that I am showing the exhibit to the defense attorney.

J   The record will reflect that.

P   Permission to approach the witness?

J   Granted.

P   Officer, now hand you what has been marked as People's exhibit #3 for identification. WHAT is this? (2)

W   It's our departmental regulation that I referred to. It governs the operation of our impound lot.

P   HOW do you recognize it? (2)

W   It's my Bible. I work with it every night. The chief handed it to me when he put me in charge of the night shift at the lot, and I have it right on my desk all the time.

P   Your Honor, I now offer People's exhibit #3 for identification into evidence as People's #3.

J   Is there any objection?

O   No, your Honor.

P   Officer, please read paragraph four of the regulation to his Honor. (3)

W   Sure. It says: "Within 24 hours of the impoundment of any vehicle, the officer in charge of the lot shall inventory any and all objects in the car that are either in plain view or in unlocked compartments."

P   WHAT did you do after you brought the defendant's car to the impound lot? (3)

W   I did exactly what the regulation says. I inventoried the car for those contents.

P   WHAT, if anything, did you find inside the defendant's car? (4)

W   I found a pistol.

P   WHERE did you find the pistol? (4)

W   In the glove compartment.

P   WHAT condition was the glove compartment in at the time? (4)

W   It was closed, but it had not been locked. It opened as soon as I gently turned the knob.

The prosecutor might continue the foundation to identify the pistol. If so, the prosecutor must authenticate the pistol as an item of physical evidence. The prosecutor should show that the pistol and its serial number match a pistol and serial number described on the list introduced during the testimony of the owner of the gun shop.

H. THE SEIZURE OF THE DEFENDANT'S PROPERTY AFTER THE DEFENDANT'S CONSENT TO A POLICE SEARCH

1. THE DOCTRINE

The inventory doctrine allows the police to search a defendant's auto even if there are no objective indications that the auto contains incriminating evidence against the defendant. The consent doctrine also permits the police to search when they lack incriminating information about the particular defendant. If the defendant consents to a search, in effect the defendant waives the protection of the Fourth Amendment. The prosecutor has the burden of demonstrating consent. *People v. James*, 19 Cal. 3d 99, 561 P.2d 1135, 137 Cal. Rptr. 447 (1977). It is even possible for the defendant to grant consent well before the time of the intrusion. In *In re Curtis T.*, 214 Cal. App. 3d 1391, 263 Cal. Rptr. 296 (1989), *cert. denied*, 498 U.S. 858 (1990), the defendant entered into a home supervision agreement including an "access" condition. The court construed the condition as granting the authorities advance consent to enter certain areas, including the defendant's bedroom. *Accord In re Binh L.*, 5 Cal. App. 4th 194, 6 Cal. Rptr. 2d 678 (1992) (juvenile probation condition); *In re Anthony S.*, 4 Cal. App. 4th 1000, 6 Cal. Rptr. 2d 214 (1992) (juvenile probation condition); *People v. Viers*, 1 Cal. App. 4th 990, 2 Cal. Rptr. 2d 667 (1991) (the probation condition legitimatizes the search even if the searching police are unaware of the condition).

The case law permits persons other than the defendant himself or herself to give effective consent to a search. *People v. Veiga*, 214 Cal. App. 3d 817, 821 n.3, 262 Cal. Rptr. 919, 920 n.3 (1989) (consent by an absent co-occupant was effective because the defendant and the co-occupant had "equal common authority over the premises"); *People v. Santiago*, 55 Cal. App. 4th 1540, 64 Cal. Rptr. 794, *modified*, 1997 Cal. App. LEXIS 545 (1997) (Carla "worked for appellant. Her duties involved more than occasional baby-sitting; she was in charge of the household approximately 40 hours per week ...."). *But see People v. Roman*, 227 Cal. App. 3d 674, 679, 278 Cal. Rptr. 44, 47 (1991) (the court cited *Illinois v. Rodriguez*, 497 U.S. 177 (1990) as authority for the proposition that the police must "reasonably believe" that the third party "possess[es] common authority over the premises"; the court added that "[t]he general rule is that a landlord has no authority to consent to a police entry of premises occupied by a tenant"); *People v. Cooney*, 235 Cal. App. 3d Supp. 1, 286 Cal. Rptr. 765 (App. Dep't Super. Ct. 1991) (the defendant's daughter had no key to the locked closet); *People v. Bishop*, 44 Cal. App. 4th 220, 51 Cal. Rptr. 2d 629, 639 (1996) ("A third party's consent to a police search of the defendant's property is invalid unless that person has authority to consent to the search, or the police reasonably and in good faith believe she has such authority"). Moreover, as in the case of alleged consent granted personally by the defendant, the prosecution must show that the police reasonably believed that the third party was consenting to the intrusion. *See Peo-*

ple v. Sena, 218 Cal. App. 3d 753, 757, 267 Cal. Rptr. 186, 188 (1990), *withdrawn*, 1990 Cal. LEXIS 2785: The third party

> made no inviting ... gesture, such as waving the officer in. ... She simply walked away as if to retrieve defendant. Under these circumstances, we consider it unreasonable as a matter of law for the officer to have inferred or assume that the [third party] had consented to his entry. ... The [third party]'s awareness of his entry and lack of protest does not validate [the] entry.

2. ELEMENTS OF THE FOUNDATION

The foundation includes these elements:

1. The police contacted the defendant.
2. The police requested the defendant's consent to search his residence, his car, or another constitutionally protected area.
3. The defendant consented. The officer's testimony about elements #2 and #3 is nonhearsay. The request is a question rather than a declarative assertion, and the consent is an operative fact. Neither the request nor the consent is therefore hearsay under Evidence Code §§ 225 and 1200. Consent may be implied or tacit, "manifested by actions. ..." *People v. Gragg*, 13 Cal. App. 4th 1447, 17 Cal. Rptr. 2d 258, 261 (1993).
4. Under the totality of the circumstances, the consent was voluntary. The consent is obviously involuntary if the police make a show of force and threaten to use force unless the defendant consents. In *Bumper v. North Carolina*, 391 U.S. 543 (1968), the Supreme Court added that consent is also involuntary when the police misrepresent that they already have a warrant authorizing a search. In the Court's words, "When a law enforcement officer claims authority to search a home under a warrant, he announces in effect that the occupant has no right to resist the search." *Id.* at 550. However, in *Schneckloth v. Bustamonte*, 412 U.S. 218 (1973), the Court announced that the police need not advise the person that he or she has a right to refuse to consent. *Schneckloth* refused to extend *Miranda* by analogy to the search context. Even a person who is both in custody and handcuffed may voluntarily consent to a search. *People v. Llamas*, 235 Cal. App. 3d 441, 286 Cal. Rptr. 467, 470 (1991). In *Ohio v. Robinette*, 519 U.S. 33 (1996), the Supreme Court announced that even if a person has been lawfully detained before the police request consent, the police need not inform the person that he or she is "free" to go as a condition to obtaining an effective consent.
5. The scope of the search was limited to the scope of the consent given by the defendant. The search conducted may not exceed the scope of the consent granted. *People v. Crenshaw*, 9 Cal. App. 4th 1403, 12 Cal. Rptr. 2d 172,

174 (1992) ("Whether the search remained within the boundaries of the consent is a question of fact. ...").

6. During the search, the police seized a particular object. The prosecutor must then authenticate the object.

3. SAMPLE FOUNDATION

The People have charged Blair Goldberg with possession of a picklock, a burglary tool, in violation of Penal Code § 466. The witness is Officer Sevilla. He has already testified that he is assigned to the Burglary Detail of the Oakland Police Department. He testifies further that there has been a series of burglaries in a large apartment complex on MacArthur Boulevard. He adds that during the afternoon of July 6, 1999, he visited the apartment complex to investigate the burglaries. The proponent is the prosecutor.

P WHAT did you do after you arrived at the apartment complex? (1)

W I went door to door on one floor where there had been a number of break-ins.

P WHAT did you do as you went door to door? (1)

W I talked to the residents of the various apartments and asked if I could look around a bit.

P WHICH residents did you talk to? (1)

W As I recall, I spoke with six of them, including the defendant.

P WHERE is the defendant now? (1)

W He's in the courtroom.

P WHERE is he seated? (1)

W He's at the counsel table to my right. He's wearing a brown suit and a brown tie.

P Your Honor, please let the record reflect that the witness has identified the defendant, Blair Goldberg.

J The record will reflect that.

P WHAT happened when you met the defendant? (1), (2)

W I introduced myself and asked whether I could look around a bit in his apartment.

P HOW did the defendant respond? (3)

W He said it was OK. However, he asked me not to look in the bedroom because his girlfriend had just been there and it was a mess.

P Before he said that it was OK to search, WHAT, if anything, did you tell him about his rights? (4)

W I told him that he didn't have to let me in. I made it clear that I didn't have a warrant. I said I'd just appreciate his cooperation.

P WHAT, if any, weapons did you display during your conversation with the defendant? (4)

W I had my pistol, but it was in my holster. I never drew it or even put my hand on it while I was talking to him.

P WHAT, if any, threats did you make if he did not allow you to search? (4)

W None.

P WHAT, if anything, did you say about a warrant? (4)

W I said I didn't have one. And I didn't say that I was going to try to get one. I just asked for his voluntary cooperation.

P   WHAT did you do after he said OK? (5)

W   I searched the apartment.

P   WHAT parts of the apartment did you search? (5)

W   I searched all the rooms except the bedroom that he told me to stay out of.

P   WHAT, if anything, did you find during the search? (6)

W   I found a picklock.

P   WHAT is a picklock? (6)

W   It's a tool that professional burglars use.

P   HOW do you know that? (6)

W   I've been assigned to the Burglary Detail for several years. I know that from my professional training and experience. For example, they show you picklocks and other specialized burglary tools during your Basic Training at the Police Academy. (This testimony is an expert opinion, and the prosecution must establish the officer's qualification as an expert under Evidence Code § 720.)

P   WHERE did you find the picklock? (5)

W   It was sitting on the top of a pile of magazines in one corner of the living room in the apartment.

P   WHERE were you standing when you saw it? (5)

W   Right in the middle of the living room by his couch.

P   From your position there, HOW clear a view did you have of the picklock? (5)

W   It was in plain view.

P   WHAT did you do after you saw it? (6)

W   I seized it. It's contraband. It's illegal to have one.

P   WHAT furniture, if any, did you have to move to seize the picklock? (6)

W   None. It was right on top of that stack of magazines. You couldn't see it from the front door; but once you were in the living room, it was right there for anyone to see.

P   Your Honor, I request that this be marked People's exhibit #2 for identification.

J   It will be so marked.

The prosecutor would complete the foundation by eliciting testimony to identify exhibit #2 as the picklock Sevilla seized.

I.   THE SEIZURE OF THE DEFENDANT'S PROPERTY AFTER A STOP AND FRISK OF THE DEFENDANT

1. THE DOCTRINE

Inventories and consensual searches require justification, but the justification does not require proof of incriminating information tied to the defendant. In many cases, though, the justification does necessitate such information. However, full-fledged probable cause is not always necessary. The quantum of individualized, incriminating information varies with the extent of the intrusion on the defendant's privacy. An arrest requires probable cause; but in cases such as *Terry v. Ohio*, 392 U.S. 1 (1968), and *Adams v. Williams*, 407 U.S. 143 (1972), the Supreme Court has declared the police may stop and frisk an individual on a lesser justification, namely, founded or reasonable suspicion. Even reasonable suspicion is unnecessary if the officer merely approaches a suspect (*People v. Clark*, 212 Cal. App. 3d 1233, 261 Cal. Rptr. 181 (1989)) to question the suspect or request identification. *People v. Lopez*, 212 Cal. App. 3d 289, 292, 260 Cal. Rptr. 641, 643 (1989), *cert. denied*, 493 U.S. 1074 (1990); *People v. Jones*, 228 Cal. App. 3d 519, 279 Cal. Rptr. 56 (1991) (a consensual encounter). No stop occurs until the suspect is somehow physically restrained or submits to police authority. *California v. Hodari D.*, 499 U.S. 621 (1991); *People v. Johnson*, 231 Cal. App. 3d 1, 282 Cal. Rptr. 114, 118 (1991); *People v. Arangure*, 230 Cal. App. 3d 1302, 282 Cal. Rptr. 51, 54, (1991). *But see People v. Gonzalez*, 7 Cal. App. 4th 381, 8 Cal. Rptr. 2d 640, 641-43 (1992) (a stop occurred when the officer issued an "unequivocal verbal command" that the defendant get back inside the car). While the courts ordinarily use the reasonable suspicion standard to determine whether the police may detain an individual, other courts have invoked the standard to uphold police action in prohibiting entry to a dwelling until they could determine whether to seek a warrant. *People v. Bennett*, 17 Cal. 4th 373, 949 P.2d 947, 70 Cal. Rptr. 2d 850, 859 (1998) (citing *Alabama v. White*, 496 U.S. 325, 327-28 (1990) and *Brown v. Texas*, 443 U.S. 47, 51 (1979)).

The typical procedure is that the officer stops the suspect, temporarily detains him for questioning, and conducts a pat-down frisk of the exterior of the suspect's clothing. *People v. Bell*, 43 Cal. App. 4th 754, 51 Cal. Rptr. 2d 115, 124 (1996) (general "questions about where Stewart was coming from and what he had been doing"). If the frisk reveals the presence of an item subject to seizure, the officer then reaches in to grab the object. The rationale for a frisk certainly permits the officer to reach in if he or she feels a weapon. *People v. Autry*, 232 Cal. App. 3d 365, 283 Cal. Rptr. 417 (1991) (in light of the AIDS threat, a hypodermic needle creates "a threatening possibility"); *People v. Valdez*, 196 Cal. App. 3d 799, 806 242 Cal. Rptr. 142, 146 (1987). Some California cases decided in the 1980's permitted the officer to reach in when the officer feels any object subject to seizure, such as the sort of plastic bag in which illegal drugs are often packaged. *People v. Lee*, 194 Cal. App. 3d 975, 240 Cal. Rptr. 32 (1987); *People v. Valdez*, 196 Cal. App. 3d 799, 806, 242 Cal. Rptr. 142, 146 (1987) (probable cause to arrest a defendant for narcotics possession "may be furnished by the officer's actual tactile perception of narcotics during a pat-search for weapons (*Lee*)"). The United States Supreme Court recognized a "plain feel" exception to the warrant requirement in *Minnesota v. Dickerson*, 508 U.S. 366 (1993). The Court emphasized that: (1) the frisk must remain within the bound of a normal weapons frisk; and (2) the officer's sense of touch must make it immediately apparent that the object felt is contraband. *See People v. Dibb*, 37 Cal. App. 4th 832, 43 Cal. Rptr. 2d 823, 825 (1995) (citing and applying *Dickerson*).

2. ELEMENTS OF THE FOUNDATION

The foundation usually includes these elements:

1. The officer encountered the defendant. However, not all encounters amount to stops. *People v. Bennett*, 68 Cal. App. 4th 396, 80 Cal. Rptr. 2d 323 (1998). There is merely a consensual encounter if the officer only approaches the individual and asks a few questions and, for his or her part, a reasonable person would feel free to go about his or her business. *People v. Terrell*, 69 Cal. App. 4th 1246, 82 Cal. Rptr. 2d 231 (1999).

2. There were articulable, objective facts indicating that the defendant had committed, was committing, or was about to commit a crime. The facts may include the defendant's appearance, actions, demeanor, and reputation, the area and time of the encounter, and informant's tips about the defendant. *People v. Lee*, 194 Cal. App. 3d 975, 240 Cal. Rptr. 32 (1987); *People v. Foranyic*, 64 Cal. App. 4th 186, 74 Cal. Rptr. 2d 804 (1998) (the defendant had a large ax attached to his bicycle at three in the morning); *People v. Avalos*, 47 Cal. App. 4th 1569, 55 Cal. Rptr. 2d 450, 455 (1996) ("Even where the police receive information from an anonymous source, if independent police investigation establishes sufficient indicia of reliability for the tip, a temporary investigative detention is permissible"); *People v. Ramirez*, 41 Cal. App. 4th 1608, 49 Cal. Rptr. 2d 311 (1996). Neither the defendant's flight (*People v. McGriff*, 217 Cal. App. 3d 1140, 1144, 266 Cal. Rptr. 429, 431 (1990)), his presence in a high crime area (*In re Bounmy*, 14 Cal. App. 4th 494, 17 Cal. Rptr. 2d 557, 562 (1993)), his membership in a street gang (*People v. Rodriguez*, 21 Cal. App. 4th 232, 26 Cal. Rptr. 2d 660 (1993)), his receipt of money in an area known for drug activity (*People v. Jones*, 228 Cal. App. 3d 519, 279 Cal. Rptr. 56 (1991)), nor his nervous conduct (*People v. Raybourn*, 218 Cal. App. 3d 308, 266 Cal. Rptr. 884 (1990)) alone is enough to justify a stop. There is some question whether it is sufficient that another police officer has requested that the defendant be arrested or stopped. *People v. Lazanis*, 209 Cal. App. 3d 49, 66 n.2, 257 Cal. Rptr. 180, 191 n.2 (1989). The prevailing view is that the test is the objective reasonableness of the suspicion of criminal activity; the officer's subjective motivation or thought process is immaterial. *People v. Conway*, 25 Cal. App. 4th 385, 30 Cal. Rptr. 2d 533 (1994); *People v. Miranda*, 17 Cal. App. 4th 917, 21 Cal. Rptr. 2d 785 (1993) ("the overwhelming majority of courts"); *People v. Sherman*, 19 Cal. App. 4th 1204, 24 Cal. Rptr. 2d 28 (1993); *People v. Uribe*, 12 Cal. App. 4th 1432, 16 Cal. Rptr. 2d 127, 129-31 (1993); *People v. Castillo*, 7 Cal. App. 4th 836, 9 Cal. Rptr. 2d 696, 699 (1992). The suspected offense need not be a felony or even a misdemeanor; a civil traffic violation suffices. *Whren v. United States*, 517 U.S. 806 (1996).

3. The facts led the officer to conclude that it was necessary to stop the defendant.

4. The officer temporarily detained and questioned the defendant. If the officer lawfully stops a vehicle, the officer may remove the occupants from the vehicle. *Maryland v. Wilson*, 519 U.S. 408 (1997); *People v. Denison*, 63 Cal. App. 4th 550, 74 Cal. Rptr. 2d 83, 88 (1998) ("if a stop is permissible

as to a passenger in a car, it is also permissible as to the driver"); *People v. Webster*, 54 Cal. 3d 411, 814 P.2d 1273, 285 Cal. Rptr. 31, 40 (1991), *cert. denied*, 503 U.S. 1009 (1992). There are no rigid time limitations on the length of the investigatory detention. *People v. Dasilva*, 207 Cal. App. 3d 43, 254 Cal. Rptr. 563 (1989); *People v. Joyce*, 63 Cal. App. 4th 308, 74 Cal. Rptr. 2d 65 (1998) (even if the traffic stop lasted longer than necessary to cite him for a traffic offense, the defendant's Fourth Amendment rights were not violated, since there was an outstanding warrant for his arrest). However, if on a mere hunch an officer continues the detention after performing all his or her duties related to a traffic infraction, the prolonged detention becomes illegal. *People v. Lusardi*, 228 Cal. App. 3d Supp. 1, 280 Cal. Rptr. 80 (App. Dep't Super. Ct. 1991). The amount of force used is a crucial factor in determining whether a stop had been converted or transformed into a *de facto* arrest. *People v. Rivera*, 8 Cal. App. 4th 1000, 10 Cal. Rptr. 2d 785, 789 (1992).

5. There were articulable, objective facts indicating that the defendant was armed. There must be a specific justification to look for weapons. The facts may include the circumstances listed under element #2 as well as the defendant's responses to the questions. *People v. Wright*, 206 Cal. App. 3d 1107, 1111-12, 254 Cal. Rptr. 369, 371 (1988); *People v. Ritter*, 54 Cal. App. 4th 274, 62 Cal. Rptr. 2d 686 (1997) (the officer observed what appeared to be the outline of a handgun in the defendant's fanny pack). Even if the officer has the right to detain the person for questioning, the officer may lack a justification for a frisk. *In re Marcellus L.*, 225 Cal. App. 3d 1169, 1172 n.2, 275 Cal. Rptr. 649, 651 n.2 (1990). Standing alone, neither the detainee's status as a parolee nor the neighborhood profile justifies a frisk. *People v. Williams*, 3 Cal. App. 4th 1100, 5 Cal. Rptr. 2d 59 (1992).

6. The facts listed in element #5 led the officer to conduct an exploratory patdown frisk. In an appropriate case, after detaining the driver of an automobile, the officer may "frisk" the vehicle's passenger compartment for a weapon. *People v. Brueckner*, 223 Cal. App. 3d 1500, 273 Cal. Rptr. 292 (1990).

7. The frisk revealed the presence of a weapon or another object subject to seizure on the defendant's person. The rationale for a frisk certainly permits the officer to reach in if he or she feels a weapon. *People v. Limon*, 17 Cal. App. 4th 524, 21 Cal. Rptr. 2d 397 (1993) (a hard, rectangular object that could be a knife). *Minnesota v. Dickerson, supra*, also permits the officer to reach in when the officer feels any object subject to seizure such as the sort of plastic bag in which illegal drugs are frequently packaged. In the words of one court, "if contraband is found while performing a permissible *Terry* search, the officer cannot be expected to ignore that contraband." *People v. Avila*, 58 Cal. App. 4th 1069, 68 Cal. Rptr. 2d 432, 435 (1998).

8. The officer reached in and seized the item. The item must be identified as physical evidence at trial.

3. SAMPLE FOUNDATION

The People have charged the defendant, Mr. Clayton, with a series of assaults. The witness is Officer Dobris. Officer Dobris testifies that there had been a series of assaults on elderly people late at night near the intersection of Mission Street and San Bruno Avenue in San Francisco. The officer testifies that he was on foot patrol in the vicinity at 11:00 p.m. on February 13, 1999. The proponent is the prosecutor.

P   WHAT, if anything, unusual happened while you were on patrol? (1)
W   I ran into the defendant.
P   HOW do you know that the person was the defendant? (1)
W   I saw him up close. I spoke with him.
P   WHERE is the defendant now? (1)
W   He's in the courtroom at the table over there. He's got a checked shirt on.
P   Your Honor, please let the record reflect that the witness has identified the defendant, Kenneth Clayton.
J   The record will so reflect.
P   WHAT initially attracted your attention to the defendant? (2)
W   As you can see, he's a young guy in his twenties. In that area there are mostly homes for the aged. It was a bit unusual to see him just loitering in that area late at night.
P   HOW was he dressed at the time? (2)
W   He was wearing what appeared to be a heavy coat. That was suspicious.
P   WHY was that suspicious? (2)
W   We'd had a hot spell in town, and it was even pretty warm at that hour of night. Most people were walking around in shirt sleeves, and he was dressed as if it was the dead of winter.
P   WHAT did you do when you first saw the defendant? (2)
W   I just eyeballed him, and then he seemed to notice that I was watching him. As soon as his eye caught mine, he did an about-face and started walking in the other direction.
P   WHAT did you do then? (3)
W   I decided that this needed investigating. I called out to him to stop.
P   WHAT did you say? (4)
W   I called out something like, "Mister, I'd like to talk to you for a second."
P   What happened then? (4)
W   After another step or two, he stopped and waited for me to catch up with him.
P   WHAT did you do when you caught up with him? (4)
W   I asked him for some ID. I told him that there had been some attacks on elderly people in the area, and I thought it was a bit peculiar that he was just hanging around at that hour of the night.
P   WHAT, if anything, did the defendant say? (5)
W   He told me that he was sorry, but he'd left his wallet at home and didn't have any identification on him.
P   HOW did the defendant act while you questioned him? (5)
W   He seemed to tense up.
P   WHY do you say that? (5)

W At the same time that he was giving me the excuse that he didn't have any ID, I noticed that he clenched one of his fists. He wouldn't look me straight in the eye either.

P HOW close were you standing to the defendant at this time? (5)

W I was only about a foot or so away.

P From that position, WHAT, if anything, did you observe about the defendant? (5)

W One of the pockets of his coats was bulging out. There was a raised line that suggested a long knife or dirk.

P WHY do you say it suggested that? (5)

W I've been a police officer for almost twenty years. I've investigated lots of crimes involving weapons like knives, and I know the shape of one when I see it.

P WHAT did you think when you saw that shape? (6)

W I concluded he was armed and that I'd better check it out before I continued questioning him.

P WHAT did you do then? (7)

W I told him that I suspected he had a knife. I then frisked him. I patted down his clothing, especially the pocket where the bulge was.

P WHAT was the result of the pat-down? (7)

W The object seemed hard and metallic. The frisk confirmed my belief that he was carrying a dirk.

P WHAT did you do then? (8)

W I immediately reached into the pocket to grab the weapon. I wanted to make sure that he didn't have a chance to use it against me.

P Your Honor, I request that this be marked as People's exhibit #4 for identification.

J It will be so marked.

At this point, the prosecutor would elicit testimony to identify the exhibit as the dirk found on the defendant's person as an item of physical evidence.

J. PROBABLE CAUSE FOR AN ARREST OF THE DEFENDANT OR A SEARCH OF THE DEFENDANT'S PROPERTY

1. THE DOCTRINE

Founded or reasonable suspicion is the Fourth Amendment test when the police intrusion is a limited stop and frisk. In many cases, however, the intrusion is a full-fledged arrest or search. When the intrusion escalates to an arrest or search, the Fourth Amendment ordinarily requires probable cause for the intrusion. The text of the fourth amendment uses the expression, "probable cause."

There is a large body of case law defining "probable cause." Prior to the Supreme Court's 1983 decision in *Illinois v. Gates*, 462 U.S. 213 (1983), it was generally accepted that there were two elements of the definition. E. IMWINKELRIED, P. GIANNELLI, F. GILLIGAN & F. LEDERER, COURTROOM CRIMINAL EVIDENCE §§ 1902-22 (3d ed. 1998). One element was the veracity or credibility test. The prosecutor had to demonstrate that there were objective facts that justified the officer in believing the information available to him or her. For example, if the information was a report from an informant, the officer could testify that he had used the informant in the past and that on each occasion, the informant's report had led to the seizure of illicit drugs. The second element was the probability requirement. Assuming that the information was worthy of belief, the information had to give rise to a certain probability or likelihood. In the case of an arrest, the information had to make it probable that the defendant had committed a crime. In the case of a search, the information had to make it likely that a particular item subject to seizure (contraband, stolen property, or evidence of a crime) was presently located at the place to be searched. It is ideal if the report is that the informant personally observed the defendant commit a crime or recently saw contraband at the defendant's residence. Or the informant may tell the police that the defendant admitted crime or told the informant about the presence of the contraband.

In *Illinois v. Gates*, the Court stressed that lower courts should apply the veracity and probability tests in a flexible fashion. The Court announced a test of the totality of the circumstances:

> The task of the issuing magistrate is simply to make a practical, common-sense decision whether, given all the circumstances set forth in the affidavit before him, including the "veracity" and "basis of knowledge" of persons supplying hearsay information, there is a fair probability that contraband or evidence of a crime will be found in a particular place.

462 U.S. at 238. The existence of probable cause depends upon an objective evaluation of the facts from the perspective of a hypothetical reasonable officer rather than the officer's personal, subjective belief. *People v. Gonzales*, 216 Cal. App. 3d 1185, 1190 n.2, 265 Cal. Rptr. 507, 509-10 n.2 (1989) ("Gonzales makes much of [Officer] Rainey's ... testimony that he did not believe probable cause existed. ... Rainey's legal assessment [is] largely irrelevant if the search was reasonable viewed objectively from a judicial perspective. Although [prior] California case law suggests the contrary ..., federal law controls application of exclusionary remedies post-Proposition 8. ..."); *People v. Holt*, 212 Cal. App. 3d 1200, 261 Cal. Rptr. 89 (1989).

The preceding paragraphs describe the fourth amendment standard which governs when the government intrusion is inspired by a law enforcement purpose. A laxer standard applies when the authorities seek an "administrative" warrant for such purposes as routine, periodic building code inspections. *County of Contra Costa v. Humore, Inc.*, 45 Cal. App. 4th 1335, 53 Cal. Rptr. 2d 647 (1996), *cert. denied*, 520 U.S. 1156 (1997).

2. ELEMENTS OF THE FOUNDATION

Although in *Gates* the Court obviously wanted to relax the standard for determining probable cause, it is still advisable for a prosecutor attempting to establish probable cause to show compliance with the credibility and probability tests. If the information available to the police satisfies the pre-1983 tests, it necessarily satisfies the *Gates* standard. For that reason, the prosecutor should normally attempt to lay the following foundation:

1. The officer had certain information in his possession. The officer's testimony about an informant's report is nonhearsay. The testimony is offered to show its effect on the officer's state of mind, namely, the production of a reasonable belief that a crime has been committed or that items subject to seizure can be found at a particular location. The information need not satisfy the technical exclusionary rules of evidence applicable at trial. *People v. Morgan*, 207 Cal. App. 3d 1384, 255 Cal. Rptr. 680 (1989) (in establishing probable cause, the police may rely on a statement by defendant's wife even if at trial the statement would be inadmissible under the marital privilege). When the officer relies on information transmitted from another officer about an outstanding warrant, the prosecution must prove that the transmitting officer received the arrest warrant information. *People v. Armstrong*, 232 Cal. App. 3d 228, 283 Cal. Rptr. 429 (1991); *People v. Ramirez*, 59 Cal. App. 4th 1548, 70 Cal. Rptr. 2d 341, 343 (1997) ("It is well settled in California officers can make arrests based on information and probable cause furnished by other officers. ... These cases, however, require that when the first officer passes off information through 'official channels' that leads to arrest, the officer must also show basis for his probable cause").

2. There were objective facts justifying the officer's conclusion that the information was credible. As previously stated, when the source of the information is an informant, the informant's past performance can support the conclusion that the information is credible. Alternatively, if the statement is contrary to the informant's own interest, the disserving quality of the statement tends to show that the statement is believable. Or the officer might independently corroborate some of the incriminating details furnished by the informant; the corroboration of some details indicates that other details are also credible. *But see Bailey v. Superior Court (People)*, 11 Cal. App. 4th 1107, 15 Cal. Rptr. 2d 17, 20 (1992) ("Independent police work here did not corroborate any suspicious activity or confirm future actions not easily predicted."); *People v. Johnson*, 220 Cal. App. 3d 742, 749, 270 Cal. Rptr. 70, 73 (1990) ("For corroboration to be adequate, it must pertain to the alleged criminal activity; accuracy of information regarding the suspect generally is insufficient. Courts take a dim view of the significance of 'pedestrian facts' such as a suspect's physical description, his residence and

his vehicles."). Further, there is authority that an officer may assume the credibility of a report from another police officer or a private citizen who claims to be a witness to or victim of a crime. *People v. Huston*, 210 Cal. App. 3d 192, 222, 258 Cal. Rptr. 393, 409-10 (1989); *People v. Brueckner*, 223 Cal. App. 3d 1500, 273 Cal. Rptr. 292 (1990).

3. The tenor of the information established the requisite probability. The most recent cases tend to define probable cause as "a strong suspicion." *People v. Guajardo*, 23 Cal. App. 4th 1738, 29 Cal. Rptr. 2d 21 (1994); *People v. Mims*, 9 Cal. App. 4th 1244, 12 Cal. Rptr. 2d 335, 337 (1992); *People v. Tuadles*, 7 Cal. App. 4th 1777, 9 Cal. Rptr. 2d 780, 784 (1992); *People v. Boissard*, 5 Cal. App. 4th 972 n.2, 8 Cal. Rptr. 2d 738, 740-41 n.2 (1992). In *People v. Hooker*, 55 Cal. App. 4th 1352, 64 Cal. Rptr. 2d 723, 726 (1997), the court stated that "'probable cause required only a ... substantial chance.'" In the case of an arrest, the information must make it likely that the defendant has committed or is committing a crime. In assessing the information, the police may consider the defendant's criminal record. *People v. Andrino*, 210 Cal. App. 3d 1395, 1400, 259 Cal. Rptr. 17, 19 (1989). The police may also factor the defendant's false, exculpatory statements into their reasoning. *People v. Carrillo*, 37 Cal. App. 4th 1662, 45 Cal. Rptr. 2d 16 (1995). In the case of a search, the information must establish that an item subject to seizure is presently located at the place to be searched. Items subject to seizure include contraband such as drugs, stolen property, and evidence of a crime. On the one hand, the information cannot be too "stale"; the information must indicate that the objects are currently located at the residence or apartment the police want to search. *People v. Mikesell*, 46 Cal. App. 4th 1711, 54 Cal. Rptr. 2d 708 (1996) (although the affidavit referred to events which had occurred two years earlier, there was also evidence of recent heavy drug traffic). On the other hand, a court may issue an anticipatory warrant on a showing that an item subject to seizure will be at a particular location at a certain, future item. *People v. Sousa*, 18 Cal. App. 4th 549, 22 Cal. Rptr. 2d 264 (1993). The information must single out a particular location as the place where the objects are situated. *Fenwick & West v. Superior Court*, 43 Cal. App. 4th 1272, 51 Cal. Rptr. 2d 294 (1996) (there was insufficient probable cause to justify searching an attorney's office to seize evidence of a corporation's wrongdoing; the attorney had represented the corporation in the past; however, there was no indication that he was the corporation's general counsel or of the nature of his past representation of the corporation). The informant might tell the police, for instance, that she personally saw bags of heroin at the defendant's apartment at a particular street address.

4. The officer acted on the probable cause. In some cases, the action consists of seeking a warrant from a judge or magistrate. Section K of this chapter discusses warranted searches. In other cases, the officer makes an arrest or conducts a search without a warrant. Sections L-O of this chapter analyze

the requirements for some common types of warrantless intrusions based on probable cause.

5. As a result of the action, the police seized an object. The prosecutor must identify the object as an item of physical evidence.

3. SAMPLE FOUNDATIONS

The People have charged the defendant, Mr. Brewster, with sale of heroin. The witness is Officer Zagel. Officer Zagel has already testified that he is assigned to the Narcotics Detail of the Los Angeles Police Department. The prosecutor is the proponent. The prosecutor is trying to establish probable cause for an arrest.

P Officer, WHERE were you on the morning of December 28, 1999? (1)

W I was at my office at headquarters in downtown L.A.

P WHAT, if anything, unusual happened that morning? (1), (2)

W I received a phone call from one of my informants, whom I call Jay.

P HOW did you know that the caller was Jay? (1)

W I have used him as informant over the past three years. In my line of police work, you need a network of contacts to get leads on criminal activity. I've met with him or spoken with him dozens of times during the past three years. I know his voice well.

P HOW often have you worked with him during those three years? (2)

W I've used him as a lead in ten different investigations.

P WHAT have been the results of those investigations? (2)

W In each case—in every one of the ten cases—if he told me that somebody had drugs or was pushing the junk, the report turned out to be true. When we arrested that person or searched that place, there were drugs right there. He's always been a reliable source of information for me.

P When you received this call from Jay, WHAT did he say? (3)

W He said that he'd just left Dugan's Bar on Flower Street where he'd had a conversation with the defendant.

P WHOM did he name as the person he'd talked with? (3)

W Greg Brewster.

P WHAT, if anything, did he say about the defendant? (3)

W He said that they had a couple of drinks and that Brewster had been bragging about his latest drug deal.

P WHAT did Jay say about the defendant's bragging? (3)

W Jay said that the defendant said he had just sold $20,000 worth of heroin to a guy who was staying at the Biltmore Hotel in downtown Los Angeles.

P WHAT, if anything, did Jay say about the defendant's conduct during their conversation at the bar? (3)

W He said that the defendant pulled out a handful of hundred dollar bills, waved them around, and said, "See—here's the proof. I ain't just bragging. The deal really went down."

P WHAT did you do then? (4)

The prosecutor would elicit the balance of the foundation.

The next fact situation is a prosecution for bank robbery. The People have charged the defendant Jennings with the robbery of the First Northern Bank in Dixon on July 1, 1999. The witness is Officer Siegan. The officer testifies that he is assigned to the Property Crimes Section of the Oakland Police Department. The prosecutor is the proponent. Now the prosecutor is attempting to demonstrate probable cause for a search.

P Officer, WHERE were you on the morning of July 3, 1999? (1)

W I was at our headquarters in downtown Oakland.

P WHAT, if anything, unusual happened that morning? (1)

W I got a call from one of my informants, Jake.

P HOW did you know that the caller was Jake? (1)

W I have used him on numerous occasions during the past five years. I have met with him and spoken with him on the phone before on many occasions. I'm very familiar with the sound of his voice.

P During those five years, HOW often have you worked with Jake? (2)

W Tens of times. I'm afraid that I can't give you a specific figure. I have relied on his reports in a lot of investigations.

P WHAT have been the results of those investigations? (2)

W In the overwhelming majority of cases, his information has proven to be true. No one's right all the time, but he's the best contact I have on the street.

P WHAT do you mean when you said "the overwhelming majority of cases"? (2)

W He's right on at least 90 percent of the time. And that's a conservative estimate.

P When Jake called that morning, WHAT did he say? (3)

W He said he'd just come from the defendant's apartment on Broad Street.

P WHAT else, if anything, did he say? (3)

W He said that he'd met the defendant there. The defendant was drinking and had been bragging about a big bank job he had pulled a couple of days before in Dixon. I had heard about that robbery just after it happened.

P WHAT, if anything, did Jake say about the defendant's conduct while Jake was at the apartment? (3)

W He said that the defendant had shown him, Jake, where he had stuffed some bank's bags containing cash in the mattress in the bedroom of the apartment. He said that the bags had "First Northern Bank" written on them.

P WHAT apartment did Jake refer to? (3)

W He said that he had just come from Apartment 3A at 1116 Broad Street.

P WHAT did you do after you received this report? (4)

Again, the prosecutor would complete the balance of the foundation.

K. WARRANTED SEARCHES BASED ON PROBABLE CAUSE

1. THE DOCTRINE

Assume that the officer in question believes that there is probable cause for an arrest or search. If time permits, the officer can contact a judge or magistrate and seek a search warrant. The law prefers that the officer obtain judicial authorization for an arrest or search. The officer has law enforcement responsibilities and may be overzealous in assessing the information. However, the judge or magistrate is presumably neutral and detached. The judge's intervention helps ensure that privacy will be invaded only if there is in fact probable cause justifying the intrusion. The officer reduces the information to a written affidavit and submits the affidavit to a judicial officer. The judge or magistrate then applies the credibility and probability tests to the information set out in the affidavit.

Because the courts want to encourage the police to seek warrants, the courts treat warranted intrusions differently than warrantless arrests and searches. Evidence Code § 664 reflects the differential treatment: "It is presumed that official duty has been regularly performed. This presumption does not apply on an issue as to the lawfulness of an arrest if it is found or otherwise established that the arrest was made without a warrant." To implement the preference for warrants, the reviewing courts in effect presume the accuracy of the underlying facts set out in the affidavit. Spear, *Search and Seizure Motions*, in CALIFORNIA CRIMINAL LAW §§ 20.17-19. The burden is on the defense. The court assumes that if the judge or magistrate decided to issue a warrant based on the affidavit, the underlying facts are true. The court applies the veracity and probability tests to those facts.

However, even a facially sufficient affidavit is vulnerable to challenge. *Theodore v. Superior Court of Orange County*, 8 Cal. 3d 77, 501 P.2d 234, 104 Cal. Rptr. 226 (1972) allows the defense to controvert or traverse the affidavit. *Id.* at § 2015. Under *Theodore*, the "defendant has the initial burden of proving that the affidavit contains material errors, and ... upon establishing this fact, the burden is then upon the prosecution to prove that affiant's belief that the erroneous statements were true and nonetheless reasonable under the totality of circumstances. ..." 2 JEFFERSON § 45.1, at 1668. *Theodore* permits the defense to challenge a facially adequate affidavit more easily than the Supreme Court allowed in *Franks v. Delaware*, 438 U.S. 154 (1978). Under *Theodore*, the only preliminary showing the defense must make is that statements in the affidavit are false and material. Recent Decision, 6 LOY. L.A. L. REV. 437 (1973); *People v. Lamas*, 229 Cal. App. 3d 560, 568, 282 Cal. Rptr. 296, 300 (1991) ("Under California law negligent misstatements must also be excised from the supporting affidavit, but only if they are unreasonable"); *People v. Bradford*, 15 Cal. 4th 1229, 939 P.2d 259, 65 Cal. Rptr. 2d 145, 181-82 (1997) (extending the same approach to omissions from the affidavit), *cert. denied*, 523 U.S. 118 (1998). In contrast, *Franks* requires the defense to make an additional preliminary showing of facts indicating that the affiant knew the facts were false or acted with reckless disregard for the truth. Jones, *Challenging the Veracity of Affidavits to Search Warrants*, 5 SEARCH AND SEIZURE L. REP. 1, 2 (Aug. 1978).

In *People v. Luttenberger*, 50 Cal. 3d 1, 784 P.2d 633, 265 Cal. Rptr. 690 (1990), the California Supreme Court declined to follow *Franks*. The court stated that Proposition 8 does not require the California courts to adopt federal discovery procedures. *Id.* at 16-17, 784 P.2d at 642-43, 265 Cal. Rptr. at 699-700. The court also clarified the defense's right to conduct discovery to establish a *Theodore* claim; the court announced that

> [t]o justify a camera review and discovery, preliminary to a subfacial challenge to a search warrant, a defendant must offer evidence casting some reasonable doubt on the veracity of material statements made by the affiant. [T]he defendant must raise some reasonable doubt regarding either the existence of the informant or the truthfulness of the affiant's report concerning the informant's prior reliability or the information he furnished.

Id. at 21-22, 784 P.2d at 646, 265 Cal. Rptr. at 703. *See People v. Box*, 14 Cal. App. 4th 177, 17 Cal. Rptr. 2d 504, 508-10 (1993) (where the defense relied on an unsworn statement by a person who was "unwilling to repeat his claims under oath," the showing was too insubstantial to require an evidentiary hearing).

2. ELEMENTS OF THE FOUNDATION

The prosecutor can use a simple, chronological organization for this foundation:

1. The officer received certain information.
2. The officer reduced the information to affidavit form. There are several methods of authenticating the affidavit. Since the officer prepared and signed it, he can identify the document. Further, if the court clerk issues an attested copy of the affidavit, the attestation would make the copy self-authenticating under Evidence Code § 1530. Finally, when the affidavit is a court record, the existence and contents of the affidavit are judicially noticeable under Evidence Code § 452(d). If the judicial officer issues a warrant based on the affidavit, the reviewing court will presume the affidavit's contents to be true and apply the veracity and probability tests to the underlying facts set out in the affidavit. The affidavit must be signed and sworn. *People v. Leonard*, 50 Cal. App. 4th 878, 57 Cal. Rptr. 2d 845, 848 (1996).
3. The officer submitted the affidavit to a judge or magistrate and requested a warrant.
4. The judge approved the request. The approval is an order or authorization. Hence, the officer's testimony about the approval is nonhearsay under Evi-

dence Code §§ 225 and 1200. When the judge approves, the judge issues a written warrant. An arrest warrant must particularly describe the person to be apprehended. A search warrant must specify the place to be searched and the objects to be seized. *Bay v. Superior Court (People)*, 7 Cal. App. 4th 1022, 9 Cal. Rptr. 2d339 (1992) (although the affidavit specified the crime being investigated, the warrant did not name the crime, the affidavit was not attached to the warrant, and there was no indication that the persons executing the warrant had read the affidavit). If the officer saw the judge sign the warrant, the officer can authenticate the warrant. Otherwise, the prosecutor can invoke judicial notice or offer an attested copy.

5. The officer executed the warrant. The officer made an arrest or a seizure pursuant to the warrant. The search warrant itself need not be present at the premises during the search. *People v. Rodrigues-Fernandez*, 235 Cal. App. 3d 543, 286 Cal. Rptr. 700, 706-07 (1991). The officer must execute the warrant in a timely manner. *People v. Seibel*, 219 Cal. App. 3d 1279, 1299, 269 Cal. Rptr. 313, 327 (1990) (Penal Code § 1534 "provides that if a search warrant is executed and returned within ten days, it is deemed to have been timely executed. ..."); *People v. Clayton*, 18 Cal. App. 4th 440, 22 Cal. Rptr. 2d 371 (1993) (the ten-day time period excludes the day on which the warrant is issued but includes the day on which the warrant is executed). Ordinarily, the officer must knock and announce before entering premises. *See Richards v. Wisconsin*, 520 U.S. 385 (1997) (there is no blanket exception to the knock-and-announce requirement in felony drug investigations); *People v. Nealy*, 228 Cal. App. 3d 447, 279 Cal. Rptr. 36 (1991); *People v. Trujillo*, 217 Cal. App. 3d 1219, 266 Cal. Rptr. 473 (1990) (it was permissible for the police to forcibly enter after they knocked, announced themselves and their purpose, and delayed 18 seconds); *People v. Miller*, 69 Cal. App. 4th 190, 81 Cal. Rptr. 2d 410 (the police must comply with the knock-and-announce rule and give notice even if the door is open, unless instantaneous entry or foregoing the notice would decrease the danger of a violent confrontation), *modified*, 99 D.A.R. 946 (Cal. App., Jan. 27, 1999); *People v. Mays*, 67 Cal. App. 4th 969, 79 Cal. Rptr. 2d 519 (1998) (when the police knocked at the front door of the residence, they did not need to repeat an announcement before entering a closed inner room); *People v. Aguilar*, 48 Cal. App. 4th 632, 55 Cal. Rptr. 2d 716, 719-20 (1996) (after the police knocked at the door to the apartment, they had no obligation to knock again at the interior bedroom door); *People v. Satz*, 61 Cal. App. 4th 322, 71 Cal. Rptr. 2d 433, 436 (1998) ("'A trespasser—or a burglar—cannot make another man's home his castle .... When police officers have reasonable cause to believe that persons within a [hotel room] are ... trespassers ..., we do not construe these individuals as householders entitled to the protection of Penal Code section 844'"); *United States v. Ramirez*, 523 U.S. 65 (1998) (the same Fourth Amendment standard applies whether or not a "no-knock" entry results in the destruction of property). In some cases, while executing a warrant on premises, the police

may have the right to detain (*People v. Ingram*, 16 Cal. App. 4th 1745, 21 Cal. Rptr. 2d 33 (1993); *People v. Huerta*, 218 Cal. App. 3d 744, 267 Cal. Rptr. 243 (1990)); *People v. Glaser*, 11 Cal. 4th 354, 902 P.2d 729, 45 Cal. Rptr. 2d 425 (1995) (the detention was especially appropriate, since the defendant appeared familiar with the premises; although the detention occurred at gunpoint, it lasted only two minutes and did not occur in a public place); and pat down (*People v. Thurman*, 209 Cal. App. 3d 817, 823, 257 Cal. Rptr. 517, 520 (1989)) occupants of and visitors to the premises. *But see People v. Gallant*, 225 Cal. App. 3d 200, 275 Cal. Rptr. 50 (1990) (although the defendant arrived at the residence during the execution of the search warrant, there was no indication that the individual was involved in the criminal activity; "a police officer may not reasonably conclude ... that everyone approaching that house is involved in the drug trade"). In the course of executing a search warrant, the officer may "search all of the residents' personal effects which are plausible repositories of the contraband described in the warrant." *People v. Berry*, 224 Cal. App. 3d 162, 273 Cal. Rptr. 509, 511 (1990). When the warrant refers to the defendant's residence and "premises therein," the police may search outbuildings and appurtenances used as a single integral unit with the main building. *People v. Minder*, 46 Cal. App. 4th 1784, 54 Cal. Rptr. 2d 555 (1996). In appropriate circumstances, the officer may even search personalty which is on the premises but owned by persons other than the residents of the premises. *People v. Reyes*, 223 Cal. App. 3d 1218, 1223-27, 273 Cal. Rptr. 61, 63-66 (1990).

After executing the warrant, the officer signs a return on the warrant and files an inventory with the court. If the prosecutor anticipates a defense argument that the officer violates these procedures, the prosecutor can lengthen the foundation to include the officer's testimony about the return and inventory:

6. The officer signed the return on the warrant and filed an inventory with the court. Since the officer personally signs these documents, he or she can authenticate them. As in the case of elements #2 and 5, the prosecutor can also invoke judicial notice or offer an attested copy.

When the defense attempts to challenge a facially sufficient warrant, the defense attorney should lay the following foundation:

1. The affidavit contains a particular statement. Like the prosecutor, the defense attorney can authenticate the affidavit in several ways: the officer's identification of the affidavit, an attestation under Evidence Code § 1530, or judicial notice under § 452(d).
2. The statement is false. In many cases, the defense attorney will call a third party to contradict the statement made by the officer in the affidavit. In other cases, the defense may be able to use the officer's own out-of-court

statements to contradict the passage in the affidavit. If the officer is unavailable at the hearing, the officer's out-of-court statements might constitute declarations against interest under Evidence Code § 1230. If the officer is available, the officer's contradictory statements might qualify as prior inconsistent statements under §§ 768-70 and then as substantive evidence under § 1235.

3. The officer made the statement recklessly or with knowledge of its falsity. Although California law does not require proof of this element, as a practical matter this showing greatly increases the likelihood that the judge will strike the statement and then grant the suppression motion. This element is usually the most difficult for the defense attorney to establish. In rare cases, the officer has made statements reflecting the requisite state of mind. The statements might be admissible as nonhearsay (circumstantial evidence of state of mind) under Evidence Code § 1200(a) or as a declaration of state of mind under §§ 1250-51. However, in most cases, the defense attorney must invite the judge to infer the requisite state of mind from the nature of the error. The nature of the error must be such that as a matter of common, human experience, the statement could not be the product of an innocent mistake.

3. SAMPLE FOUNDATIONS

The People have charged the defendant, Mr. Kuh, with the burglary of a gun store in Winters, California. The witness is Officer Gerstein. She has already testified that she is an employee of the Winters Police Department. The proponent is the prosecutor.

P WHERE were you on the afternoon of July 30, 1999? (1)
W I was on duty at our main station.
P WHAT, if anything, unusual happened that afternoon? (1)
W I received a telephone call from one of our informants, whom we call Mel.
P HOW did you know that it was Mel? (1)
W I've met with him and spoken with him over the phone on many prior occasions.
P WHAT did Mel tell you during this telephone call? (1)
W He gave me some information indicating that some of the weapons stolen from the Gregory Gun Shop two days before were located at the defendant's apartment.
P WHAT did you do after you received the call from Mel? (2)
W I immediately wrote down everything that he told me. I put it in affidavit form so that we could apply for a search warrant.
P Your Honor, I request that this be marked People's exhibit #1 for identification.
J It will be so marked.
P Please let the record reflect that I am showing the exhibit to the defense attorney.
J The record will so reflect.
P Permission to approach the witness?
J Granted.

P Now Officer Gerstein, I hand you what has been marked People's exhibit #1 for identification. WHAT is it? (2)

W It's the affidavit I just mentioned.

P HOW can you recognize it? (2)

W I recognize the contents and my signature at the bottom.

P Your Honor, I now offer People's exhibit #I for identification into evidence as People's exhibit #1.

J It will be received.

P WHAT did you do with the affidavit after you drafted it? (3)

W I walked over to Judge Garcia's chambers in the Courthouse across the street and applied for a search warrant for the defendant's apartment.

P HOW did you make the application? (3)

W I handed the affidavit to the judge and asked him to read it.

P WHAT, if anything, did Judge Garcia do? (4)

W Initially, he seemed to read the affidavit; and then he told me that he would grant the application.

P WHAT happened then? (4)

W After telling me that orally, he signed a warrant for the search.

P Your Honor, I request that this be marked People's exhibit #2 for identification.

J It will be so marked.

P Please let the record reflect that I am showing the exhibit to the opposing counsel.

J The record will so reflect.

P Officer, I now hand you People's exhibit #2 for identification. WHAT is it? (4)

W It's Judge Garcia's warrant.

P HOW can you recognize it? (5)

W I recognize the contents and his signature. I saw him sign it.

P HOW well do you know the judge's signature style?

W Very well. He was a District Attorney for several years before going on the bench, and we worked on a couple of cases together.

P Your Honor, I now offer People's exhibit #2 for identification into evidence.

J Any objection?

O None, your Honor.

J Very well, It will be admitted.

P Officer Gerstein, WHAT did you do after Judge Garcia gave you this warrant? (6)

W I carried it out.

P WHEN did you do that? (5)

W The same afternoon. As soon as he gave me the warrant, I jumped in a police car and drove over there with two other officers.

P WHERE is "there"? (5)

W I'm sorry. I mean the defendant's apartment. The warrant was for apartment 3A, 1413 Rogers Drive in Winters. That's the address named in the warrant.

P WHAT did you do when you arrived there? (5)

W We knocked, and the defendant came to the door. We showed him the warrant, gave him a copy, and explained that we were searching for certain types of pistols and revolvers.

P WHAT did you do after you told the defendant that? (6)

W The two other officers and I searched the apartment.

P WHAT was the result of the search? (5)

W We found four weapons of the type, make, and caliber that the warrant mentioned. We seized them.

P Your Honor, I request that these be marked People's exhibits #3-6.

J They will be so marked.

P Please let the record reflect that I am showing the exhibits to the defense attorney.

J The record will show that.

P Officer, I now hand you People's exhibits #3, 4, 5, and 6 for identification. WHAT are they? (6)

W They're the pistols and revolvers we found at the defendant's apartment.

P HOW can you recognize them? (6)

W When we found them, I put my initials and the date on an evidence tag and stuck it on the handle of each weapon. I recognize the caliber, shape, and markings of all the weapons.

P I now offer People's exhibits #3-6 into evidence.

J Received.

P WHAT did you do after you found these weapons? (7)

W I immediately made out an inventory of the four weapons. I gave one copy to the defendant.

P WHAT did you do after you gave him a copy of the inventory? (7)

W On the spot, I filled out the last part of the warrant, the return. I returned the warrant and the original inventory to Judge Garcia's court clerk. Then I took the weapons over to the Physical Evidence Custodian at the main station.

P Your Honor, I request that this be marked People's exhibit #7 for identification.

J It will be marked.

P Please let the record reflect that I am showing the exhibit to the opposing counsel.

J The record will so reflect.

P Officer Gerstein, I now hand you People's exhibit #7 for identification. WHAT is it? (7)

W It's the inventory of the items seized, listing the make, type, and serial number of each weapon.

P HOW do you recognize the inventory? (7)

W It's in my handwriting.

P Thank you, Officer. I now offer People's exhibit #7 for identification into evidence as People's exhibit #7.

J Any objection?

O No.

J All right. It will be received as People's #7.

Assume alternatively that the defense is attempting to challenge a warrant issued to seize drugs from the defendant Mr. Winston's apartment. The defense attorney has already established that the warrant application stated that on January 3, 1999, the defendant's landlord told an Officer Gillespie that "he" (the landlord) suspected some illegal activity in the defendant's apartment "because he saw an unusually large number of persons visiting the apartment at all hours of the day and night." The warrant authorized the police to search apartment E, 1300 Grant

Street in Auburn. The witness is Ms. Frazee. The proponent is the defense counsel.

P Please state your full name and spell your last name.

W My name is Millicent Frazee. Frazee is spelled F-R-A-Z-E-E.

P WHERE do you live?

W I live in apartment A, 1300 Grant Street here in Auburn.

P HOW long have you lived there?

W For the last twenty years—since 1979.

P WHAT is your occupation? (2), (3)

W I own and manage the apartment building I live in, 1300 Grant Street.

P HOW long have you served as manager for that apartment building? (2), (3)

W For the same time—about twenty years; since 1979.

P HOW many assistant managers, if any, do you have? (2), (3)

W None.

P WHEN, if ever, have you had an assistant manager? (2), (3)

W Never. I've always handled everything myself.

P WHO is Burton Winston?

W He's one of my tenants. He moved in January '99, as I recall.

P WHERE is he now?

W He's here in the courtroom. He's sitting right next to you.

P Your Honor, please let the record reflect that the witness has identified the defendant.

J It will so reflect.

P Ms. Frazee, WHO is Officer Gillespie? (2), (3)

W I have no idea. I can't recall ever meeting or talking with a police officer by that name.

P WHAT police officers, if any, have you ever discussed Mr. Winston with? (2), (3)

W To the best of my knowledge, I've never spoken to any police officer about Mr. Winston.

P WHAT persons, if any, have you ever discussed Mr. Winston with? (2), (3)

W Again, I don't remember anyone. I respect my tenants' privacy, and I don't go talking about them behind their back.

P For a moment let's talk about Mr. Winston. WHAT kind of a tenant was he? (2), (3)

W As far as I was concerned, he was a good tenant. He paid his rent on time, and he never had any loud parties to disturb the other tenants.

P HOW many visitors did he have at his apartment while he lived there? (2), (3)

W I really can't say. I never really noticed.

P HOW unusual was the number of visitors that he had at the apartment? (2), (3)

W I couldn't say that it was unusual at all. As I just said, I really never even noticed how many people stopped by his apartment. It just never caught my attention.

L. SEIZURES OF ITEMS IN PLAIN VIEW

1. THE DOCTRINE

The last section described the foundational requirements for a warranted search based on probable cause. In many cases in which there is probable cause, the police do not obtain a warrant. The prosecutor may invoke numerous doctrines to justify a warrantless search based on probable cause. One doctrine is plain view. The Supreme Court has approved the doctrine in decisions such as *Coolidge v. New Hampshire*, 403 U.S. 443 (1971). There is mounting support for the doctrine that an officer may inspect items in plain view when the officer is "aware of some facts and circumstances which justify a reasonable suspicion (not probable cause) that the items are the fruits, instrumentalities, or evidence of crime." 2 W. LAFAVE, SEARCH AND SEIZURE, § 4.11(C), at 34445 (2d ed. 1987). The officer may briefly peruse the item. If the perusal does not establish probable cause, the officer must return the item. Some California courts have joined the adherents to this doctrine. *E.g., People v. Clark*, 212 Cal. App. 3d 1233, 1239, 261 Cal. Rptr. 181, 183-84 (1989). However, the balance of this section is devoted to the more settled doctrine requiring probable cause for a full-fledged seizure.

2. FOUNDATIONAL ELEMENTS

A prosecutor relying on the plain view doctrine must establish these foundational elements:

1. The officer was standing in a position and place where he or she had a lawful right to be. *People v. Willis*, 71 Cal. App. 4th 530, 83 Cal. Rptr. 2d 895 (1999) (the items were in plain view through a partially opened door); *People v. LeBlanc*, 60 Cal. App. 4th 157, 70 Cal. Rptr. 2d 195, 198-99 (1997). For example, the officer has a right to stand on a public street. Or if the officer is executing a search warrant for the defendant's premises, the officer has a right to be on the premises. Or the officer might be present to conduct a legitimate administrative inspection. *People v. Castillo*, 7 Cal. App. 4th 836, 9 Cal. Rptr. 2d 696, 698-99 (1992). Or the officer may properly accompany fire personnel who enter a smoke-filled residence immediately after a fire is extinguished to investigate the fire's genesis. *People v. Glance*, 209 Cal. App. 3d 836, 257 Cal. Rptr. 522 (1989). *See also People v. Breault*, 222 Cal. App. 3d 794, 800-01, 272 Cal. Rptr. 77, 80-81 (citing *Washington v. Chrisman*, 455 U.S. 1 (1982)), *modified*, 223 Cal. App. 3d 125, 130-33, 273 Cal. Rptr. 110, 113-14(1990).
2. From that position, the officer saw the object in question.
3. The officer's discovery of the object was inadvertent. In *Coolidge*, four Justices concurred in the part of the lead opinion stating that the discovery must be accidental. Some lower courts interpreted Justice Harlan's concur-

rence as a fifth vote assenting to that statement. *Lewis v. Cardwell*, 476 F.2d 467, 470 n.4 (6th Cir. 1973), *rev'd*, 417 U.S. 583 (1974). Other courts refused to apply the inadvertence requirement to contraband, stolen property, or dangerous objects. *United States v. $10,000 in U.S. Currency*, 780 F.2d 213 (2d Cir. 1986). In *North v. Superior Court of Riverside County*, 8 Cal. 3d 301, 502 P.2d 1305, 104 Cal. Rptr. 833 (1972), the California Supreme Court held that inadvertence is not an element of the plain view doctrine. In *Horton v. California*, 496 U.S. 128 (1990), the Supreme Court resolved the split of authority over the proper interpretation of *Coolidge*. A 7-2 majority announced that evidence need not be inadvertently discovered to qualify for admission under the plain view doctrine.

To be on the safe side, though, the prosecutor should lay this element of the foundation whenever possible. It is ideal if the discovery is "accidental." However, "inadvertent" is not synonymous with "accidental"; the courts have also held the discovery to be inadvertent when before the discovery, the police lacked probable cause to obtain a warrant for the object. *United States v. $10,000 in U.S. Currency, supra.* If the police have antecedent probable cause, then it makes sense to mandate a showing of inadvertence; the requirement encourages the police to obtain a warrant. But, if the police have no antecedent probable cause, then it serves no purpose to require inadvertence.

4. As soon as the officer saw the object, it was immediately apparent that the object was subject to seizure, i.e., contraband, stolen property, or evidence of a crime. *People v. Bradford*, 15 Cal. 4th 1229, 939 P.2d 259, 65 Cal. Rptr. 2d 145, 178 (1997), *cert. denied*, 523 U.S. 1118 (1998). In *Texas v. Brown*, 460 U.S. 730, 738 (1983), the Court stated that this requirement is satisfied when it is immediately evident that "there is probable cause to associate the property with criminal activity." 460 U.S. at 738. "Courts have recognized certain containers as distinctive drug carrying devices which may be seized upon observation: heroin balloons ..., paper bindles ..., and marijuana smelling brick-shaped packages. ..." *People v. Holt*, 212 Cal. App. 3d 1200, 1205, 261 Cal. Rptr. 89, 91 (1989). *But see People v. Chapman*, 224 Cal. App. 3d 253, 257, 274 Cal. Rptr. 47, 49 (1990) ("However, a container which 'is akin to a common product like a pill bottle, a pack of cigarettes, or a plastic bag . . . may not be seized merely because it may also be commonly used to store narcotics.'"). In deciding whether the object is subject to seizure, the officer to the appearance of the object itself; the officer may consider the totality of the circumstances. *People v. Stokes*, 224 Cal. App. 3d 715, 719-20, 273 Cal. Rptr. 752, 754 (1990); *People v. Nonnette*, 221 Cal. App. 3d 659, 271 Cal. Rptr. 329 (1990), *cert. denied*, 498 U.S. 1087 (1991). In footnote 7, the *Brown* Court added: "We need not address whether in some circumstances, a degree of suspicion lower than probable cause would be a sufficient basis for a seizure in certain cases."

5. The officer then seized the object. The officer must authenticate the object as an item of physical evidence. If it is impractical for the police to seize the item as soon as it comes into plain view and they do not intend to abandon their right to seize the item, the police may sometimes reenter later to seize the item. *People v. Ngaue*, 8 Cal. App. 4th 896, 10 Cal. Rptr. 2d 521, 525-26 (1992).

3. SAMPLE FOUNDATION

The People have charged the defendant, Mr. O'Neal with bank robbery. The witness is Officer Rooney. The proponent is the prosecutor. The witness has already testified that: He was investigating a bank robbery committed by two men armed with Luger pistols; based on an informant's report, he obtained a warrant to search the defendant's apartment for cash in bank bags; and he drove to the defendant's apartment to execute the warrant.

P   WHAT did you do when you arrived at the apartment? (1)

W   We knocked. After we explained that we had a warrant and showed it to the defendant, he let us in.

P   WHAT did you do after you entered the apartment? (1)

W   From the door, we stepped right into a rather small living room.

P   WHAT happened then? (2)

W   We just looked around. As I was turning to walk into the bedroom, I caught sight of a pistol.

P   WHERE did you see the pistol? (2)

W   It was sitting on top of a suitcase on the living room floor.

P   HOW well could you see the pistol from where you stood? (2)

W   Very well. There was nothing obstructing my view, and it was daylight. I could see the pistol plainly.

P   WHAT type of pistol was it? (4)

W   It was a Luger.

P   HOW do you know that? (4)

W   As policemen, we get a lot of training in weapons. We have to be able to differentiate by sight between the common types of weapons. Any officer can ID a Luger on sight.

P   WHAT did you do after you saw the Luger? (4)

W   I seized it.

P   WHY did you do that? (4)

W   The eyewitnesses to the crimes had mentioned that the robbers used Lugers. I thought that the Luger might be evidence that the defendant was one of the robbers, but I hadn't included weapons in my warrant application.

P   Before you entered the apartment, WHAT indication did you have that you would find a Luger there? (3)

W   None.

P   WHY do you say that? (3)

W   The informant had mentioned seeing cash in bank bags, but she hadn't mentioned any weapons. We suspected that there might be other evidence of the bank job in the apartment, but we didn't have any hard evidence pointing to weapons being present.

P   Your Honor, I request that this be marked People's exhibit #3 for identification. (5)

J   It will be so marked.

P   Please let the record reflect that I am showing the exhibit to the defense attorney.

J   The record will reflect that.

P   Permission to approach the witness, your Honor?

J   Permission granted.

P   Officer Rooney, I now hand you what has been marked as People's exhibit #3 for identification. What is it? (5)

W   It's the Luger I seized in the defendant's apartment.

P   HOW can you recognize it? (5)

W   I put my initials and the date on an evidence tag on the handle. I can see them right here.

P   Your Honor, I now offer People's exhibit #3 for identification into evidence.

J   Is there any objection?

O   No, your Honor.

J   It will be received.

M.   THE SEIZURE OF ITEMS INCIDENTAL TO THE ARREST OF THE DEFENDANT

1. THE DOCTRINE

The plain view doctrine permits a warrantless seizure when the officer has both a clear view of an object and probable cause. In that setting, the probable cause is probable cause to believe that the object is an item subject to seizure. The incidental search doctrine also permits a warrantless seizure when there is probable cause in conjunction with other factors. The key factor is that the police have lawfully arrested the defendant. The arrest reduces the defendant's privacy expectation; especially when the police must transport the defendant to jail, they have a legitimate interest in ensuring that he is not armed.

2. ELEMENTS OF THE FOUNDATION

A prosecutor invoking the incidental search doctrine should demonstrate these elements:

1. There was a lawful arrest or at least probable cause for an arrest. However, in *Knowles v. Iowa*, 525 U.S. 113 (1998), where the police officer had the option of making an arrest or issuing a citation, the Supreme Court held that after issuing a citation, the officer could not conduct a search incident to arrest. The trial court had reasoned that the search incident doctrine applies so long as the officer has probable cause to make an arrest.

2. The arrest was custodial; under local law, the police were required or authorized to take the arrestee into custody for the offense. In *United States v. Robinson*, 414 U.S. 218 (1973), and *Gustafson v. Florida*, 414 U.S. 260 (1973), the Court held that any "lawful custodial arrest" justifies an incidental search. The Court reasoned that an incidental search is justified even if there is no indication that the search will yield a weapon or evidence of a crime. In *People v. Brisendine*, 13 Cal. 3d 528, 531 P.2d 1099, 119 Cal. Rptr. 315 (1975), the California Supreme Court rejected *Robinson* and *Gustafson*. The California court adopted a more restrictive view under the state constitution. The court stated that if the arrest was for a minor citation offense,

> the fact of the arrest does not justify a search of the belongings of the person cited; there can be no instrumentalities and there can be no fruits; and absent some showing on the part of the officer that he has good cause to fear for his safety, there can be no weapons search.

Id. at 540, 531 P.2d at 1106, 119 Cal. Rptr. at 322. Proposition 8 will probably require the California courts to adopt the more expansive, *Robinson-Gustafson* approach. *See People v. Sanchez*, 174 Cal. App. 3d 343, 220 Cal. Rptr. 53 (1985); *In re Demetrius A.*, 208 Cal. App. 3d 1245, 1248-49, 256 Cal. Rptr. 717, 718-19 (1989).

3. The officer searched the arrestee. Suppose that the arrestee appears to be attempting to swallow something. It is clear that the police may not use brutal force to recover the evidence. *People v. Fulkman*, 235 Cal. App. 3d 555, 286 Cal. Rptr. 728, 733 (1991). However, the courts have split over the specific question of whether the police may resort to choking to prevent the destruction of evidence. *Compare People v. Jones*, 209 Cal. App. 3d 725, 257 Cal. Rptr. 500 (1989) (no) *with People v. Cappellia*, 208 Cal. App. 3d 1331, 256 Cal. Rptr. 695 (1989) (police were permitted to choke arrested because arrestee might have died if he ingested bindles containing drugs and they opened).

4. The scope of the search was spatially reasonable. In *Chimel v. California*, 395 U.S. 752 (1969), the Court declared that the arresting officer may search the arrestee's person and the area within the arrestee's immediate control—the area from which the arrestee might grab a weapon or destructible evidence. In the case of an item such as a purse which is not immediately associated with the arrestee's person, the cases divide over the question of whether the police may conduct a warrantless search of the item after it has been reduced to the exclusive control of the police. *People v. Ingham*, 5 Cal. App. 4th 326, 6 Cal. Rptr. 2d 756, 758-60 (1992). In the case of a search incidental to the arrest of a driver, the area within the driver's immediate control includes the passenger compartment but excludes the trunk of the car. *People v. Acevedo*, 216 Cal. App. 3d 586, 593, 265 Cal. Rptr. 23, 27 (1989) *rev'd on other grounds*, 500 U.S. 565 (1991)

(the Court upheld the search on another theory). A car is deemed to be within the driver's immediate control if he was in the car shortly before the arrest and was standing at the rear of the car at the time of the arrest. *People v. Stoffle*, 1 Cal. App. 4th 1671, 3 Cal. Rptr. 2d 257, 262-63 (1991). In the case of a search incidental to an arrest of a person in a residence, the officer may conduct a "protective sweep" when the officer has a reasonable belief based on articulable facts that the area to be swept harbors another dangerous individual. *People v. Maier*, 226 Cal. App. 3d 1670, 1674, 277 Cal. Rptr. 667, 669 (citing *Maryland v. Buie*, 494 U.S. 325 (1990)), *cert. denied*, 502 U.S. 848 (1991). One California court has held that incidental to the custodial arrest of one person, an officer may conduct a warrantless search of that person's companion if the companion reacts suspiciously. *People v. Prance*, 226 Cal. App. 3d 1525, 277 Cal. Rptr. 567 (1991).

5. The search was reasonably contemporaneous with the arrest. The courts tend to apply this requirement laxly. "[A] search incident to an arrest may ... precede the actual arrest, as long as the officer had reasonable cause before the search to make the arrest." *People v. Valdez*, 196 Cal. App. 3d 799, 805, 242 Cal. Rptr. 142, 146 (1987); *People v. Nieto*, 219 Cal. App. 3d 1275, 268 Cal. Rptr. 893 (1990); *People v. Deltoro*, 214 Cal. App. 3d 1417, 1422-26, 263 Cal. Rptr. 305, 307-10 (1989).

6. During the search, the police discovered an object subject to seizure. The officer must authenticate the exhibit as the object found on the defendant's person.

3. SAMPLE FOUNDATION

For purposes of the hypothetical, we shall assume that the court decides to follow *Robinson-Gustafson* rather than *Brisendine*. The People have charged the defendant, Mr. Wilson, with burglarizing a residence in Beverly Hills. The witness is Officer Powers. He has already testified that on the morning of July 13, 1999, he received a call from one of his informants, Jake, about the burglary. The prosecutor is the proponent:

P HOW did you know that the caller was Jake? (1)

W I've used him on numerous occasions over the past five years. I know his voice well.

P WHAT have been the results in the investigations in which you've used Jake as an informant? (1)

W He always gives me reliable info.

P WHAT do you mean by that? (1)

W The info always leads to arrests and convictions. If he says I'll find drugs in a certain place, they're there.

P WHAT specifically did Jake tell you that morning? (1)

W He said that he's been drinking with the defendant and that the defendant told him that he had just broken into a house on Anderson Drive in Beverly Hills.

P HOW did you know that Jake was referring to the defendant? (1)

W He named him—Carl Wilson. When he named him, I asked him whether he meant the guy who hangs around the Double Tree bar on Pico Boulevard. He said that was the guy. I had been at the bar, and I had seen the defendant there several times.

P WHAT did you do after you spoke with Jake? (1)

W I got into the patrol car with another officer, Adamski. We headed for the area around the Double Tree bar. It took us about twenty minutes to drive there.

P WHAT did you do when you arrived there? (1)

W We walked into the bar and searched for the defendant. He was sitting at the counter.

P WHAT did you do then? (1)

W Adamski and I walked straight up to him and informed him he was under arrest for burglary. We told him we were taking him to the local police station for booking.

P WHAT did you do then? (3)

W We took the defendant outside; and before we put him into the patrol car, we searched him.

P WHEN did you search him? (5)

W On the spot.

P HOW many minutes passed between the arrest and the search? (5)

W Two or three at most.

P HOW did you conduct the search? (4)

W We patted him down and searched all his pockets.

P WHAT, if anything, did you find? (6)

W I reached into his right front pant pocket. I could feel his wallet. As I removed the wallet, a picklock fell out of the wallet.

P WHAT is a picklock? (6)

W It's a tool that professional burglars use.

P HOW do you know that? (6)

W I've investigated dozens of burglaries over the years, and I've had training at the Police Academy in the modus operandi of burglars.

P Your Honor, I request that this be marked People's exhibit #6 for identification.

J It will be so marked.

P Please let the record reflect that I am showing the exhibit to opposing counsel.

J The record will so reflect.

P May I have permission to approach the witness?

J Certainly.

P Officer, I now hand you People's exhibit #6 for identification.. WHAT is it? (6)

W It's the picklock I found in the defendant's pocket.

P HOW can you recognize it? (6)

W My evidence tag is on it, and it's got some peculiar scratches. There are seven deep scratches all parallel. I've never seen any other picklock with those unique markings.

P Your Honor, I now offer People's exhibit #6 for identification into evidence as People's #6.

J Any objection.

O No.

J It will be received.

If the court adhered to *Brisendine*, the prosecutor would have to establish specific facts justifying a search of the person for the picklock. For instance, the officer might add that Jake told the officer that when Jake met with the defendant, he saw a picklock on the defendant's person. Jake might have told the officer that the defendant bragged he was an expert burglar and took out the picklock to demonstrate his deft touch.

N. THE SEIZURE OF AN OBJECT DURING A HOT PURSUIT SEARCH

1. THE DOCTRINE

Hot pursuit is another doctrine that can sustain a warrantless seizure. Like plain view and incidental search, this doctrine rests on a combination of probable cause and other factors. The Supreme Court approved the hot pursuit doctrine in *Warden v. Hayden*, 387 U.S. 294 (1967).

2. ELEMENTS OF THE FOUNDATION

To lay a foundation for hot pursuit, the prosecutor should prove these facts:

1. The officer had probable cause to believe that a crime had been committed.
2. Some commentators suggest that the crime must be a serious one, necessitating that the police act to protect the public. In *Hayden*, the crime was armed robbery; but the Court did not expressly limit the doctrine to serious crimes. In *People v. Lloyd*, 216 Cal. App. 3d 1425, 265 Cal. Rptr. 422 (1989), *cert. denied*, 497 U.S. 1026 (1990), after observing the defendant's brother commit a crime, the police followed him. The police made a warrantless entry into the defendant's home to arrest his brother. The court justified the entry on a hot pursuit theory although the brother's crime was only a traffic violation. The court commented that

> [t]he cases which discuss limitation of the 'hot pursuit' exception to felonies, or to grave or serious crimes ... do not involve pursuit into a home after the initiation of a detention or arrest in a public place. Where the pursuit into the home was based on an arrest set in motion in a public place, the fact that the offenses justifying the initial detention or arrest were misdemeanors is of no significance in determining the validity of the entry without a warrant.

Id. at 1429-30, 265 Cal. Rptr. at 425. *See also In re Lavoyne M.*, 221 Cal. App. 3d 154, 159, 270 Gal. Rptr. 394, 396 (1990) (citing *Lloyd*, the court declares that "[s]everal California cases hold that the minor nature of an offense does not preclude" the application of the hot pursuit doctrine).

3. The officer began to search for the perpetrator shortly after the crime.
4. The officer believes that the perpetrator has entered a specific building. In *Hayden*, private citizens told the police that they had seen the suspect enter a particular building five minutes before the police arrived. It is ideal if the police have probable cause to believe that the perpetrator is in the building. However, some courts have suggested that a founded suspicion suffices. *Greer v. State*, 253 Ind. 609, 255 N.E.2d 919 (1970).
5. The police promptly entered that building.
6. During the search of the building, the police confined the search to places where the perpetrator might be hiding.
7. During the search, the police discovered an object subject to seizure. The plain view doctrine comes into play at this point.

3. SAMPLE FOUNDATION

The People charged the defendant, Mr. Ramsey, with armed robbery. The witness is Officer Solis. Officer Solis has already testified that he was on foot patrol in the downtown area of San Jose on the morning of February 2, 1999. The proponent is the prosecutor:

P WHAT, if anything, unusual happened that morning? (1)
W As I turned onto Third Street, this woman ran up to me.
P WHO was the woman? (1)
W It was Ms. Lewis, the lady who testified just before I took the stand.
P WHAT happened after she ran up to you? (1)
W She was all upset, but I told her to calm down and tell me what had happened.
P WHAT did she do then? (1)
W She said that only a few seconds before she'd been the victim of a crime.
P WHAT crime? (2)
W She said it was an armed robbery. This guy was wearing a brown hat and a long black coat. He pulled a stiletto on her and forced her to give him all her money. When she did, he took off running north on Third Street.
P WHAT did you do then? (3)
W We were standing in front of a health food restaurant. I told her to go inside and call the Central Police Station to tell them that I was taking off to try to track down the robber.
P WHAT did you do after you told her that? (3)
W I started running north on Third Street.
P WHAT, if anything, happened, as you ran in that direction? (4)
W I ran two blocks, and then I noticed some people in front of an apartment on the 2100 block. They seemed upset.
P WHAT did you do then? (4)
W I stopped and asked them if something was wrong.
P WHAT did they say?
W They said that some guy, in a brown hat and long black coat had just run by them and almost bumped into them. They said he dashed into the building and appeared to go into the second door on the right.

P   HOW many minutes had elapsed between the time you started running north on Third Street and the time when these people told you this? (4)

W   Well, I'm not an Olympic sprinter, but it was no more than a couple of minutes.

P   WHAT did you do after they told you that the man appeared to enter the second door on the right? (5)

W   I went to that door, drew my gun, and announced that I was a police officer who wanted to enter to investigate a robbery.

P   WHAT happened then? (5)

W   There was no answer. I waited a few seconds, and called out again in a loud voice. There was still no answer. I turned the door knob and discovered the door was unlocked. I stepped into the apartment.

P   WHAT happened then? (6)

W   I looked into each of the rooms to see if I could find the robber.

P   WHERE did you look? (6)

W   The first room inside the apartment was the living room. I went from there to the bedroom. The door to the bedroom was partially open. I thought he might have gone in there.

P   WHAT was in the bedroom? (7)

W   I could see the window partially open, and by the window I found a stiletto. It was laying on the carpet.

P   WHAT did you do then? (7)

W   I picked it up to take it to the crime lab for fingerprinting.

P   Your Honor, I request that this be marked People's exhibit #5 for identification.

J   It will be so marked.

P   Please let the record reflect that I am showing the exhibit to opposing counsel.

J   The record will reflect that.

P   Your Honor, may I please have permission to approach the witness?

J   Yes.

P   Officer, I now hand you what has been marked People's exhibit #5 for identification. WHAT is it? (7)

W   It's the stiletto—the one I found in the apartment and took to the fingerprint technicians.

P   HOW can you recognize it? (7)

W   I can recognize its general appearance, and it has a peculiarity.

P   WHAT is the peculiarity?

W   If you look closely, you can see there's a triangular gouge near the bottom of the handle on the right side. I can recognize it from the gouge mark.

P   Your Honor, I now offer People's exhibit #5 for identification into evidence as People's #5.

J   It will be admitted.

O.   THE SEIZURE OF AN OBJECT DURING AN EMERGENCY SEARCH

1. THE DOCTRINE

The hot pursuit doctrine illustrates a broad category of warrantless emergency searches. As in the case of a hot pursuit, the prosecutor must demonstrate both probable cause and exceptional circumstances justifying a warrantless intrusion. The exceptional circumstances must pose an immediate threat to human safety or a substantial property interest.

2. ELEMENTS OF THE FOUNDATION

The prosecutor should lay the following foundation:

1. There was an immediate threat to human safety or a substantial property interest. The threat often arises from a crime that is in progress or has just been completed. *E.g., People v. Poulson,* 69 Cal. App. 4th Supp. 1, 82 Cal. Rptr. 2d 605 (Dep't Super. Ct. 1998) (although the officers had to consider the wife's statement that she was alright, they were not bound by the statement); *People v. Miller,* 69 Cal. App. 4th 190, 81 Cal. Rptr. 2d 410 (there is no ready litmus test to determine whether there is an exigent circumstance, but there must be an imminent and substantial threat to life, health, or property), *modified,* 99 D.A.R. 946 (Cal. App., Jan. 27, 1999); *People v. Zabelle,* 50 Cal. App. 4th 1282, 58 Cal. Rptr. 2d 105 (1996) (through a wide open door, a police officer saw the defendant sitting with his eyes closed and his face on a dresser at the foot of a bed; on a broken piece of mirror, the officer also saw several dark balls which the officer believed were heroin and the officer believed the defendant had overdosed); *People v. Higgins,* 26 Cal. App. 4th 247, 31 Cal. Rptr. 2d 516 (1994) (although the woman who answered the door said that she was alone and safe, the police were justified in making a warrantless entry to investigate suspected domestic violence; the woman was nervous and obviously injured, and the police knew that domestic violence victims often deny the abuse); *People v. Wilkins,* 14 Cal. App. 4th 761, 17 Cal. Rptr. 2d 743 (1993) (the risk of further, imminent physical harm to the victim required immediate action); *People v. Dyke,* 224 Cal. App. 3d 648, 660, 274 Cal. Rptr. 66, 73 (1990):

> The presence of a handgun in a dwelling, in and of itself, obviously does not constitute an exigent circumstance. ... However, the officers reasonably believed DeBenedict, the subject of their felony arrest warrant, was secreted inside and was aware of the reason for their presence. They were not obliged to see if he ... would reach for the handgun or otherwise try to escape.

People v. Mitchell, 222 Cal. App. 3d 1306, 272 Cal. Rptr. 440 (1990) (there was a shotgun inside the home, the defendant was intoxicated, and the defendant had already brandished the weapon at a neighbor); *People v. Neighbours,* 223 Cal. App. 3d 1115, 1122, 273 Cal. Rptr. 32, 36 (1990) ("Where police officers reasonably believe warrantless entry of a residence is necessary to prevent imminent danger to a child, the entry is justified by exigent circumstances."); *People v. Cain*, 216 Cal.: App. 3d 366, 264 Cal. Rptr. 339 (1989) (the police believed that there was an injured victim in the apartment). Some courts extend the emergency doctrine to situations in which immediate, warrantless entry is necessary to prevent destruction of evidence. *People v. Camilleri*, 220 Cal. App. 3d 1199, 269 Cal. Rptr. 862 (1990). However, even a bona fide emergency does not last forever; when the emergent circumstances dissipate, the police need another basis for continuing the search. *People v. Boragno*, 232 Cal. App. 3d 378, 283 Cal. Rptr. 452 (1991). *In re Quackenbush*, 41 Cal. App. 4th 1301, 49 Cal. Rptr. 2d 147 (1996) (although a dog had bitten a person, the incident occurred two days earlier and there was no showing that the dog was dangerous). It goes without saying that the police cannot rely on the exigent circumstances as a justification for a warrantless search if the police have created the exigency. *People v. Bellizzi*, 34 Cal. App. 4th 1849, 41 Cal. Rptr. 2d 163 (1995).

2. The officer promptly entered that location to take action to meet the threat. "While an officer must have a good faith belief his entry is justified by an emergency, such an emergency need not be his sole or even primary motivation." *People v. Snead*, 1 Cal. App. 4th 380, 1 Cal. Rptr. 2d 892, 895 (1991).

3. While the officer was attempting to meet the threat, the officer observed and took possession of an object subject to seizure. The plain view doctrine comes into play. The officer must authenticate the exhibit as the object seized.

3. SAMPLE FOUNDATION

The People have charged the defendant, Mr. Meroni, with the attempted murder of his wife. The witness is Deputy Sheriff Jones. The proponent is the prosecutor.

P   Deputy, WHERE were you at approximately 5:00 p.m. on March 12 of this year? (1)

W   I was on duty at the Sheriff's Office on Panghorn Road.

P   WHAT, if anything, unusual happened then? (1)

W   We got a call on the emergency 911 line.

P   WHO was the caller? (1)

W   The caller identified herself as a Mrs. Urick. She said she was the landlady of the Malcolm Motor Lodge on Highway 113 near Court Street.

P   WHAT did she say? (1)

W   She said that it sounded as if there was a real violent argument going on in one of the motel rooms, apartment 2A.

P   WHAT did she say about the argument? (1)

W   She said she heard a man scream something like "Shut up, bitch." Then she heard a loud noise, and it sounded as if a woman cried out just then. She said that there were still loud noises coming from that room just as she was on the phone with us.

P   WHAT did you do then? (2)

W   Deputy Dunning and I jumped into the Sheriff's car and drove over there as fast as we could.

P   HOW long did it take you to get there? (2)

W   We put the pedal to the metal, and we were over there in under five minutes.

P   WHAT did you do when you arrived at the motel? (1)

W   We went straight to apartment 2A. (1)

P   WHAT, if anything, did you hear when you reached apartment 2A? (2)

W   We heard loud voices. Then there was a silent pause for a second. Then all of a sudden a shot rang out.

P   HOW could you tell that? (1)

W   I've been on the Sheriff's force for almost 15 years now and during that time, I've become real familiar with firearms. I know the discharge of a weapon when I hear it.

P   WHAT did you do after you heard that sound? (2)

W   Dunning and I drew our revolvers and ran to the door of the apartment. I cried out that we were officers and that we wanted to come in to investigate the noise.

P   WHAT happened then? (2)

W   There was no response, but I thought I could hear moaning as if someone was in real bad pain.

P   WHAT did you do after you heard the moaning? (2)

W   I kicked in the door, and Dunning and I both went in.

P   WHAT did you find when you entered the apartment? (3)

W   This woman was stretched out on the floor. She had been shot in the throat and was bleeding profusely. Right by her side was a handgun.

P   WHAT did you do after you found her and the handgun? (3)

W   We immediately called an ambulance for her. I picked up the handgun to take it to the lab for fingerprinting.

P   Your Honor, I request that this be marked People's exhibit #4 for identification.

J   It will be so marked.

P   Please let the record reflect that I am showing the exhibit to the defense attorney.

J   The record will so reflect.

P   I request permission to approach the witness.

J   Granted.

P   Deputy, I now hand you People's exhibit #4 for identification. WHAT is it? (3)

W   It's the handgun we found laying by the woman's body.

P   HOW can you recognize it? (3)

W   I've always had a good memory for numbers. In school, I was good at math. I remember the serial number.

P   I now offer People's exhibit #4 for identification into evidence as People's #4.

J   It will be received.

P.   PROPERTY SEIZED ILLEGALLY BUT IN GOOD FAITH

1. THE DOCTRINE

Suppose that the police illegally seize evidence but that they do so in good faith. The primary purpose of the exclusionary rule is to deter illegal searches by the police. If the police assumed that their search was lawful, it arguably does not serve the purpose of the exclusionary rule to apply the rule bar the admission of the evidence seized. For that reason, opponents of the exclusionary rule urged the Supreme Court to recognize a good faith exception to the scope of the rule.

The Court adopted that exception in *United States v. Leon*, 468 U.S. 897 (1984), and *Massachusetts v. Sheppard*, 468 U.S. 981 (1984). The *Leon* case is illustrative. The case grew out of a search pursuant to a facially valid search warrant obtained by California police. A court later held that the search warrant was invalid because there was an insufficient showing of probable cause. Nevertheless, the majority opinion in *Leon* authored by Justice White, held that the seized evidence could be admitted. The Court stressed that the police can act in objective good faith when they rely on a facially valid warranted search. As we shall see in the next subsection, in *Sheppard* and *Leon* the Court prescribed a number of conditions that the prosecutor must satisfy before invoking the good faith exception.

Since both *Leon* and *Sheppard* involved warranted searches and it is easiest for the police to show good faith when they rely on a judge's warrant, there was initially doubt whether the Court would extend the good faith exception to warrantless searches. The Court partially resolved that in *Illinois v. Krull*, 480 U.S. 340 (1987). In *Krull*, the police conducted a warrantless search pursuant to an Illinois statute permitting inspection of the records of licensed sellers of motor vehicles and motor vehicle parts. The federal and state courts later held the statute unconstitutional. Nevertheless, in *Krull*, the Court sustained the admission of evidence seized under the statute. The Court held that the statute clearly authorized the officers' action and that the officers' reliance on the statute was in objective good faith. Just as a police officer may rely on a warrant issued by a judge, the officer may rely on a statute passed by the legislature. *Krull* establishes that the exception applies to at least some warrantless searches.

2. ELEMENTS OF THE FOUNDATION

Warranted searches are presumptively valid; but as Section K of this chapter pointed out, the defense can sometimes successfully challenge a facially valid warrant. If the defense did so, the prosecution might then resort to the good faith exception. To invoke the good faith exception, the prosecutor must demonstrate that:

1. The officer who originally received the report about the crime neither knew that the information was false nor acted in reckless disregard for the truth. *United States v. Leon*, 468 U.S. 897, 922-23 (1984). The prosecution may

not invoke the theory of good faith reliance on a warrant if the officer in question includes in the warrant information the officer obtained in a prior illegal entry. In that event, the "error was made by the officer, ... not by the magistrate as in *Leon*." *People v. Brown*, 210 Cal. App. 3d 849, 857, 260 Cal. Rptr. 293, 296 (1989). *See also People v. Machupa*, 14 Cal. 4th 614. 872 P.2d 114. 29 Cal. Rptr. 2d 775 (1994) (*Leon* covers errors by the magistrate, as opposed to errors by the police); *Miranda v. Superior Court*, 13 Cal. App. 4th 1628, 16 Cal. Rptr. 2d 858 (1993) (the good faith exception was inapplicable where the affidavit relied on erroneous information generated within the police department); *People v. Willis*, 71 Cal. App. 4th 530, 83 Cal. Rptr. 2d 895 (1999) (parole officers are not court employees; at the time of the search, they supplied the police with erroneous information that the defendant's parole search condition was still in effect; the good faith exception was inapplicable); *People v. Ridge*, 49 Cal. App. 4th 1275, 57 Cal. Rptr. 2d 255, 258 (1996) ("case law provides exclusion of evidence serves a deterrent purpose and is an appropriate remedy when the source of misinformation leading to an unlawful search and seizure is erroneous police department computer records"); *People v. Downing*, 33 Cal. App. 4th 1641, 40 Cal. Rptr. 2d 176 (1995) (the police relied in good faith on computer data generated by the judicial branch), *cert. denied*, 516 U.S. 1120 (1996); *People v. Arron C.*, 59 Cal. App. 4th 1365, 69 Cal. Rptr. 2d 852, 855 (1997) (the error was caused by a mistake in the probation department's computer system; "the juvenile probation office is, in effect, an arm of the juvenile court").

2. The officer who applied for the warrant presented more than a "bare bones" affidavit. The affidavit might be "so lacking in indicia of probable cause as to render official belief in its existence entirely unreasonable. ..." *Id*. In *People v. Camarella*, 54 Cal. 3d 592, 818 P.2d 63, 286 Cal. Rptr. 780, 784-87 (1991), the California Supreme Court announced that the test is whether a well-trained police officer should reasonably have known that the affidavit failed to establish probable cause. The court added that in assessing the objective reasonableness of the officer's conduct, the officer may not rely on the simple fact that a warrant issued. However, "[W]here the affidavit is sufficient to create disagreement among thoughtful and competent judges, the officer's reliance on the magistrate's determination of probable cause should be deemed objectively reasonable." *People v. Spears*, 228 Cal. App. 3d 1, 19-20, 278 Cal. Rptr. 506, 516 (1991). *Compare People v. Johnson*, 220 Cal. App. 3d 742, 270 Cal. Rptr. 70 (1990) (the officer's efforts to corroborate the informant were so incomplete that the officer's reliance was objectively unreasonable) *with People v. Brown*, 224 Cal. App. 3d 1057, 1065, 274 Cal. Rptr. 432, 437 (1990) (criticizing *Johnson* for "equating mere laxity in seeking corroboration with bad faith"). The *Brown* opinion was depublished. *People v. Bradford*, 15 Cal. 4th 1229, 939 P.2d 259, 65 Cal. Rptr. 2d 145, 177-78 (1997) (concededly, the reference in the warrant to "any and all photographs" was overbroad; however, the over-

breadth related to "only one category of items listed in the warrant, and the warrant otherwise specified the items to be seized. The warrant's failure to particularize items within this category of articles to be seized did not render it so facially deficient that no reasonable officer could presume it to be valid"), *cert. denied*, 523 U.S. 1118 (1998).

3. The judge or magistrate who issued the warrant did not obviously "wholly abandon his judicial role. ..." *Id.* The judge may not act as mere rubber stamp. In *United States v. Breckenridge*, 782 F.2d 1317 (5th Cir.), *cert. denied*, 479 U.S. 837 (1986), the judge did not read the affidavit. However, the court applied the good faith exception because the judge questioned the officer and it seemed to the officer that the judge read the affidavit.

4. The warrant is not "facially deficient." *United States v. Leon*, 468 U.S. 897, 922-23 (1984). The warrant must particularize the place to be searched and the things to be seized. If the warrant does not specify those details, the officers may not "reasonably presume it to be valid." *But see People v. Alvarez*, 209 Cal. App. 3d 66O, 257 Cal. Rptr. 445 (1989) (although the warrant omitted a description of the property to be seized, the officer's affidavit contained the description; since both the magistrate and the district attorney's office had reviewed the warrant, the officer reasonably believed that it contained the required description); *People v. Bradford*, 15 Cal. 4th 1229, 65 Cal. Rptr. 2d 145 (1997) (even if the search warrant's reference to "any and all photographs" was overbroad, that reference encompassed only one category of items mentioned in the warrant; and the warrant was not so facially deficient that no reasonable officer could presume it to be valid or execute it in good faith).

5. In executing the warrant, the police may not exceed the scope of the warrant. The *Leon* Court stated that "our discussion of the deterrent effect of excluding evidence obtained in reasonable reliance on a subsequently invalidated warrant assumes, of course, that the officers properly executed the warrant and searched only those places and for those objects that it was reasonable to believe were covered by the warrant." *Id.* at 918 n.19.

At each stage of the process, the officers must act in objective good faith. The absence of any of the above elements precludes a finding of objective good faith. Moreover, as the testifying officer describes each step in the process, the officer should testify to a good faith belief in the legality of his or her action or the judge's action.

3. SAMPLE FOUNDATION

The People have charged the defendant, Mr. Wiley, with possession of heroin. On July 31, 1999, an informant told the police that the previous day she had seen a large quantity of heroin at the defendant's apartment. However, when the police drafted the affidavit for the search warrant, they neglected to specify that the informant had sighted the heroin there the previous day; the affidavit said only that she "previously visited Clevon Wiley's residence and observed heroin there. " The judge nevertheless issued a warrant. The police executed the warrant and seized the heroin. The defendant then moves to suppress the evidence. For purposes of the motion, the prosecutor concedes that the seizure was illegal; the prosecutor admits that since the affidavit did not specify the date of the informant's viewing of the heroin, the judge should have held that information in the affidavit was apparently "stale." However, the prosecutor argues that the seizure was in objective good faith. The witness is Officer Hillman, who received the informant's report, drafted the affidavit, and executed the warrant:

P   WHERE were you on the morning of July 31, 1999? (1)
W   I was on duty at the Narcotics Detail Office.
P   WHAT, if anything, unusual happened that morning? (1)
W   I got a phone call from Sally.
P   WHO is Sally? (1)
W   She is one of my informants. She gives me leads for drug arrests and seizures. I've used her many times in the past.
P   HOW often have you used her? (1)
W   At least fifteen times over the past two years. I've relied on her tips in investigations.
P   WHAT have been the results of those investigations? (1)
W   She always gives me good, solid leads. She double-checks any hearsay. Most of the info she relays to me is based on her personal observation.
P   WHAT did Sally say when she called that morning? (1)
W   She said that the day before she'd been at the defendant's apartment and seen a large quantity of heroin in the bedroom.
P   HOW did you know she was referring to this defendant? (1)
W   She gave me the address, 1440 Bencamp. I'd driven by that area and seen the defendant walking around. I knew we were talking about the same guy.
P   WHAT did you do after you spoke with Sally? (1)
W   I wrote up an affidavit for a search warrant.
P   WHY did you do that? (1)
W   I was convinced at that point that I had probable cause for a good search.
P   Your Honor, I request that this be marked People's #1 for identification.
J   So marked.
P   Please let the record reflect that I am showing the exhibit to opposing counsel.
J   The record will reflect that.
P   Officer, I now hand you what has been marked People's exhibit #1 for identification. WHAT is it? (2)
W   It's the affidavit I just mentioned.
P   HOW can you recognize it? (2)
W   I know my own handwriting. That's definitely my signature at the bottom of the page.
P   I now offer People's exhibit #1 for identification into evidence.
J   It will be received.
P   Officer, read the third paragraph of that affidavit to yourself.
W   Yes.

P WHAT, if anything, does the affidavit say about the date when Sally saw the heroin at the defendant's apartment? (2)

W Unfortunately, it says only she "previously" saw it there.

P Again, WHAT did Sally tell you when she saw the heroin at the defendant's apartment? (2)

W She said the previous day.

P WHY didn't you state that in exhibit #1? (2)

W Just carelessness. I thought I had written that in. I drafted the thing in pencil and then typed it. I'm not the world's best typist. I'm afraid that I didn't proofread it carefully. It had been a hectic day, there was a lot going on, and I just slipped up when I was typing it up for the judge.

P WHAT did you do after you typed the affidavit? (3)

W I walked it over to Judge Lorenzo's chambers.

P WHAT happened then? (3)

W She was in her office. She took a couple of minutes to read it, and I remember her asking me when I had this conversation with Sally. I told her that I had just gotten off the phone with Sally and immediately typed up the affidavit.

P WHAT did Judge Lorenzo do then? (4)

W She issued a warrant to me.

P I request that this be marked People's exhibit #2 for identification.

J It will be so marked.

P Please let the record show that I am showing the exhibit to the defense attorney.

P Officer, what is the exhibit? (4)

W It's the warrant the judge gave me.

P HOW do you recognize it? (4)

W I know the contents—the date and the rest of it. I also recognize the judge's handwriting.

P I now offer People's exhibit #2 for identification into evidence as People's #2.

J Received.

P WHAT did you do after the judge gave you this warrant?

W Officer Marshall and I executed it.

P WHY did you do that? (4)

W I assumed that we had authority to go get the heroin. I had a warrant in my hands.

P WHERE did you go after you got the warrant in your hands? (4)

W We went straight to 1440 Bencamp.

P WHY did you go there? (4)

W You can see right in the warrant. That's the place it names for the site of the search.

P WHAT did you do when you arrived at 1440 Bencamp? (5)

W We knocked and showed the defendant the warrant. He let us in and then we searched.

P WHAT did you search for? (4)

W The only stuff we looked for was heroin.

P WHY? (4)

W Again, right here In the warrant—it says that that's what we were authorized to search for. That's the only contraband we were looking for.

P WHAT happened while you were searching? (5)

W We found a large quantity of heroin.

P   WHAT did you do when you found it? (5)

W   We seized it.

P   WHY? (5)

W   I just assumed that it was perfectly proper and lawful for us to grab it. I thought I had probable cause and a good warrant for a seizure.

Q.   PROPERTY THAT WOULD INEVITABLY HAVE BEEN LAWFULLY SEIZED

1. THE DOCTRINE

The fourth amendment exclusionary rule applies not only to the evidence the police initially illegally seize but also to the fruit of the poisonous tree—evidence they derive from the initial, unlawful search or seizure. *Wong Sun v. United States*, 371 U.S. 471 (1963). Suppose, however, that the prosecutor can show that the police inevitably would have discovered the derived evidence through lawful means. The inevitable discovery doctrine can justify the admission of the derived evidence. *See People v. Superior Court of Alameda County*, 80 Cal. App. 3d 665, 145 Cal. Rptr. 795 (1978). Surprisingly, one of the leading decisions on this fourth amendment doctrine is a sixth amendment case, *Brewer v. Williams*, 430 U.S. 387 (1977). In that case, the police obtained a statement from a murder suspect in violation of his right to counsel. The statement helped the police locate the victim's body. When the defendant made the statement, volunteer search teams had already neared the location of the body. The Supreme Court held that the sixth amendment forbade the admission of the statement itself. However, in a footnote, the majority added:

> While neither Williams' incriminating statements themselves nor any testimony describing his having led the police to the victim's body can constitutionally be admitted into evidence, evidence of where the body was found and its condition might well be admissible on the theory that the body would have been discovered in any event, even had incriminating statements not been elicited from Williams.

Id. at 406 n.12.

The state courts seized on the footnote. They found that the search would inevitably have discovered the body even if Williams had not disclosed its location. Given that finding, they held that there was no constitutional bar to the admission of the evidence. Once again the case reached the Supreme Court in *Nix v. Williams*, 467 U.S. 431 (1984). In *Nix*, the majority confirmed the earlier dictum in the footnote in *Brewer*. The Court held that the prosecution may introduce illegally seized evidence if the prosecution can demonstrate by a preponderance of the evidence that the evidence would inevitably have been discovered by lawful means. The majority made clear that the good faith and inevitable discovery doctrines are independent: To rely on the inevitable discovery doctrine, the prosecutor need not show that the police's seizure of the evidence was in good faith. The primary dispute about the inevitable discovery doctrine is whether it applies only to derivative evidence like the body in *Williams*. Suppose, for example, that evidence is first observed during an illegal warrantless search and then subsequently seized in a valid, warranted search. The courts are currently split on whether the inevitable discovery doctrine applies to the direct fruits of an illegal search. *See United States v. Whitehorn*, 813 F.2d 646, 650 (4th Cir. 1987), *cert. denied*, 487 U.S. 1234 (1988). The Court of Appeals for the Ninth Circuit has indicated that *Nix* can be applied to evidence observed during an earlier invalid search. *United States v. Merriweather*, 777 F.2d 503, 506 (9th Cir. 1985), *cert. denied*, 475 U.S. 1098 (1986).

2. ELEMENTS OF THE FOUNDATION

1. It is ideal if at the time the police conducted the illegal search or seizure, there was already an ongoing investigation. In his concurring opinion in *Nix*, Justice Stevens stressed that he would not accept speculation about a future search. He stated: "An inevitable discovery finding is based on objective evidence concerning the scope of the ongoing investigation which can be objectively verified or impeached." 467 U.S. at 457 n.8. For example, in *People v. Lamas*, 282 Cal. Rptr. 296, 302 (Cal. App. 1981), there was testimony that "the officers had [already] determined to obtain a search warrant. ..." *But see United States v. Boatwright*, 822 F.2d 862 (9th Cir. 1987); *People v. Samaro*, 206 Cal. App. 3d 1131, 1144, 254 Cal. Rptr. 128, 135 (1988) ("the existence of two independent searches is not a necessary predicate to application of the inevitable discovery rule. ..."). The *Samaro* opinion was withdrawn.
2. The scope of the investigation is such that it inevitably would have led to the discovery of the illegally seized evidence.
3. The circumstances of the discovery would have been such that the seizure would have been lawful.

3. SAMPLE FOUNDATION

The People have charged the defendant Rice with murder. On February 3, 1999, the police conducted an illegal, warrantless search of the defendant's farmhouse and found a map. The map appeared to be a map of the defendant's farm. The map was marked with an "X." The "X" appeared to be situated in the northwest corner of the field beyond the fence surrounding the farmhouse. Using the map, the police went to the indicated site in the northwest quarter of the field, dug, and found the murder weapon. The revolver was buried six inches under the surface of the field. On February 1, 1999, the police had begun a systematic search of the field. On February 1, they completed a search of the southeast quarter of the field. On February 2, they searched the southwest quarter. On February 3, they were in the process of searching the northeast quarter. The police discontinued the sweep as soon as they found the map. The witness is Officer Chaney who was in charge of the sweep.

P   Officer, WHERE were you on February 3 of 1999? (1)

W   I was at the field near the defendant's farmhouse.

P   WHY were you there? (1)

W   I was in charge of a team of searchers sweeping the field for evidence.

P   WHAT type of field are you talking about? (3)

W   It's just uncultivated land.

P   HOW is it connected to the farmhouse? (3)

W   It's not. The farmhouse and two outbuildings are surrounded by a fence. They're connected by paths. However, the paths end at the fence. The field I'm talking about is beyond the fence.

P   HOW were you conducting the sweep of the field? (2)

W   Since it's a decent size and we wanted to carefully comb it for evidence, we did it a quarter each day. We divided it into quarters—the northwest corner, the northeast quarter, etc.; and we did one quarter each day.

P   WHAT equipment, if any, were you using? (2)

W   We were using dogs and metal detectors.

P   WHAT is a metal detector? (2)

W   It sets off an alarm if it detects a metal object in the soil.

P   HOW effective is a metal detector? (2)

W   There are limits. For example, if the object is buried real deep—say six feet, the detector may miss it. But if the object is buried shallow, the detector will find it.

P   HOW thoroughly were you searching the field? (2)

W   We were going step by step to comb every inch of that field. This was a big murder case, and we didn't want to overlook any evidence.

P   HOW much of the sweep did you complete? (2)

W   We had completed the southern half of the property on the first two days, February 1st and 2nd. We discontinued the search on February 3 when some other officers found a map in the defendant's house.

P   WHERE were you searching on February 3? (2)

W   That day we were in the northeast quarter.

P   WHERE would you have searched February 4? (2)

W   We definitely would have finished the northeast quarter on the 3rd, so we would have been sweeping the northwest quarter on the 4th.

P   HOW do you know that? (2)

W   The chief had assigned me four men, and I definitely had them committed until the 5th. I told them when we began that the plan was to do a quarter of the field a day. I told them then that the last day I had them scheduled to sweep the northwest quarter of the field.

P   WHAT equipment would they have used? (2)

W   I had the dogs and the metal detectors laid on for that day. It was the same equipment we had used before.

Part 2. Confessions and Admissions

R. IN GENERAL

Sections B-Q of this chapter deal with the Fourth Amendment limitations on the admissibility of prosecution evidence. This is the first in a series of sections analyzing the Fifth Amendment limitations. The Fifth Amendment includes the privilege against self-incrimination. Article I, § 15, of the California Constitution also guarantees a privilege against self-incrimination. Further, Evidence Code §§ 930 and 940 protect both the privilege not to testify and the privilege not to answer incriminating questions "to the extent that such privilege exists under the Constitution of the United States or the State of California."

In Section B. we noted that Proposition 8 affects the California courts' power to exclude illegally seized evidence. Before Proposition 8, under the state constitution the California courts had adopted many rules governing police searches that were more restrictive than the rules mandated by the Fourth Amendment. As we saw, *In re Lance W.*, 37 Cal. 3d 873, 694 P.2d 744, 210 Cal. Rptr. 631 (1985), held that Proposition 8 abolished the California courts' power to enforce more restrictive rules; they may now exclude seized evidence only when exclusion is required by the Fourth Amendment or a statute passed by two-thirds vote in each house of the legislature. However, Proposition 8 does not sweep away all exclusionary rules of evidence. The second sentence of the new § 28(d) of article I provides: "Nothing in this section shall affect any existing statutory rule of evidence relating to privilege. ..." Especially since Evidence Code §§ 930 and 940 refer to the privilege against self-incrimination, it is arguable that the language, "statutory rule ... (of privilege)" in § 28(d) exempts the privilege against self-incrimination from the operation of Proposition 8. However, in *People v. May*, 44 Cal. 3d 309, 748 P.2d 307, 243 Cal. Rptr. 369 (1988), the California Supreme Court ruled that the language includes only "legislatively created rules of privilege insulating particular communications, such as the attorney-client or physician-patient privilege." *May* holds that Proposition 8 precludes the California courts from recognizing privilege against self-incrimination exclusionary rules "based on independent state grounds."(In June 1990, the California electorate approved Proposition 115. In part, that proposition read that

> [i]n criminal cases the right[] of a defendant ... to not be compelled to be a witness against himself or herself ... shall be construed by the courts of this state in a manner consistent with the Constitution of the United States. This Constitution shall not be construed by the courts to afford greater rights to criminal defendants than those afforded by the Constitution of the United States. ...

However, in *Raven v. Deukmejian*, 52 Cal. 3d 336, 801 P.2d 1077, 276 Cal. Rptr. 326 (1990), the California Supreme Court invalidated this provision on procedural grounds.)

Sections S-X of this chapter analyze the primary limitations on the admission of a defendant's out-of-court confessions. In sequence, we shall discuss: the Fifth Amendment due process clause (S), the supervisory power (T), the *Miranda* doctrine (U), the right to counsel (V), the impeachment exception (W), and the corroboration requirement (X). Section Y considers prosecution attempts to elicit a confession from a testifying defendant.

S. INVOLUNTARY CONFESSIONS BARRED BY THE FIFTH AND FOURTEENTH AMENDMENTS DUE PROCESS CLAUSES

1. THE DOCTRINE

The introduction of confessions has long troubled the American courts. As the Supreme Court itself has noted, the courts have an ambivalent attitude toward confessions. *Moran v. Burbine*, 475 U.S. 412 (1986). On the one hand, the courts appreciate that confessions are helpful in convicting the guilty. On the other hand, the courts realize that the interrogation process is coercive and can yield unreliable "confessions" by innocent persons.

The Supreme Court's first step in attacking this dilemma was the application of the Fifth and Fourteenth Amendment due process clauses. In *Brown v. Mississippi*, 297 U.S. 278 (1936), the Court held that due process forbids the receipt of an involuntary confession. If coercion or improper inducement overcomes the suspect's will to resist, the confession is involuntary; and the prosecutor may not introduce the confession against the defendant. The voluntariness doctrine raises significant substantive and procedural questions.

One substantive question is whether the doctrine applies only when the persons applying pressure to the suspect are government agents. In *Colorado v. Connelly*, 479 U.S. 157 (1986), the Court held that only coercive police conduct violates the due process clause. Prior to Proposition 8, the California courts took the contrary view, holding that due process applies even when the pressure on the suspect was exerted by private citizens. *People v. Haydel*, 12 Cal. 3d 190, 197, 524 P.2d 866, 869, 115 Cal. Rptr. 394, 397 (1974). "The effect of the 'Truth-in-Evidence' provision of Proposition 8 ... on this issue has not been directly determined by the California Supreme Court." *People v. Sultana*, 204 Cal. App. 3d 511, 522 n.5, 251 Cal. Rptr. 115, 121 n.5 (1988), *cert. denied*, 489 U.S. 1057 (1989). In *People v. Cox*, 221 Cal. App. 3d 980, 986, 270 Cal. Rptr. 730, 733 (1990), an intermediate California court cited *Connelly* as controlling authority. Moreover, in *People v. Douglas*, 50 Cal. 3d 468, 788 P.2d 640, 268 Cal. Rptr. 126 (1990), *cert. denied*, 498 U.S. 1110 (1991) the California Supreme Court reached a result at odds with *Haydel* and consistent with *Connelly*; the court held that torture applied by foreign police does not trigger the due process clause. The court also relied on *Connelly* as authority in *People v. Clark*, 5 Cal. 4th 950, 857 P.2d 1099,

22 Cal. Rptr. 2d 689 (1993).

The next question is what types of coercion and inducement are forbidden by the due process clause. The clause unquestionably forbids physical torture. Psychological coercion such as threats can also vitiate the voluntariness of a confession. *E.g., People v. Montano*, 226 Cal. App. 3d 914, 935, 277 Cal. Rptr. 327, 337 (1991):

> Officer Kincannon aggravated the situation by using their common religion to conjure up in defendant's mind the picture of confessing to avoid going to hell. ... "[A] ... law enforcement officer conducting an interrogation of one accused of crime may not use his own or the suspect's personal religious beliefs as a tool to extract admissions of guilt. ..."

The most troublesome problems arise when the police use inducements short of threats. *E.g., People v. Benson*, 52 Cal. 3d 754, 802 P.2d 330, 276 Cal. Rptr. 827 (1990), *cert. denied*, 502 U.S. 924 (1991). Without rendering an ensuing confession involuntary, the police may tell a suspect that she would be better off cooperating or that it would be good to get the matter off her chest. *People v. Robinson*, 274 Cal. App. 2d 514, 520, 79 Cal. Rptr. 213, 217 (1969). The police may also permissibly exhort the suspect to tell the truth. 1 WITKIN § 615. However, the police overstep if they resort to misrepresentations "of such a nature as would probably result in an untrue" confession. *Id.* at § 617, at 593. *See also People v. Vasila*, 38 Cal. App. 4th 865, 45 Cal. Rptr. 2d 355 (1995) (here the police made improper promises of leniency, namely, that the defendant would be released on his own recognizance and that he would not be prosecuted in federal court); *People v. Ray*, 13 Cal. 4th 313, 914 P.2d 846, 52 Cal. Rptr. 2d 296, 311 ("psychological ploys which, under all the circumstances, are so coercive that they tend to produce a statement that is both involuntary and unreliable"), *cert. denied*, 519 U.S. 967 (1996).

The police use of coercion or improper inducement does not automatically render an ensuing confession or admission involuntary. The improper inducement must be more than a mere "but for" cause of the ensuing confession or admission. *People v. Benson*, 52 Cal. 3d 754, 802 P.2d 330, 276 Cal. Rptr. 827 (1990), *cert. denied*, 112 S. Ct. 336, 116 L. Ed. 2d 277 (1991); *People v. Mickey*, 54 Cal. 3d 612, 818 P.2d 84, 286 Cal. Rptr. 801, 814 (1991) ("such activity must be ... the 'proximate cause' of the statement, and not merely a cause in fact"), *cert. denied sub nom. Clair v. California*, 506 U.S. 819 (1992); *People v. Musselwhite*, 17 Cal. 4th 1216, 954 P.2d 475, 74 Cal. Rptr. 2d 212, 226-27 (1998) (although the police did not have the forensic reports at the time of their interview of the defendant, "they nevertheless told defendant that his prints had been lifted from the victim's skin, including her neck. Lies told by the police to a suspect under questioning can affect the voluntariness of an ensuing confession, but they are not per se sufficient to make it involuntary;" the court expressly cites *Benson*). The pivotal question is whether the suspect's ability to make a free choice was overborne by the coercion or inducement. The judge may consider the suspect's age, intelligence, and mental or physical condition. The judge will ordinarily assume that the suspect was a person of average knowledge and intelligence. If the defense claims that the suspect had a weakness making him or her particularly vulnerable to coercion, the defense should present expert testimony to prove the weakness. *People v. MacPherson*, 2 Cal. 3d 109, 465 P.2d 17, 84 Cal. Rptr. 129 (1970).

The due process doctrine poses procedural as well as substantive questions. Who may challenge a confession on voluntariness grounds? May a defendant object to the admission of a codefendant's statement on the ground that the statement was involuntary? Although only the interrogee may raise a *Miranda* objection, the pre- and post-Proposition 8 California cases allow any defendant to challenge a statement on due process grounds. Rael & Phillips, *Confessions and Admissions*, in CALIFORNIA CRIMINAL LAW § 30.14, at 625; *In re J. Clyde K.*, 192 Cal. App. 3d 710, 237 Cal. Rptr. 550 (1987); *People v. Douglas*, 50 Cal. 3d 468, 788 P.2d 640, 268 Cal. Rptr. 126 (1990); *People v. Badgett*, 10 Cal. 4th 330, 895 P.2d 877, 41 Cal. Rptr. 2d 635 (1995) (on the one hand, the defendant may challenge a third party's confession on the ground that it was the product of coercion; on the other hand, the defendant must be prepared to show that the coercion was such that it will actually affect the reliability of the evidence).

Another procedural question concerns the standard for proving voluntariness. Under *Lego v. Twomey*, 404 U.S. 477 (1972), the federal constitution standard is a mere preponderance of the evidence. However, in *People v. Jimenez*, 21 Cal. 3d 595, 580 P.2d 672, 147 Cal. Rptr. 172 (1978), the California Supreme Court decreed that state prosecutors must establish voluntariness beyond a reasonable doubt. In *People v. Markham*, 49 Cal. 3d 63, 775 P.2d 1042, 260 Cal. Rptr. 273 (1989), the California Supreme Court abandoned *Jimenez*. Relying on its reasoning in *May*, the court asserted that "the procedural rule of *Jimenez* accomplishes what a rule founded on independent state constitutional grounds, in the wake of Proposition 8, cannot—exclusion of relevant evidence based upon a standard of proof of voluntariness more stringent than that mandated by the federal constitution." *Id.* at 71, 775 P.2d at 1047, 260 Cal. Rptr. at 278. The court specifically cited *Lego* as the controlling standard. *Id. See also In re Aven S.*, 1 Cal. App. 4th 69, 1 Cal. Rptr. 2d 655, 659 (1991) (*Markham* applies to confessions by juveniles); *People v. Massie*, 19 Cal. 4th 550, 967 P. 2d 29, 79 Cal. Rptr. 2d 816 (1998), *cert. denied*, 143 L. Ed. 2d 790, 119 S. Ct. 1759 (1999).

2. ELEMENTS OF THE FOUNDATION

As the above subsection suggests, there are several ways in which a prosecutor can defeat a voluntariness challenge. The prosecutor could show that: The person pressuring the suspect was a private citizen (if *Haydel* is bad law after Proposition 8); there was no coercion or improper inducement; or the pressure did not overbear the suspect's will to resist. Suppose that the prosecutor opts for the second theory, that there was no duress or improper inducement. To establish this theory, the prosecutor should lay these foundational elements.

1. Negatively, the police did not
   a. use violence against the suspect;
   b. apply psychological pressure to the suspect; or
   c. make improper promises to the suspect.
2. Affirmatively, the police treated the suspect decently and afforded the suspect at least minimum conveniences.

3. SAMPLE FOUNDATION

Our fact situation is a prosecution for robbery. The defendant is Mr. Walters. The prosecution calls Officer Gannon as a witness. Officer Gannon identifies himself and then testifies that he is assigned to the robbery detail of the Los Angeles Police Department. The proponent is the prosecutor.

P Officer Gannon, WHERE were you on the afternoon of January 20, 1999?
W I was at our downtown station on duty in the robbery detail office.
P WHAT happened that afternoon?
W Some other officers brought in someone for questioning.
P WHO was that person?
W James Walters.
P WHERE is James Walters now?
W Here in the courtroom.
P Specifically, WHERE in the courtroom?
W He's sitting right there.
P HOW is he dressed?
W He's attired in a brown shirt and green pants.
P Your Honor, please let the record reflect that the witness identified the defendant.
J It will so reflect.
P WHAT happened after the officers brought Mr. Walters in?
W I took him to the interrogation room.
P WHAT happened then?
W I began questioning him.
P WHAT promises did you make to him during the questioning? (1c)
W None.
P WHAT force did you use during this interrogation? (1a)
W None, I never touched him.
P WHAT threats did you make? (1b)
W I didn't make any. I didn't threaten him or his family in any way.
P WHAT requests did he make during the questioning? (2)
W He asked for a cigarette, for coffee, and to go to the bathroom—that sort of thing.
P HOW did you respond to his requests? (2)
W I granted them. I gave him cigarettes and coffee. I let him go to the bathroom. I tried to make him as comfortable as possible.

T.   CONFESSIONS EXCLUDED IN THE EXERCISE OF THE COURTS' SUPERVISORY POWER

Federal Rule of Criminal Procedure 5(a), like its predecessor, commands that the police bring an arrestee before a United States commissioner "without unnecessary delay." The commissioner advises the arrestee of his or her rights at an arraignment. Therefore, a prompt arraignment rule helps ensure that the suspect knows and can intelligently exercise those rights. In *McNabb v. United States*, 318 U.S. 332 (1943), federal officers violated the predecessor of Rule 5(a). The Supreme Court announced that it possessed a supervisory power to fashion a sanction for the violation of a rule passed by Congress. The Court held that a confession obtained during a period of unnecessary delay is inadmissible. The Court reaffirmed the holding in *Mallory v. United States*, 354 U.S. 449 (1957).

Anyone generally familiar with federal and California law might be willing to wager that the California courts would follow *McNabb*. Like the United States Supreme Court, the California courts have asserted a supervisory power. *People v. Jimenez*, 21 Cal. 3d 595, 580 P.2d 672, 147 Cal. Rptr. 172 (1978); *Tarantino v. Superior Court of Marin County*, 48 Cal. App. 3d 465, 122 Cal. Rptr. 61 (1975). Further, like Rule 5(a), California Penal Code § 825 commands that arrestees be taken "before the magistrate without unnecessary delay. ..." However, the California courts have declined to adopt the *McNabb* doctrine. Rael & Phillips, *Confessions and Admissions*, in CALIFORNIA CRIMINAL LAW § 30.49 (2d ed. 1994). Rather, the California courts consider an improper delay merely as one factor in applying the voluntariness doctrine. *Id.* The delay is relevant in voluntariness analysis; by arresting the suspect and holding the suspect incommunicado for a prolonged period of time, the police can weaken the suspect's ability to resist.

However, the California courts have exercised the supervisory power to promulgate other restrictions on the admissibility of confessions. For example, in *Bryan v. Superior Court of Los Angeles County*, 7 Cal. 3d 575, 498 P.2d 1079, 102 Cal. Rptr. 831 (1972), the court held that a minor's admission in a juvenile court proceeding is inadmissible in a subsequent adult prosecution of the minor. Similarly, following *Simmons v. United States*, 390 U.S. 377 (1968), *People v. Douglas*, 66 Cal. App. 3d 998, 136 Cal. Rptr. 358 (1977), bars the use of a defendant's suppression hearing testimony as substantive evidence at the subsequent trial. *People v. Coleman*, 13 Cal. 3d 867, 533 P.2d 1024, 120 Cal. Rptr. 384 (1975), precludes the prosecution from using a defendant's testimony at a probation revocation hearing as substantive proof in a later prosecution. Finally, *People v. Hicks*, 4 Cal. 3d 757, 94 Cal. Rptr. 393, 484 P.2d 65 (1971), seemed to create a broad exclusionary rule for statements made to induce the trial court to grant probation. There is authority that *Bryan* and *Coleman* survived the adoption of Proposition 8. *People v. Humiston*, 20 Cal. App. 4th 460, 24 Cal. Rptr. 2d 515 (1993); *People v. Weaver*, 39 Cal. 3d 654, 703 P.2d 1139, 217 Cal. Rptr. 245 (1985); *Ramona R. v. Superior Court*, 37 Cal. 3d 802, 693 P.2d 789, 210 Cal. Rptr. 204 (1985).

In 1997, the California Supreme Court revisited this issue; the court reiterated that *Ramona R.* "requires that a minor's statements made to a probation officer in preparation for a fitness hearing not be used as substantive evidence against the minor at a subsequent trial of the offense ...." *People v. Macias*, 16 Cal. 4th 739, 941 P.2d 838, 66 Cal. Rptr. 2d 659, 667 (1997), *cert. denied*, 523 U.S. 1084 (1998). However, some authorities conclude that the *Hicks* rule is no longer good law. *People v. Pacchioli*, 9 Cal. App. 4th 1331, 12 Cal. Rptr. 2d 156, 161-62 (1992); *People v. Goodner*, 7 Cal. App. 4th 1324, 9 Cal. Rptr. 2d 543, 547-48 (1992).

The defense need not lay a foundation to invoke any of the exclusionary rules based on the supervisory power. The only thing the defense must establish is that the defendant made the statement at the correct type of setting: a juvenile court proceeding (*Bryan*), a suppression hearing (*Douglas*), a presentence investigation (*Hicks*), or a probation revocation hearing (*Coleman*). If the statement appears in a transcript on file with a court, the defense may request judicial notice of the record under Evidence Code § 452(d). If there is no transcript on file, the defense should obtain an attested copy of the transcript; the attesting notary's signature is presumptively authentic under Evidence Code § 1453.

U. UNWARNED CONFESSIONS BARRED BY THE *MIRANDA* DOCTRINE

In *Miranda v. Arizona*, 384 U.S. 436 (1966), the Warren Court took a step beyond the voluntariness doctrine and *McNabb-Mallory*. In the *Miranda* opinion, Chief Justice Warren stated that custodial interrogation is inherently coercive. The opinion decreed that the police take steps to dispel that coercion. Specifically, the Court held that when the police interrogate a suspect in custody, they must advise him of certain rights and obtain a knowing, intelligent waiver of the rights. There are two types of commonly litigated *Miranda* situations. In one, the prosecutor argues that for some reason, such as a lack of custody, *Miranda* did not apply. In the second, the prosecution contends that the police complied with *Miranda*, administered proper warnings, and obtained an effective waiver.

1. THE INAPPLICABILITY OF *MIRANDA*

Miranda is a limited doctrine. There are at least four different routes to the conclusion that *Miranda* was inapplicable to the questioning of a suspect.

First, *Miranda* applies only when the interrogators are government agents. *Miranda* is inapplicable to an interrogation conducted by a private citizen who is not acting as a government agent. *In re Deborah C.*, 30 Cal. 3d 125, 635 P.2d 446, 177 Cal. Rptr. 852 (1981). Likewise, *Miranda* is inapplicable to questioning by private security guards. Rael & Phillips, *Confessions and Admissions*, in CALIFORNIA CRIMINAL LAW § 30.36 (2d ed. 1994). By the same token, *Miranda* is inapplicable to a conversation between the suspect and the victim. *People v.*

Guilmette, 1 Cal. App. 4th 1534, 2 Cal. Rptr. 2d 75O, 752-53 (1991) (citing *Illinois v. Perkins*, 496 U.S. 292 (1990)).

Second, *Miranda* applies only when the defendant's statement results from police questioning. *Miranda* itself stated that no warning is needed if the suspect spontaneously volunteers a statement to the police. In *Arizona v. Mauro*, 481 U.S. 520 (1987), the defendant's wife demanded to see him. The police allowed her to speak with him, but a police officer was present and openly tape-recorded the conversation. At the later trial, the prosecutor attempted to introduce some of the defendant's statements during the conversation as incriminating evidence. The Supreme Court held that the officer present during the conversation had no obligation to warn the defendant of his right to silence. Writing for the majority, Justice Powell stated that the officer's mere presence was not the "functional equivalent of interrogation." *Compare People v. Harris*, 211 Cal. App. 3d 640, 259 Cal. Rptr. 462 (1989) (interrogating officer's comment, "I thought that you were going to come back and straighten it out," was the functional equivalent of further questioning) *with People v. Celestine*, 9 Cal. App. 4th 1370, 12 Cal. Rptr. 2d 179, 181-82 (1992) ("far more is required to constitute 'the functional equivalent of questioning' than merely advising a person he is under arrest for a specific offense") *and People v. O'Sullivan*, 217 Cal. App. 3d 237, 265 Cal. Rptr. 784 (1990) (deputy's statement, "I believe I have something here," upon discovering contraband during a strip search, was not the functional equivalent of interrogation).

Third, there is authority that *Miranda* is inapplicable when the police question for a reason other than eliciting incriminating statements. In some instances, the California and federal cases are in agreement. For example, in *New York v. Quarles*, 467 U.S. 649 (1984), the Supreme Court recognized a public safety exception to *Miranda*; the Court permitted an officer to question a suspect about a weapon without a *Miranda* warning when the weapon posed a threat to the public safety. *People v. Dean*, 39 Cal. App. 3d 875, 882, 114 Cal. Rptr. 555, 559 (1974), is to the same effect. *People v. Simpson*, 65 Cal. App. 4th 854, 76 Cal. Rptr. 2d 851 (when police execute a search warrant upon the premises of a known drug trafficker, they may question the suspect about the presence of weapons without preceding the questions with *Miranda* warnings), *modified*, 66 Cal. App. 4th 231g (1998); *People v. Cressy*, 47 Cal. App. 981, 55 Cal. Rptr. 2d 237 (1996) (the public safety exception applied to questioning about other needles and drug paraphernalia on the defendant's person, since infected needles pose health hazards; however, the questioning must be narrowly tailored); *People v. Trichtler*, 48 Cal. App. 4th 367, 55 Cal. Rptr. 2d 650 (1996) (questioning about explosive devices); *People v. Stevenson*, 51 Cal. App. 4th 1234, 59 Cal. Rptr. 2d 878 (1996) (the officer had seen the suspect place his hand to his mouth and noted white residue in the suspect's mouth and the suspect was nervous and had an elevated heart rate; the officer reasonably believed that the suspect had consumed cocaine and the officer knew that a cocaine overdose can cause cardiac arrest); *People v. Chatman*, 61 Cal. App. 4th 1030, 71 Cal. Rptr. 2d 867 (*depublished opinion*) (the public safety exception applied to routine medical questions posed to arrestees prior to jailing to ensure the safety of the arrestee, other inmates, and the police; a jail nurse asked the defendant a routine question about his last drug use). However, in other instances, the California courts have been more restrictive than the federal courts. In dictum in *Rhode Island v. Innis*, 446 U.S. 291, 301 (1980), the Supreme Court stated that *Miranda* does not apply to routine questions asked during booking. *People v. Rucker*, 26 Cal. 3d 368, 605 P.2d 843, 162 Cal. Rptr. 13 (1980), and *People v. Morris*, 192 Cal. App. 3d 380, 237 Cal. Rptr. 402 (1987) extend *Miranda* to booking questions. *Contra, People v. Valentine*, 193 Cal. App. 3d 996, 238 Cal. Rptr. 668 (1987); *People v. Herbst*, 186 Cal. App. 3d 793, 800, 233 Cal. Rptr. 123 (1986) (Proposition 8 may overturn *Rucker*); *People v. Hall*, 199 Cal. App. 3d 914, 921, 245 Cal. Rptr. 458, 461-62 (1988) ("The rule announced in *Rucker* is not federally compelled. [A] majority of the federal circuit courts have held that incriminating evidence derived from a routine booking interview is admissible despite the fact that no *Miranda* warnings were given."). In *People v. Bradford*, 14 Cal. 4th 1005, 929 P.2d 544, 60 Cal. Rptr. 2d 225, 243 (1997), the California Supreme Court approvingly cited *Rhode Island v. Innis* and refused to apply *Miranda* to an officer's "casual statement" during booking.

Fourth, *Miranda* applies only if the defendant is "in custody." The defendant is certainly not in custody when the police question him over the phone. There is authority that so-called *Terry* stop is not custody for purposes of *Miranda*. *People v. Fulcher*, 194 Cal. App. 3d 749, 236 Cal. Rptr 845 (1987); *People v. Clair*, 2 Cal. 4th 629, 7 Cal. Rptr. 2d 564, 594-95, 828 P.2d 705 (1992), *cert. denied*, 506 U.S. 1063 (1993). Section I of this chapter discusses *Terry* and the concept of an investigatory stop. In deciding whether a person is in custody, the courts consider several factors: the place, time of day, and length of the interrogation; the use of weapons or other physical restraint; whether the suspect was present voluntarily; and whether the suspect was or felt free to leave. The test is whether "[a] reasonable person, ... under these circumstances, would believe that he had been deprived of his freedom in a significant way." *People v. Benally*, 208 Cal. App. 3d 900, 911, 256 Cal. Rptr. 483, 489 (1989) (officers unlocked the door to defendant's hotel room with a passkey, announced they were police officers, and entered with drawn guns). *In re Joseph R.*, 65 Cal. App. 4th 954, 76 Cal. Rptr. 2d 887 (a juvenile was not in custodial restraint; on the one hand, earlier he had been handcuffed and placed in a police car; on the other hand, before the questioning he was released from the car, the handcuffs were removed, he was never told that he was under arrest or would be arrested, and he was informed that he need not answer the questions), *modified*, 66 Cal. App. 4th 614a (1998); *People v. Whitfield*, 46 Cal. App. 4th 947, 54 Cal. Rptr. 2d 370 (1996) (the defendant was handcuffed); *People v. Aguilera*, 51 Cal. App. 4th 1151, 59 Cal. Rptr. 2d 587 (1996) (initially, the defendant had voluntarily agreed to an interview at the police station; however, the officers did not tell the defendant that he was free to terminate the interview, the "tag-team" interrogation lasted two hours, and the questioning was intense, accusatory, and at times, threatening). *See also People v. Bellomo*, 10 Cal. App. 4th 195, 10 Cal. Rptr. 2d 782, 784-85 (1992) (the California courts disagree over the question of whether the focus of the investigation on the defendant is an indicator of custody); *People v. Alcocer*, 230 Cal. App. 3d406, 282 Cal. Rptr. 5, 7-8 (1991) (citing *United States v. Mandujano*, 425 U.S. 564 (1976), the court held that there is no need to Mirandize grand jury witnesses); *People v. Berry*, 230 Cal. App. 3d 1449, 281 Cal. Rptr. 543, 545 (1991) (the trial judge need not "admonish all witnesses ... appearing before the court. ..."); *People v. Breault*, 223 Cal. App. 3d 125, 273 Cal. Rptr. 110 (1990) (the defendant was not in custody; he was in his own home, he was told that he was not under arrest, and he was neither handcuffed nor physically restrained); *People v. Mitchell*, 222 Cal. App. 3d 1306, 272 Cal. Rptr. 440 (1990) (the court ruled that the defendant was not in custody in part because the questioning occurred on the defendant's own front porch); *People v. Mayfield*, 14 Cal. 4th 668, 928 P.2d 485, 60 Cal. Rptr. 2d 1, *modified*, 15 Cal. 4th 231A (1997) (the defendant made the statement during a telephone conversation with police negotiators; at the time, the defendant was holding a hostage at gunpoint).

Suppose that the prosecutor wants to defeat a *Miranda* objection by showing that at the time of the questioning there was no custody. Assume that the People have charged the defendant Melindez with willfully falsifying his state income tax return. The witness is Ms. Aubright, an employee of the Franchise Tax Board. She proposes to testify about some damaging admissions that the defendant made to her. The defense objects that the statements are inadmissible because Ms. Aubright did not warn Melindez in accordance with *Miranda*. The proponent is the prosecutor.

P Ms. Aubright, WHERE were you on the morning of July 22, 1999?

W At my office in downtown Sacramento.

P WHAT happened that morning?

W I received a phone call from the defendant.

P HOW do you know that the caller was the defendant?

W I have had several conversations with him—some before that date and several since. I think I can recognize his voice pretty well.

P WHAT did the defendant say when he called?

W He said that he had just received a letter from me about an underpayment of taxes. He said that he wanted to get together and discuss the matter.

P WHO first brought up the possibility of a meeting—you or he?

W He was the one who asked for a personal meeting.

P WHAT else, if anything, did he say about the meeting?

W He said that his afternoon was free and he invited me to his office in Citrus Heights for the meeting.

P WHY did he want to meet in Citrus Heights?

W He said he'd feel more comfortable there. He added that he had a lot of records at his office that might help him answer some of my questions.

P WHAT did you say then?

W I agreed to meet him at his office at 2:30 that afternoon.

P WHAT did you do after you said that?

W I spent the rest of the morning at work, but early in the afternoon I jumped in my car and drove over to his office.

P WHERE is his office located?

W 1333 Fairlawn in Citrus Heights.
P WHAT did you do when you arrived there?
W I walked in, spoke with his secretary, and asked to see him.
P WHAT happened then?
W She ushered me into a big office to see the defendant.
P WHO was in the room?
W There were two other people—two other employees of his company. It was a big room, and they were off to the side in one work area. They were physically in the room, and I guess they could overhear some of the conversation. I'm not sure.
P WHAT time of day was this?
W I got to his office a little after 2:30, so I guess it was about 2:40 when I finally saw the defendant.
P HOW were you dressed at the time?
W I had on just normal clothes. We don't have uniforms or anything like that.
P WHAT weapons, if any, were you carrying?
W None. I carry a brief case with a copy of the Revenue and Taxation Code—that's my only weaponry if you want to call it that.
P WHAT threats, if any, did you make against the defendant during this conversation?
W None. I told him that I had just come to talk to him.
P WHAT did you say about your intention to stay to question him?
W I said something like I was there at his invitation and I'd leave whenever he asked me to.
P HOW long did you speak with the defendant that afternoon?
W I think the entire conversation lasted about 10 minutes. It became immediately apparent that we weren't going to make any headway in resolving his tax problem.

At that point, the prosecutor would attempt to elicit the defendant's incriminating statements. The preceding foundation should convince the judge that the defendant was not in custody and, hence, was not entitled to *Miranda* warnings.

2. COMPLIANCE WITH *MIRANDA*

In the second situation, the prosecutor argues that the police satisfied the requirements of *Miranda*. Typically, the argument requires proof of proper warnings, the suspect's understanding of the warnings, and a waiver of his or her rights.

California police usually warn suspects in the following fashion:

(1) You have the right to remain silent.

(2) If you give up the right to remain silent, anything you do say can and will be used in court against you.

(3) You have the right to speak with an attorney of your choice before questioning, and to have the attorney present during questioning.

(4) If you cannot afford an attorney, one will be appointed for you by the court before any questioning, if you so desire. The attorney will not cost

you anything; the services are free. Rael & Phillips, *Confessions and Admissions*, in CALIFORNIA CRIMINAL LAW § 30.38, at 743.

The courts have resisted attempts to require additional warnings. For example, in *In re Gregory Z.*, 190 Cal. App. 3d 1558, 235 Cal. Rptr. 918 (1987), *withdrawn*, in which the suspect was a minor, the court refused to require the police to inform the suspect of his parents' request to see him. *Accord In re John S.*, 199 Cal. App. 3d 441, 245 Cal. Rptr. 17, *cert. denied*, 488 U.S. 928 (1988). Similarly, *People v. Hill*, 3 Cal. 4th 959, 13 Cal. Rptr. 2d 475, 839 P.2d 984 (1992), *cert. denied*, 510 U.S. 963 438 (1993), holds that the defendant need not be advised that he could receive the death penalty if found guilty of the killings being investigated. Furthermore, in *California v. Prysock*, 453 U.S. 355, 359 (1981), the Supreme Court made it clear that the police need not quote the exact language used in the *Miranda* opinion. The California Supreme Court reached the same conclusion in *People v. Mayfield*, 5 Cal. 4th 142, 852 P.2d 331, 19 Cal. Rptr. 2d 836, *modified*, 5 Cal. 4th 853a (1993). In testifying about the warnings, police often vouch that they read warnings verbatim from a card. The prosecutor can then introduce the card to corroborate the officer's testimony. If the testimony establishes that an earlier warning was reasonably contemporaneous with a later interrogation, the police need not repeat the earlier warning. *People v. Visciotti*, 2 Cal. 4th 1, 825 P.2d 388, 5 Cal. Rptr. 2d 495, 524 (1992) ("only a few hours thereafter"); *People v. Mickle*, 54 Cal. 3d 140, 814 P.2d 290, 284 Cal. Rptr. 511 (1991) (only thirty-six hours later), *cert. denied*, 503 U.S. 988 (1992); *People v. Jacobo*, 230 Cal. App. 3d 1416, 281 Cal. Rptr. 750, 753 (1991) (collecting the cases).

The second element of the foundation is proof that the suspect understood the warnings. The police usually ask the suspect point blank: "Do you understand each of these rights that I have explained to you?" Rael & Phillips, *Confessions and Admissions*, in CALIFORNIA CRIMINAL LAW § 30.38, at 743. If the suspect answers Yes, the answer is admissible to prove the suspect's understanding; the answer is both a personal admission under Evidence Code § 1220 and a declaration of present state of mind under § 1250. Further, under *People v. Hurlic*, 14 Cal. App. 3d 122, 92 Cal. Rptr. 55 (1971), the officer may testify that the suspect "acknowledged" the warnings or "indicated" that he understood. Those expressions represent proper opinion testimony. 2 JEFFERSON § 29.1, at 982. The prosecution must establish "an uncoerced choice and the requisite level of comprehension." *People v. Whitson*, 17 Cal. 4th 229, 949 P.2d 18, 70 Cal. Rptr. 2d 321, 331 (1998). In determining whether the prosecution has met its burden, the trial judge uses a totality of the circumstances approach, even when the interrogee is a juvenile. *In re Bonnie H.*, 56 Cal. App. 4th 563, 65 Cal. Rptr. 2d 513 (1997).

Finally, the police solicit the waiver itself. They sometimes ask two questions: "Do you want a lawyer?" and "Do you wish to make a statement?" If the answer to the first question is "No," and the answer to the second question "Yes," the answers are ordinarily adequate to establish a knowing, intelligent waiver. Other police make it a practice to pose a single question: "Do you wish to speak with me?"

or "Do you wish to speak with me without a lawyer?" A "Yes" answer indicates a waiver.

Suppose, however, that the suspect does not give a classic waiver response. In *People v. Ashmus*, 54 Cal. 3d 932, 820 P.2d 214, 2 Cal. Rptr. 2d 112, 131 (1991), *cert. denied*, 506 U.S. 841 (1992), the court commented that the defendant "sought to alter the course of the questioning. But he did not attempt to stop it altogether." The defendant's response might be indecisive or ambiguous. *People v. Marshall*, 41 Cal. App. 3d 129, 115 Cal. Rptr. 821 (1974), allows the police to question the suspect further to clarify the suspect's intention. However, "a request for counsel need not be unequivocal to invoke the defendant's right to call a halt to questioning." *People v. Thompson*, 50 Cal. 3d 134, 165, 785 P.2d 857, 873, 266 Cal. Rptr. 309, 325 (1990), *cert. denied*, 498 U.S. 1043 (1991). "[A]ny ambiguity as to whether a person intended to invoke his or her *Miranda* rights should be resolved in favor of an invocation." *People v. Fuller*, 3 Cal. App. 4th 1220, 5 Cal. Rptr. 2d 112, 117 (1992). Thus, if the suspect refuses to sign a written waiver form, the refusal is often considered an unambiguous assertion of the right to remain silent. *People v. Fioritto*, 68 Cal. 2d 714, 719, 441 P.2d 625, 627, 68 Cal. Rptr. 817, 818 (1968). However, a suspect's mere refusal to allow tape-recording does not constitute an assertion of the right to remain silent. *People v. Samayoa*, 15 Cal. 4th 795, 938 P.2d 2, 64 Cal. Rptr. 2d 400 (1997).

Assume that the suspect explicitly asserts the right to remain silent. In *Michigan v. Mosley*, 423 U.S. 96 (1975), the Supreme Court held that that does not cut off all questioning. In *Mosley*, the police renewed interrogation on a different subject after a fresh warning. In the past, under the state constitution, California courts have balked at following *Mosley*. In *People v. Pettingill*, 21 Cal. 3d 231, 578 P.2d 108, 145 Cal. Rptr. 861 (1978), the court pointed out that there

> are variations on this theme; there may be more than two attempts at interrogation; the interval between interrogations may be long or short; at the start of the second or subsequent interrogation the police may or may not confront the suspect with additional evidence or statements of his accomplices; and the later questioning may be conducted by a different police officer, in a different location, and deal with a different crime.

Id. at 238, 578 P.2d at 112, 145 Cal. Rptr. at 865. *Pettingill* indicated that under prior California law, in all these variations of the fact pattern the statement is inadmissible. *People v. Navarez*, 169 Cal. App. 3d 936, 215 Cal. Rptr. 519 (1985), holds that *Pettingill* survived Proposition 8. However, in *People v. Warner*, 203 Cal. App. 3d 1122, 1129, 250 Cal. Rptr. 462, 466 (1988), the court declared that "[w]e ... disagree with *People v. Navarez* ... and hold that the standard for the admissibility of statements, relating to crimes committed after the enactment of Proposition 8, given to police by a suspect who previously invoked his right to remain silent is that of ... *Michigan v. Mosley*. ..." *See also* Uelman, *The California Constitution After Proposition Eight and the Crime Victims' Justice Reform Initiative of 1990*, 17 C.A.C.J. FORUM 34, 39 (Jan.-Feb. 1990) (citing

Warner and *People v. Harris*, 211 Cal. App. 3d 640 (1989)).

Lastly, suppose that the suspect clearly asserts the right to counsel, rather than generally invoking his *Miranda* rights or specifically invoking the privilege against self-incrimination. *People v. DeLeon*, 22 Cal. App. 4th 1265, 27 Cal. Rptr. 2d 818 (1994); *People v. Lispier*, 4 Cal. App. 4th 1317, 6 Cal. Rptr. 2d 639, 641 (1992) ("a general *Miranda* invocation is not the specific expression of the exercise of the right to counsel under *Miranda* which is a prerequisite to bar all contact by all police for all potential offenses"); *People v. Goodwin*, 235 Cal. App. 3d 342, 286 Cal. Rptr. 564, 567-68 (1991) (collecting cases finding an invocation of the right to counsel), *cert. denied*, 507 U.S. 933 (1993); although the collection of cases remains useful, the *Goodwin* opinion itself was depublished on Oct. 1, 1992 and may not be cited as authority. The suspect may not make an anticipatory assertion of the right to counsel even before being taken into police custody. *People v. Calderon*, 54 Cal. App. 4th 766, 63 Cal. Rptr. 2d 104 (1997). *Edwards v. Arizona*, 451 U.S. 477 (1981), indicates that after a suspect exercises that right, the police must terminate questioning about any criminal misconduct; unlike the Sixth Amendment right to counsel, the *Miranda* counsel right is not "offense specific." Questioning can begin again only if the suspect "initiates further communication, exchanges, or conversations with the police." *Id.* at 485. *People v. Denney*, 152 Cal. App. 3d 530, 540, 199 Cal. Rptr. 623, 627-28 (1984), is in accord.

The procedures for litigating a *Miranda* objection are similar to those for a voluntariness challenge. The judge rules finally on the issue under Evidence Code § 405. The federal standard for proof of a *Miranda* waiver is a mere preponderance of the evidence. *Colorado v. Connelly*, 479 U.S. 157 (1986).

To illustrate a waiver, we shall continue the hypothetical we used to demonstrate the voluntariness of a confession. The defendant is Mr. Walters, and the witness is Officer Gannon. The officer will attempt to establish that:

1. The police administered proper warnings.
2. The suspect understood the warnings.
3. The suspect knowingly, intelligently waived his rights.

P   After you gave the defendant the cigarettes and coffee, WHAT, if anything, did you say to him? (1)
W   I read him his rights.
P   HOW did you read him his rights? (1)
W   I read them verbatim from a warning card.
P   Your Honor, I request that this be marked People's exhibit number three for identification.
J   It will be so marked.
P   Please let the record reflect that I am showing the exhibit to the opposing counsel.
J   It will so reflect.
P   I request permission to approach the witness.
J   Permission granted.

P   Officer Gannon, I now hand you People's exhibit number three for identification. WHAT is it? (1)

W   It's the warning card I just referred to.

P   HOW can you recognize it? (1)

W   I initialed it, and I had the defendant initial it as well. I see the initials and the date we wrote in pencil on the card.

P   HOW did you use the card during the questioning? (1)

W   I read from it verbatim to make certain I gave the suspect the correct warnings.

P   Your Honor, I now offer People's exhibit number three for identification into evidence as exhibit three. (1)

J   It will be received.

P   Officer Gannon, please read prosecution exhibit three. (1)

W   It says: "You have a right to remain silent. Anything you say can and will be used against you in a court of law. You also have a right to an attorney. You have a right to consult an attorney before any questioning. You have a right to have an attorney present during any questioning. If you cannot afford an attorney, one will be appointed to represent you."

P   WHAT happened after you read Mr. Walters these rights? (2)

W   I asked him whether he understood his rights.

P   WHAT was his answer? (2)

W   He said he did.

P   HOW would you describe the defendant's demeanor when he said that he understood his rights? (2)

W   He seemed calm and clear headed.

P   WHAT happened then? (3)

W   I asked him whether he wanted an attorney.

P   WHAT was his response?

W   He said No.

P   WHAT happened then? (3)

W   I asked him whether he was willing to talk about the robbery.

P   WHAT was his response? (3)

W   He told me about the robbery.

P   WHAT did he say about the robbery? (6)

W   He said he had held up the McDonald's on 4th Street, and he was very sorry he had done it. He said he desperately needed money for rent, and he couldn't figure out any other way to get it.

V.   COUNSELLESS CONFESSIONS BARRED BY THE SIXTH AMENDMENT RIGHT TO COUNSEL

1. THE DOCTRINE

In one respect, *Miranda* confers a right to counsel on suspects. *Miranda* requires that the police warn suspects in custody that they may have counsel present during any interrogation. However, in the *Miranda* doctrine, the right to counsel serves as an adjunct to the Fifth Amendment privilege against self-incrimination. In some cases, the Sixth Amendment right to counsel itself applies. Suppose, for example, that the defendant has already been formally charged and has either appointed or retained counsel. At this juncture in the criminal justice process, the defendant is an "accused" within the meaning of that expression in the Sixth Amendment guaranteeing counsel. The right to counsel comes into play and limits the police's ability to interrogate the defendant in the absence of counsel. *Massiah v. United States*, 377 U.S. 201 (1964); *People v. Arguello*, 63 Cal. 2d 566, 407 P.2d 661, 47 Cal. Rptr. 485 (1965). The limitation applies to both overt police interrogation and questioning of the defendant by an undercover informant.

The *Massiah* doctrine is an important safeguard for the defendant; but like a *Miranda* objection, a *Massiah* objection can be defeated in several different ways.

The prosecutor can argue, for example, that the questioning occurred before the right to counsel attached. If the statement was made immediately after arrest, before the filing of any charges, *Miranda* applies but *Massiah* does not. The Sixth Amendment right to counsel "does not attach until a prosecution is commenced, that is, 'at or after the initiation of adversary judicial criminal proceedings— whether by way of formal charge, preliminary hearing, indictment, information, or arraignment.'" *People v. Clair*, 2 Cal. 4th 629, 7 Cal. Rptr. 2d 564, 580, 828 P.2d 705 (1992), *cert. denied*, 506 U.S. 1063 (1993). The right is "offense-specific. That is to say, it attaches to offenses as to which adversary judicial criminal proceedings have been initiated—and to such offenses alone." *Id.* Under Evidence Code § 452(d), the prosecutor can request judicial notice of the date on court documents such as the complaint, information, or indictment (California prosecutors rarely use indictments.).

Or the prosecutor can contend that, although the right to counsel had attached, the government agents did not interrogate the defendant. In *Kuhlmann v. Wilson*, 477 U.S. 436 (1986), the police intentionally placed an inmate informant in the defendant's cell. However, the informant did not question the defendant; the informant's role was passive—he merely listened to what the defendant had to say. The informant overheard incriminating statements. The Supreme Court held that the admission of the informant's testimony did not violate *Massiah. See also In re Williams*, 7 Cal. 4th 572, 870 P.2d 1072, 29 Cal. Rptr. 2d 64 (1994) (an informant's prior working relation with the police did not make him a police agent in the pending case); *People v. Memro*, 11 Cal. 4th 786, 905 P.2d 1305, 47 Cal. Rptr. 2d 219 (1995) (the person's past history of testifying for the government did not automatically make the person a "state agent"). In contrast, in *In re Wilson*, 3 Cal. 4th 945, 13 Cal. Rptr. 2d 269, 838 P.2d 1222 (1992), *cert. denied*, 507 U.S. 1006 (1993), the informant actively engaged the defendant in conversation and inquired about defendant's criminal plan.

Alternatively, the prosecutor can urge that although the defendant was charged with a crime and had counsel for that charge, the police questioned him about different crimes. If the prosecutor later uses any incriminating statements to prove only the other crimes, there is no *Massiah* violation. In *Maine v. Moulton*, 474 U.S. 159 (1985), the Court noted that the police may continue to investigate other crimes that they suspect the defendant of. In a footnote, the Court declared: "Incriminating statements pertaining to other crimes, as to which the Sixth Amendment right has not yet attached, are ... admissible at a trial of those offenses." *Id.* at 180 n.16. As previously stated, the Sixth Amendment right to counsel is "offense specific."

Finally, the prosecutor may argue that the defendant waived his or her Sixth Amendment right. That argument poses two subissues.

The threshold question is whether the *Massiah* right to counsel is waivable. There are California cases stating that the right cannot be waived. By way of example, *People v. Jacobs*, 181 Cal. App. 3d 916, 226 Cal. Rptr. 786 (1986), *withdrawn*, states that the *Massiah* rule absolutely forbids counselless interrogation even if the defendant wishes to waive the counsel right. However, *Brewer v. Williams*, 430 U.S. 387 (1977), and *Michigan v. Jackson*, 475 U.S. 625 (1986), express the Supreme Court's view that the right can be waived. *People v. Sultana*, 204 Cal. App. 3d 511, 519 n.3, 251 Cal. Rptr. 115, 118 n.3 (1988), *cert. denied*, 489 U.S. 1057 (1989), collects the California cases and notes that "[t]he California Supreme Court ha[s] not addressed that split of authority."

If the right is waivable, the next issue is the standard for waiver. As the Ninth Circuit has noted, the lower courts are badly split over this question. *United States v. Karr*, 742 F.2d 493 (9th Cir. 1984). The Ninth Circuit noted that some courts have held that a standard *Miranda* waiver is insufficient, and passages in *Michigan v. Jackson, supra*, point to that conclusion. *See also People v. Engert*, 193 Cal. App. 3d 1518, 239 Cal. Rptr. 169, 173-74 (1987). However, other courts are unpersuaded. These courts take the position that a waiver sufficient under the Fifth Amendment is also adequate under the Sixth Amendment. *Housel v. State*, 257 Ga. 115, 355 S.E.2d 651 (1987), *cert. denied*, 487 U.S. 1250 (1988).

2. ELEMENTS OF THE FOUNDATION

Suppose that the prosecutor decides to respond to a *Massiah* objection by arguing that the police informant did not actively question the defendant. To invoke *Kuhlmann*, the prosecutor should show that:

1. Before placing the informant in the defendant's cell, the police instructed the informant not to question the defendant. They instructed him to merely talk about his own background and listen carefully to the defendant's statements.
2. The informant carried out those instructions.
3. While listening to the defendant, the informant overheard an incriminating statement.

3. SAMPLE FOUNDATION

The People have charged the defendant Scott with robbery. The defendant was indicted on July 31, 1999. As of that date, he had assigned counsel. On August 2,

1993, the police placed an informant in the defendant's cell. The informant was a Mr. Superlo. Superlo is the witness, and the prosecutor is the proponent.

P   WHERE were you on the morning of August 2, 1999? (1)
W   I was in my cell on the second floor of the detention center downtown.
P   WHAT happened that morning? (1)
W   I was called into one of the interrogation rooms on the first floor.
P   WHAT happened there? (1)
W   I met a Deputy District Attorney by the name of So. He told me that they had a proposition for me.
P   WHAT was the proposition? (1)
W   They told me that they might be willing to help me with my pending charges if I helped them nail the defendant.
P   Specifically, WHAT did they ask you to do? (1)
W   They said that all I was supposed to do was go into the defendant's cell and keep my ears open.
P   WHAT instructions, if any, did they give you? (1)
W   They said that under no circumstances was I to question the guy about the robbery or any other crime. I was just to stay in the cell, tell him about myself, and listen for anything incriminating that he might say.
P   WHAT did you say after the Deputy District Attorney told you this? (1)
W   I said that I'd do it.
P   WHAT happened after you said you'd do it? (2)
W   The guards came in and led me to the defendant's cell on the third floor.
P   WHERE is the defendant now? (2)
W   He's sitting over there at the table to my right. He's the guy in the green jacket.
P   Your Honor, please let the record reflect that the witness has identified the defendant, Wilbert Scott.
J   The record will so reflect.
P   Mr. Superlo, WHAT happened after you entered the defendant's cell?
W   I did just what the D.A. told me to do.
P   Please be more specific. WHAT did you do? (2)
W   All I did was talk about my background—primarily my own criminal record—and keep my ears open.
P   WHAT questions, if any, did you pose to the defendant? (2).
W   None. I may have asked the guy for a cigarette, but I didn't ask the guy anything about the robbery or any other crimes. I did what I was told.
P   While you were in the defendant's cell. ...

The prosecutor would continue the questioning to elicit the defendant's incriminating statement.

W. THE USE OF AN OTHERWISE INADMISSIBLE STATEMENT FOR THE LIMITED PURPOSE OF IMPEACHING THE DEFENDANT'S CREDIBILITY

Suppose that the police obtain a defendant's statement in violation of *Miranda* or *Massiah* but that the statement is voluntary in the traditional, due process sense. At trial, the defendant testifies to facts inconsistent with the pretrial statement. During the prosecution rebuttal, may the prosecutor introduce the statement for the limited purpose of impeaching the defendant's credibility? *Harris v. New York*, 401 U.S. 222 (1971), dealt with the voluntary but unwarned statement. *Harris* held that the prosecutor may introduce the statement. The *Harris* Court reasoned that if the statement is voluntary, it is probably reliable. The Court concluded that the government interest in exposing the defendant's perjury at trial outweighs the policies inspiring *Miranda*. Assume alternatively that the statement is voluntary but violative of *Massiah*. The lower courts are divided over whether the impeachment exception extends to *Massiah*, and the Supreme Court has not had an occasion to resolve the split of authority.

In California, *People v. Disbrow*, 16 Cal. 3d 101, 545 P.2d 272, 127 Cal. Rptr. 360 (1976), rejected *Harris*. The *Disbrow* court invoked the state constitution. The court stated that under California law, a statement violative of *Miranda* may not be used even for the limited purpose of impeachment. *Disbrow* antedated Proposition 8; and in *People v. May*, 44 Cal. 3d 309, 748 P.2d 307, 243 Cal. Rptr. 369 (1988), the California Supreme Court held that Proposition 8 overturned *Disbrow*. Citing *May*, the courts have held that so long as the statement is voluntary, it may be used for impeachment even when the police intentionally violated *Miranda* (*People v. Brascombe*, 62 Cal. App. 4th 444, 72 Cal. Rptr. 2d 773 (1998)), or did so "purposefully … in order to secure evidence to be used for impeachment." *People v. Peevy*, 17 Cal. 4th 1184, 953 P.2d 1212, 73 Cal. Rptr. 2d 865, 872, *cert. denied*, 525 U.S. 1042 (1998). In *Peevy*, the court held that an individual officer's deliberate *Miranda* violation does not bar resort to the impeachment exception. However, the court left for another day the question of whether the same result would obtain if it were a police department's policy of training officers to violate *Miranda* in order to obtain impeachment material. Going beyond *May*, an intermediate appellate court has permitted the use of statements admissible under *Harris* to prove the defendant's breach of a plea agreement in a revocation proceeding. *People v. Collins*, 45 Cal. App. 4th 849, 53 Cal. Rptr. 2d 367 (1996). The court reasoned that *Harris* should apply to "a defendant who agrees to testify … pursuant to a plea bargain agreement" as well as "a defendant who testifies in his own behalf."

Although *Disbrow* barred the impeachment use of a statement violative of *Miranda* and a Sixth Amendment violation appears at least as serious as a *Miranda* violation, even before the *May* decision, *People v. Jacobs*, 181 Cal. App. 3d 916, 226 Cal. Rptr. 786 (1986), held that the prosecutor may use a statement violative of *Massiah* for impeachment. Over a vigorous dissent, the majority distinguished *Disbrow* on the ground that unlike *Miranda*, *Massiah* is "not intended to prevent police misconduct." *Id.* at 921, 226-Cal. Rptr. 788. However, on its facts, *People v. Ledesma*, 196 Cal. App. 3d 657, 241 Cal. Rptr. 876 (1987), *withdrawn*, seems at odds with *Jacobs*. Although the *Ledesma* court cited Fifth Amendment concerns rather than invoking the Sixth Amendment, in *Ledesma*, the police failed to inform the defendant that his attorney was waiting to speak with him. The court not only held the ensuing confession inadmissible; the court also stated that "it was ... error for the trial court to allow appellant to be impeached by the use of" the confession. *Id.* at 880. *People v. Harper*, 228 Cal. App. 3d 843, 279 Cal. Rptr. 204, 208-10 (1991), and *People v. Cribas*, 231 Cal. App. 3d 596, 282 Cal. Rptr. 538, 541-44 (1991), *cert. denied*, 503 U.S. 951 (1992), hold that the impeachment exception is inapplicable to a confession obtained in violation of the Sixth Amendment itself rather than a mere prophylactic rule. The most recent decision, *People v. Brown*, 42 Cal. App. 4th 461, 49 Cal. Rptr. 2d 652 (1996), recognizes the impeachment exception.

When the statement violates only *Miranda*, or when the statement violates *Massiah* and the judge decides to apply *Jacobs*, the prosecutor could offer the statement during rebuttal. The only required foundation would be proof of the voluntariness of the statement. Section S of this chapter illustrates a voluntariness foundation. Even if the prosecutor may introduce the statement, the defense is arguably entitled to a limiting instruction under Evidence Code § 355. The statement is admissible as a prior inconsistent statement under § 769 but not as a substantive, personal admission under § 1220 or § 1235. By their terms, §§ 1220 and 1235 would apply here, but *Harris* makes it clear that the impeachment exception applies only to the credibility use of the statement.

X. THE BAN ON THE ADMISSION OF UNCORROBORATED CONFESSIONS

1. THE DOCTRINE

Federal and California law have long recognized a corroboration requirement—the so-called *corpus delicti* rule—for confessions. Hagie, *The Operation, Legal Basis and Purpose of the Corpus Delicti Rule in California Criminal Law*, 15 LINCOLN L. REV. 53 (1984). The courts have doubts about the reliability of confessions; and to alleviate those doubts, the courts imposed the requirement that the prosecutor present independent evidence corroborating the trustworthiness of the confession. Although many commentators refer to the *corpus delicti* doctrine as a requirement for corroboration of the confession, in reality the doctrine simply requires the prosecutor to prove the commission of a crime before offering the confession. *People v. Towler*, 31 Cal. 3d 105, 641 P.2d 1253, 181 Cal. Rptr. 391 (1982). Prosecutors have argued that the adoption of the Evidence Code impliedly overturned the corroboration rule in California. However, in the one court test of that theory, *People v. Starr*, 11 Cal. App. 3d 574, 89 Cal. Rptr. 906 (1970), the court held that California law still demands corroboration. The court conceded that Evidence Code § 351 seems to sweep away decisional exclusionary rules of evidence, but the court concluded that the language of § 351 was not definite enough to overturn a doctrine as well-settled as the *corpus delicti* rule. One commentator has argued alternatively that the corroboration doctrine did not survive the passage of Proposition 8. Crisera, *Reevaluation of the California Corpus Delicti Rule: A Response to the Invitation of Proposition 8*, 78 CAL. L. REV. 1571, 1584-94 (1990). *See also People v. Culton*, 11 Cal. App. 4th 363, 14 Cal. Rptr. 2d 189, 195-97 (1992) (Timlin, J., concurring) (citing the California Law Review article, the judge concludes that "the corpus delicti rule has been abrogated. ...").

The question of the sufficiency of the corroborating evidence is an issue for the trial judge. The corroboration must establish both a social harm and criminal causation of the harm. HEAFEY § 27.2. However, the corroborating evidence need not show the defendant's identity as the perpetrator of the crime. *Id.* at § 27.4, at 253. (Once adequate corroboration has been presented, the confession becomes admissible to prove defendant's connection with the crime. *People v. Holmes*, 12 Cal. App. 4th 1094, 16 Cal. Rptr. 2d 52, 54 (1993).) The standard of proof is a prima facie case; standing alone, the corroborating evidence need not demonstrate the social harm or criminal agency beyond a reasonable doubt. *People v. Culton*, 11 Cal. App. 4th 363, 14 Cal. Rptr. 2d 189, 191 (1992) (the standard is "minimal" and "quite modest"; the corroboration can be adequate "even [if there is] an equally plausible noncriminal explanation of the incident"); *People v. Diaz*, 3 Cal. 4th 495, 11 Cal. Rptr. 2d 353, 365, 834 P.2d 1171 (1992) ("a slight ... showing"); *People v. Jennings*, 53 Cal. 3d 334, 807 P.2d 1009, 279 Cal. Rptr. 780, *cert. denied*, 502 U.S. 969 (1991); *People v. Johnson*, 233 Cal. App. 3d 425, 284 Cal. Rptr. 579, 585 (1991) ("slight or prima facie proof"), *cert. denied*, 503 U.S. 963 (1992); *People v. Ray*, 13 Cal. 4th 313, 914 P.2d 846, 52 Cal. Rptr. 2d 296 (1996); *People v. Hooker*, 55 Cal. App. 4th 1352, 64 Cal. Rptr. 2d 723 (1997); *People v. Jones*, 17 Cal. 4th 279, 949 P.2d 890, 70 Cal. Rptr. 2d 793, 806 (1998) ("we have described this quantum of evidence as 'slight' ... or 'minimal' .... The People need make only a prima facie showing 'permitting the reasonable inference that a crime was committed.' The inference need not be 'the only, or even the most compelling one ... [but need only be] a reasonable one'"). In evaluating the sufficiency of the evidence of the harm and causation, the judge must not consider the contents of the defendant's confession. However, the judge may weigh any other direct or circumstantial evidence. Rael & Phillips, *Confessions and Admissions*, in CALIFORNIA CRIMINAL LAW § 30.16, at 626.

The legislature defined the extent to which a complainant's out-of-court statement may be used to corroborate a defendant's confession in a child sex abuse prosecution by enacting Evidence Code § 1228. Crisera, *Reevaluation of the California Corpus Delicti Rule: A Response to the Invitation of Proposition 8*, 78 CAL. L. REV. 1571, 1595 (1990). Section 1228 reads:

Notwithstanding any other provision of law, for the purpose of establishing the elements of the crime in order to admit as evidence the confession of a person accused of violating Section 261, 264.1, 285, 186, 288, 288a, 289, or 647a of the Penal Code, a court, in its discretion, may determine that a statement of the complaining witness is not made inadmissible by the hearsay rule if it finds all of the following:

(a) The statement was made by a minor child under the age of 12, and the contents of the statement were included in a written report of a law enforcement official or an employee of a county welfare department.

(b) The statement describes the minor child as a victim of sexual abuse.

(c) The statement was made prior to the defendant's confession. The court shall view with caution the testimony of a person recounting hearsay where there is evidence of personal bias or prejudice.

(d) There are not circumstances, such as significant inconsistencies between the confession and the statement concerning material facts establishing any element of the crime or the identification of the defendant, that would render the statement unreliable.

(e) The minor child is found to be unavailable pursuant to paragraph (2) or (3) of subdivision (a) of Section 240 or refuses to testify.

(f) The confession was memorialized in a trustworthy fashion by a law enforcement official.

If the prosecution intends to offer a statement of the complaining witness pursuant to this section, the prosecution shall serve a written notice upon the defendant at least 10 days prior to the hearing or trial at which the prosecution intends to offer the statement. If the statement is offered during trial, the court's determination shall be made out of the presence of the jury. If the statement is found to be admissible pursuant to this section, it shall be admitted out of the presence of the jury and solely for the purpose of determining the admissibility of the confession of the defendant.

2. ELEMENTS OF THE FOUNDATION

To establish the corpus delicti, the prosecutor must offer independent evidence that:

1. A social harm, injury, or loss occurred.
2. Criminal agency was a contributing cause of the occurrence.

3. SAMPLE FOUNDATION

The People have charged the defendant Furillo with murder. Before trial, the defendant gave the police a confession. The defense argues that the confession is inadmissible because it is uncorroborated. An earlier witness, Officer Johnston, testified that he found a body at the defendant's apartment and helped transport the body to the medical examiner's office. The witness is Dr. Gantner, the assistant medical examiner. The proponent is the prosecutor. Dr. Gantner has already described his qualifications; he has testified that he is a physician licensed to practice in California and that he is board certified in the specialty of forensic pathology.

P Doctor, WHERE were you on the afternoon of October 13, 1999?

W I was at my office downtown.

P WHAT happened that afternoon? (1)

W I received word from the front desk that the police would soon be delivering a cadaver that they had discovered.

P WHAT happened then? (1)

W I went to the receiving dock to meet the police vehicle. It arrived about ten minutes later.

P WHO did you meet when the police vehicle arrived? (1)

W There were several officers, including Officer Johnston, who just left the witness stand.

P WHAT happened then? (1)

W The police delivered the cadaver to us.

P I now show you what has been marked as People's exhibit #2. WHAT is it? (1)

W It's a photograph of the cadaver, the one that Johnston used while he was testifying. This is the body they delivered to me that afternoon.

P WHAT did you do after they delivered the body? (1)

W I had some of our attendants load the body on a cart and wheel it to Examination Room #3 on the first floor.

P WHAT did you do after the body reached the examination room? (1)

W The first thing I did was to examine the body carefully for any signs of life.

P WHAT was the result of the examination? (1)

W The person was unquestionably dead. There were no signs of circulatory, respiratory, or brain activity.

P WHAT else, if anything, did you observe about the body? (2)

W There were two observations in particular that were significant.

P WHAT were they? (2)

W One was a number of stab wounds—five, to be exact—in the back.

P WHY were those wounds significant? (2)

W It would have been physically impossible for the victim to have stabbed himself in those locations. The location of the wounds immediately ruled out any possibility of suicide as the manner or mode of death. I knew at that point that we had either a homicide or a remote possibility of an accident on our hands.

P WHAT was the other observation you made? (2)

W I carefully examined all the extremities, especially the hands. There were a number of cuts on the back of both hands—short lacerations.

P WHY were those lacerations significant? (2)

W They're what we call "defense wounds"—the sort of cuts that a victim often gets when he's trying to fight off an attacker with a knife. These wounds result when the victim tries to grab the knife away from the attacker. You often find them on the hands, fingers, and forearms. The location and depth of the lacerations both were indicative of defense wounds. Together, the location of the stab wounds on the back and the presence of characteristic defense wounds on the backs of both hands lead me to conclude that this was a homicide rather than either suicide or an accident.

Y. PROSECUTORS' ATTEMPTS TO ELICIT JUDICIAL CONFESSIONS DURING THE DEFENDANT'S CROSS-EXAMINATION

1. THE DOCTRINE

Sections R-X of this chapter analyze the limitations on the admission of the defendant's out-of-court or extrajudicial confessions and admissions. However, the prosecutor is not limited to out-of-court statements by the defendant. If the defendant testifies at trial, the defendant is subject to cross-examination, and the prosecutor may attempt to elicit the defendant's in-court confession or admission during cross.

When a defendant opts to testify, to some extent the defendant waives the protection of the Fifth Amendment privilege. To this date, the Supreme Court has not authoritatively defined the scope of the waiver. Federal Rule of Evidence 608(b) offers some guidance: "The giving of testimony ... by an accused ... does not operate as a waiver of his privilege against self-incrimination when examined with respect to matters which relate only to credibility." However, when a defendant testifies, it is hard for the defendant to confine the testimony solely to credibility matters; almost inevitably, the defendant will give some testimony about the historical merits. Suppose, for example, that the defendant is charged with a specific intent offense. On direct examination, the defendant denies entertaining the specific mens rea required for the charged offense. On cross-examination, the prosecutor may certainly question the defendant further about the mens rea element of the crime.

The unsettled question is whether the prosecutor may query the defendant about other elements of the crime that the defendant did not testify about. *See United States v. Hearst*, 563 F.2d 1331 (9th Cir. 1977), *cert. denied*, 435 U.S. 1000 (1978). The answer may lie in an interplay between the Fifth Amendment privilege and the law governing the scope of cross-examination. The courts may ultimately adopt the view that a defendant waives the Fifth Amendment privilege only to the extent of the scope of proper cross-examination permitted in the jurisdiction. Evidence Code § 773(a) limits the scope of the cross-examination to "any matter within the scope of the direct examination ...." For that reason, when a California prosecutor is arguing against a defense objection that the privilege precludes a certain cross-examination question, it is ideal if the prosecutor can point out that the question is logically relevant to an issue that the defendant's direct testimony touched upon.

2. ELEMENTS OF THE FOUNDATION

To prove a waiver permitting cross-examination questions seeking a judicial confession, the prosecutor should establish that:

1. The defendant testified about the historical merits on direct examination.
2. In doing so, the defendant explicitly or implicitly mentioned a particular element of the crime.
3. The proposed cross-examination question relates to the same element of the crime.

The prosecutor usually presents this argument at a sidebar conference after the defense objects on privilege grounds.

3. SAMPLE FOUNDATION

The People have charged the defendant Bermudez with assaulting Ms. Gertrude Wilhelm on September 28, 1999. The information alleges that the defendant committed the assault at approximately 11:00 p.m. near the intersection of Third and Mission Streets in downtown San Francisco. The defendant testified. During his testimony, the defendant denied any involvement in the assault. The defendant testified to an alibi; he claimed that on the night in question, he was in Vallejo, California. The prosecutor has evidence that she believes is admissible under Evidence Code § 1101(b). Another assault victim, Ms. Sanchez, is prepared to testify that she was attacked at 11:20 p.m. near the intersection of Fifth and Mission Streets in San Francisco on the same night. She is prepared to identify the defendant as the attacker. The prosecutor is attempting to cross-examine the defendant about the other assault to attack the defendant's alibi. The prosecutor is the proponent:

P Mr. Bermudez, is it your testimony that at approximately 11:00 p.m. on the evening of September 28, 1999, you were in Vallejo—miles away from downtown San Francisco?

W Right. And that's the truth.

P And is it also your testimony that you were in Vallejo at 11:20 that night?

O Objection, your Honor. May we approach the bench?

J Yes.

O Your Honor, I have reason to believe that this line of questioning is aimed at proving an uncharged crime by my client—an alleged attack on another woman, a woman by the name of Ms. Sanchez, in downtown San Francisco, at 11:20 p.m. in San Francisco. My client testified, but he testified only about the crime that he's presently charged with. The Fifth Amendment privilege precludes the prosecutor from asking him about a separate crime.

P Your Honor, may I respond?

J Yes.

P   It's obvious that the defendant has voluntarily testified on the merits of this case. (1) Specifically, he gave alibi testimony and denied he was in the vicinity of the charged assault at 11:00 that night. (2) It's true that on its face, this line of cross-examination relates to another, uncharged crime. However, in reality it's not only relevant to the charged crime; it's relevant to the same element of the charged crime that the defendant expressly denied on direct. (3) He says that he was in Vallejo at 11:00 p.m. You can judicially notice, your Honor, that Vallejo is a good 40 minute drive from downtown San Francisco. If he was, attacking Ms. Sanchez at 11:20 near Fifth and Mission Streets, he in all probability was not in Vallejo at 11:00 p.m. This line of cross-examination is designed to attack the alibi testimony that he expressly gave on direct.

J   I agree. Objection overruled. Proceed.

P   Mr. Bermudez, perhaps you've forgotten my question. Let me ask it again. Is it your testimony that you were in Vallejo at 11:20 the evening of September 28, 1999?

Part 3. Eyewitness Testimony

Z.   IN GENERAL

There are also constitutional restrictions on the admissibility of eyewitness testimony. There are, for example, Fourth, Fifth, and Sixth Amendment restrictions on eyewitnesses' testimony about pretrial identifications of the defendant at lineups. If the judge concludes that the eyewitness's pretrial identification of the defendant violates a constitutional restriction, the violation can conceivably result in barring the eyewitness from making an in-court identification.

AA.   THE APPLICATION OF THE FOURTH AMENDMENT TO TESTIMONY ABOUT AN EYEWITNESS'S PRETRIAL IDENTIFICATION OF THE DEFENDANT

1. AN IDENTIFICATION MADE DURING THE DETENTION FOLLOWING AN ILLEGAL ARREST

Suppose that the police illegally arrest the defendant and that during the period of detention following the unlawful arrest, an eyewitness identifies the defendant at a lineup. The Fourth Amendment exclusionary rule bars the admission of not only the illegally seized evidence but also other evidence derived from the illegal seizure. In this scenario, the eyewitness's pretrial lineup identification derives from the earlier, illegal arrest. If at trial the prosecutor attempts to elicit the eyewitness's testimony about the earlier identification, the defense may object on Fourth Amendment grounds.

The leading precedents for this doctrine are *Davis v. Mississippi*, 394 U.S. 721 (1969), and *Johnson v. Louisiana*, 406 U.S. 356 (1972). In *Davis*, the police arrested the defendant in an illegal dragnet roundup of suspects. During the period of illegal detention, the police fingerprinted Davis. At trial, the prosecutor introduced the fingerprint evidence. The Court held that the Fourth Amendment required the exclusion of the fingerprint evidence. In *Johnson*, the Court made it clear that *Davis* applies to any type of identification evidence derived from an illegal arrest. In *Johnson*, the issue was the admissibility of testimony about an eyewitness's pretrial identification of the defendant. The Court sustained the admission of the testimony, but only on the theory that the taint of the illegal arrest had attenuated because a magistrate had lawfully committed the defendant after the arrest but before the lineup.

Suppose that the judge has already ruled that the defendant's arrest was illegal. Nevertheless, the prosecutor might attempt to offer testimony at trial about an eyewitness's identification of the defendant at a postarrest lineup. To suppress the identification, the defense would have to establish that:

1. The defendant was arrested on a certain date.
2. The defendant was not released until a certain date.
3. The lineup or showup occurred between those two dates.

The defendant could testify from personal knowledge to the dates of the arrest, lineup, and later release. If the prosecutor wanted to invoke the *Johnson* theory, the prosecutor could offer testimony about an intervening, attenuating event. Under Evidence Code § 452(d), the prosecutor could request judicial notice of a court order reflecting the defendant's commitment before the date of the lineup. Or the prosecutor could cross-examine the defendant or offer police testimony to the effect that the police informed the defendant of the illegality of the initial arrest and that the defendant then consented to appear in the lineup. Either the defendant's informed consent or a commitment would probably cut off the taint of the unlawful arrest.

2. AN IDENTIFICATION BY A WITNESS WHOSE IDENTITY THE POLICE DISCOVERED BY EXPLOITING THE DEFENDANT'S ILLEGAL ARREST

There is another fact situation in which the Fourth Amendment can lead to the suppression of identification testimony. Suppose that the police illegally arrest and then interrogate the defendant. The statements the defendant makes can often be excluded as the fruit of the poisonous tree—evidence derived from the illegal arrest. However, suppose that the statements reveal the identity of a witness to the defendant's crime. Following up on the statements, the police contact the potential witness and offer her testimony at trial against the defendant. Can the defendant suppress the witness's testimony as the fruit of the poisonous tree? The federal and California courts both have indicated that in extreme cases, the witness's identification testimony can be suppressed. *United States v. Ceccolini*, 435 U.S. 268 (1978); *Bowden v. United States*, 324 F.2d 879 (D.C. Cir. 1963), *cert. de-*

nied, 377 U.S. 954 (1964); *People v. Superior Court (Sosa),* 31 Cal. 3d 883, 649 P.2d 696, 185 Cal. Rptr. 113 (1982).

Ceccolini is the leading case in point. Justice Rehnquist authored the lead opinion. On the one hand, the Court made it clear that it would be willing to exclude a witness's entire testimony as a fruit of the poisonous tree only in rare cases. On the other hand, the Court "reject[ed] the Government's suggestion that we adopt what would in practice amount to a per se rule that the testimony of a live witness should not be excluded at trial no matter how close and proximate the connection between it and a violation of the Fourth Amendment." 435 U.S. at 274-75. Justice Rehnquist listed a number of factors relevant to determining whether the witness's testimony should be altogether excluded. One is whether the police knew of the witness's identity before they illegally obtained the statement referring to the witness. *Id.* at 279. Another factor is the length of time between the defendant's statement and the contact with the witness. *Id.* The longer the period of time is, the greater is the probability that intervening events will attenuate the effect of the earlier, illegal arrest. Another key factor is the voluntariness of the witness's decision to testify against the defendant. "The greater the willingness of the witness to freely testify, the greater the likelihood that he or she will be discovered by legal means and, concomitantly, the smaller the incentive to conduct an illegal search to discover the witness." *Id.* at 276. In *Ceccolini,* the Court found that "the testimony given by the witness was an act of her own free will ...." *Id.* at 279. The Court stressed that there was no evidence that the police had coerced the witness into testifying.

To suppress an identification on this theory, the defense should attempt to establish:

1. The defendant was illegally arrested on a certain date.
2. The defendant made a statement so shortly after the illegal arrest that the statement is inadmissible derivative evidence.
3. The statement was the first notice to the police that a potential witness to the defendant's alleged crime existed.
4. The police immediately contacted that witness.
5. The police coerced that witness into testifying against the defendant.

The most difficult problem of proof for the defense is typically element #5. When the witness in question is cooperative, the witness may be willing to testify directly to his or her motivation for furnishing incriminating testimony. In other cases, however, by the time of this pretrial hearing the witness will be hostile to the defense; at the hearing, the witness may insist that he is cooperating freely and out of a sense of civic duty. If the defense attorney can find evidence of inconsistent statements by the witness, the defense attorney may be able to introduce those statements as: nonhearsay evidence (circumstantial evidence of state of mind) under Evidence Code § 1200(a), state of mind declarations under §§ 1250-51, or inconsistent statements admissible both for impeachment and as substantive proof under § 1235. The defense may also be able to use police testimony to show the witness's motivation. The police reports, for example, may reflect that the police had to interrogate the witness for eight straight hours, question the witness on five separate occasions before the witness agreed to cooperate, or threaten the witness to induce cooperation. The defense can use the reports and live police testimony to establish such facts which circumstantially suggest that the witness's decision to testify was not an act of free will.

BB. THE APPLICATION OF THE FIFTH AND FOURTEENTH AMENDMENTS TO TESTIMONY ABOUT AN EYEWITNESS'S PRETRIAL IDENTIFICATION OF THE DEFENDANT

1. THE DOCTRINE

Like the Fourth Amendment prohibition of unreasonable searches and seizures, the Fifth and Fourteenth Amendment due process clauses restrict the admission of eyewitness testimony. In *Stovall v. Denno*, 388 U.S. 293 (1967), the Court announced that due process forbids the introduction of testimony about a pretrial identification conducted in an intolerably suggestive fashion. Later in *Foster v. California*, 394 U.S. 440 (1969), the Court found the lineup in that case to have been conducted in violation of *Stovall*.

The California case law not only follows *Stovall* and *Foster*; the California decisions anticipated the federal case law. In *People v. Caruso*, 68 Cal. 2d 183, 436 P.2d 336, 65 Cal. Rptr. 336 (1968), the defendant was the only person in the lineup who matched the victims' description of the robber. The court found that the makeup of the lineup was grossly unfair. The court held that the admission of testimony about the lineup denied the defendant due process. In *Foster, supra*, the United States Supreme Court cited *Caruso*.

The due process doctrine can be stated simply: There is a denial of due process when the circumstances surrounding the lineup or showup make the confrontation unnecessarily suggestive and conducive to mistaken identification. The doctrine poses three questions.

Was the manner in which the confrontation was conducted suggestive? To answer that question, the judge must consider the conduct of all major participants in the confrontation. The fillers are the persons in the lineup other than the defendant. The defendant and the fillers all should possess the most outstanding characteristics mentioned in the eyewitnesses' description of the perpetrator. The individual fillers should not be told the identity of the suspect; otherwise, their nonverbal conduct might direct the viewers' attention to the defendant. It does not automatically violate due process to use police personnel as fillers, but it is a practice to be avoided. While they are viewing the lineup and making their individual identifications, the eyewitnesses should be separated; if they mingle, one eyewitness may influence another. The police conducting the lineup should refrain from suggestive comments. It is best if the officer in charge of the lineup is not personally involved in the investigation. As a practical matter, the courts are tolerant of less than ideal lineup procedures. *See People v. DeSantis*, 2 Cal. 4th 1198, 9 Cal. Rptr. 2d 628, 641-42, 831 P.2d 1210 (1992) ("Defendant bears the burden of showing unfairness as a demonstrable reality, not just speculation"; a photographic display was proper although the witness described the perpetrator as wearing a red jacket and the defendant was the only person depicted wearing red; the lineup in question was proper even though the defendant was the only person common to both the lineup and the photographic display and despite the fact that during the lineup, he stood on books concealed from the viewer to mask defendant's stature.), *cert. denied*, 508 U.S. 917 (1993); *People v. Wimberly*, 5 Cal. App. 4th 773, 7 Cal. Rptr. 2d 152, 160 (1992) ("California and federal courts have rejected the argument that identification procedures are impermissible suggestive if the defendant is the only person appearing in both a display of photographs and a subsequent lineup.").

If the lineup was suggestive, was the suggestive feature unnecessary? A showup, a one-on-one confrontation between the defendant and an eyewitness, is inherently suggestive. When the police present only one person for the eyewitness to view, there is an obvious suggestion that he or she is the perpetrator. *In re Hill*, 71 Cal. 2d 997, 458 P.2d 449, 80 Cal. Rptr. 537 (1969), *cert. denied sub nom. Saunders v. California*, 397 U.S. 1017 (1970), recognized this danger. *Hill* states that the police may use a showup only when there are compelling circumstances. However, in *Stovall* itself, the Supreme Court permitted a suggestive showup. The victim had been seriously injured and had been taken to a hospital for major surgery. The police took the defendant to the victim's hospital room the day after surgery. The defendant was the only black person in the room. The Court held that in the totality of the circumstances, the showup was justified. The victim was the sole surviving witness to the crime; and since the victim's death was a distinct possibility, it was critical for the police to show the suspect to the victim as soon as possible. In *People v. Yonko*, 196 Cal. App. 3d 1005, 1008, 242 Cal. Rptr. 269, 271 (1987), the court commented that "[a] single person photographic showup is not inherently unfair and violative of due process."

Even if the confrontation was unnecessarily suggestive, testimony about the identification at the confrontation is not automatically inadmissible. *People v. Contreras*, 17 Cal. App. 4th 813, 21 Cal. Rptr. 2d 496 (1993). In *Neil v. Biggers*, 409 U.S. 188 (1972), and *Manson v. Brathwaite*, 432 U.S. 98 (1977), the Supreme Court clarified the due process test. In Neil, the majority opinion, authored by now Chief Justice Rehnquist, emphasized that the central concern of the due process clause is the reliability of identification. The Court stated that the test is whether the circumstances surrounding the confrontation create a substantial likelihood of mistaken identification. If the circumstances do not create that probability, testimony about the pretrial identification is admissible. In determining whether that probability exists, the judge may consider the following factors, inter alia: witness's opportunity to view the perpetrator at the time of the crime; the witness's degree of attention; the accuracy of the witness's prelineup description of the perpetrator; the witness's degree of certitude; and the length of time between the crime and the confrontation.

2. ELEMENTS OF THE FOUNDATION

Suppose that the prosecutor decides to argue that the lineup was conducted in a proper, nonsuggestive fashion. The foundational testimony should include a description of the conduct of all major lineup participants:

1. The officer in charge of the lineup.
2. The fillers.
3. The eyewitnesses.
4. The defendant.

3. SAMPLE FOUNDATION

The People have charged the defendant Winters with armed robbery. On July 7, 1999, the police conducted a lineup at which two eyewitnesses singled out the defendant as the robber. The defense has filed a pretrial motion to suppress any testimony about the lineup identifications of the defendant. The prosecutor decides to argue that the lineup procedure was not suggestive. The witness is Officer Norris, who was in charge of the lineup. The prosecutor is the proponent.

P Officer Norris, before conducting this lineup, WHAT connection did you have with this case? (1)

W None. I wasn't at all involved in the investigation. The first I heard about it was that morning.

P WHAT happened that morning? (1)

W The deputy chief's office phoned to say that they wanted me to arrange a lineup for the defendant.

P WHAT did you do then? (2)

W The first thing I did was to read the reports about the crime. I wanted to make sure I knew the eyewitnesses' descriptions of the robber. After reading them, I knew that they had described the robber as a white male, approximately 5 feet 10 inches tall, maybe 160-70 pounds, brown hair with no evident distinguishing characteristics.

P After you learned that, WHAT did you do? (2)

W I went down to the cellblock and pulled out the defendant and five other prisoners.

P HOW did you choose the five other prisoners? (2)

W I made sure that they all pretty much matched the description of the robber.

P HOW well did they match the description? (2)

W Quite well. One guy was a little heavy set—maybe close to 200 pounds, and another was about six feet, but otherwise the group matched all the key features in the description.

P WHAT was the race of each person in this lineup? (2)

W They all were white.

P HOW were they dressed? (2)

W They all, including the defendant, where wearing the same type of prisoner uniform.

P   WHAT did you do after you gathered the defendant and the five other prisoners? (2)

W   I took them down to the Lineup Room.

P   WHERE is that room? (3)

W   In the same building.

P   HOW would you describe the room? (3)

W   There is an elevated stage where the suspect and the fillers stand.

P   WHERE do you put the eyewitnesses in the room? (3)

W   We have four different tables in the room. One eyewitness sits at each table.

P   WHO else sits at the table? (3)

W   No one else during the lineup itself. They sit there alone.

P   HOW close are the tables? (3)

W   The tables are about ten feet apart.

P   HOW many tables did you use for this lineup? (3)

W   Since there were only two eyewitnesses, Green and Schmidt, we needed only two tables.

P   WHICH tables did you use? (3)

W   I used the tables farthest apart—the two at the sides of the room.

P   HOW far apart are those tables? (3)

W   They're about twenty-five or thirty feet apart.

P   WHAT happened after you seated the eyewitnesses at those tables? (4)

W   One by one, I had the men in the lineup step forward and slowly turn around so that the eyewitnesses could view them.

P   WHAT, if anything, did you order the defendant to do that you didn't order the other five men to do? (4)

W   Nothing. I asked them all to do the very same thing.

P   WHAT, if anything, did you ask the defendant to say during the lineup that you didn't ask the other five men to say? (4)

W   Again nothing. I didn't ask any of them to say anything. The reports indicated that the robber hadn't spoken, so it was a waste of time to try for a voice identification.

P   While the six men were on the stage, WHAT communication, if any, was there between the two eyewitnesses? (3)

W   None. At least I didn't hear them talk. I didn't see them look at each other. As far as I could tell, they just eyeballed the men in the lineup.

P   WHAT happened after the lineup? (3)

W   I spoke with the eyewitnesses.

P   HOW did you speak with them—together or individually? (3)

W   I went to each table and spoke with that eyewitness individually. The other eyewitness was at the other table at the time.

P   WHAT did you say to each eyewitness? (1)

W   I didn't make any statements to them. I just asked them questions.

P   WHAT questions did you ask? (1)

W   Just three. First, I asked them whether anyone on the lineup resembled the robber. Second, if anyone did, I told them to write down the number of that person. Everyone in the lineup has a number. Third, if they identified someone then I asked them how certain they were that that guy was the robber.

CC. THE APPLICATION OF THE SIXTH AMENDMENT RIGHT TO COUNSEL TO TESTIMONY ABOUT AN EYEWITNESS'S PRETRIAL IDENTIFICATION OF THE DEFENDANT

1. THE DOCTRINE

The Sixth Amendment right to counsel completes the trilogy of constitutional restraints on the admissibility of testimony about pretrial identifications of a defendant. In *Gilbert v. California*, 388 U.S. 263 (1967) and *United States v. Wade*, 388 U.S. 218 (1967), the Supreme Court declared that the right to counsel applies at lineups. The Court reasoned that the lineup can be a critical phase of the investigation and that counsel is needed at the lineup to protect the defendant's right to effectively cross examine the eyewitnesses at trial. In *Kirby v. Illinois*, 406 U.S. 682 (1972), the Court limited the right to counsel at lineups. The Court stated that the right does not attach unless the confrontation occurs after "the initiation of adversary judicial criminal proceedings ... by way of formal charge, preliminary hearing, indictment, information, or arraignment." *Id.* at 689. Applying these precedents, many lower courts restrict the right to counsel to the lineup itself; they have held that if the police question the eyewitnesses immediately after the viewing, the defense counsel has no right to be present.

California has broadened the right to counsel at lineups in two respects. First, an early decision, *People v. Williams*, 3 Cal. 3d 853, 478 P.2d 942, 92 Cal. Rptr. 6 (1971), accords the defense attorney the right to be present during the postlineup interview of the eyewitnesses. In *Williams*, after the lineup the sheriff's officers questioned the principal witness in a nearby room. The officers refused to permit the defense attorney to attend and overhear the interview. The court held that the refusal was error. The court emphasized that the interview was the most important part of the lineup process, since the police solicited the actual identification during the interview. However, more recently, in *People v. Mitcham*, 1 Cal. 4th 1027, 824 P.2d 1277, 5 Cal. Rptr. 2d 230 (1992), the California Supreme Court held that the right to counsel is inapplicable to a postlineup interview. The court reasoned that the lineup procedure was complete when the witness filled out and signed an identification card to indicate that she recognized the defendant. The court reached this conclusion although the witness added a question mark to the card and the purpose of the interview was to clarify the question mark on the card.

Second, the California courts have extended the right to counsel to lineups occurring before the initiation of formal charges. In *People v. Fowler*, 1 Cal. 3d 335, 461 P.2d 643, 82 Cal. Rptr. 363 (1969), the court recognized the right to counsel at a preindictment lineup. *Fowler* antedated *Kirby*; but the California Supreme Court reaffirmed *Fowler* in a post-*Kirby* decision, *People v. Bustamante*, 30 Cal. 3d 88, 634 P.2d 927, 177 Cal. Rptr. 576 (1981). It is uncertain whether Proposition 8 will persuade the California courts to abandon *Bustamante* and embrace the *Kirby* limitation on the scope of the right to counsel. English & Neidorf, *Lineups and Identification*, in CALIFORNIA CRIMINAL LAW § 19.4, at 379 (1986). In June 1990, the California electorate approved Proposition 115. In pertinent part, the proposition read that

> [i]n criminal cases the right[] of a defendant ... to the assistance of counsel ... shall be construed by the courts of this state in a manner consistent with the Constitution of the United States. This Constitution shall not be construed by the courts to afford greater rights to criminal defendants than those afforded by the Constitution of the United States. ...

However, the California Supreme Court invalidated this part of the proposition on procedural grounds. *Raven v. Deukmejian*, 52 Cal. 3d 336, 801 P.2d 1077, 276 Cal. Rptr. 326 (1990). Butterworth, *Lineups and Identification*, CALIFORNIA CRIMINAL LAW: PROCEDURE AND PRACTICE § 19.4, at 436 (2d ed. 1994).

Even if the right to counsel would otherwise attach to a pretrial confrontation between the defendant and an eyewitness, the prosecutor has several theories for defeating a right to counsel objection:

- The right to counsel does not apply to photographic spreads. The right applies only to in-person, corporeal confrontations. *United States v. Ash*, 413 U.S. 300 (1973).

- The right does not apply to in-the-field, on-scene identifications shortly after the crime. *In re Richard W.*, 91 Cal. App. 3d 960, 971, 155 Cal. Rptr. 11, 19 (1979). The victim's memory is fresher at an on-scene confrontation. Further, an on-scene confrontation can quickly clear the innocent and let the police know immediately that they must continue searching for the perpetrator.

- The confrontation between the defendant and the eyewitness was accidental. The eyewitness may be sitting outside an office at the police station, and by happenstance the arresting officers walk the defendant past that office. The right to counsel does not attach to inadvertent confrontations.

- The defendant waived his or her right to counsel at the lineup. To obtain an effective waiver, the police must explicitly inform the defendant of the right to counsel at the lineup. *People v. Banks*, 2 Cal. 3d 127, 465 P.2d 263, 84 Cal. Rptr. 367 (1970). A general *Miranda* advisement is insufficient.

- The defendant lost the right to counsel because, after the police contacted the defense attorney, the attorney delayed unreasonably in coming to the site of the lineup. In *People v. Keim*, 8 Cal. App. 3d 776, 87 Cal. Rptr. 597 (1970), the court acknowledged the possibility that the defendant could lose the right to counsel by counsel's delay. However, on the facts of that case (a mere half hour wait) the court concluded that the police did not wait long enough for counsel to arrive.

- The police afforded counsel to the defendant. The counsel need not be the same lawyer who later represents the defendant at the suppression hearing or trial. In *Wade*, the Supreme Court stated that "[a]lthough the right to counsel usually means a right to the suspect's own counsel, provision for a substitute counsel may be justified on the ground that the substitute counsel's presence may eliminate the hazards which render the lineup a critical stage for the presence of suspect's own counsel." 388 U.S. 218, 237 n.27. Although the California courts have not passed on this issue, both federal courts and those of other states have upheld the practice of appointing substitute counsel for lineups.

2. ELEMENTS OF THE FOUNDATION

Assume that the prosecutor attempts to defeat a Sixth Amendment objection by showing that the defendant waived the right to counsel at a lineup. The foundation would be similar to the one for a *Miranda* waiver:

1. The police informed the defendant that he had the right to an attorney present at the lineup.
2. The defendant understood the information.
3. The defendant then waived the right to counsel.

3. SAMPLE FOUNDATION

The People have charged the defendant, Mr. Bryon, with rape. The day after the arrest, the police placed Bryon in a lineup viewed by the rape victim. It is undisputed that Bryon did not have counsel at the lineup. The witness is Officer Sheehan who was in charge of the lineup. The prosecutor is the proponent:

P WHERE were you early in the afternoon of October 16 of this year?
W I was at headquarters on Drum Street.
P WHAT were you doing then?
W I was arranging a lineup in connection with a rape that occurred the day before.
P WHO was going to be in this lineup?
W The defendant and four other guys who matched the description of the rapist.
P WHEN did you see the defendant that afternoon? (1)
W Actually, I first met with him late that morning.
P WHY did you meet with him then?
W I knew we had scheduled the lineup, and I wanted to know whether he wanted an attorney present.
P WHAT, if anything, did you tell him about his right to have an attorney at the lineup? (1)
W I said that he had a right to have one there. I told him that if he couldn't afford an attorney, we'd get one for him. I told him that the attorney could make sure that the lineup was fair and everything was on the up and up.
P WHAT else did you say to him? (2)

W I asked him directly whether he understood that he had the right to have an attorney there.

P HOW did the defendant respond? (2)

W He said he realized that.

P At the time, WHAT was the de fendant's demeanor? (2)

W He seemed calm enough. He acted as if he knew what was going on.

P WHAT else did you say? (3)

W Finally, I asked him to tell me whether he wanted an attorney.

P WHAT did he say? (3)

W He said, "No." He insisted he was innocent. To use his words, he didn't need "any damn lawyer" to protect his rights.

DD. THE PERMISSIBILITY OF AN IN-COURT IDENTIFICATION AFTER A PRETRIAL CONFRONTATION VIOLATIVE OF THE FOURTH, FIFTH, OR SIXTH AMENDMENT

1. THE DOCTRINE

At this point, we shall assume that the eyewitness in question was present at an illegal pretrial confrontation. The confrontation could violate the Fourth, Fifth or Sixth Amendment rules described in Sections AA-CC. As those sections explain, the constitutional violation will probably require the exclusion of any testimony about the eyewitnesses' identification of the defendant at the pretrial confrontation. However, the violation does not necessarily bar an in-court identification.

The Supreme Court has held that if the pretrial confrontation was unlawful, the eyewitness may still make an in-court identification when the prosecution can demonstrate an independent basis for the in-court identification, that is, a basis other than the eyewitness's exposure to the defendant at the pretrial confrontation. The Court has made it clear that the prosecution may endeavor to establish on an independent basis whether the pretrial confrontation violated the Fourth, Fifth, or Sixth Amendment. *United States v. Crews*, 445 U.S. 463 (1980) (Fourth Amendment); *Neil v. Biggers*, 409 U.S. 188 (1972) (Fifth Amendment); *United States v. Wade*, 388 U.S. 218 (1967) (Sixth Amendment). Likewise, the California Supreme Court has recognized that the prosecutor may attempt to show an independent basis for an in-court identification. *People v. Teresinski*, 30 Cal. 3d 822, 640 P.2d 753, 180 Cal. Rptr. 617 (1982); *The California Supreme Court Survey—A Review of Decisions: January 1982-June 1982*, 10 PEPP. L. REV. 167, 220 (1982).

Substantively, the test is whether the illegal pretrial confrontation created a very substantial likelihood of *irreparably* mistaken identification. That test applies across the board when there has been a violation of any constitutional exclusionary rule. As a generalization, there is a much greater probability that the judge will preclude an in-court identification when the pretrial confrontation violated the Fifth Amendment. Violations of the Fourth or Sixth Amendment rules might have little impact on the trustworthiness of an in-court identification, but a grossly suggestive lineup violative of the Fifth Amendment can have a lasting, distorting impact on the eyewitness. As a matter of procedure, once the defense establishes an illegal pretrial confrontation, the burden shifts to the prosecution. The prosecution must show that there is an independent basis for an in-court identification, and the *Wade* Court stressed that the prosecution must make that showing by the rigorous standard of clear and convincing evidence.

2. ELEMENTS OF THE FOUNDATION

To demonstrate an independent basis, the prosecutor should show these foundational elements:

1. The eyewitness had the ability to perceive the perpetrator at the time of the crime. It is best if the eyewitness also has some special training in carefully observing people.
2. At the time of the crime, the eyewitness had a good opportunity to view the perpetrator. The quality of the opportunity depends on such factors as the lighting conditions, the length of the period of time the eyewitness viewed the perpetrator, and the eyewitness's physical proximity to the perpetrator.
3. If possible, the prosecutor should also show that there is an independent basis for an in-court identification in addition to the eyewitness's observation during the crime. In some cases, the eyewitness was familiar with the perpetrator before the crime.
4. The eyewitness disclaims any reliance on the view at the illegal pretrial identification. In laying this element of the foundation, the prosecutor may elicit the fact that after the crime and before the illegal confrontation, the eyewitness gave the police an accurate description of the defendant. The accuracy of the description is circumstantial evidence that the witness is not relying on the exposure to the defendant at the illegal confrontation.

3. SAMPLE FOUNDATION

To illustrate the foundation, we shall continue the hypothetical of the defendant Bryon charged with rape. The witness is Ms. Folsom, the alleged victim. The judge has already ruled that the pretrial lineup Ms. Folsom attended violated Bryon's Sixth Amendment rights. The prosecutor is now trying to establish an independent basis for an in-court identification.

P Ms. Folsom, I notice that you are not wearing glasses. HOW good is your eyesight? (1)

W It's perfect. It's been 20-20 my entire life. I've never worn glasses a day.

P WHAT is your occupation? (1)

W I'm currently a student.

P WHAT are you studying? (1)

W Art, specifically painting.

P HOW does that background affect the way you view people's faces? (1)

W It makes you a very acute student of faces. I do a lot of portrait painting, and I'd like to think that I have a very good eye and memory for facial features.

P I know this is difficult for you, but I'd like to take you back to the evening of October 15 of this year. WHERE were you? (2)

W I was in my apartment. I had been reading, and I guess I just fell asleep on the couch.

P WHAT happened after you fell asleep? (2)

W A man entered my apartment through an open window and raped me.

P WHAT were the lighting conditions in your apartment at the time? (2)

W I don't like dark rooms. I had all the lights on in the living room and the bedroom where the rape occurred.

P HOW long of a period of time did you have to view the man who raped you? (2)

W He was in my apartment at least twenty minutes.

P HOW close were you to him? (2)

W He was right on top of me during the rape, and the rest of the time he was only a few feet away.

P HOW well did you see the man during the rape? (2)

W Very well. He occasionally turned his back to me, but most of the time I could see his face. He wasn't even wearing a mask or anything to cover his face.

P HOW often, if ever, had you seen the man before that night? (3)

W I recognized him as a janitor at Stewart's, a pharmacy that I go to all the time. I probably viewed him tens of times before the night of the rape.

P WHAT happened immediately after the rape? (4)

W I called the police, and they came right over.

P WHAT happened when the police arrived? (4)

W I was outraged. I'd been attacked and violated, and I wanted to help them get the animal who did that to me as soon as possible. I gave them a detailed description of the rapist.

P At that time, HOW did you describe the rapist? (4)

W I told the police that the man was white, about thirty, six feet tall, approximately 190 pounds, black hair, brown eyes, a fat nose, thin lips, and a mole on his right cheek.

P WHERE is that man now? (4)

W He's sitting right there at the counsel table to your left.

P HOW is he dressed? (4)

W He's in a gray jumpsuit.

P Your Honor, please let the record reflect that the witness has identified the defendant as the rapist.

J The record will so reflect.

P Ms. Folsom, I want you to think carefully now. In identifying the defendant today, to WHAT extent are you relying on your opportunity to view him at the lineup on October 16? (4)

W I'm not. I don't need to rely on that.

P WHAT are you relying on?

W I had a good chance to view him during the attack. And I knew him before that from the drug store. That's what I'm basing my identification on.

Chapter 12

SUBSTITUTES FOR EVIDENCE

A. INTRODUCTION

The previous 11 chapters analyze the legal restrictions on the process of admitting evidence during a trial. However, there are substitutes for conventional evidence: The parties may stipulate to certain propositions, the judge may judicially notice a proposition, or the jurors themselves may be taken outside the courtroom to view a scene or object that is relevant to the case. This chapter discusses the limitations on those substitutes.

B. STIPULATIONS

1. THE DOCTRINE

It is very common for the parties to stipulate before or during a trial. A stipulation can save both parties' time; and by stipulating in the jury's presence, a party can attempt to create the impression in the jurors' minds that he or she is a reasonable, fair person.

There are several types of stipulations. For example, the parties may stipulate to continuances. Or the parties may enter into a stipulation of law that certain testimony shall be admitted at the trial. *In re Kerry O.*, 210 Cal. App. 3d 326, 258 Cal. Rptr. 448 (1989). However, we are concerned primarily with two types of evidentiary stipulations. The first is a stipulation of fact; the parties agree that a certain fact existed or that a certain event occurred. If the parties enter a stipulation of fact, neither party can ordinarily introduce evidence to contradict the stipulated fact. The second type of stipulation is a stipulation of expected testimony; the parties agree that if a particular person were present in court as a witness, the person would give certain testimony. The parties are not stipulating that the testimony is admissible, truthful, or correct; the parties may introduce evidence to contradict what the person would testify to or object to particular passages in the stipulation. The parties are agreeing only what the person's testimony would be if the person appeared and testified in court.

The procedure for introducing stipulations varies. Some judges commonly permit the attorneys to recite oral stipulations. Other judges prefer that the parties reduce their stipulation in writing. Written pretrial stipulations obviously reduce the possibility for disagreement at trial over the content of the stipulation.

The final procedural question is whether the judge accepting the stipulation must personally question the parties. May the judge accept the attorneys' assurances that the parties assent? In civil actions, the judges routinely do so.

The answer is more complex in criminal cases. In *Boykin v. Alabama*, 395 U.S. 238 (1969), the Supreme Court held that since a defendant waives certain constitutional rights by pleading guilty, the trial record must reflect that the defendant knowingly waived the rights. The California Supreme Court reached the same result in *In re Tahl*, 1 Cal. 3d 122, 460 P.2d 449, 81 Cal. Rptr. 577 (1969), *cert. denied*, 398 U.S. 911 (1970). In many cases, the defendant stipulates to a trial on the basis of the preliminary hearing transcript. This practice is sometimes called a "slow (guilty) plea." Butterworth & Horne, *Pleas and Case Settlement*, in CALIFORNIA CRIMINAL LAW: PROCEDURE AND PRACTICE § 10.19 (2d ed. 1994); Trask & Polis, *Pleas and Case Settlement*, in CALIFORNIA CRIMINAL LAW § 10.8 (1986). *People v. McCoy*, 8 Cal. App. 4th 1464 n.2, 11 Cal. Rptr. 2d 145, 146 n.2 (1992) ("A *Bunnell* submission, or 'slow plea,' is a bargained-for submission to the court on the preliminary hearing transcript, unaccompanied by defendant's testimony or argument of counsel."); *People v. Huynh*, 229 Cal. App. 3d 1067, 1079, 281 Cal. Rptr. 785, 792 (1991) ("An example of a slow plea of guilty plea is when a defendant, usually in exchange for a promised sentence, submits to court trial based on a preliminary hearing transcript containing unchallenged prosecution evidence and the defendant does not argue its sufficiency."). Even when the defendant does not stipulate to the truth of all the facts recited by the prosecution witnesses at the preliminary hearing, the defendant is entering into a stipulation of expected testimony; the defense is agreeing that if the same witnesses appeared at trial, they would give the testimony they gave at the earlier hearing. The argument was made that since this practice is practically a guilty plea, the courts should apply *Tahl* by analogy. The California Supreme Court accepted the argument in *Bunnell v. Superior Court*, 13 Cal. 3d 592, 531 P.2d 1086, 119 Cal. Rptr. 302 (1975). *But see People v. Rodgriguez*, 70 Cal. App. 4th 1272, 83 Cal. Rptr. 2d 265 (1999) (the defendant was charged with being a felon in possession of a firearm; his tendered stipulation to convicted felon status was not tantamount to a guilty plea, since the stipulation did not dispose of all the elements of the charged offense).

In *Bunnell*, the court announced:

> [I]n all cases in which the defendant seeks to submit his case for decision on the transcript ..., the record shall reflect that he has been advised of his right to a jury trial, to confront and cross-examine witnesses, and against self-incrimination. It shall also demonstrate that he understands the nature of the charges. Express waivers of the enumerated constitutional rights shall appear. In cases in which there is to be a submission without a reservation by the defendant of the right to present evidence in his own defense he shall be advised of that right and an express waiver thereof taken. If a defendant does not reserve the right to present additional evidence and does not advise the court that he will contest his guilt in argument to the court, the defendant shall be advised of the probability that the submission will result in a conviction of the offense or offenses charged. In all ... submission cases the defendant shall be advised of the direct consequences of conviction such as the permissible range of punishment. ...

Id. at 605, 531 P.2d at 1094, 119 Cal. Rptr. at 310. In *People v. Wright*, 43 Cal. 3d 487, 729 P.2d 260, 233 Cal. Rptr. 69 (1987), the California Supreme Court clarified the scope of the *Bunnell* rule; the court explained that a submission on a preliminary hearing transcript does not amount to a slow guilty plea if at the hearing, the defense counsel conducted "substantial cross-examination" or argued "the legal significance to be accorded" the facts. *Id.* at 496, 729 P.2d at 260, 233 Cal. Rptr. at 69. The court has likewise clarified the status of the *Bunnell* doctrine. The court has announced that the *Bunnell* rule is not of constitutional dimension; it is a judicially declared rule of criminal procedure. *People v. Orduno*, 80 Cal. App. 3d 738, 145 Cal. Rptr. 806 (1978), *cert. denied*, 439 U.S. 1074 (1979).

When *Bunnell* applies, the record must affirmatively show the advisement and waiver. *People v. Wright*, 43 Cal. 3d 487, 729 P.2d 260, 233 Cal. Rptr. 69 (1987). However, in advising the defendant, the judge need not quote the exact language used by the *Bunnell* court. *People v. Lucky*, 41 Cal. 3d 315, 710 P.2d 959, 972, 221 Cal. Rptr. 880, 893 (1985), *aff'd*, 45 Cal. 3d 259, 753 P.2d 1052, 247 Cal. Rptr. 1 (1988), *cert. denied*, 488 U.S. 1034 (1989). *People v. Lizarraga*, 43 Cal. App. 3d 815, 118 Cal. Rptr. 208 (1974), held that when the defendant contemplates stipulating to a prior offense allegation, it is sufficient for the judge to advise the defendant that he has the right to demand a trial, to force the prosecution to produce the record of conviction, and to contest its validity. However, *Lizarraga* has frequently been criticized. *People v. Balderrama*, 221 Cal. App. 3d 282, 286, 270 Cal. Rptr. 432, 434 (1990) (collecting cases).

2. ELEMENTS OF THE FOUNDATION

The procedure for entering a stipulation includes these steps:

1. One attorney announces to the judge that there has been a stipulation.
2. The judge then inquires of the other attorney whether there has been a stipulation.
3. The second attorney answers in the affirmative.
4. The proponent of the stipulation establishes the tenor or content of the agreement. If the stipulation is oral, the proponent simply states the nature of the agreement on the record. If the stipulation is in writing, the proponent introduces the writing.
5. When required, the judge personally questions the party or parties before accepting the stipulation. The judge ensures that the party understands the nature and consequences of the stipulation. *See People v. Knight*, 6 Cal. App. 4th 1829, 8 Cal. Rptr. 2d 827, 828-29 (1992) ("Where submission upon the preliminary hearing transcript is tantamount to a plea of guilty, a defendant must be advised he is giving up his right against self-incrimination. It has been held that ... a defendant must [also] be advised of the potential maximum and minimum term of imprisonment."); *People v. Limones*, 284 Cal. Rptr. 418, 421 (Cal. App. 1991) (" defendant must be

advised of the probability that the submission of the preliminary hearing transcript without a reservation of the right to present additional evidence or contest his guilt in argument would probably result in a conviction. ").

After the judge accepts the stipulation, the judge informs the jury of the stipulation and instructs the jury on the legal effect of the stipulation.

3. SAMPLE FOUNDATIONS

The first fact situation is a suit for breach of contract. The plaintiff, Marshall Industries, alleges that on January 10, 1999, it entered into a contract with the defendant, Rowl Company. The complaint alleges that under the terms of the contract, Rowl Company promised to excavate a site, lay a foundation, and build a two-story shopping center for the plaintiff. In its answer the defendant raises the affirmative defenses of impossibility and financial impracticability. The answer alleges that a week after beginning excavation, the defendant discovered a subsoil condition that made it prohibitively expensive for it to do the promised construction work. The proponent is the plaintiff.

P   Your Honor, I would like to announce that the parties in this case have reached a stipulation as to their actual knowledge of the existence of the subsoil condition that the defendant discovered in March 1999. (1)

J   (To the defense attorney.) Is that true? (2)

O   Yes, your Honor. (3)

J   What is the nature of this stipulation? (4)

P   We have stipulated that before the defendant's discovery of the layer of granite in March 1999, none of the employees of either the plaintiff or the defendant had actual, subjective knowledge that the layer of granite existed.

J   (To the defense attorney.) Is that the tenor of the stipulation?

O   Yes.

J   And both of your clients consent to this stipulation?

P   Yes.

O   Yes, your Honor.

J   Has this agreement been reduced to writing?

P   No, your Honor.

O   No—it's an oral stipulation.

J   Very well. If that is the case, I shall accept the stipulation of fact. Ladies and gentlemen of the jury, the plaintiff and the defendant have just entered into an agreement or stipulation. All parties agree that before the defendant discovered the layer of granite at the construction site in March 1999, none of the employees of the plaintiff or defendant had actual, subjective knowledge that the granite was there. Will both parties state for the record that I have correctly described the stipulation for the jury?

O   Certainly, your Honor.

P   I concur.

J   And ladies and gentlemen of the jury, because of the stipulation, you will not hear any evidence on that issue. However, I am instructing you that you are simply to assume the truth of the stipulated fact. All right, let's proceed with the evidence.

The second fact situation is a criminal prosecution for theft. The People allege that the defendant, Mr. David Miles, stole $1,700 from a local Vons Department Store. An acquaintance of the defendant saw him leave the department store in a furtive, hurried fashion immediately after the alleged theft. Unfortunately for the prosecution, that person is now vacationing in Florida. Rather than forcing the witness to return or seeking a continuance, the parties enter into a stipulation of expected testimony. On this occasion, the parties decided to reduce the stipulation to writing before trial.

Stipulation of Expected Testimony

It is hereby stipulated between the People and the defense, with the defendant's express consent, that if Robert Prothero, 766 Somerset Street, Daly City, California, were present in court and sworn as a witness, he would give the following testimony:

I know the defendant, David Miles. We have been members of the same labor union for the past three years. I can recognize him by sight. On the afternoon of July 28, 1999, while I was walking by the entrance to the Vons Department Store on H Street in downtown Millbrae, I saw the defendant exit the store. As soon as he stepped outside, he looked both ways—up and down the street. He seemed to be nervous. Then he stuck his hand in his right pants pocket; there was a big bulge in the pocket. As soon as he removed his hand from his pocket, he began running away from the store.

_____
/s/ Deputy District Attorney

_____
/s/ Defense Counsel

_____
/s/ Defendant
Dated: November 1, 1999

The parties now offer the stipulation at trial. The prosecutor is the proponent. Since the parties are not stipulating to a trial on the preliminary hearing transcript, _Bunnell_ does not apply directly. However, the judge decides to conduct an abbreviated _Bunnell_ inquiry.

P   Your Honor, I want to announce that the parties in this case have reached a stipulation as to the expected testimony of an unavailable witness. (1)

J (To the defense counsel.) Is that true? (2)

O Yes, your Honor. (3)

J What is the stipulation? (4)

P Your Honor, I request that this be marked People's exhibit number four for identification.

J It will be so marked.

P Please let the record reflect that I am showing the exhibit to the opposing counsel.

J It will so reflect.

P I now offer People's exhibit number four for identification into evidence as People's exhibit four.

J (To the defense counsel.) Is this the stipulation?

O Yes, your Honor.

J Mr. Miles, please hold the exhibit in your hands while I ask you a few questions.
   (5)

D Yes, sir.

J Have you ever seen this document before? (5)

D Yes.

J When? (5)

D My attorney showed it to me when he asked me to sign it.

J Are you familiar with its contents? (5)

D Yes.

J Is that your signature on the bottom of the page? (5)

D Yes.

J Has your lawyer advised you that you do not have to enter into this stipulation?
   (5)

D Yes. He told me that.

J Has your lawyer informed you that you have a right to insist that the prosecution
   produce Mr. Prothero at this trial? (5)

D Yes.

J Do you realize that if Mr. Prothero appeared at this trial, he would have to testify
   under oath? (5)

D Yes.

J Do you understand that if he testified at trial, he would have to testify in view of
   the jury? (5)

D Yes.

J Do you realize that if he testified at trial, you would have an opportunity to cross-
   examine him? (5)

D Yes.

J Do you understand that you are losing these rights by agreeing to this stipulation?
   (5)

D Yes, sir.

J Has your counsel advised you that even if you stipulate to Mr. Prothero's testimony, you can introduce evidence to rebut or contradict what Mr. Prothero says?
   (5)

D Yes.

J Has your counsel told you that even if you stipulate to Mr. Prothero's testimony,
   your counsel can make objections on evidentiary grounds to the testimony? (5)
   (As a practical matter, there will rarely be evidentiary objections after the entry of

the stipulation; the parties usually eliminate any objectionable material during the bargaining over the content of the stipulation.)

D Yes.

J Do you consent to this stipulation? (5)

D Yes.

J Well, then the stipulation will be accepted. The exhibit will be received.

P Your Honor, I request permission to read the exhibit to the jurors.

J Permission granted.

P Both parties, the People and defense, have agreed and stipulated that if Mr. Robert Prothero, 766 Somerset Street, Daly City, California, were present in court, he would give the following testimony: "I know the defendant, David Miles. We have been members of the same labor union for the past three years. I can recognize him on sight. On the afternoon of July 28, 1999, while I was walking by the entrance to the Vons Department Store on H Street in downtown Millbrae, I saw the defendant exit the store. As soon as he stepped outside, he looked both ways—up and down the street. He seemed to be nervous. Then he stuck his hand in his right pants pocket; there was a big bulge in the pocket. As soon as he removed his hand from his pocket, he began running away from the store."

O Your Honor, will you please instruct the jury about the stipulation?

J Yes. Ladies and gentlemen of the jury, the prosecutor has just read a stipulation of expected testimony. The parties have agreed as to what the testimony of Mr. Prothero would be if he appeared here and testified under oath. The stipulation does not admit the truth of the testimony, and it does not add anything to the weight of Mr. Prothero's testimony. The defense may attack, contradict, or explain Mr. Prothero's testimony. In deciding how much weight to attach to Mr. Prothero's testimony, you may consider the fact that you have not had an opportunity to personally observe his demeanor.

C. JUDICIAL NOTICE

1. THE DOCTRINE

Like the stipulation technique, judicial notice is an alternative to the presentation of formal evidence. The judge relieves the parties of the duty to present evidence by noting a fact and informing the jury of the fact's existence. In some jurisdictions, the expression, "judicial notice," is also applied to the process by which the judge learns of the applicable law. The judicial notice mechanism is not confined to trial. Before trial, in ruling on a demurrer, the judge may notice facts which supersede inconsistent allegations in the complaint. *City of Chula Vista v. County of San Diego*, 23 Cal. App. 4th 1713, 29 Cal. Rptr. 2d 89 (1994). After trial, on appeal, the appellate court may invoke the doctrine to notice developments, reflected in the trial court records, which occurred after the appeal was filed. Hunter, *Problems with the Record on Appeal*, CAL. LAWYER 59, 60 (Dec. 1995).

Judicially Noticeable Propositions

In California, the governing substantive statutes are Evidence Code §§ 450-60. Those statutes govern judicial notice of law and adjudicative facts.[1] The key provisions are §§ 451-52. Those sections list the types of facts and laws that a California judge may notice. The list in §§ 451-52 is not exhaustive. Section 450 states that a judge may judicially notice a proposition if authorized to do so "by law." Evidence Code § 160 defines "law" as including case law. The Law Revision Commission comment to § 450 points out that read in light of § 160, § 450 authorizes the courts to expand the list of judicially noticeable propositions.

Even without such expansion, the list in §§ 451-52 is lengthy. The list includes both factual and legal propositions. For example, subdivision 451(f) mandates judicial notice of "[f]acts and propositions of generalized knowledge that are so universally known that they cannot reasonably be the subject of dispute." The Assembly Committee comment to § 451(f) explains that "'[u]niversally known' does not mean that every man on the street has knowledge of such facts. A fact known among persons of reasonable and average intelligence and knowledge will satisfy the ... requirement. " Subdivision 452(g) permits judicial notice of facts that are matters "of ... common knowledge within the territorial jurisdiction of the court. ..." The Assembly Committee comment to § 452(g) defines the expression, "the territorial jurisdiction of the court." In the case of a Superior Court, that area is the county; and in the case of a Municipal or Justice court, the area is the judicial district. Finally, § 452(h) authorizes notice of "propositions that are not subject to dispute and are capable of immediate and accurate determination by resort to sources of reasonably indisputable accuracy. " For example, the judge may judicially notice the fact that there was a rapid rise in real estate prices in California

---

[1]Like Federal Rule of Evidence 201, the statutes do not restrict the courts' informal notice of so-called legislative facts. As the court stated in *Auchmoody v. 911 Emergency Servs.*, 214 Cal. App. 3d 1510, 1518-19, 263 Cal. Rptr. 278, 283 (1989),

> [T]he Law Revision Commission Comment to Evidence Code section also provides that, "Under the Evidence Code, as under existing law, courts may consider whatever materials are appropriate in construing statutes, determining constitutional issues, and formulating rules of law. In many cases, the meaning and validity of statutes, the precise nature of a common law rule, or the correct interpretation of a constitutional provision can be determined only with the help of ... extrinsic aids."

Nevertheless, the courts sometimes cite the judicial notice statutes to justify their consideration of material relevant to the construction of a statute. *Johnson v. Superior Ct.*, 25 Cal. App. 4th 1564, 31 Cal. Rptr. 2d 199 (1994); *In re Ramon A.*, 40 Cal. App. 4th 935 n.1, 47 Cal. Rptr. 2d 59, 61 n.1 (1995); *People v. Barrera*, 70 Cal. App. 4th 541, 82 Cal. Rptr. 2d 755 (1999) (the legislative history of an amendment to the judicial disqualification statute); *People v. Herrera*, 67 Cal. App. 4th 987, 992 n. 2, 79 Cal. Rptr. 2d 539, 543 n. 2 (the legislative history of Senate Bill No. 721), *modified*, 68 Cal. App. 4th 623e (1998); *but see Duarte v. Chino Community Hosp.*, 72 Cal. App. 4th 849, 85 Cal. Rptr. 2d 521 (1999)(the court refused to judicially notice studies by the California Law Revision Commission, since the Commission's publication was not an expression of the legislature and the studies indicated an intent to change existing law, not simply clarify it).

during the 1970's and 1980's. *City of Oceanside v. McKenna*, 215 Cal. App. 3d 1420, 264 Cal. Rptr. 275 (1989); *Golden Sec. Thrift v. First American Title*, 53 Cal. App. 4th 250, 61 Cal. Rptr. 2d 442 (1997) (dictionary definitions); *Medina v. Hillshore Partners*, 40 Cal. App. 4th 477, 46 Cal. Rptr. 2d 871 (1995) (street gangs generally claim home territory, the gangs attempt to prohibit rival gang members from entering the area upon threat of severe physical injury, and gang activity spawns violence); *Roy Supply, Inc. v. Wells Fargo Bank, N.A.*, 39 Cal. App. 4th 1051, 46 Cal. Rptr. 2d 309 (1995) (commercial banks follow the custom of providing customers with monthly statements and canceled checks); *Acosta v. Los Angeles Unified School Dist.*, 31 Cal. App. 4th 471, 37 Cal. Rptr. 2d 171, *modified* (Apr. 14, 1995) (gymnastics, especially a front catch on the high bar, is a hazardous activity). *But see Jordache Enterprises, Inc. v. Brobeck, Phleger & Harrison*, 18 Cal. 4th 739, 748 n. 5, 958 P. 2d 1062, 1068 n. 5, 76 Cal. Rptr. 2d 749, 755-56 n. 5 (1998) ("We ... deny Jordache's request for judicial notice of three Brobeck partners' biographical data, extracted from a popular national directory of attorneys and law firms"). Subdivision 452(h) embodies the verifiable certainty principle that allows the court to notice propositions documented in scientific treatises. The Assembly Committee comment to § 452(h) states that the subdivision liberally allows judges to notice facts "accepted as established by experts and specialists in the natural, physical, and social sciences. ..." *See* 1 PAUL GIANNELLI & EDWARD IMWINKELRIED, SCIENTIFIC EVIDENCE § 1-2 (3d ed. 1999); Sevilla, *A Lazy Person's Approach to Introducing Defense Evidence*, 16 C.A.C.J. FORUM 22, 22-24 (Jan.-Feb. 1989). *But see Ford v. Pacific Gas & Elec. Co.*, 60 Cal. App. 4th 696, 70 Cal. Rptr. 2d 359 (1997) (the court refused to take judicial notice of a recent scientific article concerning the alleged connection between electric and magnetic fields (EMF) and cancer). While subdivision (h) is often applied to scientific propositions, by its terms it is not limited to that type of fact. For example, it can encompass the fact that a certain type of election was not held in a given area (*Professional Engineers in California Gov't v. Wilson*, 61 Cal. App. 4th 1013, 72 Cal. Rptr. 2d 111, 119 (1998)) or the terms of a redevelopment agency's development agreement with an Indian tribe. *People ex rel. Lungren v. Community Redevelopment Agency*, 56 Cal. App. 4th 868, 65 Cal. Rptr. 2d 786, 788 (1997).

Similarly, the list in §§ 451-52 includes legal propositions. Subdivision 451(a) requires the judge to notice "[t]he decisional, constitutional, and public statutory law of" California and the United States, and § 452(a) permits similar notice of the laws of other states. (Under these provisions, the California courts have noticed even unpublished opinions. *Thomsen v. City of Escondido*, 49 Cal. App. 4th 884 n.6, 56 Cal. Rptr. 2d 902, 908 n.6 (1996).) At common law, some courts balked at judicially noticing administrative regulations and local ordinances, but § 452(b)-(c) breaks with the common law and authorizes the judge to notice those species of law. *E.g., People v. Hawkins*, 10 Cal. App. 4th 565, 12 Cal. Rptr. 2d 633, 636-37 (1992) (regulations of the Commission on Peace Officer Standards and Training); *People v. Ochoa*, 231 Cal. App. 3d 1413, 282 Cal. Rptr. 805, 811 (1991) (welfare regulations); *Traverso v. People ex rel. Dept. of Transp.*, 46 Cal.

App. 4th 1197 n.14, 54 Cal. Rptr. 2d 434, 442 n.14 (1996) (local zoning ordinance). Subdivision 452(f) even permits judicial notice of the law of foreign countries or organizations of nations. *See Balcom v. Hiller*, 46 Cal. App. 4th 1758, 54 Cal. Rptr. 2d 536, 540 (1996) (a standing order issued by a British court); *Chong v. Superior Court (HBZ Finance Ltd.)*, 58 Cal. App. 4th 1032, 68 Cal. Rptr. 2d 427, 429 (1997) ("We take judicial notice of the treaty between Britain and China on the status of Hong Kong, a binding international treaty").

The most controversial provisions authorizing judicial notice of law are § 452(c)-(d). Subdivision 452(c) authorizes judicial notice of "[o]fficial acts of the legislative, executive, and judicial departments of the United States and of any state of the United States." *E.g.*, *Carleton v. Tortosa*, 14 Cal. App. 4th 745 n.1, 17 Cal. Rptr. 2d 734, 739 n.1 (1993) (the court judicially noticed a publication of the California Department of Real Estate as an official act of the executive department); *Schmidt v. S. Cal. Rapid Transit Dist.*, 13 Cal. App. 4th 23 n.10, 17 Cal. Rptr. 2d 340, 344 n.10 (1993) ("various legislative materials, including committee reports"); *Thorning v. Hollister School Dist.*, 11 Cal. App. 4th 1598, 15 Cal. Rptr. 2d 91, 93 (1992) ("resolutions, reports, and other official acts of a legislative body," including "[o]fficial minutes of meetings of a legislative body"); *City of Atascadero v. Merrill Lynch*, 68 Cal. App. 4th 445, 80 Cal. Rptr. 2d 329 (1998) (settlement agreement and release between county and securities broker), *modified*, 69 Cal. App. 4th 909d (1999); *Planned Parenthood v. Williams*, 10 Cal. 4th 1009, 898 P.2d 402, 43 Cal. Rptr. 2d 88 (1995) (government maps and surveys); *Adkins v. State*, 50 Cal. App. 4th 1802 n.2, 59 Cal. Rptr. 2d 59, 62 n.2 (1996) (executive acts of the Governor in declaring emergencies). Since a county is a legal subdivision of the state, a county commission record could qualify as an "official act." 1 WITKIN § 98, at 85; *Masters v. San Bernardino Cty. Employees*, 32 Cal. App. 4th 30 n.1, 37 Cal. Rptr. 2d 860, 864 n.1 (1995) (the bylaws of the county employees retirement association, adopted by the San Bernardino County Board of Supervisors); *Washington v. County of Contra Costa*, 38 Cal. App. 4th 890, 45 Cal. Rptr. 2d 646 (1995) (county reports and inspections). Thus, the judge could judicially notice a land use plan promulgated by a county commission. Subdivision 452(d) permits judicial notice of "[r]ecords of ... any court of this state or ... any court of record of the United States or any state of the United States." Similarly, the judge may judicially notice the minutes of various administrative proceedings. *Sacramento v. Water Resources Control Bd.*, 2 Cal. App. 4th 960 n.2, 3 Cal. Rptr. 2d 643, 647 n.2 (1992) (the minutes of a hearing of the Regional Water Quality Control Board); *Social Serv. Union v. City and County of San Francisco*, 234 Cal. App. 3d 1093, 285 Cal. Rptr. 905 (1991) (the official minutes of a civil service commission); *In re Visciotti*, 14 Cal. 4th 325, 926 P.2d 987, 58 Cal. Rptr. 2d 801 (1996), *modified*, 14 Cal. 4th 1089A (1997) (State Bar proceedings).

Subdivision 452(c) obviously applies to records reflecting judicial judgments and orders. *E.g.*, *Temple Community Hospital v. Superior Court*, 20 Cal. 4th 464, 467 n. 1, 976 P. 2d 223, 226 n.1, 84 Cal. Rptr. 2d 852, 855 n. 1 (1999) ("we take notice of the trial court's order granting Valleylab's motion for summary judgment"); *County of San Diego v. State*, 15 Cal. 4th 68 n.7, 931 P.2d 312 n.7, 61 Cal. Rptr. 2d 134, 142 n.7 (1997) ("the appellate record from that action"); *Conservatorship of Rodney M.*, 50 Cal. App. 4th 1266 n.6, 58 Cal. Rptr. 2d 513, 515 n.6 (1996) ("superior court file"); *Citizens for Open Access v. Seadrift Ass'n*, 60 Cal. App. 4th 1053, 71 Cal. Rptr. 2d 77, 84 (1998) ("judicial notice may be taken of a prior judgment and other court records"); *Forty-Niner Truck Plaza v. Union Oil Co.*, 58 Cal. App. 4th 1261 n. 7, 68 Cal. Rptr. 2d 532, 541 n. 7 (1997) ("We accept Unocal's request to take judicial notice of the unpublished" order in a federal district court case); *Zelda, Inc. v. Northland Ins. Co.*, 56 Cal. App. 4th 1252 n. 1, 66 Cal. Rptr. 2d 356, 358 n. 1 (1997) ("judicial notice of the underlying superior court action"). *State Water Resources Control Bd. v. OAL*, 12 Cal. App. 4th 697 n.1, 16 Cal. Rptr. 2d 25, 26 n.1 (1993) (a "ruling of the Sacramento Superior Court"); *Brown v. Watson*, 207 Cal. App. 3d 1306, 1315 n.5, 255 Cal. Rptr. 507, 513 n.5 (1989) (records in a Texas lawsuit); *McAdory v. Rogers*, 215 Cal. App. 3d 1273, 264 Cal. Rptr. 71 (1989) (an order and briefs in an appellate case); *People v. Hayes*, 52 Cal. 3d 577, 611 n.3, 802 P.2d 376, 396 n.3, 276 Cal. Rptr. 874, 893 n.3 (1990) (an amended complaint), *cert. denied*, 502 U.S. 958 (1991). The point of agreement is that the subdivision allows the judge to notice the existence of the record. *In re Luckett*, 232 Cal. App. 3d 107, 283 Cal. Rptr. 312, 313 (1991) (the court judicially noticed the existence and results of Luckett's prior 43 appellate actions to support its: conclusion that he was a vexatious litigant under Code of Civil Procedure § 391). The point of disagreement is whether the judge may notice the truth of findings and recitations of fact in the records. *Id.* Justice Jefferson states his position:

> Even though judicial notice of the truth of facts asserted in documents in a court record, such as orders, findings of fact and conclusions of law, and judgments, is usually appropriate, it is not appropriate for judicial notice to be taken of the truth of a factual assertion in a court order, such as a minute order, if that assertion of fact is not predicated upon the court's finding based upon an adversary hearing that involves the question of the existence or nonexistence of such fact.

2 JEFFERSON § 47.2, at 1759; *Gilmore v. Superior Court*, 230 Cal. App. 3d 416, 281 Cal. Rptr. 343, 344 (1991) ("The superior court took notice not only of the existence of that opinion and the result reached, but also relied upon our statement of the facts surrounding the homicide to establish the truth thereof."). In *Sosinsky v. Grant*, 6 Cal. App. 4th 1548, 8 Cal. Rptr. 2d 552, 558-65 (1992), the opinion notes that some cases indicate that a judge may judicially notice the truth of certain findings of fact by tribunals. However, the court questions the soundness of those cases. The court points out that to be judicially noticeable, a proposition must be indisputably true. The court states:

> [N]either a finding of fact made after a contested adversary hearing nor a finding of fact made after any other type of hearing can be indisputably

deemed to have been a correct finding. Taking judicial notice of the truth of a judge's factual findings would appear ... to be tantamount to taking judicial notice that the judge's factual findings must necessarily have been correct and that the judge is therefore infallible. We resist the temptation to do so.

Id. at 1568, 8 Cal. Rptr. 2d at 564. *See also Bach v. McNelis,* 207 Cal. App. 3d 852, 255 Cal. Rptr. 232 (1989) (a judge may not judicially notice the truth of assertions in declarations filed in judicial proceedings); *Stormedia Inc. v. Superior Court,* 20 Cal. 4th 449, 457 n. 9, 976 P. 2d 214, 219 n. 9, 84 Cal. Rptr. 2d 843, 848 n. 9 (1999)("When judicial notice is taken of a document, however, the truthfulness and proper interpretation of the document are disputable"); *Fowler v. Howell,* 42 Cal. App. 4th 1746, 50 Cal. Rptr. 2d 484, 486 (1996) ("a court may not take judicial notice of the truth of a factual finding made in another action"); *Mangini v. R.J. Reynolds Tobacco Co.,* 7 Cal. 4th 1057, 875 P.2d 73, 31 Cal. Rptr. 2d 358, 361-63 (although the court can judicially notice official records and acts, "we do not take judicial notice of the truth of all matters stated therein"), *cert. denied,* 513 U.S. 1016; *Williams v. Wraxall,* 33 Cal. App. 4th 120, 39 Cal. Rptr. 2d 658 (the court will not judicially notice the truth of hearsay statements in decisions or court files, including pleadings, affidavits, testimony, and statements of fact), *modified,* 34 Cal. App. 4th 199b (1995).

Although the Evidence Code §§ 451-52 contains a long list of proper subjects of judicial notice, there are limits to judicial notice even in California. Thus, the courts will not judicially notice private correspondence (*In re Jackson,* 3 Cal. 4th 578 n.6, 11 Cal. Rptr. 2d 531, 539 n.6, 835 P.2d 371 n.6 (1992)) or business documents. *Carleton v. Tortosa,* 14 Cal. App. 4th 745, 17 Cal. Rptr. 2d 734, 739 n.1 (1993); *Gould v. Maryland Sound Industries, Inc.,* 31 Cal. App. 4th 1137, 37 Cal. Rptr. 2d 718, 722-23 (1995) (the existence of a contract between private parties).

Procedures for Judicial Notice

While §§ 451-52 prescribe the substantive test for judicial notice, §§ 453-60 regulate the procedure. Section 453 states that judicial notice of a proposition listed in § 452 becomes mandatory if a party makes a timely request and "[f]urnishes the court with sufficient information to enable it to take judicial notice of the matter." *Evans v. Pillsbury, Madison & Sutro,* 65 Cal. App. 4th 599, 76 Cal. Rptr. 2d 679 (1998) (mandatory judicial notice of an attorney's declaration was not required; although the declaration was part of the trial court's file, the declaration was not a mandatory subject for judicial notice; and the trial judge had not been asked to take judicial notice of the declaration); *People v. Moore,* 59 Cal. App. 4th 168, 69 Cal. Rptr. 2d 56 (1997). Subdivision 454(a)(2) provides that when the judge rules on a judicial notice request, "[e]xclusionary rules of evidence do not apply except for Section 352 and the rules of privilege." Suppose, for example, that a plaintiff requested judicial notice of a scientific proposition under

§ 452(h). The plaintiff could submit to the judge excerpts from a scientific treatise even though the same excerpts would be objectionable hearsay if the plaintiff attempted to present the treatise directly to the jury. Some judges still insist on the authentication of any material submitted in support of a judicial notice request. *See Quelimane Co. v. Stewart Title Guar. Co.,* 19 Cal. 4th 26, 46 n. 9, 960 P. 2d 513, 524 n. 9, 77 Cal. Rptr. 2d 709, 720 n. 9 ("None of the materials submitted by plaintiffs is authenticated, however. (Evid. Code §§ 1401, 1530.)"), *modified,* 19 Cal. 4th 253b (1998). For that reason, to be on the safe side, it is a good practice to submit the material with a supporting affidavit from an expert. The notary public's signature on the affidavit is presumptively authentic under Evidence Code § 1453(c). If the judge ultimately decides to judicially notice a proposition, § 457 comes into play. That section states that upon request, the judge must "instruct the jury to accept as a fact the matter … noticed."

2. SAMPLE FOUNDATIONS

The initial fact situation illustrates the first basis for judicial notice, matter of common knowledge. The fact situation is a tort action arising from a traffic accident. The plaintiff, Ms. Garnet, alleges that the defendant, Mr. Simmons, was speeding and carelessly struck her as she was crossing the street. The plaintiff has already called Mr. James Farnsworth as a witness. Mr. Farnsworth testifies that he observed the accident. He testified that the defendant's car struck the plaintiff at the intersection of F and Girard Streets in downtown Millbrae. Mr. Farnsworth also expresses his opinion that the defendant was driving thirty-five miles an hour just before the accident. Mr. Farnsworth leaves the witness stand, and the following occurs. The plaintiff is the proponent.

P   Your Honor, I now request that you judicially notice two propositions.
J   What are they?
P   The first is that in this state, unless otherwise posted, the speed limit in a business district is twenty-five miles an hour. That limit is stated in Vehicle Code § 22352(b). I have here a copy of the Vehicle Code volume containing § 22352. The volume purports to be published by public authority, and it is therefore authenticated under Evidence Code § 644. I believe that the speed limit is judicially noticeable under Evidence Code § 451(a).
J   I concur. What else would you like me to judicially notice?
P   The second proposition is that the intersection of F and Girard Streets in downtown Millbrae is part of our business district. That fact is a matter of common knowledge locally, and it should therefore be judicially noticed under Evidence Code § 452(g).
J   Once again I agree.
P   Your Honor, would you please instruct the jury about the judicially noticed propositions?
J   Yes. Ladies and gentlemen of the jury, I am now judicially noticing two facts. The first fact is that in California, unless otherwise posted, the speed limit in a business district is twenty-five miles an hour. The second fact is that the inter-

section where the accident occurred—F and Girard Streets—is in Millbrae's business district. Since these facts have been judicially noticed, you will not hear any formal evidence about these facts. You must accept these facts and assume them to be true even though you will not hear any evidence of these facts.

The next fact situation illustrates the second basis for judicial notice, verifiable certainty. The second situation is a continuation of the first. The plaintiff ultimately wants to offer the testimony of Officer Ripley. Officer Ripley had his police car parked near the intersection when the accident occurred. His police car was equipped with a radar speedmeter. The speedmeter clocked the defendant's car at thirty-six miles an hour just before the accident. As Section L in Chapter 5 points out, part of the foundation for an offer of scientific evidence is proof of the theory's validity and the instrument's reliability. Since the radar speedmeter is a scientific instrument, the plaintiff must lay those two elements of the foundation in our hypothetical. However, since those facts are readily verifiable certainties, the plaintiff need not present live testimony; the plaintiff can use judicial notice to supply the first two elements of the scientific evidence foundation. Before trial, the plaintiff could obtain this affidavit.

STATE OF CALIFORNIA   )
)   AFFIDAVIT
CITY OF DAVIS   )

I the undersigned, being duly sworn, depose and say that:

1. My name is Glenda Schneider, I reside at 7144 Lake Boulevard, Davis, California.
2. I teach electronics at the University of California, at Davis. I have taught that subject there for the past seven years. I have a B.S., a master's, and a doctorate in that field from Michigan State University.
3. The underlying theory of the radar speedmeter is the Doppler shift principle. The principle is that if a beam of microwaves of known frequency strikes an approaching or receding object, the beam changes frequency. The change in frequency is proportional to the speed of the object. This theory has been experimentally verified by hundreds of experiments throughout the world. It is accepted as a valid theory by all experts in the field.
4. The radar speedmeter applies the Doppler shift principle. The speedmeter consists of a transmitter and a receiver. The transmitter generates and sends out the beam of microwaves. The receiver measures the frequency change after the beam strikes an object and bounces back to the car containing the radar speedmeter. Like the underlying theory, the radar speedmeter instrument has been subjected to numerous experiments. The conclusion of the ex-

periments is that if the speedmeter is in proper, working order and operated properly, the instrument will accurately measure speed to within a few hundredths of a mile per hour. At one time or another speedmeters have been used by law enforcement agencies in every state in the United States. Experts in my field almost universally accept the reliability of radar speedmeters.

/s/ Glenda Schneider

On September 17, 1999, before the undersigned, a Notary Public for the State of California, personally appeared Glenda Schneider, known to me to be the person whose name is subscribed to the within instrument, and acknowledged that she executed the same.

/s/Mildred Adams
Notary Public
My license expires October 17, 2004

In addition to using affidavits from experts, the party can sometimes use an affidavit from a professional school librarian. The librarian's affidavit is attached to Xerox copies of the title page and the pertinent pages from a learned treatise in the scientific field. The librarian's affidavit states the librarian's position, lists the credentials of the author of the treatise, and finally asserts that the treatise is a standard, authoritative text in its field. The party then uses the excerpts from the treatise to establish that the principle's validity or the instrument's reliability is a verifiable certainty. The plaintiff could submit the affidavit to the judge with a notice of motion for judicial notice and supporting points and authorities. For a sample notice and set of points and authorities, *see* Sevilla, *A Lazy Person's Approach to Introducing Evidence*, 16 C.A.C.J. FORUM 22, 24-25 (Jan.-Feb. 1989).

The plaintiff would use the points and authorities and affidavit at trial in this fashion. As soon as the judge granted the first request for judicial notice, the plaintiff could make this request before calling Officer Ripley as a witness. The plaintiff is still the proponent.

P Your Honor, I have one last request for judicial notice.
J What is it?
P May we approach the bench?
J Yes.
P Your Honor, I request that you judicially notice the validity of the theory underlying radar speedmeters and the general reliability of speedmeters. Both facts are verifiable certainties under Evidence Code § 452(h).
J (To the opposing attorney.) Did you have advance notice that the plaintiff was going to make this request?
O Yes, your Honor. He gave me notice a week ago.

P   Your Honor, I request that this be marked plaintiff's exhibit number nine for identification.

J   It will be so marked.

P   Please let the record reflect that I am showing the exhibit to the opposing counsel.

J   It will so reflect.

P   I now offer plaintiff's exhibit number nine for identification into evidence as plaintiff's exhibit number nine.

J   (To the opposing attorney.) Have you seen this exhibit before?

O   Yes. The plaintiff's attorney gave me a copy about a week ago.

J   Do you have any objection?

O   Yes, your Honor. This affidavit is gross hearsay.

P   Your Honor, at this point we're litigating the propriety of judicial notice. As my memo of points and authorities points out, under Evidence Code § 454(a)(2), the hearsay rule doesn't apply to your determination whether these facts are verifiable certainties.

J   You're right. The objection will be overruled, and the exhibit will be received.

P   The exhibit establishes that the validity of the underlying principle and the reliability of the instrument are verifiable, scientific certainties. For that reason, judicial notice is appropriate.

J   I will grant your request.

P   I request that you inform the jury of these facts.

J   Yes. Ladies and gentlemen of the jury, I am now going to judicially notice two more facts. One fact is the validity of the theory underlying radar speedmeters. As you may know, the police in this jurisdiction use radar speedmeters to measure the speed of cars. The technical theory underlying speedmeters has been accepted by scientists. Secondly, the speedmeter itself is a reliable instrument if it's in working order and operated correctly. You are to assume the validity of the theory and the general reliability of the instrument. I understand that we are about to hear some testimony about a radar speedmeter clocking of the defendant's car. I want to make it clear that I am not deciding whether this speedmeter was in good, working condition or whether the officer used the correct procedures. You will have to listen to the testimony and make those decisions. I am instructing you only that you must assume the validity of the scientific principle and the general reliability of speedmeters even though you won't hear any evidence on these topics.

D.   JURY VIEWS

1. THE DOCTRINE

Sometimes the attorneys want the jurors and judge to view an object or location that cannot feasibly be brought into the courtroom. In most cases, the attorney will be content to offer either a witness's oral description of the object, a diagram of the object, or a photograph. However, in some cases, the object is so complex and plays such a pivotal role in the case that the attorney wants the trier of fact to personally observe the object or location. This procedure is known as a jury view.

The California statutes authorize views in criminal and civil cases. Penal Code § 1119 permits a view

> [w]hen, in the opinion of the court, it is proper that the jury should view the place in which the offense is charged to have been committed, or in which any other material fact occurred, or any personal property which has been referred to in the evidence and cannot conveniently be brought into the courtroom. ...

The decision whether to permit a view is committed to the trial judge's discretion; the operative verb in § 1119 is "may." Code of Civil Procedure § 651 is the civil counterpart to Penal Code § 1119. Section 651 empowers the judge to order a view of any of the following:

> (1) The property which is the subject of the litigation.
> (2) The place where any relevant event occurred.
> (3) Any object, demonstration, or experiment, a view of which is relevant and admissible in evidence in the case and which cannot with reasonable convenience be viewed in the courtroom.

Evidence Code § 813(b) specifically permits jury views in cases such as eminent domain proceedings in which the trier of fact must determine the value of property.

In most jurisdictions, the sense impressions the trier of fact gathers during a view do not qualify as substantive evidence in the case. However, California subscribes to the minority view. Evidence Code § 140 defines "evidence" as including "things presented to the senses that are offered to prove the existence or nonexistence of a fact." The Law Revision Commission comment explains that § 140 includes jury views. Hence, the information the trier of fact gains during a jury view constitutes independent evidence under the Code. 2 WITKIN § 852, at 817.

2. ELEMENTS OF THE FOUNDATION

The proponent of a jury view usually makes a pretrial motion for a view and submits declarations in support of the motion. The declarations should show that:

1. Certain property exists.
2. The property is logically relevant to the pending case.
3. It is impossible or inconvenient to bring the property into the courtroom.
4. The features of the property are so complex or detailed that an oral description, diagram, or photograph would be inadequate.
5. The property is in substantially the same condition as at the time of the relevant event. If the property has changed materially, the judge usually exercises discretion by denying the motion. If the property has changed markedly, a view might mislead the jury. When there is potential for misleading

the jury, Evidence Code § 352 cuts against granting the motion. However, if it can be made clear to the jury how the property has changed, the judge can still grant the motion. *People v. Hardy*, 2 Cal. 4th 86, 825 P.2d 781, 5 Cal. Rptr. 2d 796, 849, *cert. denied*, 506 U.S. 987 (1992).

3. SAMPLE FOUNDATION

The fact situation is a personal injury action arising from a collision in February 1999 on a winding, rural road in Yolo County. The plaintiff moves for a jury view of the section of road where the collision occurred. In support of the motion, the plaintiff submits two declarations. Both declarations refer to the same section of road mentioned in the pleadings. For that reason, both declarations lay the first three elements of the foundation. The date of the hearing on the motion is August 1, 1999.

Declaration

1. My name is George Wasterson. I live at 1444 Court Street, Woodland. California.
2. I am a professional photographer. I am the proprietor of the Wasterson Photography Studio, 1456 Court Street, in Woodland. I have owned that company for 15 years. While I was on active duty in the United States Army between 1981 and 1988, I received formal training in photography. I have since taken seven photography classes at California State University in Sacramento.
3. On July 1, 1999, an attorney, Ms. Eileen Richards, contacted me by phone. She asked me to meet her at the intersection of Rural Route 4 and Range Road outside the city limits of Woodland. (1), (2), (3) I met her there later that afternoon.
4. While we were at the intersection, Ms. Richards explained to me that she represented the plaintiff in a civil action arising from a collision at the intersection. She also explained that she was interested in showing the jurors the 200 yards of Range Road immediately to the west of the intersection with Rural Route 4. She asked whether I could photograph or videotape that section of road.
5. I carefully inspected the two hundred yards of road in question. I walked the stretch of road twice and drove it twice. I then advised Ms. Richards that in my professional opinion, neither still photographs nor a videotape would be adequate. The section of road in question is not only winding; the road is also uneven—any car traveling that section of road is constantly riding up and then down and then up again. Even if I took 100 still photographs and submitted them to a jury, the stills would not adequately convey to the jury the sense of traveling down that stretch of road. In addition,

since the road is both curvy and uneven, even a videotape would convey only a limited sense of perspective of a driver on that stretch of road. I declare under penalty of perjury that the above statements are true and correct.

Executed this 14th day of July, 1999, in Woodland, Yolo County, California.

_____
/s/ George Wasterson

Declaration

1. My name is Doris Kingman. I reside at 723 Range Road in Yolo County, California. I have lived at that residence for the past 37 years.
2. I am intimately familiar with the intersection of Range Road and Rural Route 4 outside Woodland in Yolo County. It is the intersection closest to my house. I have driven through that intersection thousands of times.
3. I can recall the condition of the 200 yards of Range Road immediately to the west of the intersection with Rural Route 4 as of February 1993. I generally remember the condition of the road and the foliage on both sides of the road. I inspected that area again today. To the best of my recollection, the condition of the foliage and road today is substantially the same as the condition in February 1999.

I declare under penalty of perjury that the above statements are true and correct.

Executed this 29th day of July, 1999 in Woodland, Yolo County, California.

_____
/s/ Doris Kingman